CATHEDRAL

THE GREAT ENGLISH CATHEDRALS
AND THE WORLD THAT MADE THEM
600–1540

CATHEDRAL

THE GREAT ENGLISH CATHEDRALS
AND THE WORLD THAT MADE THEM
600–1540

JON CANNON

CONSTABLE · LONDON

Constable & Robinson
3 The Lanchesters
162 Fulham Palace Road
London W6 9ER
www.constablerobinson.com

First published in the UK in 2007 by Constable,
an imprint of Constable & Robinson Ltd

This edition published in 2011 by Constable & Robinson

 A copy of the British Library Cataloguing in Publication Data is available from the British Library.

ISBN: 978-1-84901-679-7

1 3 5 7 9 10 8 6 4 2

Frontispiece: The Virgin Mary ascends to heaven in this roof boss on the pulpitum, entrance to the choir at York Minster; the lantern of the central tower rises above
Pages 30–1: An earl of Arundel and his wife, from a tomb moved from the site of Lewes priory to Chichester cathedral after the Reformation; the touching holding of hands is a Victorian 'restoration', and the inspiration for Philip Larkin's poem 'An Arundel Tomb'
Pages 258–9: Cusps on the fourteenth-century tomb ascribed to Bishop Stapeldon's brother at Exeter turn into tiny mourner's heads

CONTENTS

To my mother and father
to Liu Hong, Ann, May and Lily
and to Millibar: here's your 'churches book'

NAMES DATES AND NOTES

Modern conventions for medieval dates and names vary somewhat, especially as both the date of New Year and the calibration of the calendar itself have changed, as have the prevailing opinions on how medieval toponyms and other names are best given. I have followed the dates and names given in my sources, using the *Oxford Dictionary of National Biography* to arbitrate in any disputes.

It is important that readers can follow a particular point further, or find my authority for a given fact; but also that the pages of what is essentially a general work are not overloaded with references. I have tried to devise a system that meets both needs, if giving slightly more importance to readability. Where a point in the chapters of general history in the first part of the book relates directly to something I say in one of the cathedral essays that follow, the citation is not repeated: it will be found in the cathedral essay. Architectural and historical facts that are widely available in standard sources are left entirely unreferenced. Where one source is repeated many times in a given chapter or cathedral essay, its first citation summarizes future use; it is only repeated thereafter for direct quotes. Indeed, only direct quotes have been granted page numbers within the sources referenced. The referencing system I have adopted, or rather adapted, saves space by giving author and date alone, but can involve some page-turning when establishing which volume an individual article comes from. I apologize to those for whom this generates some extra digging; I hope they understand that my main aim has been to make such digging possible at all within the bounds of a project whose primary aim is not academic. Likewise, I have tried to avoid peppering the pages with cross-references.

Except in a few instances, all of which are flagged, I have made it a rule to restrict direct quotes to medieval sources. Translations are as rendered in my secondary sources, though on a few occasions, all of which are credited, new translations have been commissioned.

ACKNOWLEDGEMENTS

Without the extraordinary love, support, encouragement and patience of Liu Hong, Ann and May, Charmian and Cyril Cannon, Lin Leng Shi, Liu Fu Tai and Lin Yan Shi, this book would have been impossible to complete. Without the generosity, hospitality and congeniality of Michael and Caroline Mitchell, Susan Wightman and all who sail in Libanus Press it would have taken three times as long; without Nick Robinson (whose idea it was) and Toby Eady it would simply not have existed. Lydia Greeves and Katy Carter, my editors, Bill Smuts, who drew the diagrams and (at Constable & Robinson) Pete Duncan and Charlotte Deane have had a transformative impact on the book and again I cannot thank them enough; in addition to the services rendered above, Libanus Press designed it with beauty, craftsmanship and near-infinite patience. Indeed, the help given by all these people, in their various ways, has been more important even than that unwittingly provided by Bach, Bob Dylan, Burning Spear, the Clash, Monteverdi, T.S. Eliot, Geoffrey Hill and Russell Hoban – which is saying something. I dreamed I saw St Augustine.

I would also like to thank James Peddle for coming up with the title; Kirstie Jackson for Latin translations; Jennifer Alexander for showing me round Lincoln; John David for showing me round the York masons' yard and chapter-house tracing-floor; and Lucy Rutherford for an introduction to the York Glaziers' Trust. Richard Plant was good enough to read and comment on the entire manuscript; portions have also been read by Lesley Abrams, Jenny Alexander, Tim Ayers, Brian Ayers, Sarah Brown, James Clark, John Goodall, Pamela King and John Maddison. I cannot express enough my thanks to them all, nor emphasize enough that any errors in the book are my own. Tim Ayers, Anna Eavis, John Goodall, John McNeill, Richard Plant and the helpful list members at 'Medieval Religion' have all been valued sources of good conversation.

PREFACE

An overpass on the A36 is not the most obvious place for an encounter with a vanished world. But Salisbury, through which this road passes, is no ordinary city. An enormous church dominates the view from the road. This cathedral is so familiar that we tend to take it for granted. Yet it is as emphatically a 'tall building' as anything in Hong Kong, New York or Frankfurt. And no building in those cities dwarfs everything around it so completely. To rival Salisbury, these places would need to be dominated by a single enormous skyscraper, with no other structures of comparable size for a day's journey in any direction. The cathedral compares more closely with the pyramids, or with the Ministry of Truth, the colossal structure conjured up in Orwell's *1984*. Yet Salisbury manages to be beautiful, too.

At the same time, the comparison is an apposite one. Medieval Salisbury cathedral was a centre of great power, set apart from other churches by the fact it was the seat of a bishop. As a bishop's church, it had ultimate authority for religious life in an area roughly equivalent to modern Wiltshire, Berkshire and Dorset. Church teaching dominated what people believed about the world and their place in it. Major churches such as Salisbury also delivered much of what we would call education and social services, and were important land-owners. Their courts played a key role in the legal system. Salisbury's bishops were often, in their own right, prominent political players on the national and international stage.

But Salisbury cathedral was not merely an expression of power. As a religious building, it *meant* something. Through the rituals performed there each day, God confirmed His contract with humanity. Without the authority of its bishop, man's side of this contract would break down: not just in Salisbury, but throughout the diocese too. Its architecture and decoration conjured up a complex series of images that between them embodied an entire world-view.

The cathedral is, of course, part of a city, the core of which remains as planned in medieval times.[1] When first laid out, this was a new town, a medieval Crawley or Milton Keynes, both created and owned by the bishop himself. The cathedral

The columns of the twelfth-century Galilee at Durham bear the marks of the years they spent in the open air, perhaps during a stand-off between bishop and monks over the building's location

complex forms a city-within-a-city, a place apart, accounting for about a third of the settlement in which it stands. The close is surrounded by a high, castellated wall. The town beyond had no such protection:[2] it is the cathedral that matters.

The Heavenly Jerusalem, here depicted at Worcester cathedral, was a potent image for medieval people, inspiring much cathedral architecture

A walk through the city today makes it startlingly clear just how much the cathedral was the master of this place. The house plots in the medieval city are about 15 metres wide: a reasonable size for a building that might house an extended family and a small business. But the houses inside the cathedral close are of another order entirely:[3] their plots are around 40 metres wide. Here lived the men who ran the cathedral and administered Church life throughout the diocese. These houses are in turn dwarfed by the 75-metre long bishop's palace, which sits in glorious isolation between the cathedral and the Avon, and by the cathedral itself, 144 metres long and topped by a spire 123 metres high. Not until the nineteenth century would buildings overtop the medieval cathedrals. Yet, in terms of size and wealth, Salisbury is only an average cathedral and it has lost much since it was built.

If the city of Salisbury represents the secular world, and the cathedral close stands for the religious life, the cathedral church is an evocation of the supernatural. For medieval people knew that the world would end, probably quite soon, and that at that moment their souls would be consigned to either heaven or hell. They also knew that, if they were among the 144,000 lucky individuals to be granted a place in heaven,[4] they would be residing for eternity in a city. They even knew that city's name, because it was given in the Bible: the heavenly Jerusalem, Holy Zion.

Heaven was a city like no other. The Bible supplied a few details of its appearance. It was an ordered place, but also a bewildering one: a 'house of many mansions', Jesus had called it.[5] The Book of Revelation described it as built of jasper, crystal, gold and other treasures, yet also as being 'clear as glass', generating its own light 'like unto a stone most precious', with great gates orientated on the cardinal points and walls of extraordinary height. This was a structure of ravishing beauty, 'prepared as a bride adorned for her husband'.[6]

In the lower half of this picture stands Salisbury cathedral, surrounded by its park-like close, in which sit the expansive homes of the men whose church it was. The city beyond was also their creation

Heaven was a many-towered garden paradise in which ceaseless worship took place: Jan van Eyck's Adoration of the Lamb, *in St Bavo's cathedral, Ghent*

Just like the heavenly Jerusalem, Salisbury cathedral was colossal, with many side chapels and ancillary buildings. It contained polished and painted stones of diverse hues; had diaphanous walls which glowed like jewels; and grand entrances oriented west, north and south. All this was intended to provide an appropriately impressive setting for a sacred and theatrical series of rituals. Vestments and rich scents added to the multimedia impact of the whole. Worship was the single most important activity any human being could undertake and here the privileged and exclusive community of the cathedral worshipped, for up to eight hours every day.

In a world where no other buildings matched these for size, and which had no theatre, cinema or art galleries, there was no other experience that could match the impact of the cathedral. The church was an assault on all the senses, designed to give people a direct experience of the numinous, to make faith as real as stone.

Buildings like Salisbury are a challenge to people today. It is hard to write about them objectively. They are, after all, still cathedrals, still the seats of bishops, still used for worship. The English cathedrals may no longer be the local representatives of papal power, but the traditions that created them are alive and well; much about their modern form would be recognizable to those who built them; and the break with Rome itself is still a live issue in the European body politic if, thankfully, no longer the cause of warfare.

Less often remarked upon are the wider achievements of the cathedral-builders. Both Salisbury and its cathedral are still thriving places eight hundred years after the town was laid out and the church built. This alone is enough to make modern town planners green with envy. Although this 'city of God' may have changed radically since it was created, it still offers a vision of urban community that is a challenge to the modern world. Many hugely important aspects of life today, including much of our education system, the building blocks of our Civil Service, the organization of many other corporate bodies and, to an extent, the very idea of the city itself, were forged in cathedrals such as this. It is no accident that there is a copy of Magna Carta displayed in the chapter-house at Salisbury: some of

Lichfield: even the outside of the cathedrals glowed with coloured glass and rich statuary

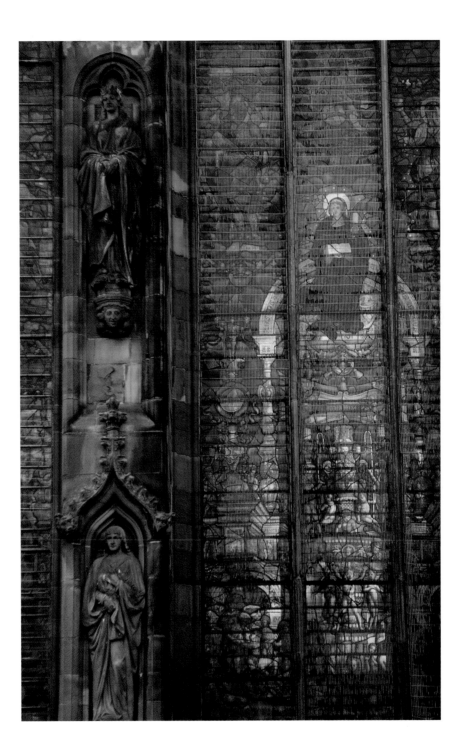

The cathedrals have become icons of the English landscape: Constable's Salisbury Cathedral from the Bishop's Grounds (c. *1825*)

those involved in negotiating, drafting and distributing that document helped build the cathedral.

Today, the cathedrals are major tourist attractions as well as places of worship. Salisbury welcomes 300,000 visitors a year[7] and the view of it from the close or from over the water-meadows along the Avon has come to typify England at its best. For many, perhaps most of its visitors it is more significant as an art gallery, museum and national monument than as a place of worship. Many must quietly wonder what on earth such a building is doing here at all; how and why people in a world both materially and technologically poorer than ours could create such a structure; and how it was used.

It requires an effort of imagination to answer these questions. Salisbury was created in a world that is very foreign to us. Even the power of the architecture has been blunted. The pointed arch that is such a feature of Salisbury was revolutionary when the cathedral was built. It is now used to signify 'church' everywhere from Beijing to Buenos Aires. It is hard to imagine a time when it was a novel and radical departure; yet it was part of a way of building, known as gothic architecture, that was unlike any before or since. And no matter how deep our personal faith, few of us could imagine what it is like to grow up in a world where people have never met anyone else with any other faith, let alone people with none at all;[8] where the doctrines of religion are simply *fact*. There was an unquestioned belief in the possibility that God could intervene invisibly and miraculously in people's lives, even if this heavenly assistance was a little less reliable than the powerful and invisible force of gravity that we take for granted, or the equally unseen current of electricity. When fire engulfed St Peter's abbey, Gloucester, in 1300, 'many folk ran together from all sides, and many prayed, and the entire fire was soon brought under control, so that this may be ascribed more to a miracle than to the great help we received.'[9] In other words, half the monks rushed to get water and the other half prayed as hard as they could; and it was the second group who were thought to have done most to put the fire out.

Unquestioning faith in miracles of this kind might cause even the most devout modern Catholic a moment's pause. And many in the west today would perhaps be put off by such credulity, preferring to admire religious traditions and mythologies that are a little less close to home. Yet this was a world that contained much of beauty, much that should be loved by anyone who appreciates stories, ideas and images, or is interested in the roots of western culture. It was an astonishingly rich, subtle and multi-faceted culture.

If we could take a time machine to the Salisbury of 1220 we would find much that was appalling as well as much to admire. The aim of this book is to be that time machine. We know the names of many of those involved in the building of Salisbury and its cathedral. We know something of their political and religious interests; we know about their lives. Once one knows how to read it, Salisbury is a monument to a specific moment in the past: to the concerns of a narrow group of educated and powerful men in the 1220s. Other cathedrals are monuments to other periods, and to the interests of other individuals. Many, having been reconstructed and extended over the last thousand years, cover a huge range of such moments. For the medieval world was anything but monolithic. Faith changed. Political upheavals, some of them violent, engulfed the cathedral builders. Art and architecture evolved. The cathedral as an institution, a community of some two hundred people, developed too.

The more we know of this history, the easier it is to understand these buildings. They are a window on the past, presenting a lost world that is at once thrilling, frightening and challenging. They are also underestimated as crucibles of modernity, midway in the evolutionary path between ziggurats and skyscrapers. In these pages, I hope, the world that made them will come alive, and readers will discover the true significance of the view from the A36.

Medieval English cathedrals and other churches covered by this book

NORWICH Medieval cathedral
Ripon Medieval great churches that have become cathedrals since 1540
● Monastic
○ Secular

CARLISLE
DURHAM
Ripon
YORK
Chester
LINCOLN
Southwell
LICHFIELD
NORWICH
COVENTRY
Peterborough
WORCESTER
ELY
HEREFORD
Gloucester
Oxford
St Albans
Bristol
ST PAUL'S (LONDON)
BATH
ROCHESTER
WELLS
Southwark
SALISBURY
WINCHESTER
CANTERBURY
EXETER
CHICHESTER

N

INTRODUCTION

The society that created the cathedrals was based on agriculture. Wealth and power were dependent on land ownership. The biggest towns, London, Bristol, York and Norwich, were islands in a sea of massive fields, carefully managed commons and woodland, and countless scattered settlements. It was an intensely hierarchical society, but not a simple one. And it was full of churches. Many of these are still standing, among them thousands of parish churches and almost all the cathedrals; but an extraordinary variety of other religious buildings has been lost. Small chapels, wayside shrines and hermitages; leper houses and hospitals; communities of monks and nuns, some tiny, others enormously wealthy: almost all have disappeared.

Labour on the land dominated medieval life: Adam, depicted at Canterbury cathedral

The state was really two parallel, interlocking entities: one lay and one religious. On the lay side the dominant power was the king, his prestige dependent as much on the extent of his landholdings as on any abstract notion of nationhood: it was he who ultimately bestowed on others the right to possess land. For much of our period, when the realm of the king of England included a substantial area of France, these estates could in theory be on either side of the Channel. Even at the level of the king, however, power had a religious dimension. Indeed, in this world, *everything* had a religious dimension.

The religious part of the state, the Church, was a pan-European institution that placed ultimate authority on earth in the pope. His senior representative in England was the archbishop of Canterbury, Primate of all England,[1] a man matched in power only by the king, a man as wealthy as the greatest aristocrats in the land. The lay and religious parts of the state ran separate legal systems; they even did business in different languages. Most of the people in this book would have used English when talking to 'the man in the street', an Anglo-Norman form of French among the nobility and Latin for Church business.[2] By the early sixteenth century, one-sixth of the adult population worked for the Church.[3]

As today, there were two archbishops in the country, each presiding over a province that was subdivided into dioceses or sees. Each diocese was governed by a bishop. The northern province, based at York, had just three such suffragan dioceses (today it has thirteen). But the archbishop of Canterbury, in addition to his power in the nation as a whole, had authority over fourteen (now twenty-nine). These archbishops also each had a see of their own.[4] That of York was enormous, including present-day Northamptonshire, Derbyshire and Lancashire as well as Yorkshire itself. By contrast, the see of Canterbury was tiny, basically consisting of eastern Kent.

English sees were, on the whole, richer than those in much of the rest of Europe and, for the size of the country, there were fewer of them. In Italy, for example, there were 235 bishoprics; none was as wealthy as the three richest in England, and four-fifths were poorer than any English diocese. Twelve of Europe's forty richest sees were in England.[5] This relative wealth was an important factor in the building of exceptional churches. Without the financial resources to support them, none of the grandiose projects of the Middle Ages could have got off the ground.

As a bishop's church, the cathedral was the place where he had his *cathedra* or throne and which acted as his headquarters; medieval people often simply called the cathedral their mother church. For most of our period, there were nineteen cathedrals in England. But there were only seventeen sees because Bath and Wells, and Coventry and Lichfield, were joint sees, with a cathedral church in two cities.

Like the provinces of Canterbury and York, these sees varied enormously in size. The see of Lincoln was as large as a small country; that of Rochester barely took up half a county. New sees could be created, and cathedrals relocated within them, but these were major decisions. The cathedrals mattered because of the unique authority of bishops and archbishops. Their powers were partly political and pastoral, concerned with maintaining standards in the churches of the see and governing religious life there. But they were also quasi-magical: only bishops could create priests, bless oils and dedicate churches, in other words, provide the necessary conditions for the sacraments to be performed. These sacraments, especially the Eucharist, without which salvation was impossible, were sacred obligations of all humanity.

Within the Church, there were two ways of life. Those who devoted themselves to a life of prayer, poverty, celibacy and seclusion, living communally and in obedience to a written Rule, were known as monks. Secular churchmen, on the other hand, lived 'in the world'. They could live alone and possess their own property; before the twelfth century, most ignored the requirement of celibacy and married; they could also live in a loose kind of community known as a collegiate church. They dominated the administrative side of the Church: most bishops and parish priests were seculars.[6] Indeed the concept of priesthood lay at the heart of the lives of these men. A priest is a man set apart, ritually created by a bishop, and thus able to perform the Eucharist and other sacred tasks. Monks can be priest, but for secular churchmen the priesthood, and the contact with laymen that it implied, was a defining feature.

Each cathedral, as well as being the seat of a bishop, was home to a religious community. From a practical point of view, it made sense for these to be communities of priests, many of whom could support the bishop in running the diocese. Nine English cathedrals (Chichester, Exeter, Hereford, Lichfield, Lincoln, St Paul's,

Again and again, cathedral art emphasizes the power of bishops: here, on the twelfth-century font at Winchester, bishop-saint Nicholas performs an act of charity outside his cathedral

Monastic Durham on its peninsula. The monks' convent is clearly visible, cut off by the cathedral church from the bishop's castle-cum-palace and the town (contrast secular Salisbury, p. 12)

Salisbury, Wells and York) followed this collegiate-church model. These were the secular cathedrals, each of which had a core community of canons, or senior priests. Each canon was supported by income from a portion of church lands known as a prebend, and all had a seat on chapter, a word which refers both to the community's daily meeting but which was also used to describe the canons as a corporate body. Their leader, second in seniority to the bishop, was the dean.[7] The other ten English cathedrals (Bath, Canterbury, Carlisle, Coventry, Durham, Ely, Norwich, Rochester, Winchester and Worcester) were monastic. These cathedral priories, as they were known, had a community of monks headed by a prior. The bishop was considered to hold the role of abbot, the title given to the prior's superior in most other monastic houses.[8] The monks were supported communally from the cathedral's lands; all were members of chapter. The creative tension between these two models of the religious life is one of the themes of this book.

It is the tension between exclusion and engagement, idealism and practicality.

Like all corporate bodies, then and now, these institutions aspired to greater wealth and independence. In this the cathedral chapters behaved much like the other religious communities of their diocese. Many preferred to behave as if their bishop was more an honoured figurehead than a hands-on leader. Some won exemption from their bishop's considerable powers; the greater monastic houses, including some cathedral priories, even acquired mitred status, which gave their leader procedural parity with their bishop and virtual autonomy as far as internal affairs were concerned. Some religious houses might also be designated the mother church for a given area, replacing the bishop in various ways. This privilege applied to certain monasteries in the far south and west of the large see of Lincoln,[9] and the collegiate churches at Ripon, Beverley and Southwell were all 'deputy cathedral' local mother churches within the sizeable diocese of York.

For medieval west Europeans, the Church was what we think of as the Catholic or Roman Church. It embodied the only form of religion, the only world-view, of which most medieval people had any direct experience. But it was also a broad Church, containing an enormous variety of ideas, institutions and people. There were churchmen who cleaved to a vision of their religion as a force for good, a vision every bit as radical and hard to realize in reality as were the idealistic political systems of more recent years.[10] On the other hand, there were church-men who lived venal and worldly lives but were also as politically effective as the most adroit modern politician or corporate leader. Everywhere in this Church there were great tensions: between one cathedral and another, between monastic houses, between monks and seculars, bishops and kings. Often these tensions were a driving force in politics and architecture alike.[11]

Architecturally, although there was much variation, all churches had certain things in common. All were surrounded by an enclosure, whether it was the parish churchyard or the gated close of a cathedral. All were oriented east-west, with open access to the westernmost parts and a more exclusive and sacred area to the east, which was believed to be the direction in which Jerusalem lay. This area was separated from the rest of the building by screens.

Certain kinds of architecture were considered appropriate only for the richer religious communities, including the cathedrals. These features are known as 'great church' architecture and had come to include, from the eleventh century, a three-storey internal elevation, an elaborately-planned east end, more than one richly-decorated façade and, from the mid-twelfth century, vaults in stone throughout the building. A great church might also have more than one tower

The Eucharist, at which Christ was held to be physically present, was the miracle at the heart of cathedral architecture

and various elaborations to the transept, or north-south arm. This might have aisles, for example, or a second transept might stand in the eastern half of the building. Finally, as well as being used as a burial ground, the enclosure or close around a great church contained the living quarters and offices of its community.

The great church is a vivid expression of the sophisticated visual hierarchies and codes within which medieval people operated. The lack of widespread literacy was compensated for by an extraordinarily rich visual culture, full of emblems, symbols and cross-references. One reflection of this was the rigidity of the distinction between ambitious parish church and great church. The three-storey elevation became such a powerful indicator of a church's status that there are several examples of architects designing a two-storey elevation only to have someone, presumably their patron, insisting that a middle storey be inserted when building was already under way. This happened at Exeter cathedral and St Werburgh's abbey, Chester.[12] In England as a whole, only one ordinary parish church boasted a three-storey elevation, vaults throughout the building, a reasonably complex east end and aisled transepts. This was St Mary Redcliffe in Bristol, an extraordinary piece of architectural *lèse-majesté* built in the 'millionaire's suburb'[13] of England's second city.

While there were practical aspects to the development of such features as the three-storey elevation and the stone vault, the driving force behind their existence was an aesthetic and symbolic one. Unlike a castle, or even a palace, great churches have no practical function except, perhaps, as places of burial: they are entirely monuments to the cultural and spiritual realms. The architecture provides an appropriate setting for worship and for experiencing the mysterious and invisible: the existence of God, the presence (at every performance of mass) of angels, and the miraculous process by which bread and wine become Christ's body and blood at the Eucharist. The architecture is thus concerned with appearances and messages to an extent impossible to parallel in the modern world; and this in turn makes it an unusually effective, if distorting, mirror of the times in which it was created.

A medieval pilgrim approaching a cathedral passed through several layers in an unspoken hierarchy of sacredness that he would have understood intuitively. First, he entered the diocese; then the lands that belonged to the bishop or his community; then the limits of the cathedral city itself; then the walled enclosure of the cathedral close. Going into the cathedral, he would walk towards its east end. Here, near the high altar, was stored the consecrated host on which the Eucharist depended. The sacred zone around it was virtually out of bounds to our pilgrim, but he could have access to the cathedral's miracle-working collection of relics or its saint's shrine, which stood nearby, often in a screened enclosure known as a feretory. Everything he passed on the way had a role. Only certain doors, often insignificant side doors, were appropriate for the ordinary layman to use. Only certain people could be commemorated in a monumental tomb inside the church and these could only be placed in appropriate locations.[14]

The most important furnishings in the church ran down the central axis of the building. Separating nave from east end was the great image of the crucifixion known as the rood, with the nave altar beneath it, and a substantial screen known as a pulpitum. Further east there was the choir, with its often richly-carved stalls, and the presbytery around the high altar itself, where fittings could include an elaborate reredos behind the altar. If there were any saints' shrines, or a lady chapel, these were usually positioned further east still, beyond the high altar. The church might contain twenty or thirty side-altars, each lavishly fitted out. Everywhere there would be statues, which were often brightly painted, wall paintings and stained glass. Indeed, the church was an assault on the senses: from the scents of beeswax candles and incense to the sonorous echo of chanting; from the slow theatre of the liturgy to the rich texture of tapestried cloth, the architecture was a backdrop to a lavish artistic display.

All these interiors have been much altered since the Middle Ages. To appreciate what a medieval church would have looked like one has to learn both what it has gained and what it has lost. Most of the stained glass, monuments and fittings in English churches were installed after 1800: however important they are as works of their period, to discover the medieval world one has to mentally strip them away and recreate the building as it was from the traces of its medieval furnishings and decoration.[15]

The fact that we have lost most medieval glass and large-scale sculpture means that gargoyles, corbels, bosses and other small decorative features from the period tend to get undue attention. But this is like trying to read a book by glancing only at incidental illustrations and marginal doodles. Such images were only

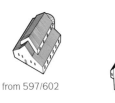
from 597/602

mid-9th century

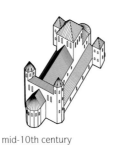
mid-10th century

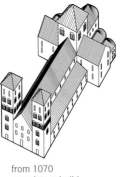
from 1070
complete rebuild

The cathedrals were rebuilt or extended many times over the centuries. At Canterbury, England's mother church, we know about almost every stage

appropriate on a small scale; they exist at the edges of an artistic world-view that placed the saints, God and the liturgy centre-stage. Compared to later Christian culture, though, they are remarkable for their breadth of subject matter. Images of nature, sin and daily life were reminders of the bestial instincts that human beings, led by the Church, had to conquer, and of the rich, semi-mythological culture they inhabited. Indeed, these people did not necessarily think of monsters as creatures of the imagination. Reports of the huntsmen who rode black goats through the park of one unpopular abbot of Peterborough were taken seriously.[16]

A mermaid, warning against vanity and lust, performs a perpetual striptease above the worshipping heads of the Exeter canons

Through such images all medieval life finds its way into the cathedrals. From the labours of the months carved in the east end of Carlisle cathedral,[17] for example, one could write an entire book on medieval peasants and their world. This book, with its much larger compass, could thus take a lifetime to write and be encyclopaedic in scale. I have adopted various strategies in order to make sense of the cathedral-as-history and to deal with the vast amount of potentially relevant information.

My focus is the nineteen churches that were built as cathedrals in the High Middle Ages. This separation of one particular type of institution from all other great churches makes little sense in terms of pure art history,

from 1096   from 1174   1370s to 1490s

but it lends focus to this exercise in architecture-as-history, especially as most of these buildings have survived. Only two, St Paul's and Coventry, have gone. As a control to this sample I have also covered the nine medieval great churches (Bristol, Chester, Gloucester, Oxford, Peterborough, Ripon, St Albans, Southwell and Southwark) that were converted to cathedrals at or after the Reformation. All were important former monasteries or collegiate churches. My aim is thus not to give a detailed account of formal architectural development or an archaeological analysis, nor is it to write a history of medieval England. This book is about the places where history and architecture overlap. It is about the parts of cathedrals most richly charged with the times in which they were created and aims to see what happens when the cathedrals themselves are treated as if they were historical documents. There are thus some formally important structures that I pass over very briefly; and likewise there are major historical events that do not happen to be reflected in cathedral architecture. The story of the cathedrals is more concerned with the Church and its history, and the specific status of bishops within the Church, than with other things, and so that is the main focus of the book too. I also concentrate on England. In the Middle Ages, the cathedrals of Wales came under the wing of the archbishop of Canterbury, who had the four Welsh bishops as his suffragans despite the fact Wales itself was not part of England until the 1290s. But the story of the Welsh cathedrals is deeply interconnected with that of Welsh history and culture and I have chosen to omit these buildings rather than treat them as an adjunct to English history. Scotland too is excluded. It was a separate nation throughout the Middle Ages, the Scottish Church was independent of the archbishop of York from the twelfth century and acquired its own archbishop in the fifteenth.

Throughout I use 'medieval' to mean the period from 1066 to the 1540s, with the four hundred years before this treated as a crucial preamble. I have given particular attention to subjects such as saints' cults and iconography (that is, the messages encoded in a building's glass, sculpture, paintings and architecture), because these are such potent bridges between architecture and history. I have tended to take the accounts of medieval writers, including their descriptions of miracles, at face value, because the cathedral builders generally did so. On a more prosaic level, I have paid special attention to certain kinds of building activity. A complete end-to-end rebuild requires enormous political and economic resources; the creation of (for example) a new east end only marginally less so. Such events are thus of particular interest to the hunter for architecture-as-history. For example, the building histories of secular and monastic cathedrals are rather different, a fact that has not been noted before, and a major theme of this book. It is precisely in this kind of synthesis that I hope to add something new.[18]

Outside and in, the cathedrals were a riot of colour: the polychromy that covered Exeter's west front has recently been reconstructed

The cathedrals were built by real people, men with budgets and constraints working within institutions as confusing, politically complex and, just occasionally, empowering as any modern corporation. This, to me, goes much further in explaining their existence than the practical details of how they were put up. The medieval cathedrals were breathtaking technical achievements for their age, but no more so than the long barrows were for the Neolithic, or digital and biological technologies are for our own day. At all times, human beings have poured disproportionate amounts of their resources into such achievements, stretching their technical abilities in the process.

This book is extraordinarily dependent on the achievements of others. It condenses, and in Part One synthesises a new story out of, a huge amount of scholarship and original research, much of it carried out over the last thirty years or so. In generalizing, and banning the words 'perhaps' and 'maybe', except *in extremis,* I fear I have thrown out many subtleties. I hope that in using a very broad brush to paint a picture that already exists as hundreds of exquisite miniatures, I have not simply created a big mess; perhaps even distorted the very ideas I aim to represent. I can only apologize if this is the case.[19]

In particular, without the extraordinary series of cathedral histories produced over the last twenty to thirty years,[20] the relevant volumes of the *Conference Transactions of the British Archaeological Association*, the *Victoria County History* and Nikolaus Pevsner's *The Buildings of England* series, this book simply could not exist. Such texts formed the backbone of my research; but they are the beginning rather than the end of the story. The amount of scholarship focused on medieval architecture has increased enormously in the last few decades, and shows no sign of abating. Many major contributions were published as I wrote, more are round the corner; meanwhile, projects like the online *Oxford Dictionary of National Biography* have transformed the research process. As much intellectual energy is being put into the cathedrals as at any time since they were built.

Like the English landscape itself, each medieval cathedral is a complex creation, deeply rooted in a specific history and a specific place. Each has thus acquired a distinctive voice, a character as rich and complex as a human personality.[21] It is a voice that was frozen in time when the monstrous juggernaut of cathedral-building was stopped in its tracks around 1540 by the Reformation, and then muffled by the subsequent centuries of iconoclasm and change.[22] My aim has been to distil and attempt to explain each individual voice, and to put across the story that emerges when they are all put together. I hope to entertain and enthuse as well to inform; to tell a story that shakes the dust off these sometimes self-important buildings; to reveal a rich, strange and wonderful world whose traces are all around us still.

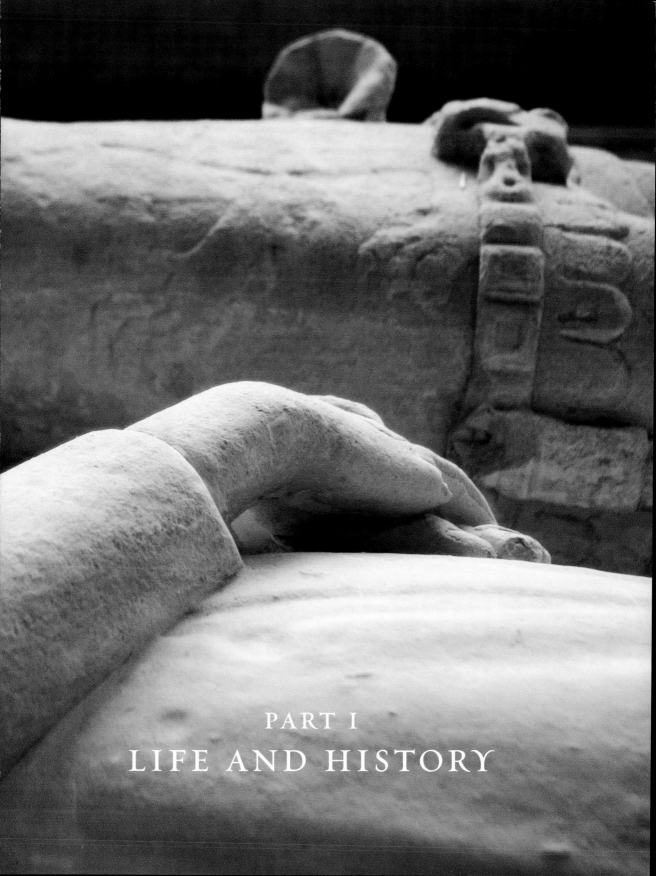

PART I

LIFE AND HISTORY

Chapter One

BIRTH

The little parish church of St Martin stands on the edge of Canterbury. Its walls are partly made of thin, flat red bricks; in every other respect it is unremarkable. Yet by reaching out and touching these walls one is in intimate contact with a revolutionary moment in English history.

St Martin's was built for a foreign Christian, Princess Bertha of the Franks, in the late sixth century. She had married Ethelbert, the pagan, Anglo-Saxon King of Kent, and needed a church and a priest so she could practise her faith. An abandoned Roman church was found on the edge of the ruined city of Durovernum Cantiacorum, present day Canterbury, and restored to use. The priest, Liudhard, she brought with her was no ordinary cleric: he was a bishop. The rebuilt St Martin's was thus a bishop's church, and a bishop's church is a cathedral.

Bertha came from a world in which some forms of urban life and Church institutions had survived the fall of Rome. But Britain had effectively reverted to the culture of the Iron Age and the area we now call England had been colonized by Anglo-Saxons from pagan northern Europe.[1] Christianity only really seems to have survived in the highlands of the west. Here, the Church was essentially monastic. One or even several bishops might be attached to each monastery. Though powerful, it seems these men did not necessarily have specially ambitious churches of their own.[2]

The late sixth century was an important time for the Anglo-Saxon kingdom of

Thirteenth-century foliage in the nave arcade at Wells, a church deeply conscious of its Anglo-Saxon roots

At first glance St Martin's, Canterbury is an ordinary thirteenth-century parish church: but its walls of red Roman tile witnessed the birth of English Christianity

Kent. Bertha's husband Ethelbert was an overlord among the Anglo-Saxons, the senior king south of the Humber.[3] His kingdom was wealthy; his very marriage one sign of its cosmopolitan connections. Many such Anglo-Saxon kingdoms were beginning to compete culturally and were developing ambitious and sophisticated monuments in the process: monumental barrows; great royal halls of wood, such as that uncovered at Yeavering in Yorkshire; dramatic ship burials, such as that at Sutton Hoo in Suffolk.[4] Perhaps Ethelbert wanted to be one step ahead of his peers.

Pagan Anglo-Saxon art could be exquisite, but stone buildings were something new

It is the thin red bricks that makes St Martin's so special, because this style of construction is decidedly roman.[5] It is unclear which parts were built by the Romans, which by Bertha and Liudhard, and which by their successors, the followers of St Augustine. But this very uncertainty is significant. All the possible builders might have used Roman techniques; all of them would have seen themselves as more or less connected to Roman culture. And in the Roman Church, bishops mattered.

The Roman Church and the Roman Empire were interconnected. Christianity had been declared the official religion in 312 shortly before the legions left Britain, and the popes had remained in Rome when the western empire was destroyed in the fifth century. Like the empire, the Church was divided into provinces and dioceses, and its Pope and archbishops compared to the emperor and provincial governors of ancient Rome.

But in the late sixth century this Church was under threat. Pagan invaders from the north reached the gates of Rome. The pope, Gregory the Great, began a missionary counter-offensive. He decided to start by converting the heathen people of Britain, a land that had been lost to both Rome and the Church.[6] In 596 he selected a group of twelve monks from a monastery he had founded and chose as leader a man named Augustine. Then he sent them off to convert the Anglo-Saxons. These men had little missionary experience and they must have felt as if they were being asked to jump off the edge of the world. They returned after a few months, 'appalled at the idea of going to a barbarous, fierce, and pagan nation, of whose very language they were ignorant.'[7] Gregory promoted Augustine to the rank of abbot; he selected more monks to accompany him, so there were forty in all; he armed them with letters of introduction to the rulers they might meet en route; and he sent them off again.

The monks took a year to reach England. They probably landed near Ebbsfleet in late 596 or early 597. King Ethelbert asked them to wait on Thanet, but ordered that they be provided with everything they needed. Soon the king came to Thanet. Unsure of the powers of the visitors' god, he met the monks in the open air, where magic was less effective than indoors. Even so, the sight of a procession of tonsured, chanting monks, carrying a silver cross and a painting of Christ, must have been unnerving. The monks preached to the king about their god's power over death. Ethelbert gave them a place to live in ruined Cantiacorum which seems, unlike some Roman cities, to have not been entirely deserted. Tiny St Martin's became the temporary centre for their mission.

The Roman Augustine baptising the Kentish King Ethelbert in a suitably roomy font: from a thirteenth-century illustration

By his death in 616 both Ethelbert and other leading local Anglo-Saxons had converted. This alone is remarkable enough: they were, after all, abandoning gods whose existence they had never previously questioned. But they had also taken on a cultural package that came with Augustine's mission and which had revolutionary implications. The Anglo-Saxons were effectively illiterate; their legal system operated without written records. Now, Anglo-Saxon laws were written down, a task which first involved working out how to transliterate the English language.[8] In about 602-604 bishoprics were founded in the former Roman cities of Canterbury, London, and Rochester, all of which were at that time in Ethelbert's territory. Augustine was made an archbishop so that he could consecrate bishops. And work began on a cathedral for each of these new sees.

Canterbury was the most remarkable achievement of this initiative. Ethelbert and Augustine turned the half-abandoned Cantiacorum into a symbolic model of Rome itself.[9] A monastery was founded outside the walls, dedicated to St Peter and St Paul (today known as St Augustine's): it would be a burial church for kings and archbishops, and a centre for the monastic life. A cathedral was built inside the walls, dedicated to Our Saviour, to be the focus of Church authority and pastoral work. This arrangement was closely modelled on that in Rome. These were new buildings in stone in a country where all new buildings were of wood; set in a symbolically revived city in a land whose towns were in ruins. They were also centres for law and literacy in an effectively illiterate culture; a deliberate balancing of the public authority of bishops with the spiritual purity of monks; and an

Seventh-century Canterbury was a small Anglo-Saxon settlement in the battered remains of an abandoned Roman city

evocation of the great city of St Peter. In all these respects Augustine and Ethelbert's refounding of Canterbury contains the DNA for a millennium of English cathedrals.

This infant Church demanded real investment from the local elite. Anglo-Saxon nobles had traditionally placed magnificent grave goods in their barrows. Those who became Christians founded new churches instead, endowing them with gifts of land. They lost vital resources as a result, but created living institutions, places where their souls could be prayed for forever. Tracts of land given to Canterbury by seventh-century noblemen of the kingdom of Kent are still owned by the Church of England today.

At first, though, it was by no means certain that Christianity would triumph. Augustine had to travel almost to the Severn to find any British Christians and, when he did, his overtures resulted only in mutual antagonism. And after the converted kings of Ethelbert's generation died, several of their successors reverted to paganism. The bishops of London and Rochester fled: only the archbishop of Canterbury held his ground. It was the 690s before the king and his inner circle in every Saxon kingdom had been converted and each of these kingdoms provided with a bishop and a cathedral.[10] Gregory the Great had proposed a Britannia reborn, its church administered, like the Roman Empire, from provincial capitals at York and London. York was not a stable archbishopric until 735; and London now lay on contested territory between two minor Anglo-Saxon kingdoms, its cathedral temporarily abandoned. In spite of attempts as late as the 1190s to relocate the archbishopric to London, Canterbury remains the capital of the English Church to this day, sixty miles from its intended destination, a major institution resulting from thwarted plans that date back over a millennium.

The fragmentary remains of that ground-breaking church of about 602 lie beneath Canterbury cathedral today. Its status was indicated by its size: at perhaps 27 to 31 metres long,[11] it was just a few metres longer than the nearby monastery of St Peter and St Paul and about a third longer than other English churches of the period. It was architecturally very similar to early churches known from parts of Italy and north Africa. Built of Roman bricks, it was likely to have had a rectangular nave surrounded by small rooms and open on the east side to an apse, whose entrance was marked by a pair of classical columns. It is hard to overstate how revolutionary this simple architecture would have been: no one who saw it can ever have seen a new stone building of any kind, let alone a church.

Five of the seven earliest cathedrals were set in the middle of abandoned Roman towns.[12] These were symbolic acts. It is fitting that Augustine had as his namesake St Augustine of Hippo, the man who, in *The City of God*, coined a rich and lasting analogy between the city and the Church. Nothing we would recognize as an urban settlement would exist for centuries more. Yet it seems we owe to these men the rebirth not just of the cathedrals, but also of the *idea* of the city. York, London and Winchester, to name but three, would not be the places they are now without them. The creation of the first stone buildings since the Romans left, buildings that were also the bases for spreading both a new religion and many other new ideas, is a key moment in the evolution of the English landscape.

——

Within a couple of decades of Augustine's arrival, a second phase of missionary activity opened up, one in which the thriving Irish Church played a vital role. It began in Northumbria, the lands north of the Humber, an Anglo-Saxon territory that, until the early seventh century, was split into the northern kingdom of Bernicia and the southern one of Deira.

The conversion of Northumbria at first followed a familiar pattern. The Anglo-Saxon king, Edwin, married one of Ethelbert's daughters in 625. She was a Christian and brought with her Paulinus, a companion of Augustine. Within two years Edwin had built a cathedral in the ruins of Roman York. In 634 Paulinus was made bishop, but Edwin had died the year before and the kingdom reverted briefly to paganism before an archbishopric could be created.

Northumbria, however, looked north and west towards the Britons and the Irish rather than south and east to Europe. The Christian Oswald, who became king in 634, and his successors drew on the traditions of the Irish Church, as transplanted to Iona in Scotland, to continue Paulinus's project. The churches that resulted were thus the creations of Irish missionaries, working with Anglo-Saxon kings, rather than of missionaries from Italy. They incorporated ideas from Irish, Anglo-Saxon and Gaulish culture as well as from Rome.[13] Not for the last time, reformers had introduced a European art form only for it to be quickly modified by the traditions of the British Isles. This art is called 'insular', but it is a polyglot art, anything but inward-looking.

Soon, missionaries, initially from the Irish Church, were converting Anglo-Saxons, and founding cathedrals across much of southern England and the Midlands, from Essex to Wessex and Mercia; while in Northumbria the fact there were significant differences between the Christian traditions now present in the

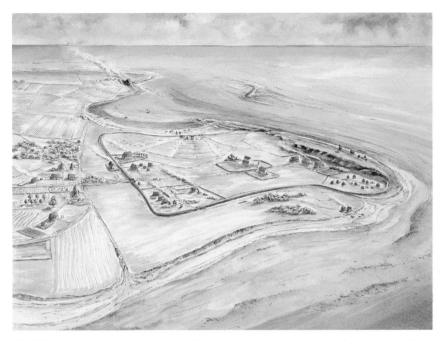

The Irish monastery-cum-cathedral at Lindisfarne was an important centre of power in seventh-century Northumberland

north was becoming a growing issue. The region's second cathedral, for example, founded at Lindisfarne in 635, was originally as Irish in character as that at York was Roman. A daughter house of the monastery on Iona, Lindisfarne's setting on an island that was cut off at high tide was intended to evoke monastic isolation rather than civic grandeur. In reality, it was close to the Bernician royal seat at Bamburgh and thus no more a desert fastness than ruined York was a thriving metropolis, but the symbolism was important. One early abbot-bishop of Lindisfarne, Finan, built 'a church in the Isle . . . suitable for his episcopal see', if made 'not of stone, but of hewn oak thatched with reeds after the Irish manner'.[14]

The differences between these traditions, in particular a dispute about the date of Easter, came to a head around 664 when a British Christian king found himself celebrating Easter on the same day that his Roman Christian queen had her Palm Sunday. If the liturgy was divinely ordained, then one calendar or the other had to be wrong. At a historic church council in Whitby, the Northumbrian Church agreed to accept Roman authority. Meanwhile Theodore, a prominent Greek theologian, had become archbishop of Canterbury and held a synod at

Hertford in 673 at which, for the first time, all the bishops of England gathered together. They agreed to the overall authority of their archbishop and signed a statement that focused on the unique powers of bishops.[15] So now, long before there was a single kingdom of the English, the Church was a functioning institution in which bishops played a key role. The Roman model had won; and with it, the cathedrals.

The only true architectural time-machine to these seventh-century cathedrals is Northumbrian. For its existence we have to thank the most worldly, irascible, vainglorious character of the early English Church: Wilfrid, monk, bishop and saint. Wilfrid had joined the monastery of Lindisfarne in the 640s when he was fourteen. After only a few years he had taken himself off to Rome – a journey of many months – returning a committed member of the Roman party. He was made abbot of a British monastery at Ripon, played a key role at the Synod of Whitby, and became bishop of York at the age of just thirty in 665.

Wilfrid was good at making enemies. In 678 he was expelled from Northumbria, attacked for 'the number of his monasteries, the vastness of the buildings, his countless followers arrayed and armed like a king's retinue'.[16] His vast see was broken up into three smaller ones. For thirty years, Wilfrid fought to be reinstated: he made the long journey to Rome twice in search of papal support, each time returning in triumph only to alienate the local rulers and be expelled once again. During each of these journeys he stopped to convert the pagans he encountered en route, first in Frisia, in what is now Holland and Germany, and then among the South Saxons of south-east England, the last unconverted Anglo-Saxon kingdom, where he founded the precursor of today's Chichester cathedral. He died in his seventies in 709, only a few years after returning from Rome for the last time. In these last years a compromise was reached: he was allowed to retain the title of bishop of Northumbria but was given jurisdiction only over the much smaller see of Hexham. Here are the beginnings of another constant in our story: the endless power struggles involving bishops, kings, and popes.

Wilfrid's crypts at Ripon and Hexham are remarkable remnants of the first English cathedrals

Wilfrid's churches were built in the 660s and 670s with the help of craftsmen from

Italy and Gaul. They mark the beginning in Britain of the 'great church': the architecturally magnificent creation of a mighty abbot or bishop. They included a new cathedral at York, with rich decorations and glazed windows, which has entirely vanished; a new monastery at Hexham, which became Wilfrid's cathedral at the end of his life; and a new monastery at Ripon, where he was eventually buried. Ripon finally became a cathedral in 1836.

These churches were magnificent, offering a glimpse of the 'glories of Rome',[17] 'supported by columns of various styles . . . with walls of remarkable height and length' and 'many winding passages and spiral staircases leading up and down.'[18] At Hexham and Ripon, their stone crypts survive. These crypts are tunnel vaulted and accessed through narrow subterranean corridors that allowed monks and lay people to approach from different entrances. A sense of being close to the distant past is enhanced by surviving chunks of Roman cement lining their vaults and by the Latin inscriptions and marks of Roman stone-dressing which peek out of the walls: for they were built from material that had been recycled from nearby ruins. The crypts are powerful today; in the seventh century, they must have been mind blowing.[19]

People call this period the Dark Ages, but the makers of these churches were fostering intellectual and artistic life, and furthering administration and law, as well as practising their religion. Within a century of the first missionaries, a rich and scholarly culture had developed. It was associated with men like the monk-scholar Bede, whose *A History of the English Church and People* is almost the only written source on the conversion of the English and such figures as the Lindisfarne monk-bishop Cuthbert and the Northumbrian princess Etheldreda (illustrated p. 325), founder of the monastery at Ely. The two last, both protégés of St Wilfrid, would become the greatest English saints before Thomas Becket. Many other figures of the early Church, including Augustine and Bede, were also later regarded as saints. Then there is Alcuin, the priest who abandoned the cathedral at York for the court of Charlemagne and was one of the great thinkers of his age, and Cuthbert's successor, Bishop Eadfrith of Lindisfarne, who created the Lindisfarne Gospels. This illuminated manuscript, as ambitious as a cathedral, embodies the

St Cuthbert, greatest of early saints, about to enjoy a miraculously-delivered meal of chopped dolphin

sophistication of this culture better than any surviving building.

While no structure goes back so directly to the seventh century as the crypts at Ripon and Hexham, several cathedrals founded in the seventh and eighth centuries, Canterbury, Hereford, Lichfield, London, Rochester, Winchester, Worcester and York,[20] exist today. Others are but distant memories. Places such as Selsey, Dunwich and Dorchester-upon-Thames, for example, do not obviously come to mind as cathedral cities. Yet all three were the seats of bishops for centuries. The history of English bishoprics before 1066 is a complex one, reflecting the expansion and eclipse of lost kingdoms, such as East Anglia and Mercia, the trauma of Viking invasion, and the growth of the kingdom of Wessex, from which the English royal line descends. The great monasteries (later cathedrals) at Ely, Peterborough and St Albans were refounded by the kings of Mercia, who even briefly established an archbishopric at Lichfield; the Wessex sees of Ramsbury and Sherborne later became the diocese of Salisbury; the cathedrals of Lindisfarne, Hexham, Lindsey (perhaps located in Lincoln) and Leicester, all accessible to invaders from the north and east, were lost to the Vikings.

Women played an important part in this world: women like Bertha, Ethelbert's queen, and the future cathedral saints Frideswide of Oxford, Werburgh of Chester and Etheldreda of Ely, all three aristocratic women who chose monasticism over marriage and got into trouble with pagan suitors as a result.

Yet it was to be hundreds of years before the cathedrals truly had the authority to which they aspired. The contrast between bishops' and other kinds of churches was a slim one; the parish church did not exist yet. Indeed apart from the greatest monastic houses, it is often hard to be sure what kind of community served a church. The landscape came to be filled with medium-sized minster churches,[21] served by groups of priests with pastoral responsibility for substantial areas, perhaps some 15 to 20 miles across.[22] Such churches could be architecturally ambitious, whether built of wood or stone. Each was part of a wider diocese, but the bishop's churches to which they theoretically were junior were not necessarily larger or richer, and in practice the authority of English bishops took time to expand far beyond their duty to bless sacred oils and make priests.[23]

'In the beginning was the word': the opening page of the gospel of St John in the Lindisfarne Gospels. This miraculous creation of cathedral art probably spent the middle ages on the high altar at Durham cathedral

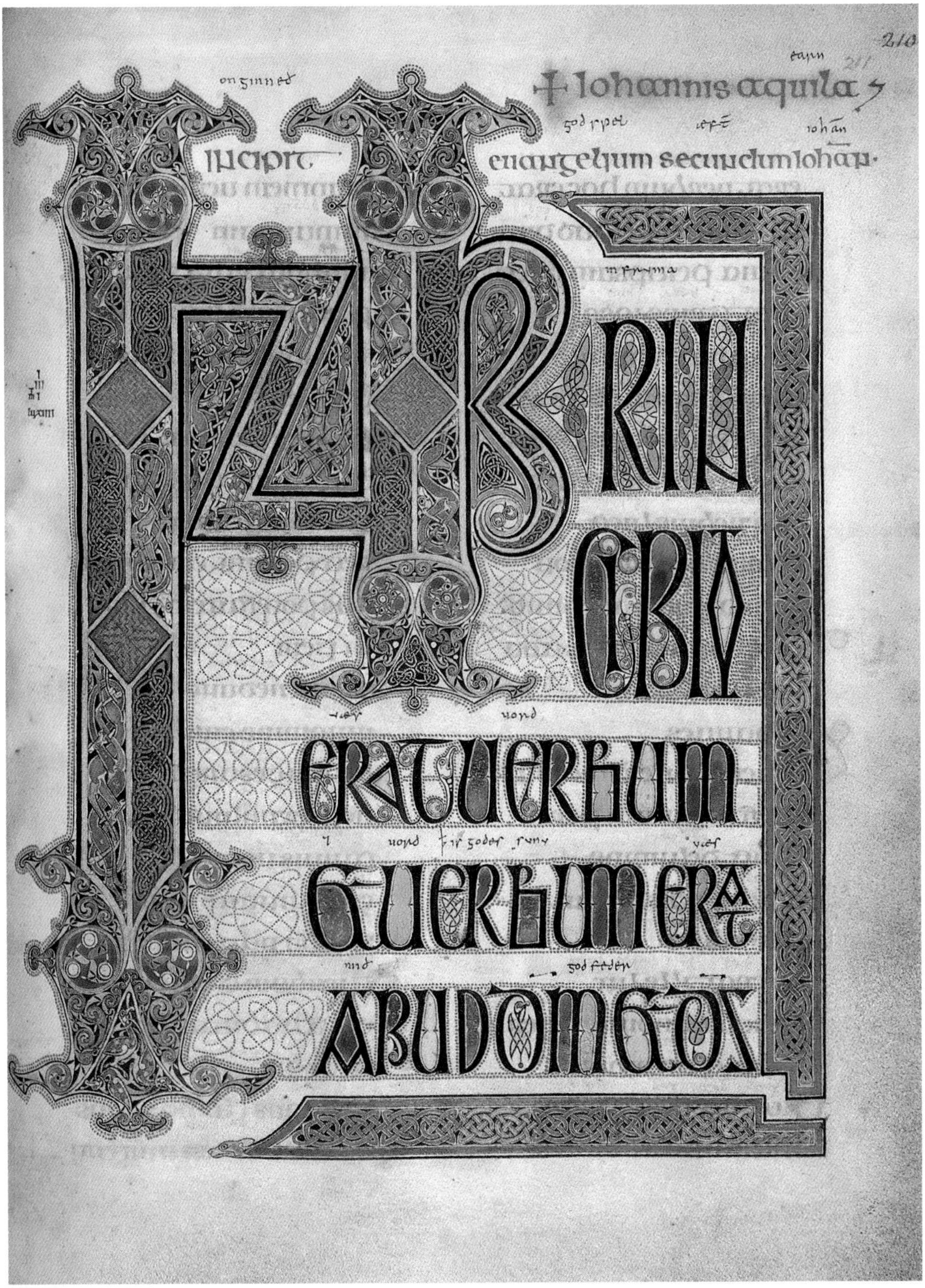

on ginneð god ryðet iefe iohan

INCIPIT euangelium secundum Iohan·

in ðryma

INPRIN
CIPIO
ERAT UERBUM
ET UERBUM ERAT
ABUD DM ET DX

The Viking attacks and invasions, which started in the late eighth century and dominated the next hundred years, caused a major fracture in the story of the cathedrals, but led ultimately to the next great wave of building. The Viking impact was greatest in the north and along the eastern coast. The monks fled Lindisfarne in 875 and became a peripatetic cathedral, circulating the north for decades. In time, too, many Vikings embraced Christianity. But the cost was high. Three hundred years after the achievements of the seventh century, several cathedrals had been abandoned; monasticism was at a low ebb, and was effectively wiped out in the north.

Then, in the late tenth century, a group of influential bishops in southern England began a movement to rebuild and reform religious life through monasticism. The cathedrals of Canterbury, Winchester, Worcester and Sherborne became communities of monks headed by a bishop and such abandoned communities as Bath, Ely, Ripon and Peterborough, all of which later became cathedrals, were also refounded as monasteries. The most vivid architectural achievement of this revival was the Anglo-Saxon cathedral we know most about: the Old Minster at Winchester.[24]

King Edgar of Winchester: one of the magnificent manuscripts produced at Anglo-Saxon England's 'capital city'

Winchester was the capital of the kings of Wessex, the men who had gradually conquered all the other Anglo-Saxon kingdoms and who now governed a united England. With streets laid out by Alfred the Great in an early exercise in town planning, Winchester was the closest thing England had to a capital city. Indeed, it only finally lost the treasury and exchequer to London in the late twelfth century.

In 959 a new king, Edgar, took the throne. Over the next few years, he appointed three prominent monks to key posts in the English Church: Dunstan of Glastonbury became archbishop of Canterbury; Oswald of Fleury in Gaul was made bishop of Worcester (and later also archbishop of York); and in 963, Ethelwold of Abingdon became bishop of Winchester.

Oswald and Dunstan had worked abroad, at monasteries that were spearheads of a pan-European movement to revive the Church. Ethelwold had been Edgar's tutor. He

The Old Minster was a magnificent church; its foundations are marked in the close at Winchester cathedral

was 'terrible as a lion to malefactors'.[25] What Oswald and Dunstan took a generation to achieve at Canterbury and Worcester, he did in a single day, just a year after becoming bishop.

Like many churches of the period, Ethelwold's cathedral, the Old Minster at Winchester, was staffed by married priests. Ethelwold and his contemporaries wanted to replace such men with a disciplined, celibate community. For them, religious life focused on the necessary, magnificent and correct performance of the liturgy, and the creation of a caste of ritually pure people was central to this mission. Monks thus stood at the centre of the Church. The result was an aggressive corporate takeover of the cathedral.

In 964 Ethelwold and the king brought the monks of Abingdon abbey to the Old Minster and had them wait outside the door while High Mass was being performed. As the priests within sang 'get you discipline, lest you perish from the right way', they burst into the church.[26] The priests were asked to choose between abandoning their families and becoming monks, or leaving the community altogether. With their replacements standing in front of them, and the service unfinished, it must have been a tense moment: all the clerics left; only three later became monks. Disgruntled canons later tried to poison Ethelwold.[27]

Over the next twenty years or so, Ethelwold created a modern monastic complex around the Old Minster, separated by walls or fences from the rush and disorder, as it was put, of the nearby town. He also dramatically expanded his cathedral church, transforming a small, 350-year-old building into a rambling great church some 76 metres long, with four great towers perhaps over 30 metres high. The architectural highlight of this church was its substantial western block, from the gallery of which the king could see and be seen during services. This west end also created a dramatic setting for the tomb of Bishop Swithun, who had died in 862 with a saintly reputation, and for the graves of the Wessex kings, all of which had previously been positioned outdoors. The renewed Old Minster had 'many chapels with sacred altars . . . so that whoever walks in these courts with unfamiliar tread, cannot tell whence he comes or wither to return'.[28] It was one of the largest churches in northern Europe, yet the original church of 662 still stood at its heart. It had been added to and extended dramatically but not rebuilt.[29]

This ambitious building programme was punctuated by dramatic events. On 15 July 971, when Edgar had the remains of St Swithun moved inside the Old Minster, screens had to be put up to control the watching crowd. A huge storm left everyone soaked and gave rise to the idea that rain on 15 July, St Swithun's day, means it will be wet for forty days thereafter. Two years later, King Edgar turned thirty, the age at which a man could be ordained as a priest. He and Archbishop Dunstan devised a grand coronation service in which the king would be anointed, just as if he were being made a priest. They wanted to emphasize the sacredness of the power of kings. It was the forerunner of the coronation ceremony in use today.

Just a year after that, Edgar and Ethelwold gathered all the heads of the English religious houses together in Winchester, where they signed up to the *Regularis Concordia*.[30] This key text of English monasticism detailed the liturgical practices and daily regimes that monks throughout the country were to follow. It again reflected Edgar and Ethelwold's interest in emphasizing the sacred nature of kingship: over a third of the foreword was devoted to this theme. The extended cathedral at Winchester was specifically designed with the *Regularis* in mind. The three apses that surrounded its high altar, for example, enabled pairs of choirboys to sing from hidden positions on Maundy Thursday, as this liturgy prescribed.

Dunstan, Oswald and Ethelwold stood at the leading edge of two hundred years of Church reform that had monasticism at its core. Between them these monk-bishops revived and reformed religious houses across the land and invented the monastic cathedral. This new type of institution, a cathedral staffed by monks, lasted until the Reformation; only Sherborne would be lost, when the bishop relocated to Old Sarum after the Norman Conquest, leaving the monks and (thankfully for us) their cathedral behind.

The Norman invaders of 1066 liked to emphasize the poor state of the Church

By the early eleventh century, Canterbury cathedral was a magnificent structure, perhaps incorporating remains of Augustine's seventh century church

they found in England. Yet, during the eleventh century, the large districts served by minsters had begun to be broken up into smaller areas served by local parish churches, a process in which England was ahead of much of Europe.[31] Energetic bishops had been imported from Normandy and the Low Countries, several of whom, such as Giso at Wells and Leofric at Exeter, had reformed their churches, or moved the seats of their sees to better sites, as the Normans would do (St Germans and Crediton were merged and moved to Exeter in 1050; Ramsbury was absorbed into Sherborne in 1058). The richly-endowed monastery at Coventry was founded by 1043: the Normans later made it a cathedral. And the eleventh-century Anglo-Saxons were energetic builders. Apart from a few reused fragments at St Albans (later a cathedral) and Worcester,[32] there is little of this period standing above ground, but there were building projects at several of the churches in this book, and we know about the impressive pre-Conquest Canterbury cathedral, with its east and west apses, one for the high altar, one for the archbishop's throne and altar of Our Lady, and its four towers. Canterbury had been expanded several times since 602 but, like Winchester, it had an ancient building at its core, in this case the venerable church of St Augustine, preserved like a kind of sacred relic.[33] And at Sherborne abbey, the cathedral for western Wessex

This exquisite angel from the 8th-century shrine of St Chad at Lichfield was discovered in 2003

from 705 to 1075, monasticised by Bishop Wulfsige before 1001 and enlarged by Bishop Aelfwold sometime in the period 1045–58, it is (just about) possible to stand inside a cathedral of late Anglo-Saxon England.[34]

Today Sherborne abbey looks like a mixture of twelfth- and fifteenth-century work. But buried within it, like a skeleton, is much of the Anglo-Saxon cathedral priory, including two Anglo-Saxon doors which once opened onto a substantial western block designed to hold a shrine to Wulfsige, who had acquired a saintly reputation. This eleventh-century church escaped rebuilding because the Normans moved the diocese to Old Sarum; Sherborne was 'agreeable neither for the density of its population not for the attraction of its position'.[35] It remained a great abbey church until the Reformation.

Such buildings could be magnificent inside. At Ely we know about just a few of the possessions of what was one of Anglo-Saxon England's wealthiest abbeys: the images of St Etheldreda and her sisters which presented a 'great spectacle to the populace'; special textiles for use on feast days, including the pall in which Edward the Confessor, the king whose death led to the Norman invasion, was wrapped when he was offered to the monastery as an infant; a crucifix, 'big as life', given by Stigand, the last Anglo-Saxon archbishop of Canterbury; and a chapel with a life-sized image of the Virgin and Child in gold and silver, covered with gems.[36] Yet only a single bronze pin survives of all this. With architectural obliteration comes cultural amnesia: it is easier to find Anglo-Saxon architectural references in the architecture of the Norman cathedrals than it is to find the Anglo-Saxon cathedrals themselves.

By the Norman Conquest there were fifteen cathedrals in England.[37] The pattern of sees and their cathedrals was the result of several reorganizations; it was to change several times more, yet we can still trace the history of this lost England in the modern cathedral landscape. Had it not been for short-lived, early Anglo-Saxon kingdoms, there would be no Rochester or Chichester cathedrals. The massive dioceses of Durham, York, Lincoln and Lichfield owed their existence to the great lost kingdoms of Northumbria and Mercia and are reflected in their turn in the modern regions of the East and West Midlands, Yorkshire and the North East. And extraordinary survivals like St Martin's Canterbury and the Ripon crypt are testaments to an architectural and cultural revolution that transformed a polyglot island on the fringes of Europe into a powerful cultural force and led directly to the great age of the cathedrals.

WHAT TO SEE

Revolution

St Augustine's mission: St Martin's, Canterbury; fragmentary remains of other early churches can be seen, for example, at Reculver in Kent and at St Augustine's abbey, Canterbury.

Northumbria: the crypts at Ripon cathedral and Hexham priory church; the Lindisfarne Gospels in the British Library, London. The most complete building of the period is the tiny church at Escomb, County Durham.

A new England

Monastic reform: The remains of the Old Minster in Winchester City Museum and the outline of the former church in the cathedral close.

Anglo-Saxon cathedrals: For upstanding remains of an Anglo-Saxon cathedral visit Sherborne abbey: the north west doorway is the most obvious structure. Such Anglo-Saxon churches as Bradford-on-Avon, Wiltshire, Brixworth, Northamptonshire, and Deerhurst, Gloucestershire, give a strong impression of the character of mature Anglo-Saxon architecture.

Chapter Two

INVASION

CONQUEST 1066–1130

Every cathedral in the country was rebuilt after the Norman Conquest. Despite later alterations, the scale of our greatest churches and, in many cases, large parts of the churches themselves still date back to this period, over 900 years ago. This colossal rebuilding, which was completed in about forty years, provides a vivid window on the times. The bishops and other magnates responsible had been massively enriched by the Conquest; many also had a personal agenda, a need to proclaim status, power and authority.

In the year 1066, Edward the Confessor, King of England and William, Duke of Normandy were both working on great new abbey churches. Edward spent a third of his revenue on the rebuilding of Westminster abbey, which stood next to his new royal palace west of London. The church that resulted did not look Saxon: it was 'erected after that kind of style which, now, almost all attempt to rival at enormous expense':[1] the style evolving in Normandy. Indeed it was a homage to the abbey of Notre-Dame at Jumièges whose former abbot, Robert, had earlier been made bishop of London and archbishop of Canterbury by the king. Edward was familiar with Normandy. He had been exiled from England for almost thirty years by the Danes and had spent much of his youth with William and his family at the Norman court. Robert was one of a small group of Normans who accompanied him on his return in 1041.

Girning romanesque beasts and energetic hunters lurk on the doors added by the Norman warlord-bishop Alexander the Magnificent to the Lincoln west front

William, too, was building. Work on the abbey of St-Etienne, near to his palace at Caen, was being overseen by its abbot, Lanfranc, a reform-minded monk from northern Italy who was also an important and influential scholar. Architecturally, this new monastery was to be an advance on both Jumièges and Westminster.[2]

In December 1065, Edward fell ill. He had wanted Westminster abbey to be a burial church for himself and his descendants: now there was a rush to get it completed. It was consecrated on 28 December 1065; just a few days later Edward died, leaving no son and heir. Harold Godwinson, the powerful earl of Wessex, had been chosen by the dying king as his successor and was crowned the same day. But, some years earlier, Edward had promised William the throne and only two years before, Earl Harold had made a similar pledge. William put his building plans on hold and prepared an invasion force. But before he could cross the Channel, the Danish king, another claimant, invaded northern England. Harold's army defeated the Danes in Yorkshire, but then had to rush hundreds of miles south to Hastings to confront the Normans. The speed with which the exhausted Anglo-Saxons were defeated helped convince William that his invasion was justified by 'the secret and wonderful counsel of God'.[3]

William had sought the support of the papacy for his plans: he was, after all, toppling an anointed king. Abbot Lanfranc had been sent to Rome, where he emphasized his master's commitment to Church reform. It helped that Stigand, the last Anglo-Saxon archbishop of Canterbury, was guilty of pluralism, holding the titles archbishop of Canterbury, bishop of Winchester and others simultaneously. The timing was perfect. The papacy was entering an expansive phase

A workman rushes to add the final touches at the east end as Edward the Confessor's cortège approaches the west end of a barely-complete Westminster Abbey, evoked in the Bayeux Tapestry

driven by a reformist agenda. The pope gave Lanfranc the support he needed; William flew a papal banner over his army.[4]

William, duke of Normandy, was crowned king of England in the new Westminster abbey on Christmas Day 1066. Aggressive reform of the English Church was now inevitable; and Westminster and Caen (work now restarted on the latter church) were the bridgeheads of a new architecture. Like that of the Anglo-Saxons, Norman architecture was romanesque, using semicircular arches and other features descended from the building styles of the Roman Empire. But the Saxons also loved to place bold patterns and other decoration over the surface of a building and they used triangular as well as round arches. The architecture of Normandy, by contrast, was regular and spare, clearly articulating the form of the building itself. Once across the Channel, though, the Normans began to absorb new influences. As a result, the cathedrals and other buildings produced in the decades after the Conquest would gradually, especially from the 1080s, become something new: an Anglo-Norman architecture.

This great rebuilding could not get fully under way until England was peaceful and secure. The years immediately after the Conquest were uncertain ones. A northern rebellion in 1068 was put down so savagely that little was left standing within a 30-mile radius of York; the Danes attempted to invade again in 1069 and, two years later, there was a Danish-supported insurgency in the Fens. The reparations that followed this uprising left the Anglo-Saxon monasteries of Ely and Peterborough, both later cathedrals, financially crippled for years. Even the Anglo-Saxon saints fought the Conqueror. After the new sheriff of Cambridge declared 'I have never heard of Etheldreda', the royal saint and her virgin sisters appeared in a dream where they took it in turns to impale his henchmen on their staffs;[5] while, in Durham, the king himself ran terrified from the cathedral after being overcome by a strange fever, presumably conjured up by St Cuthbert.[6]

In these challenging years, 1070 was something of a turning point. A team of papal advisers helped depose Archbishop Stigand and two other particularly corrupt Anglo-Saxon bishops. Lanfranc came from Caen to be archbishop of Canterbury. At about the same time, the Anglo-Saxon nobility was aggressively purged so that, by 1087, most of them had been replaced by Normans. The feudal system was imposed, in which all lords owed the king specific services, usually military, in exchange for their lands. That same year, the Normans started to build: they started at the top.

Canterbury's magnificent cathedral, which perhaps included parts of Augustine's seventh-century church, had been badly damaged in a fire in 1067.

In 1070, Archbishop Lanfranc demolished it completely, building a near-copy of his church of St-Etienne in its place.[7] It seems unlikely that this was the only option open to him: no other cathedral fire in this book led to the complete obliteration of the building affected. Lanfranc's new cathedral was 'rendered almost perfect' within seven years.[8] Even if this just refers to the east end and the part of the nave that contained the monks' choir, it is perhaps the fastest cathedral-building campaign of the English middle ages. All this was a powerful demonstration of Lanfranc's power and a green light to any of his bishops who might want to do something similar. It was also the act of a man who was unhappy with his new home. 'The language was unknown to me and the native races were barbarous,' Lanfranc complained.[9] He suspected the English saints, saying that he doubted the quality of their sanctity[10] and disliked some of the elaborate liturgical practices he found. Tellingly, there was not enough room in his new church for the many shrines from the old building to be lavishly displayed,[11] just as his own standard liturgy pointedly simplified some of the practices of the *Regularis Concordia*.[12]

Architecturally, the new Canterbury cathedral was a Norman import.[13] Even the stone of which it was built had been shipped across the Channel from quarries at Caen. The architect may well have been the same man who designed St-Etienne; a few adaptations made it more suitable for activities of 'greater solemnity . . . by reason of the primatial see which is there'.[14] For example, in a highly effective display of power, the high altar and archbishop's throne were placed in the east end over a crypt that lifted them dramatically above the rest of the church, pushing the monks' choir into the nave.[15] Lanfranc also built himself a large archbishop's palace, on the site where the palace is today, for which a street near the cathedral had to be demolished.

At the same time, Lanfranc and William began reforming the Church as a whole. It cannot have been easy: the archbishop's monks may have respected his learning, but their culture was being supplanted, their relatives divested of their lands. 'I endure so many troubles and vexations every day – such hardness of heart, greed and dishonesty – that I am weary of my life,' Lanfranc complained. But he was determined, making changes 'often with good reason, but sometimes simply by the imposition of his own authority'.[16] Churchmen from Normandy and elsewhere began to be moved into key posts.[17] The latest good practice was collated into a manual, the *Decreta Lanfranci*, which was adopted by at least fifteen monastic and cathedral communities across England.

Many Normans wanted to thin the ranks of the Anglo-Saxon saints as

Lanfranc's new cathedral at Canterbury obliterated England's most ancient and sacred church

aggressively as they had decimated the English nobility. The new abbot of Evesham, a former pupil of Lanfranc, simply put the monastery's relics on a bonfire on the basis that those that were genuine would not burn (one skull broke into a sweat and was rescued).[18] Some saints, though, were of widely-accepted significance, and this may explain the scale of the next building in our story. St Alban was a respected early Christian martyr. The conqueror himself had sworn an oath on relics of the saint in 1066.[19] The new abbot of St Albans, who was Lanfranc's nephew, began rebuilding the abbey church, not a cathedral until 1878, in 1077, the year Canterbury was completed.

The entire project may be a pointed completion of a failed Anglo-Saxon attempt to move the ancient church, built around St Alban's tomb, uphill to a new and more striking site overlooking the main road from London to the north.[20] While the remains of St Alban went too, the bones of lesser figures, such as King Offa, were pointedly left behind.[21] The new abbey was enormous. It was a third longer than the cathedral at Canterbury. The regime was developing architectural ambitions of its own. Normandy, the fountainhead of this architecture, would soon become an architectural backwater.[22]

In 1072 and 1075, in line with papal policy, ambitious plans were announced to move a number of rural cathedrals to new locations, many of these sites were more urban, but ready defensibility or a Roman origin appeared key. Not all these moves were initially successful. The decision to relocate the cathedral for East Anglia from Elmham to Thetford resulted in the bishops battling for a decade to take over the nearby abbey of Bury St Edmunds before redirecting their efforts to Norwich, which was finally settled on in the late 1080s. The cathedral at Sherborne was moved to heavily-fortified Old Sarum, where a new, if rather small, cathedral was built;[23] but 150 years later it was moved again, to Salisbury. The base for the poor diocese of Sussex was relocated just a few miles, from Selsey to Chichester, even though the more centrally located Lewes might have been a more sensible choice. And Lichfield was moved to Chester, only to move again, probably in the 1090s, to Coventry. None of these churches was rebuilt until the 1080s or 1090s. By contrast, the most audacious move of these years, from Dorchester to Lincoln, was also the most successful.

This move was presided over by the one Norman bishop who was on the scene when Lanfranc took up his post: Remigius, a monk from Fécamp in Normandy. Here was a small man in a hurry. He was short, big-hearted, charming, 'swarthy of hue but comely of looks'.[24] In 1066, it was said, he had personally funded one boatload of knights and himself joined battle at Hastings.[25] He was given a bishopric in 1067, before there was even a Norman archbishop, when all his colleagues were Saxon appointees and when the success of the invasion itself was unclear. And he had eagerly accepted his mitre from Stigand, even though both King Harold and King William had managed to avoid being crowned by the suspect Anglo-Saxon archbishop.[26]

Remigius had gone from middle management at a monastery to head of one of the largest dioceses in Europe in a single leap. And this appointment was no sinecure. His see stretched from the Thames to the Humber but Dorchester cathedral was just half a mile or so from its south-western boundary. The archbishop of York was attempting to take over a large northern part of the diocese; yet here and elsewhere much of the see was still effectively frontier country. Yorkshire and the Fens were both still hotbeds of resistance and the Danes were plotting invasion from the east coast.[27] Furthermore, the reformers were questioning the bishop's position: as well has having been consecrated by Stigand, he was suspected of having bought the job in the first place. In 1071 he accompanied Lanfranc, the archbishop of York and others to Rome to have the issue resolved.

William and Lanfranc must have trusted in Remigius's abilities, for they kept him in his post and quickly thrust him into the cutting edge of Church and

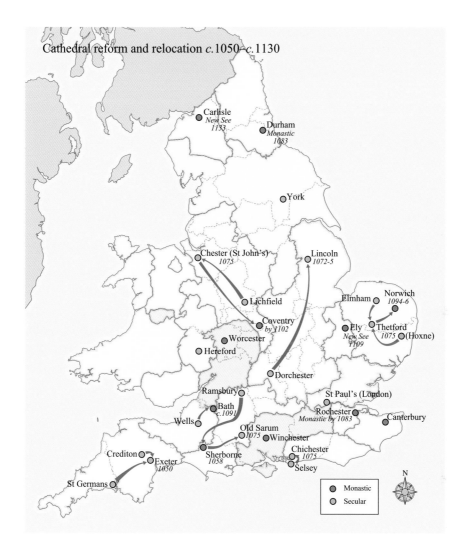

Carlisle
New See
1133

Durham
Monastic
1083

York

Chester (St John's)
1075

Lincoln
1072-5

Elmham

Norwich
1094-6

Lichfield

Coventry
by 1102

Ely
New See
1109

Thetford
1075

(Hoxne)

Worcester

Hereford

Dorchester

Ramsbury

St Paul's (London)

Bath
c.1091

Rochester
Monastic by 1083

Canterbury

Wells

Old Sarum
1075

Winchester

Crediton

Exeter
1050

Sherborne
1058

Chichester
1075

Selsey

St Germans

Monastic

Secular

N

national politics. Between 1072 and 1075 it was decided to move the seat of his see some 125 miles north-east to Lincoln, a major trading town at the junction of two of England's most important roads, a main route leading north towards Hadrian's Wall and the Fosse Way, which went cross-country. Lincoln was also, cannily, just inside the territory that the archbishop of York wanted to wrest from the see.[28]

Lincoln's Roman walls enclosed an area on the edge of a limestone ridge where the Normans were already constructing a castle. The cathedral was built here as well, and a special enclosure made for both church and castle that involved destroying 166 houses of well-to-do Anglo-Saxons.[29] Unusually, Remigius was given a military role, with responsibility for twenty knights in the castle.[30] On the whole, his new church was another descendant of St-Etienne. The exception was the west end, which was itself a kind of castle.

Five enormous arches, set in a wall 19 metres high, still greet the visitor to Lincoln today. They are embedded in the west front of a cathedral that has been enlarged many times since the 1070s; behind them is a hidden warren of office-like spaces, suggesting a large and complex structure.[31] This massive west end appears to have been a fort-like headquarters for the bishop, complete with machicolations and garderobes, its entrance as imposing as a Roman triumphal arch 'a strong church in a strong place . . . suited to the times, invincible to enemies'.[32]

Yet the military details were more symbolic than practical. The elegant niches at the corners of the west front meant that it was almost useless as defensive architecture,[33] while its arches seem very well suited for the display of banners, as required on Ascension Day in the liturgy used in the church, known as the Lincoln Use.[34]

The apparently secular associations of Lincoln's west front are remarkable in themselves. But the building is more interesting than that. In evoking the image of a castle, it is a symbolic building, alluding to the power of the bishop, temporal as well as spiritual, and evoking the heavenly Jerusalem. Some have even wondered if the effect of a triumphal arch was a deliberate reference to Lincoln's Roman heritage.[35] This was something new: architecture with a message. The Normans had upped their own architectural ante once again.

This new cathedral was also given an advanced constitution, and with its landholdings being rapidly expanded by the king and other great men, Lincoln soon lost its brief status as a frontier outpost and was well on the way to being the effective headquarters of a vast, fertile diocese.[36]

The 1070s are fascinating years. The invasion was still fresh in people's minds, its success not a foregone conclusion. Yet a handful of ambitious churches had been begun.[37] Canterbury gave other patrons carte blanche to demolish and rebuild hallowed structures; St Albans indicated that the resulting buildings could be ambitious; while Lincoln seems to be trying to talk about temporal and spiritual power, a direct report from the coalface of conquest. But stylistically all these buildings are similar to those in Normandy. They are no preparation for what came next.

From 1079, a former royal chaplain named Walkelin, who was now bishop of Winchester, began the construction of one of the largest buildings ever created. The design of this cathedral moved the architectural achievements of the regime into a new gear. From now on there was nothing to prove. The regime had gone from conquering to conqueror.

Having been a canon at Rouen cathedral, Walkelin knew about the running of these great churches. Now he had the third most important job in the English Church, after the archbishoprics of Canterbury and York, and one of the richest sees. In spite of the recent development of Westminster, Winchester was still the dynastic capital of England, a status that was reflected in an extraordinary range of buildings, including the Old Minster. The royal treasury was here; key decisions were made about the English Church here;[38] and this is where, from 1086, the compilation of Domesday Book began. William the Conqueror rebuilt the Saxon royal palace and was creating a new castle in the city. Walkelin flattened the Old Minster.

More than twice as long as Lanfranc's Canterbury, the new Winchester cathedral remains the longest cathedral in Europe. But in its day it was one of the largest roofed structures in the world.[39] Only two other buildings in Christendom, both of them grand churches with major roles, came close: St Peter's in Rome and the cathedral of Speyer, one of the spiritual hearts of the Holy Roman Empire. As the architectural historian Eric Fernie has put it, Winchester is not

Remigius' castle-like west front of Lincoln is a report from the front line of Conquest politics

just a great church: it is a building with imperial pretensions.[40]

Today, Walkelin's building is low-slung as well as enormously long. But it once had a dramatic profile, sprouting up to ten towers, and a massive western block some 15 metres long, all of which have since gone.[41] Yet to walk into Winchester's transepts or crypt (illustrated p. 444) is to walk into England in 1079, raw in tooth and claw.

Outside, the architecture is relieved by little bits of ornamentation. On the inside, the building is almost painfully plain and massive. There was no paint on the walls[42] and the unmoulded arches had cushion capitals, like bulging muscles supporting great weights. This is as close as medieval architecture got to the vast, shadowy spaces of Piranesi or the brutalism of the 1970s.

Winchester has both fully-aisled transepts and a crypt, an expensive combination matched by no other English church. It is also a polyglot building, as if its creator had hoovered up the most impressive design ideas from all over Europe. The many-towered profile comes from the Holy Roman Empire, the square-ended chapels perhaps from Flanders and many of the dimensions from St Peter's, Rome. It also includes some motifs that were coined at Edward the Confessor's Westminster abbey.[43] It is as if Walkelin had sent his mason on a Grand Tour, asking him to return with an account of the biggest and best of everything; or, more accurately, to infuse an architecture that was first invented in Normandy with a collection of more grandiose ideas from the Holy Roman Empire.[44]

For all its conquering power, this church celebrates rather than rejects its Anglo-Saxon past. It had a very unusual east end, with a substantial chapel extending east of the main building, and a large west end; both partly recall those at the Old Minster. Saints' relics, the bones of kings and other treasures from the old church were all moved into the new building. Its architecture aggrandized its Anglo-Saxon liturgy, even as Lanfranc was consigning his to the dustbin.[45] Every Easter William ceremonially wore his crown in the church, just as Edgar and his successors had in the Old Minster.[46] The regime was no longer on the defensive.

Winchester marked an important constitutional step, too. Bishop Walkelin had wanted to eject the monks and make his cathedral secular, but Lanfranc stopped him. Lanfranc had already encouraged his close associate, Bishop Gundulf, to throw out the secular canons at his cathedral in Rochester, where, in 1080, work

Winchester's north transept is a work of crushing power; yet it aggrandised Anglo-Saxon traditions even as it asserted Norman dominance

began on a small monastic cathedral with distinctively Germanic features, such as a flat (as opposed to apsed) east wall.[47] Dunstan and Oswald's Anglo-Saxon monastic cathedrals were, it seems, not merely being defended; they were being expanded.

Over the next decade, a new cathedral rebuild was initiated on average every eighteen months. Soon St Paul's, London and York had joined Winchester and Canterbury in the list of key churches that were also building sites; by the 1090s perhaps ten English cathedrals were at some stage of complete reconstruction. At no point before or since have so many cathedrals been rebuilt simultaneously.[48]

At York, the rebuilding of the cathedral had a political dimension. The first Norman archbishop, Thomas of Bayeux, had challenged Lanfranc over the question of which archbishop had primacy. In 1071 he went to Rome with Lanfranc and Remigius in pursuit of a solution. The resulting decision basically went in Lanfranc's favour, but Thomas continued to claim that certain parts of the southern province and, theoretically, Scotland as well came under his jurisdiction. The issue of primacy was not completely resolved until the twelfth century.

Thomas used his cathedral to make a point.[49] The ancient church was demolished and, as if drawing attention to York's importance in Roman times, the new building placed precisely in the middle of the city's Roman fortress. The new church was second only to Winchester in size but had no aisles, apart from a narrow passageway that skirted the choir. The result was a colossal empty space ending in an enormous apse. This is a church that wants to be as different from other churches, especially Canterbury, as possible. Unlike previous buildings, the underlying agenda is not about the Conquest: it is about intra-church rivalry. Today, Thomas's building has almost entirely disappeared beneath later work that was also designed to underline York's importance.

The building of St Paul's, too, had a competitive edge. With the new palace at Westminster and, like York, a long memory of its significance as a Roman capital, London could expect a church that matched that of Winchester: it got one that was at least as big, but built without the same resources. Described in 1148 as 'incompletable', the bishop as 'of an unrestrained mind,'[50] St Paul's took almost a century to rebuild. Indeed no new church on such a gargantuan scale would ever be attempted again.[51]

It would be fascinating to know what the Anglo-Saxons made of all this. The most hallowed structures in the land knocked down; parts of thriving settlements flattened; new architecture on a scale not seen before. The rebuilding of the monastery of St Peter and St Paul founded by Augustine at Canterbury seemed to stop for a few years, expressing a stalemate of which we know nothing, at the very point when demolition of the seventh century part of the Saxon church was about to begin. At Worcester, in 1084, one of the last Anglo-Saxon bishops in England wept as he demolished his own cathedral, making a stinging attack on the vanity of such projects. Yet he went on to build the largest church in western England (illustrated p. 454), with a crypt as ambitious as any in the land. What marked out this church most were its decorative features, some apparently of Anglo-Saxon origin.[52] Its bishop, Wulfstan, trod a similarly fine line between old and new, supporting Church reform while doing much to preserve his native culture. His circular chapter-house (illustrated p. 455) and investment in chronicle-writing would become defining features of future great churches. Worcester also marks the coming of age of a microclimate of architectural experimentation in the West Country:[53] when St Peter's abbey at Gloucester, a cathedral since 1541, was begun five years later it subtly and experimentally trumped Wulfstan's church.

Walkelin of Winchester's brother Simeon became abbot of Ely in 1082, triggering the rebuilding of another major Anglo-Saxon monastic house. The result was a rather smaller, less severe version of Winchester. With its venerated saints and cathedral-like powers over its lands, the monastery at Ely was a cathedral in all but name: when a see was finally created here, in 1109, by carving a chunk out of the see of Lincoln, the scale of the building did not need to be altered. The abbey of Bury St Edmunds, on the other hand, an equally mighty institution, began its own Winchester-sized church after fighting off attempts to turn it into the cathedral for East Anglia: this was an architectural celebration of *not* being a cathedral.

It is hard not to detect a heady atmosphere of politico-architectural one-upmanship in all of this. It as if every self-respecting bishop felt obliged to rebuild and the need to watch the initiatives of his peers very carefully. In this sense, the bishops' chief concern was no longer their relationship to the Saxon masses: it was their relationship to each other. And as the bishops acted to defend their cathedral's interests, rather than simply to impose their authority, so bishop and community came to rely on each other. The Normans were 'going native'.

In the 1090s, the architecture of invasion moved into another new gear: decoration. As at Worcester and, to an extent, Winchester, a new spirit of innovation and reform drew on a growing ease with Anglo-Saxon culture, fuelled further by the fact that, across Europe, monasticism was at its high point of influence and wealth. All this was summed up in a building that is at once the climax of the muscular, powerful aesthetic coined at Winchester and the source of decorative ideas for centuries to come: Durham.

Durham was the most important town in the North East, that part of England that was barely England at all. With Scotland just up the road, it was a kind of buffer state, keeping its eyes on the kingdoms to north and south. It was also the inheritor of a proud Northumbrian heritage of its own and here it had a sacred trump card: the incorrupt body of monk-bishop St Cuthbert. Cuthbert was regarded as a kind of patron saint for the region. He had guarded and guided the community in their years of wandering after the Vikings drove them out of Lindisfarne. But, like all saints, he combined atavistic power with a certain flexibility: he could be endlessly reinvented. As could his church.

Durham had been the focus of a major rebellion in the 1070s. As late as 1079, its first Norman bishop had been murdered and his Anglo-Saxon attackers were able to melt into a fog, perhaps more human than meteorological, conjured up by St Cuthbert. The Norman monk, William of St-Calais, was appointed bishop in 1083, but it was another decade before he started rebuilding.

St-Calais was a trusted political operator, as often with the king as in the North East. In spite of this he found time to replace the secular community of his cathedral with a group of monks. But, instead of bussing in new blood from Normandy, he welcomed a group of Anglo-Saxons from Evesham in Worcestershire. Even his prior, Turgot, was Anglo-Saxon, and was granted an exceptional range of powers in church and diocese alike.[54] Together they sponsored a rebirth of the cult of Cuthbert, writing a new life of the saint and encouraging people to remember that Cuthbert had himself been a monk, that the reform was really a return to Durham's roots. Some 'facts' that supported their agenda were slipped in along the way. The myth of Cuthbert's misogyny, for example, appears to be an invention of this period, emphasizing the greater ritual purity of the monks over the married secular churchmen they replaced. Women were allowed to enter the cathedral only as far as a line across the nave, which is still there today.

St-Calais spent much of the late 1080s and 1090s embroiled in political machinations at Court. Yet by 1093 he had created a unique community, at once an exemplar of Church reform and authentically Anglo-Saxon; at once new and old, Norman and English. Now he announced that he would help fund a complete rebuild of the cathedral, itself less than a century old. But St-Calais was a busy man and his prior may well have been more engaged than he with the detail. The resulting structure, a great hymn to the power, sanctity and authority of its founder saint, draws on all local traditions: Anglo-Saxon in general,

Northumbrian in particular; north European in general, Norman in particular.

Its choir is a colossal model of a saint's shrine, supported by six elephantine columns incised with spirals (illustrated p. 308). These spiral columns made it an image of the shrine of St Peter at Rome, blown up to huge proportions. The choir was entirely vaulted in stone. This in itself was a relatively new technique, but at Durham projecting ribs, perhaps intended as miniature supporting arches, were added to follow the main lines of the vault. These created an impression of effortless strength and obscured some of the messier joins that were hard to avoid in such vaults. The effect was to make the space even more shrine-like. These may be the first rib-vaults in Europe (illustrated p. 314). Ultimately the technique gave rise to what is known as gothic architecture and dominated the roofing of churches for half a millennium.

Like those at Winchester, Durham's walls were not painted: the effect was meant to be as spare and muscular as it is now. Other Norman cathedrals, such as Worcester, were bright with white plaster which sometimes, as at York, was used on the outside as well as the inside, and picked out with thin red lines in imitation of finely-jointed masonry. All these decorative schemes complemented the impressive clarity of the architecture itself.

By the 1090s the problematic relocations of the 1070s were resolved and some further initiatives completed. Lichfield cathedral had moved to the secular church of St John's, Chester, but somewhere between 1087 and 1102 the seat of the see was moved again, to the wealthy abbey at Coventry. In 1090 there was a new relocation, from secular Wells to another rich monastery, Bath. Two further monastic cathedrals had thus been created. Rebuilding soon began at Bath as it did at Lichfield, whose exact relationship to the bishop of this period is unclear, but there is as yet no evidence for new work at Coventry: nothing earlier than the 1120s has been found in excavations there. Rebuilding also began at Chichester cathedral and at the important abbey of St Werburgh's, Chester, which became a cathedral in the sixteenth century. Architecturally, all these buildings would have been revolutionary just twenty years earlier: now they are virtually Norman-by-numbers.

This is true on a grand scale of the solution to the East Anglian problem, in which the bishops gave up trying to acquire Bury St Edmunds, abandoned Thetford, which was being used as a temporary base pending acquisition of Bury, and settled for the prosperous town of Norwich. Here an enormous new church was built. Begun in 1096, it was almost twice the size of Lanfranc's Canterbury, and the way it was created could have been taken from an aggressively interpreted textbook on building Norman cathedrals. Take one ambitious senior monk from Normandy (Herbert de Losinga, said to have bought his title to the see). Eject the married priests from an ancient Anglo-Saxon community and replace them with observant French Benedictine monks. Flatten the very heart of a thriving urban community to create a site for a castle and a cathedral.

This new monastic cathedral is stylistically almost indistinguishable from Ely, which was started in the 1080s, and the later abbey church at Peterborough, and each of these churches takes a step away from Winchester's barely-veiled violence and a step towards greater sophistication, lightness and elegance.[55] But Norwich's nave, fourteen bays long compared with Canterbury's eight, St Albans' eleven,[56] or Winchester's twelve, is a piece of one-upmanship. And in the spirit of Durham and its precursors the building performs clever architectural tricks, in this case the employment of references both to Anglo-Saxon architecture and to shrines, as well as the reuse of an ancient bishop's throne. These features reminded visitors that the see was ancient and its bishop's authority sacred, even if the cathedral was new.

By the late 1090s, all but two English cathedral cities contained a vast building site.[57] The exceptions, Exeter and Hereford, lay on the western fringes of the

Norwich is a mature work of Norman Romanesque. Thick spiral columns (right) mark out the nave altar

Norman realm; work on both had probably begun by 1115.[58] Much of England was being architecturally re-branded, with new castle-and-cathedral combinations dominating Lincoln, Durham, Norwich, Rochester and elsewhere. In spite of the impact of this architecture of invasion, the political urgency of the 1070s had faded. Indeed, non-cathedral great churches were beginning to be founded in some numbers by newly-enriched Norman aristocrats.

Indeed, the earliest Norman cathedrals were already old-fashioned. How could Lanfranc's Canterbury, meant to be mother church of England, hold a candle to Winchester, York, St Paul's, Durham, or even Norwich, each of which could contain it almost twice over? What had all that architectural harshness been for, anyway? The rank-and-file great churches now beginning to be built across England were being created to an architectural standard that had been set in the 1070s and 80s. But, back at Canterbury, the next stylistic leap forward was brewing.

By 1094 there was a new king, William II (more often known as William Rufus), and a new archbishop, Anselm. Men that had played no part in the invasion now ruled both Church and nation. And whereas William I and Lanfranc were perhaps the most effective archbishop-king double act in medieval history, the relationship between William II and Anselm was very different. 'Yesterday I hated him much, today I hate him more, and tomorrow and henceforth I shall hate him with even greater hatred' said the king of his archbishop.[59] Indeed, across Europe, the Church was asserting complete independence of lay dominion: Anselm and other church leaders were becoming both grand and belligerent.

Anselm was no ordinary archbishop. His theological writings were read throughout Europe and are still discussed today; after his death many claimed he was a saint. He had followed in Lanfranc's footsteps, from the mountains of what is now northern Italy to the Normandy abbey of Bec, where he had become abbot. Even his monks found his 'exaggerated . . . cultivation of those virtues which were more fitting for a monk of the cloister than for the primate of so great a nation'[60] a bit much. He was a man of principle, lacking in *realpolitik*: a third of his sixteen years in office were spent in exile or on extended trips to Rome, seeking papal support for his arguments with the king. But he did not lack intellectual bravery: he even essayed a philosophical proof of the existence of God.

A year after Anselm became archbishop, Pope Urban II proclaimed the first crusade. To help the king's brother Robert of Normandy go to Jerusalem, Anselm exchanged the next seven years' income from his rich manor of Petteham in Kent for £100 in cash from the monastic community. This was a very good deal for the monks, who spent the windfall on a grand new project.[61] The diminutive east end of Lanfranc's church, barely twenty years old, was demolished and a palatial new structure put in its place. Here were more traces of the future: by the Reformation, every one of the Norman cathedrals (apart from Norwich) had had its east end lavishly rebuilt, sometimes twice over.[62]

To call this building an east end is to undersell it. It is as long as Lanfranc's entire cathedral and, at 58 metres, three times longer than the east end it replaced. It was almost a second church. It outdid Winchester's east end in size, York's in innovative plan and Durham's in ornamentation. 'Nothing like it could be seen in England, either for the brilliance of its glass windows, the beauty of its marble pavements, or the many-coloured pictures which led the wandering eye to the very summit of the ceiling.'[63]

The monks found their new home, of which the crypt is the main survival (illustrated p. 275), 'delightful as a paradise of pleasure',[64] perhaps partly because it included some very high-profile burying of post-Conquest hatchets. Even before he became archbishop, Anselm had advised Lanfranc not to look down on the Anglo-Saxon saints. The new building had ample room for the display of their relics, with special chapels devoted to the shrines of such saints. And a great altar to the Virgin stood at the heart of the enormous crypt, replicating something of the grandeur of that which had stood in the western apse of the Anglo-Saxon cathedral.[65]

The rebuild was also a measure of the grandeur of contemporary monasticism, which was now at its peak as a centre of cultural and spiritual life. By moving the choir out of Lanfranc's nave into a church-within-a-church that even had its own set of transepts, an idea coined only recently at the great abbey at Cluny in France, the cathedral had been made into a celebration of monastic exclusiveness.[66]

Other decorative ideas, such as intersecting blank arcades, were translated from their Durham birthplace,[67] where they had been infused with masculine Anglo-Saxon energy, and transformed into something light-hearted, playful, Continental. These arcades dance round the exterior, while the extraordinary crypt had patterned columns whose decorations were carefully choreographed so as to climax in a display of spiral columns around the altar, as at Durham. All this was a potent reminder that Canterbury's special authority, which Anselm fought bitterly to protect, made it England's Rome. Lions and other beasts cavort on the capitals of these columns, their detail picked out in paint. These delicately carved motifs had jumped straight out of the exquisite manuscripts being produced in the monastery's newly revived scriptorium.[68]

The carvings in prior Ernulf's crypt at Canterbury (left) echo the motifs created in his scriptorium (right); they set a new standard for sophistication in carved decoration

Anselm's prior, Ernulf, was in charge of both the new east end and the new scriptorium.[69] He completed his work within the seven years in his budget and went on to build at Peterborough and Rochester. But his successor, Prior Conrad, spent over twenty years ornamenting the 'Glorious Choir',[70] and installed five bells in the central tower, bells so enormous that sixty-three men were needed to ring them.[71] He also commissioned elaborate pieces of liturgical clothing, such as a cope woven with gold thread and hung with 140 little silver bells.[72] The dedication of the east end in 1130 must have been a spectacular event.

The new east end of Canterbury stands at the end of an era of vaunting ambition among the cathedral builders. It looks forward rather than back, to an era of sophisticated decorative experiments and intellectual endeavours; an age in which bishops behaved like warlords as a triumphant monasticism fragmented beneath them.

———

It is hard to overstate the architectural achievement of the eleventh-century cathedral-builders. It surpasses even the contemporary wave of castle building, in that most of the eleventh-century castles were wooden structures. Nothing quite like it would be seen again. Every one of these rebuilds involved the complete obliteration of the previous church. Total demolition was a choice, based on a rejection of the previous building so complete that even its foundations were useless. By contrast, between 1130 and the Reformation only one rebuilding, that of Salisbury, would be so radical.[73] Just six complete end-to-end rebuilds were attempted over these centuries, almost all involving the incorporation of large parts of the previous church; the resulting cathedrals were between 125 and 155 metres long, only three-quarters the size of Winchester.[74]

Moreover, without the relocations of the eleventh century, places like Lincoln, Norwich and Chichester would today be market towns rather than cathedral cities, while the signature buildings that still dominate many English townscapes would be quite different in appearance. Some of these churches, of which Norwich, Durham and the slightly later abbey at Peterborough are the most complete, survive almost in their entirety. In other cases, such as Worcester and Canterbury, the church itself has been rebuilt (sometimes several times over) but still retains the basic footprint that was defined in the eleventh century. Lanfranc's audacious demolition of 1070 was a true 'year zero' for the cathedrals.

Perhaps the most flabbergasting aspect of this building programme is the sheer amount of wealth it must have involved. The Normans invested far more in England than in their ancestral estates on the other side of the Channel, which became a comparative architectural backwater.[75] The story about the wood demolished in three days by Bishop Walkelin so as to build Winchester cathedral, or the complaint that 1097 was a bad year because of the scale of forced labour on Westminster Hall, hint at the economic impact.[76] This achievement was institutional as much as architectural. As impressive as the architecture of Lincoln cathedral is the fact that a whole community was successfully moved over 100 miles, away from most of the lands that sustained it. The cathedral retained large estates in far-off south Oxfordshire but, thanks to large donations of land from the king and others, became rapidly wealthier as it built up a more convenient endowment nearer Lincoln. Without the wholesale transference of wealth from the Anglo-Saxon nobility to a much smaller and newly aggrandized Norman elite, the whole enterprise would surely have been impossible. By the 1080s, fewer than two hundred men, many bishops among them, owned half the land in England.

The cathedrals, then, were tied up with a seismic social shift. They were also monuments to the new feudalism. As landowners, even bishops owed the king military service. Men such as Remigius of Lincoln had gambled much on the invasion and been richly rewarded as a result; his castle-like west end is a very public statement that his new standing included his responsibility for twenty knights. At the other extreme, centres of resistance such as Ely and Peterborough were made to support a disproportionately high number of knights: at Ely there is even a story that they lived in the monastery, at a ratio of one knight for every monk.[77]

Yet there are also continuities with the past. The relocations continued a process that had begun before the Conquest, when bishops had started moving their sees to more urban sites. And only the cathedrals and most important monastic houses were rebuilt in the eleventh century. Most Anglo-Saxon minster churches survived this period; the process of dividing their lands into parishes continued either side of the Conquest.[78] Indeed the two most innovative buildings of the earlier years, St Albans and Winchester, were both at least partly responses to Edward the Confessor's Westminster abbey, which they both had cause to be institutionally threatened by.[79] And, in Europe as a whole, there were parallels for such mighty churches: the new regime had moved England into the architectural front rank, but on the other side of the Channel the cathedrals of Speyer and Mainz and the new abbey at Cluny stood alongside St Paul's and Winchester as the largest buildings of their age. All these buildings were in a mature Romanesque idiom. This way of building redefined architecture until the Reformation.

The invasion may have provided the spur for cathedral-building, but the triumph of monasticism across Europe, a much longer process, is its context. The monk-led reform at its heart started well before the Conquest, in the 990s. Of the cathedrals that were rebuilt on a gigantic scale, four, Winchester, Ely, Durham and Norwich, were monastic; only St Paul's and York were secular and these two were both responses to institutional challenges set at monastic Winchester and Canterbury. Of the smaller cathedrals all were secular apart from Rochester and Lanfranc's Canterbury. In other words, it was monasticism as much as the fact they were cathedrals that accounted for the huge size of some rebuilds. The support given to monasticism by monk-archbishops Lanfranc and Anselm was also an important factor. Lanfranc could have made the monastic cathedrals into a footnote of Anglo-Saxon history: instead, he defended Winchester, added Rochester to the list and supported the creation of Durham. After the foundation, from the late 1080s, of Coventry, Bath and Norwich, and the raising of Ely to cathedral status in 1109, by the 1130s half of England's cathedrals were monastic.[80] One result was that, a century later, several of the smaller secular cathedrals would require rebuilding as bishops' churches par excellence.

There were important organizational changes, too, which affected both secular and monastic cathedrals. At Lincoln and Old Sarum the latest models for the organization of secular cathedral chapters were imported from France, principally from the cathedrals of Rouen and Bayeux. Both these churches had passed over the opportunity to be staffed by monks;[81] both quickly began to develop secular chapters of exceptional size and to provide members of their community with support from separate prebends. These changes would prove vital to the funding of the great gothic cathedrals.[82]

And at Durham, York, Exeter and Wells and the archbishop of York's collegiate churches of Southwell and Beverley, the Normans rejected a potential 'third way' in which secular priests lived communally and to a rule, like monks. The communally-organized secular chapter at Durham went monastic: the others remained secular but became *less* communal as separate prebends were carved out for each member of chapter. At Wells, the communal buildings were deliberately demolished. The result was an emphatic cultural and constitutional contrast between the communal monastic and more individualistic secular communities. It also meant that, as secular cathedrals grew in size and complexity, they gradually became more and more unlike other kinds of secular church. By the late twelfth century, the only collegiate communities in England that remotely approached the secular cathedrals in size were those at Southwell and Crediton.[83] More typical was the contrast between Ripon and York, the former a local minster, the latter a metropolitan cathedral. In 1070, both had seven priests; the number at Ripon did not change, but the community at York grew to thirty-seven; by the late 1130s it had begun to employ vicars (see p. 180), thus freeing the canons to pursue careers in politics and administration.[84]

The Norman invasion had sparked off a forty-year burst of mind-boggling architectural energy and investment. At its artistic peak in the 1090s, a couple of buildings, notably Durham and the Canterbury crypt, achieved effects that can still stir the emotions in a way that is as deeply felt as it is indefinable. Yet both are ultimately statements of monastic exclusivity, spiritual purity, sophistication and power. This world was about to fragment.

TRANSFORMATION 1130−70

The men and women present at the dedication of Anselm's east end in 1130 lived in a world that had moved on from that of the late eleventh century. William Rufus died in 1100 in the New Forest, probably in a hunting accident although some said it was murder. He was buried beneath the new central tower at Winchester, which was so upset at being associated with a man who was no friend of the Church that in 1107 it collapsed and had to be rebuilt. This was the last royal burial at Winchester.[85] Anselm died two years later. Henry I and Queen Matilda, the new monarchs, were present at the dedication. So, too, was David I of Scotland, Matilda's brother, who was to be a minor player in the struggle for the throne that followed Henry's death, a struggle that would ultimately lead to civil war and the end of the dynasty established by William the Conqueror. In the process many English bishops, buoyed up by lavish living, became virtual warlords. Yet changes were round the corner that would lead to the next great wave of architectural transformation.

The architectural traces of this are, among the cathedrals, more subtle than dramatic. Many of the cathedral rebuilding projects that had begun in the late eleventh century were still under way; once the east end of a church was functioning, work proceeded more slowly. Most of these stuck doggedly to designs of the late eleventh century until the gothic revolution at the very end of the century forced them to change their language.[86]

The energy that had gone into the cathedrals was now making its mark elsewhere. Across England, abbeys, priories, nunneries and parish churches were founded or rebuilt in their hundreds, possibly their thousands. This was part of the religious and institutional revival, with monasticism at its heart, that had been gathering pace since the tenth century and which was described vividly as 'a white mantle of churches' crossing Europe.[87] It has been estimated that there were 50 religious houses and perhaps 1,000 monks and nuns in England in 1066. By 1216 there were some 13,000, in 700 houses of various orders. After this the expansion gradually levelled off. Not until the fifteenth century would the epicentre of architectural activity again be so far from the cathedrals themselves.[88]

At the same time, 'a new kind of monster' was abroad.[89] These warlord-bishops were apparently more concerned with dynastic politics than any profound religious calling. Such men, often interrelated, played a key role in the civil war that followed the death of Henry I in 1135. Stephen, Henry's nephew, initially seized the throne and reigned with his French queen Matilda. Henry's daughter and only surviving child, also Matilda, was the rival claimant and the waters were further muddied by her uncle, David I, who seized the moment to pursue claims to Northumberland.

Alexander the Magnificent, bishop of Lincoln 1123–48,

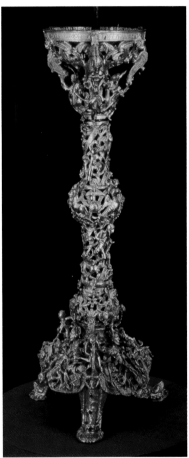

The Gloucester candlestick, now in the Victoria and Albert Museum, shows the riches of twelfth-century fittings

took his cathedral's martial architecture literally, using it as a base from which to assist the earls of Gloucester and Chester in the breaking of Stephen's siege of Lincoln castle in 1141, a key moment in the war. The lavish new doors and the memorable, strip-like frieze of carved scenes that Alexander added to Remigius's west end (illustrated pp. 50, 363) are almost all that remains of his post-siege reconstruction, which left the church 'more beautiful than before and second to none in the realm'.[90] Alexander's uncle, Roger of Salisbury, bishop of Old Sarum and chief justiciar of England, built castles at Devizes and Sherborne and other 'wondrous . . . buildings' across his see 'without any sparing of expense'. Poore, the first of several Sarum bishops with this surname,[91] began a luxurious and highly influential rebuild of Old Sarum, only to be stopped in his tracks by his public disgrace of 1139. King Stephen, fearing that the bishop was about to side with his rival, Queen Matilda, seized both Roger and all his castles.[92] 'Men said openly that Christ and his saints slept'[93] under Poore's warlike nephew Nigel, bishop of Ely and treasurer of the Royal Exchequer. The prior's door at Ely,[94] perhaps built under him, marks a new sophistication in the decoration of this abbey-turned-cathedral. Nigel and Alexander of Lincoln, it was said, 'loved display . . . disregarding the holy and simple manner of life that befits a Christian priest, they devoted themselves . . . utterly to warfare',[95] as they 'filled the land full of castles'.[96]

Matilda was one of the key figures in the dynastic wars of the mid-twelfth century

Towering over all of these men is Henry of Blois, bishop of Winchester (1129–71), abbot of Glastonbury and sometime papal representative. Another nephew of Henry I, he helped his brother Stephen obtain the throne and held the balance of power at key moments in the war. His Winchester Bible is one of the most breathtaking manuscripts of the entire medieval period (illustrated p. 446); his palace of Wolvesey castle included both pleasure gardens and a private zoo; he rebuilt several churches in his see, and founded the Hospital of St Cross at Winchester which, with its almost exhaustingly opulent church, still provides a home for the elderly and a dole of bread for passing pilgrims. His cathedral architecture includes, appropriately enough, two strong-rooms in which some of the treasures with which he showered Winchester could be securely stored and perhaps displayed.[97] The treasury's twelfth-century entrance arches have an ornate swagger that comes as something of a shock in the brutal simplicity of an eleventh-century transept.

Henry was an arbiter of taste. His liking for rich stone-carving and the black, shining marbles of Tournai helped to foment a fashion for the polished stones that were to become a signature motif of English architecture.[98] Never backwards in coming forwards, he ensured many of his gifts, such as the magnificent ring he gave to the abbot of St Albans, had his own name on them.[99] On a visit to Rome he purchased classical statues and had them shipped back to England to decorate his palace at Winchester.

By the time Henry of Blois became bishop, artists were drawing on motifs from far-flung civilizations, from ancient Rome, Byzantium and even the Islamic world. A taste for ornate carving emerged, for buildings thick with antique allusions, for richly-painted frescoes (illustrated pp. 273, 445) and exotic, coloured stones, for

Henry of Blois is depicted carrying a gift for one of his churches in these sumptuous enamelled plaques, made in Mosan, Belgium

the use of pointed as well as round arches. The bishops who sponsored this art often had vast estates in places such as Normandy and Anjou as well as in England and their sense of identity was similarly transnational. Men of the Church, they were part of an institution that spanned Europe.

Indeed the twelfth century was one of the most outward-looking eras in English history. British churchmen were at the forefront of the twelfth-century Renaissance, in which a huge range of non-Christian intellectual traditions, from ancient India, Persia, Greece and Rome, many of which had been preserved in Arabic writings, were rediscovered, not least as a result of the crusades.[100]

These were men such as Adelard, a native of Bath and one of the first people in Europe to see the value of Arabic philosophical texts; Robert of Lotharingia, the German bishop of Hereford, who adapted the astronomical works of ar-Zarqala, a scholar in Moslem Spain, so they were relevant to the latitude of the English Marches; and William fitz Herbert and Hubert Walter, archbishops of York and Canterbury respectively, who brought beautiful Islamic artefacts home from journeys to Sicily and Palestine.[101] Some of the earliest uses of Arabic numerals in Europe are in manuscripts in Hereford cathedral library. At Norwich, Herbert de Losinga encouraged his novices to read Ovid and the mid-century cloister, where these boys might have been educated, was covered in carvings from classical mythology.[102]

Such men were equally curious about Anglo-Saxon culture. The old English practice of writing chronicles had been kept alive at Worcester and played a key role in the revival of the form at the abbeys, later cathedrals, of Peterborough (where the church was being rebuilt after a traumatic late eleventh century), Gloucester and elsewhere.[103] Monk-historians, of whom William of Malmesbury was the most important, wrote lives of recently-deceased Anglo-Saxon bishops, such as Wulfstan of Worcester. There were 'discoveries' of 'old' English saints, among them Ithamar at Rochester and Amphibalus at St Albans, and *Lives* of more solid figures, such as Oswald of Worcester, were translated from Anglo-Saxon into Latin so that French-speaking monks could understand them. At Ely and Durham and St Frideswide's, Oxford, the monks hesitantly examined the Anglo-Saxon relics they had inherited, at once ashamed to be questioning their veracity and desperate to establish whether what tradition said was true. Etheldreda's sister Withburga was so upset at having her inviolability questioned that she smashed the windows of the church with lightning, showing 'by means of the terror of heaven that she was displeased at being so handled in public'. All were of course found to be 'flexible and beautiful' in their tombs.[104] And in

Oxford, as well as in Paris and Bologna, advanced schools were developing that were independent of any religious house at all.

Even as it reached its apogee of power and influence, monasticism was fragmenting. As the home of the most liturgically and architecturally magnificent version of the Benedictine life yet seen, the abbey at Cluny in France exceeded the most fevered dreams of the tenth-century bishops Dunstan, Oswald or Ethelwold. But Cluniac houses were entirely independent of their local bishop, answering only to Cluny itself.[105] The precedent had been set for the creation of new kinds of monastic organization.

For centuries monastic houses everywhere had based their regimes on the Rule, or guidelines for monastic living, written by the sixth-century monk St Benedict.

This Arabic casket from Sicily may have been brought to York by William fitz Herbert

Now half a dozen or more improved versions of Benedict's vision were developed. New orders were spawned. Among the most important of these were the Augustinians and the Cistercians. Enormously attractive to lay patrons, in other respects these two orders could not be more different, the one open and flexible, the other closed and puritanical.

An Augustinian community consisted of a group of priests living communally to a rule: just the kind of arrangement that had been rejected in the first decades after the Conquest. Many Anglo-Saxon minster churches were converted to Augustinian houses. Their members, known as canons regular, could, as priests, engage with the world by running hospitals or administering the sacraments, while still living the spiritually pure, communal lives of monks. Because they were priests, and unlike some other new orders, the Augustinians were by definition subject to their local bishop. It was a winning formula, and over fifty new Augustinian houses were founded in Henry I's reign alone;[106] they include the future cathedrals of Bristol, an offshoot of the intellectual, Paris-based Victorine Augustinians; Oxford, a former minster and key to the creation of a scholarly focus in the city; and Southwark, another reformed minster, standing on the south side of London Bridge. St Thomas's, the hospital that was associated with Southwark, survives to this day, although it now lies a little way upstream at Lambeth. In 1122–3 an Augustinian, William de Corbeil, became archbishop of Canterbury.

This high tide of Augustinian influence is marked by the creation of England's one-and-only Augustinian cathedral. North-west England was isolated and impoverished, far from the effective reach of bishops. In 1133, Henry I created a new see in the strategically vital town of Carlisle. The cathedral of the new see, which had to wait until the end of the century before it could even afford a permanent bishop, was to be a community of Augustinian canons; Carlisle was small compared to other English cathedrals, but it was still the largest church in the area and the biggest Augustinian church in the north. It was also the last major change to the landscape of English bishoprics until the Reformation, marking the end of an evolutionary process that had been under way since 597.[107]

There was nothing flexible about the Cistercians. The order was born at Cîteaux in France in 1098 and presented a striking challenge to the Church establishment. Originally intended as a back-to-basics reform movement within the Benedictine order, the Cistercians soon became an independent organization, setting up isolated monasteries from which they launched polemical and political attacks on the likes of the warlord-bishops. At York, a group of such reform-minded monks had walked out of St Mary's abbey after a dispute with the abbot and headed for an isolated valley where, in 1132, they founded Fountains abbey. Bernard of Clairvaux, the order's chief propagandist, railed against the excesses of twelfth-century architecture and urged Alexander of Lincoln 'not to regard the passing glory of the world',[108] while simply calling Henry of Blois 'the old whore of Winchester'.[109] As for William fitz Herbert, Bernard told the pope he was a 'man rotten from the soles of his feet to the crown of his head'.[110] In fact poor William was just an archbishop of York, by nature 'likeable, with a certain lightness of morals',[111] who happened to be in the wrong place at the wrong time.

The Cistercians of Fountains (and others) chose to pick a fight with William in an attempt to clean up the process of electing bishops. William had been selected in the 1140s as a compromise candidate in an election on which no one could agree. The events that unfolded as a result were a dummy run for those that would soon transform both English architecture and the English Church.[112]

William's struggle went as far as Rome where the new pope, himself a Cistercian, tried to have the abbot of Fountains made archbishop in his stead. William went to Rome twice in the mid-1140s to fight his corner, on one occasion going on to sunny Sicily to stay with the island's chancellor, who was a fellow Yorkshireman.

By 1154 William was free of many of his opponents and returned to York to a hero's welcome. So many people crowded onto the bridge over the Ouse to greet

The Cistercians espoused a back-to-the-land asceticism

him that it collapsed, but the archbishop made the sign of the cross and no one was hurt.[113] A couple of weeks later, while celebrating mass in the cathedral, William fitz Herbert suddenly became ill. He died on 8 June 1154, amid rumours that the Eucharistic wine had been poisoned.

A saint's cult later developed around Archbishop William. It is less clear what his story signified in the 1150s and 1160s.[114] But – given the events to come – the popular interest in his plight suggested by the Ouse bridge miracle and the sacrilegious nature of his apparent murder are both intriguing. Equally suggestive is the unsavoury story of the cult of St William of Norwich. In 1144 a young boy was found murdered and the local Jewish community blamed. Here the cult developed rapidly and dramatically; there were violent attacks on local Jews as well as miraculous healings. This was unequivocally a popular cult, led by the priests and people of Norwich, perhaps fuelled by a range of ethnic tensions in a city the Normans had done much to divide.[115]

Such outbreaks of cultic enthusiasm are new to our story. As far as we can tell, even the cults of comparatively recent figures like Anselm and Wulfstan were products of their respective monastic communities. Perhaps in the stories of the

St William of York, shown in a fifteenth-century window at the minster. The Ouse bridge miracle can be glimpsed below

two Williams we can discern the traces of a significantly broadened popular engagement with religion. Likewise the many new parish churches and other religious houses depended for their existence on the generosity of local knights and lords across the country, the same kinds of people who flocked to join the crusades.

The authorities must have reacted to such events in varying ways. At Norwich, the bishops initially kept the boy William at arm's length and Norwich's architecture was never to focus heavily on him. At York, on the other hand, a remarkable building campaign began.

Archbishop Roger of Pont l'Evêque's new east end and west front at York minster in the 1160s is, more than anything else, York's response to the challenge set by Anselm's new east end at Canterbury. But, like the story of Archbishop William, its story becomes intriguing when one bears future events in mind. This east end has almost completely disappeared, but we know it took the rich architecture of the age in a new direction, with a novel plan and an unprecedented use of rich decoration and polished stones. Its use of early gothic features such as the pointed arch was one in the eye for the Cistercians, whose Burgundian masons had brought a sober version of the nascent style with them. Now the same teams of masons were asked to work on a building that embodied all the architectural licentiousness built in the aftermath of the death of Archbishop fitz Herbert. Something of the flavour of what resulted can still be seen at Ripon, where Roger of Pont l'Evêque built a miniature version of the same architecture, partly as a setting for the shrine of St Wilfrid.[116] When, later in the century, gothic east ends were created at Canterbury and Lincoln that were palpably suffused with the power of new saints, it was to York's east end of the 1160s that they turned for inspiration.

These dramatic events, new religious movements, revived saint's cults, and the adoption of a new kind of architecture, were all writ large in the revival of cathedral building after 1170. In the meantime, the landscape in which bishops worked had literally been shifting around them. The new monastic orders were one dimension; another was the creation of parishes. In the 1000s secular religious communities, roughly comparable in size and influence, were everywhere and the authority of bishops was comparatively weak. By 1200 there was a huge gulf between the parish church, on the one hand, and the greater monasteries and cathedrals on the other. Between these two types of church stood countless new religious institutions, including hospitals and leper houses as well as smaller monasteries, many staffed by members of young and competing monastic orders. This was a situation with a powerful centrifugal tendency that could only be countered if the authority of bishops became more effective.

The cathedrals had to become uncontested centres of power in a varied, rapidly changing situation. They were supported by a papacy that wanted to advance the independence of the Church, an institution that was developing its own laws and taxes, answering only to God and the pope. As the ambitions of this Church Militant increased, episcopal power needed to develop a broader reach. The events that resulted were to shake the body politic to its core, if ultimately lead to a new kind of Church Triumphant. The next architectural revolution was brewing.

WHAT TO SEE

Invasion

The 1070s: the nave, tower and transepts of St Albans; the west front of Lincoln.

The 1080s: the crypt and transepts of Winchester; the crypt of Worcester.

The 1090s: the crypt of Canterbury and almost all of Durham and Norwich.

Transformation

Warlord bishops: Grand doorways added to Durham and Lincoln; Henry of Blois' Hospital of St Cross in Winchester.

New orders: the Augustinian chapter-house at Bristol and east end of Christ Church, Oxford. Of the great Cistercian houses, much of Fountains abbey is of this period. Of course neither this nor the other evocative Cistercian ruins are in any sense bishop's churches.

Chapter Three

TRIUMPH

MIRACLES 1170–1220

In 1170, Thomas Becket, archbishop of Canterbury, was murdered in his own church by knights who believed they were acting on the wishes of the king, Henry II. But the scandalous assassination itself was the least of the story. What mattered was the reaction to it: and the extraordinary architecture unleashed as a result.

Thomas Becket had been a contrary and intransigent personality in life: hardly an obvious candidate for saint-hood, except that he defended the independence of the Church and began to display an ascetic streak in his final years. Yet his transformation into a maker of miracles began almost immediately. Within forty-eight hours of his blood and brains being scattered on the cathedral floor, contact with them had cured a paralysed woman. Unlike England's existing major saints, Becket was not some hieratic emblem from a hazy past; he was here and now; he was *news*. Alone among post-Conquest saints, Becket became an all-pervasive presence in the cultural fabric. Soon miracles were taking place in unprecedented numbers.

The murder of Becket, from a fourteenth-century boss at Exeter cathedral

No other cult in this book developed so fast or spread so far. Like all truly popular movements it was unpredictable, powerful and fluid, awash with half-expressed and contradictory politics.[1] Within the Becket story one can detect the

Foliage of heaven? The fantasy genus known as stiff leaf; from an Early English capital in the thirteenth-century lady chapel at Bristol cathedral

The monks could barely control the flood of laymen seeking miraculous cures at Becket's tomb

traces of issues local to London and Kent as well as wider tensions within the Church and between Church and state. And behind it all lie powerful, if vaguely articulated popular opinions about where the best interests of ordinary people lay. At the same time, people rushed to join the third crusade, announced in 1189.[2] Something charismatic and dangerous, the first stirrings of which had been discernible earlier in the twelfth century, had awakened in popular religious culture. A new age of saints had begun.

Even churchmen might have reeled at this outpouring of religious enthusiasm. By 1174, though, the establishment had recovered its nerve. Becket was canonized; Henry II made a very public display of penance at Becket's tomb in Canterbury; a new archbishop was appointed after a long delay. Such acts drew the political sting from the cult even as they rendered it official.

But then Anselm's glorious choir, now forty years old, burnt down. This set the monks quite a challenge. They needed to match the magnificence of the structure they had lost. But they also had the opportunity to respond architecturally to the new cult. Unprecedented events deserved unprecedented architecture. Only one other building, the new east end at York, showed the way.

Canterbury's new east end exploited every architectural trick possible. Polished and coloured stones were used on an unprecedented scale. Shades of ivory and rose are everywhere in this edgy, experimental architecture, creating emblems in stone of the violent moment of martyrdom and the sacramental themes that flowed from it. The windows, vast for their date, place stained-glass images of the recent events alongside more traditional subjects. The new work was constructed

A single candle marks the site of Becket's shrine; around it stands the Trinity Chapel

above and inside the remains of Anselm's east end, large parts of which were still standing, as if recreating its much-loved predecessor. Yet the plan was literally inflated by the presence of the new saint. After 1180, in a dramatic change of mind, it ballooned to the east to create a palatial new setting for Becket's shrine, the Trinity Chapel. This was reached by a sequence of aisles and flights of steps, a bewildering experience for pilgrims, increasing the drama of arrival at the series of Becket-related shrines that were developing along the route (illustrated p. 277). At the heart of the chapel were planned a series of furnishings whose power and significance fed off each other like some spiritual combustion engine: the high altar, the throne of the archbishops, Becket's shrine itself.[3] And the entire structure was built, to quote the building's biographer, the Canterbury monk Gervase, in 'a different fashion from the old', based around the potential of the pointed arch.[4] Architectural paraffin was being poured on a spiritual and political conflagration.

We are used to gothic architecture. But in the 1170s there was not a building in Europe in which the round-headed arch was used to the exclusion of the pointed-headed one; while techniques that were fundamental to its impact, such as the rib vault, were themselves only a few decades old. Canterbury's new east end was as shockingly potent and modern as the saint himself.

Gothic had been invented in France,[5] where it was increasingly being used to create elegant buildings with strong vertical accents. Canterbury proposed something quite different. This is a world of emphatic horizontals, richly patterned and coloured. Just a century earlier, Lanfranc's Canterbury had given the bishops of England a green light to demolish and rebuild their cathedrals; Anselm's had licensed the use of richly-carved decoration. Now the post-Becket rebuilding encouraged adoption of an entirely new style, and its adaptation to the needs of a new age of saints. English gothic architecture was thus born in an atmosphere of spiritual and political urgency, and as a response to the challenge of the miraculous. Transitional, the term usually used to describe it, is too passive a name for a style that would, in a few decades, crystallize into Early English. It is 'early gothic', actively exploring and experimenting with the effects that could be stimulated by the engineering and aesthetic possibilities of the rib vault and the pointed arch.[6]

Meanwhile, everywhere in England, the guardians of existing cults looked to their laurels, at once excited by the new interest being shown in the saints and threatened by Becket's popularity. A number of churches attempted to breathe new life into old cults, from Oxford's local patron Frideswide to mighty Cuthbert at Durham. Elsewhere new saints appeared on the scene, some apparently manufactured by the Church authorities, others connected to outbreaks of popular fervour. The result was a wave of saint-inspired new architecture which included major building projects at Durham, Lincoln and Wells, and a colossal series of ambitious new east ends. Between 1170 and 1250, every cathedral, indeed almost every building in this book would have its east end rebuilt or extended.[7]

At Durham the monks produced a new *Life* of the venerable St Cuthbert, claiming he had cured people let down by visits to Becket's shrine; against the wishes of both the monks and, they believed, the saint himself, Bishop du Puiset made it possible for female pilgrims to visit the church by building the exquisite Galilee. Intended for the east end of the cathedral but eventually built at the west end, the Galilee's hall-like space is divided by four parallel arcades of breathtaking elegance and verve, a fitting setting for a range of features that might attract lay visitors: a new shrine to St Bede, a miniature version of the high altar accessible to women, and special masses for the Virgin Mary.

As if that were not enough, a new cult was fostered around Godric of Finchale, a local hermit and former merchant and pilgrim who died in 1170. After waiting two years for Godric to produce a miracle, the monks grew impatient. Complaining that Becket had started working miracles as soon as he had died, they decided to test the potential of the dead man by taking his metal coat to Kelso in southern Scotland, where it was applied to a sick child. The cure was immediate and Godric briefly became a northern Becket, with some two hundred more cures claimed to his credit over the next few years. In the same year as Godric started his spate of cures, Cuthbert also began to generate new miracles. Other new lives of the saints were written in these years too, several of them by the raconteur, writer and politician Gerald of Wales, though some of the characters tackled, such as William at Norwich, Remigius at Lincoln and Ethelbert at Hereford (see p. 347, 355, 374), were obscure, controversial, or lacked a strong cult.

Some of those who could not beat Becket, joined him: the monastic houses at Peterborough and Southwark, both on key roads leading towards Canterbury, both dedicated the hospitals at their gates to the new saint. Southwark had the advantage of being close to London Bridge, the scene of Becket's triumphant return to the capital after his exile. At Peterborough, on the main road south from northern England, one of Becket's biographers became abbot: he

Durham's elegant Galilee was partly a response to the new age of saints

stole some Becket relics from Canterbury and at about the same time seems to have ordered the monks to expand and complete the west end of their unfinished abbey in the gothic style. The Scots baker William of Perth, murdered near Rochester en route to Canterbury, was the ultimate homage to Becket's power. After contact with his corpse had healed a mad woman, his body was taken to Rochester and he became a cathedral saint. He is the only adult layman of the English Middle Ages to be so honoured.[8]

Only one building took Canterbury on its own terms and outflanked it, architecturally and spiritually. By the 1190s, Henry II had found a new spiritual right-hand man, filling something of the void left by the intemperate Thomas Becket. As part of his expiation for the murder, Henry had founded the first house of Carthusian monks in the country. To help build it he plucked a charismatic monk, Hugh of Avalon, from obscurity and relative seclusion in the foothills of the Alps and brought him to Witham in Somerset.[9] Hugh was to be responsible for the next attempt to build a cathedral based on the pointed arch. In 1186 he was installed in the moribund see of Lincoln, whose church had been battered in the civil wars of the mid century, shaken by an earthquake and left without an effective bishop for eighteen years.

But Hugh was no ordinary man (see p. 361), and these were no ordinary times. He became the king's spiritual adviser, capable of dramatic acts of *lèse-majesté* that only one with a holy reputation could get away with. In a diocese that had seen little of its bishops, and at a time when great churchmen were distant figures,

St Hugh, here shown in a modern setting in a painting by Robert Mason, had a reputation as a living saint

he travelled from village to village, blessing children, inspecting parishes, living plainly. In the febrile post-Becket atmosphere, his reputation spread like wildfire. One story recounts how he stopped to confirm a peasant who was too exhausted to walk to church; then slapped him for his laziness. And this was at a time when few monasteries bothered to ensure there was a priest in the parish churches for which they were responsible. Hugh was said to have been late for his first meeting with Richard I, who was to succeed Henry II, because he had found the unburied body of a pauper by the side of the road, and stopped to dispatch the man properly. Hugh also seemed to be overcome by a combination of religiosity and possessiveness when in the presence of holy relics. He is said to have added to his private relic collection by cutting a protruding sinew from the incorrupt arm of St Oswald at Peterborough and biting a chunk from the body of St Mary Magdalene.[10] When he died in 1200 his corpse was taken on a miracle-fuelled progress north from his London palace, on the site of what is now Lincoln's Inn, to his half-rebuilt cathedral. 'Here lies Hugh, model of bishops, flower of monks, friend of scholars, and hammer of kings', was inscribed on his tomb.[11]

Hugh had the common touch. In spite of his intense personal asceticism – he had conquered all sexual desire, with a little divine help – he saw nothing wrong with letting the laity indulge their senses if it helped bring them closer to God. He put his personal weight behind a project to rebuild the east end of Lincoln cathedral with great magnificence. If Canterbury was a church built as a result of the death of a holy man at the hands of the king, Lincoln would go one better. Here there would be a church built by a living holy man, a man who could rebuke kings in public and get away with it.

St Hugh's work at Lincoln is as mad and outrageous as its builder. Of his new east end, only the choir remains, its three bays and eastern transept stuck between the later Angel Choir and the main transept. But this piece of architecture, 30 metres long, is the most certifiable piece of large-scale architecture in any English cathedral and marked the beginning of an extraordinarily ambitious and influential complete rebuild. Hugh himself had assisted with laying some of the masonry of the east end. At the same time he had miraculously healed some of the cathedral's masons. The building itself was thus charged with the possibility that its creator was another Becket, this time holy in life rather than in death. A flood of donations, many of them tiny contributions from people who could

The restless detailing of St Hugh's choir, viewed across Lincoln's Angel Choir

barely afford to give, helped fund the project.

Lincoln is partly a homage to Canterbury and, before it, to the earlier east end at York: here are the pointed arches, the polished shafting, the inventive, disorientating plan. At Canterbury, in particular, continental ideas are given a very English twist by an interest in surprise over regularity, pattern over purity of form, horizontals over verticals. But, at Lincoln, it is as if Canterbury's eccentricities had received an electric shock. The decoration here is manic: not a surface is left unornamented and motifs change with almost obsessive restlessness. Painted openings that appear to be carved arches adjoin the real thing; wall arcades are allowed to crash into the corners. It is as if no one had thought through the implications of a tumult of decorative ideas. And up above, the 'crazy vaults of Lincoln' (illustrated p. 360) swing with drunken abandon from one side of the building to another. These vaults would prove to be Lincoln's most significant contribution to the future, suggesting for the first time that vaults could include ribs that were there purely as ornament.

Another project, begun before Lincoln, is as plain as St Hugh's east end was fancy. At Wells, Bishop Reginald fitz Jocelin had started, soon after 1174, to completely rebuild the former Anglo-Saxon cathedral. Unlike Lincoln, the design of this church was pointedly different from Canterbury, and with good reason. It was part of a remarkable movement that marked the turning of the tables on the century-old triumph of monasticism.

The college of priests at Wells had a chip on its shoulder. At the Norman Conquest they had been an exemplary institution. But the Normans had stripped Wells of its cathedral status, creating a new monastic cathedral in the Benedictine abbey at Bath. In the mid-twelfth century, the bishops rediscovered the value of their secular chapter at Wells, who supported their bid to win control of mighty Glastonbury abbey, the cuckoo-in-the-nest of the Somerset diocese. The resulting fracas, ultimately resolved in Rome, re-established Wells as a cathedral, albeit jointly with Bath. During this process a new church was built that was both obtusely defensive and a proud statement of its own episcopal aspirations.

The new 'wannabe-cathedral' at Wells survives as the nave and transepts of the current church. It is a strange and remarkable building (illustrated pp. 218, 433). On the one hand, it is breathtakingly modern: it has been called the first building anywhere to entirely dispense with the semicircular arch. Yet it rejects almost all of the signature features of Canterbury: there was no attempt at creating a saint's cult [12] and there are no shafts of polished stone or heady architectural effects. Its handsome, highly individual architecture was the setting for a veritable manifesto in stone of the community's past and future status as a cathedral. Tombs, chapels and fittings from the old Anglo-Saxon cathedral were remade and reused in an emphatic evocation of the church's historic identity.

The relationship of Wells with Bath was only one of the reasons for its stylistic contrariness. The other lay just six miles away. Glastonbury abbey had everything Wells did not: enormous age; one of the greatest gatherings of relics anywhere; and an ambitious new church, rebuilt by Henry of Blois. This building was filled with the very motifs, polished stone and arches carved with the romanesque zigzag ornament known as chevron, that Wells so conspicuously rejected.[13] Wells' architectural bid to be emphatically both a cathedral and *not* a monastery was successful. By the 1250s, it had neutered the independence of Glastonbury[14] and won not only formal parity but de facto superiority over its sister cathedral at Bath, a superiority expressed as much through architecture as through any explicit constitutional arrangement.[15]

Lichfield, too, had been upstaged by a new monastic cathedral after the Conquest; it too began to achieve equal status with its rival, Coventry, from the mid- to late twelfth century. During this process its east end was rebuilt at least twice before a century-long reconstruction of the entire church began. Lichfield's architecture displays a growing sense of confidence as work proceeds. As at Wells, its eventual superiority over Coventry was never formalized; but it was inevitable that bishops of joint sees would gravitate towards their secular cathedral, whose chapter could support them in their work. In the 1190s one bishop even tried to make Coventry itself secular, forcibly expelling his monks even as they resisted, laying 'violent hands upon him, spilling his blood before the high altar'. The monks returned a few years later.

These developments were part of a wider pattern. The bishops of Rochester also tried (and failed) to de-monk their cathedral after just a century as a monastic house; and, by 1189, even Canterbury's status as a cathedral was under threat. The Cistercian Archbishop Baldwin tried to move his seat to Hackington just outside the city, where he had plans for a new kind of secular arch-cathedral, with space for the king, all his suffragan bishops, and sixty to seventy canons. This new and striking statement of archiepiscopal power would have sidelined the ancient monastery, home of English Christianity. The monks fought back vociferously and Baldwin moved the planned location of the new cathedral to a site on the south side of the Thames near Westminster, given to him for the purpose by the bishop of Rochester. This church, which would have been Lambeth cathedral, would have finally fulfilled Gregory the Great's dream of centring the English

Church in London.[16] But Baldwin went away on a crusade and died in the Holy Land; instead Lambeth palace was created, providing the archbishop of Canterbury with a much-needed base near Westminster to this day.[17] Eventually, in 1201, Archbishop Hubert Walter promised never to threaten the monks in such a way again: to cement his commitment he built one of the largest great halls in England at his palace next to the cathedral. The monks rewarded him with a magnificent tomb and the new, but deliberately archaic-looking, throne of St Augustine, both of which still stand in Canterbury cathedral.

The alternative metropolitan cathedrals of Hackington-by-Canterbury and Lambeth-by-Westminster are among the great, unrealized building projects of the Middle Ages; they sit alongside Wells and Lichfield as emphatic statements of the interests of the secular Church. Yet by 1199 another complete secular cathedral rebuild was being mooted. The bishops of Old Sarum, to which Sherborne cathedral had been moved in the 1070s, were finding that their site was wildly impractical; it was decided to relocate the cathedral to nearby Salisbury.

The rebuilding of no fewer than five secular cathedrals was thus proceeding or being planned: Wells after 1174; Hackington/Lambeth from 1189; Lincoln from 1192; Salisbury from the late 1190s; Lichfield as work-in-progress. While the scale of this rebuilding does not compare with that of the years after the Conquest, it still means that about half the secular cathedrals were being rebuilt at once, and was the last time that several complete cathedral rebuilds would be carried out simultaneously.[18] Wells, the first of these, is especially significant as, unlike Lincoln, it was an emphatic rejection of the heady mysteries of monk-led architecture. Indeed the cool, rational, model episcopal style it proposes was eventually to be realized in the most elegant way at Salisbury.[19] But work there was delayed for twenty years because, in the 1200s, after the death of Richard I and the succession of his brother John, Church and king fell out even more dramatically than they had in the 1160s.

St Augustine's throne at Canterbury marked a new compact between the archbishop and his monks

King John outdid his father, Henry II, by fighting not just with his archbishop, but with the entire English Church. As a result, there was little new English cathedral architecture in the first decade of the thirteenth century. The only major initiatives were connected to the king. His favourite saint, Wulfstan of Worcester, was canonized in 1203. His right-hand man, Peter des Roches, bishop of Winchester, created a magnificent, if oddly hesitant, retrochoir at his cath-edral.[20] This early gothic structure may have been intended as the hall-like setting for the shrine of St Swithun, but the saint's shrine was never moved into it. Des Roches also rebuilt the priory of St Mary Overie at Southwark (which became a cathedral in 1905). Less ambitiously, some of the most sober of late eleventh-century cathedrals, such as Winchester, Norwich and Durham, were given a coat of plaster in the late twelfth or early thirteenth century and brightened with delicate and sometimes elaborate painted decoration. But there were no other major new projects. Instead, there was a general strike.

In 1205–6 the monks of Canterbury secretly elected a new archbishop, sending their candidate to Rome to be blessed before King John could intervene. This calculated demonstration of Church independence immediately sparked a dispute with the king. Eventually the pope, the energetic and reform-minded Innocent III, imposed his own candidate, Stephen Langton, a prominent English intellectual based in Paris, over the heads of both parties. But the king refused to recognize Langton and expelled the rebellious monks of Canterbury from their monastery. In response, in 1208 the pope laid an interdict upon the king, suspending all Church sacraments and public worship in his realm.

In response to the interdict, the cathedrals and all other churches closed their doors. No bells rang: at first mass was not said at all; later, only once a year and behind closed doors. The liturgy ceased for the first time in centuries. At Old Sarum, 'St' Osmund inconveniently cured a paralysed beggar right in the middle of this ritual strike and, caught between a rock and a hard place, the community rushed to the choir, where they performed the obligatory Te Deum in silence.[21] The archbishops of York and Canterbury (the latter followed by his monks) and the bishops of Bath and Wells, Lincoln, Rochester, Ely, Old Sarum and Hereford fled to France around 1209, accompanied by up-and-coming associates such as Richard Poore, dean of Old Sarum, and Elias of Dereham, an associate of Stephen Langton. Many of these men ended up in Paris where, in an atmosphere charged by events at home, they were exposed to the latest theological and artistic ideas.

Meanwhile the monks at Rochester took the opportunity to indulge in a ferocious bout of forgery aimed at undermining some of the rights of the absent bishop, Glanville, who wanted to get rid of them. The magnificently irascible east end there (illustrated p. 400), the setting for the shrine of William of Perth, is one of the period's most intriguing and hard-to-date buildings; yet work here petered out before it was completed. Indeed, in cathedrals across the country building was stopped in its tracks, causing stylistic jumps of about ten years to be discernible in many buildings.

When work at Canterbury stopped, much of its fittings and decoration were incomplete; Becket's shrine, for which the Trinity Chapel was designed, was still located at his tomb in the crypt. At Wells, carved details change subtly half-way down the nave: the masons simply reached a suitable stopping-point and then abandoned the building until their bishop returned. The planned relocation of Old Sarum to Salisbury was put on ice. Chichester had no bishop throughout the period of the interdict: the early gothic retrochoir was completed, but the planned vaulting of the entire church had to wait until Richard Poore of Old Sarum became bishop in 1215. At Lincoln the story is less clear, but there are early thirteenth-century changes of design between the east end and the transepts, where building work was continuing under the saintly Hugh of Avalon's successor Hugh of Wells, and between the transepts and the nave. Similar jumps include that at Hereford between the new retrochoir, which is early gothic, and the lady chapel, which is Early English; between the west front and the Galilee porch at Ely and, in churches that did not become cathedrals until after the Reformation, between the design of the west front and its beguilingly confused completion at Peterborough (illustrated p. 388) and between the nave and the west front at Ripon. At St Albans, the fact the monks were fined 1,100 marks by the king perhaps explains why an elaborate new west front was abandoned. It was not completed until the 1880s.[22]

A dramatic five years followed the lifting of the interdict in 1213. With his

Between the lavish Romanesque west front and the poised Early English Galilee porch at Ely lurk the years in which the Church went on strike

barons now plotting to oust him, King John needed to make peace with the Church. He capitulated, promising to pay the pope £12,000 in compensation, and an annual subsidy thereafter. As a result, England was for a number of years a feudal fief of the papacy.

Though vilified in life, King John was given a magnificent tomb at Worcester

It is perhaps no surprise then that the archbishop of Canterbury helped broker Magna Carta in 1215. In spite of this, Elias of Dereham and other cathedral churchmen preached that King John should be deposed and replaced by Prince Louis of France, who eventually arrived with an invasion force. The king fled, losing much of his treasury in the Wash;[23] the exhausted monarch died soon after; Louis of France withdrew. John's body was rushed to Worcester to be buried alongside his much-loved St Wulfstan; Peter des Roches, bishop of Winchester, was left to run the country while John's young son Henry was hastily crowned at Gloucester abbey (now the cathedral).

The English Church had gone from a Church militant suffused with miracles to a Church-in-exile. But the result of this five-year collective sulk, followed by another five years of chaos and recovery caused by the struggle between John and his barons, was the victory of the Church. The building sites left behind by Archbishop Stephen Langton and the brothers Jocelin (bishop of Wells) and Hugh of Wells (bishop of Lincoln)[24] each offered a contrasting and radical vision of the new architectural possibilities. Such men were to take cathedral building in a newly assertive direction on their return, replacing nervous exploration with a fixed and graceful assertiveness.

———

These churches must have looked as if they had been parachuted in from a parallel universe or, more specifically, from heaven. The stylistic ideas they embodied were astonishingly varied: the Canterbury east end, Wells transepts and Durham Galilee, for example, display strikingly different ideas about everything from capital design to the articulation of arches. Even so, among this feverish inventiveness, certain ideas were gradually becoming standard: long, thin 'lancet' windows arranged in simple patterns; a new type of carved foliage known as stiff leaf; and lavish use of shafts of polished stone. These were to be the building blocks of the Early English style; yet, as late as the 1220s, they still had the power to shock and excite those who saw them. St Hugh's biographer Hugh d'Avranches, for example, saw the dark gleam of the polished stones at Lincoln and described how, 'people's minds are in suspense as they wonder whether it is jasper or marble'.[25]

But perhaps the most remarkable result is the complete disappearance of the semicircular arch.[26] This had, after all, been the defining motif of most architecture since Roman times. Gothic, a unique and purposefully ravishing architectural language, would dominate architecture for the next three hundred years. And, although all the cathedrals were rebuilt after 1070 in a romanesque style, it is gothic that we associate with them. In England, it went hand-in-glove with the troubling birth of a new age of saints and the emergence in its wake of a new assertiveness among the bishops and their supporters in the secular Church.

In spite of the short-term victories of the monks at Canterbury, Rochester and Coventry, the tide of history was with the secular cathedrals. By 1250 secular Old Sarum had been relocated to Salisbury, where the new building was a cool-headed attempt at creating a model cathedral; secular Lichfield and Wells had achieved parity, and even dominance over monastic Coventry and Bath; and another archbishop of Canterbury had tried (but failed) to create an enormous new collegiate church at Maidstone (on which Elias de Dereham was to have worked).[27]

These developments were not intended to attack monasticism per se: secular bishops such as Peter des Roches and Richard Poore themselves founded monastic houses.[28] The aim was to glorify and expand the authority of bishops, and to ensure they had at their disposal the highly-skilled manpower they needed to fulfil their role. The bishops were developing administrative machines of ever-increasing effectiveness, not only within the Church but also on behalf of the king and the senior aristocracy. They needed educated men to support them. Such men were no use buried in a monastery: only in a secular cathedral, or failing that in a collegiate church whose patronage was in the bishop's pocket, could a bishop's own staff sit on chapter and work with him in the diocese.

The deep understanding of canon and civil law required of such men made it increasingly important that they had attended the advanced schools that were proliferating in Oxford and Paris, in which secular churchmen also played a key role.[29] Canterbury and the other cathedral priories were quickly becoming little more than important monastic houses that happened to have a bishop: it was the canons of the secular cathedrals who were at the political coalface. After 1184 no Benedictine was ever again archbishop of Canterbury; and only one monk of any order after the late thirteenth century.[30]

As administration developed, a series of institutions were invented which have long outlasted the drama of these years. The exchequer was a creation of the twelfth century: it still has its chancellor. Within the Church, canonization; the process of saint-making was institutionalized, ensuring bishops and popes had the authority to make or break cults. Among the schools of Oxford, Bologna and Paris, the idea of a university, in which groups of teachers accepted a certain amount of corporate control in return for recognition of their student's qualifications, emerged. At Oxford the schools were obliged to operate under a chancellor from 1214 and incorporated as a formal institution from 1231: Oxford university had been born; Cambridge followed soon after.

A pattern is discernible in many of these developments: febrile evolution in the late twelfth century, followed by a pregnant pause during the interdict and subsequent strife, leading to crystallization and a kind of corporate control in the 1220s and 30s. At Oxford, for example, St Frideswide was being co-opted as a saintly mascot for the city's scholars in the late twelfth century,[31] but it was in the earlier thirteenth century that the schools became an institution. Late twelfth-century canonizations such as those of Becket, one of the fastest in history, and Wulfstan, who reacted furiously from beyond the grave when uncanonically translated,[32] seemed designed to demonstrate the authority of that process, but in the crop of new cathedral saints created in 1220 and afterwards, that authority was unquestioned. And throughout this process, the secular cathedral chapters in England were completing their massive post-Conquest growth: Lincoln acquired its last new prebend in 1196, Wells in 1220. Such communities had grown from six

The universities and the gothic cathedrals emerged at the same time

or seven to several dozen members over the course of about a century.

Other, important features of medieval culture that became firmly established at this time would, like the gothic style, endure until the Reformation. One is the spread of celibacy among secular churchmen. Such men were almost always married in 1100, and their sons also often went into the Church (in 1090–1127, a quarter of the canons of St Paul's were married).[33] By 1200 it was taken for granted that they would be celibate. No longer could monks view secular churchmen with disgust, as if they were ritually impure. It is a remarkable fact that the victory of gothic happens just as many of those involved stop having a sex life.[34]

But the religious revival of the period involved ordinary people as well as churchmen. It played a role in the emerging idea of chivalry, a culture in which lay aristocrats could find in their worldly, martial activities some of the virtues of the religious life; and in a burgeoning cult to the ultimate saint, Jesus's mother Mary. The Church regarded chivalry with suspicion. Marian devotion, on the other hand, was encouraged. A daily mass in St Mary's honour, 'seeing as it is done in all the noble churches of England,'[35] was gradually introduced, a development that went hand-in-glove with the building of a suitably enriched lady chapel, often at the easternmost end of the building, as a setting for this mass.[36]

The twelfth-century renaissance likewise paid dividends for centuries to come. It was driven by an exceptional openness to other cultural traditions, even if the riches that resulted were as often gained by the sword as by the pen. The men behind it, monks and secular churchmen alike, had a level of direct contact with other traditions, be they Jewish, eastern Orthodox or Islamic, that would not be repeated until the age of exploration in the fifteenth and sixteenth centuries. Through it they discovered the learning and culture of the ancient world, and caught up with advances being made in other cultures. From Arabic numerals to Aristotle, the results are with us still.

Thus the gothic style germinated in a soil that contained a combination of nutrients. Many of these enabling factors were common to Europe as a whole but, in England, rather as happened at the time of the Norman Conquest, they were given a vital and politically-charged edge by specific circumstances. The scalping of an archbishop in the country's mother church by the king's men led to English gothic being born with miraculous blood on its hands. At Canterbury, Lincoln, Wells and elsewhere, the architecture is urgent enough for it to sometimes seem as if that blood is barely dry.

By the 1220s, it must have seemed to English churchmen that their time had come. A scandalous king had died, having capitulated to the demands of the Church. In his stead, England was ruled by a triumvirate dominated by the Church: Pandulf Verraccio, the pope's representative in England, Peter des Roches, bishop of Winchester, and the leading magnate Hubert de Burgh. The young king, Henry III, would himself grow up unusually pious.

After the fierce struggles and heady events of the late twelfth century, the English Church had held its breath for a decade. Now it was ready to exhale, self-confident and triumphant. One result was the creation of many quintessentially English landmarks: the city of Salisbury and its cathedral; the Wells west front; the great south transept of York minster, still impressive from the narrow streets around Minster Gates; the three great mouths of Peterborough abbey, gaping over the city's shopping centre. The dramatic story that starts with a religious general strike and ends with a religious king has left an enduring imprint.

Where building projects had been halted by the interdict, they were restarted with a new boldness and vigour. The interior of Wells cathedral had been searching and exploratory in tone, but the new west front was a trumpet blast; the decision to move the cathedral from Old Sarum was finally implemented, resulting in a poised and self-assured new cathedral at Salisbury. In other cases, the triumph is more a matter of style than of scale. Between the building of the nave and west front at Ripon, or the west front and Galilee at Ely, architecture that was searching for a voice suddenly finds it.

Salisbury's cool elegance: the essence of the 1220s

At the same time, something creative shuts down. The exploratory designs of later twelfth century are replaced by a language of motifs as ordered and defined as a papal edict, a language that was to evolve only slowly in the ensuing twenty to thirty years. This was the tightly-defined architectural canon of Early English, the key motifs of which: pointed arches, large, single light windows, shafts of polished stone and still-leaf capitals, were distilled from the inventive architecture of the later twelfth century.

The year 1220 was the turning point. The young Henry III, still only thirteen, was given a second coronation. This was a rather more orthodox affair than the first ceremony at Gloucester, when the queen had had to use her bracelet as a temporary crown. A month later, the fiftieth anniversary of Becket's murder was the occasion for a lavish event that marked a new harmony between Church and state. By this date the long-delayed fitting-out of Canterbury's east end had finally been completed. Now the saint's remains were translated to a grand new shrine, which stood in the heart of the palatial Trinity Chapel. Key figures at the translation included Archbishop Stephen Langton, Bishop Richard Poore of Salisbury[37] and the ambitious Elias of Dereham, all of whom were given the special privilege of viewing the dead man's body. The young king was also there. St Hugh of Lincoln was canonized in the same year; his shrine stood in the east end that he had built.

The two projects that stand out from this era, both of them in the West Country, are Salisbury cathedral and the west front at Wells. Salisbury was the initiative of the Paris-educated Richard Poore, scion of a family of churchmen. He triumphantly realised the frustrated relocation plans of the 1200s, rewrote his cathedral's constitution and codified its liturgy. He was also responsible for the new town that was laid out to the north of the cathedral close. Like others dating from this period, such as Portsmouth, Leeds and Chelmsford, the new settlement thrived and forms the core of the present city. He assembled a chapter of brilliant men that included a future saint. He even tried to get Old Sarum's first Norman bishop, Osmund, canonized. The influence of the renewed cathedral, it was said, shone 'like the sun in full orb, shedding her beams on every side so as to make up for the shortcomings of other churches'.

Poore's efforts on Osmund's behalf were unsuccessful, a setback that, in some ways, reflects the mindset of Poore and those like him. For Poore, saints' cults were of huge importance, but he saw them as only one element in the overall scheme of things. Architecturally, Salisbury is built for the performance of the liturgy rather than the glorification of a saint; its focus is on the high altar and the miracle of the Eucharist, a sacrament whose importance was emphasized by formalization of the doctrine of transubstantiation in 1215. In that sense, and in the balance and grace of its architecture, the cathedral is a polite riposte to the heady effects of the late twelfth century. Yet it also reflects the ideas of its intellectual patrons. Some of the dimensions of the cathedral at Old Sarum, for example, are invisibly coded into the new church, as if passing on the authority of the past. Detailed aspects of Poore's model constitution are also written into the cathedral's architecture. For example, fifteen altars are built into the church: precisely enough to ensure that the minimum required number of resident canons would each have somewhere to perform their obligatory daily mass.

Salisbury's design was gracious and ordered: its muted colour scheme is still visible in many parts of the building. Silver-grey carpets of grisaille fill windows with geometrical patterns; walls are painted to imitate ashlar; bursts of painted foliage or stone carving are restricted to specific locations. The decoration becomes richer, in controlled stages, as it comes closer to the high altar in the east end. Indeed the very restraint and forensic rationalism that pervades Salisbury can be read as the product of university-educated secular churchmen reacting against the heady indulgences of monk-influenced works, such as those at Canterbury and Lincoln; men whose interest is to support the authority of their bishop rather than to invoke miracles.

Intellectual restraint, though, was not a feature of the new project at Wells. Bishop Jocelin, a native of the city, discarded the rather defensive principles that had been followed in his rebuilt church since the 1170s. In about 1220, in a wave of episcopal enthusiasm fuelled by key victories over Glastonbury and Bath, he and his chapter leapt from we *ought* to be a cathedral to we *are* a cathedral by commissioning the Wells west front, with its tiers of stone statues. This is the largest single display of medieval sculpture in England. As a construction project requiring the creation of over 176 life-size figures, it must have employed a significant proportion of the men capable of such work.[38]

This facade was designed as a setting for spectacular events of ritual theatre. Its top register is carved with images of the very event, the bodily resurrection of the faithful, that the townspeople believed would one day occur in the layman's cemetery that stretched below the west front. And once or twice a year, at Palm Sunday and other festivals (see p. 96), the facade came alive. Passages hidden in its walls allowed choristers and trumpeters to secrete themselves behind and above the statues, making it seem as if the figures, that were painted to look as real as possible (illustrated pp. 418, 434), were singing and playing. Such events must have

The Wells west front is a great trumpet-blast of episcopal triumph

been spine-tingling. In the 1170s, with no in-house saint's cult and no chance of matching the saints of Glastonbury, Wells had tried instead to draw attention to its history. Now it was turning the liturgy itself into a spectacle, while looking out to the ordinary people of the see.

Wells remains a prodigy. The related screen-facades of secular Salisbury, Lichfield and Exeter are not on the same scale; the ambitious sculptural displays at Salisbury and Exeter were never completed (or not to their original plans);[39] comparable projects at Lincoln and York may also have been left unfinished. Yet almost every secular cathedral has some feature on its west front that can be interpreted as a setting for choristers and liturgical events. There are few close comparisons among the monastic cathedrals. Only Coventry acquired a screen façade, though an equally ambitious design was attempted at Peterborough abbey. These sculpted facades are the clearest embodiment of the outward-looking quality that was beginning to set the secular cathedrals apart architecturally.

The phrase public-spirited is too anachronistic to use of the churchmen of the 1220s. Yet a concern with impressing the laity can be detected in these buildings. The stained glass at Canterbury and the translation of Becket in 1220 seemed calculated to reach out to a wide public.[40] Archbishop de Gray, former chancellor of England, created a new saint in the shape of St William of York, who was canonized in 1227, and rebuilt the transepts at his cathedral at the same time, creating a striking new entrance for lay visitors (illustrated p. 465), one which steered pilgrims past his own tomb (and, he intended, those of his successors) to the tomb-shrine of St William in the nave. Perhaps the possibility that large numbers of people might want to witness a Palm Sunday procession, if it was theatrical enough, was one of the influences on the design of the west front at Wells. At Lincoln some of England's earliest rose windows face over the cathedral close on one side and look over the diocese on the other: they were quickly called the dean's eye and the bishop's eye, emblems of the cathedral's all-seeing authority.[41] The new west fronts at the churches of Ripon and Peterborough, both later cathedrals (illustrated pp. 388, 394), placed a new emphasis on the part of the building that was most visible from the town, just as the York south transept had done. At Ripon, as at York, the new work led directly to the site of a shrine, in this case of St Wilfrid; at St Albans, another future cathedral, the shrine of St Amphibalus was moved from the east end to a more accessible location in the nave.

Yet the greatest achievements of the era are focused on the secular cathedrals. Four, Lichfield, Lincoln, Salisbury and Wells, were in the process of being rebuilt. The constitutions of Lichfield, Exeter, York, Chichester and Salisbury were overhauled, as was that of monastic Worcester. Secular churchmen were canonized, among them Edmund Rich, the high-minded archbishop of Canterbury and former canon of Salisbury (1246), as well as St William of York. Secular Chichester was vaulted and extended; secular Hereford's lush lady chapel was completed; while the west front at Ripon sits alongside the east end at Southwell and the grand rebuilding of Beverley minster as projects supported by the archbishops of York and constructed in their three great secular sub-cathedrals. Only Beverley would never become a cathedral in its own right.

There were fewer grand projects at the monastic cathedrals – apart from three churches with important Anglo-Saxon saints. At Worcester, a refined east end was begun in 1224 as a suitable setting for the tomb of King John and the shrines of Saints Oswald and Wulfstan. At Ely, an extraordinarily lush east end, packed with poetic architectural evocations of St Etheldreda (illustrated p. 326), was built by monk-bishop Northwold. In the richly-burgeoning spirit of its architectural decoration,[42] it was a key link in the chain of design ideas that would lead, in the 1250s, to the Lincoln Angel Choir. At Durham, inspired by Richard Poore (who was bishop there after he left Salisbury), the sumptuous Chapel of the Nine Altars (1242) separated monks from laity while making a grand backdrop for the shrine of St Cuthbert. Elsewhere, monastic projects stumbled: the long-drawn out completion of the retrochoir at Winchester and the failed attempt to rebuild the east end at Norwich being the most extreme examples.

The defining moment of the era came in 1215, when Pope Innocent III, Parisian intellectual and friend of Archbishop Stephen Langton, had announced a plan to 'root out vices, foster virtues, correct errors, reform morals, stamp out heresies and strengthen the faith, laying discord to rest and establishing peace, curbing oppression and protecting liberty'.[43] Some 1,200 bishops and abbots from across the western Church descended on Rome for the Fourth Lateran Council: the corporate hug to end them all. Such was the excitement that the bishop of Amalfi was crushed to death in the crowds. Among those who attended were Richard Poore of Salisbury and Archbishop de Gray of York; the bishop of Carlisle and the abbot of Peterborough went too.

At the council, Innocent III issued a series of detailed recommendations. Many dealt with issues that had been the concern of Church reformers for centuries, such as liturgical correctness and clerical celibacy, setting the seal on the recent achievements in both areas. Other decrees were more radical. There are signs of concern with the welfare of the laity: the kind of thing that had made Hugh of Lincoln so exceptional was now becoming mainstream. The Fourth Lateran Council, for instance, laid down the minimum standards of knowledge that every priest should have, no matter how small his parish. These were not ambitious: it was thought he should be able to recite the Creed correctly, for example. The council also stated that lay people had a minimum obligation to confess their sins and receive communion once a year. These decrees are direct demonstrations of the extent to which the Church was beginning to assume some level of control over the lives of ordinary clergy and their flocks.

Leading bishops everywhere were making the first Church-wide effort to ensure that every parish had a priest. In England, Hugh of Wells, bishop of Lincoln; Richard of Wych, bishop of Chichester; Richard Poore, bishop of Salisbury and the bishops of Worcester and Ely put huge pressure on the monastic houses in their sees to ensure that they installed priests in the parishes from which they derived an income. At the same time, it became compulsory for the canons of the secular cathedrals to employ an in-house vicar to perform the liturgy on their behalf. The reformers were concerned to ensure these priests had some security of tenure and, in 1222, at the Council of Oxford, they were guaranteed a 'minimum wage' of five marks a year; soon they began to form informal sub-communities of their own within their cathedrals.[44] For the monasteries in particular, this principle of wider responsibility came as something of a challenge to institutions that had become used to the idea that prayer was their raison d'être and a sufficient justification for appropriating the income from large areas of land.

Men like Richard Poore issued pastoral guidance for their priests, advising them to remind mothers not to let their children play near water, and encouraging people to get married in churches rather than taverns. Too many men, Poore counselled, seduced simple girls with mock marriages, putting rings of plaited reeds on their hands and taking them to the nearest pub. The Church was finally extending its reach down to village level, partly because it could and partly because it had to, as the centrifugal events of the twelfth century had demonstrated. As late as 1381, English bishops were still issuing manuals for priests based on the Fourth Lateran Council.[45]

———

The developments of the 1220s are in many ways a continuation of those of the late twelfth century, but with an important difference. At the heart of the shift from an exploratory and febrile architecture to a more fixed and reasonable one lay the idea of authority, and thus of the power of bishops. These men were the focus of the Church's political authority and embodied the chains of ritual and ceremony that bound it together. They would have noticed signs of the changing times in Rome as well as in their own sees: it is around this time that the Vatican emerged as a separate state and the popes, finding that they too needed a larger bureaucracy to match their expanding administrative reach, started using secular cathedral chapters across Europe to fund posts in their new city-state.

This victory of episcopal power found its clearest expression in the great secular cathedral rebuilds of the era. Those at Lichfield, Lincoln, Salisbury and Wells were by the end of the century joined by equally grand projects at Exeter and York. As a result, six of the eight secular cathedrals became entirely gothic in style, while their monastic peers remained largely romanesque. It is no coincidence that for many people today these buildings remain the archetypal cathedrals, for they articulate a new vision of the great church. The great romanesque rebuilding of the late eleventh century had ultimately been an expression of a resurgent monasticism (given added emphasis by the politics of invasion), whereas the gothic one of the thirteenth century articulates the idea of the great church as spectacular centre of episcopal authority. In other words, the primary message of these churches is not that they are grand monastic houses that are also the seats of bishops; it is that they are *cathedrals*. Architecturally and institutionally, the age of gothic is also the age of triumphant episcopal power, of the great church as bishop's church.

It is no surprise that the secular cathedrals should most fully realize this vision.

In the post-Conquest rebuild they had rarely matched their monastic peers in size; most now seemed on the small side. More crucially, the interests of their chapters overlapped more fully with those of their bishops than at their monastic counterparts, making corporate support for a complete rebuild and artistic engagement with episcopal messages easier to achieve. This was, we know, critical at Salisbury and Exeter, to name but two.

The aura of corporate power that surrounds these works is reflected in the number of chapter-houses and bishop's palaces that were constructed. The bar had been raised in the 1200s when Archbishop Hubert Walter of Canterbury built a massive new hall at his palace, a hall rivalled only by that of the king at Westminster. Soon several other magnificent residences were under way, among them the palaces at York, Wells, Lincoln and Worcester. The first centralized chapter-house had appeared at monastic Worcester in the twelfth century, but this uniquely English and unfailingly spectacular building type was from then on, among the cathedrals at least, exclusively the preserve of the secular Church.[46] By 1250 work had begun on polygonal chapter-houses at Lincoln, Lichfield, Wells and Salisbury. An expensive dispute with Bath led to the construction of the chapter-house at Wells being abandoned for some years, but work started again on a magnificent scale in the 1280s. Yet more ambitious buildings followed at York, Southwell and Hereford. The exception that proves the rule is Exeter. Built hard on the heels of reforms that confirmed the chapter's unusually communal nature, the chapter-house was, exceptionally in this period, to a rectangular design that was more like the chapter-houses of monastic cathedrals in style.

These buildings embody corporate pride, but there is an element of hubris in the enormous cloisters that appeared at secular Wells, Exeter (both later rebuilt) and Salisbury in this period.[47] One of the cloister walks might have been used as a corridor to the chapter-house or bishop's palace, but the other three must have lain largely silent and been used just once or twice a year during key processions. This was in marked contrast to the situation in a monastery, where the cloister was central to the monks' daily life. Yet, by the end of the Middle Ages, secular Lincoln, St Paul's, Hereford, and Chichester had also equipped themselves with cloisters, leaving only Lichfield and York with the cloister-free arrangement that had once set the secular cathedrals apart from the monastic churches.

Another defining development of these years is the way in which the Church further institutionalized the new universities. During the thirteenth century, Cambridge emerged from a range of possible candidates as England's second university. These colleges introduced solid, well-funded institutions among the loose confederations of teachers that were the first universities; many survive to this day. Bishops played a key role in their development, founding three of the six new colleges created at Oxford and Cambridge in the thirteenth century.[48] For the next three centuries, the bishops of Winchester, Lincoln, Norwich and Ely in particular would invest hugely in the creation of these academic-cum-religious colleges. This pattern reflected their geographical proximity to the universities concerned. The bishop of Lincoln was invariably Oxford's chancellor, in spite of its position on the edge of the diocese.[49] Cambridge was almost in the centre of the diocese of Ely and here the chancellor was likewise usually the bishop of Ely. In other words, the universities had developed an umbilical relationship with the cathedrals. They were after all a subset of the secular Church.

But monasticism had not quite run out of steam. In the heat of the late twelfth and early thirteenth centuries was forged the last and most radical of the reformed monastic movements of the Middle Ages. These orders, the Franciscans, Dominicans and other smaller groups, are collectively known as the mendicants. They were to inspire devotion and hatred in equal measure among the Church establishment. Caught up in this story is the last great building campaign of these years, and one of the era's most compelling personalities.

But a different kind of institution had got there before them. At Oxford, Cambridge, and many other urban centres, communities of friars, also known as mendicants, were setting themselves up. This new kind of monk posed a radical, and to many very appealing, challenge. Only the Cistercians had been as genuine in their commitment to poverty but, unlike the Cistercians, the mendicants were profoundly engaged with the lay world. They moved from place to place, preaching and ministering to ordinary people. And they had as their leaders charismatic men of wide appeal: the Spaniard (and future saint) Dominic, founder of the Dominicans, who died in 1221, and the Italian (and future saint) Francis of Assisi, founder of the Franciscans, who died in 1226.

Pope Innocent III gave these orders his seal of approval not least because, even as the pattern of parishes was being fixed, the cities were outgrowing them. The mendicants could work in areas

Pope Innocent III gives the Franciscans his blessing: from Giotto's fresco in Assisi

where parishes were now too large for their growing populations; in other words in just those communities where such missionary activities seemed most important. But the cities were where the cathedrals were located and Innocent III had declared that the mendicant orders should operate free of episcopal control. For many bishops, they were nothing but a threat. Yet their expansion was rapid: England had nearly 150 houses by 1300.

The Dominicans had come to Canterbury in 1221 and Archbishop Stephen Langton saw no problem when, three years later, the Franciscans also arrived, wilfully penniless and asking nothing but the most basic food to sustain them. But in Hereford the bishop saw the Dominican house that was founded there in the 1250s as a threat to the cathedral's monopoly on the proceeds of burials in the city.[50] He strongly opposed the building of their new priory and raised further objections when, later, they wanted to expand it. In Worcester, for similar reasons, the cathedral's monks forcibly exhumed the body of a pauper from the Franciscan burial ground, and then had a fight with the mendicants over exactly where the unfortunate man should be laid to rest.[51] As late as 1311 the monks of Norwich complained that the friars were attacking the monastic way of life.[52] Partly to meet the mendicants on their own ground, there was a move to create monks who were competent and well-informed teachers, able to preach in the vernacular (though few did) and not be overshadowed by the skill and learning of the friars. To this end, Gloucester abbey (now the cathedral) belatedly set up the first monastic quasi-college at Oxford in 1277, a move that was soon supported by other Benedictine houses.

The mendicants are one of the most tantalizing 'noises off' in our story. Their urban churches, with hall-like naves where crowds of laymen could gather to listen to a preacher, have disappeared more completely than those of any other order. Every tendency towards plainness and spaciousness and a focus on lay congregations thereafter might or might not be indebted to them. The cathedrals responded by setting up outdoor preaching crosses and aggrandized settings for lay burial, such as the Carnary chapel at Norwich and the Pardon churchyard at St Paul's. And when a bishop was pro-mendicant, the combination of populism and power he embodied could quickly give him a saintly reputation. Richard of Wych of Chichester was one such, his perceived holiness helping to generate the funds for a wave of additions to Chichester cathedral, some built in his lifetime.

Robert Grosseteste of Lincoln was a more controversial pro-mendicant. This scholarly secular priest was one of the great thinkers of the Middle Ages, producing a host of philosophical and scientific works. He was probably the first chancellor of Oxford university. On becoming bishop of Lincoln, he maintained his academic interests, installing a company of Greek translators in his palace. He was deeply attracted to the mendicants, acting as lector to the young Franciscan community at Oxford and stopping just short of becoming a monk himself.

Robert started his time at Lincoln brilliantly, but soon became jaded by the politics and, as he saw it, corruption that went with such a role. When he attempted to carry out an inspection of the work of his own chapter, with the help of his mendicant-dominated inner circle, the canons tried to stop him. Grosseteste fell out very badly indeed with this urbane group of administrators. He took the dispute to Rome. But the more he saw of the Papal Curia, the more convinced he became that there was corruption at the very heart of the Church, that the venal world of preferments and legalisms that had evolved there was very far from the spiritual ideals of St Peter and the early Church. He told the Curia so, in a speech that made him *persona non grata* in Rome.

Hated by his own chapter, Grosseteste was hugely popular with the people of his diocese, for much the same reason as the mendicants: he was principled, lived an ascetic life and was visibly concerned with meeting the spiritual needs of ordinary people. He was often assisted by friars when touring the parishes and wrote an influential manual inspired by the Fourth Lateran Council for the use of parish priests.

By the time of his death in 1253, it must have already been clear that Grosseteste was another near-saint; rumours of miracles surrounded his tomb. Yet in spite of, or perhaps because of the fact that he embodied much of what was new and radical about the 1230s and 1240s, he stood no chance whatsoever of being canonized. The heady days of unpredictable saints like Becket and Hugh, or men of the people like Godric of Finchale and William of Perth, had gone. The new age of saints had entered its official phase, with cults sanctioned by canonization and comparatively anodyne figures, whose struggles focused on exemplary episcopal practice, celebrated. Archbishop and saint Edmund Rich (canonized 1246) and bishop-saint Richard of Wych of Chichester (canonized 1262), were good bishops, loyal to the Church. Just as Early English is at once a regularizing and a neutering of the early experiments with gothic, so the vital spark of the 1180s had been replaced by something more manufactured. Interesting figures like Grosseteste might have stood a chance fifty years earlier: by the 1250s, he was out on a limb.

Robert Grosseteste, intellectual and hammer of the pope, from one his writings

Grosseteste's arrival in Lincoln in the 1230s came just as one of the most lavish rebuildings of the entire Middle Ages was coming to an end. Following the completion of St Hugh's east end, and the subsequent rebuilding of the transepts, work had continued west until the entire church was rebuilt, leaving only Remigius's five great arches in the west front as a memorial to the cathedral's romanesque predecessor. The new nave that resulted built on the strengths and resolved the eccentricities of the previous designs. It may be the most straightforwardly beautiful interior of all the major English cathedrals, combining the balanced poise of Early English with a new richness and, as a result of a sobering up of Hugh's 'crazy vaults', including the first tierceron vault in the country. Before this date, all vaults simply had four ribs, in effect very narrow arches, which followed and projected from the main lines of the groined ceiling, thus appearing to support it. By adding extra ribs, a rich symmetrical palm-tree effect was created and the underlying form of the ceiling itself was obscured. These extra ribs were purely decorative. The future of architecture lay in just such a primacy of decoration over structural clarity.[53]

During the Grosseteste years, the rate of construction at Lincoln slowed. The central tower collapsed, it was said because the new building disliked the bishop, and was rebuilt.[54] Yet within two years of Grosseteste's death, and with the cathedral only newly complete, the canons knocked down half of St Hugh's sixty-year-old east end and rebuilt it on an even grander scale. The creation of the jaw-droppingly ostentatious Angel Choir from 1255 was, quite simply, unnecessary. But the community had found itself with a windfall of new and potential saints. As well as St Hugh, a cult of uncertain proportions hovered around Remigius, the

Lincoln's Angel Choir: one of the most lavish buildings in England

first Norman bishop, and, in the 1250s, he was joined by Little St Hugh, whose unofficial cult was in the same anti-Semitic mould as that of St William of Norwich. Now there was Robert Grosseteste as well. However unpopular the man had been in life, the prospect of a new saint could only be a 'good thing'. There were repeated attempts to have Grosseteste canonized until 1307.

The Angel Choir is as poetic and ravishing a piece of clerical extravagance as the Wells west front (illustrated p. 367). Like Wells, on which it built, it was an attempt to fuse theology, faith, theatre, liturgy, sculpture and architecture in one charged creation. Like the nave, it has a tierceron vault. Like Henry III's Westminster abbey, begun twelve years earlier, it uses another new technique, window tracery, an innovation from France that opened up a whole range of new decorative possibilities. Window tracery and the tierceron vault are the two key innovations from which later gothic architecture evolved.

There was a third element too which, although not entirely new, was now being explored with a new thoroughness. The Angel Choir's sculpture was laden with symbolic meaning; the structure itself was shaped like a saints' reliquary, only with the decoration on the inside. The most influential version of this idea, of architecture-as-fitting, church-as-shrine, had been the design in 1242 of the new Ste-Chapelle in Paris. But key elements of it were native to England: the Wells west front is a screen writ large[55] and, as far back as Durham, churches had imitated shrines. But now such ideas were driving a baroque approach to architecture that was far from the austere world of the mendicants or the classical clarity of the 1220s. The resulting buildings are crowd-pleasers, albeit ones that remind the viewer, whether he be pilgrim, churchman or angel, of the exclusivity and sacredness of Church power. In such ideas lay the seeds of a new style, Decorated gothic.

Lincoln is a joyous building, but perhaps an overblown one. The optimism of the 1220s was under strain. By the 1250s Henry III was turning out to be inflexible and at times dangerously wrong-headed. Robert Grosseteste, the last great figure of the new age of saints, had, with his Franciscan friends, publicly attacked the very foundations of the Church Triumphant. More change was afoot, though it would come gradually at first.

Pious Henry III was a great patron of architecture

There is something joyous about the architecture of Wells and Lincoln. It has none of the hell-fire and brimstone associated with later medieval religion. The Wells west front presents a bowdlerised vision of the end of the world, a place where everyone is saved and the scary demons of hell are passed over. Similarly, the angels in the Lincoln choir smile to themselves as if amused by some super-natural joke.[56]

These two great buildings are the product of a society that is basically at peace. England became gradually more prosperous throughout the thirteenth century, reaching a population peak around 1300 that was not to be equalled again until the seventeenth century. By then there were over six hundred towns in the country, perhaps twenty of which contained more than five thousand people. London, the capital, had a population of perhaps eighty thousand. Most of the population, though, lived in the country. The cathedrals managed their large estates carefully. They controlled large areas of farmland. Churchmen and aristocrats alike hunted game in extensive deer parks, such as the three that surrounded the archbishop of York's palace in bucolic Southwell. Carvings in the chapter-house here, built after 1288, depict in detail the plants and animals that sustained the church's wealth.

Dogs pull a rabbit from its burrow in the Southwell chapter-house

The crises of the later thirteenth century seem parochial compared to the epic struggles of previous years. There were inherent contradictions between the ultimate claims of the Church and those of kings, but they expressed themselves as periodic squabbles over the appointment of this or that bishop rather than all-out struggles for supremacy. At a practical level, both the episcopal bureaucracy and the royal administration worked well enough.

But the themes that would dominate the future were already in the air. In 1259 Henry III gave up all claims to the lands in France that had been lost in John's reign, making England the sole extent of the king's domain for the first time since the Conquest. Henry was a pious king with a passion for building. He gave free timber from the royal forests to many of the cathedrals. Some six hundred royal

Westminster Abbey, Henry III's great project, changed architecture forever

oaks alone were used to make the roofs, doors and choir-stalls at Salisbury, all of which survive.[57] Indeed, throughout his reign, Henry spent about 10 per cent of the state's annual income on architecture, three times more than his predecessor King John. It was perhaps something of a substitute for the political authority that was never quite in his grasp.[58] He rebuilt the Anglo-Saxon Westminster abbey, turning it into a mausoleum for the English kings, at the same time promoting the cult there of his predecessor Edward the Confessor. Between 1245 and 1272, he spent well over £40,000 on this lavish, regal church, roughly the equivalent of the state's entire annual income for two years.[59] For the first time, the most influential building in England was a work of a king rather than an archbishop.

The king's belief in his divine powers threw his limitations into high relief. His plan of 1258 to help the pope take Sicily was so misguided that the barons effectively took power from his hands, ultimately triggering a brief civil war in 1264 led by the controversial earl, Simon de Montfort. Simon was deeply loved by his supporters and his death triggered a cult at Evesham where, in 1265, Henry III's son, the future Edward I, defeated the rebels. Many blamed Henry's problems on his appointment of large numbers of Savoyard and other foreign advisers. In 1259 Londoners even entered St Paul's to murder two Roman clerks who were occupying a stall there on behalf of an Italian appointee.[60] This issue had striking architectural results at Hereford, where the Savoyard bishop, Peter d'Aigueblanche, placed twenty of his countrymen on the cathedral staff. This led to such intense local resentment that the Gascon dean was murdered at the high altar in 1252. Aigueblanche died in 1268, having built a new north transept as a setting for his tomb and for those of future bishops. To this day, the transept remains an achingly cosmopolitan imposition in an otherwise very local building. Hereford sometimes has a homespun feel: the exaggeratedly metropolitan language of its north transept comes as something of a shock (illustrated p. 350).

Seven years after Aigueblanche's death, Thomas de Cantilupe became bishop of Hereford. A man who had played a key role in the council that ruled England in the king's stead during the civil war, he was also the most interesting cathedral cult of the late thirteenth century. Cantilupe was more of a dutiful administrator than a holy man; he owed his cult more to Church in-fighting than to great issues of principle. He had a strong sense of propriety and of the behaviour appropriate to his lordly status. His archbishop, John Pecham, was a bitter enemy of the worldly and legalistic culture that churchmen such as Cantilupe inhabited and the two men fell out over the precise demarcation lines between bishop and arch-bishop. As a result, Pecham excommunicated Cantilupe. The bishop went to

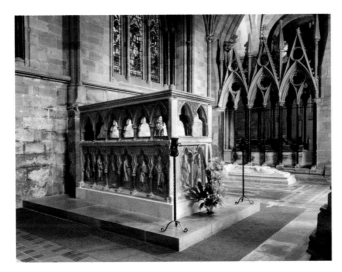

The tomb-shrine of Thomas Cantilupe at Hereford was designed to help stimulate rumours of sainthood. The tomb of the controversial Savoyard bishop d'Aigueblanche can be seen behind it

Rome to clear his name but died while he was there.

A dramatic cult subsequently arose around this unlikely saint, one that seems to have been at least partly manufactured by his supporters on the Hereford chapter. Cantilupe's remains were translated to a shrine-like tomb in Aigueblanche's new transept at Easter 1287, an act calculated to advertise the bishop's possible saintliness to a wider world; the first miracle conveniently occurred in the cathedral just days before the translation and, despite the fact that it was only loosely associated with Cantilupe, the news of this wondrous event was broadcast with great haste. The resulting cult was brief but intense: it was at once the last gasp of the new age of saints and a clear indication that something new was afoot.[61]

Henry III was not above xenophobia himself. He aggressively taxed the Jewish community, some of whom played a vital role as moneylenders to cathedral projects.[62] From 1253 he also attempted to restrict the Jews' freedom of movement, helping to create an environment in which anti-Semitic cults, such as that of Little St Hugh at Lincoln, could flourish.[63] As with the cult of St William of Norwich a century earlier, the Church at first seems to have held this saint at arm's length, accepting the child's body but not making a fuss of it. This changed when Edward I finally expelled all English Jews in 1290. It seems the king himself supported the creation of a new shrine to Little St Hugh at about this time: the setting for it, perhaps originally emblazoned with royal arms, still survives as part of Lincoln cathedral's choir screen. Certainly, the cult served Edward's political interests.

Yet it was internal tensions within the cathedrals that had the most dramatic architectural effect. Everywhere, secular chapters were struggling to exact concessions from their bishops, to create a situation where they were constitutionally almost as independent as a monastic community. The palatial secular chapter-houses of the thirteenth century can be remarkably brazen in the extent to which they set in stone the precise constitutional arrangements that resulted. Often these buildings were constructed soon after bishop and chapter had come to a major settlement. At Wells, no new canons were created after 1220, and the bishop granted the chapter ever-increasing independence from 1258. The chapter-house, dating from 1286, has one stone seat for every canon and barely differentiates that of the bishop from the others. At York, the archbishop himself was excluded from chapter, on the grounds that he did not possess a prebend, and here the chapter-house appears not to have a separate throne for the archbishop at all.

Just as indicative of corporate exclusivity and pride were the castellated close walls built at London, York and Exeter in 1285, at Wells in 1298 and at Lichfield from 1299. At Wells, Bishop Robert Burnell, chancellor of England, created one of the most sumptuous of surviving medieval bishop's palaces.

Meanwhile a quiet revolution had taken place in architectural style. Apart from the final completion of the lavish new nave at Lichfield, and the start of work on a grand new east end at St Paul's, both under way in the 1260s, there were few ambitious projects in progress. But the ornamental gauntlet laid down by Westminster abbey and the Lincoln Angel Choir was taken up by dozens of designers. The white heat of canonical authority, which had tempered the architecture of the early thirteenth century into a tightly defined set of motifs, had lost its immediacy. Everywhere, people started to play with new decorative possibilities. Designers of traceried windows initially only used a single 'canonical' pattern, based on the simple patterns formed when a single circular light is placed above two narrow ones, but in the course of the 1260s and 1270s started to find they could in fact create just about any design they wished. At the same time, those who carved in wood and stone began to depict foliage in a variety of styles apart from stiff leaf. As for roofs, just how many tierceron ribs per bay could a vault have, given that these ribs were purely decorative? In the Lincoln nave of the 1230s there are seven; in the Wells chapter-house of the 1280s there are nine; at Exeter, built a few years later, there are eleven.[64] The glorious palm-tree effect created by the spreading ribs on these roofs is among the most memorable, and distinctively English, of medieval architectural experiences.

Gradually, as tierceron vaults became standard, stiff leaf disappeared and window tracery diversified, a new style was born, one that had grown gradually out of the old and which emerged in the 1260s and 1270s: today, we call it Decorated. But this most restless of styles continued to spawn new motifs, around 1300 moving into a new phase. Now the sweeping tierceron ribs were broken up by adding short decorative ribs, called liernes, allowing an almost infinite variety of patterns to be created. At the same time the ogee arch appeared, its sinuous double curves perhaps the most emphatically ornamental arch shape imaginable. The new style replaced Early English only gradually. The Angel Choir (1250s), for example, is ornamented with stiff leaf and has simple tracery patterns. But the Wells chapter-house (1280s) is adorned with naturalistic and other types of foliage and has inventive window tracery that incorporates little ogee arches. In the Angel Choir, the architectural language is rooted in Early English, even if the thinking behind it has moved on. The Wells chapter-house is something new.[65]

In the last decades of the thirteenth century, two projects on the grandest scale were begun. One, the rebuilding of Exeter, was the last complete cathedral reconstruction, to a single design, to be successfully completed in the Middle Ages.[66] Starting in the 1270s and gradually gathering momentum, the rebuilding of Exeter became as sustained and focused a campaign as the rebuilding of Salisbury and Wells had been, or of the great Norman cathedrals before them, even though Exeter's Norman towers were left proudly intact. The other project of these years, the rebuilding of the nave at York from 1291, obliterated all traces of pre-gothic architecture in the minster. Unlike Exeter, this project extended for some two centuries: rebuilding of the nave (illustrated p. 328), which proceeded rather slowly, led to the creation of a new west front and ultimately to the replacement of Pont l'Evêque's east end of the late twelfth century and all the church's towers, a process only completed in 1475.

Archbishop le Romeyn's rebuilding of York's ancient nave (illustrated p. 467), barely touched since the late eleventh century, is the most prescient of these projects. The York nave, like most of the cathedral gazes imperiously and pointedly over the southern province and towards the Continent, taking many of its ideas direct from France and Germany. The icy beauty of the structure that resulted is what strikes us today, but originally it was a visual feast, replete with messages. The emphasis on rebuilding a nave rather than an east end or a west front was novel and would return in later centuries. Here, for the first time in a cathedral, the lay community erupts into the heart of the church. But this is not a populist building: it is a lordly one. In a development of an idea that was first coined at Westminster abbey, the minster's arcades and stained-glass windows are decorated with images of dozens of heraldic shields, bringing the noble northern families figuratively within the church. Even more remarkably, lifelike images of knights and other civilians stand in the middle of each bay of the triforium. The windows of the aisles filled up with rich stained glass, almost all sponsored by senior local churchmen or aristocrats, and occasionally by some of the more privileged local merchants and craftsmen. To enter the York nave in the early fourteenth century would have been to be surrounded by a chivalrous and aristocratic company of knights. The nave evoked the powers of the lordly community as vividly as the chapter-houses and choirs reflect the authority of their peers in the Church.

We cannot be sure that this scheme was unique, as no other complete decorative programme for a cathedral nave survives.[67] But it does suggest that the nave could be used as a powerful emblem of a lay congregation, and that the once-controversial culture of chivalry could be celebrated in one of the most important churches in the land. The nave also reflects the northern nobility's pride in their provincial church. Even as the nave filled with stained glass, these same families would be deeply involved in a bloody war that would sap the strength from the English monarchy, a war during which York would temporarily be capital of England and the minster's exquisite new chapter-house the meeting place of Parliament.

In retrospect, there were other portents of what was to come. In 1272, thirteen people died in a violent rebellion in Norwich. We are told the 'whole cathedral' was burnt down, but this is medieval propaganda from the cathedral authorities that means 'damage to gatehouse, spire, chapter-house, some other conventual buildings and fittings'. Once the riots had been quelled, the city was forced to hand over 3,000 marks in reparations to the cathedral priory. These were spent on a series of reconstructions between 1270 and the mid-fourteenth century that gradually became almost aggressively defensive, as if anticipating further trouble. There was unrest elsewhere as well. In 1264 the citizens of Winchester set fire to the gate of the priory, part of the church and some houses, while in 1283 the precentor of Exeter was murdered in the close by people from the town,[68] leading the authorities to wall the enclosure shortly afterwards.

But perhaps the most direct reflection of the changing times is the eighty years it took to rebuild the east end of St Werburgh's abbey, Chester, although it was not an especially big project. One reason for this drawn-out campaign, which involved no fewer than five changes of design, was that Edward I kept taking masons away from the project to build his Welsh castles, part of his concerted campaign to conquer the principality. England was at war on a scale unmatched

Norwich's Ethelbert gate was a pointed reminder to the citizens that the cathedral community could be fierce if attacked

since the Conquest, and Chester was the strategic bridgehead into Gwynedd. In the late thirteenth century, more was being spent on royal castles, some £75,000 in twenty-four years, than on cathedrals.[69] From now on war, riot and unrest would become common. The next, and perhaps most remarkable, historical turning-point was brewing.

WHAT TO SEE

Miracles

The new age of saints: the east end of Canterbury cathedral; the transepts and nave of Wells; St Hugh's choir at Lincoln; the Galilee at Durham.

The interdict: perhaps most palpably embodied in the (not firmly dated) mixed-up west front at Peterborough, begun to one design and completed to another.

Triumph

Almost every building in this book contains high-quality work of this period. Highlights include Salisbury; the west front of Wells; the east ends at Ely and Worcester and the nave and Angel Choir at Lincoln.

Prosperity

The nave at Lichfield; the chapter-house and nave at York minster; the chapter-houses at Wells, York and Southwell.

Chapter Four

CHANGE

In the early decades of the fourteenth century, cathedral architecture developed an almost feverish variety and intensity. Extraordinary artistic achievements took place in an atmosphere of deepening political crisis, especially surrounding Edward II, troubles that darkened into a long decade of war, famine and economic catastrophe.

In retrospect, Walter Langton, bishop of Coventry and Lichfield, might have seen the problems coming. He had been Edward I's treasurer and greatest confidant, but he was no friend of the king's son, the future Edward II, who seemed to him over-reliant on favourites. Langton's years at Lichfield cathedral were marked with lavish building, including a sumptuous new shrine to St Chad, a wall around the close, and a bishop's palace that imitated Caernarfon castle. The palace was decorated with paintings showing the exploits of Edward I;[1] Langton would go on to build a lady chapel in his cathedral that, like the other great buildings of the ensuing decades, was in thrall to another achievement of Edward I: the exquisite private chapel of St Stephen at Westminster palace. Here, the walls were also filled with glass, and the stonework was enriched in a playful, witty spirit; the Decorated style at its most sophisticated.

But, in the early years of the fourteenth century, Edward I's invasion of Scotland began to go awry and his reputation suffered. Work on St Stephen's chapel was stopped and its masons dispersed. And Walter Langton acquired

One of the exquisite leaves in the Decorated chapter-house at Southwell, built in the 1290s

influential enemies at court. The king died in 1307, on his way north. Langton was arrested as he was going to London to arrange the royal funeral and his estates were confiscated. Much of his income went into the pockets of Edward II's favourite, Piers Gaveston. Work at Lichfield ceased.

Edward II's relationship with Gaveston eventually triggered a baronial revolt and led to Gaveston's execution in 1312.[2] Soon afterwards Langton, whose expertise and experience were much needed, was rehabilitated and work restarted at his cathedral. The church, where building had been under way fitfully for over a century, was completed with the creation of its three distinctive spires; they must have made the castle-like complex look like a vision of Avalon. And at the east end of the church Langton began his new lady chapel, as a spectacular backdrop to St Chad's shrine. The chapel is a cage of glass and stone that rises the full height of the building, shimmering in the distance as one enters the church (illustrated p. 358). Such eye-catching pieces of architectural panache, created by men caught up in tumultuous political events, were the shape of things to come.

Over the next decade, the political situation deteriorated. Langton went in and out of political favour. Edward took up with new favourites, such as Hugh Despencer, and began to lose the war against the Scots. The English were slaughtered at Bannockburn in 1314 and soon after the Scots invaded northern England. Over the next eight years they were to destroy both the palace of the bishops of Carlisle and the fittings in the east end of Ripon minster. Soon York itself, Edward's base, was under threat. Archbishop Melton, creator of the Heart of Yorkshire west window at York minster, was defeated in battle. Warlord-bishops, who put more effort into fortifying their palaces than enriching their cathedrals, were appointed in the border sees of Durham and Carlisle.

Langton died in late 1321, leaving £604 for the completion of his lady chapel. Edward II promptly pocketed the legacy, though he had little time to spend it: the country was sliding into civil war. It was to be several decades before Langton's lady chapel was joined properly onto the rest of his church.

In 1322, Edward II defeated the barons who were opposing him and executed their leader, Thomas of Lancaster. The dead earl immediately became the subject of a saint's cult: the king ordered an image of him that had been put up in St Paul's cathedral to be taken down. For the next four years, during which even Edward's wife deserted him, king and barons fought over much of southern England. Edward II was eventually captured and imprisoned in Berkeley castle, Gloucestershire, where he died, almost certainly murdered, in 1326. He was given a grand burial at St Peter's abbey, Gloucester (illustrated p. 338).[3] He was the first English king to be deposed and murdered by his own aristocracy. A tear had been made in the very fabric of feudal society.

Political violence generally increased in these years. The bishop of Exeter, a supporter of the king, was murdered in the same year as Edward II. There were crises at Canterbury in 1327, where the burgesses dug ditches around their cathedral, stopping all pilgrim traffic;[4] at St Frideswide's, Oxford, which was besieged by people from the town in 1336;[5] and at Carlisle in 1345, where riots broke out and soldiers garrisoned there killed a man in the cathedral close.[6]

Economic and other pressures fuelled unrest. The country was overpopulated, its inflexible agricultural system unable to keep up with the demands being placed upon it. Every year between 1316 and 1322 brought either a disastrous harvest or an epidemic of animal diseases, causing widespread famine. By 1320 prices were higher than at any other time before the Reformation, but wages had not increased. In fact, during the ensuing decade they actually fell, in the case of stonemasons from 4s 5d to 3s 4d a day, while the top layer of society became even richer as their labour costs decreased in relation to prices in general.[7]

There was a brief, intense building boom, orchestrated by a series of bishops whose standing with Edward II shot up and down as rapidly as the king's own political fortunes. The result was the 'long 1320s', the era from the first famine

Famine and war were endemic in the early fourteenth century; from a fifteenth-century Netherlandish chronicle of England

of 1316 to the final takeover of Edward III in the early 1330s. This was arguably the most artistically brilliant 'decade' in English architectural history.

The extraordinary achievements of these years include the fittings in the choir at Exeter, commissioned by Bishop Stapeldon after 1316. Still the most breathtaking series of cathedral fittings in England, they are dominated by a bishop's throne (illustrated p. 333) that is almost as high as the church itself and originally included an equally enormous reredos that is now lost. Exeter brilliantly sidestepped its lack of a saint's cult by turning the entire cathedral into a kind of shrine to its own liturgy and, by extension, to the authority of its bishops. Stapeldon's story was one of the more dramatic of the period. As chancellor, and one of Edward II's most loyal servants, in 1326 he was recognized in London by a mob opposed to the king and decapitated with a bread-knife.

Around the same time, Bishop Droxford of Bath and Wells, Keeper of the Privy Seal, and his dean began rebuilding the east end at Wells, using the same mastermasons, Thomas of Witney and, later, William Joy, who built much of Exeter. Witney's lady chapel is the highlight of the new east end. It is shaped like a stretched octagon and approached through a sequence of spaces of such subtle complexity that entering them can be compared to walking through some exquisitely complex work of polyphonic music.[8] But the lady chapel has a secret: a

Exeter's west front is one of the finest displays of Decorated sculpture anywhere

hexagonal space at its entrance that was intended as the setting for the shrine of Bishop March, an unlikely potential saint who had been a casualty of the last years of Edward I. Droxford, who had himself fallen out with Edward II, pushed unsuccessfully for March's canonization from 1324 until his own death in 1329.

Meanwhile, in East Anglia, the bishops of Norwich and Ely had become political rivals. Both had accompanied Edward II on key missions to Paris and Avignon. Bishop Hotham of Ely became chancellor in 1317, only to be blamed by the king for his losses in Scotland; he was replaced as chancellor by the monk-bishop John Salmon of Norwich.

From around 1316 Salmon and his monks set about rebuilding parts of Norwich cathedral that had been damaged in the riots of 1272. Their designs show a remarkable concern with the events of forty years earlier. The Ethelbert gate's defensive intent is only thinly

The womb-like world of the Wells retrochoir and lady chapel

disguised (illustrated p. 119). The Carnary chapel was part of a bid to attract pious lay people back to the cathedral. But the monks also began to rebuild their cloister, where works like the Prior's Door, their private entrance to the cathedral, were as sumptuous as a piece of metalwork.

But this work at Norwich was eclipsed by the glorious architecture produced at Ely, where Bishop Hotham worked closely with his prior and sacrist (illustrated pp. 316, 322). In 1321 they began to build yet another lady chapel, a square stone box whose walls are covered so thickly with intersecting curves and carved decoration that they can seem to flicker. Even today the chapel seems half-alive; when built, it must have felt more like a hothouse than a work of architecture.[9] Just a year after work began, the cathedral's ancient central tower collapsed. Barely missing a beat, Hotham and his monks started on a replacement that is probably England's greatest architectural *coup de théâtre*: an enormous octagonal gothic dome, the widest vaulted space in England before Wren's St Paul's. Above this structure, known as the Octagon, rises a gravity-defying lantern. Hotham built a choir next to the Octagon that would double up as his mausoleum, perhaps employing William Ramsey, an up-and-coming mason who had worked on the cloister at Norwich, on some of the work. Yet, somehow, he and his monks also

The Prior's Door at Norwich was brilliantly carved and painted

found the resources to rebuild much of their convent, including such sumptuous gems as the private chapel of prior John Crauden.

The works of Hotham at monastic Ely and Droxford at secular Wells have much in common. The two bishops were both senior figures who had retired in disgrace and at both communities other key men, especially the sacrist at Ely and the dean at Wells, played an unusually engaged and influential role in the design of new work.[10] Perhaps most strikingly, these buildings are laden with architectural metaphor: both contain profound and poetic explorations of the ideas evoked by the Virgin Mary. This architecture-for-troubled-times, it seems, is directing its attention on the unique intercessionary powers of the Church and its saints while also ravishing the onlooker with unparalleled aesthetic effects.

Indeed, there was a brief return to the new age of saints at this period. Only now the cathedral cults were unofficial, and had a virulent edge focused on royal politics. Hidden factions and potential mass movements seem to lurk behind figures such as Edward II and Thomas of Lancaster. Bitter enemies in life, the two men both attracted miraculous rumours like lightning rods once they were dead. The tomb-shrine of Thomas Winchelsey, archbishop of Canterbury and opponent of the king, was still being visited at the Reformation.[11] At the other extreme, a brief and unlikely cult flickered around James Berkeley, bishop of Exeter for just a few months after Stapeldon's murder, in whose older brother's castle the king had been killed.

None of these men was ever canonized but, between about 1270 and about 1350, every known saint's shrine in England was renewed, with a peak of activity in the 1320s to 1340s when there were high-profile translations at Hereford and St Paul's; survivals of the period include the reconstructed shrines in Christ Church, Oxford, Chester and St Albans, all later cathedrals.[12] At Lichfield, Wells and Ely, shrine spaces were integrated with brilliantly creative lady chapels, each an architectural homage to the virtues of Mary, the ultimate saint.[13]

For all the brilliance of these buildings, there is desperation in the search for spectacular effects. This architecture is obsessed with message: the linked power of bishops and liturgy at Exeter; warnings to the townspeople at Norwich; the Virgin and her personification in St Etheldreda at Ely. Perhaps there really was a 'chilling of men's devotion towards the church and the saints and the works of God' at this time, as a bishop of Lincoln noted, suggesting that 'the adversities and pressures of this age, which increase daily, work against this devotion'.[14] At the very least, these buildings, whose design depended on lavish, one-off details to an even greater extent than the miracle churches of the late twelfth century, were constructed by people whose wages were falling, but paid for by people who were getting richer. Perhaps the bishops wanted to keep their populations busy.

There were other remarkable works in this period too. A magnificent new east end, dedicated in 1314, was built at St Paul's and the shrines of two bishop-saints there were sumptuously renewed in 1326, perhaps to divert Londoners' attention from the more dangerous cult of Thomas of Lancaster.[15] The choir and feretory at Winchester were refurbished and partly rebuilt with help from a young Thomas of Witney. For a couple of decades the bishops of Salisbury stopped fighting with their chapter and created that church's perfect spire instead. York's nave and west front, designed for one of the greatest displays of sculpture in the land, crawled towards completion, while the bishop of Rochester, Hamo de Hethe, a supporter of the beleaguered Edward II who even refused to do fealty to Edward III when he was proclaimed king in 1327, was responsible for the magnificent door now leading to the cathedral's Chapter Library (illustrated p. 398).

Yet not everything was spectacular. While campaigning hard for the canonization of Thomas Cantilupe, Bishop Swinfield of Hereford used funds from the shrine to refurbish the pilgrim route around his cathedral and to build new towers (illustrated p. 352) and a series of retrospective tombs to previous bishops. Building standards slipped as the cult collapsed, resulting in work as aggressively local as the cult itself. Even more self-effacing, perhaps as a conscious reaction to the excesses of the era, is the new nave at neighbouring Worcester. This tied the monks' thirteenth-century choir to their twelfth-century west front in a design that draws heavily on that of these older parts of the church. Much the same could be said of the restrained 'alternative' vision of Decorated architecture in the new east ends of the abbeys at Chester and St Albans (both later cathedrals).

The world turned upside down: a fourteenth-century motif, symbolised by the most unthinkable role reversal of all: a wife beating her husband

Indeed the really stupendous cathedral buildings of the era were the products of a small group of bishops close to the royal court. Men like Droxford of Wells, Stapeldon of Exeter and Hotham of Ely were political players;[16] their sophisticated West Country and East Anglian experiments outposts of court culture, even if regional masons supplied much of the detail. Indeed, these Decorated buildings were so individual that they barely comprise a style at all: each seems determined to coin new kinds of motif, keeping a restless eye on its peers as it does so. The artistic climax, which was reached simultaneously in London and Gloucester, would come even closer to the court and its concerns.

The presence of a dead king at Gloucester had turned the city into a temporary outpost of Westminster. Edward II's tomb is the most breathtaking medieval monument in England; and it sits on an aesthetic fracture line. For, somewhere in the years between the murder of Edward II and the coming to power of Edward III, there was a moment of artistic crystallization. Out of the ferocious twists and turns of the old, a new style was born fully formed.

After Edward II's death, and with Edward III still only a boy, the queen and her lover Roger Mortimer ruled England for three years. In 1330 Edward III seized power. Over the next ten years, he put great energy into mending the wounds in the body politic. He made offerings at his father's shrine in Gloucester and sought the canonization of Thomas of Lancaster, drawing the teeth from both cults as he did so. He went to war with France in 1337 and successfully intervened in Scotland, recalling the glory years of Edward I. He exploited the culture of chivalry to foster a martial spirit of unity between king and barons, for example, by setting up the Knights of the Garter. This chivalrous order had a constitution that imitated a secular religious community and was based at the innovatory college of St George in Windsor Castle, founded by Edward in 1348.[17]

In about 1331 the abbot of Gloucester decided to use the income from Edward II's shrine to rebuild his east end. A team of masons was sent from the court to work on it. The south transept that resulted, and the choir that followed directly on from it, have much in common with the works of the previous ten or twenty years. Here are further cages of glass, integrating stained glass, woodwork and sculpture so as to create an architecture of spectacular intent. Here again the plan plays with polygons, in this case bowing the east window outwards like an enormous transparent altarpiece, and there are more spectacular glimpses across and between spaces. Here, too is the marked influence of Edward I's chapel of St Stephen in Westminster, work on which was restarted by Edward III, and before it ideas from thirteenth-century France. And here the building once again carries a message, in this case about the sacred nature of kingship and the feudal hierarchy.

Yet the Gloucester east end is also a striking contrast to its predecessors. The fashion for constant changes of pattern and curvaceous ogee arches was rejected. Instead a grid of straight lines was stretched like a fragile skeleton over the entire structure. It is as if someone had taken the architecture of Ely, Wells or Lichfield and applied a ruler to it. Even the colour scheme has changed. The glass at Gloucester (illustrated p. 341) gives everything an icy hue of blue and silver, replacing the rich red, gold and green that had made buildings such as the lady chapels at Wells (illustrated p. 439) and Ely the most richly colourful of the Middle Ages.

In some ways, Gloucester is another upping of the ante, another brilliant contribution to a restless conversation. In others, it is an end to that dialogue, an entirely new aesthetic language distilled from the flood of decorative ideas. And, after Gloucester, it is as if architectural taste breathes a huge sigh of relief; as if something that has been hunted for with an almost neurotic brilliance has suddenly been found.

Gloucester's choir cast thin bars of stone over a cage of glass

The designer of Gloucester's east end would have known of the West Country experiments of the previous decade, especially those by William Joy. He also knew the work of Michael of Canterbury, who had worked on St Stephen's Chapel, Westminster. But it seems men further afield were also on the same track. In the same year, William Ramsey, now one of the key figures in East Anglian architecture, came to London to build a new chapter-house and cloister at St Paul's cathedral where he adopted exactly the same suddenly narrowed and disciplined range of motifs. Edward III's works at Windsor castle from 1350 used them too. This style, invented apparently overnight in about 1332, was to dominate architecture for two hundred years, until masons had forgotten that there was any other way to build.[18] The style is called Perpendicular. It replaces the extravagant and mildly deranged architecture of those close to Edward II with something that, initially at least, was comparatively martial, sensible and reserved – and intimately linked to the new regime. Architecture had gone straight: Decorated had been nothing if not licentious.

A whole new vocabulary of motifs was coined. The sinuous ogee was replaced by the staid four-centred arch. Emphatically horizontal transoms, previously only used in the great halls of castles and other secular buildings, were used in window tracery. One simple motif, the rectangular panel, was repeated over and over again to form a decorative grid that could be stretched over everything, of whatever size, from windows and wall surfaces to vaults (the fan vault, invented at Gloucester, was the result) and fittings.[19] This simple idea was the heart of the style and resolved what had emerged as a core concern during the Decorated period: how to unify the small and the large and blur the boundaries between fittings and architecture. The discovery of such a simple way of doing this was a kind of aesthetic eureka moment which had dramatic implications for all aspects of architecture.

Many other themes that would dominate the future are first seen in these years. Kings would be deposed three more times over the next century or so, while the English economy remained on a war footing until the late fifteenth century. The king and his circle, rather than Canterbury, had become the epicentre of architectural ideas. The belated rebirth of the new age of saints continued in its new and unsettlingly politicized form until the Reformation. The uncertainty of the times seems to have also fuelled new religious practices. The feast of Corpus Christi became the focus of a rich popular religious culture, while increased interest in the doctrine of purgatory led to the founding of hundreds of new chantries. The founding of chantries, normally seen as a typically late medieval practice, actually peaked in the early fourteenth century; similarly, the lay guilds and confraternities so characteristic of the fifteenth century seem to have had their roots at this period in a popular desire to organize elaborate Corpus Christi processions. Popular religion and the founding of chantries would remain key themes.[20]

An equally remarkable but more provincial building acts as a postscript to this story. The rebuilding of the east end of the abbey of St Augustine's, Bristol, now the cathedral, was begun at some point between 1298 and the 1320s as a mausoleum for the Lords Berkeley, who were deeply involved in the struggle against Edward II. The resulting work, by a brilliant and independent-minded designer, is a castle great hall in stone. It has a guiding taste all of its own that has been systematically applied to every detail. Like the early Perpendicular buildings, it explores repetition and the straight line rather than curvaciousness and variety; yet it is at times almost wilfully eccentric, as if coining mischievous architectural jokes. And the core of its message is the most brashly stated of all the great architectural manifestos of these years, for it is nothing less than a great display of feudal and chivalrous values, conceived as a purpose-built family mausoleum. Like the York nave and Langton's Lichfield, St Augustine's is full of the culture of chivalry. Borrowing went the other way as well. Aristocratic and royal architects were drawing on the visual effects of the great churches and using them to create meaning-laden architectural spectacles in their castles, as at Caernarfon, Dunstanburgh and Windsor. We are far from the Church-centred messages of the first new age of saints.

By the 1340s, a great wave of new architectural ideas had washed over the country, leaving behind the template for a new style. There was no shortage of activity. All the buildings discussed here were under construction, though many were nearing completion or going forwards only in fits and starts. Thomas de Cantilupe, his cult at Hereford now fading, was belatedly canonized in 1349 and translated to a shrine that had been awaiting him since 1320. And in Norwich, work was continuing on the cloisters, where in 1346–7 the sacristan invested in an illustrated account of the Apocalypse. His masons were working on something special: several hundred vividly carved bosses, focused on the story of the Last Days. Perhaps someone was wondering if the end of the world was nigh.

During the fourteenth century the world of chivalry comes bursting into church architecture: King Arthur's knights Galahad and Gawain are shown here

In the summer of 1348, those who had carved the images of the Apocalypse in the Norwich cloister must have wondered if Death and Pestilence had indeed come to ride with Famine and War across the English countryside. On 25 June they sold off 159 carved stones and went home. Their master-mason, William Ramsey, one of the inventors of Perpendicular, was dead; all building work had been put on hold. The Black Death or plague had arrived. Soon a third of the population and forty per cent of all churchmen would be dead.

It must have seemed to the bishops that their parish priests were dying as fast as they could be created. In diocese after diocese, bishops performed mass ordinations only to have to do so again just a few months later, 'owing to the loss of so many priests in so many churches'.[21] Their chapters were hit hard, too: at Lincoln four dignitaries, three archdeacons and fourteen other canons died.[22] At York the sub-dean had to be replaced three times in three months.[23] At Peterborough abbey and other monastic houses the number of monks halved, in many cases never to return to the level they had reached before the plague.

At Winchester, Bishop Edington helpfully reminded the people of his diocese that 'sickness and premature death often come from sin'[24] and recommended that they perform penance by processing barefoot. Monks and laymen came to blows after the city's cemeteries overflowed with bodies. With no one to farm the land, the economic crisis deepened: in 1350 the communar of Norwich received less than £9 from estates whose produce was normally worth about £50 a year.[25] The cathedral's income may have been cut by as much as eighty per cent; in the city itself, 7,000 people were said to have died: some entire parishes were wiped out.

To cope, long-held religious taboos had to be suspended. The pope authorized dying laymen to confess to each other, and even to confess to a woman, if no priest could be found. Such edicts were widely distributed: in the diocese of Ely, for example, that concerning confessing to laymen was read out in every parish church 'in the mother tongue' – the use of English notable in itself.[26] At Lincoln, bishops were permitted to ordain married men in an emergency.[27] Considering the architectural and institutional efforts made over many centuries to underline the separation of the priesthood from the laity, such steps were extreme indeed.

The mortality of 1348 was followed by a huge shortage of labour, enabling everyone from agricultural labourers to priests to dictate their own terms. 'So numerous were priests before the pestilence', wrote Henry of Knighton in Leicester, yet 'now scarce any would accept a vicarage of £20 or 20 marks.

[and] . . . There came crowding into Orders a multitude of those whose wives had died in the plague, of whom many were illiterate.'[28] The first-ever wage controls were enacted in 1351; in 1353 chaplains' wages were fixed at 7 marks a year.[29] Yet, because of Edward III's campaigns in France, the country was still on a war footing, requiring heavy taxation. It was also deeply fractured. The stealing of the head of St Hugh from Lincoln cathedral in 1364; the theft of building materials for the Winchester nave; and the series of internal scandals that engulfed St Frideswide's, Oxford, and St Werburgh's, Chester, in the late fourteenth century[30] were all signs of a society in turmoil and perhaps no longer in thrall to its own institutions. What is remarkable about these years is that the state did *not* collapse completely. Perhaps, after the 1320s and 1330s, people had simply come to expect that times would be hard. Plague was to strike eleven more times over the next century and a half.

Architecturally, the impact of the plague can be compared to that of the papal interdict during the reign of King John, with one important difference. The interdict occurred when a great wave of architectural activity and inventiveness was at its peak; the Black Death during its endgame. Almost everywhere, there are signs of tools being downed suddenly, with a stylistic jump when work restarts. William Joy, one of the key designers of the 1320s, was a victim of the plague: the west front at Exeter, his last project, was left unfinished. William Ramsey, in addition to his work at Norwich, was in 1348 acting as a consultant on the updating of the Lichfield choir, connecting it to Walter Langton's lady chapel. Instead the building jumps from high Decorated to a faintly cack-handed Perpendicular. Ely lady chapel is an almost perfect example of the Decorated style, but has a vault and main windows that are early Perpendicular. At York, the east end of the 1360s is a kind of reinvention, in Perpendicular, of the nave, still under way in 1348 in spite of having been begun in 1291. At Hereford the unfinished base of an early fourteenth-century chapter-house was continued in up-to-the-minute Perpendicular in the 1360s.

In contrast, work on the east end of Gloucester abbey continued without apparent pause. By the 1360s, pilgrims to the tomb-shrine of Edward II saw the new style

There was a grisly side to late medieval religion, typified by the effigies of church-men as dried up-corpses to be seen at Exeter (above), York and Wells

grandly displayed. Edward III also used the style at Windsor castle, where ambitious works had kept the style alive while the plague raged. Yet Perpendicular was no overnight success, especially in the north and east of the country. Those involved in the prolonged rebuilding of Carlisle cathedral and Chester abbey long remained in thrall to a curvaceous Decorated, stripped of its past wit; masons at Ely were still installing Decorated windows in the choir into the fifteenth century; the spectacular clerestory built in the Norwich choir after the spire fell in 1361–2 and, at Lincoln, the new base for the head shrine of St Hugh – the stolen head had by now been recovered – and other enrichments by treasurer Welbourn are effectively Decorated structures with details that pay lip-service to the sober new ideas from the south.

It was in the 1360s that the great patron-bishops suddenly re-awoke and began building for 'memorable, just, urgent . . . and legitimate reasons', as it was put at York minster.[31] As if making up for lost time, major building campaigns were begun in England's three most powerful bishoprics: York and Canterbury, the seats of the archbishops, and Winchester, now settling into a late medieval role as the preferred see of most royal chancellors. New naves were begun at Winchester and Canterbury, a new east end at York. These were all campaigns with exceptionally powerful patrons, all campaigns that proceeded in fits and starts.

When the new work began, the eleventh-century naves at Canterbury and Winchester must have been battered and antiquated buildings. Canterbury was in a 'notorious and evident state of ruin', according to Archbishop Sudbury;[32]

The peasant's revolt: the priest John Ball (centre) and Wat Tyler (right) gather with their followers outside London

and the fact that Winchester's massive romanesque west end was completely demolished and not replaced suggests it had structural problems. In spite of this the focus on the western half of these great churches is interesting. Ever since Anselm's work at Canterbury in the 1100s, new east ends have dominated our story, with new naves constructed only in the course of a complete rebuild. Apart from the York nave of the 1290s, with its emphatic evocation of an aristocratic lay community, no cathedral nave had ever been rebuilt without a new east end being created first. This new attention to the lay end of the building in the 1360s is remarkable: it turns previous architectural priorities on their heads.

As these projects proceeded, the world at large was also being turned upside down. The Canterbury nave had begun as an initiative of the monks in the late 1360s; Archbishop Sudbury had stepped in after an abortive fundraising campaign, only to be murdered by a revolutionary mob in 1381. As chancellor of England, one of the few of the era who was not also bishop of Winchester, the mild-mannered Sudbury was blamed for the hated poll tax, the 'evil subsidy' imposed to help fund war in France.[33] The men of Kent, en route to London as part of uprisings in Kent and East Anglia, denounced the archbishop in his half-rebuilt nave before moving on to the capital, where he was found and beheaded. The body lay unburied for two days. The revolt had been triggered by a combination of unfairly imposed wage controls and the poll tax: the rebels' demands included the abolition of serfdom.

Canterbury was not the only cathedral to suffer. The martial Bishop Despencer of Norwich put down rebels in Norwich and Peterborough and celebrated his success with a magnificent new altarpiece, the Norwich retable, in Norwich cathedral. At Ely, where the Church was the main landlord, a townsman used the cathedral nave to address his fellow citizens, denouncing the 'traitors' who ran the local courts. A riot ensued in which prisoners were freed from the bishop's prison, many of the cathedral's legal records were destroyed and a local judge murdered.[34] Within two years the great Ely Porta, a colossal fortified gate to the monastery, was under way, providing a secure venue for the storage of official records and the holding of prisoners.[35] Something similar had happened at Worcester in 1349, when the citizens broke

Around the edge of the Despencer altarpiece in Norwich cathedral are the coats of arms of the families who put down local rebels in 1381

Worcester's Edgar Gate was part of a new breed of heavily-fortified close gatehouse

into the convent 'in warlike manner with arms' and assaulted the prior;[36] and at Lincoln after a rebellion in 1386. Both cathedrals quickly built massive defensive gatehouses. The events of 1381 were dramatic, but they were also signs of the times.

The murder of the archbishop of Canterbury by a crowd of commoners with political grievances, and with no saints' cult in sight, is itself a sign of how much things had changed since the Becket years. But radical ideas were abroad in religion as well as in politics. The ideas of John Wyclif, a radical theologian at Oxford, were becoming hugely influential, and were even cited by some of those involved in the revolt. Wyclif and men like him questioned the whole panoply of ideas and beliefs represented by the cathedrals, among them the powers of the priesthood, the sanctity of the Eucharist and the cults of the saints. They even criticized the rich images and elaborate liturgy on which cathedral art depended.

At first Wyclif's ideas seemed to be little more than a new intellectual fad. Archbishop Sudbury had declared that, though they were 'ill to the ear', they were nevertheless true.[37] But it began to be clear that they could be political dynamite. Sudbury's successors Courtenay and Arundel made increased efforts to control these Lollards, endeavours that culminated in 1401 when the first Lollard heretic was burned at the stake. 'God . . . has . . . brought me into this land for to destroy thee and the false sect that thou art of', Arundel had said.[38]

By 1417, when Sir John Oldcastle was burnt at the stake, Lollard ideas had reached the heart of the establishment

After the events of 1381, Archbishop Courtenay had paid more attention to the strengthening of his castle at Saltwood in Kent than to the Canterbury nave, but Archbishop Arundel piled resources into the nave's completion and ensured it contained coded pleas to lay piety. These were focused around a rebuilt lady chapel near the nave altar. Here Arundel created a chantry chapel for himself, making much of the fact it allowed lay people to hear mass when other parts of the church were closed off. Arundel and his successors would put huge efforts into ensuring the Church supported and encouraged appropriate lay involvement in religion. By 1420 the finished nave (illustrated p. 280) was being used for great gatherings. An estimated 100,000 pilgrims attended the jubilee of Becket's translation in that year.[39]

Archbishop Arundel preaching to laymen in support of Henry IV

The new nave at Winchester, too, was delayed by history. Bishop Edington was no great aesthete, but as royal chancellor he had direct access to court masons using the new style. As early as the 1360s they had coined an era-defining new idea at one end of the nave, in the shape of a chantry chapel for the bishop. Instead of being, for example, located at an existing altar, Edington's masons placed his tomb and an altar for the chantry priest inside a roofless rectangle of stone screens, covered in an elegant grid of Perpendicular panels. Such an enclosure could potentially be inserted into the church wherever there happened to be space for it. As the architectural expression of one of the key motors of the doctrine of purgatory, and a classic Perpendicular solution to the old design problem of how to characterize chantries architecturally,[40] these 'cage' chantries are one of the defining inventions of the period. As well as freeing up space at altars, they made it possible to stage chantry masses in a manner that was visually distinct. By the 1540s well over forty such structures,[41] often reflecting their founders' interests and tastes, had been added to the English cathedrals: the six at Winchester form a veritable history of the men who ran late medieval England.

Edington did little more than build his chantry at one end of the nave and start rebuilding the west front at the other. But his successor William Wykeham went much further. Here was another royal chancellor: a man who had made his name overseeing royal building projects. The many buildings of his episcopacy have a powerful and consistent visual identity, thanks to his partnership with the mason William of Wynford. But the two men's attempts to continue the new nave were diverted by ever-increasing distractions. The stockpile of building materials was stolen and, towards the end of Edward III's reign, Wykeham became embroiled in political storms before becoming a trusted advisor to Richard II. Finally, he diverted his energies from cathedral-building to the founding of two important new institutions.

Architecture of purgatory: the Edington chantry at Winchester

The staff and scholars of New College stand around their patron, William Wykeham

In the 1370s Wykeham founded a grammar school in Winchester and a new university college, now aptly called New College, at Oxford, with the expectation that young men would graduate from one to the other. His aim, apart from ensuring that his own soul was prayed for constantly in both college chapels, was to help create a flow of orthodox and professional young men who could fill the priesthood of a depleted Church.

Winchester college, which is still thriving, was the first school to be set up with the resources and institutional complexity of a great church while being independent of one. It is thus a crucial bridge between the Church schools and the modern education system. New College, also still with us, was exceptional, too. It was larger than any previous university college. Bishops had been founding religious houses and academic colleges for years, but never on a scale like this, or with such thorough attention to planning and constitutional arrangments.[42] Wykeham returned to his nave in 1390; with the support of his convent, it was almost complete by the time of his death in 1404.

By this date an extraordinary image of the End of Time was under way in York. It was the crowning glory of the new lady chapel. This chapel was the first result of a project that had been mooted before the Black Death, as the end of work on the nave came in sight: to rebuild Roger of Pont l'Evêque's twelfth-century east end so as to ensure the entire minster would have a 'uniform beauty', as it was put at the time. In 1365 Archbishop de Thoresby began a focused and well-funded campaign. His mason was instructed to follow the design of the nave closely, though he updated its details to Perpendicular.

This lady chapel, which rose the full height of the church, is today visually indistinguishable from the choir to its west, work on which proceeded more slowly. It is the work of an archbishop who, as a deputy to the bishop of Worcester, had seen the full extent of suffering in 1348;[43] now de Thoresby's Lay Folks' Catechism – a little book in English that was a kind of ready-reckoner for the 'basics' that any Christian soul should know – displayed a special concern for the beliefs of ordinary people, while also specifically reminding them that laymen were not to administer the sacraments.[44] De Thoresby filled his east end with a paean to the history and venerability of the minster. The brasses he installed to

The Winchester nave is a work of handsome, crystalline Perpendicular

former archbishops were fake tombs that formed a kind of heritage vision of the cathedral's history. There was heritage interpretation too, in the shape of the Tables of the Vicars Choral, painted boards on which the story of the minster was written out for the edification of interested visitors.[45] St Paul's, Canterbury and other great churches eventually had similar accounts on display. But the entire space, lady chapel and choir alike, is dominated by the great east window, one of the largest in Europe, where the emphasis was the future rather than the past. Its 144 openings, one for every thousand souls for which there would be room in heaven, were filled after Thoresby's death with a vivid depiction of Genesis and the Book of Revelation, with a heavy emphasis on the horrors of the latter (illustrated p. 471).[46] As it was installed, yet more dramatic events unfolded.

Archbishop Arundel of Canterbury helped engineer the deposition of the increasingly tyrannical Richard II in 1399 and his replacement by the archbishop's own uncle, Henry Bolingbroke, who now became King Henry IV. Unlike Edward II, with whom Richard had identified, the king left no son and heir. The dynastic crisis that resulted would dominate much of the fifteenth century.

Soon the judgement of Henry too began to falter and in 1405 Archbishop Scrope of York, in an unusual mood of populism, encouraged the citizens to join a group of northern barons in a rising against the king. Henry IV met Scrope and his people's army near the archbishop's palace outside York, took him prisoner, and had him beheaded. The archbishop became the focus of the biggest saint's cult since the 1320s and 30s, a cult the authorities worked hard to suppress.

Then, in 1407, the minster's central tower collapsed, and the king tried to repair relations with York by sending one of his own master-masons, William Colchester, north to work on its replacement. The offerings received at Scrope's shrine were redirected to fund the project. Such a situation was bound to arouse strong feelings. One of Colchester's masons was murdered, yet the resulting tower, which had been paid for from the proceeds of an illegal saint, was emblazoned with the heraldry of his enemy Henry IV. Stylistically, the tower was an emphatic piece of southern Perpendicular on a building where the authorities had spent half a millennium trying not to imitate London or Canterbury; equally remarkable is the way in which it ignores the cult that funded it. We are indeed a long way from the 1170s.

By now, despite the years of troubled kingship and economic crisis, Perpendicular had taken over completely. The Winchester and Canterbury naves, the former designed by William Wynford, the latter, probably, by Henry Yevele, the king's master-mason, were mature, sure-footed and beautiful where their predecessors had still had an experimental air. The east end of York suggested a northern version of this sober, crisp and masculine style, softening it with lace-like patterns and rounded forms. In contrast to the fevered interiors of the earlier fourteenth century, colour was now used more sparingly and subtly. The Winchester nave, for example, featured bare stonework: only decorative details such as bosses were picked out in bright paint. The York glass, like that at Gloucester, is flatter and cooler than earlier designs.[47]

For much of the rest of the fifteenth century, the archbishops of York and Canterbury continued to keep pace with one another, adding further towers and other extras to their churches. Both buildings only began to look as they do today within a few decades of the Reformation. Indeed, among the cathedrals as a whole, towers are the only large-scale projects of the fifteenth century. In their way, they demonstrate how much had changed.

Perpendicular towers can be stupendous. Memorable examples were built at Durham and Wells and the abbeys, later cathedrals, of Bristol and Gloucester; there is also the new spire at Norwich and the western lantern at Ely. Invariably added to ancient crossings that were not designed to bear their weight, they are also remarkable works of engineering. The first man to attempt to build a new central tower on top of the Canterbury crossing, which had become unstable having had every structure that abutted it updated or rebuilt over some four hundred years, was Richard Beke, a former bridge engineer.[48] Yet great towers of this period are just as much a feature of parish churches. Exceptional architecture was no longer the preserve of the cathedrals and monastic houses.

Indeed, in some cases, such as the towers of Carlisle and Southwark (later a cathedral), what was built does not compare with what was achieved at parish level. Much the same could be said of the refurbished nave at Rochester and the newly-constructed one at Ripon minster (illustrated p. 395): they are indistinguishable from, indeed arguably *less* impressive than, some of their equivalents on parish churches. The master-mason behind the Ripon nave designed ambitious towers at Louth parish church, Lincolnshire, and Durham cathedral alike. The grand new tower at Gloucester abbey was soon surrounded by comparable structures built by wealthy wool merchants on the churches of the Cotswolds. Indeed, Perpendicular additions were made to almost every parish church and many were entirely rebuilt. A building boom was sweeping the country whose epicentre was not in the cathedrals and whose patrons were far beneath the rank of bishop.

These buildings were expressions of an enormous popular religious revival. Partly driven by a belief in purgatory that was itself fuelled by the uncertain times, people at all levels put huge resources into enriching their local churches.[49] The Lollards, Wyclif's followers, may have questioned the need for priesthood or the Eucharist; others accepted the mysteries of their faith but demanded increased participation in the practice of it. There was a newly personal edge to this faith, vividly expressed in the works of lay mystics such as Margery Kempe, who was interviewed by Archbishop Arundel himself.

Cathedrals, too, were now being personalized. New structures and fittings were so extensively branded with the badges of those who had funded them, ostensibly to encourage prayer for the patron's soul, that piety blends into self-advertisement. Those who commissoned Durham in the 1090s or the west front at Wells in the

The central tower of Gloucester stands proud on top of the ancient church beneath

1220s have left no trace in the architecture. By contrast, in the late Middle Ages Bishop Fox used the bosses of his Winchester presbytery to list the bishoprics of his career, as if creating a curriculum vitae on a roof vault. Thomas Brouns, bishop of Rochester, left £20 'to the fabric of the nave of the cathedral church' in 1445, 'provided that work is made in such a way as to be a memorial, with sculptures on it showing my arms and my name'.[50]

Lay involvement in religion was matched by a secularization of professional areas, such as royal administration and the law, which had previously been dominated by senior churchmen.[51] The first layman to be royal chancellor was Sir Robert Bourchier, who was appointed in 1341; eight more laymen would follow in this post before the Reformation.[52]

At the same time, cathedrals were becoming foci for new kinds of popular ritual, many of them associated with the increasingly influential guilds and religious confraternities. By joining one of these, lay people could imitate something of the loose and ritualized spiritual brotherhood of the religious college. Such organizations, which had been growing since the fourteenth century, protected their members' trading practices and funded religious activities and celebrations, often focused on the feast of Corpus Christi. The guild of St George in Norwich, for example, claimed Henry V as its founder and included many of Norwich's most notable citizens. Together with others in Norwich, several of which were associated with the cathedral, the guild held mass processions in which sacred stories were re-enacted; these performances were one aspect of the scriptural dramas that are today known as the mystery plays. The processions converged on the west front of the cathedral four times a year.[53] By 1452 the guild had a membership of some two hundred, including the prior of Norwich. An element of theatricality also appeared in the liturgy. The canons of Lincoln bought props for the plays they would perform on Christmas Day and during the feast of St Anne;[54] there and at Norwich, great images were suspended from the nave vault during key feasts.[55]

In the mid-fifteenth century, Bishop Lyhart of Norwich created the most emphatic statement yet of the power of the nave.[56] Lyhart completed the upgrading of the west front begun by his predecessor, Bishop Alnwick, and created a spectacular new vault that ran the length of the nave within. It is studded with 252 bosses, giving an account of the biblical history of the world from Creation to the End of Time. Unlike the abstruse, theological subtleties of Norwich's fourteenth century Prior's Door, these carvings were designed to educate the laymen who gathered beneath them and borrowed scenes from the religious dramas in which they participated and the *biblia pauperum*, the wood-engraved religious primers that were become increasingly popular. At this date, the east end still had a wooden roof, which must have made Norwich look bizarrely back-to-front.[57] Stone vaulting had partly been invented to aggrandize east ends: we have come a long way.

This flowering of popular piety was closely linked to the development of forms of self-governance in the emerging cities of England. Bristol was given county status in 1373, to be followed by York in 1396, Norwich in 1404; Chester followed in 1506. The guildhalls, medieval examples of which survive in Norwich, London and Carlisle, provided an architectural landmark that celebrated the citizens themselves. At Peterborough in 1401–2 and Rochester in 1423, the monks were persuaded, after years of struggle, to build separate parish churches for the towns-people, who had previously worshipped at a parish altar within these great monastic churches. And everywhere, powerful urban bodies developed their own elaborate rituals, loosely borrowed from religious processions; rituals that could even be used in anger. The mayor of Bristol and his men fought the canons of St Augustine's over the right to process over what is now College Green;[58] while in 1443 the people of Norwich staged an imitation of a religious procession to cover a major insurrection against the cathedral. The genie of 'the city', one that the cathedral builders had worked so hard to evoke, had firmly and finally emerged from its bottle.

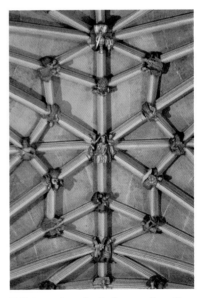

Perpendicular had now been in existence for a century. It would survive until the Reformation. Although the roots of the style lie in the early fourteenth century, its spread and success coincide precisely with the period historians call late medieval, a time when so many of the portents of the modern world are first discernible.

Nothing like this style had occurred before. The comparative lack of architectural evolution at this period is just one of its unique characteristics. Yet this innate stylistic conservatism becomes easy to understand in the context of the era. The very variety of buildings being commissioned, combined with the greater range of people involved in the rebuilding and decoration of churches large and small, must have provided an inherent drag on novelty. Gone were the days when a handful of interconnected patrons and masons could dominate

Religious primer for the laymen of an alien-ated city: vault bosses in the Norwich nave

architectural innovation as they had done in the 1080s-90s, 1170s-90s and 1310s-30s. The new and now ever-present threat of heresy may also have helped create an atmosphere that prioritized orthodoxy over experimentation. In practical terms, Perpendicular was versatile. Its flexibility and repetitive modularity meant it could be applied to a great variety of buildings and to interiors of different scales without the need to constantly re-invent the stylistic wheel.

Perpendicular is also uniquely English. This, too, may have its roots in the early fourteenth century when, for the first time, English design became influential among the top echelon of European patrons. Some papal tombs at Avignon seem to be by English designers working in the Decorated style and Nikolaus Pevsner, the architectural historian, saw the roots of all late European gothic in the experiments of those years.[59] Architecture had ceased to quote directly from continental buildings in the direct way that many earlier cathedrals had done. York in the 1290s was the last English cathedral to do that.

This confidence in an English vision comes through in many buildings of the period. Cardinal Henry Beaufort, warrior-bishop of Winchester and uncle of the king, had his portrait painted by the northern Renaissance master, Jan van Eyck (illustrated p. 450). Yet his swaggering chantry chapel in Winchester cathedral shows no signs of an interest in the new way of seeing embodied in that painter's work. Robert Sherborn, later bishop of Chichester, built a Renaissance-style college for English churchmen visiting Rome in 1501, but made Perpendicular architecture at home. No one would guess from the architecture of the Oxbridge colleges that English bishops took an eager interest in humanism, founding chairs in Greek and Hebrew, and studying in the Renaissance atmosphere of such universities as Bologna and Padua, because their buildings are both utterly gothic and utterly English. As an Italian visitor put it in 1500, 'the English . . . think there are no other men than themselves, and no other world but England'.[60] In a sense Perpendicular, architecture of humanists, merchants and lords, and hammer of heretics, is as complete and self-defining a fifteenth-century art form as the celebrated Renaissance traditions of Florence, Venice and Rome.

It was forged precisely as Edward III's military successes ushered in the Hundred Years War and cut England off politically from the Continent while also focusing attention on its distinct identity. Since the time of Edward I, monarchs had essentially been rulers of England rather than lords of a series of great estates on both sides of the Channel. Henry VI, in his thirty-nine years of power, never set foot in Scotland or Ireland, had a day in Monmouth to count as his experience of Wales, and never returned to France after the age of nine. The adoption of

Perpendicular likewise marches very neatly with the rehabilitation of English as the national tongue. English had been a lower-class vernacular. French had been spoken at court, Latin in the Church; before the fourteenth century, literature and records were invariably in one of these two languages. Now, things changed. Parliamentary business was first recorded in English in 1362; English was the language of Chaucer in the 1380s. This new national consciousness was personified in the iconic St George, whose cult, like the new style itself, had been promoted to serve the political interests of Edward III in the 1350s before it spread to the wider population. In 1381, the revolting peasants carried a red cross on a white background to symbolize their ultimate loyalty to the Crown. Never before had a saint been embraced as an emblem of 'the English'.[61] St George's flag remains the backdrop to national events to this day.

In retrospect, the Crown had won the power struggles of the twelfth century. Papal authority had been undermined by squabbles in the 1370s over which candidate was really 'God's vicar on earth' and by the resulting schism, in which rival popes ruled from Rome and Avignon simultaneously. By 1400, the king normally got his way in appointing bishops, rather than finding himself in a struggle with the pope. Papal taxes tended to find their way into the coffers of Westminster rather than those of Rome or Avignon. In 1414 there was even a precursor to the Reformation, when Henry V cut off foreigners' claims on the English Church by dissolving monastic houses whose mother house was not English.[62] The funds released in this way helped finance William Wykeham's New College. Lollard sympathizers at court had a century or more to dream of the riches that might be freed up from a wholesale dissolution of monasticism itself.

Few new monastic houses were created at this period. It did no harm that the Statute of Mortmain (literally 'dead hand') of 1279 had sought to control the flow of land into monastic houses, encouraging new forms of spiritual investment, but the cultural focus had also moved on. People who wanted to set up religious institutions on a large scale founded colleges or, occasionally, houses of ascetic orders such as the Carthusians. Few saw the point in giving to the rich cathedrals and Benedictine houses on the grand scale that had been common in the past.[63] The late fourteenth century rebuildings of the naves of Winchester and Canterbury belatedly rendered these two cathedral priories the only ones in the land that were end-to-end gothic buildings in the manner of their secular peers. In any case, the focus of architecture had diversified. There were other things to consider apart from the creation of overpowering great churches. The focus was on new types of institution, rather than new cathedral churches, and the flexiblity of the religious college was perfectly suited to this.

These collegiate foundations were evolving at a bewildering rate. They could be founded purely to pray for their founder's souls (Burghersh chantry, Lincoln cathedral) or, while retaining a chantry element, to educate (New College); to create a chivalric brotherhood (St George's, Windsor); or as a war memorial (All Souls, Oxford). Bishops, amongst others, founded lavish university colleges and grammar schools. Lincoln and Magdalen colleges, Oxford, for example, were founded by Bishops Flemming of Lincoln and Waynflete of Winchester in 1427 and 1448 respectively, to help the fight against heresy.[64] Waynflete also founded two grammar schools and played a key role in setting up both Eton and King's college, Cambridge. Most of the secular cathedrals, including Hereford, Salisbury, Wells and St Paul's, instituted programmes of theological lectures or created purpose-built libraries, often above their cloisters. This was the period when the secular cathedrals incorporated the sub-colleges of their vicars (for example, at Hereford in 1395, with a close built for them in 1472), chantry priests (York, 1455) and choristers (Wells, 1354) into formalized institutions, building or rebuilding their bespoke collegiate complexes within the cathedral close.[65] Such cathedrals also showed an interest in public works, financing the market cross in Chichester and its lost cousin at Lichfield, 'for poor market folks to stand dry in', as Dean Denton put it.[66] The water conduit and revamped market place at Wells, large portions of which survive, were the work of Bishop Beckington.

There was even a hint of the secular triumphalism of the 1190s to 1240s. Richard III tried (and failed) to found an enormous college for a hundred chaplains at York minster. Bishop Carpenter of Worcester founded and rebuilt his college at Westbury-upon-Trym, turning it into a model establishment, not far from the economic powerhouse that Bristol had become. Yet in secular and monastic

Chantry chapels are rich architectural worlds-in-miniature: the chantry of Treasurer Sugar at Wells

cathedrals alike, constitutional turf wars between bishops and chapters had largely fizzled out (at Worcester no new constitutional issues arose after 1394; at Lincoln after 1438). The monastic cathedrals were constitutionally virtually unchanged since the eleventh century, but their secular siblings had continued to develop. Now both, with their sub-institutions and many lay residents, had become complex, self-replicating beasts, at once impressive and complete unto themselves. Yet this seemingly 'solid state' is tinged with defensiveness: the Church needed to keep its members on the straight and narrow. The chantry priests' college at York and the vicars' college at Wells had special bridges that were designed to ensure their members walked into church rather than wandered into the town, where they might be distracted by lay culture, or worse, talk heresy (see p. 182).

The early decades of the fifteenth century, from the 1410s to the 1440s, had marked perhaps the biggest slump in cathedral building in the whole Middle Ages. No major projects were begun; those underway, such as at Canterbury and York, continued fitfully. It was a period of economic stagnation when craftsmen commanded high wages.[67] Only when the political situation turned from dynastic crisis to outright civil war in the 1450s did cathedral building truly come back to life, like some architectural Frankenstein's monster.

The violence came threateningly close to some cathedrals. The bishop of Salisbury was murdered in 1450, that of Chichester in 1451, resulting at Salisbury in the fortification of the gatehouse that protected the close from the town. At nearby Wells Aiscough's nervous colleague Beckington also built massive gateways to both the bishop's palace and the cathedral close. As a result of the security problems of the 1320s, 1380s and 1450s, many cathedral closes now greeted the visitor with a massive defensive gatehouse.[68]

The Wars of the Roses, 1455–87, were the most serious civil wars of the English Middle Ages and they spawned a great crop of architectural cathedral furnishings replete with political symbolism and propaganda. At the core of these events, which were accompanied by widespread civil unrest, lay the competing claims to the throne of the Houses of Lancaster and York. The cathedrals of Canterbury and York both mysteriously acquired major stone fittings that just happened to demonstrate that Henry IV and his line, the House of Lancaster, were the rightful rulers of the country. These pulpitums, which dominate the naves of each building,[69] are magnificent, swaggeringly handsome Perpendicular affairs. They carry statues of a carefully chosen company of English kings, apparently supporting the dynastic claims of the House of Lancaster.[70]

The pulpitum at Canterbury was the crowning glory of a long campaign to make the cathedral a kind of Lancastrian Westminster abbey. The cloister, south porch and south-west tower were rebuilt, and the south transept recast in the Perpendicular style; their vaults bear bosses that are a 'who's who' in heraldry of Lancastrian society. In addition, Henry IV was buried in the east end and several of his relatives in a purpose-built chapel in the south transept.[71] All this must have been a source of some embarrassment to the Yorkist Edward IV, who was in the cathedral when he heard of the final defeat and capture of Henry VI and thus of the victory of the House of York. He later installed a magnificent pro-Yorkist royal window in the north transept. The crossing and transepts at Canterbury, scene of Becket's martyrdom, were thus visually dominated by a potted history of the dynastic traumas of the mid-fifteenth century.

Events at York were even more dramatic. Here the figure of Henry VI on the pulpitum became the focus of a saint's cult after the king's murder in 1471. Orders were issued forbidding anyone from making offerings here or at a similar image in St Paul's, and the statue was destroyed. The current Henry is a modern replacement; he remains the only non-medieval statue on the screen.

At the same time as these galumphing (if exquisitely carved) works of political propaganda, an anti-heretic innovation appeared. Lollardy had not gone away. In 1457, for example, three men in Cambridgeshire claimed that priests had no more power to make the body of Christ appear than they had to create straw, and that the pope was Antichrist. They were ordered to walk around Ely at Pentecost with a faggot on their backs.[72] In 1462 a Bristol man was punished for claiming that the statues before which people offered candles were nothing but stones, that baptism was as good in a river as in a font, and that one should give to the poor rather than to the saints.[73] It is as if the great tide of Church hegemony, which had reached its high point in the early thirteenth century, was gradually withdrawing.

The colossal Great Screens at Winchester, St Albans abbey and St Mary Overie in Southwark (both St Albans and Southwark were later cathedrals) virtually fill the east ends of their respective buildings, completely blocking the view of any saint's shrine behind. The great silver Christ that dominated St Albans and Winchester, and which may also have been present at Southwark, dramatized the new practice of raising the host, just as its value was being questioned and the popes were emphasizing the importance of the Eucharist as the one sacrament that could never be administered by a layman.

Further pro-orthodox fittings came in a crop of enormous new saints' shrines, built for St Osmund at Salisbury (around 1457); St William at York (1472); and St Swithun at Winchester (1476). The canonization of Osmund, which took place in 1457 after a delay of nearly three hundred years (see p.100), was perhaps designed to refocus attention on the sacred authority of bishops within years of the murder of Bishop Aiscough; while the translation of William of York into his new shrine, as well as marking the final completion of York minster, must have helped draw attention away from political 'saints' Scrope and Henry VI. Only fragments of St William's shrine remains, but it was one of the largest in Europe; while that of St Swithun, which is also lost, must have been impressive enough not to be upstaged by the colossal chantries of Cardinal Beaufort and Bishop Waynflete, which still stand to either side of its site. The presence of such mighty structures would have transformed the experience of these buildings.

A phalanx of kings, subliminal propaganda in the Wars of the Roses, dominate the York nave

This burst of architecture as propaganda had inspired fresh creativity from the cathedral-builders: it was a fitting precursor to a final flowering of creative energy, in which a new dynasty built on a grand scale in an effort to establish its role as the bringer of peace.

REBIRTH 1485–1538

Thanks to his Welsh origins, his Lancastrian blood and marriage into the House of York, Henry VII was able to portray himself as a peacemaker, uniting the competing dynasties of Lancaster and York as well as England and Wales. He also happened to be a supremely effective king.

Under him, the initiatives of the 1450s were transmuted into a small return to the glory years of the cathedrals. But the focus of this flowering was not so much in the cathedrals themselves as in the king's personal projects: Henry VII's combined lady chapel, shrine to Henry VI and dynastic mausoleum, now simply known as Henry VII's chapel, at Westminster abbey; and completion on a grand scale at the enormous chapels of King's college, Cambridge (which was begun by Henry VI), and St George's college, Windsor castle, (mostly built by Edward IV).

These unique structures can be seen as attempts to derive a new kind of cathedral-scaled collegiate chapel, they sit happily in any list of the greatest architectural experiences of medieval England.

These Tudor buildings, mostly of the early sixteenth century, show a rebirth of interest in the golden age of the 1320s. While unequivocally Perpendicular, they are as breathtakingly ornate as any of the structures of that era. They also coin a few motifs, such as the Tudor arch, a subtle variant on the four-centred arch, that make it possible to identify a late Perpendicular style. But it is symptomatic of the times that new work at the cathedrals was small in scale compared to the royal projects. The Booth Porch at Hereford is a delightful structure, but it is simply an extension to the existing cathedral porch and the little lady chapel above it, albeit one that is full of references to West Country Decorated architecture. The tiny, ornate universes created in chantries such as that of Bishop Oldham at Exeter and Prior Bird at Bath are even closer to being fittings rather than architecture. Built in the sixteenth century, both chantries have roofs covered in the ogee-dominated patterns beloved by Decorated designers. Also from this period are the fine lady chapel between the nave and south transept at Rochester, which was never completed, and Bath cathedral priory. Rebuilt as a kind of overblown chantry chapel at two-thirds of its previous size, the priory is the last complete rebuilding in this book. At Bath and, a little later, at Peterborough abbey, master-masons such as the Vertue brothers and John Wastell produced spectacular and enormous fan vaults, drawing on ideas that had virtually lain fallow since the fan vault itself was invented in Gloucester in the 1360s.[74] The yet-more spectacular fan vaults worked on by the same men at Henry VII's chapel and King's college chapel were the final great masterpieces of medieval English architecture.

At Canterbury, Cardinal Archbishop Morton completed the lovely Bell Harry tower, surely the most perfect and finely judged cathedral tower in England. Its slim poise and elegance owe as much to the cardinal's self-importance as his aesthetic judgement: the decision to heighten it, and to liberally sprinkle the building with carvings of the cardinal's cap, seems to have coincided with Morton's promotion to that 'heady' office. It has come to something when Canterbury, of all the cathedrals, lies at the climax of a tradition rather than the beginning of one, reversing the role played by this great church in the first centuries of our story. Much the same could be said of the political situation. Henry VIII, soon to be head of the English Church, an idea that would have scandalized Becket, Lanfranc or St Augustine, introduced reforms that were to bring medieval cathedral building to an end. Yet he helped complete its last two

Climax of English gothic: the pendant fan vaults at Henry VII's chapel in Westminster Abbey

great monuments, King's college and Henry VII's chapel.

Exeter, Salisbury and Wells are among the secular cathedrals which experienced an institutional heyday in these years, and there were increases in the numbers of monks at some monastic cathedrals. Yet attempts to gradually 'Perpendicularise' several great churches came to a halt. The cathedrals of Winchester and Norwich

Henry VII: from his effigy by Pietro Torrigianio in Westminster abbey

and the abbeys of Gloucester, Bristol and Chester might today be largely Perpendicular structures had the Reformation not intervened. Winchester for example had Wykeham's nave and Waynflete's great screen; now Bishop Fox, another Winchester-based chancellor, began to rebuild the choir and transepts. At the same time he added new choir screens and set above them the bones of the Anglo-Saxon kings. Moved and re-displayed many times as the Old Minster was partly rebuilt around them, these relics were now housed in new, proto-Renaissance caskets.

Explicitly continental motifs were filtering back into English art. The king once again made the most extravagant gesture by commissioning a fabulous monument from Michelangelo's friend Pietro Torrigiano for his chapel in Westminster abbey. The north European Renaissance touched Chichester, where Bishop Sherborn employed Lambert Barnard, who knew about artistic developments there, as his in-house painter; and at Winchester Prior Silkstead had the lady chapel painted with images of the life and miracles of the Virgin in a northern Renaissance style. Continental late medieval influence can be seen in the works of Prior Gondibour at Carlisle, and of Bishop Alcock, another great builder-bishop, in his chantry at Ely. One of the earliest pure Italian Renaissance motifs in England, little more than an arabesque carved in wood, can be found in a fragment from the screen to the Winchester chantry chapel built by Bishop Langton in about 1501. If what had happened in 589, 1070 and the 1170s was anything to go by, an influx of new continental ideas into cathedral art was a sign that revolution of one kind or another was around the corner.

But perhaps the most evocative Tudor monument in an English cathedral stands at Worcester. Henry VII's eldest son, Arthur, looked set for greatness. Young, handsome and well educated, he was married to Catherine of Aragon and running Wales from Ludlow castle. But Arthur died from a mysterious fever in 1502 when he was just sixteen. The king and queen were so devastated they could not bear to attend the funeral.

Soon a magnificent three-storey chantry chapel, the size of a small church, had been built around the prince's tomb. The heraldry carved on this structure repeats the dynastic claims of the Tudors again and again, while carved saints and angels transform the chapel into a Te Deum in stone. The building itself has as much elegance, poise and flair as anything from the long gothic heyday of the cathedrals, 1170 to 1330. It makes a fitting endpiece to this story, suggesting as it does that English design was by no means exhausted in the decades before the Reformation and that the powerful visual tradition that had been reinventing itself ever since the 600s, and which was to be stopped in its tracks by the turmoil of the 1530s, still had plenty to say for itself. And if Arthur had lived, what would we not have lost?

The future King Arthur II died at just sixteen years old

WHAT TO SEE

Unrest

Decorated: Exeter, with its west front and choir fittings; the lady chapel at Lichfield; the east end of Wells; the Octagon and lady chapel at Ely; the east end of Bristol, Edward II's tomb in Gloucester.

Perpendicular: the south transept, east end, and cloister at Gloucester.

Politics

New naves: Winchester and Canterbury and the nave vault at Norwich.

New towers: Durham and Gloucester.

New colleges: Winchester college, New College and Magdalen college Oxford, all founded by bishops of Winchester.

Chantry chapels: particularly good collection at Winchester; also Exeter, Wells, Hereford, St Albans.

Political saints: the apocalyptic glazing scheme in the east window of York, installed while the Scrope cult unfolded; the sober central tower there, funded by it.

Propagandist fittings: the Great Screens at Winchester, St Albans and Southwark (much restored); the pulpitum and Lancastrian tombs at Canterbury; the pulpitum at York.

Rebirth

Bath; the fifteenth-century retrochoir, or 'new building', at Peterborough; the Bell Harry tower at Canterbury; Prince Arthur's chantry at Worcester.

Chapter Five

END

Between 1538 and 1541, the world that created the cathedrals finished forever. These years were at the epicentre of the events in the 1530s and 1540s known collectively as the Reformation. This turning-point, centred on Henry VIII's decision to break with the pope, was almost as radical in its consequences as the arrival of the mission of Gregory the Great had been nearly a thousand years earlier.

It is hard to overstate the scale of the losses involved. As a result of the dissolution of the monasteries, an entire type of institution vanished. Thousands of works of art were lost. Lucky survivals such as the twelfth-century Gloucester candlestick (illustrated p. 73) and Bishop Despencer's Norwich retable (illustrated p. 135) hint at the wealth of precious objects that would have enriched every great

Lambert Barnard's paintings at Chichester prefigure the Royal supremacy; he lived to see his cathedral decorations painted out in favour of sober moralisms

The dissolution of the chantries brought an end to an institution which had created much cathedral art, such as Bishop Beckington's Perpendicular chantry chapel at Wells

church in the land. Barely a trace remains of the nave roods, high altars and saints' shrines that would have been the main landmarks of any visit to a cathedral.[1]

Although the material loss was huge, the long-term consequences for English society were even more far-reaching. A whole way of seeing and an extraordinary creative tradition died in the mid-sixteenth century. Cathedrals still existed and a few new ones have even been built since. Likewise both monasticism and Catholicism are alive and well, if no longer at the cutting edge of social change. But the forces that created the extraordinary structures in this book were wider than a specific faith: they were expressions of an entire society, and that has gone forever. The significance of what survived, and the extraordinary eloquence with which the Reformation is played out in cathedral architecture, is perhaps less often realized.

———

So that he could legally marry Catherine of Aragon, his elder brother's widow and, later, when she failed to produce a male heir, legally divorce her, Henry VIII had become embroiled in a major battle with the pope, a battle which helped convince him that England should be free of papal authority altogether. As far as the king was concerned, the doctrinal implications of this decision were limited: theoretically, there was no need for change in the Church. But, thanks to the heretic tradition that was already changing the face of Europe and that had now been in England for some 150 years, some saw far wider implications in what Henry was doing.

The king replaced the pope as head of the Church in 1534. In 1536 the smaller monastic houses were dissolved. From 1538 the saints' shrines were dismantled: Becket, whose belief in the supremacy of Church over king had led to his martyrdom, was given a show trial and found posthumously guilty of treason. England's greatest shrine was taken apart piece by piece. In the years that followed, the king's commissioners moved round the cathedrals and remaining monastic houses, destroying relics, taking apart shrines, and taking away cartloads of jewels and precious metals in a colossal windfall tax.

Much such work was done under the cover of darkness. The giant shrine of St Swithun in Winchester, only about sixty years old, was 'made an end of' at 3 a.m. one Saturday morning: 'there was no gold nor ring nor true stone in it, but all counterfeits',[2] it was reported. Etheldreda's much more ancient tomb at Ely, said to be a re-used Roman sarcophagus, turned out to be 'made of common stone and not of white marble', 'which makes the truth of all the rest to be suspected'.[3]

In 1538, the greater monasteries were dissolved. This included all ten cathedral priories and dozens of other monastic houses, a few of which, such as Glastonbury and Bury St Edmunds, were easily the match for the mightiest cathedrals. With the monasteries went a huge network of what we would call social services. Travellers and merchants had been able to rely on the countrywide availability of free and safe hospitality; local grandees had somewhere to store their valuables; and unknown numbers of the poor were kept alive with handouts from their local religious community. At the same time, not all was totally lost. The bishops of the former monastic cathedrals remained in place, their estates largely intact, and some ancient monastic schools, such as those at Ely and Canterbury, were refounded out of the income of the dissolved monastery. The king's schools at these two cathedrals can thus claim to go back in an unbroken line to the very dawn of English Christianity.

The death of monasticism was also the victory of the secular church. Of the ten cathedral priories, all except Coventry and Bath were turned into secular cathedrals in 1541, their monastic buildings destined to be destroyed or converted into canons' houses,[4] their lands divided up to form prebends. The achievements of men like St Ethelwold of Winchester, Gundulf of Rochester and St-Calais of Durham, all of whom had turned secular cathedrals into monastic ones, had been reversed. Yet a surprising number of monks from the former cathedral priories simply stayed on as canons. Fifteen of the twenty-three professed monks of Ely became canons and other officers of the new secular cathedral.[5] Interestingly, dissolution had come at a time when there was a resurgence of interest in the cloistered and ascetic life. As late as 1534, ten new people had made a commitment to the monastic life at Ely and Winchester. Worcester and Norwich also witnessed an increase in recruitment in the early sixteenth century.

Initially, at least, these radical changes of the mid sixteenth century were carried out with remarkable ease. Perhaps medieval monasticism, like the dinosaurs, pre-Copernican astronomy, or the former communist states of the Soviet bloc, had simply outlived itself; or perhaps those involved quietly awaited the return

Thomas Cromwell, vice regent of England, here portrayed by Hans Holbein, was one of the architects of Reformation

of the true faith. The last prior of Ely, who joined the secular chapter after 1539, lived to see his 'old ceremonies and doctrines of the church of Rome' briefly return under Queen Mary.[6]

As had happened in the reforms after 1066, new sees were created, this time in an attempt to match the English dioceses more closely to centres of population. The new dioceses of Peterborough and Oxford reduced the size of the see of Lincoln; those at Bristol and Chester belatedly reflected the economic clout of these cities. In other cases, such as Gloucester and, perhaps, Peterborough, the demographic imperative for a new diocese was weaker, but the local monastic church contained royal burials of importance to the regime. At each of these sees, a former monastic church was turned into a secular cathedral. As a result, the churches of three of the wealthiest Benedictine abbeys (Gloucester, Peterborough and Chester) and two important Augustinian houses (Bristol and Oxford) have survived to the present day.[7]

Meanwhile, the nine secular cathedrals came through the reform comparatively unscathed. Their canons were simply expected to swear allegiance to king rather than pope, and to excise all references to Thomas Becket or the pope from their service books. From the late 1540s they were permitted to marry. The imposition of a single standard liturgy in 1549, Archbishop Cranmer's *Book of Common Prayer*, unified practice across all these institutions. The prayer book, partly derived from Richard Poore's Use of Sarum of 1220, underpins traditional Anglican worship to this day. Poore would recognize much about the secular cathedrals: what he would make of the triumph of the collegiate principles he did so much to reform is another matter.

The academic colleges were preserved, too. Indeed, they thrived; and their architecture defines much of modern Oxford and Cambridge. Through them, and their feeder schools at Eton, Winchester and elsewhere, a panoply of medieval concepts has spread into the education system. So, we still have colleges, and colleges still have deans and refectories, and every child in the country goes to school according to a calendar of terms base on the medieval religious year. Moreover, the architectural ideas of men like William Wynford have had a defining influence on the design of colleges of higher education the world over: from the Victorian University of Adelaide in Australia to the modernist University of Sussex, these institutions are grouped around cloisters. Even my 1960s state school in Devon followed such principles. It had a central quadrangle with covered walkways leading to the communal dining-hall on one side and to the far larger block, which contained the school itself, on the other: cloister, refectory, church.

The story of the Augustinian priory of St Frideswide in Oxford embodies this process. Cardinal Wolsey was archbishop of York as well as papal cardinal,[8] and the king's right-hand man. In 1524 he decided to found an academic college at Oxford; it was planned to outclass even King's at Cambridge. Cardinal college had a cloister that was a third bigger than that of Salisbury cathedral.[9] The base for the tower possibly intended for it could have supported a skyscraper.

To help fund the college, and give it a suitable chapel, Wolsey dissolved St Frideswide's priory next door. But in 1529, with demolition of the church under-way, Wolsey fell dramatically out of favour with Henry VIII. The project in Oxford stopped dead in its tracks. The walks of the colossal new cloister were incomplete; much of the nave of St Frideswide's had gone, but the rest of the church was still standing. Interestingly, Henry VIII did not abandon the project. Renaming it Christ Church college, he made what was left of the church into the college chapel and then, in a final twist, in 1547, the chapel was asked to double up as a new cathedral for Oxford. St Frideswide's or Christ Church cathedral as it is now known, is the monastic house that was quite literally half-consumed by the Reformation. Wolsey's unfinished cloister is one of the most recognizable features of Tom Quad to this day.

Some important collegiate churches, including the quasi-cathedral at Southwell, were also allowed to remain in business. Ripon and its sister church at Southwell later found themselves near areas of heavy industrialization and population growth; in 1836 and 1884 respectively they became cathedrals for new sees covering Nottinghamshire, Derbyshire and northern Yorkshire. And, in a few cases, local communities adopted former monastic and collegiate churches as their parish churches. When it became clear towards the end of the nineteenth century that London had become too vast to be covered by a single diocese, two of these, St Alban's and St Mary Overie, Southwark, both of them in a very poor state after centuries of serving communities that were far too small for them, were converted into cathedrals for new sees. Over the ensuing years several medieval parish churches in places like Sheffield and Portsmouth followed suit.

As a result of all these changes, twenty-six medieval great churches are the seats of bishops today. These survivals pale into insignificance besides what has been lost, but they are precious nonetheless. Gloucester, Peterborough and St Albans were always in the first rank of monastic houses. Without them and Bristol, the story of English architecture would look very different, while St Frideswide's, Oxford, although never a major institution, was the focus of an extraordinary and dramatic story. These buildings were lucky; they were in the right place at the right time.[10] Substantial portions of a handful of other great churches, such as Malmesbury abbey or Whitby abbey, survive as parish churches or ruins. Only archaeology can recover the hundreds of other equally interesting structures that have vanished entirely.

In other words, although the vast majority of English monasteries disappeared, a few of the larger ones have been preserved and, crucially for the aims of this book, an important class of medieval building has survived almost entirely. All but two of the buildings known to people in the Middle Ages as cathedrals are still cathedrals today. The losses are St Paul's, which was rebuilt after the Great Fire of London in 1666; and the cathedral priory at Coventry, which found itself with no role in a see that already had a secular cathedral at Lichfield and was situated only a few hundred metres from two enormous medieval parish churches. The mayor pleaded that the cathedral be saved, for 'the lack and decay wherefore shall be . . . a great defacing of the said city,'[11] but no sustainable future could be found for the building. Bath cathedral priory was luckier: it had always dominated its city and was given to the local community in 1572. As a result, although rebuilding works here stopped at the Reformation, they were to continue afterwards when the former cathedral had adopted a new guise as a grand parish church, known today as Bath Abbey.

There was idealism behind the reforms of the mid-sixteenth century, not least a conviction that the wealth of the monasteries could be better spent on education than on prayer. Religious statelets such as the sees of Ely and Durham (and the more secular County Palatine of Cheshire) were dismantled. But many of these far-sighted plans were watered down. Most of the lands freed up by the Dissolution were simply privatized: given to the gentry and aristocracy in an enormous redistribution of wealth that helped buy their loyalty. And in spite of the fact that there were rebellions such as the Pilgrimage of Grace and important martyrs among those who opposed the process, including John Fisher, bishop of Rochester, who became a Catholic saint, there was no revolution. Instead, the estates that had once supported the cathedrals now helped fund the prodigy houses of the later sixteenth century and the English country house replaced the great church as the focus of architectural invention.

Inside the Church, though, there was a revolution. Until the 1540s the Reformation was in a sense simply a wave of Church reform, like so many that had washed over England from the time of Gregory the Great onwards. Monasteries had been dissolved before; and cathedrals converted from secular to monastic or monastic to secular. At root all these issues, from the relationship of king to pope to the question of where best to locate cathedral churches, had been of concern in 1070 or even, to stretch a point, 598. The dominance of king over pope and of secular over monastic principles had been in the air for a century or more. But in the sixteenth century the spirit of reform quickly took the Church in directions most of its originators never dreamt of.

In the reign of Edward VI, from 1547, the full force of European Protestantism, in all its strictness, hit England. The Rood of the North Door, statue of St Uncumber and other miraculous images at St Paul's were taken down in a night of violence during which two workmen were killed and 'divers others sore hurt'.[12] At Ely 'all images . . . were to be so totally demolished and obliterated with all speed and diligence, that no remains or memory might be found of them for the future'.[13] As a result, windows that have lost their stained glass light Ely's breathtaking architecture and hundreds of empty statue niches stud the walls of the lady chapel there. Ely today is like a magnificent cover on a book that has had all its pages ripped out. Lambert Barnard, the artist who had painted colourful sprays of foliage all over the walls of Chichester cathedral, was asked to whitewash over his own work and to replace it with stern religious homilies. At Canterbury,

Iconoclasm was carried out with sober, systematic violence: from a Flemish engraving of 1566

dismantling 'that cathedral ocean of images'[14] was a major undertaking: the angel that had been a feature of the city skyline since the twelfth century was pulled down by a hundred men with a rope, only to bury itself in the ground where it fell. At Ripon minster someone hid forty-nine service books and six carved images, fragments of which were found buried beneath the choir stalls in 1871.[15]

At the same time some of the truths that had fuelled cathedral architecture were overturned. Communion was no longer seen as a supernatural event and the doctrine of purgatory, which had lain behind the building of the chantries, was rejected. The chantries themselves were dissolved in 1547. As a result, the chapels financed by Bishop Longland at Lincoln and Abbot Malvern at Gloucester never received their burials. Some later collapsed through neglect and lack of use, among them the magnificently-painted chantry of Lord Robert Hungerford at Salisbury and the miniature fan-vaulted church built by Bishop Stillington at Wells. But most survive, ornate and empty, each a *Marie Celeste* of the Reformation. They include our next poignant monument, the Gardiner chantry at Winchester.

Stephen Gardiner, bishop of Winchester, spent most of the 1540s in the Tower of London, issuing daring written denials of the new faith. In 1556 he was buried in his cathedral in a purpose-built chantry chapel. Illegal at the time of its construction, this is perhaps the last and strangest monument of the English Reformation. Within this *samizdat* chantry, old world and new collide in the most bewildering of aesthetic juxtapositions. The richly-vaulted roof is gothic, but the altar retable is one of the first 'pure' classical architectural compositions in the country. Once again, a historical turning-point was coinciding with the import of a new European style. Unlike the flood of Norman churches that followed the Conquest, it was some time before a classical great church was built. St Paul's, the only Renaissance great church in England and as much a model cathedral of its era as any of its predecessors, was built 120 years after the Reformation.

The second great wave of iconoclasm took place about a century after the reign of Edward VI, during the Civil War and the Commonwealth. Puritans, and often Roundheads too (and sometimes greedy royalists, seeking treasure rather than Taliban-like purification), attacked images everywhere. The bishoprics were abandoned and many cathedrals simply locked: others became venues for Non-conformist meetings. Some hardliners proposed demolishing them completely. A

Like a radio tuned to two stations at once, an elegant Renaissance altarpiece explodes inside the spiky gothic of Bishop Gardiner's samizdat *chantry at Winchester*

swathe of destruction follows the front line of the Civil War across the Midlands. Lichfield cathedral, bombarded by the armies of both sides, lost its roof and its spire (illustrated p. 359); Southwell and Peterborough were denuded of almost all their medieval fittings.[16] At Lincoln, the stained-glass windows, which must have been mind-bogglingly beautiful, were taken down in 1664–5 and the lead, over 7 kg of it, used to make bullets: a dramatic case of ploughshares into swords.[17]

Not all change was destructive. The new cathedrals of 1541 were given appropriate new fittings and the subsequent ebb and flow of religious correctness was reflected in further fittings and decorations in the years to come. Many of these were swept away by the Victorians in the nineteenth century, by which time the churches themselves were often in a disastrous structural condition. Today Chester and Peterborough, Worcester and Lichfield are almost bare of medieval fittings; they are instead great repositories of Victorian art.

Yet the medieval saints have not been completely lost. Their relics were the glue that tied together politics, architecture and faith. Those of St Chad of Lichfield were looked after by recusant Catholics and are now in the Roman Catholic cathedral at Birmingham; for similar reasons, Catholic Downside abbey has relics of St Thomas Cantilupe. The bones of St Frideswide, mixed with those of a Cistercian nun who married after the Dissolution, are buried somewhere in Christ Church, Oxford. The bases of the shrines of St Alban and St Werburgh have been reconstructed from fragments; among the cathedral shrines, the Head Shrine of St Hugh at Lincoln is astonishingly intact. Tombs have survived in greater numbers, and with them traces of some of the more intriguing cathedral cults. The shrine-like tomb created at Hereford in the 1280s to help advertise the saintly potential of bishop Thomas Cantilupe is one. At Salisbury, the tomb-shrine of St Osmund was a virtual copy of Becket's first shrine at Canterbury. An object of devotion for centuries before Osmund was finally canonized in 1457 and moved into a grand new shrine, this bed-like structure of polished stone is with us still. And at Gloucester there is the great shrine-like tomb of the uncanonized Edward II. The saints inspired some of the greatest cultural achievements in English architectural history and their shrines were the focus of scenes of shamanic intensity and blind superstition. These survivals embody both what was appalling and what was, in a very literal sense, magical about this lost world.

Perhaps the most electrifying story of these saints comes from Durham, where the hard-headed commissioners of the king were struck almost dumb to find the venerable Cuthbert still incorrupt when they came to take his shrine down in 1539 or early 1540. They must have been shaken to the core. They had, after all, grown

Candles by the former site of the shrine of St Richard at Chichester: recent years have seen a quiet revival of interest in such sites

up in a world that took such miraculous events for granted and would have had to make a conscious effort to reject such beliefs. At the Reformation, Cuthbert's fate was left undecided for two years before he was reburied on the site of his shrine. He was the only saint to be treated in this way. The flagstones around his tomb bear the dips created by four hundred years of pilgrims' knees. More extraordinary is the fact that one of the greatest and most revolutionary churches in Europe was designed around the burial place of this saint and that his bones, alas no longer incorruptible, still lie there.

At Durham, Chichester, Hereford and St Albans, people are being drawn back to the sites of medieval shrines, irrespective of their religious beliefs. At Hereford in 2007-8 the (presumably empty) tomb of Thomas Cantilupe was turned back into a shrine, complete with a relic of the saint. As St Albans a steady stream of visitors leave offerings at the shrine-base, recently reconstructed with the help of Lottery funds. Since 2002, this shrine too has even contained a putative fragment of the saint. In the North East, Cuthbert has become a standard bearer for a New Ageist take on 'Celtic Christianity'. It seems the saints of England have been quietly reinvented once again; their cathedrals are with us still.

WHAT TO SEE

Christ Church cathedral and college, Oxford; Stephen Gardiner's chantry at Winchester and, in the Triforium Gallery, fragments of sculptures and fittings destroyed after the Reformation.

Chapter Six

WORKERS AND WORSHIPPERS

Getting dressed was quite a task for the archbishop of York: especially if he was just back from a trip abroad. On such occasions, ceremony demanded, he was to be greeted in full procession outside the west door of the minster. The archbishop had to put on his grandest vestments. His bejewelled ring signified his marriage to the Church. His golden staff symbolized his pastoral authority. His cope was more a piece of architecture than an item of clothing; by the fifteenth century such vestments would be stiff with jewels and metal decorations and covered with images of saints. Over it he wore the pallium, a scarf of purest lambs-wool: only the pope could confer this, and only an archbishop could wear it. On top of his head was his mitre, his cap of office. One medieval bishop's mitre, covered in jewels and embroidered in gold, is known to have cost £82. This was as expensive as a small building.[1] Equally striking were the rest of his clothes: the white silk gloves over which his rings were slipped; and the padded pontifical stockings, covered in rich embroidery. The archbishop's feet were rarely cold.

The procession coming towards him was an equally extraordinary sight. Above it towered the west front of the cathedral, covered in brightly-painted statues. This cliff of images was the perfect setting for the display beneath. Indeed, it had

The translation of a bishop-saint was a once-in-a-lifetime experience. A bishop censes as the incorrupt body of his predecessor is lifted from its burial place. Around him are churchmen of various types, from a Benedictine monk to an archbishop. Only the most important of laymen have been permitted to join this exclusive gathering; but a crowd of ordinary people pack the aisle beyond and peer through the choir screens: The exhumation of St Hubert, *by Rogier van der Weyden*

been partly designed as a backdrop to such events. The cathedral bells tolled thunderously; blasts of noise came from a portable organ. Painted embroideries of red, gold, green and blue shone. It was a hierarchical and magnificently decorous array. As above, so below.

Emerging from the door in the centre of this facade were the people who lived and worked at the cathedral. At a glance, the archbishop could distinguish each by their clothing and their position in the procession. At its head where the cathedral's senior officers and some other members of chapter. Behind them where the foot-soldiers of the church, the men who, as well as being responsible for a range of minor administrative tasks, performed the liturgy that was the minster's raison d'être. Altogether, there were enough of them to ensure that the full liturgy, which took six to eight hours, was enacted every day at the high altar, that there was also a daily mass at each of the cathedral's other altars, and that all those who had founded chantries were duly honoured.

The archbishop studied the procession closely: and not only for its aesthetic delights. Behind the grandeur, there was much for him to worry about. York minster may have been the archbishop's cathedral church, but his status within it was largely ceremonial. The archbishop had a three-layered job. He was head of one of the two provinces of the English Church, with authority over three sees. Secondly, he was bishop of one of those dioceses and, lastly, he was nominal head of his cathedral community. In addition to this, like any senior member of the medieval establishment, the archbishop had to manage the large estates on which he depended for an income. With each of these roles came a complex range of administrative and ritual responsibilities and constant political battles, not least with the community of his own cathedral.

The papal curia was the ultimate court for a thousand years of English churchmen: a fourteenth-century Italian image of Pope Boniface VIII and his cardinals

This archbishop of York had no voice in chapter and he might visit his cathedral only rarely. 'The dean in the church is greater than anyone after the archbishop; and in chapter he is greater than them all,' it was said of York.[2] He spent much of the year moving around on business, accompanied by his staff of officials, servants and secretaries. He had seven palatial houses in his diocese; one medieval bishop of Lincoln, who had thirteen such manors, travelled on average 30 miles a day. At all times, this bishop was accompanied by at least two clerks, two chaplains, two messengers, several legal advisers and much of the rest of his inner circle, and sometimes he was escorted by a company of knights.[3] Yet he was not indestructible. A serious dispute with his chapter could send him or his staff off on the six-month journey to Rome to seek a decision from the pope on the issues at stake.

So there could be much sensitivity in how the archbishop was greeted on the occasions he made a return to his cathedral. Everything mattered, from the clothes the participants wore to the gestures they made. It was important, for example, that the dean's vestments did not outshine those of the archbishop: this could be a very real issue. At Worcester cathedral in the late fourteenth century it was the custom for the prior to wear a bishop's mitre. Some priors even had this right conferred on them, a mark of the status and independence, in internal matters at least, of their convent. But a prior wearing a mitre instantly raised procedural issues: the bishop and the prior could not be seen in the same cathedral wearing mitres of equivalent grandeur. At Worcester, the argument over mitre design went all the way to Rome. The bishop had to watch his prior carefully to see if he had indeed removed the gold fringe and jewels which, it had been decreed, made his mitre look too much like the bishop's one, or whether his staff contravened the papal decree which restricted its colours to blue and silver.[4]

And then, at the climactic moment when an archbishop met his dean, how would they greet each other? Would they exchange a kiss of peace? This question became a major issue between Henry II and Thomas Becket and the resulting loss of trust had catastrophic consequences. No wonder the monks at Norwich cathedral priory sought papal guidance on this tense moment. In 1445, they were told that their prior was only obliged to exchange kisses with his bishop if the bishop had been away for more than two months.[5] Such rulings must have led to much nervous checking of dates. All this procedure may seem overblown, but it mattered in a world without fast transport or mass communication. Badges of status and ceremonial arrivals and departures made authority visible in the same way that press conferences and news reports do today.

Within his diocese, the bishop had much authority. No one could preach without his licence and he could carry out inspections of churches and religious communities of every kind. In the sixteenth century, Bishop Atwater of Lincoln carried out these inspections, known as visitations, in over a thousand parishes, taking over seven years to do so. He had thus covered about 60 per cent of his diocese.[6] Each church was obliged to offer his officials hospitality and to pay a fee for the privilege of being inspected. Before the bishop of Worcester inspected his own cathedral priory in 1461, he 'got food and drink for himself and his servants for two days', after which the community paid him the visitation fee of four marks and the real work began.[7]

In return, the bishop might issue a detailed report, covering everything from the physical state of the church to the moral standards of those who served it. Bishop Atwater found that a quarter of the parishes in the see of Lincoln had no priest at all. In a tenth of them the priest had some kind of established relationship with a woman, which was almost as worrying. After studying each of these relationships more carefully, the bishop decided that half were not suspicious: the women were simply employed to do the laundry or the cooking. But the others, many of them presumably marriages in all but name, were deemed immoral.[8]

On a monastic visitation, the bishop's officials might look critically at the house's accounts, and conduct detailed private interviews with members of the community. The final report could be fiercely censorious. When the bishop of Worcester visited Great Malvern priory in this way in 1282, he preached to the monks on the theme 'I will descend on you'. Having completed his investigations, he accused the prior of keeping twenty-two women on various houses and farms connected with the priory and ordered that he be deposed. But Great Malvern priory came under the jurisdiction of Westminster abbey, which was both distant and powerful. To prove a point, the abbot in Westminster waited a full five years before acting on the bishop's recommendations.[9]

Such struggles plagued the lives of medieval bishops and disagreements could even lead to violence. When the archbishop of York carried his cross upright in the province of Canterbury in 1279, thus implying that the two archbishops were of equal status, armed men fell on him at Rochester and broke the cross in two.[10] In theory all bishops were alike in their powers: in practice, their standing varied hugely, not least because there were enormous variation in their material wealth. The cathedral priory at Durham was the dominant religious house in this north-east corner of England and the cathedral's estates included almost all of what is now the county of Durham as well as substantial lands elsewhere. The bishop was thus one of the country's chief magnates. The bishop of Chichester, by contrast, had a comparatively small and poor diocese in which the mighty archbishop of Canterbury owned more land than he did. Moreover, the archbishop claimed his estates were independent of the bishop's authority. Two of the largest religious communities in the diocese, Lewes priory and Battle abbey, also claimed this 'episcopal immunity', so the bishop of Chichester was left with a rump of comparatively poor parishes and smaller religious houses.

The feared visitations could be emasculated in other ways as well. At York, the dean and chapter negotiated an arrangement with their archbishop in 1290 by which his powers of inspection at his 'home' church were almost completely neutered. The archbishop could only visit the chapter once every five years and when he did so he had to be accompanied at all times by two of the cathedral's canons. Any questions he wanted to ask had to be put in writing first, and no one could be interrogated against their will.[11] At Wells, in 1258, the bishop even surrendered the power to appoint canons. These agreements, common in the thirteenth century, turned the role of the bishop in his own church into a largely ceremonial one. At the same period, many independent-minded chapters, York and Wells included, financed palatial new chapter-houses from their own resources, ritual meeting-rooms which symbolized the corporate pride of their community. These expensive and beautiful works of architecture literally fixed in stone, by the way the seating was positioned, for example, constitutional arrangements that might otherwise be impermanent.

Carved heads of senior churchmen separate the stalls of the dignitaries in the Wells chapter-house

In spite of their corporate independence, some members of chapter might be personally and professionally extremely close to the bishop. He might have given prebends to members of his *familia,* or inner circle of trusted advisors; as for the archdeacons, who were his immediate juniors as far as diocesan work was concerned, in the secular cathedrals they often had a right to a seat on chapter.[12] The archdeacons each looked after the bishop's interests in a separate 'patch' of his diocese. They were grand men in themselves: those of Richmond (York) and Chester (Coventry and Lichfield), whose territories covered much of Lancashire and Cheshire in the wild north-west of England, ran their patches almost as if they were independent sees. The archdeacon of Canterbury effectively administered the diocese on the archbishop's behalf. These archdeaconries were subdivided into smaller areas that were taken care of by rural deans. Each of these men employed clerical assistants and servants, so the total number of people dedicated to a cathedral's diocesan work could be large. Bishop West of Ely is said to have had a hundred people on his staff.[13] As the administrative machinery got more and more complex, bishops needed deputies simply to keep on top of their workload. One late medieval bishop of Lincoln had two suffragan bishops, a vicar-general, an official principle, a commissary general and a chancellor.[14]

This administrative machine became so competent that almost all a bishop's powers could be delegated to such officials. This was especially true in places where the diocese was small, the bishopric was wealthy and his cathedral was monastic. Most late medieval bishops of Winchester were royal chancellors, spending their working lives at the service of the king in London and elsewhere. The bishops of Ely and Durham, too, often served as royal chancellors or treasurers. Four successive bishops of Worcester in the late fifteenth-century were Italian cardinals who rarely if ever set foot in England, let alone getting as far as the Severn valley.

Thus a bishop's working life was a mixture of high ceremony, tedious litigation and administration. It was a demanding role. Herbert de Losinga, bishop of Norwich, complained of having become an 'old and practised warrior whose wrestling is . . . against flesh and blood, against viscounts, against county magistrates, against informers'.[15] But such pressures did not stop them from living well.

When John Stafford was made bishop of Bath and Wells in 1424, he was greeted with a great feast, at which the bishop and those at the high table enjoyed one more course than the rest of the company. They consumed swan, heron, crane and venison followed by a light second course of almond rice (moulded into the form of a rabbit), as well as peacock, teal, curlew and gull, with pasties and dates. Dessert featured more meat, eggs, poultry, cheesecake, 'cold brawn' and fruit, washed down with a sweet wine.[16] The satisfied bishop might then have taken himself to bed. In 1399 the bishop of Bath and Wells did exactly that, slumbering in a tapestry-lined room under the favourite green bedspread, decorated with white lilies, that he was careful to have carried from manor to manor.[17] The bishop was expected to give as well as to receive. Royal officials came to Wells in

Churchmen join a lord's table in his great hall: such was the setting for much of the day-to-day machinations of a bishop's working life.

1337, concerned about disafforestation on the bishop's lands. It would not have done to let such an inspection get off to a bad start. Bishop Ralph of Shrewsbury found hay for 32 horses and accommodation for 268 men. The party consumed 86 gallons of wine and 672 loaves and a number of fish-banquets were held featuring eels from the Somerset Levels and cod, pollack, hake, haddock, bream, gurnard, plaice, salmon and pike from the Severn and the Irish Sea. A quarter of a Mendip sheep was supplied for the visitors' pages.[18]

The scale of all this good living can still be glimpsed at a few places. The magnificent bishop's palace at Wells is one of the country's finest medieval residences. The offices of the modern bishop of Southwell occupy just part of a half-ruined palace that was once used by the archbishop of York as a stopover on the way to London. Grand houses such as these, lay and religious alike, were centred on a great hall where daily business was done, most meals were eaten, and banquets were staged. Two of the largest great halls in England were built by bishops Hubert Walter at Canterbury and John Salmon at Norwich. Most bishops also maintained a sizeable palace on the edge of London for their visits to parliament or the court. Here the Holborn palace chapel of the bishops of Ely, now St Etheldreda's, Ely Place, and the ruined hall of the bishop of Winchester in Clink Street, Southwark, a kind of medieval no. 11 Downing Street, survive. Yet many well-known features of modern London grew out of these grand places. Whitehall is on the site of the palace of the archbishops of York and Lincoln's Inn replaced that of the bishop of Lincoln. Bishops had their own game parks, their own farms and their own fishponds, and defended encroachments on them aggressively.

All this grandeur was essential to maintaining one's place in a society where informal networks of patronage were essential and where life was accompanied by a keen sense of social and spiritual hierarchy. When a council in Westminster

By the end of the medieval period much tithe payment was in cash rather than kind: a painting of 1615 by Pieter Breughel the Younger

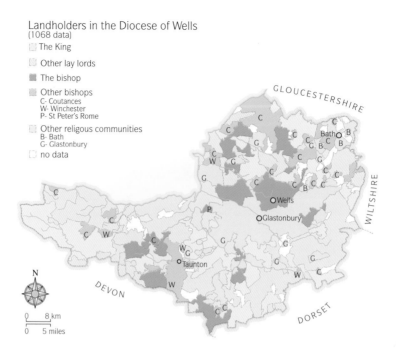

Landholders in the Diocese of Wells
(1068 data)

☐ The King

☐ Other lay lords

■ The bishop

☐ Other bishops
C- Coutances
W- Winchester
P- St Peter's Rome

☐ Other religous communities
B- Bath
G- Glastonbury

☐ no data

advised an archbishop of York on the kind of travelling arrangements that were
appropriate for him and his senior churchmen, they had to consider practicalities
as well as matters of rank, for each man needed to transport his staff and much of
his paperwork in order to do his job effectively. The archbishop was told that he
could travel with a train of up to fifty horses; that each of his suffragan bishops
could be followed by twenty or thirty beasts; and that his archdeacons needed to
get by on just five to seven.[19] Such decisions are very comparable to the wrangling
over office cars and other perks that goes on in corporations today.

Like all medieval institutions, the cathedral depended on land for its wealth.
The estates, which were divided between a bishop and his chapter, built up over
time, and could be quite widely scattered. York minster, for example, derived
income from lands in both Gloucestershire and Hampshire. But many great
churches had a compact core patrimony, such as Worcester's Hundred of
Oswaldslow. The bishop of Bath and Wells, Salisbury and others owned the cities
in which they were based. Norwich cathedral priory was managing a lucrative
flock of four thousand sheep in 1480 and nearly doubled it over the next forty
years: the bishop criticized the monks for even grazing sheep in the cloister.[20]

These lands gave the cathedrals other worldly responsibilities, too. They maintained peripatetic courts with which to deal with the complaints of their tenants; they also had feudal obligations to the king, being obliged to support a given number of knights according to the size of their landholding. A religious house could hold an entire manor, which might be large enough to include several villages, and receive from it specified proportions of its agricultural produce and of the labour of those who lived there; or it might simply rent a group of urban houses out for cash. Agricultural work could be overseen directly by the cathedral community or contracted out, put 'to farm', in which case the tenant managed the property and paid the cathedral a proportion of his proceeds from selling what was grown or raised. Cathedral priors and deans alike became sophisticated land-managers: Prior Eastry of Canterbury,

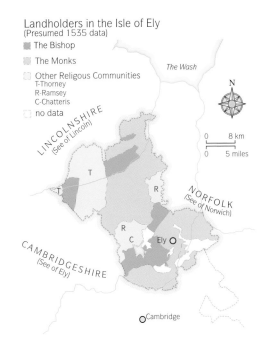

Landholders in the Isle of Ely
(Presumed 1535 data)
■ The Bishop
▨ The Monks
▢ Other Religous Communities
 T-Thorney
 R-Ramsey
 C-Chatteris
▢ no data

for example, invested cannily in the local land market and so improved the productivity of the estates under his management that for a period Canterbury had a year's surplus cash in its coffers.[21]

At the bottom of this system were the humble peasants who worked the land. Even they were members of a complex hierarchy. The ninety-five cottars of the township of Ely were comparatively well off, for peasants: yet they had to work hard for their feudal overlords, eke out a living from their lands and still find the wherewithal to give three hens at Christmas and thirty eggs at Easter to the cathedral priory. Every townsman was also required to maintain two furlongs of the Alderheye causeway, ensuring this crucial dry route to the Isle was well looked after.[22] Lower down in the hierarchy where the serfs, who owned little more than a house and a patch of land and lived a subsistence lifestyle based on hard labour for others; and beneath them where the landless, who were as good as slaves (but without the job security). Although they are almost invisible in this book and its sources, this peasantry comprised the overwhelming majority of the population. It is hard to imagine what they made of the colossal churches that dominated both their landscape and their lives. Such a society arguably depended for its stability on the belief that certain powers were sacred.

A church might own large and profitable flocks of sheep: a shepherd from a misericord at William Wykeham's Winchester college

The bishop's authority, after all, derived ultimately from God via St Peter, the man whom Jesus, God incarnate, had called 'the rock on which I will build my church'.[23] St Peter was the first bishop and the model for all subsequent bishops. The pope, St Peter's successor, was also a kind of bishop, as was an archbishop. The pope appointed archbishops (often after a tussle with the local king) and approved the appointment of bishops (again, often after drawn-out negotiations with the king and the cathedral community, who claimed the right to elect him). Knowing that Henry I intervened in one such process, telling a cathedral community, 'I order you to hold a free election, but nevertheless, I forbid you to elect anyone except Richard my clerk', it is easy to be cynical.[24] But the appointment of bishops was about far more than a simple chain of command.

The bishop had spiritual powers that were focused on the sacred event of the Eucharist. The miracle at the centre of the mass, the transformation of a disc of unleavened bread and a chalice of rough wine into the body and blood of Christ, enshrined a sacred contract between humanity and God. Only a priest could administer this sacrament, and only a bishop could create a priest. Priests were set aside from other men, for they had powers that were not even granted to the angels: 'Oh, how very great is their power', said St Laurence Justinian, 'A word falls from their lips and the body of Christ is there substantially formed from the matter of bread . . . the angels abide by the order of God, but the priests take him in their hands, distribute him to the faithful, and partake of him as food for themselves.' Every speck of dust associated with the Eucharist was taken seriously: the chrism cloth used to administer it had to be burned or recycled appropriately.

Priests were required to perform mass once a day, every day, at a suitably blessed altar in every religious community and in every one of the eight thousand or more parish churches that dotted the landscape by the end of the thirteenth century.[25] Ordinary people perhaps took Communion once a year or so (though they may have watched services far more frequently than that), but that did not decrease its significance. Such ceremonies were the liturgical glue that held the Church together and bound God to humanity; they formed the spiritual infrastructure of society itself.

It is this that gave every medieval bishop such significance and made the cathedrals so powerful. For bishops were not only essential to the Eucharist; they had a range of other sacramental powers. Bishops blessed the holy oils essential to many religious ceremonies, from baptism to the blessing of the sick; and they consecrated churches and thus rendered them ritually 'fit for use'. Again and again cathedral architecture reflects the sacred nature of episcopal authority. The Great Screen at Winchester, for example, was designed so that a silver image of Christ would frame the celebrant at the moment he raised the host and the divine spark entered the little disc of unleavened bread. Similarly, the most spectacular bishop's throne in Europe stands in the choir at Exeter whose cathedral of St Peter is a great hymn to episcopal power. Without bishops, the Church would have stopped in its tracks, and humankind stand exposed to the bitter winds of a life outside God's grace. That is why the cathedrals mattered.

They also provided employment and housing for a large number of people. The ninety or so men who greeted our archbishop were only some of the people who lived at York minster. Most English cathedrals supported around two hundred full-time staff and there would also have been bailiffs and servants on their manors.[26] Many of these were laymen, from the three men who swept the floor at Lincoln,[27] through the lay brothers who assisted the monks at Ely, to the well-connected local landowners and stewards who gave the prior of Canterbury advice and support.[28] By the end of the Middle Ages, some advisers and retired local gentry were even living with their families in the cathedral close, at Norwich, for example.[29] Such people might be members of a separate 'precinct parish', with an altar inside the cathedral set aside for their worship. The close had become a tight community of lay and religious people whose lives were united by the great church at its heart. Nonetheless, although politically important and practically useful, such laymen were peripheral. The people who really mattered in the affairs of a cathedral such as York were the members of chapter and, in particular, their elected officers. They governed the day-to-day life of the minster.

York was a secular cathedral (see p. 21), staffed by canons who followed privileged careers in Church or state. Those who made up the York chapter did very nicely from the income of their prebends. That of Masham, worth over £166 a year, was the richest in England.[30] With incomes like this, the chapter dominated the city financially, even though York itself was one of the wealthiest towns in the country. In 1290, the dean's income was £373, while the entire worldly possessions of the richest man in York were worth just £26 forty years later. The personal wealth of the archbishop might be anything from £800 to £5,000: his peers were not the merchants of York, but men like the Earl of Northumberland.[31] But, however large his retinue, the Earl of Northumberland was an individual. Apart from the royal court, there were no other institutions of the wealth and complexity of a cathedral chapter. The way in which the minster eclipses every other building in York is a palpable expression of the fact that it was the corporate headquarters of one of the richest organizations in the country.

The canons were educated men. At Hereford in the fourteenth century, for example, 30 per cent of them had doctorates. A house-sized building had to be constructed in 1414 when Canon John Newton of York, former master of Peterhouse, Cambridge, gave his books to the minster: today this former library is the cathedral shop.[32] These men worked all over the country; indeed some travelled all over Europe. Perhaps a fifth of them might work for their bishop as archdeacons or other senior advisors. Others were employed by other bishops, in England or overseas, and a significant number worked for the king or were representatives of the English Church, or papal officials, in Rome. Hereford's prebends were comparatively poor, its community comparatively resident. Some members of York's chapter, by contrast, can rarely have met each other.

It has been estimated that a half to two-thirds of York's annual income of around £2,000 went into the pockets of men who never visited the see. Of thirty-four new canons appointed at the minster in 1306–15, just ten were chosen by the archbishop: another dozen were appointed by the king and worked in London, where they formed a 'vast and close-knit affinity' of Yorkshiremen at the heart of fourteenth-century English government.[33] Pluralism, the practice of having more than one post, was also rife. Fourteenth-century precentors of Lichfield included a Frenchman, three Italians and a clerk of the king's pantry;[34] these men's canonry in the English Midlands was just one among a portfolio of posts through which they funded a lavish lifestyle. Pluralism could get out of hand. One dean of York was also dean of Lincoln and precentor at Lichfield:[35] each was an important post in its own right, with an income on which a man could live well.

In spite of holding posts elsewhere, these men could have a surprisingly strong sense of identity with their cathedral community. Some might even make a formal commitment to become residents. This was an expensive process as they had to live in the close, worship in choir daily, and entertain all-comers for a pre-set period, often six months, to qualify, but being a resident brought considerable benefits. Residents received a share of a separate common fund that might be worth £40 to £100 a year and there were many other perks, such as the 21 loaves and 30 gallons (137 litres) of ale a week that were given to the resident canons at St Paul's, or the sum of about £26 that was paid at York for attendance at certain key services.[36] These men were busy. Much of the administration of the cathedral fell to them, and they were obliged to entertain other churchmen and important lay visitors. But they lived well. Archbishop Cranmer talked of resident canons as 'good livers' with 'superfluous belly cheer'.[37] A home even came with the job; these men had large houses in the close each of which, like a miniature bishop's palace, would contain a *familia* of minor officials and liveried servants.

Among these resident canons were the dignitaries, the cathedral's senior officers.[38] These were the men who managed cathedral life. At York they were the precentor, the chancellor, the treasurer and the dean. The precentor oversaw the endless round of the liturgy, and trained young choristers. The chancellor ran the cathedral's secretariat, drawing up accounts, taking minutes, issuing proclamations and keeping files; he was also responsible for the cathedral's grammar school. The treasurer looked after the cathedral's possessions, taking care of any precious objects and the furnishings of the church itself.[39] He was responsible for maintenance of the church and of other buildings in the close and on its lands. Presiding over all these officers was the dean, the president of chapter. If the bishop was non-executive chairman of the cathedral, the dean was its chief executive, with a lifestyle to match. One sixteenth-century dean of York arrived at the cathedral's Christmas

Men like this canon of Wells arguably formed the first professional middle class

service accompanied by some of his staff: fifty gentlemen in tawny coats corded with black velvet and thirty yeomen in coats corded with taffeta.[40]

York was well known for its large number of non-resident canons, but the minster was only the most extreme example of a practice that existed across England. The majority of canons at the secular cathedrals, from those at Exeter, which had the smallest chapter (only twenty-four canons) to those at Lincoln, which had the largest (sixty-three), were never there. Exeter shared with Hereford the distinction of attracting comparatively high rates of residency, but even here the chapter-houses were largely empty. The existence of an institution whose members are predominantly absent is remarkable enough, but the fact they were all churchmen, whose lives were theoretically dedicated to communal acts of worship, makes it even more surprising. This was a real problem, but it had a very practical solution: each canon employed a junior churchman to stand in for him and keep up the daily worship that lay at the core of cathedral life. These men were the vicars choral. At York there were about thirty-six of them, all of whom lived on site and prayed in the cathedral every day.

A visitor to the minster on a typical day would only see such vicars in the church. They worshipped at the high altar for six to eight hours daily, ensured other masses were performed and carried out lesser administrative tasks in what time remained. A canon was a rare beast: perhaps one (that week's hebdomadary canon) might lead the daily high mass: otherwise they were merely glimpsed, moving grandly from one task to another, followed by a small cloud of clerks. In spite of this, on important days, if all the vicars, choristers, chantry priests and resident canons gathered together, as many as eighty people might be packed into the choir.[41]

It was the vicars who performed the church's primary function: worship. Yet they had no power within the cathedral, no seat on chapter: they were merely ciphers for the canons. We first come across them in the early twelfth century, a period when cathedral chapters were rapidly expanding.[42] At first they even lived with their canon. By around the turn of the century, canons began to be obliged to pay their vicars a wage and guarantee them some job security. Later, sometimes at the prompting of the bishop or chapter, but sometimes as a result of

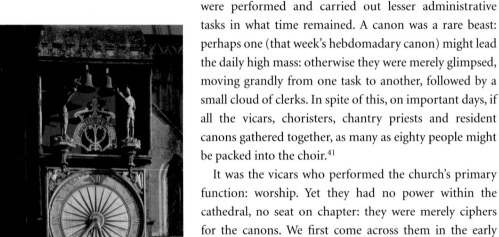

Clocks like that at Wells helped the various communities of the close keep up with a complex liturgical timetable

their own initiative,[43] they became a community within a community. They occupied their own close within the wider cathedral close, with their own hall and chapel and later even acquired their own lands and elected their own warden. The earliest of these vicars' closes was founded at York in the late 1240s: by the mid-fifteenth century every secular cathedral had one and, in a wave of institutionalizations that started in Wells in 1348 (illustrated p. 440) almost all had been formally incorporated. Thus the vicars choral evolved from a group of spiritual stand-ins into a miniature religious college. The vicars' closes were also a way of dealing with a group of people who could be hard to discipline. After all, here were groups of from thirty to fifty youngish men, employed in work of mind-numbing boredom, living together, and forbidden contact with the opposite sex.

It must have been a strange life, being a vicar choral. The day was dominated by acts of worship: yet these men had none of the cachet, the 'otherness' of monks; none of the public engagement of parish priests, and none of the standing of canons. When not in choir they might be found wearing 'the wanton and outrageous clothes of laymen, with the collars of their doublets stuck up too high over the collar of their gowns and cloaks which were cut too low', as was complained of at Wells in 1459.[44] At Salisbury in the fourteenth century they were fined for playing ball in the close, and for wearing boots made of red and green squares. One of them, John Wallope, was always arguing, it was complained. Worse than that, he had slept with three women and talked heresy while everyone ate.[45] The girlfriend of one of the York vicars had even given birth in his room.[46] Such problems went to the heart of church life. At York in 1403 about half a dozen vicars could be persuaded to actually sing when they were in choir; the other twenty-eight or so talked amongst themselves or simply did not bother to turn up.[47] The young 'poor clerks' at Lincoln were told not to talk during services. They were also admonished not to rush their chanting so as to get back to catching pigeons and lighting fires in the bell tower.[48] No wonder many vicars' closes had covered ways directing their members directly into the cathedral.[49] Yet vicars are known to have stayed at their cathedrals for almost all their lives, in spite of the fact that it was almost unknown for them to rise to the level of canons.[50]

Punishment in cathedral schools could be severe: from a window in York minster

The vicars choral were just one of the sub-communities connected with the cathedral. Another was composed of the chantry priests, employed to sing regular masses for the souls of bishops and local grandees who had left money for this purpose. Some chantry priests were simply moonlighting vicars choral, but others had been employed separately. By 1391 there were seventy-four chantries being performed at St Paul's cathedral, each of which needed an altar space once a day, and also sixty-three obits, whose donors were commemorated in an annual remembrance mass, usually on their 'deathday'.[51] Soon twenty-seven priests were being employed full time in addition to the vicars. Each priest was supported by the endowment of the founder of the chantry. Many cathedrals formed these chantry priests, too, into a separate sub-college. The first was established at St Paul's in 1318 and was followed by others at Wells, Salisbury, York and Exeter. These chantries were often performed at existing altars, and this had to be fitted into the cathedral's already complex liturgical timetable. Thus it is not surprising to find that the cathedrals were among the first to invest in accurate clocks, which began to appear in the early fourteenth century: famous examples can still be seen at Wells and Salisbury; that at Norwich, with its moving models of the sun and moon and its mechanical procession of monks,[52] has long disappeared.

All cathedrals also ran a choir school, at which a handful of promising young men with good singing voices might be educated for nothing as a quid pro quo for their attendance at services. Fee-paying students, who were not expected to sing in the cathedral, were also accepted. Wells was not alone in running both a choir school and a grammar school. A professional lay schoolmaster was employed, and there was a 'beautiful dwelling' for the pupils to live in. In 1460 Bishop Beckington issued the children with careful instructions on everything from their sleeping arrangements to their table manners. When eating bread at meals, they were 'not to gnaw at it or tear it with their nails'; and they were to sleep three to a bed, nose-to-tail.[53]

There were many informal schools outside the Church, but it was the model of the religious college that was used as the basis for the first formally constituted independent schools. Independent grammar schools, such as Winchester college, and university colleges, such as New college, Oxford, were organized as collegiate religious communities. Other collegiate churches had other functions; many celebrated chantries for their founders and provided a pool of prebends with which high-flying churchmen could be rewarded. By the Reformation there were perhaps 210 collegiate churches of various kinds in England as a whole.[54] Some were very small, but up to fifty, including the cathedrals, were wealthy enough to employ vicars choral: an indication that their members were free to do things other than worship.

Yet even among the collegiate churches, of which they were a subset, the secular cathedrals stood apart. Before the late fourteenth century, when large academic colleges began to be founded, the secular cathedrals were substantially larger and richer than any other collegiate foundation. The only colleges that came close to being exceptions to the rule all had a special relationship with the bishop of their see. For example, only Southwell, Ripon and Beverley had their own formally-constituted vicars' colleges; and only Southwell and Crediton had more than a dozen canons.[55] Southwell, Ripon and Beverley were 'deputy cathedrals' of the archbishop of York; while Crediton was itself a former cathedral.

The members of these communities formed a group of well-educated men who were institutionally based and potentially available to work anywhere in Europe. Their very existence must have made it easier for complex administrative processes, whether lay or secular, to develop and for the machinery of government to evolve. Here was a professional class of mandarins, lawyers and theologians in the making.

Benedictine monks, such as the mid-twelfth century Canterbury monk Eadwine, dominated European learning for centuries

An archbishop returning to York, a secular cathedral, might thus study those who greeted him for all kinds of political nuances. Many of his archdeacons and other staff, though, were also canons, so he would have been catching the eyes of men who worked with him or for him. Many were men he had appointed and some of them would have followed him throughout their careers. And he knew that all the canons, whether resident or not, were men like him, caught up in a complex, demanding, well-rewarded and highly political world in which Church and state merged. All this stands in sharp contrast to the way monastic cathedrals functioned. A bishop returning to a monastic cathedral was greeted by a crowd of near-strangers dressed in black.

The monastic cathedrals (see p. 22), like all other monastic houses, were huge, highly-disciplined communes, made up of men who had foresworn personal property and most forms of contact with the outside world. Worship was the main purpose of their lives, and this centred round performing the liturgy together six to eight hours a day, every day. When not worshipping, they studied, worked for the monastery, preached, taught or performed acts of charity. Every aspect of a monk's life was strictly regulated according to the community's Rule, which laid down how the monks should live. All but one of the monastic cathedrals followed the Rule written by St Benedict in the sixth century.[56] Unlike canons, monks were not obliged to be priests, though many were; in practice what defined them was their devotion to this life apart. All the monks had a seat in chapter, making the monastic cathedrals rather more democratic, as well as more centralized and communal, than the secular ones.

As in a collegiate church, the community elected the man who governed them. This prior was the equivalent of the dean and, like the dean, he had a handful of senior officers to assist him. These were the obedientaries, the monastic equivalent of the dignitaries.[57] A prior would normally report to an abbot, but in the cathedral priories the bishop was the titular abbot. Such bishops usually had little time to see to the running of the community and after the end of the twelfth century were rarely monks by profession.

The senior officials in a monastery had more or less the same roles as those in the secular churches, though their titles were different. The obedientary most often involved with building works, for example, was the sacrist, who also stage-managed the liturgy. But the obedientaries also included many lesser officials. At Ely there were about twenty in a total community of fifty monks. Each had a budget assigned to him that was often based on the income from a specific land-holding. These men were responsible for ensuring that the daily needs of the community were met. Enormous quantities of food had to be gathered and prepared; clothes had to be made and washed. Some roles were more esoteric. The Ely sedge-master obtained the sedges that were essential for repairing thatched roofs and the fuel for keeping peat fires alight. Other monks might assist these men and there was usually a small army of lay servants as well. The servants were men if at all possible, as contact with women could ritually pollute the monks, and it was they who did the actual cooking and cleaning, leaving the monks to concentrate on worship and on running their convent. Secular cathedral communities employed such people too but, as they were less communal, they needed fewer of them.

The cathedral priories were more like other monastic houses than the secular cathedrals were like other collegiate churches. Without taking into account the finances of the bishop, which were separate, the six richest cathedral priories lie scattered in a list of the twenty wealthiest monasteries in England, a list that includes the abbeys of Glastonbury, Westminster and Bury St Edmunds. All these powerful and wealthy religious communities were Benedictine and there was a good deal of contact between them. From 1215, the leaders of each house met each other regularly at the order's general chapter. They also followed the same routines. A monk from the monastic cathedral of Durham who visited other great Benedictine abbeys, such as St Peter's, Gloucester (which became Gloucester cathedral in 1541), or St Mary's in York (whose ruins stand by the Ouse), would find that the layout of the monasteries and their daily routines were basically identical. The most significant difference was that Durham happened also to be the seat of a bishop.

The monastic communities could be large. Canterbury, the largest monastery in England, had between eighty and a hundred monks for most of our period; at the other extreme, Rochester had no more than twenty-four to thirty. Most communities had forty to seventy monks, and there would have perhaps been twice as many laymen associated with them. The smallest of all was Carlisle. The last new cathedral of the Middle Ages, Carlisle was exceptional in that it was Augustinian rather than Benedictine. Its members followed a rule that was a kind of third way between the monastic and the secular; they were all priests, dedicated to serving the laity, but lived communal, disciplined lives, like monks.

What the monastic cathedrals gained in sanctity, idealism and community, they lost in flexibility. None of the key features of a Benedictine monastery changed between 1000 and 1500. By contrast the secular cathedrals evolved gradually over time: the emergence of vicars' colleges is one example of this. The monasteries had much less room for manoeuvre and issues arising within monasticism could easily spill over into the fracturing of the order and the formation of new ones. The Cistercians, Augustinians, Carthusians, Dominicans and Franciscans all started as a result of dissatisfaction with the monastic status quo (see pp. 77, 107).

The changing fortunes of the monastic and secular cathedrals are one of the dominant themes of this book. The traditional Benedictine monasteries kept learning and culture alive for many centuries, and were seen from the ninth to the twelfth centuries as the key to any programme of renewal and reform within the Church. They played a crucial role after the Norman Conquest, when the number of monastic cathedrals was expanded and monk-bishops were commonplace: men like Remigius of Lincoln, de Losinga of Norwich and archbishops Lanfranc and Anselm of Canterbury. It was the monastic cathedrals, such as Norwich, Durham, Ely and Canterbury, that had the grandest romanesque architecture. But it was through the secular cathedrals that the skills of learning and administration transformed themselves into the building blocks of the world as we know it. The great gothic cathedrals, Lincoln, Salisbury, York, Wells, Lichfield and Exeter, are mostly secular. By 1250 almost all bishops were secular churchmen, even at the monastic cathedrals.

To this day secular cathedral closes, as at Wells, Salisbury and Chichester, are quite different from their monastic counterparts, as at Canterbury, Worcester or Durham. A secular cathedral did not need a cloister, though all except two had built them by the end of the Middle Ages.[58] At the monastic cathedrals, by contrast, the cloister is at the heart of things. The communal buildings, the dormitory, refectory and chapter-house, are all grouped round it, generating a sense of inward-looking enclosure. At the secular cathedrals, the canons' houses are set in generous plots of land and little vicars' closes are located among them. There was no canonical plan for the secular cathedral close. Some, such as Lincoln and York, appear to have evolved relatively piecemeal while others, such as Wells and Salisbury, were carefully designed. The layout of the monastic close, by contrast, was set from the ninth century and differed only in detail or where there were practical reasons to do so, such as the lie of the land, or convenient access to running water.

These closes, secular and monastic alike, have changed considerably since the Reformation. The area around the west front and towards the town usually contained a cemetery for lay people. There would also have been various buildings and other structures in this important part of the close, of which only a few survive. They might have included a preaching-cross, as at Norwich and St Paul's (both gone); a substantial detached bell-tower, which was a feature of many cathedrals, including Salisbury and Worcester (only those at Chichester and Rochester survive); one or more chapels, as at Worcester, Exeter, St Paul's and Norwich, which might also be used as ossuaries (only the chapel at Norwich survives); a parish church, as at Ely and Rochester (Rochester survives) and even shops, as at St Paul's and Norwich. There might be one or more anchorites' cells, too, in which those who had renounced the world lived in silence and solitude; there were three female anchorites in the close at Norwich.[59] The close

Lack of a practical need for one did not prevent the canons of Salisbury from building England's largest medieval cloister

could be a busy place. As the venue for lay processions, funerals and Palm Sunday rituals alike, it could regularly come alive in noisy, dramatic ways. The cathedrals encouraged this activity and burials, from which they derived an income, even more so.

The area around the east end of the church and between it and the community's buildings was far more exclusive. The members of the community might have separate burial grounds here: some secular cathedrals buried their vicars separately from their canons. Such areas might include gardens and other landscaping. Two important monasteries, Westminster abbey and the cathedral priory at Norwich, had contemplative gardens between the monks' cemetery and the lady chapel.[60] There were two further gardens in the close at Norwich. One was used for growing medicinal herbs, the other was a place where important visitors could relax.[61] Presumably this was not unusual. Indeed, the degree to which the community landscaped its surroundings is one of the great unknowns of the cathedral closes, secular and monastic alike. The records give occasional hints of tree planting, among them the elm trees planted outside the Wells west front as it neared completion and the two hundred hawthorns that were transplanted to the bishop's palace at Lichfield in the early fourteenth century.[62]

All this would have been normal to the lay visitor: what would have struck him or her instantly was the difference between a monastic and a secular close. The monastic cathedrals, like other monastic houses, greeted the visitor with a row of charitable and public-service buildings, places where travellers could stay, or paupers receive doles of food or fuel. Secular cathedrals had nothing like this. It would have been immediately obvious that the secular close was a community of exclusive homes, a gated garden city whose mayor was the bishop.

The monks of Chester ate communally in their refectory

Whatever the type of community connected to it, the close was dominated by one building: the cathedral church. Here the situation outlined above was reversed: it was the secular cathedral churches whose architecture tended to reach out to the layman. All except one (Coventry) of the great sculpted screen-like west fronts are on secular cathedrals (Wells, Lincoln, Salisbury, Lichfield, Exeter, York); the west fronts of the monastic cathedrals were undemonstrative by comparison

(Norwich, Winchester, Canterbury Durham, Worcester),[63] as was the tight complex of claustral and other buildings adjacent to them. At some monastic cathedrals, such as Ely and Winchester, lay people entered by a small door in the transept; by contrast grand porches welcomed visitors to Hereford and Salisbury. And, partly because this was the only building that embodied the community as a whole, the secular cathedrals put far more effort into their chapter-houses. Like the cloister, the chapter-house of a secular cathedral was often empty; but at least it had a practical function as the venue for chapter meetings.[64] With one exception – and it is Worcester, where the idea was invented – the spectacular polygonal chapter-houses all belong to the secular cathedrals, where they were expensively constructed in the thirteenth and fourteenth centuries; with one exception – and it is Exeter, the most communal of secular cathedrals – the rectangular chapter-houses belong to the monastic cathedrals, and most appear to have been refurbished rather than rebuilt after the twelfth century.[65]

Such distinctions break down if great churches that were not cathedrals are also included; but that is the point. The screen facades, chapter-houses and gothic rebuildings associated with the secular cathedrals are partly a product of their unique character. The peers of the monastic cathedrals were other great monastic houses: the secular cathedrals had no exact peers. Their architecture was far more likely to be shaped by the things that set them apart: by the fact that they were bishop's seats, that they were mother churches to a diocese, and that they combined great corporate pride with a lack of any real communal life.

While many of the people who worked for the bishop of a secular cathedral held prebends in the cathedral church, none of the bishops' staff at a monastic one were also members of the monastery. The bishop himself had very little influence in the monastery. He might at best hope to guide the selection of the prior and was rarely involved in the appointment of any of the other senior monks. The bishop had to ensure that all the business of administering the diocese, all the work that was unique to him as a bishop, was funded out of his own part of the cathedral budget. Likewise the monks, though they had many worldly responsibilities as landowners, did not have to concern themselves with diocesan matters.[66] In the years after the Conquest, when bishoprics were created at existing monastic houses such as Coventry, Bath and Ely, the convent's income was divided up so that both monks and bishop had revenue coming in, a process that often caused rancour among the monks.

This money funded the bishop's *familia* and the other staff who ran the diocese and worked for him in the bishop's palace; where they lived was up to them. They

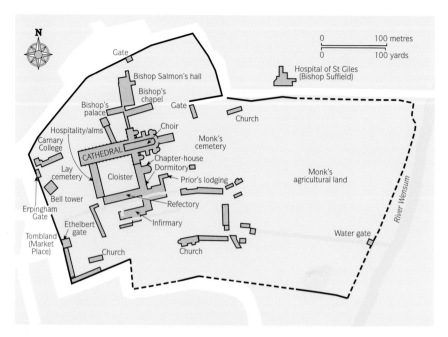

The following labels appear on the map:

N

Gate

Bishop Salmon's hall

Bishop's chapel

Bishop's palace

Gate

Hospitality/alms

Carnary College

CATHEDRAL

Choir

Church

Monk's cemetery

Chapter-house

Dormitory

Lay cemetery

Cloister

Prior's lodging

Monk's agricultural land

Bell tower

Erpingham Gate

Refectory

Ethelbert gate

Infirmary

Tombland (Market Place)

Church

Church

Hospital of St Giles (Bishop Suffield)

Water gate

River Wensum

0   100 metres

0   100 yards

The close at monastic Norwich was dominated by the cloister and associated buildings

had no official role in the cathedral; they were paid directly by the bishop or had portfolios of prebends and other sources of income from other churches. Many bishops of monastic cathedrals founded small colleges of their own to help them dispense such patronage: the bishop of Norwich founded one next to the cathedral close;[67] the bishop of Durham had Howden; the archbishop of Canterbury Maidstone and Wingham; the bishop of Worcester, Westbury-on-Trym. In spite of this, the bishop's household in a monastic cathedral was the polar opposite of the monastery itself: the least regulated, least formalized of all groupings of churchmen.[68]

This disconnection between a bishop and his monastic community was the opposite of what was intended when monastic cathedrals were created by the reformers of the tenth and eleventh centuries. At that time monasticism was seen as the focus of good religion, and the model of the bishop who was also monk and abbot was a meaningful one. But the monastic calling did not sit easily alongside a Church that was claming increasing influence over the lives of ordinary people: as Archbishop Stephen Langton put it in the early thirteenth century, only a rare monk made a good bishop.[69] It also made little difference to the diocese at large.

Site of Mountery College
(Chantry priests)

Canons' houses

Canons' barn

Canons' houses

Vicars' close

Canons' houses

Deanery

Chapter-house

Canons' Cemetery

Choir

Vicars' cemetery

CATHEDRAL

St. Andrew's Well

Lay cemetery

Gate

Library over

Choristers

Cloister

Lady chapel by-the-cloister (Stillington chantry)

The New Works

Gate

ponds

Gate

Market place

Gate

Bishop's palace

Bishop's chapel

moat

Bishop Burnell's hall

millstream

Chilcote Stream

N

0   100 metres
0   100 yards

Bishop's barn

Lawpool

The canons' houses and sub-colleges of the close at secular Wells made it a privileged city-within-a-city

With enough resources, the bishop could run his business in the see smoothly whether or not his staff happened to be members of the cathedral community. But it made a big difference in the cathedrals themselves. In the monastic cathedrals, the bishop came to be more of a bolt-on figure: in the secular ones, however independent the chapter, the bishop was far more integrated with the community and was the defining feature of its identity.

Were the archbishop of Canterbury to return to *his* cathedral from a trip overseas, then, he would have been met by a procession of near-strangers. Exceptionally, at Canterbury the archbishop played a key role in selecting the senior obedientaries.[70] But behind them stood the lesser obedientaries, then the other monks and lastly the acolytes, young men preparing to commit themselves to the monastic life.

Everything about the monastic life was prescribed. Even the acolytes were only allowed a very few personal possessions. As well as bedding and clothing in specified quantities they could have a comb, shaving materials, and needle and thread; also writing boards and implements.[71] At Durham the monks were locked in from 5 p.m. to 7 a.m. each day. Every night, the sub-prior checked their sleeping arrangements; St Benedict had pointed out that beds should be regularly checked to make sure no one had personal property secreted away. A register was called before the midnight service. Even eating was a ritual. Before their evening meal, which finished at 5 p.m., the monks queued to wash their hands at communal wash-basins and to dry them on freshly-laundered towels before entering the refectory; while they ate they were read passages from the Bible.[72] These washing areas can still be seen in the cloisters at Worcester and Norwich and at Gloucester abbey; elaborate hydraulic systems ensured that the very cleanest water reached these lavatoriums first (illustrated p. 279).[73] At Carlisle and St Werburgh's abbey, Chester (later a cathedral), the refectory pulpit can still be seen. Conversation was heavily restricted at all times: some basic matters were communicated with hand signals so the monks did not have to break their silence.

At least the food was reasonable. The monks of Ely ate two main meals a day (reduced to one for Lent and other fast days). In addition they were given bread and a warm drink before bed. For supper in winter they might eat a filling pottage with black peas, beans, leek and cabbage in a vegetable or, in spite of their commitment to vegetarianism, meat base. On Wednesdays and Fridays they ate fish from the Ouse weirs, the prior's fishpond, or from the sea, brought salted from Lynn or Cromer. Dessert included a milk pudding known as a tansies. The menu changed each day: meat rissoles or pancakes for supper on Sunday; fried and battered fish on Tuesday; whelks baked with spices on Wednesday; Fenland eels with pepper, cumin and saffron on Saturday.[74] The cath-edral priory of Norwich bought 7,000 to 13,000 eggs a week to feed its hungry horde, as well as pepper, cloves, cinnamon, cumin and sometimes ginger. Many other herbs were grown along-side the nuts and fruit in the priory garden.[75] A single day's consumption at Winchester had a cash value of 8s 6d, rising to 10s 9d on festival days.[76] This was a reason-able increase if it reflected what was consumed during Whitsun in Durham in 1346. This feast, for local friends as well as the monks, required 1,000 herrings, 42 salmon, 14 ling and a host of other fish (salt and fresh) as well as more than 10 oxen carcasses, 13 swine, 14 calves, 3 kids, and 26 suckling pigs. The cooking used 5 stone (32kg) of

Winchester monk with a chessboard: the cathedrals are covered with carvings that warned churchmen against lax behaviour

hog's lard, 4 stone (25kg) of cheese, butter and milk, a 'pottle' (over 2 litres) of vinegar, the same amount of honey, 14lbs (just over 6kg) of figs and raisins, 13lbs (almost 6kg) of almonds, and 8 lbs (3.5kg) of rice. Lay valets, ushers and cooks served the food.[77]

Everything was organized communally: there were communal barbers, shoe-makers, laundrymen and tailors. The repetitious, mannered, disciplined perform-ance of the liturgy had spilt over into daily life. Yet the very relentlessness of this routine was demanding in itself: the Canterbury monk Eadmer explained how, if a man 'becomes a monk, his faults press upon him . . . the man who seemed humble and long-suffering shows up now as impatient and proud. If he blames the monastic life, it is as though the coin were to say to the fire, "you made me false!" The fire did not make the coin false, it showed it up for what it was.'[78]

Still, there were some comforts. In the thirteenth century, the pope gave special permission for the members of many English monastic communities to wear hoods in choir during winter. By the fifteenth century, many monasteries fed their monks late in the morning, giving them time for another meal (rather than just a drink and a snack) before bed, and let them eat meat as long as it was prepared separately. Many dormitories came to be divided into individual cells, just as religious faith in general was becoming more private. In the common house at Durham, monks in need of a break could find wine and an open fire, and in Lent there were figs and walnuts too.[79] Most monks got a few shillings pocket money every year to spend as they pleased (their *peculium*) and each possessed a wooden drinking cup known as a mazer, a goblet, a bowl and a silver spoon.[80] There was also regular bloodletting or *seyney*, which medieval people thought was essential for health. 'Excess' blood was removed through the application of leeches. To recuperate, the monks of Norwich repaired to their infirmary; they may also have had brief breaks at daughter houses such as Yarmouth. The monks of Durham could repair to Finchale. During the fourteenth and fifteenth centuries, life became even more comfortable when many monastic cloisters were glazed, a previously unheard-of luxury. The stained glass that was installed could be used to describe the history of the monastery or to celebrate its chief benefactors, as was done at Worcester and elsewhere.[81]

This softening over time especially affected the senior obedientaries. The prior of a monastic cathedral was a lordly figure who was expected to live magnificently. At Ely, for example, Prior Crauden's richly-ornamented chapel was part of a complex that included private rooms, guest rooms and a hall. Similarly splendid priors' apartments were added to other monastic cathedrals, Winchester and Norwich among them, in the thirteenth and fourteenth centuries. The prior of Canterbury, like most cathedral priors, was permitted to wear a bishop's mitre by the end of the Middle Ages. Effectively head of England's largest and oldest monastery, he had a lifestyle to match. He had his own stables with a farrier, groom and stableman, where horses were always ready for the ride to Gravesend. This was the first leg on the two-day journey to London, which would be completed by taking a barge up-river the next day. The prior had his own kitchen, which served his table with 176 dishes every day, his own laundry and even his own butcher's boy. His archbishop may have had Lambeth palace; but the prior of Canterbury had his own inn on Tooley Street in Southwark.[82]

At Worcester, Prior William More enjoyed the networking aspect of his job hugely, holding otter hunts and inviting minstrels and jugglers to the feasts he held for important citizens and their wives. In 1536 his reputation for good living over-took him and he was banished to Gloucester, though the county gentry fondly remembered how they were 'familiarly entertained by him'.[83] Yet it was a stressful role. The prior was the mediator between the monks and the bishop, and the entire community ultimately depended on him. He was also responsible for the good management of the large estates that supported the monastery, and thus had considerable sway over the lives of many of their inhabitants. It is no wonder that at least two twelfth-century priors of Canterbury embraced greater asceticism when they retired: one became a Carthusian, the other a hermit.[84]

The monastic ethos encouraged caution and consensus, 'Arduous business should be dealt with by the counsel and assent of all the brethren and nothing should be determined against the will of the convent', as Prior Eastry put it.[85] But the monks had a long collective memory and could be implacable when threatened. At Canterbury they spent much of the Middle Ages watching their archbishop for signs that he was going to create his own, separate secular cathedral somewhere else; or watching the archbishop of York for signs that he was claiming equal status with Canterbury; or keeping a competitive eye on St Augustine's, the rival monastery in Canterbury itself.

Prior Simon Senhouse built himself a palatial residence at Carlisle

Usually to prove their entitlement to various lands or privileges, they became skilled forgers of official documents, especially in the earlier centuries when monastic scriptoriums were still the main places where books were made. Of 351 surviving charters ostensibly given to monastic houses by William the Conqueror, 61 were invented in the century after his death.[86] As a shocked Archbishop Stephen Langton told the pope in 1238, 'Holy Father, there is not a single sort of forgery that is not perpetrated in the church of Canterbury'.[87]

Intra-church litigation could be expensive, especially as rich bishops were prepared to take disputes to the papal curia in Rome if necessary, either attending themselves or instructing representatives to act for them. One abbot of Gloucester's trip to Rome in 1449 cost £400.[88] This was almost a third of the monastery's entire income for the year, and certainly enough to stop any major building project in its tracks. Disputes over property at Norwich went to the royal justices forty-nine times between 1191 and 1303, which works out at a major legal case concerned with property alone every two years or so.[89] Not surprisingly, cathedral libraries show a concern with law that is second only to that with theology and charters were kept in elaborate filing systems: yet the study of law itself, expected of a canon, was for a long time seen as rather too worldly for a monk. It was only in 1336 that Pope Benedict XII commanded that one in twenty monks should have legal training at a university. By this time, thanks to an initiative at St Peter's abbey, Gloucester, the English Benedictines had founded an Oxford college (today known as Worcester college). Yet of thirty-nine higher degrees awarded to Canterbury monks, just seven were in canon law rather than theology.[90]

By the fifteenth century, though, some of the monks were living more like lawyers. The senior obedientaries of a cathedral priory had by then built separate houses for themselves and their staff within the close. They were also often the only officers of the monastery permitted to leave the convent without asking permission and without a second monk to chaperone them. At Worcester they even ate in their own houses, rather than coming to refectory with their brethren, while at Durham, although they took meals in the refectory, they were served better food, from a separate hatch, and had their own part of the room in which to eat.[91] These men were responsible for large budgets, but their career path was far more limited than that of a secular canon. Secular canons could jump from cathedral to cathedral and post to post; monks almost always stayed in one place. One monk at Durham became an obedientiary thirty-six years after he first joined the monastery. Prior Cawston of Canterbury had been living in the community for fifty years when he died in 1504 at the age of seventy-six. Over the years he had been chancellor, third sub-prior, feretrar or shrine keeper, sacristan, treasurer, coroner, master of the infirmary and 'collector of the names of the living and dead monks'.[92]

Such posts are typical of those held by the lesser obedientaries. In time, these minor officials became more and more numerous, until they eventually comprised a third or more of the convent, making it possible for a monk to change jobs every five years or so. Many of these posts inevitably involved contact with the outside world. The sacristan at Ely, for example, was the most powerful figure in Ely township and a major purchaser of foodstuffs and goods from a wide hinterland. Such men were given dispensations from all but the most important religious services. Eventually a distinction emerged between the cloistered monks, who made up perhaps a half to two-thirds of the convent and who devoted themselves to worship and holy living, and the others, many of whom needed to leave the convent on business or spent much of their time with laymen. This was a pale echo of the gulf that separated canons from vicars, but it could also be seen as a major watering-down of the original ideals of St Benedict.

WORSHIPPING IN THE CATHEDRAL

Every Palm Sunday, a procession left Wells cathedral. This procession was even more remarkable than that which greeted the returning archbishop of York. Palm Sunday marks Christ's entry into Jerusalem, and the start of the week before Easter, the holiest week of the Church year. The cathedral's community was preparing to enter their church with all the theatre and ceremony they could muster; and their west front was to represent the very gates of Zion.

Usually, the community processed inside the church. The nave even had little markers in the floor, about four paces apart, to help the men of the cathedral line up for what was a daily ritual.[93] Using the aisles of the church, they would process round the entire east end, sprinkling holy water on side altars and other locations as they did so.[94] They then entered the choir to perform the main services of the day.

The Palm Sunday the ritual was more elaborate. The procession snaked out of the church into the cloister and then emerged onto the burial ground outside the west front, breaking into two as it did so. A small group headed for the west door, holding aloft a consecrated host in a rich reliquary.

The rest of the community made their way to a point west of the church, in the middle of the lay cemetery, and turned to face the 176 life-size statues on the west front (illustrated p. 430). The bright paint on the sculpture made the figures look like actors wearing too much make-up. But there were real people hidden in this cliff of stone. Choristers crouched in passages hidden in the thickness of the wall, next to openings secreted behind painted stone angels. At the climactic moment of the procession, the choristers sang, and the architecture sprang to life.[95]

The procession moved towards the church. 'Lift up your heads, O ye gates . . . and the king of glory shall come in,' sang its members. 'Who is the king of glory?', the choristers replied from their hiding-places, making it seem as if the painted figures of the west front were the gatekeepers of Zion. 'Even the lord of hosts, he is the king of glory', answered the procession. Then the doors of the church opened and the procession went in, passing underneath the elevated host as it did so. The people holding the reliquary then took up the rear. Christ had entered Jerusalem; and, for a few minutes, architecture, theatre and ritual had fused.

Such spectacular displays were the most theatrical and charged performances medieval people could witness. They were made all the more remarkable by their rarity; they were the markers of the key points in the Church's year. But worship inside the cathedral never ceased. The men who had been involved in the procession spent most of their lives standing in the choir-stalls, chanting. Only the choristers made much use of service books: no one could become a monk or priest without knowing most of the psalms and other important texts by heart.

The office of nocturn took place at around 1.30 to 2.30 a.m., or at dawn during summer. The community rose in silence in the middle of the night, picked up their candles, slipped on their woollen night-shoes and processed into church. In the winter, they went back to sleep before attending matins at dawn. After this there were the morning services, which included lauds, prime, sext and a morrow mass, after which anyone who had business to do could leave. In between the

Above the lowest row of statues can be glimpsed the trumpet-holes positioned high on the Wells west front

services there was time for a brief breakfast snack, which might just be a warm drink, and around two hours was available for smaller services. The most important of these was lady mass, usually celebrated at about 8 a.m. in the lady chapel. But every priested member of the community had to say a mass of their own daily, and an ever-increasing number of chantries had to be fitted in too. This part of the day thus put huge pressure both on logistics and on the building itself. At St Albans abbey, so many extra altars were needed during the thirteenth century that a new one was added in the nave almost every ten years.

All this was done by about mid-morning. Everyone washed, changed their shoes and went to the chapter-house for a meeting so ritualized it was almost a liturgical event in itself. In the monastic cathedrals at least, a chapter of the monks' rule or the order's statutes were read. A senior member of the community would give a reading. A long list of the dead, the 'mind', was read out: some of these people were past members of the community, some benefactors of the church. Confessions were made and punishments handed out, in extreme cases involving the flogging of an errant monk in front of his peers; individuals were then given tasks for the day. Only after all this was done would any business be seen to. The chapter might discuss important new statutes or hold an election for a vacant office, from the bishop down to a minor dignitary. The community then gathered for a grand procession to the high altar, where the most important services of the day, centred on high mass, were performed. Dinner was between

Christ approaches Jerusalem on Palm Sunday: cathedral west fronts were the scenes of ritualized re-enactments of such events. From Winchester's Benedictional of St Ethelwold

midday and 2 p.m., depending on the season. It was the main meal, and in summer could be followed by a brief sleep before the community settled down to a few hours' work, reading or study. Late in the afternoon everyone returned to the church for vespers, then changed into their night-clothes, had a drink and a light meal, and ended the day with compline at about 7 p.m.

This liturgy varied from church to church in subtle and complex ways. The liturgical traditions of some cathedrals went back to well before the Norman Conquest; at others they were comprehensively renewed several times over. The result was that cathedrals tended to evolve local variants on standard rituals, known as the Use of that particular church. The Use was never set in stone. An energetic bishop or precentor might revise or codify it. Of the two greatest achievements of Richard Poore, bishop of Salisbury, the revision of the liturgy was far more influential than the building of Salisbury cathedral. His Use of Sarum is the basis of the Anglican liturgy today.

In all these Uses, each day of the year had its own significance. Every saint had his or her day, or feast, and some were celebrated on other days as well, such as the date of their death, or the date their body was moved into a shrine. As there were thousands of saints, each cathedral had to choose which ones they were going to focus on in their particular calendar. These choices can be used to trace the local significance of certain saints, or the institutional affiliations of the cathedral concerned: saints from Maine, France were honoured at Durham centuries after William of St-Calais had come from Le Mans to be bishop of Durham, bringing local cults with him.[96]

The year had certain fixed points. Sundays were more important than other days. Certain feasts, such as the most important of those associated with St Mary or St Peter, were universally celebrated. And the festivals of Christmas, Easter and Pentecost (Whitsun) were major points in the turning of the year, each of them surrounded by a constellation of holy days and practices, from the elaborate rituals of Good Friday to now obscure festivities such as Candlemas and Rogationtide.

The feasts associated with any in-house saint were especially significant. By the end of the Middle Ages, only Exeter and Wells did not possess a major relic: usually the body of an individual who had been associated with the cathedral in life and whose miraculous powers were widely accepted. Some saints, such as St Swithun at Winchester or St William at York, were of little significance outside the diocese. At the other extreme, institutions such as Ely and Durham were virtually defined by their saints, and celebrated several separate feast days associated with them.

As a result of this complex pattern, Worcester, for example, celebrated over a hundred feast days a year, which meant that on at least three days in every week there would be a more elaborate liturgy, better food in refectory, and less time for other activities.[97] But the calendar itself was universal. Medieval people might talk about the feast of the assumption of the Virgin Mary and Candlemas in the same way that we might refer to the dates in our diaries. At Christmas and Easter, everyone had a week off, and there were also free days at Whitsun.[98] Indeed, these 'holy-days' are still holidays; they are the year's key turning-points, except that Whitsun has been upstaged by a later summer break. While Glastonbury Festival may be a long way from the feastivals, when monks were given extra wine and a better menu after a hard day in choir, the word has its origins in medieval religion.

Theatrical rituals where associated with these feasts. At Pentecost, a dove and an angel were lowered from the vault at Lincoln.[99] On Maundy Thursday, local paupers had their feet washed by the cathedral community. Hereford cathedral was decorated with ornamental hangings at All Saints and Christmas, and with rushes and ivy at Easter.[100] Good Friday vied with Palm Sunday for spectacle: at Durham and elsewhere the monks crawled to the Cross.

At first, services were accompanied by simple plainchant. But gradually this began to change. The first organ is mentioned in 1133: it would have provided loud bursts of noise, rather than a discernible tune. Like bells, organs were initially used to add drama to ceremonies outside the church and were only later moved inside for use during services.[101] Polyphony, in which music is divided into a number of simultaneous parts, also originated as an improvised embellishment to the most important services, especially those devoted to the Virgin Mary.[102] By the fifteenth century, most cathedrals employed professional song-masters who taught choristers to sing polyphonically and who could compose passages of music. One such was Master Walter Braytoft, who was at Lincoln in 1395.[103] Many later cathedral lady chapels, such as that off the transept at Canterbury, can be seen as architectural responses to the development of polyphony. Indeed, it is possible that the powerfully inventive tradition of lady-chapel architecture may even have stimulated the development of ever-more elaborate Marian liturgies, helping bring about the invention of polyphony itself.

Notation for liturgical singing; the thirteenth-century Hereford breviary

Worship ate up resources. Vast numbers of candles were needed to light the choir. The sacrist at Norwich spent £30 a year, two-thirds of his annual budget, on the purchase of 500 to 600 kg of candle-wax.[104] Church candles had to be made of bees-wax, as the bee was believed to sacrifice itself, Christ-like, in the making of its wax. There was also the question of keeping the building itself in good repair. Lincoln cathedral employed three carpenters full time. In addition to maintenance work, these men were expected to provide warm water for the washing of altars on Maundy Thursday, were responsible for installing the Lenten veil, and had to supply furs and crowns for the Three Kings at Christmas.[105]

Thus daily life in the cathedral was an endless, repetitive round. Indeed, both architecture and liturgy depended on the ability of innumerable individuals to repeat the same tasks with enormous accuracy many times over. For every bishop's visitation that complains of rushed chanting and half-empty choirs, there is one, such as that of Norwich cathedral priory in 1423, which simply reports the excellence of the monks' observance of their Rule.[106] This, rather than the political storms with which bishops had to contend, was normal life in the cathedrals.

LAYMEN

Let us imagine another procession, this time at Whitsun. The people in it have come from parishes all over the diocese. They have now converged and are heading towards their cathedral. A priest leading each group carries a banner bearing the name or emblem of the parish. The villagers walk behind him. They have come to help fulfil the contract that binds each cathedral to every human soul in its see. Each household has made a small payment, sometimes called a 'smoke farthing', as every home with a hearth was obliged to contribute, to its parish priest. This money, perhaps 6d to 9d per parish, is being taken to the cathedral to be exchanged for consecrated oil, the Chrism oil that makes it possible for the priest's flock to live and die within God's grace.

Medieval religion is often thought to be very non-participatory. It is seen as an exclusive affair for monks and priests, who did the praying while everyone else was toiling, or fighting, before dying young of some ghastly disease. The truth is that there was plenty of participation: it was just very different from today. Most lay people took Communion just once a year, at Easter, but this only made the event more sacred and more charged with supernatural power. But they took part in processions, formed religious confraternities of their own, made offerings to churches, and, above all, sought miraculous experiences at saints' shrines.

Laymen and churchmen process a saint's relics through the streets, hoping to ward off plague

At St Paul's, the Pentecostal processions were apparently so popular that the diocese had to be divided into sub-sections. People from each group of parishes came to the cathedral on a different day and they each took a different route through London.[107] The processions were granted the privilege of entering the cathedral through its west door, led by the mayor and aldermen. In the diocese of Lincoln, on the other hand, only the nearby archdeaconries of Lincoln and Stow were still processing to the cathedral by the fifteenth century. Elsewhere Chrism oil was distributed from more local centres, such as Leicester, where, on one four-teenth-century occasion, the men of Wigston Magna were reported to have got into a bloody fight while on their way to make a donation.[108] And at Carlisle in 1372 only the parish priests were obliged to process to the cathedral with the offer-ings of their flock, the members of which stayed at home. The offerings were left on the high altar, presumably as a sign of subjection to the bishop and his church.[109]

We do not know how many people witnessed the ritual events of the cathedral. The liturgy was a sacred duty no matter how many lay people were present; and, in any case, on ordinary days interested laymen would be more likely to head for their parish church than a cathedral if they wanted to be present at a service. Yet a small crowd of citizens was gathering for the evening service at Canterbury when Thomas Becket was murdered, and a fourteenth-century statute for Wells mentions that lay people in the nave should genuflect when the host was raised in choir.[110] In both cases their presence seems taken for granted. Similarly, the archbishop of York was expected to preach 'to the people' in the minster on Palm Sunday,[111] and one of the reasons why Old Sarum was abandoned for Salisbury is that the garrison of the castle there kept denying admittance to the 'crowds' arriving for the celebration of the key festivals.[112] The appointment of Thomas Winchelsey as archbishop of Canterbury in 1293 was announced from the

Priests were the vital link between God and humanity: Ash Wednesday, from a French book of hours

pulpit of the nave: breaking news, indeed. In 1400 a new retable there was dedicated by the archbishop and three bishops and 'shown to the people'.[113] This perhaps explains the size of the cathedral naves. The fact that they were empty most of the time was not the point. They were only expected to be full for the occasional important event. Only two schemes of nave iconography, at York minster (particularly) and Norwich, survive. They are perhaps 150 years apart, but both reach out emphatically to lay culture.[114] In the meantime many naves became the venue for a range of day-to-day activities – St Paul's seems to have been packed with professional letter-writers, jurymen seeking work, and others – and some, such as that at St Albans, doubled up as parish churches.[115]

The congregation was meant to see mass being celebrated, if from afar. The ceremonies taking place at the nave altar were partly performed for their benefit. After the twelfth century, it was rare for a cathedral choir to be walled off, as those of Winchester and Rochester had been: instead, their enclosing screens were designed so that people could peer through them. And when no services were in progress, people could go into the choir itself: at Wells there was a collecting box for donations in front of the tomb of Bishop Shrewsbury.[116]

The processions in particular functioned as a kind of symbolic glue between Church and lay society. By turning the act of walking together into a ritual, people were able to act out their relationships to each other, to the Church, and to their faith. Every year, over three days, the citizens of Ripon, peasants, churchmen and knights together, processed around the minster's lands, their position in this great communal hike defined by their rank. They carried a dragon before them on the first day; had a cross in front of the beast on the second; and moved the dragon to the rear on the last, symbolically enacting Christ's victory over sin. The third day ended with the local knights meeting church officials in the chapter-room[117] to reconfirm their tenure of minster lands. The knights were then permitted to lead a final procession, in which they bore the shrine of St Wilfrid himself around the fields.[118] At St Paul's the canons and vicars went even further, censing the mayor, citizens and people of London during their Whit week processions.[119] Such privileges became especially popular in the century before the Reformation.

At Durham, another place where cathedral, saint and land were strongly inter-connected, citizens came to the cathedral in groups according to their trade on the feast of Corpus Christi, bearing banners that announced the occupation of each group. In front of the procession was carried a crystal shrine containing the host, taken from its usual home in the city's main parish church. The clergy processed from the cathedral to meet the townspeople, bearing with them the sacred corporax banner, at the heart of which was the square cloth that St Cuthbert had used to perform the Eucharist. This banner was so heavy that four men had to carry it. Everyone trooped into the cathedral, banners aloft and torches lit. They filed around the church, past the shrine of St Cuthbert, and then processed back into the city, where the crystal shrine was locked away in the parish church until the following year.[120]

The cathedral reached into the lives of ordinary people in all kinds of other ways. The Church was responsible for all moral issues, such as cases of adultery

Two adulterers, sentenced by a Church court to process naked through the town

and all crimes committed by churchmen. It also had a judicial role as a landlord. Until relatively recently, there was a court room inside most cathedrals where the bishop's legal representatives heard cases that could not be resolved further down the Church's legal system. Occasionally, the bishop himself was involved: Bishop Atwater of Lincoln, perhaps a bishop who was unusually engaged with his see, is known to have attended 84 out of 133 recorded hearings.[121] Spaces for such courts survive most visibly at Exeter (St Edmund's chapel at the west end),[122] and Norwich (the Bauchun chapel).[123] The Norwich court was convened 65 times in 1510–11, on each occasion bringing lay people with very earthly concerns into the east end of the cathedral.[124] In Lincoln, the bishop had serious breaches of Church law announced publicly three Sundays in a row in the parish churches of the archdeaconry in which they had taken place.[125] The same network was a vital conduit for the news: by asking that prayers be said for this or that event, the bishop could swiftly give the laity a steer on national events.

Sentences passed in Church courts usually involved some level of public humiliation. After Sir Rannulph de Rye had attacked the church of Gosberton, Lincolnshire, he was instructed to join the main Sunday procession in Lincoln cathedral outside the west front. He was to carry his arms and lay them on the altar-step in expiation.[126] When Sir Peter de Mauley was found guilty of adultery in 1325, he was asked to fast every Friday in Lent and other days for seven years; to go on pilgrimages to the shrines of St William in York, St Thomas in Hereford, St John in Beverley and St Wilfrid in Ripon; and was scourged – flogged – seven times before the Sunday procession in Southwell minster.[127]

Excommunication was the severest punishment of all. A person who was excommunicated stood outside God's grace entirely, could not receive any of the sacraments and, in theory, was to be shunned. When Thomas Cantilupe wanted to get the better of the Earl of Gloucester in a dispute over hunting rights, he confronted him in a forest, dressed in full regalia and accompanied by his chaplains, and began to perform an excommunication.[128] The earl fled. But when the archbishop of Canterbury excommunicated Thomas, he insisted that he was innocent because the excommunication had been uncanonically performed.

The justice of the Church also had another, more compassionate side to it: the offering of sanctuary. This practice, in which the church was regarded as an unassailable refuge, originated as a way of breaking the destructive grip of tit-for-tat blood feuds in Saxon culture. Durham cathedral still has its sanctuary knocker. This allowed a felon who grasped it thirty-seven days' grace in which to find passage overseas, although he also had to submit to being questioned and give satisfactory answers. Well over half of the known sanctuary-seekers at Durham were accused of murder or homicide, but their number also included animal rustlers, debtors and others. At some other cathedrals, such as Norwich, those seeking sanctuary had formed a small community within the close; at Winchester they even had their families with them.[129]

The compassionate face of the Church also came through in the acts of charity that cathedral priories, like all other monasteries, were committed to. Monks were obliged to provide food,

Durham's sanctuary knocker – an exquisite work from the time of Bishop du Puiset – provided protection for generations of felons on the run

clothes and shelter for the needy, and the almoner, who was responsible, attracted many donations from lay people. At Norwich, between 240 and 275 loaves were given away each day at the gate of the close, as well as clothes, shoes, ale, meat, fish, eggs and peat turves for fuel.[130] The poor gathered outside the gates of the bishop's palace at Rochester when Bishop Fisher had his main meal of the day, because this ascetic man always ensured the leftovers were passed on to them. Two people died and several others were left very unwell after the bishop was the victim of an attempted poisoning, perhaps by the Boleyn family, in 1531.[131]

Some of the charitable doles founded by bishops and others were strikingly generous. Bishop Ridel of Ely donated 48.5 hectares from which 1,200 poor people were to be fed each year on his death-day.[132] Similarly, Henry III demanded that 15,000 paupers be fed in St Paul's churchyard. News of these hand-outs must have spread rapidly and ensured that small crowds gathered outside the relevant churches on key days.[133] Yet it has been estimated that only one village in five in medieval Cambridgeshire could reach a monastery within a day, which means that the vast majority were effectively denied any help.[134] And some charitable acts, although effective, also had a substantial element of ritual to them. Every year, the prior of Durham washed the feet of thirteen poor men, kissing each foot as he finished drying it. After the prior had ritually humbled himself in this way, each man received thirty pence, seven red herrings, bread, drink and wafers, and a bench on which to sit while watching divine service.[135]

The monastic cathedrals were also obliged to provide hospitality, matching what they offered to the status of their guests. Visits from royalty and other great men could be very expensive, and those monasteries that were on main roads, such as St Albans, could suffer financially as a result. Peterborough abbey spent over £1,543 on entertainment during a visit by Edward II: the king was presented with an embroidered robe and insisted that his favourite, Piers Gaveston, had one too.[136] At Durham, the keeper of the guest chamber ensured there was clean linen every day as well as provender for horses: strangers, it was said, should lack for nothing 'what degree soever he was of'.[137] Ironically the institutions that survived the Reformation, the secular cathedrals, were not nearly so public-spirited.

SAINTS

When one East Anglian farmer found his oxen were sickening, he invested in the longest candle-wick he could get and corralled the animals together in a field. Then, presumably with some assistance, he wrapped the wick around the entire herd. The long wick was then made into an elaborate, wheel-shaped coil and surrounded with wax to make an enormous candle, which the farmer took to the shrine of St William at Norwich. He had it lit, and left a donation. The herd got better.[138]

Our farmer had measured the cows for William. He was not alone in doing this. Anything could be measured for a saint, from a sick child to an entire town. Every year, the city of Dover sent a candle whose coiled wick was the length of the city boundary to Becket's shrine at Canterbury, to be lit as a special privilege at masses of St Thomas and funerals of Canterbury paupers. One thirteenth-century knight, who felt he had ashes in his eyes, was slowly going blind. He desperately wanted to still be able to see the elevation of the host and to play chess, so he measured himself for St Thomas of Hereford and sent the resulting candle to the cathedral along with a wax pair of eyes. Three days later his sight was restored.[139]

Saints could move towns. At St Albans, the Roman city gradually fell into ruins as the population drifted away to live around the church that had been built in an extra-mural cemetery, over the tomb of the proto-martyr himself. Their cults helped fund the rebuilding of parts of churches, as at Lincoln (St Hugh) and Hereford (Thomas Cantilupe), and they were the symbolic protectors of whole tracts of land. The shrine of St Oswald at Worcester was used to repulse an approaching army in 1139 and in 1390–1, after the saint had helped the surrounding countryside through 'a time of exceeding dryness', 20kg of wax torches were bought as a thank-offering.[140] The ground-up bones of St Wilfrid at Ripon minster had the power to keep cattle from pain, while a hole in the wall of his ancient crypt was used as a chastity-tester.[141] In such ways, people saw the saints as their most potent point of connection with the cathedrals, offering the

A reconstruction of the scene at the shrine of St Swithun in Winchester (above) and the same scene today (below). The site of the shrine is marked by a sculpture of 1962

possibility of a raw, immediate and personal connection with the supernatural.

Saints' cults took on many guises. Some were ancient: by the Norman Conquest, figures such as Etheldreda of Ely and Cuthbert of Durham were part of the fabric of national culture, their powers taken for granted regardless of however infrequently they were associated with miracles. Elsewhere, the cathedral authorities effectively manufactured their saints. Not all such attempts succeeded. The canonization of Thomas Cantilupe at Hereford is a textbook case of one that did; whereas the failure of the authorities at Wells to have Bishop March recognized as a saint has left a shrine-shaped gap at the heart of one of England's most exquisite buildings. And some cults happened without official encouragement: that of Archbishop Scrope at York was so politically controversial that it was initially driven underground; he was never canonized.

The relics, too, took many forms, not all of which inspired mass enthusiasm. The relic collection at Coventry included the arm of St Augustine of Hippo, a barrel of mixed relics, and 'Our Lady's milk in silver gilt'.[142] But where a cathedral held the entire body of a saint who had been associated with it in life, powerful talismanic associations could grow up. Figures such as Erkenwald, who refounded St Paul's, or Swithun, patron saint of Winchester, had been reforming bishops; by the twelfth century, although their names had little resonance in the wider world, they had a solid reputation within their respective dioceses. When a bishop died, signs of potential saintliness, such as the sweet scent of paradise emerging from their tombs, or the failure of their remains to decay, excited passionate attention, potentially triggering events of revivalist proportions.

The Church developed the process of canonization, the final proof of sainthood, partly as a way of staying in control of such cults. The associated paperwork, such as that for Thomas Cantilupe of Hereford, includes some of the most fascinating of medieval documents. Without this official approval, a saint often inhabited a kind of half-life where the local church, or local people, very much wanted to assist canonization but were forbidden from moving the saint's body to a shrine, or celebrating his day as a major feast. It was in just this liminal period that the cult was often at its height.

For the Church, simple credulity was not sufficient proof of a miracle. When a twelfth-century woman claimed that her blindness had been cured by St Hugh of Lincoln, 'it was essential carefully to ascertain the truth about this and other miracles, and not have any proclaimed or published unless they were confirmed,'[143] as Hugh's biographer pointed out. Miracles were real, but no educated churchman expected them to occur very often. The commissioners charged with checking

Thomas Cantilupe's claims to saintliness ensured they had corroboration of each story from at least two independent witnesses.

These miracles are the greatest challenge for most modern readers. They are also what give the stories of the saints their power. Discussion of whether they really happened is beside the point although, of course, we only know about the successes. We are told about the herds that were cured by being measured, not about those that were not. But people believed miracles were real, and acted accordingly. And most of us have found that certain kinds of complaint, from vague aches and pains to infertility, can be affected by state of mind as well by medical intervention. A striking number of recorded miracles could be given a psychological interpretation, among them the curing of the woman who could not suckle and of the mad girl, 'wearied out with much shouting and screaming', who lay at the head of the tomb-shrine of St Osmund at Salisbury.[144] St Hugh of Lincoln cured nine cases of insanity; four each of blindness and 'dropsy'; three each of paralysis and muscle contraction. He also enabled two mutes to speak, brought a 'dead child' back to life, and helped a 'barren woman' to conceive:[145] any one of these problems might or, of course, might not have been connected with emotional trauma or severe shock.

The saints had powers in death that far exceeded any influence they had had in life; and they could be endlessly reinvented, acquiring qualities that had little connection to their actual achievements. St Cuthbert may have been a good man and an important leader of the Church, but in death he was reinvented, several times over, first as a twelfth-century monk-misogynist; then as a fourteenth-century warrior-saint; finally as a sixteenth-century confounder of Protestants. Each reinvention suited the needs of Durham cathedral at that particular time.

Most saints' cults flowered briefly and then ran at a loss to the cathedrals, though they added enormously to their prestige. Staff were needed to make the shrine secure, to take donations, and to perform the associated liturgy. Pilgrims had to be offered hospitality; if they were very important, they had to be hosted in style. In the year of his translation, 1220, Thomas Becket attracted perhaps the largest amount donated over a year for an English saint: a colossal £1,142. But, in that same year, the cellarer spent £1,154 catering for the visitors who had made these donations: in purely financial terms, one of the greatest religious events of the Middle Ages ran at a loss. At Canterbury, ten people were dedicated full time to the cathedral's shrines. There were two at the shrine where Becket's body was held; two at the separate shrine of his original tomb; two each at the lady altars in the crypt and the nave; one at the corona, where Thomas's head

Sometimes St Mary seems to upstage even God: an unrestored alabaster at Wells (left) and an image of her protecting the souls of humanity in a book from the library of Exeter's Bishop Grandison (right)

probably had a separate shrine; and one at the site of his martyrdom. Two others were employed at the shrines of St Dunstan and St Alphege. These attendants slept by the shrines and opened them each morning by a ring of their bell, at 6 a.m. in the winter and 5 a.m. in summer. The shrines were again shut at lunchtime, and at dusk the attendants searched 'each dark place and suspect corner' for a thief or rabid dog before closing for the night.[146]

Pilgrims were directed along a predetermined route that linked these various cultic foci. In order to manage the conflicting needs of pilgrims and liturgy, a complex series of internal walls, stairs and passages was developed around the Martyrdom in the north transept. The monks had to cross the transept every time they processed from cloister to choir and the Martyrdom was also of enormous importance for pilgrims. Very important visitors received special attention: the prior himself showed the great humanist scholar Erasmus around the cathedral, indicating the relics with a white rod and giving him the opportunity to kiss them.[147] Pilgrim numbers were particularly high during saints' feasts, when many churches also held major market-fairs: the tat available at St Etheldreda's fair at Ely has given us the word tawdry, based on 'Audrey'; the short form of Etheldreda. The crowds who flocked to see the exhumation of St Erkenwald at St Paul's in 1140 were so huge that the cathedral's doors were torn off their hinges: the canons were forced to complete their translation 'in the middle of the night, in order to avoid a disturbance of the people'.[148] Contemporaries talked of 100,000 people descending on Canterbury for Becket's jubilee in 1420, at which a general pardon of pilgrims' sins was offered. In a normal year, the average take at the shrine was about 4d a day, with offerings varying from a few shillings to fractions of a penny. In 1420 the take was £644, so the claim may not be an exaggeration. At the other extreme, on an ordinary weekday in November at Ely, perhaps as little as a fraction of a penny was left at the shrine of St Etheldreda.

Shrines in general grew larger and more magnificent during the Middle Ages, and stylistically they were always a step or two ahead of the latest designs for the tombs of bishops and royals. The coffin itself lay on top of a high stone pedestal, or shrine base, in which there were recesses; these allowed pilgrims to get as close as possible to the sacred remains above. The coffin was completely covered, though the lid could be winched up 'when any man of honour . . . disposed to make prayers' or to 'offer anything to the shrine' visited, as well as during key moments in the daily liturgy.[149]

The space around such shrines could become crowded with objects. In 1307 the papal commissioners listed 2,204 items in the area where St Thomas Cantilupe's tomb-shrine stood, ranging from night-gowns to ships made of cloth, wax, wood and silver. Even as the commissioners watched, a further eighty-five objects were left and a group of Irish sailors, saved from a storm by praying to St Thomas, turned up carrying two silver ships. Edward I sent a wax model of one of his gyrfalcons to Canterbury; and Henry VII donated a life-size kneeling silver-gilt image of himself, to be positioned 'as nigh to the shrine as may well be'.[150]

In addition to candles measured for this or that cause, people 'bent pennies', vowing the coin to the saint if a crisis was averted, and these were affixed to the shrine. In 1538 Bishop Shacton of Salisbury forbade the 'decking of images' (not just saints' shrines) with gold, silver, clothes, lights or herbs and the leaving of 'candles, oats, cake-bread, cheese or wool'.[151] The shrine of St Erkenwald in St Paul's had 130 precious stones attached to it, and the monks of Durham gratefully displayed the 'unicorn horn, elephant tooth, or such like thing' given to St Cuthbert.[152] Pilgrims might spend considerable amounts of time at a shrine: Julia, who had been cured of madness by St Osmund, had spent four or fives nights at his tomb at Salisbury; after he cured her, she returned each year to give thanks.[153] The canons of Lincoln complained about a madwoman who had chained herself to the shrine of St Hugh in search of a cure and wailed during services. Details such as these leave an impression of voodoo as much as High Church.

Shrines were not the only focus of attention. At Norwich, St William rarely attracted more than £1 a year in offerings by the late fourteenth century, but £20 to £50 might be left at the high altar, and offerings were also made at images of St Leonard, St Sitha of Lucca and St Mary; at the tombs of the saintly (but never sainted) bishops, Walter Suffield and John Salmon; at the rood in the nave; and at a collection of relics of uncertain size and content, often housed in glorious portable reliquaries that could be taken on procession.[154]

All this was a bid for the saint concerned to intercede in heaven, as intercession could result in the curing of maladies or a change of fortune on earth. Here, one saint was more powerful than all others: Mary, mother of Jesus. St Mary was the focus of such rich theological ideas and liturgical practices that she often seems to subtly upstage God himself. Every church had its lady chapel. Sometimes there were two, as at Canterbury and St Augustine's, Bristol, one more focused on lay people and the other on the community's daily lady mass. Intense cults might develop around images of Mary. One image at Worcester developed a miraculous reputation in the fifteenth century; in 1513, £93 was offered by pilgrims there.[155] At once mother and virgin, Mary was Queen of Heaven and the main mediator there on behalf of humanity. Our Lady was the inspiration for many of England's most spectacular interiors, from the Ely Octagon to the polygonal chapter-houses. Her

Marian ideas suffuse certain medieval buildings: the York chapter-house, like the Virgin, was the 'rose of roses'

LIFE AND HISTORY

liturgy, in turn, was rich in architectural metaphors (see p. 420), encouraging buildings that evoked corporeal fecundity and spiritual purity – the contradictory impulses at the heart of her cult – in equal proportions.

(see p. 420)

DEATH

It is an exaggeration, but not a major one, to say that everything in this book, the endless liturgical round, the institutions that supported it, the cathedrals themselves, were about one thing: death. Without the allure of heaven, the threat of hell and the certain knowledge that history would end with the physical resurrection of the body, these buildings would not have been created. This is, in short, a society focused on the hereafter. It is not surprising that the funeral procession of an archbishop was as grand as any he had known in life. When one archbishop of Canterbury was taken from Lambeth to his cathedral, two hundred horsemen and his entire household accompanied the carriage. A hundred torches lit the procession.[156] A bishop was buried in full regalia, with a chalice. His tomb became a kind of talisman for the cathedral itself, to be solemnly translated should the church be moved or rebuilt, as happened at Exeter and Salisbury.

Former bishops were prayed for, especially if the bishop had founded a chantry, and their tombs might be asperged in processions. That of Bishop Sherborn at Chichester was kept hidden behind a curtain for most of the year and only revealed on his deathday and other key festivals, when the cathedral's eight boy choristers and others sang for his soul. The bishop's will specified the treats of milk, egg and saffron that the boys could consume when their duties were over.

A nobleman might earn an equally prestigious burial by giving the community his best horse, as John Neville did in 1328. As the equivalent of a top-of the-range car with extras, it was agreed the steed would be delivered to Peterborough abbey saddled and bridled. But the sacrist there declared Neville's horse was not good enough and asked for an extra forty shillings.[157]

For medieval people, the dead had not vanished into oblivion. Their bodies were a visible part of everyday life[158] and, from the early fifteenth century, could even be

The final procession: a funeral enters a church

Bishop Sherborn of Chichester intended his tomb to be the scene of lavishly cloying scenes on his annual 'deathday'

vividly realized in stone on their monuments, worms and all (illustrated p. 133).[159] The saints were in paradise and could actively intervene in people's lives on earth. Less exalted souls were in purgatory, but good works or prayers carried out on earth in their name might yet earn them a place in heaven. By founding a chantry, a rich man might ensure his soul was prayed for throughout eternity, a practice linked to much remarkable architecture. Many colossal structures, such as Archbishop de Gray's south transept at York minster, had their patron's tomb at their heart, a regular chantry mass associated with it. Later the 'cage' chantry developed, a specific architectural form created to house both tomb and altar in a structure that stood alone (see p. 137).

This sense that the dead were all around, and that their concerns were deeply interwoven with those of the living, explains much about the way cathedral communities saw themselves. When the weekly 'mind', the list of dead members and benefactors, was read in the chapter-house, the monks knew that their names would one day be added to the list. A group of canons at Wells in the late thirteenth century paid for the magnificent new chapter-house and then had their names incorporated in the stained glass below images of the Resurrection (illustrated p. 436). The cathedral's cemeteries, where it was believed the Resurrection would one day take place, were the venue for fairs and lay processions. People spent their lives preparing for their deaths in the certain knowledge that, once dead, they would remain connected to the community from which they came.

Lay people's wills tell us more than any other source about the standing of a cathedral in its community. Of forty-two wills made at Worcester between 1450 and 1500, twenty-two asked for burial in the cathedral cemetery and ten in the cathedral itself, usually specifying a location in front of the image or altar of a specific saint.[160] At Norwich, on the other hand, just 0.5 per cent of the many wills surviving from the 1370s to 1500 ask for burial in 'my mother church'. About a third of the citizens left money to the cathedral, but half made bequests to one of the town's friaries and a massive 95 per cent to their local parish church.[161] The cathedral was a worthy enough cause, but it took exceptional circumstances for it to become the focus of most people's attention.

WHAT TO SEE

Choirs: Exeter: pulpitum, stalls, bishop's throne, sedilia, possible section of reredos in the chapel of St Andrew and St Catherine, bishop's tombs, glass. Lincoln: pulpitum, stalls, Remigius' shrine-like founder's tomb, which doubled as the Easter sepulchre, fragments of shrines. Winchester: stalls, Great Screen, choir screens and tombs.

Closes: The monastic complexes at Canterbury and Durham and at the abbeys, later cathedrals, of Gloucester and Chester. The well-preserved secular closes at Salisbury, Wells and Chichester.

Shrines: The best example in the country is at St Albans; others can be seen at Lincoln and also at Chester and Oxford. The tombs of Thomas Cantilupe at Hereford and Edward II at Gloucester are vivid examples of cults-in-the-making, that of St Osmund at Salisbury of an early tomb-shrine.

Chantry chapels and monuments: Almost every building in this book holds good medieval tombs. Highlights include the sequence of archbishops' tombs in Canterbury, which is a virtual history of medieval England and its art; the tomb of Bishop Aigueblanche and other tombs and chantry chapels in Hereford; the tombs of builder-bishops Stapeldon, Grandison and others at Exeter; the bishops' tombs in the east end of Salisbury; the fine collection of effigies at Wells; and the chantry chapels in Winchester, England's best series, and at St Albans abbey.

Chapter Seven

BUILDERS AND PATRONS

There is something vaguely illicit about climbing above the vaults of a cathedral. It is like going backstage at a theatre, or being told the secret of a conjuror's trick, or discovering the mysteries of a peculiarly elaborate form of underwear. Yet here we can see how the cathedrals were built.

From the ground, for example, the Ely Octagon appears to defy explanation. But if you climb into the roof spaces, all is revealed. The vault hangs from a huge wooden skeleton in which some pieces of oak are 19 metres long.[1] The timbers are scoured by the marks of ancient axes. An impression of weightlessness is replaced by an awareness of the engineering and physical labour involved.

We know a lot about this building. Ely's sacrist, Alan of Walsingham, made a 40-mile journey to Chicksands in Bedfordshire with 'John the Carpenter' in 1322, and there spent £9 on twenty carefully-selected oak trees.[2] William Hurley, soon to become master-carpenter to the king, was paid £8 a year to devise and build the timber vault.[3] A separate team of masons, probably from Norwich, built the stone octagon on which the 450-ton wooden skeleton sits.[4] The project depended on a legion of labourers for felling, hewing and carrying; we can see the marks they left on the timber, but the men themselves are faceless.

The marks made by labourers' axes are still visible on the timbers supporting Ely Octagon

Masterpiece of the mason's art: the early gothic Wells nave updated local romanesque practice to produce one of England's most distinctive interiors

These anonymous toilers are the unsung heroes of the medieval cathedrals. They loaded a cart with building materials and guided it for days over muddy tracks, they levelled the land for building, and they cut the blocks of raw stone into manageable pieces. Any peasant who owed labour service to bishop or chapter might be brought in to do such work. At Exeter, from nine to seventeen labourers and from two to four carters worked alongside the twenty skilled workers; some might earn 8d to 11d a week depending on conditions.[5]

Every aspect of construction presented logistical challenges that could only be resolved through hard toil. To build Exeter cathedral, a staggering 12,000 cartloads of stone were transported from quarries at Barley Hill outside the city between 1299 and 1325–6.[6] At Ely, the bridges and causeways that led across the fens had to be strengthened before building began; the stone that came along them had already been dragged overland on sledges from the quarry at Barnack in Northamptonshire and ferried on barges down the River Nene.[7] No wonder the cost of carriage could be three times that of the stone itself.[8]

The peasants of Wingham, Kent owed carrying-service to the archbishop of Canterbury: cathedral building depended on the toil of such men

Everything needed for the job had to be carried there or made on site. At Walter Langton's bishop's palace in Lichfield, oaks had to be felled, at a cost of 4d a day, to fuel the kilns in which solder was made.[9] To vault the York lady chapel, 10,000 nails had to be sourced; they cost 13s 4d;[10] at Ely, they simply built their own smithy, manned by John Amyot, the blacksmith.[11] Nothing went to waste. At Exeter, old wheels and dead horses were sold off and carts returning empty to the quarries generated income by carrying wine or even corpses for burial.[12] Yet the economic footprint of such a project could be surprisingly wide. Lanfranc's Canterbury cathedral of the 1070s got most of its stone from Caen in Normandy. The two great oak trees that were cut up to form the ribs of the York lady chapel vault were probably British (much oak came from Ireland), but the 580 boards that filled the gaps between them would have been made of pine from the Baltic coast, from Estonia, northern Poland and perhaps north-east Germany, just as our pine comes from Scandinavia today.[13]

There was little in the way of technology to reduce the hard work involved. Indeed, apart from a little electronic assistance, the techniques used by cathedral stonemasons remains almost unchanged to this day. All things considered, it is not hard to sympathize with the Marxist view that the cathedrals are as much a monument to proletarian labour as they are to the bishops and master-masons.

CRAFTSMEN

For the lucky few born near a major quarry, cathedral-building was one of the medieval world's few paths to self-betterment. It was a waste of effort to transport undressed stone from quarry to building-site. Instead, master-masons ordered their stone in quantities that had already been dressed, or cut into cubes.

Ely Octagon is built of scores of ashlar blocks of various dimensions arranged in over 130 rows. Each block was extracted from the quarry by splitting the rock along naturally-occurring faults or beds; each was then smoothed and squared before transportation. A greater level of skill was required to make the hundreds of more finely-shaped pieces of stone that went into the massive arches and large windows that pierce the Octagon walls. For example, the stone tracery of each window at Ely is made up over fifty thin, curved pieces which had to fit together perfectly when completed. Even more skilled were the men who crafted the twenty decorative niches that are sprinkled across the walls, enriched by stylized sprigs of carved foliage known as crockets. But only the most skilled might be entrusted with carving the twenty statues which once filled these niches. It is not surpising, then, to find that there might be as many as five to a dozen different rates of pay on a cathedral building site.[14]

All these tasks were united by an underlying need for accuracy. Even the statue-carvers were limited creatively in that they had to follow conventions about the clothing and symbols associated with a specific saint. But cathedral architecture depended more than anything else

By working at a local quarry, medieval villagers might become stonemasons

on the ability to reproduce identical yet complex shapes in stone over and over again.

Some designers made the specification of such requirements into an art. At Durham in the 1090s, for example, the master-mason prescribed the precise size and quantity of blocks he would need to build the church.[15] Blocks of standardized dimensions, 850 pieces of one size, 600 of another, make up the plinth that surrounds the east end and transepts. Similarly, the great spiral, zigzag and diamond patterns on the columns of his church have been created from five standardized block designs: 850 blocks of one size and shape; 600 of another; 230 of a third; and further quantities of two more. Some of the blocks are cut by a deep square-sided groove of precise dimensions: by arranging these in different ways, all the patterns on the columns can be generated. It is as if the church was a vast kit.

The work of preparing such blocks might be done at the quarry, but the more skilled shaping was more likely to be carried out on the building site, where work could be supervised. Decorative motifs, such as the profile of a moulding or designs for a tracery pattern, formed a master-mason's architectural signature and were kept under his control if at all possible.

A quarry worker with aptitude might eventually join a lodge or group of masons working on a major project on site. In time, he could become a mason. The names of cathedral stonemasons suggest something of these men's career paths.[16] When a man left his home to work elsewhere, he was simply called by his place of origin. John of Burwell, who carved the central boss in the lantern vault at Ely, was thus from one of the Burwells in Suffolk and Lincolnshire. When such toponyms are plotted onto a map, they tend to cluster around major quarries. Clearly it was possible for a villager to work at a nearby quarry, pick up the fundamentals of a trade, and then move on to seek wider fame and fortune in a mason's lodge.

It is not clear how far or fast such men could rise. Every master-mason had done his time cutting and carving stone, suggesting the possibility of considerable economic mobility. But even masons rose slowly. Even today it takes young stonemasons four years to progress from simply squaring-off stones to carving them into mouldings.[17] And most of the work available to a mason was small-scale and dependent on unreliable sources of funding. The grand building projects that are the focus of this book were the exceptions rather than the rule; for many, opportunities might have been limited to small projects at local parish churches or the halls of better-off knights.

A major building project was a honey-pot, attracting pre-existing lodges and men with basic stone-working skills from a wide area. Not all came willingly: some rich patrons could 'impress' stonemasons into working for them. William of Wykeham, later bishop of Winchester, is said to have impressed nearly every mason and carpenter in England to the king's works at Windsor in 1359, making it hard for other projects to continue.[18] But this was unusual and required royal approval. The lodge that created the lady chapel at Ely probably came from Lincolnshire,[19] where a tradition of lavishly-carved stone furnishings already existed. But the chapel may have taken thirty years to complete, enabling some of these men to find almost a lifetime's employment on a single site: surely an attraction in itself. When their work was done, the masons might disperse again, taking new ideas with them. The fourteenth-century niches on the east wall of St German's priory in Cornwall, and the tomb in the contemporary chancel of the collegiate parish church at Bere Ferrers in Devon, were the work of men who had picked up motifs from Thomas of Witney at Exeter cathedral and were now work-ing on local churches elsewhere in the diocese. The brothers John and James Woderofe, one of whom worked on the Erpingham gate at Norwich, the other on the new monks' door, may have gone on to work on East Anglian parish churches such as Beccles.[20] Or a top-level master-mason might be brought in to do designs for a lesser church and the construction then be left in the hands of a talented junior from his lodge. The east end of Southwell minster was perhaps designed by the master-mason who had been in charge of key parts of Lincoln cathedral.[21] At Lincoln everything is perfect, but at Southwell some of the stone carving is average and its construction is full of bodges, as if a lesser talent was left to oversee the actual building work.

In any case, a mason might find himself employed for a season or two and then laid off. Little could be done in the winter months when stones could become brittle with frost, the days were short, and water penetration could ruin newly-built walls. Work went slowly, and a core of masons might be kept on as much to retain their skills as anything else.[22] At all times, the lodge might in any case only employ a small number of men on a wage, bringing in other masons when funds permitted and paying them

Southwell's east end is a sophisticated design but its detailing is crowded and slightly second-rate

by the piece. This is the reason for the mason's marks that can be seen cut into the stonework of many great churches: they ensured that the pieceworkers were properly paid. At Carlisle, there are over twelve hundred of them, but some are repeated thirty-three times or more. A careful study of their distribution reveals much about the working lives of these men. A team of perhaps thirty-six worked over each summer season. About seventeen of them cut moulded stones for the piers of the choir. They were split into two teams, for the two sides of the choir, and each team had its own foreman. Once the arcades were up, only nine of these reasonably skilled masons were kept on; less skilled men, more suited to setting in place stones that had already been cut replaced them.[23] Those that were unlucky would go off in search of more work or, as they did in winter, simply return to their lands and their families.

Some specialist stonemasons could ensure the market came to them. The Isle of Purbeck was the principal source of a very hard limestone which could be polished to a dark, marble-like gleam.[24] All the carving and marbling of this stone was done close to the quarries. Patrons who wanted such effects could leave detailed specifications of what they needed at the marblers' shops and warehouses in London and the work would be delivered in due course.[25] Purbeck marble was common throughout the age of the cathedrals, from the mid-twelfth century to the Reformation. Polished to a dark ebony glow and carved into pipe-like shafts, it is a defining feature of thirteenth-century architecture, but it could also be half-polished, resulting in the warm tones of the piers at Exeter, or sumptuously carved – demanding work on this hard stone – as in the mid-fifteenth century chantries of Bishops Waynflete and Beaufort at Winchester.

The marbler's bread and butter was the production of standardized, off-the-peg items, from flat tomb slabs to carved effigies. The tomb of Prior Selyng of Canterbury was carved by a marbler working in St Paul's churchyard and cost £4 13s 4d; Archbishop de Gray of York was honoured with a generic bishop's effigy which is not wearing the correct vestments for an archbishop and has had to be cut down to fit a tomb chest of slightly different dimensions.[26]

In spite of the ability to buy in some work that had already been carved, the cathedral building site was a busy place. During the summer, from dawn to dusk, apart from time for meals, a midday sleep and the occasional unpaid holiday,[27] men might be seen 'working so vehemently with bustle and noise that a man could hardly hear the one next to him speak'.[28] They worked in conditions that gave them as much natural light as possible, either in low temporary sheds open to the elements, the lodges after which a mason's team was named, or in the open air. Equipment was limited and simple. The stained-glass workshop at Norwich in 1436 was a hut containing a large pair of compasses, a hammer, a stool and a few smaller items, such as pieces of lead and solder; large working tables with a plaster surface would also have been present.[29]

With men coming from up to 200 miles away to work on a major project, there was a rich mix of dialects and accents on site, and there might well be a mix of languages too. There could be foreigners among the workforce. Italians worked on the thirteenth-century marble pavement at Canterbury cathedral, with its complex inlay. 'Brice the Dutchman' carved some of the Norwich cloister bosses.[30] Although it is often thought that the medieval common man was deeply rooted in a particular locality, in fact he could spend much of his life far from home. The most cosmopolitan could switch between elements of English, Latin and French, depending on whom they were talking to and what they were talking about.

Perks of the job might include free food from a monastic kitchen, or the provision of working gloves. The workmen who installed York's great east window were paid 4s a week, but they got a £5 bonus at the end of the year, and an enormous £10 each, one year's salary, if the work was done in time.[31] When the first stones of one of York's western towers were set, in 1432–3, the masons were given a celebratory meal.[32] Figure-carvers might be given a cloak or gown, a perk that could also be used as a badge, to show they were in the employ of a specific cathedral. Highly-skilled men such as these might be living in rented rooms, but most ordinary masons probably slept together in temporary lodgings. This might have been one of the functions of the makeshift lodge for twelve men that was built in the north transept at York during the rebuilding of the choir.[33]

The building site could be a dangerous place. The master-mason William of Sens was invalided off the building of the east end of Canterbury cathedral after 1180; and the sacristan there, John Grove, fractured his skull after a fall at the west end in 1425.[34] Chips of stone flew from the chisels, and limestone can make the eyes sore, though ingestion of small quantities is reasonably harmless: it is, after all, made from calcium, the stuff of our bones.[35] The making of pigments for stained glass and wall-painting was rather different. The apprentices who darkened colours by adding lead oxide ground with glass dust must have done great long-term damage to their health. Other substances used to aid drying or contribute to the colour included silver nitrate, red wine, vinegar and urine.[36]

Indeed, the stuff of which cathedrals are built itself sometimes seems to be half alive. Magnesian limestone comes from the ground damp with quarry sap; it has to be allowed to dry out before it is crisp enough to cut. It even changes colour with the rain. The Tadcaster stone used at York minster looks a hard off-white after rain but glows like set honey in sunshine. Many cathedrals are direct reflections of the local geology and its history, their masonry cut from beds which were once the floors of long-vanished seas; their polished limestones squirming with fossilized crustaceans. Worcester, to which stone could be delivered by water thanks to its site overlooking the Severn, reflects the varied geology through which the river passes. Its yellow-white limestone came from the Cotswolds, the red sandstone from the vales, and the green Carboniferous sandstone from the far north-west of the county.[37] In some parts of the building these stones are arranged in striped layers to striking effect, though they may originally have been plastered over. What looks like a decorative pattern may simply be an attempt to ensure stability by evening out the different stones used.

There were many other crafts represented on a building site, and the boundaries between people with different skills were not as clear-cut as they are today. Because wooden templates had to be cut for each moulding and each shaped stone, and vaults could themselves be built of wood, stonemasons and carpenters worked particularly closely together. Indeed, at the top of their game, the two professions were interchangeable. Men like William Hurley at Ely were equally at home creating wooden architecture on a grand scale in the Octagon as in carving the choir-stalls that stood beneath it. Thomas of Witney was brought to Exeter precisely because he could create elaborate fittings in both wood and stone.

But the cathedrals were multimedia creations. A smith from Dereham and his boy produced the hinges for the chapter-house door at Norwich. These would have been elaborate pieces of work, from which decorous metal tendrils spread across the door itself. They cost £4 6s, but the bill included a further 2s 6d, half the cost again, for transport and installation, which involved a further four assistants.[38] A painter and his assistant worked for fourteen weeks on decorating the cathedral clock at Norwich in 1316–17, using five hundred leaves of gold. They were paid 9s 6d a week 'and not more, because they stayed at the table of our lord', presumably meaning that the prior ensured they were fed and watered.[39] Cathedral and monastic seals, which validated legal contracts, official announcements and payments, had to

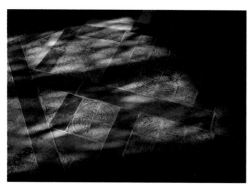

The creation of elaborate glazed tiles, as here at Gloucester, was just one of the many crafts that went into making the cathedrals

be particularly carefully made. It took eight weeks, and £7 6s 8d, to create the new seal of Canterbury cathedral priory in 1233.[40] The eight different matrices needed for the design were as hard to imitate as a hologram in a banknote.

The making of stained glass was perhaps the most striking and sophisticated of these skills; yet very few of the materials for it were manufactured in England. High-quality coloured glass was bought in France; even the white glass that was made in England was considered inferior. This does not seem to have affected the skills of the artists, of whose work so much has been destroyed. Only at Canterbury and York and, to a lesser extent, Gloucester and Wells, is it possible to get a real idea of the impact medieval stained glass would have had. Even at these churches, the effect has been muted by time. Many individual pieces of glass have been replaced or restored and leading needs replacing every century or two. The amount of leading inevitably increases every time breakages are repaired. The black lines that originally enhanced the legibility of the window can begin to obscure it. In 1304 Exeter's new east end was glazed with some 1,204 metres of glass by Walter the glazier at a cost of £4 10s.[41]

Cathedral-building was thus a collaborative enterprise, in which men of many disciplines came together. But there was also a strong sense of hierarchy and relative status. The east window at Wells might include some of the most subtle and considered subjects for stained glass to be seen anywhere, evidence of close collaboration between glazier and clerical patron. Yet it seems that William Joy, who devised the pattern of stone tracery into which it would be set, could come up with whatever tracery pattern he preferred, rather than developing one that complemented the arrangement of figures suggested by the glazier.[42] The man at the top of the tree, whose skills were surrounded by a special mystique, was thus the master-mason, the medieval equivalent of an architect. He, above all others, strode through the building site with lordly authority.

MASTER-MASONS

The master-mason could be a mighty figure, entering the masons' yard 'in his finery, gesturing with his rod on a piece of stone, and ordering "cut it for me so!"'[43] Men like the master-carpenter William Hurley, who worked at Ely, or his contemporary Thomas of Witney,[44] who worked at Winchester, Exeter and Wells in the fourteenth century, were men of property in their own right, their wealth placing them among the richest laymen of their day, their status comparable to that of a minor cathedral canon.

In 1311, Thomas of Witney was living in Winchester with his wife Margery and working at the cathedral, where he produced the presbytery arcade and the stone screen around the feretory platform, where the shrine of St Swithun stood. He first went to Exeter as a consultant, to help select wood for the bishop's throne, but from 1317 he was master-mason, on an annual salary of £6 13s 4d.[45] Perks included rent-free accommodation. His great bishop's throne there is the size of a small building and made entirely of wood; yet he was equally at ease continuing the construction of the cathedral itself. By 1323 he was in Wells, working on the cathedral's new east end; he became the third richest layman in the city. He passed responsibility for the project on to his junior colleague, William Joy, in 1329; Joy was made responsible for work in Exeter by 1342. Thomas of Witney received the full salary for his work at Exeter all the time he was at Wells and probably kept his family at home in Winchester throughout. From here, his son became a master-mason in his turn.

Witney was a master-mason at ease with creating wooden fittings; William Hurley, a master-carpenter who could produce architecture in wood. At Ely he could command £8 a year and free board and lodging;[46] once the Octagon was complete, he was kept on at £1 a year to finish the choir-stalls and keep a weather eye on the innovative Octagon itself. By the 1330s he was riding high, able to command fees of £40 or £50 for his work for various aristocratic patrons, among them Hugh Despencer at Caerphilly Castle.[47] By 1336 he was the chief carpenter and surveyor of all the king's works south of the Trent and Humber, for which he earned an additional £18 a year and was given a robe that marked him out as a senior royal servant. He was even involved in Edward III's Scottish wars, taking a wooden engine to the siege of Dunbar in 1338, a trip that took eleven weeks.

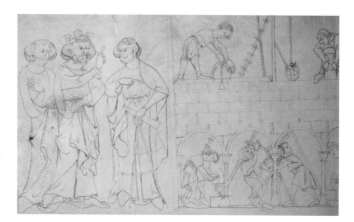

The patron, in this case an imagined King Offa at St Albans, inspects a building site

If Witney's wealth matched that of the richest city layman or merchant, Hurley's was comparable to that of a minor cathedral canon or knight. He even adopted a coat of arms, the ultimate indicator of status, and he and his wife Idonea eventually moved into a house provided by the Crown inside the Tower of London.

Such men were at the top of their trade, involved in more than one large project at the same time and employing other more junior master-masons to oversee day-to-day work. When John of Evesham became master 'for the rest of his life' at Worcester in 1359, he was paid 3s a week and given a loaf of white bread each day. This was reduced to 1s a week once free accommodation had been found for him. By this date, the new nave had been under way for over fifty years; John of Evesham thus had little creative work to do and his contract suggests that instructing others in his craft was as important as working on the building itself.[48]

The genius who designed the Gloucester south transept carved a unique image of himself staring in horror as a promising assistant falls from his vault

We only know about these men from chance mentions in account rolls and other documents; we know almost nothing about master-craftsmen from earlier centuries. The men behind the great post-Conquest building boom, for example, are virtually anonymous. Robert, who designed St Albans in the 1070s, was said to have 'excelled all masons of his time'[49] and we know he owned a house in the city in 1135. The large number of Germanic details in the cathedrals of that period may suggest an influx of craftsmen from across the North Sea as news of the building boom spread.[50] By the late Middle Ages, we know a lot more; the earliest English architect of whom it has been possible to write a biography is Henry Yevele, who worked for the king and his circle in the late fourteenth century and probably designed both the Neville screen at Durham and the Canterbury nave.[51]

Despite the mind-boggling achievements of these men, they were not infallible. The works that we have today tend to be those that were well constructed. The spire at Salisbury is the tallest standing structure surviving from the Middle Ages only because we have lost the even loftier spires that once stood on top of Lincoln cathedral and St Paul's, and because the medieval spires that were designed for Cologne and Ulm were only built in the nineteenth century.

Exceptionally, at York, the workplace of a top-flight master-mason survives.

Shortly after the chapter-house was finished, probably in the early fourteenth century, the room above its vestibule was turned into a working space. By the end of the century it had become the centre of operations for the cathedral's master-mason and his team.[52] It is just a large bare room equipped with a toilet and fireplace. But to have such features and a stone-built room was itself a mark of real status; and it is not everywhere that one can sit in the very garderobe where a medieval master-mason might have had his best ideas. The main feature, though, is the gypsum-covered floor on which the master-mason would have engraved his designs full-size. These giant blueprints were then used to create the templates for individual pieces of stone. As each design was finished with, another would be scratched on top of it until the tracing floor became illegible. At this point a new layer of gypsum would be put down. The room was probably also used for filing the wooden templates created for each piece of stone. The tracing floor at York contains perhaps 150 years of designs, ranging from details for the fourteenth-century choir to windows for St-Michael-le-Belfry, the church built next to the minster in the 1520s.[53] The simplest way to make the gypsum flat was to walk on it: and the imprint of dozens of socked medieval feet, perhaps those of the masons themselves, can still be detected as subtle marks in the floor today.

Yet the master who installed the Bishop's Eye in the south transept at Lincoln cathedral appears to have worked in the cramped, dark conditions of the Angel Choir's triforium. Here, on a column, he sketched out his first idea for the tracery of the rose window.[54] The finished article, with its flowing lines flickering within two great pointed ovals, stretched tracery techniques to their limits.

Other master-craftsmen might also reach the giddy heights of the master-mason. By founding a chantry in the cathedral and filling a window there with stained glass, Richard Tunnoc, bell-founder and prominent citizen of York, was ranking himself with the minor aristocracy. His window seems intended to provide maximum visibility both to his piety and to his trade. Above images of Richard himself, self-abasingly presenting a little model window to St William, there are dozens of tiny gold and silver bells and scenes of his staff at work. In such images, piety and advertisement blur.

A 'working drawing' for a new rose window at Lincoln, engraved in the triforium of the Angel Choir

PATRONS

Not far away from Richard Tunnoc's bell-making window at York an equally striking scene is played out in glass. Sinners bend in supplication before knotted
whips; little piles of coins and the figures of stonemasons fill the borders. This is
the window installed by William Langtoft, the archbishop's penitancer. It was his
role to listen to confessions from lay people, often extracting a donation to the
cathedral in expiation. This money went directly into the cathedral's fabric fund,
which Langtoft administered.[55] The minster, it would appear, is literally built on
the guilt of medieval Yorkshiremen.

Or is it? The Ely Octagon cost £2,400; yet there, the pittancer, whose budget was
a focus for donations from lay people, gave just £16.[56] Similarly, the income from
collecting boxes and other offerings at Exeter in the 1280s came to just £2 a year,
and the sale of no fewer than twenty-four indulgences in 1324–5 realized little
more than £25.[57] Although these sums may have had a symbolic significance they
were a drop in the ocean for the rebuilding then underway. So, who paid for the
cathedrals? And to what extent did such people influence their design? The
answer starts at the top of the cathedral hierarchy, with the men whose job made
a cathedral a cathedral, and who were among the most cash-rich people in the
nation: the bishops.

A bishop's cash resources outstripped those of all other churchmen. In theory, too, unlike lay lords, he had no descendants to pass his riches on to. In the eyes of the Church, the cathedral was his spouse; he even wore a ring to symbolize this fact. So it is not surprising that, in the few cases where we know how a building project was financed, the input of the bishop was fundamental. Bishop Northwold spent £5,040, estimated to be three-quarters of the total cost, on the new east end built at Ely in the 1230s. A century later,[58] Bishop Hotham spent almost £2,035 on the choir, which was to be the setting for his tomb.[59] The completion of Lichfield, after a century's work, in the 1300s and the completion of the Canterbury nave around 1400 were only possible as a result of massive personal contributions from bishops Langton and Arundel respectively. Cathedral-building depended utterly on a bishop's support.[60]

The men who financed many of these projects, Hotham of Ely among them, were coming towards the end of high-flying careers in which they had played senior roles in national life. They were leaving a legacy to community and see as well as performing a lordly act of piety appropriate to their station, and giving future generations a permanent reminder to pray for their souls. Bishop Alnwick of Lincoln had a bitter battle with his dean and left just £20 to the cathedral, where he was buried in 1449. But he left enough money to his previous church,

One of the exquisite ivories commissioned for private use by Bishop Grandison of Exeter

Norwich, to refurbish the west front and build the tomb that he hoped would be his final resting-place. The tomb, in the nave, is empty but it is clear where his heart lay.[61]

Some bishops clearly had a personal enthusiasm for architecture. Archbishop Lanfranc of Canterbury and the thirteenth-century Bishop Hugh of Lincoln came to their respective churches fresh from building at St-Etienne in Caen and Witham Friary in Somerset respectively. Richard Poore was successively bishop of Chichester, Salisbury and Durham, initiating major works at all three cathedrals. William Wykeham of Winchester, perhaps the most interesting architectural patron in this book, formed a lifelong partnership with the master-mason William of Wynford, and an unmistakable aesthetic vision, shot through with a kind of glorious sobriety, runs through all his works. Wykeham and his mason dined together thirteen times in

1393.[62] Robert Sherborn, the late fifteenth-century bishop of Chichester, did not have anything like Wykeham's wealth, but managed to make contributions to building works at St Paul's, St Frideswide's, Oxford, and his own cathedral, as well as overseeing the construction of a Renaissance college for English priests in Rome. From Hugh du Puiset in twelfth-century Durham to William Waynflete in fifteenth-century Winchester, builder-bishops such as these had a disproportionate impact on the architecture of their times.

Building work could cement relations between bishop and community after troubled times, as Richard Poore found when he was sent to Durham to sort out the convent's debts and initiated the Chapel of the Nine Altars. Or it could be a way for a new bishop to show he meant business. Archbishop de Thoresby of York, for example, completed the rebuilding of the nave, a project that had been under way for a century and began energetic work on a new east end. He was equally involved in reforming his diocese and improving standards among parish priests. On the other hand, interest in new building could be an expression of relative political impotence. At York and elsewhere, the bishop was virtually excluded from chapter. It must have sometimes been the case that bishops built because it was the only thing they *could* do in their cathedral.

The bishop's authority was less uncertain in his diocese. A whole battery of fund-raising techniques depended on him. The new east end at St Paul's, begun in 1258, is a typical example. Here a letter was circulated to bishops throughout the country advertising remission of sins for any individual who gave a donation for building works. This indulgence was then passed on to all the parishes of each see, encouraging lay contributions. These letters even reached as far as Scotland and Cologne and new indulgences were announced several times over the ensuing decades. All offerings in the cathedral itself were likewise directed to 'the new work': most churches had collecting boxes for offerings (Wells, for example, had five). And collections were made across the see, with the clergy of London specifically asked to make donations.[63] Bishops taxed their own communities too. At secular Salisbury in the 1220s, the income from each prebend was taxed at the rate of 25 per cent a year for seven years and at monastic Winchester in the 1390s the sub-prior was asked for £100 a year, the convent collectively 100 marks a year, about a third less. One bishop of Norwich even sat outside the west front 'receiving gifts' after a fire in 1171:[64] an encouragement few could ignore.

When it came to the architecture itself, bishops could insist on signing off every detail of the design, as Archbishop Morton did during the construction of Canterbury's Bell Harry tower in the 1490s. The master-mason, John Wastell, drew up two alternative designs for the tower's pinnacles and gave them to the prior, to be forwarded to the archbishop with a covering letter.[65] Presumably it was Morton's intervention that doubled the height of the tower at around the time he was promoted to cardinal. But a bishop's aesthetic influence, it seems, was usually less hands-on than that.

The bishop must have signed-off proposals for new work and agreed major changes, such as the decision to double the size of the east end at Canterbury in mid-build in 1180, and the initiation of a new east end, the Lincoln Angel Choir in the 1250s, just when rebuilding of the cathedral had been completed. Both these were expensive decisions that centred round the architectural response to controversial new bishop-saints. More usually, the bishop might suggest general motifs and approaches. The private palaces and chapels of these men, for example, are often idiosyncratic. The tower-like palace from which Herbert de Losinga overlooked the building of Norwich cathedral was surely based on a suggestion of the bishop himself and was part of a concerted attempt, presumably his idea, to portray Norwich as inheriting the authority of previous East Anglian cathedrals.

But it was perhaps more usual for the bishop to simply agree the brief for the church. Such discussions do not even need to have been long or detailed. When Anselm of Canterbury and his prior, Ernulf, decided to rebuild the east end of Canterbury in 1096, it was the prior who did most of the work.[67] All the archbishop had to do was give his support for a building that was large enough to be a kind of church-within-a-church for the monks and had the space for the revival of various rites and cults practised at Canterbury before the Conquest. Perhaps he also endorsed or suggested the idea that the design should include some architectural references to Rome. Anselm was in exile for much of the time thereafter, so the detail and its execution were perhaps down to Ernulf and his masons.

Other bishops barely built at their cathedrals at all. Many advanced their interests more effectively by founding monastic houses, such as those at Titchfield, Selbourne and elsewhere built by Peter des Roches of Winchester; or academic colleges, such as that at Oxford founded by Bishop Flemming of Lincoln. Cardinal Beaufort, bishop of Winchester, gave £200 to the fabric of Hyde abbey in the city:[68] perhaps there we could have discovered as much about his architectural interests as we now can at Winchester cathedral itself.[69] And at all times and in all places, ambitious projects were the exception rather than the rule. Franciscans such as Bishop Gainsborough of Worcester, who had to borrow the money for his own installation and arrived 'half naked' and without a horse, would have scorned such grandeur.[70] At the other extreme, Henry of Blois, bishop of Winchester in the twelfth century, lavished his wealth on bibles, jewellery and painting. He also built magnificently, leaving behind the existing parish church at East Meon, the opulent Hospital of St Cross and, further afield, a new Glastonbury abbey. Yet there is little of his architecture remaining at the cathedral. The archbishops of York seem to have initiated new work at the collegiate churches of Southwell, Ripon and Beverley in step with that at York minster itself; while Thomas Langley is an example of a bishop of Durham who gave lavishly to the minster as well as to his own cathedral.

As a result, it is not possible to make a straightforward link between a bishop and the precise details of a resulting building. After all, to be remembered as the builder of part of a church, the bishop only needed to have paid for most of it. Late medieval construction at Winchester was almost entirely posthumously funded. Bishops Edington, Wykeham, Beaufort, Waynflete and Fox left large sums to the church which were used to rebuild the west front and the nave and to begin rebuilding the east end, as well as to construct a magnificent sequence of chantry chapels for the donors themselves. Were it not for the Reformation, which interrupted building work, Winchester might have ended up as entirely Perpendicular.[71] We tend to ascribe particular stages of this building to the bishop concerned, but it is equally possible that it became a tradition for late medieval bishops to leave money to the fabric fund, to be spent to an agenda set by the convent.

Many of these observations are hypothetical. We can only work out by inference who might have taken the initiative, and how they might have communicated their ideas. But the question of whether the bishop or his community took the lead is in some ways academic. Whether or not the bishop personally

The tomb of bishop Droxford, still covered in original colour, is prominent in the Wells east end – exceptionally, his dean, John de Godley, has a tomb of identical design

influenced the content of a building, the power of his office was key to its identity and often the main subject of its architecture. Whether it was the chapter or Bishop Jocelin that initiated the west front at Wells is in a sense immaterial. This tour de force reflects the atmosphere of episcopal triumph that was abroad in the 1220s and which would have excited bishop and chapter equally. The many references to St Peter's built into the eleventh-century cathedrals, such as the twisted columns of Durham and of Anselm's crypt at Canterbury, express something important about the historic identity of these churches, something that meant as much to the community as to the bishop. The Lincoln Angel Choir is a monument to a succession of saintly bishops; Exeter's choir fittings eschew such cults in a frothy celebration of the sacred nature of the liturgy and of episcopal authority. While such projects needed the bishop's support, the initiative could have just as easily come from his chapter: the result is the same. The chronicler Matthew Paris gives a particularly honest account of the way things were. 'Out of respect, these works are ascribed to the abbot, for the person on whose authority a thing is known to have been done, may be taken to have done it.'[72]

THE CHAPTER

Whoever initiated the rebuilding of a cathedral, it was the chapter that did the work. It was they who had to take on administration of the project and live with the inconvenience it caused. If there was a major dispute between bishop and chapter, work could grind almost to a halt, as happened at Lincoln during the episcopacy of Robert Grosseteste. By the same token, the construction of the Salisbury spire seems to have coincided with a rare period when, under bishops de Martival and de Gandavo, bishop and chapter were *not* at loggerheads.

And in almost every great project where we know about the funding, the chapter is the biggest financial contributor after the bishop himself. Particularly in the secular cathedrals, where canons could be scattered far and wide and have hugely varying incomes, some encouragement was needed. In 1255 Pope Alexander IV censured the non-resident canons of York who had refused to contribute to building works.[73] In 1361 the canons were taxed as little as one-twentieth of their income over three years, yet, even so, non-payers were being threatened with excommunication in 1368.[74] In other cases, as at Exeter, where

Some monks moved from monastery to monastery, in demand for their artistic skills

bishop and chapter both agreed to a 50 per cent tax on their incomes, these men might have been giving their money willingly for a project that was dear to their hearts.

Indeed, building was written into the job descriptions of these men. Building maintenance was part of the role of all monastic sacrists and most secular cathedral treasurers, while the dean or prior took line-management responsibility. The bishop might only be involved with major financial decisions and major projects. The massive contributions made by Archbishop Arundel that ensured the completion of the Canterbury nave tend to overshadow the fact that Prior Chillenden had been putting in £400 or so every year. He is the man behind Canterbury's nave, just as priors Ernulf and Conrad are remembered as the men behind Anselm's east end.

Men like Alan of Walsingham, sacrist at Ely, had to worry about logistics, about the right fuel and materials reaching the site on time. Where projects were slow and extended, as in the rebuilding of St Werburgh's abbey, Chester, simply keeping work going seems to have been challenge enough. But if the men in charge had an aptitude for what they were doing, they could have a profound influence on the architecture.

This is certainly true if one reads between the lines of Alan's career. We will never know if there was a eureka moment when he had the idea for the Octagon, a design that brilliantly synthesizes both the practical and the symbolic aspects of the cathedral. We do know that, as well as being a monk, Alan was also a skilled goldsmith. We also know that subsequent master-masons, among them John Cementarius and John Attegrene, were paid a quarter of the wages of master-carpenter William Hurley.[75] One wonders if these masons were employed primarily to design details such as window tracery and for their management expertise, while Hurley's technical abilities were fundamental to the creation of the Octagon's wooden vault, and Alan himself had the overall vision.

Elias of Dereham was apparently made a canon of Salisbury specifically to oversee the construction of the new cathedral in 1220. His career at this point shows a man of considerable financial and administrative acumen; a man that bishops trusted with their most private financial information. He worked with William of Colchester, artist-monk and sacrist of St Albans, to stage the translation of St Thomas at Canterbury in 1220, where by his 'council and invention everything necessary to the making of the shrine, to its setting up and translation was done'.[76] He knew Adam Lock, designer of the Wells west front, well.[77] Perhaps, then, rather than coming up with specific design ideas himself,

Elias was a trusted project manager and diplomat; but also a man who had taste, and who knew which craftsmen to appoint and how to brief them.

We know men such as Elias were the exception to the rule because medieval chroniclers went out of their way to remark on their abilities. Elias was also exceptional because he was probably not a craftsman and yet his involvement, and that of men like him, resulted in some of the most significant and historically eloquent architecture. The input of clerics was more normally restricted to the iconographic programmes that filled the cathedrals with meaning. Dean de Godley at Wells, for example, was probably the brains behind the subtle meditation on the Virgin enshrined in the glass there. Similarly, the complex messages encoded in such great iconographic programmes as the Wells west front and the Lincoln Angel Choir are emphatically the work of educated churchmen, giving us a glimpse of the mindset of the scholarly clerics and mystical monks who sat on chapter.[78]

Clerical involvement was not always so benign. The design of de Thoresby's lady chapel at York and of the Worcester nave, which was overseen by the prior and his senior monks, both reflect an understandable insistence by the patron that the proportions and forms of older parts of the building be respected. Such an approach would be seen as laudable today: yet, five hundred years later, these are among the least memorable cathedral interiors. Salisbury's many subtle imperfections seem to arise from clerical interference: one can imagine men like Richard Poore and Elias of Dereham insisting, against their master-manson's common sense, that the building reflect aspects of Old Sarum, or of Poore's constitution for the cathedral. Design by committee rarely works. And in-fighting within the convent could slow work down, as happened at Norwich. After a new-broom prior relieved the sacrist, Worstead, of responsibility for the rebuilding of the cloisters, the cost per bay fell from £34 to £11. Five years later the prior himself fell from favour and in 1335 Worstead, now pittancer, was placed in charge again, only to be relieved of responsibility and then re-appointed a few years later.[79]

A cathedral needed constant maintenance, as did its conventual buildings, and associated palaces and manor farms. This is where smaller donations were genuinely useful. At Rochester, the chrism and synodal pennies received from parish priests went towards the maintenance of the conventual buildings.[80] Vicars at Lichfield who failed to appear for services on time were fined and the income went straight into fabric maintenance.[81] At Winchester, the income from two Hampshire manors was earmarked for such work. Much of the repainting and renovation visible in the church between the building of the retrochoir in the

1200s and the start of work on the nave in the 1360s could have been paid for in this way, with little involvement from the bishop.[82] Some quite substantial changes could thus be made without the need for rebuilding or the participation of the bishop. For example, in the thirteenth and fourteenth centuries, the window tracery of many monastic churches was updated.[83] At Durham, almost every Norman window was filled with gothic tracery and documents show that even the massive south-transept window (1398) was to be 'of such design as the prior decides': no mention of the bishop.[84] With little overlap of personnel between the convent and the bishop's staff, changes such as these were perhaps easier to organize than an ambitious rebuilding and contributed to the comparative architectural sluggishness of the monastic cathedrals after their post-Conquest heyday.

It is also worth keeping in mind that these men had architectural concerns beyond the cathedral. Henry of Eastry was prior of Canterbury for forty-six years, from 1285 to 1331, and his obituary listed his building works as among his greatest achievements. But the cathedral was not the main focus of his efforts. Of some £6,000 that Eastry spent on building, £3,739 went on the priory's manors. Of the £2,184 devoted to the church and monastery, only a little was spent on the cathedral itself. By comparison Prior Eastry spent £3,624 on lawsuits, defending Canterbury's interests in London and Rome.[85]

Indeed, the architectural impact of a member of the cathedral community seems to have been inversely proportional to the amount of time they spent *in* the cathedral itself. Senior monks like Alan of Walsingham, who did have an impact, had major responsibilities in the wider world; the more cloistered monks, on the other hand, had little involvement in building work or its design. This is even truer of the secular cathedrals. The invisible cogs of the worship-machine, the vicars choral, chantry priests and choristers, rarely played any part in the visual impact of the church in which they worshipped. The contribution of the lay population is even more hazy.

LAYMEN

It is difficult to judge lay interest in cathedral building projects. When the collecting boxes at Exeter yielded £2 a year, we do not know if this sum represented hundreds of farthings left by the devoted peasantry or donations of £1 each from a couple of wealthy aristocrats.[86] In any case, although it would have helped with maintenance, such a small sum would have had little impact on a rebuilding budget. Yet bishops clearly wanted to involve lay people in the building of the cathedrals: there was more to the issuing of indulgences and other pleas than just a desire for funds.

Whether lay people wanted to give is another matter. Of the 2,500 wills surviving from London between 1258 and 1358, only forty-nine leave money to St Paul's, although the new east end was underway at the time. But 134 people left money for the maintenance of London Bridge.[87] Overall, there is an impression of a lack of active enthusiasm. The cathedrals of Worcester and Hereford had a monopoly on lay burials in their respective cities, but there is nothing to suggest that the income they derived from this made much difference to what they were able to do architecturally. The lay population was more likely to take an interest in, for example, their parish church; their donations tended to be more useful for maintenance than for grand projects.

Laymen, then, had no direct impact on a cathedral's architecture. But they could commission fittings and hope to be buried within its walls. Wealthy businessmen like the bell-founder Richard Tunnoc (see p. 468) funded individual stained-glass windows at York. When Agnes de Olme gave a hundred shillings to the minster in 1361, together with the cost of a pilgrimage to Santiago de Compostela, she expected this donation would give her both a window and the

The fifteenth-century cloister at Hereford made a grand setting for lay burials from the city

Richard Tunnoc, bellfounder and Mayor of York, donating a window to the minster

Joanna de Bohune was granted a prominent monument in the lady chapel at Hereford cathedral, after her donations helped enlarge the choir there

right to burial in the nave.[88] The minster, though, always had control of overall aesthetics. Although Agnes de Olme would have been able to choose the subject of her window, its design needed to match a pre-set compositional framework.[89]

Agnes is an example of the lay women who began to make contributions to the cathedrals after about 1300. Often, these were specifically for burial in or close to the altar in the lady chapel, as is shown by lay female burials at Hereford, Worcester, Canterbury and Lincoln.[90] Women also funded major works of art, albeit usually as memorials to their husbands. The dowager Lady Ros, for example, paid for the enormous St William window at York minster around 1414.[91] Other women were less self-effacing. Sadly we have lost the large and richly-decorated chantry in Salisbury cathedral that was built by Lady Margaret Hungerford, at a cost of £497, after 1459, in which her effigy upstaged that of her husband.[92]

Poorer cathedrals were disproportionately dependent on such donations. In 1327 Joanna de Bohun, Lady of Kilpeck, who had outlived two husbands, left the income from the church of Lugwardine to the chapter of Hereford cathedral. They used this money to fund ten more vicars, enough new staff to ensure the lady mass was properly performed and not 'as in a parish church'.[93] In return, Joanna was buried in the lady chapel, very close to the intended shrine site of St Thomas. The effigy on her tomb clutches a model of Lugwardine church, reminding future generations of her gift.

Almost all these fittings and monuments were given by members of local aristocratic families, who compared in rank to the canons and bishops of the cathedrals. Many of these people involved themselves with their local cathedral throughout their lives, through membership of its confraternity for example. This was a kind of medieval friends' organization with spiritual benefits, which offered prayers for the souls of its noble members. Most churches, including Durham, Lichfield, St Hugh's Lincoln and St Albans abbey, ran such an organization. Local magnates could also offer significant benefits-in-kind. At Gloucester, for example, the cost of making lead for a new roof in 1234 was reduced when a wealthy landowner granted the abbot permission to fetch dead wood, essential for running a forge, from a nearby forest for a specified period of time.[94]

Even such prominent men could not assume that they would have more than a commemorative brass or a floor slab in the church after they died. Monumental burials in the cathedral were carefully controlled. So it would be interesting to know who persuaded the monks of Winchester to let the father of Piers Gaveston, Edward II's favourite, be buried inside the cathedral, where he is apparently the only layman to have a tomb with an effigy on it. Many monastic houses, on the other hand, were partly monuments to their lay founders. Perhaps the most remarkable example of this kind of relationship was at St Augustine's, Bristol, where the community enjoyed the support of the Berkeley family almost continuously for four hundred years: a long time even by medieval standards. Yet it seems the family demanded little for their financial support; only the works of the early fourteenth century there reflect their interest in any specific way. We must have lost many other buildings that were similarly in the pocket of one noble family.

Kings, too, often built great churches, but only Henry III emerges as a major patron of the cathedrals. As well as spending the equivalent of two years' tax income on Westminster abbey and involving himself deeply in its design, Henry gave much timber from his forests for other great churches. The roof, choir-stalls and doors at Salisbury, most of which survive, took 1,443 oak trees, most of them 'good oak'. Of these, 581 were a gift from the king's West Country forests.[95] Henry also donated a ruby, some rich silk fabric known as samite and, fittingly in a church architecturally focused on the Eucharist, a silver pyx for the high altar. He made contributions in kind to many other projects too.[96]

The saints' cults, which attracted popular support, are the exception that proves the rule. Although in general they ran at a loss (see p. 208),[97] when these cults took off the financial windfall could be dramatic. It seems likely

The arms of the lords Berkeley pepper their 'mausoleum' church of St Augustine's, Bristol

that a flood of tiny donations, many made up of land rather than cash and thus capable of yielding income forever, was stimulated by the cult of St Hugh at Lincoln. Before the cult of Thomas Cantilupe took off, Hereford's fabric fund, based on one canon's share of the common fund and the income from sporadic indulgences, was purely devoted to maintenance. But within a year the cathedral found itself with £178 in donations to 'St' Thomas; and in 1290-1 receipts at the shrine made up three-quarters of the fabric fund. Both towers were rebuilt and most of the pilgrim route through the nave and east end was refurbished as well.[98] The cults of Edward II at Gloucester and Archbishop Scrope at York had similar effects. All these men, and Becket too, were not yet canonized when donations reached their peak; yet if their architectural legacy is anything to go by, they attracted the most dramatic cults in our story. Even if indirectly, they support the principle that only bishops, and sometimes kings, could pay for cathedrals.

TIME AND MONEY

It is a myth that it took centuries to build a cathedral. The difficulty was not in the construction itself but in maintaining the financial and political support needed to see it through. Lanfranc's Canterbury was apparently built in seven years. It is true it was a small cathedral, but it was only about a third shorter than giants such as Winchester. Similarly, the altars of Salisbury's east end were ready within five years of work beginning and Durham's ambitious Norman east end was built in about a decade.[99]

Where the bishop and his chapter had a strong desire to ensure construction was completed quickly, and possessed the wherewithal to raise the necessary funds, the only restrictions were logistical; a great gothic church could be built in two or three generations. Installing fittings and completing towers, west fronts and other non-essentials, as well as conventual buildings, might take rather longer. Lincoln did not have its full complement of towers and spires for nearly a century after the body of the church was complete. The Norman eastern half of Ely took about twenty years,[100] but the west front was not finished until the early thirteenth century. The evidence from three contemporary projects of contrasting elaboration suggests that, given a reasonable flow of funds, forty to sixty years was a good average building time. 'Plain' Wells was begun after 1174; when work stopped in the 1240s, the west front was almost complete but the chapter-house had barely been started. 'Rich' Lincoln, begun in 1192, was completed in the 1230s; at this point the cathedral had a chapter-house but lacked towers. 'Plain' Salisbury was built from 1220 to 1258. The completed work included a chapter-house, a cloister and the base of a tower, but there was no spire or sculpture on the west front. Averaged out, each bay at Exeter took three years; each bay at Salisbury, one.[101]

Focused, well-funded campaigns led to the greatest architecture, but they were few and far between. Of the handful of complete rebuilds that took place after the great Norman rebuilding, those at Lichfield, York and to a lesser extent Lincoln[102] were prolonged affairs that lacked architectural unity. There were more focused campaigns, resulting in few design changes, at Wells, Salisbury, Exeter and Bath. But the east end of every English cathedral was replaced and enlarged to some extent during the Middle Ages, providing more space for altars, separating clergy from laity more emphatically, or adding a grander shrine space or lady chapel.

Buildings in sees that were poor or troubled might be constantly under scaffolding. Chichester and Carlisle, two of England's poorest cathedrals, are each the result of a constant process of patching and reworking, done with beguiling leisure and understatement at Chichester and doggedly, in the face of storm, fire and war, at Carlisle. This was probably true of many smaller great churches and is the truth behind the myth that these places took a century to build. Only two cathedrals, York and Lincoln, both of them in exceptionally large and wealthy dioceses, managed to rebuild themselves several times over, as if the flow of funding on a grand scale had become embedded in the institution and, perhaps, the wider local economy. In most other cases, major building projects only occur once or twice in a cathedral's history, and are often the result of exceptional combinations of circumstances.

All this construction was enormously expensive. The Ely Octagon alone cost at least £2,406; the adjacent choir £2,034. Salisbury cathedral cost £28,000;[103] bay-for-bay, Westminster abbey, the most lavish building of its age, a figure twice as much.[104] These are enormous sums by the standards of an age when a decent

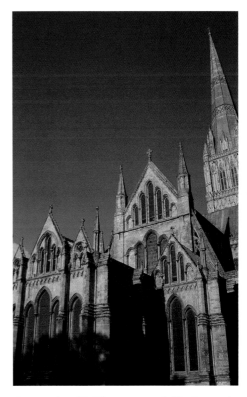

Construction of Salisbury was speeded by the use of many repeated details

annual income for a priest or a master craftsman was £5 to £8, and a wealthy canon's prebend might be worth £50. On the other hand, these figures were not excessive compared with other kinds of spending among the elite. Archbishop de Gray of York was said to have given the king £5,000 in exchange for the chancellorship of England; and another £10,000 for the archbishopric.[105] His transept at York was thus by no means the most expensive outlay of his life.

Architectural splendour usually reflects institutional wealth. The richest cathedrals (in declining order) were Canterbury, Ely, Winchester and Durham, all of which were monastic. The secular cathedrals of York, Wells and Lincoln are next on the list. All these places have truly exceptional cathedrals. Yet there are some surprises further down the pecking order. St Albans abbey, for example, has architecture that is plain and patched in the extreme, despite the fact it was among the ten wealthiest monastic houses in the country. Begun in the 1070s, it is one of the very earliest of the Norman great churches, and much of it survives.

All these cathedrals must have locked up in stone a significant part of the disposable income of the society that created them. Much English history since the Reformation could perhaps be characterized as the story of what happens when that wealth is liquefied.

BUILDING THE CATHEDRAL

However long it took to build a church, and whatever combination of people and circumstances lay behind its design, the actual process of putting it up changed little between the 1060s and 1540s. The foundations were dug, often for the entire building, and the walls were started, often being taken up to sill level. After that, the priority was to get the east end up and running. As soon as there was space for altars in the new church, the old building was knocked down. Work on the west end of the church might then be allowed to drag on for decades, perhaps with a masons' lodge of reduced size.

Wooden scaffolding and arched wooden forms supported the arches and vaults that were erected as building progressed. The voissoirs, or stones of the arch, were laid over the forms and the wooden support removed once the keystone was put in place. Building then usually proceeded upwards and westwards in stages. The men building the arcades were always a bay or two ahead of those constructing the triforium or gallery and they, in their turn, were always working a couple of bays ahead of the team working on the clerestory. Funds and materials were managed so that, if at all possible, any pauses or stoppages happened at a stable moment in the building process, such as when the east end, transepts and crossing had been completed, together with enough bays of the nave to buttress them. The last part of the church to be built was the vault, which was usually constructed under the protection of a wooden roof.[106] Stained glass was put in as soon as possible after the vault was finished and paintings, sculpture and other fittings could then be installed.

It was critical that the liturgy was interrupted as little as possible. In the case of complete rebuilds, the old church might be left intact next to the building works until the last minute, as happened when Winchester and Wells were rebuilt; more often the new building was simply put up around the old one, which was kept in use until the new one was ready and then demolished. This was essential if it was only the east end that was being rebuilt, as happened at Southwell, York minster and many other places. Alternatively, the new structure might be built on the stumps of the walls of the old: new naves were often constructed in this way, as at Exeter and Canterbury.[107]

In terms of engineering, the most important development of the Middle Ages was the invention of the rib vault around 1100. This revolutionary technique ultimately led to the development of the gothic style, and the creation of window tracery: all were standard architectural practice by 1250. The twelfth century also saw the development of the water-powered sawmill, which enabled stone to be cut to a manageable size more quickly, and advances in the tooling of chisels, which meant stone-carvers could create more delicate effects.

Number symbolism was sometimes incorporated into the design of a cathedral. This was usually an initiative of the patron rather than the master-mason. A piece of parchment listing the dimensions of St Peter's, Rome, seems to have been doing the rounds during the late eleventh century when various cathedrals were being rebuilt. Many key dimensions of that church are repeated at Winchester, Ely, Durham and other English great churches. The tight geometry of Salisbury cathedral is apparently encoded with references to the size and shape of the cathedral of Old Sarum. Only university-educated men would be likely to come up with this kind of informed, self-consciously clever symbolism.

The geometrical ideas of the masons, on the other hand, tended to reflect the years they spent with set squares and compasses rather than the curricula followed by clerics at Oxford or Paris. One of the most consistently recurring of proportional relationships, for example, is one to the square root of two (or 1:1.4142). This formula may seem as if it requires an understanding of sophisticated mathematics, but it can be simply demonstrated by drawing a diagonal across a square. The relationship between the length of the diagonal and each side of the square will be in the ratio of one to the square root of two. Entire buildings, among them Norwich and Durham cathedrals, appear to have plans based on this ratio; at Norwich, the cloister is the square, and from it is generated the length of the church. One result is that apparently abstruse mathematical relationships, in which many have since seen all kinds of mysteries, can be a simple side-effect of the way masons worked. These men would not have been surprised to be told that their work contained number patterns of which they themselves were unaware, for they took it as read that the elegance of geometry was a natural outcome of the harmony of a created universe.

———

The cathedrals thus depended for their appearance on an extraordinarily small group of people: bishops, priors and deans, master-masons and other top craftsmen, a sacrist or treasurer. And the most vivid and eloquent works of cathedral architecture seem to cluster around certain hotspots, when building activity increased across the board. These periods, the 1070s to 1100s; the 1180s to 1230s (with a ten-year gap for the interdict), and the 1320s and 1330s,[108] lie at the core of this book. During such periods, it seems, an elite group of craftsmen went from project to project, funded by a small group of patrons whose interest in architecture was raised by the critical mass of works under way. Perhaps a dozen men, all interconnected, thus created the architectural miracle of the 1320s. Both Thomas of Witney and William Hurley had worked on the royal chapel of St Stephen in the Palace of Westminster early in their careers,[109] and they were sponsored by high-flying bishops, many of whom had been Edward II's chancellor. The buildings created in these periods of greatest activity are those that seem most determined to impart a message set by the clerics and their designs seem most often to fulfil challenging briefs in subtle and satisfying ways.

Such periods were the exception to the rule. Most of the time, at most cathedrals, rebuilding was not underway. And work was often more a matter of maintenance and updating, or of respectful extension, than of making an ambitious statement. During the mid-twelfth century, or from about 1250 to about 1320, or from the 1380s to the 1450s, large-scale architectural work was relatively scarce. Those communities that did initiate major projects were unlikely to have had much experience of ambitious works. As a result, they were more likely simply to take the advice of their master-mason and be content with what he produced, provided it was up-to-date and came in on budget.

All this suggests a sociology of cathedral-building that can do much to explain the big picture. This is even truer of the many contrasts between the secular and monastic cathedrals. At the extremes, the differences are striking. During the great rebuilding that followed the Conquest, the monastic cathedrals became larger and more elaborate than the secular ones: the giants of the era are Winchester, Canterbury (after 1096), Durham and Norwich. The exceptions are York and St Paul's, both churches with 'something to prove'.[110] After this period not a single one of the monastic cathedrals mustered up a complete rebuild. Worcester and Canterbury became gothic in disconnected stages. Bath is the one exception; its rebuilding, right at the end of our period, left it significantly reduced in size. There is thus nothing to compare with the focused, end-to-end efforts that produced complete gothic churches at secular Wells, Exeter, Salisbury, Lincoln and, rather more slowly, Lichfield and York. In any case, new east ends, rather than complete rebuilds, were the most common major projects after the twelfth century. Only the east end of monastic Norwich was not completely rebuilt while the list of those that were refashioned more than once is dominated by the secular cath-edrals, such as Lincoln, Lichfield and York.

Even the greatest of the gothic monastic cathedrals, Winchester, Ely, Worcester and Canterbury, are not stylistically uniform and retain substantial parts that are romanesque. In Ely's case, this applies to the entire nave and transepts. In contrast to the all-gothic secular cathedrals, they went up in stages, with long periods when there was little activity apart from maintenance. This was so, for example, at Winchester for much of the thirteenth century, and at Canterbury in the four-teenth. This was precisely the period when the secular rebuild was at its height, leaving no romanesque fabric at all at Wells, Lichfield or Salisbury[111] and none visible on the interiors of Exeter, Lincoln and York. The ambitious idea of building a rib vault throughout the church may have been conceived at monastic Durham, but this innovation was never achieved at monastic Ely, Rochester or Carlisle while the vaults at Winchester and Norwich were only completed in the sixteenth century. In contrast, all the secular cathedrals have a rib vault and, because these stone roofs are so visually arresting, even comparatively humble churches such as Hereford and Chichester, both of which were built in several phases, come across at first impression as being substantially gothic. The central-ized chapter-house, first seen at Worcester, was similarly a monastic invention, but it was the secular cathedrals that ran with this design. Only two do not have ambitious centralized chapter-houses; the cathedral priories, on the other hand, all kept to the rectangular design.[112]

Some of the reasons for this are cultural. The gap between the secular cathedrals and other collegiate churches was a great one, whereas the monastic cathedrals were on a much more equal footing with the great monasteries that were not cathedrals. Thus, the secular cathedrals were far more likely to be shaped architecturally by what made them unique: the fact that they were bishop's seats. But the explanation is also to do with the structures of the institutions themselves. The creators of the monastic cathedrals had envisaged monk-bishops; they had built great churches to express the spiritual might of monasticism as much as because these buildings were also episcopal seats. The secular cathedrals of the same period, on the other hand, were smaller. In size, they were much more comparable to the minsters that then dominated the great church landscape. But the monk-bishop idea did not last and it was episcopal power rather than monasticism that eventually set the agenda. By 1200, the secular cathedrals were still diminutive but had a hugely enhanced significance, particularly as they now operated in a landscape where small parish churches rather than minsters accounted for the vast majority of other places of worship.

More importantly, by this date they also had the institutional wherewithal to see through a rebuilding programme. Monastic cathedrals appear to have devolved far more architectural work from bishop to community, with the prior and sacrist, in particular, taking a lot of responsibility for maintenance and renewal. The examples from Winchester and Durham above suggest how far this could go. In such a situation, and given the disconnection between bishop and monastic chapter, there was less likelihood of a grand architectural solution; the result was a patchwork of small changes. The exceptions prove the rule. At Canterbury, whose east end and nave are both ambitious works of gothic architecture, the archbishop had unusual powers of appointment over the key members of the priory; at fourteenth-century Ely, where bishop and chapter co-operated on a huge investment in building, Bishop Hotham had placed allies in the key posts of prior and sacrist.[113] By 1300, Worcester had gothic stone-vaulting at both the east and west ends of its church: construction of the nave, a large project that seems to have been in the hands of the monks, could thus have been seen as an ambitious kind of mainten-ance. Ironically, when building activity across the Middle Ages is viewed as a whole, the monastic cathedrals seem to have put more resources into architecture than the secular ones. Yet the way these resources were spent resulted in a series of much-expanded romanesque churches rather than dramatically rebuilt gothic ones. What resulted were monuments to the glory days of monasticism; the gothic secular cathedrals by contrast were a spectacular hymn to the power of bishops.

In the end, all these buildings are the result of patrons and craftsmen talking to each other, sometimes quite literally, in two slightly different languages. Both groups want to create architecture that suits the grandeur of the liturgy and evokes the experience of heaven. But the masons are interested in formal problems: the outline of a moulding, ways of handling the junction between vault and wall, new decorative effects. Patrons, on the other hand, may have taken no interest in the detail of the design, though they became more engaged during the hotspot years, limiting their engagement to laying down a sophisticated theological scheme, or prescribing a few generalized forms and preferences. What they understood was how the building *worked*, what it was *for* and what they wanted it to *say*, rather than the formal detail of how that was expressed. In this sense the modern obsession with changing style, although so useful for dating, is a distraction; what these two groups of men excelled in was something different. They were engineers of the imagination, the creators of colossal 'machines for worshipping in',[114] whose invisible presence, like the angels, saints and God himself, is everywhere in these buildings. Their achievements astonish to this day.

WHAT TO SEE

Many of the places that most vividly conjure up the mason's life, in particular existing cathedral masons' yards and conservation studios, or the old tracing floors, are not normally open to the public. Other places and topics in this chapter are more easily illustrated.

Going behind the scenes: tours at Ely, Salisbury and Wells take visitors into triforiums, roof spaces and towers.

Stonework planning: Durham and its patterned columns.

Patron/designer partnership: Winchester college, Winchester nave and New college, Oxford.

Stained glass: York, Canterbury, the east window at Gloucester, the east end at Wells (much restored), Ely stained-glass museum.

For a tour of the works of one patron: there is much connected with Bishop Henry of Blois to be seen in and around Winchester: the Winchester Bible in the library and the treasury in the north transept of the cathedral; the Hospital of St Cross and Wolvesey castle, the remains of the bishop's palace, in Winchester; East Meon church about 20 miles east of Winchester.

POSTSCRIPT

We have now travelled at breakneck speed through nearly a thousand years of history, the millennium of the cathedrals, from St Augustine's house-sized building in half-abandoned Durovernum Cantiacorum in *c.*600 to mighty Canterbury cathedral, still being enriched before the Reformation. The seventeen purpose-built cathedrals and nine other great churches we have visited dominate the cities in which they stand to this day. These buildings offer a series of frontline reports from the cutting edge of history, albeit from a particular perspective and in a form that is not always easy to interpret. The mission of St Augustine, the Norman Conquest and the Reformation, all events in which cathedrals, as centres of political power, had a role to play, flag the beginning, middle and end of our story. Through the cathedrals we have discovered some of the intervening plot developments, in particular the emergence of England in the years after the Viking invasions, the development of a new age of saints (which soon became a new age of bishops) from the mid-twelfth to the early thirteenth century, and the forging of new aesthetic themes in the traumatic decades before the Black Death.

As buildings, the cathedrals are often direct reflections of the way the communities that lived in them were organized and managed. So tailor-made was the Wells chapter-house that the canons would have been in difficulty if someone had endowed an extra prebend, or reformed the traditional hierarchy. When reform was eventually imposed, in the mid-sixteenth century, these extraordinary buildings were left as silent and spectacular monuments to past certainties. By the same token the cathedrals embody a kind of symbolic reality, often making concrete

A bishop looks out from the sixteenth-century Perpendicular Prince Arthur's chantry at Worcester

communal events, from full meetings of chapter to massed gatherings of laymen, that rarely occurred in reality.

Cathedral architecture offers a glimpse into a vanished world. Just as significantly, it helps us understand why, in today's very secular world, the medieval cathedrals matter, aside from their status as works of art and their ongoing significance to Christians. The simple answer is that they were fundamental to the development of most western educational and administrative traditions.

Here, the secular cathedrals played a particularly unsung role. While the monastic houses kept education and intellectual life alive in the early years of our story, it was the collegiate churches, of which the secular cathedrals were the ultimate expression, through which universities developed and a formal institution made of the grammar school. Thanks to their comparative flexibility, the medieval world found a way of turning state administration from the doings of a handful of men with the ear of the king into a complex and professional machine. The law was professionalized in the same way. Ultimately, monasticism died as a cultural force, while the collegiate principle continued to thrive.

Indeed, as town corporations and guilds became wealthy and independent from the fourteenth century on, paving the way for much that we take for granted in modern civic life, what other model was there for a complex, self-governing corporate body apart from that offered by the Church, especially in its more pragmatic, collegiate incarnation? The English Parliament came into being during the thirteenth century and became ever more politically significant over the ensuing years: again, the chapter of a religious community offered the only model for a voting body with influence over its executive. The polygonal chapter-houses which were the venues for this restricted form of democracy were even, as at York and Westminster abbey, sometimes the venue for Parliament itself. All kinds of institutions, many still with us, are thus descended from the religious college, which helped create everything from the Civil Service to civil society. The cathedrals are the forgotten midwives of the modern world.

The secular chapters created a more publicly-focused cathedral art than their monastic counterparts. People expected cathedrals in general to reach out to laymen. Adam, the Cistercian abbot of Dore, criticized 'the meaningless paintings in churches, especially in cathedral and parish churches, where public stations take place'.[1] But, in the monastic cathedrals, the complete separation of the chapter from the staff of the bishop could allow the monks to sink back into a self-contained and ancient otherness, the bishop's chair in the choir incidental to their concerns. No one on a monastic chapter had any diocesan responsibility, the bishop had no built-in support on chapter for major architectural initiatives and the maintenance of the building was taken care of by the prior and sacrist. This distinction is a rule to which there are many exceptions, but the 'closed' west fronts of Canterbury, Norwich or Winchester could not contrast more with the emphatically 'open' display of those at Exeter, Wells or York.

The cathedrals also helped invent the city. Indeed, they evoked the very idea long before England had any real cities and created the focus around which many subsequently grew. As the seats of bishops, they also helped coin the more specific idea of the capital, of the city as the focus of a region's political power. Today, the cities have overtaken them. Newcastle, Birmingham and Leeds dwarf their medieval equivalents, Durham, Coventry Lichfield and York, and have in turn had cath-edrals created for them.[2] Yet the closes that surround medieval cathedrals still propose a small-scale, community-based urbanity that is something of a challenge to modern planners. The cathedral closes were in effect garden cities, even if they were also exclusive gated communities.

The cathedrals were centres of an oppressive political authority, but they were also the products of a culture that put spiritual activity at the heart of every aspect of life. There is a worldly, organic quality to cathedral art; even these self-important buildings did not shy away from addressing the corporeal realities of sex and death. Their art is at once inclusive and hierarchic-al. Its all-embracing aspect, at least, can sustain us in subtle and numinous ways, having much to offer in an age when man's relationship to the natural environment is in crisis.

It is often said, for example, that the modern world is obliterating a sense of place, replacing it with a world that can seem rootless, homogeneous and anodyne. The cathedrals, by contrast, are deeply rooted in their localities. St Albans is only the latest structure in a shifting pattern of ancient cult sites; Wells, set gloriously in the choppy hinter-land between the high Mendips and the sodden Levels, has almost literally grown from its source, St Andrew's well. Yet it was only one of three ancient religious communities that grew up beside springs in Somerset. Ely and Durham domin-ated entire landscapes, economically and spiritually, and their cathedrals suggest this. Durham is a cliff on top of a cliff; Ely a great vessel on the swell of its island hill.

A buttress off the Wells lady chapel reaches out a steadying arm towards St Andrew's well, tap root of England's most perfect cathedral

Ancient cathedral politics have had a surprising impact on modern England. The sees of Lincoln and Lichfield are at once the ghosts of ancient Mercia and the predecessors of modern regional identities in the east and west Midlands. The very existence of the sees of Rochester and Chichester is a result of relatively short-lived political situations in the far-off seventh century. Both the Anglo-Saxons and the Normans liked to locate their cathedrals in former Roman cities, among the 'immense palaces . . . beautiful baths, remains of temples and sites of theatres' that were still visible, for example, in twelfth-century Chester.[3] St Albans, Gloucester and Lincoln are just three of the surviving buildings that seem architecturally imbued with the Roman context of their setting.[4]

The cathedrals are at once deeply rooted in their own landscape and its history and profoundly connected to the wider world. They stood on the edge of a universe whose centre was hundreds of miles away, in Rome and Palestine, and were designed to evoke such distant structures and places as St Peter's, Jerusalem and Galilee. William Blake wrote of building Jerusalem in England's green and pleasant land; men like Richard Poore and Thomas of Witney actually did so.

This spiritual geography carried with it constant reminders of an era more aware of its dependence on the earth for survival. Cathedral archives provide glimpses of a natural landscape that is at once fuller and more vivid, as well as less controlled and more dangerous, than our own. For the manor of Stuntney to have provided Ely with 23,000 eels a year, the fen must virtually have been boiling with them;[5] certainly the air of the Isle would have been sweet with the scent of the peat fires kept in fuel by the monastery's sedge-master. When the canons of Southwell had one of their occasional sittings in their chapter-house, they were surrounded by realistic carvings of the specific plants and animals that provided for their glittering careers. The cathedrals also mark changes in our relationship with the earth. Just as the twelfth century marked a peak in the process, in which the great churches played a vital role, of clearing wastelands and planning towns, so the cathedral's depiction of foliage shifted from the battling tendrils of high romanesque to the gracious, tamed fantasy genus that is stiff leaf.

This deep connection with the land is one of the roots of the fecundity that is perhaps medieval art's unique characteristic. At the core of the architecture that resulted is a knowing combination of suffering and growth, memorably embodied in the image of the green man. Found carved on bosses, corbels and elsewhere, and much sought out by modern cathedral visitors, the green man is fecund, yet rarely happy. Such images are a subset of those of the suffering Son of Man and his virginal mother that once dominated these churches, and a suitably earthy reflection of the idea of incarnation that lies at the heart of Christianity and its art. Yet they also illustrate how medieval people approached such ideas in terms of the natural world with which they grappled daily. Metaphors in which decay and suffering are intertwined with happiness and growth were far from obscure: they were as clear and sustaining as daylight.

This is far more relevant to understanding the minds of the cathedral-builders than the modern division of medieval art into distinct styles, however effective it is for dating parts of a building. Those who saw these buildings engaged with them as the venue for sacred events and as huge repositories of meaning. The early thirteenth-century poet Hugh d'Avranches wrote a life of St Hugh of Lincoln which shows how the educated visitor expected to coin clever metaphors from everything they set eyes on: the white ashlar walls of the half-rebuilt Lincoln cathedral were emblematic of

Medieval art sees death and fecundity as indivisible: a green man from a misericord in Norwich cathedral

'modesty hewn by doctrine' he said; and the many-layered decorative openings of St Hugh's choir 'like a honey comb', sweet with inner meaning.[6]

This engagement with nature and the land turns out to be one of the more unexpected ways in which the medieval world is anything but a distant country. Cathedral wealth was based on the ownership of great estates, gifted by kings and nobles from as early as the seventh century. Much of this land is still in the hands of the Church, which remains one of the largest landowners in England.[7] Even the cathedral priory of Norwich, whose monastery was dissolved in 1541, still possessed two-thirds of its medieval lands when they were placed in a central Church of England 'pool' in the 1870s; the same was true of St Paul's and Canterbury.[8] This gives the Church of England, an institution such generous donors as Eudo the steward of twelfth-century Norwich, let alone King Ethelbert in seventh-century Kent, would find hard to recognize, a wealth and power that many might feel quite outstrips its significance in an increasingly secularized and multi-faith society.[9] If the Church of England were to be invented today, it would not be nearly as wealthy; and I doubt any modern regime, religious or non-religious, has put comparable investment into vainglorious architecture. In a literal, and very earth-bound sense, the world that made the cathedrals is with us still.

PART II

THE CATHEDRALS

BATH

Bath is the cathedral that shrank. What we see today – a parish church, rather than a cathedral – is a rebuild, begun in the 1480s and only completed after the Reformation. The first cathedral, which was built in the 1090s, was one and a half times bigger. As a result this former abbey church, which shared the status of cathedral for Somerset with Wells, is a monument not to the Normans, or even particularly to monasticism, but to the gutsy world of late medieval religion.

The Norman cathedral at Bath itself replaced a venerable Saxon church which had been turned into an important Benedictine monastery by St Oswald in about 967–70 (see p. 44).[1] In 1090, with a mixture of piety and chutzpah, the first Norman bishop, John of Tours, decided to relocate his cathedral from secular Wells to this monastic house, despite the fact that Wells was better located in the see, and at least as important a settlement. Perhaps, as William II's physician, the bishop had his eye on the business opportunities of a place famous for its healing waters; perhaps he was simply attracted by Bath's Roman origins. Whatever his reasons, Bishop John 'anointed the king's hand' with silver and gained possession of the entire city. He soon began rebuilding his church.[2]

Like its Saxon predecessor, Bishop John's church has almost entirely vanished: the only surviving traces above ground are the stumps of columns and hints of blocked arches at the east end of the present building. They prove that the church as it

The cathedral that shrank: Bath's west front dominates the heart of this otherwise Georgian city

stands is only as long as the nave of that built by John of Tours; indeed, his monastic enclosure took up an entire quarter of the city and included the healing springs themselves.[3] This really *was* a cathedral. Its building also marked the start of an architectural story that reflected the often troubled relationship between Bath and Wells.

From the late twelfth century Wells staged a fifty-year fight to regain cathedral status. Eventually the churches were made joint seats of the bishop, with Wells very much the senior partner. Little is known architecturally of Bath cathedral priory thereafter, although a lady chapel was built in the thirteenth century.[4] It seems the bishops lavished the wealth that went with owning two cities on Wells rather than Bath.

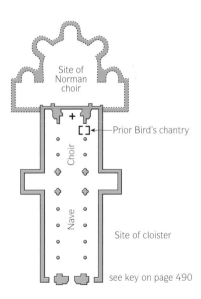

see key on page 490

Work on Bath's spectacular fan vaults ceased at the Reformation, and they were only completed in the nineteenth century

In 1500 Oliver King, bishop of Bath and Wells, intervened in a sluggish rebuilding programme initiated by the monks. Declaring that the 'present prior is slack', he decided to 'restrain . . . the pleasures' of the convent: he took £300 from the monastery's annual budget, leaving the monks just £180 to live on,[5] and brought in the royal masons Robert and William Vertue.[6] They soon boasted that there would be 'none so goodly neither in England nor in France' than the vault devised for the new church.

The Vertues' plan was to create an enormous fan vault. This type of vault, an invention of the 1360s, was most common in chantries – Bishop King's predecessor Bishop Stillington had used it, for example, to vault his ambitious cruciform chantry at Wells – but it had rarely been seen outside the West Country or on a monumental scale.[7] The Vertues applied the idea of a fan vault to an entire great church. The idea was taken up at the same time at Henry VII's most ambitious projects: his chapel at Westminster abbey and King's college chapel, Cambridge, both cathedral-sized buildings housing lavish chantries, with spectacular fan vaults.[8] Bath, it seems, is at once a reduced-size monastic cathedral and a massively expanded chantry chapel. Both these traits make it a potent reflection of late medieval priorities.

King's unusual west front is a typically late medieval structure, a reply – 300 years late – to the magnificent west front at its sibling cathedral in Wells. Where Wells is corporate, anonymous, at

Bath the great crowned olive trees (symbolizing Oliver King)[9] and the cardinals' hats (for his absentee successors Castellesi[10] and Wolsey) leave little doubt as to who was in charge. Wells shows only grandeur and happiness; Bath focuses on sin, and the disembodied, wound-punctured limbs of Christ. Yet its dominant image of Jacob's Ladder is highly original: for lay people, the story was a bold statement of renewal, an encouragement to give to the Church, while for the monks it was a warning against pride, and a pointed criticism of the heel-dragging that had forced Bishop King to intervene in the first place.[11]

Bath was the last attempt at a complete cathedral rebuild in the English Middle Ages; at the Dissolution much of its western half remained unfinished, while the flat east wall was still attached to the ruined east end of its Norman predecessor. The last prior, Holloway ('a man simple and not of the greatest wit'), had continued work on the building, but was perhaps more interested in alchemy than architecture. He claimed, it is said, to have discovered 'Our Stores, our Medicine, our Elixir and all', but 'When this Abbey was suppressed he hid [them] in a wall.'[12] Returning to the abandoned church, he found the hiding place empty, lost his reason and spent the rest of his life half-blind, wandering the countryside with a boy as his guide.[13] Luckily, the west front and choir had been completed under Prior Bird, who took on the building project after Bishop King's death in 1503. Bird's lovely chantry chapel of 1515 is Bath's one and only surviving medieval fitting.[14]

The half-rebuilt church was bought by the MP for Bath, whose son gave it to the town in 1572: the former cathedral priory was now to be an Anglican parish church. Work restarted after a nationwide fundraising campaign authorized by Queen Elizabeth I herself, during which the charming legend that Bishop King's west front came to him in a dream was invented.[15] Renaissance tastes are visible only in the galumphing west doors of 1617. The nave was given a sloping plaster roof: the vaults were finally completed, following the original intentions, by George Gilbert Scott in the 1860s.

Bath today is an architectural postscript to the medieval world, and a vivid reminder that a great medieval city separates Roman from Georgian Bath. It is the only English cathedral to have a complete Perpendicular interior, as exemplary of its style as Durham is of Norman, Salisbury of Early English and Exeter of Decorated, its small scale in comparison with them itself symptomatic of the changing times. While its west front embodies a world view on the brink of Reformation, its architecture crashes right into that revolution and comes out the other side unscathed.

WHAT TO SEE

St Peter and St Paul, Bath
Anglo-Saxon church c. 675; Benedictine monastery from c. 967–70; monastic cathedral from 1090; see held jointly with Wells from 1170s/1240s to the Reformation; dissolved 1539; parish church from 1572.

Church: sculpted west front with Jacob's Ladder and other motifs; Bird chantry chapel; fan vaults.

Setting: a great medieval church in the middle of Georgian Bath; its predecessor would have come picturesquely close to the banks of the Avon.

BRISTOL

The east end of Bristol Cathedral is like no other building. Its airy, hall-like spaces are the result of its having aisles that reach to the full height of the nave, separated by rows of enormous arches. Everywhere in this structure, its designer coined one-off motifs, features so unusual that argument rages over their date. What is not in doubt is his genius.

This building speaks a unique and convincing language of its own. It is a language infused with ideas that come from far outside the normal interests of the Church: ideas that take us deep into the curious amalgam of machismo and piety known as chivalry. It only became a cathedral in 1542.

Before the Reformation Bristol was an Augustinian community in the diocese of Worcester, and perhaps the most important monastic house in Bristol. Unlike the other three wealthiest cities in England, the city had no single dominant religious institution.[1] By the early fourteenth century it had also evolved a powerfully independent and idiosyncratic local architectural tradition.

Like many other 'average' abbeys of the medieval world, St Augustine's depended for its patronage on a single secular family, the lords Berkeley, who made their reputation in twelfth-century Bristol, but then retired to the rural glory of their castle at Berkeley itself, 18 miles to the north.[2] The abbey was founded in the 1140s, though the presence of the Anglo-Saxon Harrowing of Hell sculpture, one

Bristol's east end may have been born in a fit of feudal defensiveness, but the result is aesthetically a world unto itself

of the largest surviving carvings of its period, suggests that it was not the first church in the area.

St Augustine's was a daughter house of the abbey of St-Victor in Paris, then famed for its learning and led by the mystical theologian Hugh St-Victor. The abbey's founder, Robert Fitzharding, Henry I's 'man in Bristol' and first lord Berkeley, had laid out large portions of the city. Even then, Bristol was 'almost the richest city' in the land,[3] trading amongst other things in English slaves for export to Ireland, a trade which Bishop Wulfstan of Worcester (d. 1095) had worked hard to stamp out.

Henry II took an interest in the abbey in the 1160s, the period from which the lower half of the Great Gatehouse and the chapter-house date; the walls of the latter, covered in rich and sophisticated

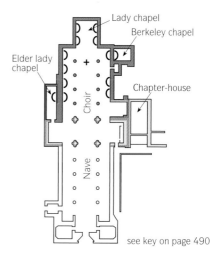

Lady chapel
Berkeley chapel
Elder lady chapel
Chapter-house
Choir
Nave

see key on page 490

carved patterns, are like an enormous tapestry of stone.[4] Sometime between 1218 and 1222, Adam Lock, designer of the Wells west front, was lent to St Augustine's by the dean of Wells to build a lady chapel: the resulting Elder Lady Chapel is a little Early English gem (illustrated p. 82), in spite of being built from not-quite-fitting parts[5] by a mason then running one of the biggest projects in Europe.

But it is for its extraordinary east end that this church is most celebrated. More like a castle than a place of worship, the eastern half of the church (the nave, which dates from after 1868, does not concern us here) was built in the early fourteenth century, completely replacing its predecessor and sidelining Adam Lock's lady chapel by creating a grand new one in its eastern bays. Other 'hall-churches' existed in England, though none on this scale; but every castle had a great hall of precisely this description. The aisle vaults sit on bridge-like flying buttresses built inside the church, from which spring tiny vaults-within-vaults – a remarkable design that appears again to be a reference to castle great halls, the elaborate wooden roofs of which produced comparable visual effects. The large transoms in the church's windows, a revolutionary motif rarely, if ever, seen in a church before, were again almost universal in the windows of great halls.[6]

The building, in other words, is meant to conjure up the image, not of a church, but of a castle great hall. This audacious idea has its roots in the strange and wonderful world of chivalry, which enabled the knightly class, whose raison d'être was fighting, to imitate some of the aspirations of the priestly class, whose raison d'être was praying. Chivalry gave the aristocracy a powerful, semi-ritualized culture of its own. Some of its literature sought analogies between the courtly life and the religious one, and during the crusades, military orders such as the Knights Templars had attempted a fusion of the monastic and the martial life: the Temple church in London is another gothic 'hall church'.

The castle imagery of Bristol's architecture therefore had echoes deep within the literature associated with chivalry, especially the stories of King Arthur, in which great hall and church become one in the shape of the grail hall.

St Augustine's is a monument to this culture. Its walls are lined with purpose-built tombs in extraordinary, identical star-shaped recesses like emblazoned helms, positioned along the processional routes which were censed daily by the passing canons. Its decoration and stained glass are thick with knightly heraldry (there are thirty-five Berkeley coats of arms alone)[7] and military saints such as King Edmund of England.[8] This knightly great hall-cum-church even has a 'kitchen', in the shape of the Berkeley chapel ante room – surely the strangest medieval space in England – which is equipped for the cooking of Communion wafers.

This building is so unlike all others that there is considerable argument over its date and significance. It was begun by a senior canon, Edmund Knowle, in 1298; he later became abbot. If the design is of this period, it was one of the most influential in all medieval history, presaging most aspects of late medieval gothic in northern Europe.[9] Arguments rage over how quickly building work proceeded, and even whether there was more than one designer. The dominant message in its architecture is not that of the abbots, but of the lords Berkeley. It was certainly finished by 1353. Their intriguing history during these years unfolds as we watch the 'starburst' tombs of this grand family mausoleum fill with their effigies; and in this history may lie clues as to the east end's most likely builder.

Here, by the Berkeley chapel, are the tombs of Thomas II, Lord Berkeley (d. 1321) and his wife, Lady Joan Ferrers (d. 1309). Thomas had a brilliant

The stellate tomb recesses delight in the tension between stiff polygons and swinging convex curves

In Memory of her renowned Anceſtors
RICHARD TOWGOOD S.T.B. Dean of this Church
And ELIZABETH his Wife

political and martial career, bringing the family profile to giddy new heights.[12] Maurice, their son, was lord in his own right for less than two years before he was imprisoned for his role in the rebellion against Edward II; he remained in captivity until his death, in 1326, his estates sequestered by the Crown. His tomb is here, too, presumably installed by Thomas III, who succeeded him; and here also is the tomb of Thomas III's wife, Lady Margaret Mortimer, daughter of Roger, Lord Mortimer. As the lover of Queen Isabella, Roger was the leader of the rebellion against Edward II; he and Isabella jointly ruled England after the overthrow of the king in 1326. It was just after Thomas became lord that the king was murdered in Berkeley castle and the family estates were returned.

From 1330, when Edward III took power from Roger Mortimer and Queen Isabella, Thomas – already a man whose father had been murdered by the king, and whose father-in-law had instigated a civil war and, briefly, run the country – also stood accused of regicide.[13] From the late 1320s Thomas began an aggressive programme of self-promotion and renewal. By the late 1330s he had rebuilt his estates, cleared his name, won the trust of Edward III and founded lavish chantries at St Augustine's and elsewhere. The exquisite chapel and great hall he built at Berkeley castle are apparently by the

A riot of romanesque patterning in Bristol's Augustinian chapter-house

THE CATHEDRALS

same masons as St Augustine's. Between them, these men must have played some role in turning their family foundation into a castle-like mausoleum. But its uniqueness is equally an expression of its function: with their income dependent on Berkeley lands, and their church containing the tombs of the dynasty, the canons would have seen themselves as a prayer factory for the benefit of Berkeley sons.

The late medieval period was something of a heyday for Bristol, which in 1373 became the first city outside London to be made a county in its own right. The ever-increasing power and political autonomy of the citizens caused tension between abbey and town, the mayor and the canons even coming to blows outside the church in 1496.[14] Throughout this period, the fourteenth-century lady chapel filled with the tombs of fifteenth-century abbots, among them men who rebuilt the central tower and the cloister, and recased the Norman transepts in spiky-but-dull Perpendicular architecture. Abbot Newland added a handsome two storeys to the Norman gatehouse, and wrote a brief history of the Lords Berkeley, later supplemented by a history of the abbots.[15]

In spite of Bristol's status – it was now the most important trading city in England after London – Henry VIII's decision to create a new see (with St Augustine's as its cathedral) came late in the day, in 1542; the church would probably otherwise have been utterly lost. The first bishop, Bush, built himself a grisly proto-Renaissance cadaver tomb; a proud local merchant rescued some stone screens from the dissolved Carmelite church and installed them around the choir of his city's new cathedral,

having his merchant's mark added to them in the process.[16]

The case is not closed on Bristol's east end: it may yet turn out to be a creation of the canons in the 1290s. It matters not only because it is so unclassifiable, and so exceptionally suffused with lay, aristocratic interests; but also because it is such a convincing and beautiful work of architecture. Its designer is unknown.[17] To move along the aisles at processional pace, as contrasting, interlocking vistas open up across the vast arches and directions of view compete among the pierced vaults, is to be in the presence of architecture that is as brilliant, if not as grandstanding, as any of the other, more celebrated architectural miracles of the earlier fourteenth century.

WHAT TO SEE

St Augustine's, now Holy Trinity, Bristol Augustinian priory, founded 1140; secular cathedral from 1542.

Church: ornate Norman chapter-house; Early English Elder Lady Chapel; breathtaking Decorated east end, with some original glass and Berkeley tombs.

Carvings: Anglo-Saxon Harrowing of Hell; chapter-house walls; Elder Lady Chapel stiff-leaf and animal carvings; first-rate incidental sculpture throughout the east end.

Close: the monastic buildings are now swallowed up by episcopal offices and an independent school.

CANTERBURY

England's premier church was always riven with conflict. Everything from the great issues of the era to the most obscure dispute over a mill or a meadow was laid at its door. Canterbury fought kings and popes. It fought its siblings, the archiepiscopal church in far-off York and St Augustine's abbey, a quarter of a mile away. The monks fought their archbishops and they fought among themselves. Canterbury's buildings were razed by fires and rocked by earthquakes, its archbishops were banished and murdered, its visitors came in state and on their knees. Some came in search of miracles, others to do away with everything it stood for.

All the themes of its history were thus embodied in a few violent seconds one evening in December 1170. Human blood and brains were splashed across the floor of the north transept; a political battle for control of the Church became an event of international significance.

The story began when a low-born Londoner of Norman extraction became archbishop. Thomas Becket was the first English-born archbishop since the Conquest, and one of the first non-monks to hold the post.[1] He had worked for the previous archbishop, and gone on to be Henry II's chancellor. He was a quick, charming man, perhaps given to bouts of stress-related illness. He had revelled in the courtly life of hunting, fighting (he once led 700 men into battle) and lavish display. Henry must have hoped that he and Thomas would form one

of history's great archbishop-and-king double acts.[2] But instead Becket took to wearing hair shirts and engaging in long bouts of prayer,[3] and the new archbishop fell out with the king very badly indeed over the independence of the Church. 'Many violations of public discipline – theft, rape and homicide – were regularly being committed by

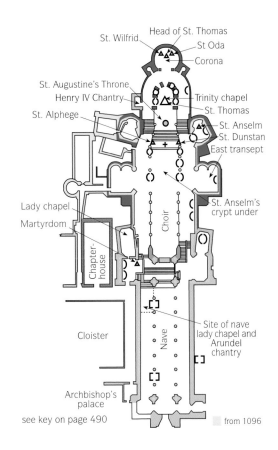

Bell Harry, England's most beautiful cathedral tower, tops a church whose walls stand witness to medieval history

see key on page 490

from 1096

271

clerks', who – thanks to the independent system of justice run by the Church – could then escape punishment.[4] Henry wanted churchmen to face the same court as anyone else; for Becket, the Church was above such worldly institutions.

The archbishop was unbending. In the end he went into exile in France for seven years. Here he practised a life of prayer and austerity: 'some said that he was a damnable traitor to his kingdom; others that as a defender of the Church he was a martyr'.[5] When, in December 1170, Becket returned to England, his reputation had transmuted from archbishop-in-a-flounce to holy man. 'A crowd of poor people gathered to meet him, some striving to be first to receive blessing from their father as he landed, others humbly prostrating themselves on the ground, some wailing, some weeping for joy, and all crying out together.'[6] The same thing happened when he reached London, where a crowd of three thousand gathered.

But the king refused to see him, and the archbishop had isolated himself from his peers, having excommunicated most of the English bishops for usurping his rights while abroad. Under a very grand kind of house arrest in his Canterbury see, Becket began to wonder if 'this affair could not be brought to completion without bloodshed'.[7] Via his rival, Roger of Pont l'Evêque, archbishop of York (see p. 80), Becket informed the king that, in spite of having returned home, he had no intention of compromise on any of the issues that divided them. This was the last straw. The king 'went . . . white with fury, and said that he "who has eaten my bread, who came to my court poor, and I have raised him high – now he draws up his heel to kick me in the teeth! He has shamed my kin, shamed my realm; the grief goes to my heart – and no one has avenged me."'[8]

Four of the king's knights decided to take action. They went to Canterbury with a small armed force, probably hoping to imprison the archbishop, or at

least force him to back down. Becket stood firm in his palace as they arrived, but his monks pleaded that 'it was not right for him to be absent from Vespers, which were just then being celebrated'.[9] They took him into the north transept of the cathedral. Becket and his companions had reached the steps to the choir when the barons caught up with them, 'instilling terror in the onlookers by the sight of them and the clatter of armour'.[10] 'Where is the archbishop?' shouted one of the knights. Becket stepped forward and descended the steps. 'Here I am,' he said 'no traitor to the king, but a priest. What do you want from me?'[11]

A small crowd of local people, monks and clerks had gathered. The situation required swift action. Becket was manhandled to the ground. One of the knights 'applied himself particularly fiercely'. 'Pimp!' said the archbishop, 'you who by right owe me fealty and obeisance.' 'I do not owe you fealty or obedience against fidelity to my lord king', spat the knight. Then he hit Becket hard.[12]

One of the blows severed the crown of Becket's head: indeed it was so severe that the sword was dashed on the pavement. A knight put his foot on Becket's neck, and 'horrible to say, scattered the brains with the blood all over the pavement', causing a grisly gash of red and white to cover the flagstones. 'This fellow will not get up again', he said. The shocked knights fled.[13]

Although 'everything was disturbed and confused', many in the crowd 'daubed their eyes with blood . . . made away with as much as they could', and 'eagerly dipped in parts of their clothes they had cut off'.[14] It must have been obvious to them that the violent death of England's senior churchman, in the heart of England's senior church, was not mere murder: it was martyrdom. There are no fewer than five eyewitness accounts of those violent few moments in the north transept, and what is most remarkable to us in what they record is perhaps what was most obvious to them: that given the choice between rushing to get help, pursuing the murderers, or rubbing their eyes with the warm blood of their dead archbishop, those present did the latter.

'He who once died at Jerusalem to save the whole world had come again to die at Canterbury for the English Church', Herbert of Bosham said of Becket's return from exile.[15] The archbishop 'who in other things had imitated Christ' had died of five wounds, it was noted, one of which had sliced off the very part of his body which 'the oil of holy chrism had dedicated to God'. Not only were Becket's last days tinged with Christ-like echoes, but the murder itself seemed full of symbolism: 'Blood white from the brain, and the brain equally red from the blood, brightened the floor with the colours of the lily and the rose, the virgin and the mother, and the life and death of the confessor and martyr.'[16] Here was everything: flesh and blood, bread and wine, sacrifice and purity.

The next day there were 'many armed men gathered . . . outside the city wall'. They were determined to get hold of the archbishop's body – to 'pull it asunder through the city with horses . . . or hang it on a gibbet, or tear it to pieces . . . and dispatch it in a swamp', to avoid the body attracting a miraculous reputation.[17] But they were too late. One townsman had come back from the church with his shirt dripping with blood. His wife, who suffered from paralysis, 'asked to be washed, and the blood to be mixed in the water, so that she might derive health and benefit'. She was cured there and then. The miraculous cat was out of its blood-soaked bag.[18]

At first the church was closed – polluted by human blood – and royal officials forbade veneration of the dead man. But miracles kept happening, firstly in Canterbury and then further afield. By Easter the church had reopened to all comers, with dramatic effect. 'In the place where Thomas suffered, and where he lay the night before the high altar, awaiting burial, and where he was buried at last, the palsied are cured, the blind see, the deaf hear, the dumb speak, the lame walk, folk suffering from fevers are cured, the lepers are cleansed, those possessed of a devil are freed, and the sick are made whole from all manner of disease.'[19] A political row had spilled over into a charismatic event of dramatic proportions.

Visitors flocked to Canterbury. They visited the 'Martyrdom' in the north transept, where the murder took place. They moved on to the tomb of the archbishop himself, in the easternmost part of the crypt (illustrated p. 84). They spent time in the Trinity Chapel above it, the easternmost structure

This image of St Paul and the Viper in Anselm's crypt may have been commissioned by archbishop Becket himself

in the cathedral, where the live Becket had often prayed. They viewed his vestments and the abandoned weapons of the barons. They took away miraculous totems in their thousands: little phials filled with water, mingled with a drop of the holy man's blood – red and white again. Soon the city was 'so crowded with the throng of those working in stalls and shops and those coming and going, that almost everywhere it seemed as busy as a market place. Nights hardly less than days, winters hardly less than summers.'[20]

The cult spread extraordinarily fast.[21] At Peterborough and perhaps Southwark, chapels were apparently dedicated to Becket even before he was canonized. Becket's childhood home, parish church and parents' tomb in London became cult sites in their own right. By the 1180s there were churches dedicated to him in Sicily and Aragon, and soon as far as away as Poland. In Sweden, Becket's cult was second only to the local St Olaf, and no fewer than three Icelandic sagas feature him as their central figure. Forty-five near-identical caskets, apparently produced in a kind of Becket relic factory in the late twelfth century, have been found everywhere from Spain to Austria.[22]

During 1173–4 the authorities got a grip on the situation. With the blood of an archbishop on his hands, Henry conceded some of the key legal points of his dispute with Becket. The pope declared St Thomas a saint, in one of the half-dozen fastest canonizations ever.[23] After two years' tussle with the monks of Canterbury, a new archbishop was appointed, a former monk and friend of Becket.[24] Finally, the king made a dramatic gesture: he walked barefoot through Canterbury, not thinking 'of the hardness of the path, or the tenderness of his feet, or the spectacle to the common people all about'.[25] Henry II bared his chest, squeezed his head and shoulders into openings in Becket's tomb, and allowed the assembled bishops and each of the eighty monks of

Canterbury to give him a good (if, one imagines, respectfully administered) flogging. He then spent the whole night in prayer.

By giving his full and public support to the martyr cult, Henry had also drawn the political sting from it, though its spiritual momentum continued to expand unabated. By the time the new archbishop arrived in London, on 3 September 1174, it must have seemed as if the most traumatic aspects of the events of 1170 were firmly in the past. But two days later, 'by the just but occult judgement of God', the ornate east end of the cathedral, which had been completed only fifty years earlier, was burned to the ground.[26]

———

The east end was soon to be rebuilt in a manner that matched the extraordinary events that had taken place within it. At this point, Canterbury was a church dating from the 1070s. But it was by no means the first church on this site (growth of the cathedral: illustrated p. 27). This is, after all, where Roman Christianity in England began, and the place from which it was governed. The church of 602, founded by Augustine and dedicated to Our Saviour (hence Canterbury's alternative name, Christ Church), lies beneath the modern cathedral; its archbishop was the most powerful man in the country after the king himself.

Augustine's church, one of the most important structures in this book, was effectively an Italian import, perhaps just 30 or so metres long.[27] But what really marked it out was its setting: in combination with St Augustine's abbey (then the abbey of St Peter and St Paul), built outside the city walls, a little model of far-off Rome had been built in ruined Durovernum Cantiacorum (see chapter one).[28] In the centuries afterwards this church only increased in size and significance. Archbishop Dunstan (d. 988) began the process of turning it from a community of priests into an observant Benedictine monastery. Archbishop Alphege (d. 1012) was acclaimed a martyr after he died having been taken hostage by the Danes.[29] By the Norman Conquest no fewer than fifteen of Canterbury's archbishops were likewise regarded as saints.[30]

This Canterbury cathedral had been enlarged and enriched several times since the seventh century, yet it still retained parts of St Augustine's church, the tap root of English Christ-ianity, at its core. By 1066 it was some 65 metres long,[31] and was a building whose architecture fully matched its significance (illustrated p. 47). The shrines of St Dunstan and St Alphege stood on either side of the high altar in its grand eastern apse; the archbishop's throne stood in a great apse at its western end.

The Normans destroyed this church utterly: few architectural slates have been quite so summarily swept clean. By the time the last Anglo-Saxon archbishop, Stigand (so corrupt he helped justify the Norman invasion in himself), was deposed in 1070, his cathedral was apparently already a pile of ashes, as a result of another fire with uncannily good timing.[32] By 1077, Stigand's Norman replacement Lanfranc had completely replaced Christ Church as a slightly larger copy of the Norman abbey of St-Etienne at Caen.

Although Lanfranc's building (see pp. 53–5) has been rebuilt so many times that only a few stretches of wall remain visible, this 90-metre long Norman church remains the underlying template for the modern cathedral.[33] Lanfranc's nave has proved large enough for all future needs – the current structure stands on its foundations – and his north-west tower was only demolished in 1831.

As well as rebuilding his cathedral, Lanfranc set

The crypt of Anselm's 'glorious choir' is a numinous romanesque homage to Our Lady

to work on winning back various lands whose ownership had been neglected by Stigand. As finances improved, the community expanded: eventually the number of monks doubled, from about sixty to perhaps 140 (before plateauing at sixty or seventy for the rest of the Middle Ages).[34] In addition to its status as the archbishop's church, Canterbury was now home to the largest and richest monastic house in the country.

Lanfranc's act unleashed the great Norman rebuilding of the cathedrals. But for his replacement, Anselm, the eastern half of the new church was woefully inadequate: indeed it appeared designed to squeeze out certain pre-Conquest relics and rituals. It also forced the growing community of monks to worship in an enclosure that took up much of the nave. From 1096, therefore, Anselm and his priors rebuilt the twenty-year-old east end, creating as they did so a church within a church, a 'paradise of pleasure',[35] itself the size of a small cathedral. The cathedral was now 133 metres long; but what was most revolutionary about this building was its decoration – then the richest display of stone carving in England. In the massive crypt, where the Anglo-Saxon celebration of the cult of the Virgin was revived, the forest of spiral columns is a deliberate evocation of St Peter's shrine in Rome. At a time when the dispute between York and Canterbury over which was England's primatial church was at its height, the crypt was a symbolic reminder of Canterbury's claims.

It was thus into the roof of this east end, built by Archbishop Anselm eighty years earlier and since the site of Becket's tomb and scene of miracles, that sparks from a nearby house fire were blown in an 'extraordinarily violent south wind' in September 1174.[36] They smouldered invisibly in the space between roof and painted ceiling. Soon sheets of lead on the outside of the church were curling and melting in response to a great heat beneath them, creating more space for the wind to get in. A small fire had become a large one before anyone had even noticed it. 'The people and the monks assembled in haste' to douse the flames, but soon 'they abandoned the attempt in despair'. The timbers of the roof collapsed into the church, setting alight the woodwork beneath, so that the 'glorious choir itself fed and assisted the fire that was destroying it'. Even the walls themselves were scorched, and the columns cracking. Soon the church was 'a despicable heap of ashes . . . a dreary wilderness . . . laid open to all the injuries of the weather'. 'The people were astonished that the Almighty should suffer such things . . . they tore their hair and beat the walls . . . of the church with their heads and hands, blaspheming the Lord and his saints.'

The east end of the church was ruined. Its enormous crypt survived; the outer walls above stood almost to roof height; but the rest was damaged beyond repair.

Almost immediately a series of masons was interviewed, and one of them, William of Sens, was retained, 'on account of his lively genius and good reputation'. His place of origin is interesting: Sens, in northern France, had been Becket's place of exile, and its new cathedral was one of the most up-to-date in Europe, a potent display of the aesthetic possibilities of the new architecture of the pointed arch (illustrated p. 85).

'The new work is of a different fashion from the old', commented the Canterbury monk Gervase, who witnessed these events, with a very unmedieval lack of hyperbole; everything was 'of a more noble fashion'. He was right: this noble fashion, which we call gothic, was almost new to England; the new cathedral was one of the most architecturally up-to-date in Europe.

It was also unusual, with enormously long columns that gave it a leggy appearance, and dripping with polished and coloured stones to an extent previously unknown. Experimentalism in

The twists and turns of the post-Becket east end at Canterbury seem designed to bewilder visiting pilgrims

such a high-profile building is remarkable enough, but there were practical reasons as well as ingenuity behind the strangeness of the structure. First, it went up on top of its predecessor's crypt, ingeniously incorporating both it and the surviving choir windows of Anselm's east end into a design that was nearly 4 metres higher than its predecessor.[37] By trying to fit a higher, more up-to-date and even more palatial building on top of the walls of the old one, William of Sens had given himself a series of design challenges that would tie any architect up in knots.

But as one moves east in this church, the knots unravel, and the oddness of the design resolves itself into something suffused with a tangible,

almost numinous power. This is the result of one of the most dramatic (and, presumably, expensive) changes of mind in English architectural history: the decision in about 1180, when work on the east end was well advanced, to let the full implications of the Becket cult run architectural riot in England's primatial church.

A previously unplanned extension now burst through the newly built east wall of the building.[38] This new structure, itself the size of a second church, covered the location of St Thomas's tomb-shrine in the crypt of Anselm's east end and replaced the small Trinity Chapel above. It was the final climactic lengthening of the cathedral, resulting in a church which remains about 156 metres long. Canterbury cathedral had quite literally been inflated by the power of the events that had taken place within it.[39] Becket's tomb was now at the centre of a large underground hall, an extension of the crypt of Anselm's church.[40] Above it, a palatial new Trinity Chapel extended behind the high altar, the planned setting for both a new shrine to the saint and the archbishop's throne. Altar, throne and shrine thus formed a linked trinity of power in themselves, a palpable reminder of the significance of the cath-edral as a whole. Beyond all this, yet another new chapel was built at the far east end: a unique, circular, tower-like building known as the Corona, which was probably the setting for a sepa-rate shrine to Becket's severed crown.

In this eastern extension, unfettered by Anselm's structure, all eccentricities are resolved. The result has some of the earliest securely dated flying buttresses – one of the key markers of gothic engineering – anywhere, and windows that were enormous for their date, soon to be filled with scenes of events from Becket's life in stained glass – scenes so recent that they come close to reportage.

The change of design coincides with the replacement of William of Sens by William the Englishman after the French master suffered a fall in 1180. However, the two parts of the building are in one style, and rather than being the result of a change of master-mason, the expansion is more likely to mark a decision by the church itself to make as much of Becket as possible. Indeed what was apparently a kind of internal coup in 1179 resulted in the appointment of a strongly pro-Becket prior.[41] The new east end was to be an appropriate setting for miracles, a link between St Thomas in particular and archbishops in general, and an aggressive promotion of a militant Church.

There is a kind of glorious horror to this archi-tecture. Everywhere, rose-red and creamy-white stones are combined. The violence enacted on the transept floor in the winter of 1170 was thus colour-coded into the building itself;[42] history quite literally turned to stone. Even the plan of the building seems designed to exceed expectations, stage-managing the emotions of the crowds who came here, people rich and poor, already tense with the anticipation of miracles. Other cathedrals follow one or another plan of a type that pilgrims might recognize from their own parish churches, albeit on a grander scale. But Canterbury stretches east, and then further east, via several dramatic flights of steps, in ever-increasing stages of dis-orientation. 'Still further up the church, further upwards, for behind the high altar is an ascent into what one may call still another church', as Erasmus put it; and at the furthest east, in its crown-like circular chapel, 'the entire face of the saintly man, [stood] overlaid with gold and ... precious jewels'.[43] Just as architecture had never been quite so in thrall to a saint and his shrines, so moving through the building itself was a kind of pilgrimage.

The new east end was completed in 1184, exactly ten years after it was begun. But it was another thirty-five years before its decoration was complete, and St Thomas's body was translated to its intended location. Instead, the monks of Christ Church went to war against their archbishop, and archbishops and monks together went to war with the king.

In 1185 Archbishop Baldwin decided that his cathedral would work much better with no monks in it. He began to lay the foundations of a new Canterbury cathedral on a suburban site, less than a mile outside the city, only to be frustrated by the monks. He tried moving the unfinished 'Hackington cathedral' to Lambeth but died while on crusade; the project was continued by his successor Hubert Walter. These men wanted to create a mighty new secular arch-cathedral, with space for the king and all the bishops, abandoning what would then have become Canterbury abbey forever.[44]

These projects may have had an institutional logic, but they ran against the grain of 500 years of history. The monks reacted with ferocity. Baldwin's plan would have left them as just another rich Benedictine monastery. They sulked (imprisoning themselves inside their convent for eighteen months) and they fought (taking the case to the papal court in Rome). Eventually they won. In 1205 Hubert Walter declared that no such college would ever be built; he had already tacitly accepted the decision by building a colossal new hall in his palace adjacent to the cathedral,[45] and – probably in 1201–4 – by installing an 'antique'-looking throne for himself, St Augustine's Throne, in the east end (illustrated p. 92).

Then, in 1206, the new east end had to be mothballed for several years. A dispute over the election of a new archbishop became a full-scale row between the pope and King John, and all eighty Canterbury monks went into exile in France with their archbishop. The interdict had begun: from 1207 to 1213 almost all worship at Canterbury cathedral ceased, and the rest of the English Church followed suit almost immediately.

The fall of John, the return of Archbishop Stephen Langton and the accession of Henry III in 1216 created an atmosphere of triumph across the English Church. The inlaid floors and stained glass windows of the Trinity Chapel were completed, and a magnificent shrine built. A great translation ceremony in 1220 marked the final completion of the plans of the 1180s; the event was masterminded by the senior cleric Elias of Dereham (soon to oversee the creation of Salisbury cathedral), with help from the painter William of Colchester, sacrist at St Albans abbey. In front of a twelve-year-old Henry III and seventeen bishops (every English bishop not either ill or recently deceased), Archbishop Langton moved Becket's body to its sumptuous new setting, heralding a victorious new age for bishops and their churches (see chapter three).[46]

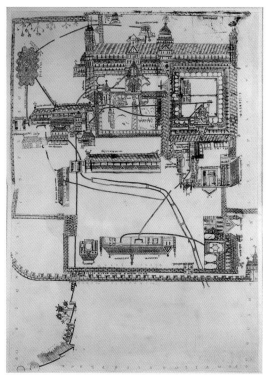

The mid-twelfth century 'waterworks' drawing shows the extent of the vast conventual complex

Thomas's would remain far and away the most significant cult in the country until the Reformation; he may have had the only shrine that genuinely turned a profit for its church.[47] An extraordinary £1,142 was received in offerings in 1220;[48] at the Reformation, St Thomas was second only to the pope himself as a target of the reformers.

Canterbury cathedral's architecture had now been keeping pace with events since 602. At times it almost seems to have been making that history, dictating the terms in which it would have the past remembered. Now, for 150 years from the 1220s, it fell into a kind of architectural torpor. Apart from the tombs of the archbishops,[49] there is little to be seen in the cathedral of their extra-ordinary personalities and dramatic life stories: Winchelsey (d. 1313), for example, even became a cult figure in his own right. Building work tended, in fact, to be delegated to the priors,[50] which was perhaps why it was focused more on the enormous, metropolis-like monastic complex, which had itself been the focus of enormous investment almost continuously since the days of Lanfranc, and which reached its full extent in the thirteenth century. The priors of Canterbury were effective rulers of this enormous city-within-a-city; many were energetic builders whose work throughout the cathedral and its complex is as visible as that of the archbishops. Prior Eastry (d. 1331), for example, ran the

Perpendicular masterpiece: Henry Yevele's nave at Canterbury

monastery for forty-six years and under four arch-bishops, and spent almost £6,000 on architecture, mostly on Canterbury's manors and the conventual buildings (see p. 240), but most visibly today in a grandly refurbished chapter-house and an exquisite set of choir screens by the royal mason Michael of Canterbury. Likewise, some sixty years later Prior Chillenden, 'the greatest builder of a prior that ever was in Christ's Church',[51] put about £400 a year into the new nave. Chillenden also rebuilt the cloister, created a kind of upmarket pilgrim hotel, and placed a magnificent, now lost, reredos behind the high altar, as well as improving the conventual buildings.[52] Perhaps the priors' effective mainte-nance was one of the reasons why no major rebuilding took place for so long in the cathedral itself.

But in the late fourteenth century the cathedral's architecture came back to life. Building projects would continue for the next century and a half, a long Indian summer, but one rocked by storms and earthquakes cultural, political and literal. And now the messages of the building concerned kings more than archbishops, and heresy rather than the power and independence of the English Rome (see chapter four).

In 1369 England's mother church still had the wooden-ceilinged nave designed in 1070, perhaps enriched a little later.[53] Visiting bishops from other cathedrals – not least York, whose own ancient nave had just been replaced – must have felt as though they had come from a palace into a shed. The monks finally decided to replace it in time for the bicentenary of Becket's martyrdom in 1370, but after raising a miserable £44 7s 11d they abandoned the campaign. At the end of 1378 Archbishop Sudbury finally demolished the nave, and gave at least 2,000 marks to the project, but he was murdered in the Peasants' Revolt of 1381.

Work continued, only for the church to be damaged by an earthquake.[54] Archbishop Arundel saw all this as an opportunity. He had helped replace Richard II with his own relative, Henry IV; he had supported the use of the death penalty to combat the new threat of heresy. To him the nave was a place designed to encourage conventional piety, a place where ordinary people might witness the key mysteries of their faith.[55] He gave 1,000 marks to the works, and placed his own chantry chapel between the nave's ancient lady chapel and the nave altar, making a point of citing lay access to mass in his reasons for doing so.[56] The nave, which cost between £6,000 and £11,000, was funded by grants from archbishop and priory alike and supported with various 'tax breaks' from the Crown.[57] It is very probably the design of the royal master-mason Henry Yevele, master of the new Perpendicular style (see p. 229). Even without its stained glass and chantry chapels – to the heretic-bashing Bishop Buckingham of Lincoln, the king-making Archbishop Arundel, and the local magnate Sir William Brenchley[58] – the nave is an articulate work of great formal beauty, its quietly inclusive grandeur as far from the fevered east end as the political 1390s were from the charismatic 1170s.

The new nave led to a Perpendicular rebuilding of the cloister next door, which abutted it on the south side, and as this was completed the monks turned to recasing and stylistically updating the transepts. Major changes were also made to the tower crossing which stood between them, followed by the upgrading of the approach to the church from the city: the south-west tower was rebuilt and the boxy south porch added (a large freestanding bell tower was built here too, only to be 'possessed by an evil spirit' during at storm in 1458).[59] All this work was completed by the 1480s. During this process a new fan-vaulted lady chapel was built off the north transept, perhaps for the performance of the polyphonic music which now graced the Marian liturgy: a professional choir was employed by 1438 (see p. 202).[60] The entire interior of the church was therefore now gothic in style, and its western half was entirely Perpendicular, apart from Lanfranc's north-east tower.

Yet the messages contained in much of this Perpendicular updating of the cathedral were much more concerned with kings and politics than with archbishops or liturgy. The building came to be filled with the propaganda of dynastic struggle, thanks to the dying wishes of the Black Prince. He had been educated at Canterbury and asked to be buried there; his chantry chapel is in the crypt.[61] His early death in 1376 was the root cause of the dynastic crisis that eventually erupted into the Wars of the Roses, and his presence at Canterbury made it a magnet for the competing houses of York and Lancaster. The situation was exacerbated by the monks' enthusiasm for their royal burial: contrary to the prince's own wishes, they installed his tomb not in his chantry chapel but in a much more high profile position in the Trinity Chapel. Keen to underline its legitimacy, Henry IV's regime then turned Canterbury into something of an 'alternative Westminster': Henry himself was buried there, almost opposite the Black Prince, as were several of his nearest relatives. Henry even cooked up a bizarre theory linking his coronation to a miraculous oil associated with Thomas Becket.[62]

The shifting allegiances of the aristocracy at this time are played out in 1,000 or so[63] fifteenth-century carved bosses. In the cloister and, from the 1420s, the south transept and south porch, these were dominated by the heraldry of the Lancastrian families then in the ascendancy, while those in the north transept, done by 1482, are mostly Yorkist. And as England slipped towards civil war, the extraordinary 'propaganda' pulpitum of the 1450s was created, using a carefully judged selection of English kings to mount a defence of Lancastrian legitimacy. The capture of Henry VI and resulting victory of the house of York were announced to the new Edward IV while he was in the cathedral –

perhaps, one imagines, staring at the pulpitum itself – and in 1482 he ensured that it was overlooked by the grand Royal Window. Thus the warring factions of the fifteenth century glare at each other over the Canterbury crossing, power-hungry aristocrats gathering around the Martyrdom.[64]

The Tudor dynasty presented itself as uniting the warring factions of Lancaster and York: Canterbury too needed to pull itself together. The cathedral had been lengthened twice and rebuilt almost entirely since 1077; its central tower must have looked oddly out of place. It was not until the late 1490s, when Henry VII was on the throne, that Canterbury finally had a tower in keeping with the rest of the building. The creation of a new central tower on top of the 400-year-old crossing was a major engineering challenge, and it may be no coincidence that the first man to try it (as early as the 1430s) was master-mason Richard Beke, most famous for building London Bridge.[65] Work ground to a halt in the mid-fifteenth century, perhaps as a result of another earthquake, this time in 1449; when work restarted, by the 1460s, it proceeded only slowly. It was mainly Archbishop Morton, who became a cardinal in 1493, who created the tower we see today, commissioning its design (see p. 233), doubling its height and completing its building within five years. This expansion of a major project whose stability could not be guaranteed is one of the medieval world's last great acts of architectural chutzpah, and the result, light and decorous in spite of its enormity and weight, is indeed 'the completest beauty of its kind'.[66]

———

By the Reformation Canterbury was 'a cathedral ocean of images'.[67] The nave was packed with paintings, including a series of boards that told the history of Christ Church. The choir, built to present the shrine of Becket and St Augustine's throne in glorious isolation, was now packed with the tombs of royalty and archbishops; they spilled out into the rest of the church. At Easter a collection of lavish Renaissance tapestries filled the east end, whose aisles walls had been recently covered with robust paintings of saints' lives. Its shrines include the twin altars of Dunstan and Alphege, each surrounded by four great candelabra, as well as the obscure relics of Blaise, Swithun, Wulfgate, Bregin, Feologild and many others, including such delights as the 'Height of Mary'. Around and behind the high altar were silver depictions of Christ, the Apostles, Our Lady and the Holy Ghost, a brazen eagle for the readings of the Gospel, and a Paschal candlestick of copper and gilt.[68]

But the church's Ground Zero was Becket's shrine, layered and enriched over the intervening centuries. The Venetian ambassador – surely well-placed to judge – said 'it surpasses all belief' in 1500.[69] Twelve candles burned perpetually on a beam above it, their light dancing off flowers made of gold. Stuck to the shrine itself were coins donated by kings and other nobles, the huge 'Regale' Ruby given by Louis VII of France, and other offerings, from models of ailing birds to a life-size silver Henry VII (see p. 208).

All this vanished from 1541, when the Canterbury monks' nightmare of the 1190s, when Archbishop Baldwin had wanted to dispense with their involvement in the cathedral, became a reality: abandoned by their saint, the convent was transformed into a secular college. Two years earlier, when Becket's shrine was taken down, twenty-six cartloads of jewels had been hauled off to London.

Today, the violent forces that created this building have been sucked dry and replaced by the calm of the museum piece: a 'huge dry flinty rock', as a Puritan put it.[70] Yet Canterbury retains the

Canterbury's mid-fifteenth century lantern was topped by a delicious sixteenth-century fan vault

power to go up a gear, from object of beauty to the architectural equivalent of a heavy sword on a tonsured head. The crypt is perhaps the easiest place to access this power, but once recovered it is everywhere.[71] There is a kind of sprawling menace about this church: in its east end, suffused with a potent chemistry of violence and miracles; in the unspoken civil wars of its crossing; and in its obliteration of the primordial buildings whose remains lie beneath it. But it is in this dramatic story that Canterbury's significance lies: it has been at the cutting edge of history for a thousand years, and thanks to its architecture, the revolutions of Augustine, Lanfranc, Becket and Henry VIII are with us still: raw, vivid, astonishing.

WHAT TO SEE

Christ Church, Canterbury
Secular cathedral 597/602; Benedictine monastic cathedral c. 1000; secular cathedral 1541.

Church: Norman crypt; early gothic east end; Perpendicular nave and central tower.

Fittings and glass: collection of archbishops' and royal tombs, mainly in the east end; twelfth- and fifteenth-century stained glass, especially in the east end; choir screens, archbishop's throne and decorative pavements in the choir. Wall paintings in the crypt and elsewhere.

Close: largest and best preserved monastic complex in the country.

CARLISLE

This determined little building is testimony to the violent centuries it took to establish Cumbria as part of England; indeed, its very existence is a side-effect of twelfth-century border politics. In its architecture can be traced various false starts, setbacks and rude interruptions, as well as the dogged persistence needed to complete the building in the face of adversity.

When William II annexed Carlisle in 1092, the area was loosely part of the kingdom of Scotland, nominally within the see of Durham, and separated from centres of power by the Solway Firth, the Pennines and the Lakes. Yet Carlisle had proud origins as a city on the edge of the Roman Empire, a strategic location just south of Hadrian's Wall. Early British Christians came here, and St Cuthbert visited in 685. He founded a church nearby and was given a tour of the Roman 'sights'. After that, Carlisle's history is hazy.

The Normans effectively refounded Carlisle.

Much-battered Carlisle, seen here from the west, was England's poorest cathedral in its newest see

William II rebuilt the castle, replanned the town, and moved in settlers. In 1122 or 3 Henry I gave land on which to build a new church.[1] He and the archbishop of York approached the head of a nearby new Augustinian priory, Athelwold, to be its prior. But the new city, in its isolated and strategic location, needed to be more than a monastic outpost. In 1133 Henry announced that a new diocese had been created, and Athelwold became a bishop. King David I of Scotland took the city four years later, turning its massive new castle into his palace. One man's northern outpost can easily become his opponent's southern stronghold.[2]

The surviving Norman parts of the cathedral – the battered transepts and the stump of the nave – seem symbolic of the insecurity of border politics: their brusque architecture is full of changes of mind that no one had the time or money to put right.[3] Carlisle's new cathedral paled into insignificance besides its grand, ancient siblings in the northern province, Durham and York.[4] But it was probably the highest building in Cumbria's county town, and along with the castle a very visible outpost of the state in an isolated region.[5] It was also institutionally unique, for it was not just England's last monastic cathedral but its only Augustinian one, the peak of a great wave of new Augustinian communities. By Augustinian standards, its church was exceptionally large, and the only one in the province with an aisled nave.[6]

Bishop Athelwold was a 'vigorous' man.[7] By the time of his death in 1156/7, Carlisle was under the English kings again, and the administrative framework of a diocese had been created, with an archdeacon, a prior and rural deans – men who could be the bishop's standard-bearers and tax collectors in a small but mountainous see, roughly covering the northern Lake District.[8] But he was

The glorious, if much restored, choir roof at Carlisle (c. 1355), is influenced by designs in Scotland and the Low Countries

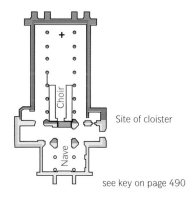

Site of cloister

see key on page 490

personally wealthy,[9] and funds were never created to finance the bishop's post itself. It took fifty years to find another man willing to be bishop: in the end, the post went to a Croatian refugee.

Bernard de Ragusa, archbishop of Dubrovnik, had been expelled from his homeland. He befriended Richard I during the crusades and became bishop in 1204, his post funded by the king. But the archbishop of York objected to having another archbishop in the province; and Ragusa was exiled for opposing King John.[10] After the interdict (see p. 93), the Scots occupied Carlisle and 'encouraged' the canons to elect a bishop favourable to them. The English soon took control again, and the new bishop was ejected.[11]

In the 1220s Hugh of Beaulieu, a Cistercian, took on this poisoned chalice. He had attended the Fourth Lateran Council (see p. 104) in 1215, and was treasurer of England. Yet he struggled to drag the church of Carlisle into the thirteenth century. To provide the bishopric with a permanent source of income, without which the job of creating a cathedral was incomplete, he took lands from the canons. He died on his way back from Rome in 1223, only to be remembered for this 'deceitful and iniquitous division'.[12] It was 1249 before the canons finally accepted the enormous cut in their income that it must have entailed.

Carlisle's truncated nave is extraordinarily spare for a twelfth-century design

Hugh built a bishop's palace near Carlisle, and it was probably at his instigation that the new east end of the cathedral was begun, its choir almost 4 metres wider than its predecessor and twice as long.[13] This design in the distinctive northern version of Early English had expensive features such as blank wall arcades and stone-vaulted aisles. A new aisle to the north transept was also built; perhaps it was hoped to replace much of the church.[14] But work was still under way in 1253, and in 1285;[15] and then came 1292, a hard year even for Carlisle. That winter, the then bishop died after a journey from London in deep snow. In May, a hurricane threw travellers off their horses, forced the sea inland, and fanned the flames of a fire in the city started in revenge by a young man who had been disinherited by his father. Soon, little was left of city or cathedral: 'muniments, organs, bells, wood, glass and stalls were burnt to ashes'.[16]

Fundraising aimed at restarting the building project began almost immediately;[17] but now war broke out with Scotland. Warrior-bishops were appointed: men like Bishops Halton and Kempe were also wardens of Carlisle castle. The king himself used the cathedral as his base in 1307 and thereafter. But the war was not going well for him, and in 1316 the Scots attacked Carlisle itself. It was a hard time for the cathedral: in 1318 it received just £20 in income, because travel was simply too dangerous for taxes to be gathered. The army stored its provisions in the cloisters (the soldiers tunnelled their way into the prior's cellar and stole twenty barrels of the king's best wine).[18] The bishop's palace at Rose castle, south of the city, suffered major attacks in 1314 and 1322.[19]

When the English eventually began to get the upper hand, in the late 1340s, work on the cathedral restarted, to designs now a decade or more old. A series of experimental 'skeletal vaults' was abandoned, and the upper parts of the church were given simple detailing and a wooden ceiling rather than a vault.[20] Those parts of the church not completely ruined by fire, such as the aisle walls with their blank arcading, were kept; others were even re-erected, in an extraordinary exercise.[21] The thirteenth-century arcade arches, having not been erected for a century after they were carved, sit on top of fourteenth-century columns. The overriding aim was to complete a project that was now over a century old. Most of the building was finished by the late 1350s.[22]

Yet Carlisle feels like a great northern Decorated church, comparable in style to buildings such as Selby abbey and York minster, even if it is in fact half-rebuilt from the remains of fire and war, using thirteenth-century stones. The reuse of the Early English vaults and arches gives the interior a rich effect, complemented by a couple of fourteenth-century set pieces: a showy east window featuring a Last Judgement, the end of time, and a fine set of capitals, featuring the Labours of the Months, or time itself.

When, in 1380, the tower fell down, even Carlisle seems to have run out of energy. The Perpendicular tower does its job of being higher than Carlisle castle, but little more; the tower arches and recased transepts beneath have little finesse.

But the cathedral was entering an unheard-of period of stability, with a sequence of well-born bishops and priors. Border raids continued, but outright warfare had ceased; Carlisle became the centre of a buffer zone known as the West March. The region's very poverty, caused by a lack of arable land, shielded it from the famines and agricultural crises of the era.[23] The prior, like many better-off border people, built himself a quasi-defensive pele tower; the two-dozen-or-so canons, mostly local well-born men, updated their refectory.[24] The cathedral even developed a belated cult around an image of the church's patron, the Virgin Mary. She had miraculously intervened in an attempted Scottish assault of 1385; an image of her was a centre for local pilgrimage in the fifteenth century.[25]

During this century the east end was enriched: it had new choir-stalls by about 1430, and was given new windows,[26] choir screens and a complete repaint under Thomas Gondibour, prior from 1465 to 1500. Richard III had been warden of the West March before he became king and gave £5 for stained glass. Gondibour added to the choir-stalls a series of educational 'strip cartoons' facing the choir aisles, showing visitors the lives of St Anthony, founder of monasticism; St Augustine of Hippo, reputed founder of the Augustinians; St Cuthbert, local missionary and saint; and the twelve disciples, each with the verse he was said to have contributed to the Creed. Much of this work looks north: Gondibour's screens, like work of the period in Scotland, are more Continental Flamboyant than English Perpendicular, while the wooden choir ceiling (c.1355) is of a characteristic Low Countries design, imported via Scotland.[27] Carlisle has long been easier to reach from the north than from the south.

Many of the canons of the priory reappear after the Dissolution as members of the secular chapter of 1541. The nave, which had been used as a prison for Scots soldiers, fell into ruin in the mid-seventeenth century and the five westernmost bays were demolished. The south transept – once the canons' exclusive entrance from the cloister – was made into the grand public entrance of the Anglican cathedral in the nineteenth century.

Carlisle cathedral was, and remains, a peculiarity. Its grand choir dwarfs its truncated, ancient nave; it was institutionally unique, with a community who were at once priests and monks, ruled by a bishop; and it was England's smallest and poorest medieval cathedral, standing in its youngest see. Yet had a key battle or royal marriage gone in a different direction, we might now think of it as Scotland's southernmost cathedral, and the Lakes as the mountains of the borders.

WHAT TO SEE

St Mary, now Holy Trinity, Carlisle
Augustinian priory, founded 1122 or 3;
Augustinian monastic cathedral from 1133;
secular cathedral from 1541.

Church: battered, truncated Norman nave; choir a clever rebuild across two centuries
Fittings and carvings: stained glass in the top of the east window (Last Judgement); carved choir capitals (Labours of the Months); stalls, misericords and screens; repainted and much altered choir ceiling.

Later enrichments: impressive collection in the treasury; magnificent Low Countries limewood altarpiece in the north transept.

CHESTER

Before Liverpool, there was Chester, the great port of the north-west, sucking up outside influences, eager to innovate, its residents with a reputation for hospitality and skulduggery in equal measure. And at the heart of it stood the great monastery of St Werburgh's, which became a cathedral in 1541.

The origins of St Werburgh's are obscure. The great Roman fortress city of Deva may have had Christian churches; the Britons who inhabited the area thereafter certainly did. By the time of the Norman Conquest, Chester was a large and prosperous place, with conspicuous Roman ruins (see p. 256) and two churches. St John's stood outside the walls by the River Dee, while St Werburgh's occupied an entire quarter of the Roman city. It held the fragmentary remains – incorrupt ten years after she died in Hanley, but dust by the time they reached Chester[1] – of the saintly Mercian princess Werburgh, perhaps brought there by Aethelflaed, queen of Mercia. She had refounded the Viking-decimated city, perhaps including its twin minsters, in 907.[2]

William the Conqueror made Cheshire into a kind of buffer state to northern Wales, with power focused on a single aristocratic ruler, Hugh d'Avranches. This earl of Chester spent the next twenty years taking possession of a vast territory, including most of the county. He also became grotesquely fat, having 'indulged himself to excess in hunting, war, women, mountains of food, reckless

expense, and lavish generosity to the knights and clerks of his household'.[3]

The founding of a great abbey was among the acts expected of such a magnate. In Hugh's case local politics were also at play. The first Norman bishop of Lichfield had moved his cathedral to secular St John's, Chester in 1075.[4] Hugh decided to turn the city's other minster, St Werburgh's, into a monastery.[5] In 1092–3 he persuaded Anselm, abbot of Bec in Normandy and future archbishop of Canterbury, to come and help. Anselm parachuted in a group of Norman monks and an abbot to join St Werburgh's thirteen married, Anglo-Saxon priests. The priests were allowed to stay on until they died, when they were replaced by more monks. By the thirteenth century the community had

By the early nineteenth century, Chester looked more like a battered tooth than a church (right); its current appearance (left) is largely a re-invention

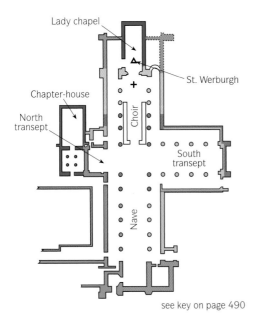

Lady chapel

St. Werburgh

Chapter-house

North transept

Choir

South transept

Nave

see key on page 490

grown to about forty monks, before levelling off at twenty-five or so.[6] Hugh and many of his followers made donations of land and were buried in the new church. A Norman abbey was thus transplanted into north-west England, inheriting an Anglo-Saxon saint and an endowment of recently acquired Anglo-Saxon land.

The new abbey of St Werburgh was vastly wealthier than the new cathedral of St John. The bishop must have felt rather upstaged, and at some point between 1087 and 1102 he moved his bishopric to Coventry.[7] But he did not lose possession of his church at Chester, and based one of his archdeacons at St John's. Sometime during this period, both St John's and St Werburgh's were rebuilt. Work at St Werburgh's began between 1089 and 1092: the battered romanesque arches in the north transept are the main visible remnants of a standard issue Norman great church.[8]

The monks lived in a city that was a crossroads of ideas and influences. As a St Werburgh's monk called Lucian described it in 1194, the city

attracted ships from Ireland, Aquitaine, Spain and Germany, as well as marauding Welsh-men. The monks were seldom 'free from crowds flocking round them'. Their saint was Chester's patron. Her very name, Lucian believed, meant 'preserver of the city'. When the city was under attack, her shrine was placed on the walls; when it was threatened by fire, it was carried through the streets. The citizens were famous for their friend-liness, helpfulness, idleness and 'borrowing other people's property without leave'.[9] It seems the modern stereotype of the Scouser has ancient roots.

This account of the people of Chester comes from Lucian's *Description and Praise of the City of Chester*,[10] a very original work which in itself showed how well-read the Chester monks were. But he was parochial compared to the fourteenth-century librarian at St Werburgh's, Ranulph Higden. By 1327 Higden had completed his *Polychronicon*, his 'universal history', which became the most popular encyclopaedia in medieval England. Despite his great learning, Higden had barely ever left the abbey enclosure, except on a special visit to the king. Edward III asked him to come 'with all your chronicles . . . to speak and to advise with our council on certain matters which will be explained to you'.[11]

St Werburgh's benefited for nearly two centuries from the patronage of the earls of Chester: its chapter-house contained the tombs of Hugh d'Avranches and his descendants. But in the 1280s the earldom of Chester was brought under Crown control: Henry III gave the title to his son, making Cheshire a County Palatine – a prince's county. Within a few years, Chester became the mustering point and logistical key to the conquest of Wales; and Edward I made the future Edward II prince of Wales as well as earl of Chester.[12] As a result of Edward I's actions, St Werburgh's lost its key patron. The princes of Wales were increasingly distant from their county. Although the east end of the abbey was rebuilt from the early thirteenth century on, a programme that would gradually become a rebuilding of the entire church, it proceeded in fits and starts.[13] Workmen were taken from the abbey to build Welsh castles in 1277, 1282 and 1284, and during this time there were several changes of design in the choir alone. A triforium was inserted into a half-completed two-storey elevation: it is so like those in Burgundy that it may have been designed by the king's Savoyard castle builders. Monastic penny-pinching is probably behind the decision to lower the height of the church in mid-build, leading to the oddly flattened arches of the windows in the choir aisles.[14]

With the conquest of Wales complete, the County Palatine became something of a backwater. In the late fourteenth century, Adam of Usk called the city 'a nest of wickedness', while the Welsh poet Lewys Glyn Cothi complained of the 'crafty mobs of Chester, who 'have left me barer than a salmon swimming a stream'.[15] The Black Prince, Edward III's eldest son, tried at least twice to prevent men from carrying arms with them wherever they went; yet for almost a hundred years, the princes of Wales did not even bother to appoint a justice of the peace.[16]

The problems penetrated St Werburgh's itself. In 1344 Abbot Benington had the abbey mitred, making it independent of the bishop of Coventry and Lichfield, 'so that he might give himself up to dissolute living'.[17] Four senior monks acted as whistleblowers and had to be given refuge in other monasteries. There were at least three more serious scandals between the 1350s and the 1420s: two monks were even assigned to supervise Abbot Sutton, sleeping in his bedchamber to as to 'safeguard his reputation'.[18] No wonder building work appeared to slow to a halt sometime in the 1350s, leaving much of a Norman church standing west of the choir.

The monks of St Werburgh's constantly had to be reminded that they were meant to lead lives of

The ruined east end of St John's, Chester's other great church, briefly a medieval cathedral

cloistered prayer: in 1315 they were criticized for giving their leftovers to their hunting dogs rather than the poor, and for having too many servants and their own private apartments.[19] Their city-centre monastery held an annual fair outside the abbey gates, during which the monks had a complete monopoly on trade in the city; the abbey also doubled up as an important parish church.[20]

The lives of these monks are everywhere apparent at St Werburgh's: in the urbane and cosy cloister, for example, where there are little desk spaces for each of them and glazed windows for comfort. Their refectory, now the cathedral restaurant (illustrated p. 188), has a pavilion-like pulpit from which they would be read to as they ate. Their chapter-house is St Werburgh's highlight: the bundled ribs of its vestibule vault rush from floor to ceiling without hindrance from a capital, and the (much restored) arrangements of blank and open lancets on the east facade make a delicious play of light and shade. Few medieval fittings have survived in the church, but the sumptuous choir-stalls (of around 1380) are a reminder of the monks' cosmopolitan tastes. Five of their misericords were considered so indecent by the Victorians that they were destroyed. There are rarely depicted scenes of courtly love and chivalry from *Tristram and Isolde*

Chester's choir-stalls (c.1380) are among the finest in England

and *Sir Yvain* – products of a community that had the right to hunt freely anywhere in Cheshire, and was regularly implicated in minor sex scandals.[21]

Late in the fifteenth century, when the city became exceptionally wealthy, Abbots Simon Ripley and John Birkenshaw gave much of the church a Perpendicular makeover. Ripley paid for a new stone pulpitum, and completed the south transept and central tower by 1493; his successor updated many features of the east end, reroofed the north transept, completed the nave clerestory, built the south porch and the west front, and began (but never completed) a grand south-west tower. The luxurious cloister was being rebuilt in 1527–9: within ten years it would become useless.[22]

In 1539 the monastery was dissolved, and the church became a cathedral the following year. Just ten of the twenty-eight monks left, and the last abbot became the first dean. Chester had also joined Bristol, Norwich, London and York as a city with county status in 1506, while the status of the

wider County Palatine of Cheshire was normalized by Henry VIII. The new see was a step forward, for the area had been far from episcopal control for centuries.[23] Eventually both Manchester (1847) and Liverpool (1880) became sees of their own.

By the nineteenth century the church had become 'a great mouldering sandstone cliff'.[24] Chester's battered cathedral became a focus for local pride, and it was restored and rebuilt by the area's rich industrialists.[25] As a result, none of the church's high vaults is medieval. Most of the window tracery has been replaced. The memorable tower-pierced profile is a Victorian invention, and indeed some parts of the church have been completely rebuilt.[26]

The engines of an empire have thus left St Werburgh's a monument as much to the Victorian as to the medieval period. It is in some ways a fitting fate: the history of Chester cathedral has for centuries been intimately linked with that of the area around it. St Werburgh's is an enduring reminder that Chester preceded Manchester and Liverpool as the economic, political and cultural centre of the North West.

WHAT TO SEE

St Werburgh, now Christ Church and St Mary, Chester
Anglo-Saxon church; refounded in the tenth century; Benedictine monastery from 1092–3; secular cathedral from 1540.

Church: choir-stalls; reconstructed shrine of St Werburgh (made from fragments found walled up in the nave in 1889); Victorian tombs and fittings.

Close: one of England's best-preserved monastic complexes: chapter-house (vestibule); refectory (reader's pulpit); cloisters (monks' carrels). The former monastic and lay cemeteries are now city parks.

CHICHESTER

A thousand years of saline winds, sinking foundations, ravaging fires and relative poverty have somehow left Chichester one of England's more loveable great churches. Yet in a sense it shouldn't exist at all.

In the early 680s, Northumbria's irascible, vainglorious Wilfrid (see p. 40) had one of his periodic grand huffs. He travelled south in exile, looking for a place to make his mark. Only one Anglo-Saxon kingdom had yet to be won over to Christianity: that of the South Saxons – modern Sussex – based along a stretch of coast in southern England. Wilfrid proceeded to build a cathedral at Selsey, at what is now Church Norton on that marshy coast. Yet there was already a community of Irish monks at Bosham;[1] and within a few years, the South Saxon kingdom had been swallowed up, first by Mercia and then by Wessex, reverting to paganism for twenty years as it did so.[2] If Wilfrid had not come, or had arrived a few years later, the cathedral would have had no cause to exist.

For its first four hundred years the see flickered in and out of existence. Nearby Bosham was a royal centre of some importance, but in other respects Chichester was cut off behind the thick, sparsely populated forest of the Weald and the high ridge of the South Downs.

It was probably King Alfred who refounded a city on the site of Roman Chichester.[3] The Normans moved Wilfrid's cathedral there in 1075. Even this may have been a compromise: Lewes would have been a more logical choice, being at least as important and more centrally located; but the bishop's lands were centred around Selsey.[4]

Chichester was the third poorest cathedral in England, after Carlisle and Rochester. The diocese simply covered Sussex; it was squeezed between the mighty sees of Canterbury, St Paul's and Winchester; both Canterbury cathedral and the Cluniac priory at Lewes held more lands in the see than it did, and they and Battle abbey were exempt from the bishop's control.[5] The bishops were left with a rump of rural parishes and smaller religious houses to oversee.

The 'committee-man's romanesque'[6] of a late eleventh-century Norman cathedral still dominates the choir and nave. The church's east end was probably complete by 1108; rebuilding continued into the mid-twelfth century.[7] It was damaged by fire

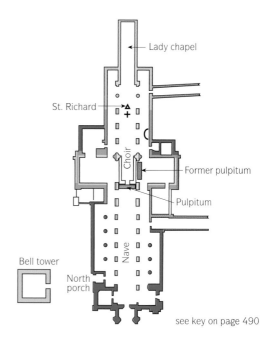

see key on page 490

in 1114 and again in 1189, patched up on both occasions and rededicated in 1199. Yet by the early thirteenth century Chichester's inadequate foundations had made the entire building slump like some dying monster. After further works it was dedicated for a third time in 1279.[8]

Buried in this complex story are several choice moments of architecture-as-history. The effects of the fire of 1189, for example – a few hours of violent conflagration – can be recreated by following the scars of the post-traumatic architectural surgery. Chichester's clerestory is early gothic, that is, late twelfth century. Its predecessor must have been burnt beyond repair. But the gallery beneath is Norman: the fire can barely have touched it. And the arcade below that is schizophrenic: Norman on the aisle side, but with an early gothic facelift towards the nave. All this suggests a fire that got a grip on the roof timbers, sending them crashing to the floor, where they set light to wooden fittings, thus damaging the clerestory and the inner face of the arcade disproportionately, while leaving the gallery and aisles relatively undamaged.[9]

The canons of Chichester took the opportunity presented by the fire to rebuild their east end, using huge quantities of polished stone. For their new retrochoir they took the design suggested by the post-fire work further west, creating a sumptuous piece of early gothic, with pointed and round-headed standing together in polite balance.[10] Plans to add a stone vault to the building were perhaps halted by the interdict (see p. 93), when the bishopric lay vacant, and restarted in newly matured Early English by builder-bishop Richard Poore, who was promoted from dean of Old Sarum to bishop of Chichester in 1215; two years later he became bishop at Old Sarum itself, and began to

The charm of Chichester's nave belies its troubled history: an early Gothic makeover after a fire of 1189; the addition of vaults only exacerbated longstanding instability

create Salisbury cathedral. By 1240 the church was vaulted from end to end, funded by successive bishops, the issuing of indulgences, and a tax on the canons, as well as generous gifts of wood from Henry III.[11] But the vaults added a huge extra weight to the unstable walls.

The man who inherited this problem was eventually canonized. St Richard of Wych (Richard of Droitwich) is textbook material for a medium-sized saint's cult: popular among the people of his see, and in favour with church authorities for his stand against royal interference.[12] He was himself the disciple of another saint: as an official of Edmund Rich, archbishop of Canterbury, he was with Rich at his death en route to Rome in 1240, and arranged his burial. Rich was canonized in 1246. Richard went into a period of deep crisis after his friend's death, and nearly became a Franciscan friar. But in 1244, when Henry III tried to give one of his administrators the bishopric of Chichester, the new archbishop of Canterbury nominated Richard of Wych in his place.

Richard reached Chichester to find that the king had closed the gates of the city to him, and that the lands on which his income depended would not be released to him. For two years he lived in a country rectory, where he tended his garden and toured his see, enacting reforms in the spirit of the Fourth Lateran Council (see p. 104), and presumably making himself popular among the parishes of Sussex as he did so. Eventually Richard was allowed possession of his cathedral, and sometime after 1246 he began to add a row of chapels along the outer aisles of its nave. There is no parallel to these in any other English cathedral, but they are commonplace across the Channel in France, where they partly help to support vaults: they perhaps helped support those of the sagging nave.[13]

In 1253, Richard was making his way through Sussex and Kent preaching a crusade when – while in Dover, dedicating an altar to his beloved St

Chichester from the east, its fourteenth-century lady chapel extending to the right

Edmund Rich – he fell ill and died. Soon prayers to him were causing church candles, snuffed out by Sussex storms, to reignite, and bringing back to life boys who had been run over by carts. He was buried in one of the few nave aisle chapels completed in his lifetime – perhaps unsurprisingly, that dedicated to his friend St Edmund. When he was canonized in 1262, the canonization bull asked that Richard be reburied in a more fitting place. But the then bishop was caught up in the civil war between Simon de Montfort and Henry III, and no shrine was ready until 1276, when the saint was translated to the retrochoir,[14] whose architecture already provided a fitting setting for it.

There is a palpable jump in the scale of Chichester's architecture after Richard's death, just when his cult was probably at its peak. His row of nave chapels was completed on a more ambitious scale, and the church's slumped roofline and unstable vault were made good with flying buttresses, a new parapet and roof. A new series of porches reflected the hierarchies of medieval life: a small one for lay people on the north side facing the city; a magnificent one for the bishop on the south side facing the close; and a grand ceremonial porch at the west end. The lady chapel was lengthened around 1304.

Work had been under way on and off since the late eleventh century. Now it began to slow. A jaunty Decorated window in the south transept and a set of choir-stalls with entertainingly second-rate misericords were paid for by Bishop Langton in 1337.[15] The north transept became unstable in 1371; once they had repaired it, the masons went on to add a spire to the tower, causing a renewed structural crisis, and the building of the surviving stand-alone tower for the heavy cathedral bells.

By the Reformation, Chichester's close had grown into a maze-like tiny city, hermetically sealed from the outside world. It remains one of the most evocative secular cathedral closes in England, with its grand bishop's palace and associated park; villa-like plots for prebends' houses; and a little vicars' college built in 1397, with a dog-leg alley by which they reached the church. The uneven three-walk cloister is a fittingly pragmatic series of corridors 'joining the dots' between various parts of the close; the 'chapter-house' is merely an upstairs room off the south transept. The city itself retains its medieval hospital – a spectacular survival, still run as an almshouse by the dean and chapter – and its market cross, given by Bishop Otter.

Robert Sherborn, bishop from 1508, brought an ostentatious sentimentality to pre-Reformation Chichester – as well as to Portsmouth, Rome, St Paul's and Oxford, all of which benefited from his taste for building.[16] Like many of his canons,[17] he

Patching in greensand, limestone, flint and brick make a geological palimpsest of the chapel of the bishop's palace

Christ's face, awed by his own powers, as depicted on the Lazarus panels at Chichester

was a Wykehamist who had moved smoothly from Winchester college to New College and on into administration and diplomacy.

At Chichester he engaged Lambert Barnard, a jobbing artist familiar with the north European Renaissance, as the cathedral's in-house decorator. He had the painter fill the south transept, which was probably where the general chapter met,[18] with pictures of scandalous hubris and political guile (illustrated p. 155). Here Henry VIII is portrayed as head of the church and Sherborn lines himself up as a second St Wilfrid. The bishop preached a sermon in favour of the king in 1535, and died the following year.[19] His tomb (illustrated p. 216) is a garish recess of deep blues, golds and reds, in which the elderly bishop poses as a beautiful young man

of waxy alabaster. The tomb was curtained off for most of the year, but on Sherborn's deathday, boy choristers and professional singers (the latter had been endowed by him) would gather before it, the choristers bearing glass cups filled with sweetened egg and milk coloured with saffron. After singing for Sherborn's soul, the boys could eat their treat; 'a poor remembrance I have made', he called it.[20]

Lambert Barnard was asked to paint in Chichester cathedral several more times before his death in about 1567, by which time he had considerable experience of the changeable winds of artistic correctness. Sherborn had him cover the church (and some of his palaces) with decoration, such as the delicate swathes of foliage, peppered with Wykehamist proverbs ('Manners makyth man'), which covered the vaults. Under Edward VI, Barnard was paid to paint these over, replacing them with sober biblical texts (illustrated p. 155); then under Mary he was asked to paint back the crucifixion over the high altar, only later to paint it out a second time, replacing it with the Ten Commandments.[21]

It is something of a wonder that Chichester cathedral has managed to stay up at all. It is more like a pair of heavily patched jeans than a work of architecture. Its spire, north-west tower and many windows had to be replaced by the Victorians after their predecessors collapsed; walls and gates separating it from the town have been torn down, though the bell tower remains, a rare survival.[22]

Chichester's greatest treasure is, in its way, characteristic of the entire building. In 1820 restorers found two carved panels behind the choir-stalls: they are probably from the twelfth-century choir screen.[23] They feature two scenes from the story of Lazarus, whom Jesus raised from the dead.[24] The figures in these scenes – from lowly gravedigger to mighty Messiah – are graded hierarchically by

size. There is real feeling in Christ's grave, yet terrified, eyes – a sense of how it might be to feel human, yet have the power of a God. Like Chichester itself, these carvings have only just escaped oblivion. They are at once reminders of the authoritarian power embodied by the cathedrals, and the touchingly humane expression of that power which Chichester exemplifies.

WHAT TO SEE

Holy Trinity, Chichester
Secular cathedral; see founded 681, moved to Chichester 1075.

Church: romanesque 'Lazarus' panels; early gothic 'plastic surgery' in the nave; new-build retrochoir; Bishop Sherborn's painted propaganda and tomb.

Close: bell tower, wavering cloister, half a vicar's college, sites of prebendal houses, bishop's palace and delightful gardens.

Elsewhere in the city: Hospital of St Mary (access must be arranged in advance) and Market Cross.

COVENTRY

On a hilltop in central Coventry stand three of the most contrasting cathedrals to be found anywhere. Two of them are well known: the current cathedral, finished in 1960 and designed by Sir Basil Spence; and next to it the dark shell of St Michael's, a medieval parish church of enormous size that was made a cathedral in 1918 and heavily bombed in 1940. But to see the third, the hunter of medieval cathedrals has to visit the Priory Visitor Centre, completed in 2001. Within it are displayed the fragmentary remains of the monastic cathedral of St Mary, Coventry's first cathedral, rediscovered in excavations of 1909. This was the only cathedral in the country to be completely destroyed at the Reformation, and the only one of Coventry's buildings that comes within the scope of this book. Reconstructing the essentials of this lost church is essential to any survey of medieval cathedrals.

Before the 1540s there were also three huge churches on this site: the cathedral, St Michael's, and another large parish church, Holy Trinity, which unlike its siblings is still intact. Each of these churches was topped by a spectacular spire: the cathedral may even have had three spires. Between them they made the centre of this hugely prosperous mercantile city one of the most spectacular gatherings of 'tall buildings' in medieval England.[1]

The cathedral priory of Coventry was based in a monastery founded by Earl Leofric and Lady Godiva, possibly in about 1020.[2] A church founded by the semi-mythical Osburga may have preceded it.[3] Leofric was one of King Cnut's most trusted advisers: he and his (now more famous) wife had one relic, the head of St Osburga; to complement

this, the archbishop of Canterbury gave them the arm of St Augustine of Hippo, which he had bought in Pavia.

It was sometime between 1087 and 1102 that this Benedictine monastery became a cathedral. The bishopric of Lichfield had moved to Chester in 1075, but Bishop Robert Limesey welcomed the opportunity to move to a more stable part of the country and acquire a rich monastic house as he did so. The earliest romanesque masonry yet found

Sir Basil Spence's cathedral is the third to share a hilltop site in Coventry

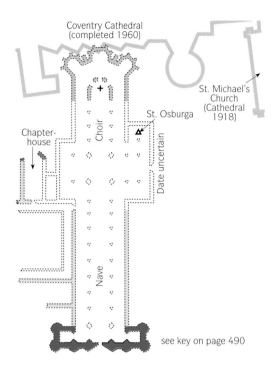

Coventry Cathedral
(completed 1960)

Chapter-
house

Choir

St. Osburga

St. Michael's
Church
(Cathedral
1918)

Date uncertain

Nave

see key on page 490

buildings. The monks fought back, 'spilling his blood before the altar', but the bishop won the day. The monks returned in 1197, only to fall out with the canons of Lichfield in 1222, and again in 1321, over the appointment of a new bishop. On both occasions the dispute had to be referred to Rome.[5] Procedurally both churches were equal, but by the fourteenth century – and in spite of the city's increasing importance as an economic power-house – Coventry was increasingly behaving like a middling-sized abbey in which the bishop happened to have a seat, while the real focus of episcopal activities lay at Lichfield.[6]

The sad consequence of this came at the Reformation: there was only a need for one cathedral in each diocese, and it was the monastic churches that had their necks on the block. The

The stumps of what was once England's grandest monastic cathedral west front are still visible

at Coventry dates from the 1120s, so it is not known whether Limesey rebuilt his church, as would seem likely given that both St John's at Chester and Lichfield – the previous seats of the see, and both still 'in the pocket' of the bishop – were rebuilt in the late 1080s or 1090s. In 1148 Lichfield was returned to cathedral status, creating the bishopric of Coventry and Lichfield: the resulting struggle for precedence between monastic Coventry and secular Lichfield lasted two centuries, the tension between the two becoming a recurrent theme in Coventry's history.

In the 1130s or 1140s the monks forged a series of charters to demonstrate their independence of the bishop, perhaps inventing the legend of Godiva's naked ride to bolster the reputation of their foundress.[4] In 1189 Bishop Hugh Nonant tried forcibly to replace them with canons. He and his men broke in, demolishing several of the monastic

Medieval Coventry was one of the most impressive gatherings of churches in the land: from a reconstruction of 1971

saint Osburga, whose feast day was given increased liturgical importance in 1410 – a sign that she was being given a higher profile around this time. There were elaborate late fifteenth-century vaults in this part of the church, too.[8]

Thus is revealed a Coventry cathedral that was a match for any in the land: comparable in size to Worcester, larger than Lichfield, and with perhaps the grandest west front of any monastic cathedral. This impression is borne out by the finest of the objects found in excavations at Coventry: a fragment of chapter-house arcading bearing an exquisitely painted scene from Revelations. It is a battered fragment, redolent of wealth, piety, art, industry and destruction. The Midlands hilltop from which it came has seen more than its fair share of each.

city of Coventry's greatness was its undoing. With two vast parish churches next to the cathedral, and the secular community at Lichfield already the seat of a bishop, no function could be found for St Mary's cathedral church. The site was sold for £400; by 1581 much of the church was in ruins.[7]

The foundations of the chapels at the east end of the ruined church are visible just a few yards from the wall of the modern cathedral. The grand stumps of its west front can be seen in the Priory Visitor Centre to the west. These, and the results of several excavations on the site, suggest that the church had a screen facade like that at Lincoln; a Norman nave; a much gothicized romanesque chapter-house with an apsidal end; and an unusual early fifteenth-century apsidal east end, perhaps built in connection with renewed interest in the obscure in-house

WHAT TO SEE

St Mary, St Peter and St Osburga, Coventry Benedictine monastery founded by 1043; became monastic cathedral from between 1087 and 1102; see held jointly with Lichfield from mid-twelfth century until the Reformation; dissolved 1539; fell into ruin.

Church and close: fragmentary ruins; Priory Visitor Centre.

Later cathedrals of Coventry: bombed-out ruins of the late medieval parish church, made a cathedral in 1918; Sir Basil Spence's replacement, completed in 1960.

DURHAM

The goldsmith stood alone at the top of the ladder. Three men watched him from the church floor: Dr Leigh, Dr Henley and Master Blythman, sober commissioners of King Henry VIII. It was a clear, cold day in the winter or spring of 1539–40, and they were surrounded by piles of jewels, newly prised from the saint's shrine.

They had 'disgarnished' many such shrines, though this was the most important. They knew of St Cuthbert's many miracles. They knew that the body of this man, who had died in 687, had been seen at least twice since its burial – in 698 and 1104 – and that both times it had looked as fresh as if Cuthbert had just fallen asleep. They also knew that every 'saint' they had yet taken from a shrine had proved to be 'nothing but dust and bones'.[1]

The goldsmith found an iron-bound box on top of the shrine. He started to smash his way in, but stopped. There lay Cuthbert, dressed for mass. His face was as clear as day; a fortnight's stubble greyed his chin. The goldsmith gazed down at the figure, astonished and unnerved. 'Alas, I have broken one of his legs!' he exclaimed.

Dr Henley had grown used to the old-fashioned sensitivities of such workmen. 'Cast down the bones!' he ordered. 'I cannot', came the reply, 'the sinews and skin hold and he will not come asunder.' Dr Leigh called the impressionable goldsmith down, and mounted the ladder. What he saw

St Cuthbert was endlessly reinvented to suit changing times: this illustration to his late twelfth-century Life *pointedly emphasises the fealty the bishop-saint was owed by his monks*

wrongfooted him, and he spoke to his colleague in Latin so the goldsmith could not understand him: 'He is lying whole', he said to Dr Henley. You can almost hear the catch in his throat.

'*Cast down his bones*', Dr Henley repeated. Now Leigh climbed down, and Henley climbed up himself, and 'did handle him and did see that he laid whole'. This wasn't meant to happen.

They brought the box down. Cuthbert wore exquisite vestments, 'fresh, safe and not consumed'; various precious objects accompanied him. And,

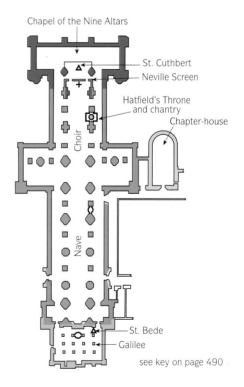

see key on page 490

305

Durham has the most dramatic setting of any English cathedral

'contrary to their expectation', the 900-year-old body was 'whole and incorrupted'. They took the coffin and its precious contents to a vestry, ensured that it was locked, and composed a letter to the king. Some situations need to be delegated upwards.

We don't know what Henry's reply was, or even if there was one. He may have passed the buck to the bishop of Durham, who was in any case president of the Council of the North.[2] For two years the body was kept locked away, if more exposed to the elements than it had been for centuries. Cuthbert was caught in a kind of impasse, a cusp between the ages of faith and reason. Then, in 1541, a solution was finally found. The shrine was levelled to the ground, some of the bones of other Durham saints were added to the coffin, and a new wooden box placed around them all. Then everything was reburied – after two and a half days' hard digging – exactly on the site of the shrine.[3] No other cathedral saint received such treatment.

———

Durham cathedral would have been a glorious sight on the day the commissioners arrived. Over the previous half millennium, it had been enriched and ornamented in Cuthbert's honour, its adornment reaching a peak of intensity around the spot where they stood.[4] Narrow doors guarded the feretory, leaving the visitor only half prepared for what was within. It was dominated by the enormous shrine, 'one of the most sumptuous monuments in all England', with its base of 'fine and costly marble' carved with dragons, beasts and religious scenes, 'gilted with gold'. High above, within a protective cover that could be winched clear of it, lay the coffin, 'decked with gold and precious stones'.

Elsewhere in the feretory were a number of large cupboards, 'painted and gilded with little images very seemly and beautiful to behold'. These contained some of the cathedral's other relics. The nearby 'Irons' displayed some of the more remarkable gifts donated over the years, such as the Durham Emerald, valued at £3,336 13s 4d in 1401,[5] enough 'to redeem a prince'. And there was more, including an altar where mass could be said, 'several sorts of imagery work of alabaster', and a great hanging crown of candles so bright that monks could read by it at night.

The commissioners were lawyers – officials on a mission for the king. As far as they were concerned, everything they found was simply a spectacular windfall tax for the Crown. Yet it seems that – to the commissioners, and even to the king – Cuthbert was different.

They were right. On one side of this great cathedral stood a castle – the bishop's palace – and on the other a monastery of fifty to sixty monks, a major institution in its own right (illustrated p. 23). Both claimed to have inherited the authority of Cuthbert. The complex was squeezed onto a cliff-edged peninsula, at whose base ran the River Wear; beyond, for 10–20 miles on either side, lay the country between the Rivers Tyne and Tees we call County Durham, which, thanks to the saint, was almost entirely owned by the cathedral. Durham's influence stretched wider than this: the diocese included everything north to the Scottish border, and its landholdings spread into Lincolnshire and Lothian. But the core of these lands – including modern County Durham, and everyone who lived there – was simply thought of as 'St Cuthbert's'. Even its name set it apart: for many, this was 'Haliwerfolk', 'the county of the people of the saint'.[6]

This church, then, was much more than the centre of a diocese: it was the talismanic repository of its history. St Cuthbert's relics had come to define the identity of a region and to justify the enormous powers of its cathedral. By stripping the church of its contents, the commissioners were tearing away its memory. Yet the architecture remains, and by following it back in time, layer by layer, we can still recover something of its story. At each stage, Cuthbert's cult, endlessly reinvented, lay at its heart.

As recently as the fifteenth century, up-to-date window tracery had been put into many of the cathedral's windows and then filled with a resplendent series of scenes in stained glass: the Te Deum in the south transept, the story of St Cuthbert in the cloister. The central tower had been built, giving the building its regal profile. Windows and tower remain, though the stained glass has gone.

Going further back, the thirteenth and fourteenth centuries had been the heyday of power for the bishops of Durham. They had become effectively the princes of a semi-autonomous region, a buffer

Fourteenth-century prince-bishops installed a bishop's throne that almost upstaged the saint himself

save Bishop Hatfield, the lands of St Cuthbert and indeed the whole kingdom at a time of crisis. In 1346, with the English army in France, the Scots gathered an army of 30,000 and attacked from the north. The abbeys of Lanercost and Hexham were quickly taken; Durham was next. The Scots army gathered near the prince-bishops' out-of-town palace of Beaurepaire.[8] Bishop Hatfield brought 16,000 men to face them.

Back at the cathedral, the prior had a vision. He was to remove from the cathedral the Corporax cloth used by Cuthbert to administer the Eucharist and take it to the battlefield. The monks processed towards the armies and took up position on the ground, prostrate and praying hard. The Scots attacked, 'running and pressing by them with intention to have spoiled them'. But the soldiers 'had no power . . . to commit any violence . . . to such holy persons'.[9] The course of the battle mysteriously altered, and the bishop's army was victorious. Fifteen thousand Scots and Frenchmen lay slaughtered, including four earls, three lords and the bishop of St Andrews. The bishop of Durham and the monks accompanied local aristocrats, including Ralph, Lord Neville and his son John, to the cathedral, to offer their thanks. Cuthbert had repulsed an invasion of his land; it was of course just by-the-by that the monks' prayers had subtly upstaged the bishop's military prowess.

The Lords Neville built a cross on the site of the battle, and paid for a magnificent new reredos – the Neville screen – in the cathedral itself. Although now stripped of its statues, it is the one really stupendous fitting of medieval Durham to have survived. This wonderful confection of tabernacles, once filled with statues, was probably designed by the royal mason Henry Yevele. It was shipped in pieces from London to Newcastle, and then brought overland to Durham, where by 1380 it had been put back together like a huge kit.

Durham's extraordinary concentration of polit-

between England and Scotland at a time when the two kingdoms were at war and Haliwerfolk became a County Palatine (see Chester, p. 292). Such generalissimo-bishops[7] could get above their station: Anthony Bek, who died in 1311, was the first ordinary mortal to consider himself worthy of burial *inside* Cuthbert's church. Thomas Hatfield (d. 1381) equipped the building with an extraordinary stone bishop's throne, perched on top of his own chantry chapel, assertively several feet higher than the shrine to its east.

When the wars with the Scots were at their height, St Cuthbert saved the day, stepping in to

ical and spiritual power may have ultimately been owed to its saint, but it did not guarantee a happy institution. The bishop and the monks inhabited separate universes. The bishop's castle – with its extraordinary romanesque chapels and swaggering late medieval halls – is dominated by the keep, another work of Bishop Hatfield. In it the bishop held court, entertained kings, and – with a small army of officials – saw to the business of running his mini-state. The monastery had great power and wealth in its own right, but it saw itself as an exclusive world apart, with its library, dormitory, refectory, chapter-house and other buildings housing a tightly regulated life of quiet grandeur. Here everything was prescribed, from the liturgy to the menu (see p. 193), cooked in the great kitchen of 1366 (another highlight built during Hatfield's episcopate, and now the cathedral shop).

For much of the century or more before Hatfield's day, the monks and bishops of Durham fought both each other and the archbishop of York, the tensions occasionally erupting into moments of violence or expensive trips to the papal curia. After one such spat in the 1220s Richard Poore, bishop of Salisbury, was asked to sort out Durham's debts. He left Salisbury, where his new cathedral was well under way, and moved to the far north-east. As its new bishop Poore brought peace to Durham, cleared the debts, and began fundraising for a building campaign at his new church. As a result, St Cuthbert would be used to help pull his own community together, and one of the most dramatic shrine settings in England would be created.

Poore was a modernizer, with strong ideas about the running of a religious community. He had attended the Fourth Lateran Council in Rome in 1215 (see p. 104); Salisbury cathedral is a virtual manifesto in stone for how that epochal gathering's ideas might be worked out architecturally. His ideas had supporters among northern monks, for in 1221 the Northern Province of the Benedictines

The monks claimed that the English victory at Neville's Cross was due as much to St Cuthbert's miraculous intervention as any military might

had met for the first time, aiming among other reforming measures to standardize the liturgy and increase the separation of monks from laity. It was time to create a structure that would increase the number of altars in the cathedral, positioned where few but monks could reach it – and at the same time to make it easier for pilgrims to reach Cuthbert's shrine nearby.[10]

The fundraising took time: the Chapel of the Nine Altars was eventually begun by the prior in 1242. The vault of the old church's semicircular apse was disintegrating; vault and apse were demolished, along with the eastern ends of the choir aisles that stood each side of them. Cuthbert's feretory, which the apse had held, was bulked out to form a square platform. Below and beyond this a new structure was begun, to be accessed from the choir aisles. This 'chapel' was basically an enormous transept, positioned at the far east end of the building like a great, long hall. Nine altars stretched out along its sheer eastern wall, surrounded by rich late Early English architecture: polished marbles, innovative window tracery to north and south, and a great rose window at the heart of it all.[11] The result was one of the most distinctive thirteenth-century east ends, one dominated by glimpses of St Cuthbert's shrine glittering on its platform and overlooking the great new space beneath. By demolishing the cramped aisles that previously led to the shrine, access to the relics had been improved. The new structure beyond provided an exclusive and magnificent new area in which the monks could celebrate masses uninterrupted, while dramatizing the setting of the shrine itself.

Some eighty years earlier an even more audacious attempt had been made to 'repackage' Cuthbert, resulting in the exquisite galilee. Hugh du Puiset (d. 1195) its builder, was a typically grandiose twelfth-century bishop, who built throughout his see and installed at the cathedral candlesticks that were as big as houses:[12] Durham's 'Paschal Candle',[13] studded with crystals and images of beasts, could only be lit by reaching through a special hole in the roof vault.

To du Puiset and the monks, the Becket cult, which exploded in the 1170s, was a threat. A new *Life* of Cuthbert was produced, updated to include recent miracles[14] such as the story of a little boy who plumped for Durham over Canterbury and was healed. Women feature among the protagonists of these miracles, even though they had been shut out of the cathedral since the 1080s. Now du Puiset tried to add an extension to the feretory, a predecessor to the Chapel of the Nine Altars, that

The spectacular Neville Screen; the feretory and the Chapel of the Nine Altars stand behind it

women could be allowed to use. The monks must have reacted with glee when it refused to stay up: Cuthbert had made his wishes clear.

But du Puiset simply took the stones of his near-complete building to the west end, and the resulting Galilee, which had to be built out over a precipice, is still with us today. Complete by 1185, it is contemporary with many influential early gothic buildings. It contains no pointed arches, yet is the embodiment of gracefulness and light. Here the lady mass could be said, and women could worship at a painted copy of the high altar of the cathedral,[15] much of which is still visible, despite the attentions of the commissioners and their colleagues. At the same time, the monks sponsored a new cult in the shape of the hermit Godric of nearby Finchale, at the site of whose tomb a daughter house of Durham was eventually created (see p. 87).[16]

We have travelled back through the layers that resulted in the church the commissioners saw, leaving the bulk of the romanesque cathedral until last. It is an ironic fact that, by stripping away the intervening centuries of enrichment in paint, glass, gold and silver, the reformers were unwittingly making the cathedral look more as its builders intended: a colossal, unpainted exercise in the formal power of pure architecture, albeit one with a saint at its core.

It is now late August 1104; picture again a scene around the shrine, this time with ten monks present. This is exactly the same place in which the commissioners would stand, but the surroundings are very different. There are no 'irons' here, no enormous reredos towers to one side, and no cavernous view over the Chapel of the Nine Altars spreads out on the other. Instead we are inside the curved apse of a Norman church, and the shrine is smaller and simpler – only the riches within it are the same. These monks had spent the last twenty-one years rebuilding their cathedral: its eastern half

was now complete. It was time to move Cuthbert into his new home.[17]

The day of this translation – 29 August – had been broadcast far and wide. But the monks felt both 'anxious and ashamed', for they had decided to check the relics before this event took place. Cuthbert's body may have been their raison d'être, but it had not been glimpsed for centuries. They had prepared for this moment with prayers and fasting, and they waited until dark to open the coffin. Within, a sheet of fine linen hid the outline of a body. 'An eager desire' overcame them, mingled with fear.

The monks lifted the cloth, and 'a marvellous sweet and pleasant odour' arose. There lay St Cuthbert, on his side, richly clothed. He had an aquiline nose, a strongly dimpled chin, and appeared like 'a person asleep rather than dead'. 'They shrank back. . . fell on the ground, and repeated the penitential psalms amid a deluge of tears.' Eventually, they recovered enough to look again. They could see a skull inside the coffin, as well as the body of Cuthbert: this belonged to St Oswald, Northumbrian king and founder of their see. They could also see a loose collection of bones, belonging to St Bede, who wrote down Cuthbert's life. These bones of lesser saints were preventing Cuthbert from lying on his back; they lifted him carefully out of the box and placed him on a bed of tapestries and robes in the middle of the choir. Then they removed the bones from the coffin – the bones which, placed in separate reliquaries of their own and displayed for all to see, the commissioners were to remove from cupboards near the shrine 400 years later. Chanting the Te Deum and various psalms, the monks returned St Cuthbert to his coffin.[18]

The next night they examined the coffin more soberly. Within it they found a chalice and paten with a cloth – the Corporax Cloth, later to save England from invasion – a small but exquisite Gospel book, and other things. There were more cloths, exquisite ones in which the saint was wrapped: a dalmatic woven with two colours, so as to produce 'ever-new and diverse patterns', and a sheet so foreign-looking that its 'character is not fully understood'. Even the coffin had 'the likeness of men' carved upon it. The body itself was 'firm, pliable and unimpaired . . . the veins full of moisture . . . the flesh agreeably soft'. Gently, they washed their saint.

By now, 'men of all ranks ages and professions, the secular and the spiritual' were gathering outside the church, anticipating the imminent translation. The abbot of Séez arrived and complained that Cuthbert's condition should be verified independently. The monks were affronted, and their bishop intervened. Bishop Flambard ('the Torch') had kept aloof from all this, but now, even as expectant crowds gathered, he invited a group of forty-six VIPs to a special viewing. The sceptical abbot would be allowed to touch the body; everyone else would be watched like hawks to ensure that not a thread went missing.

Soon, the assembled churchmen had joined the monks around the body. The Norman abbot lifted the 'venerable head . . . bending it backwards in different directions'; he 'drew the ear backwards and forwards in no gentle manner'; he placed the body in a 'sitting posture from its quiet abode'. Eventually, he agreed that the body 'consisted of solid sinews and bones', he agreed; it was 'clothed with the softness of flesh'.

It was a moment of triumph. 'The holy body of the father was placed upon the shoulders of a fit number of bearers . . . a band of singers resounded far and wide with heavenly hymns', and the monks moved through the church and burst into the sunlight. An immense crowd awaited them. Some wept; many prayed loudly; the 'bearers of the sainted body' could barely 'advance through the dense throng'. Eventually, they arrived outside the newly built apse, and awaited their bishop.

Ranulph Flambard was one of the great characters of Norman England: with a combination of guile and daring, he had escaped both an assassination attempt and imprisonment in the Tower of London. He had clawed his way into the highest ranks of society through sheer force of character; he was William II's right-hand man. He considered this a fine moment for a sermon: and soon, although 'the day had far advanced', the bishop kept preaching, 'touching many points not at all appropriate to the business in hand, and fairly wearing the patience of many of his hearers'. Suddenly, although there had been 'no sign of bad weather whatever in the sky', 'a torrentous fall of rain appeared from nowhere'. The brethren 'snatched the coffin . . . and hastily conveyed it into the church', noting that none of its precious ornaments had even become damp. This had been a divine downpour. Of all the unspiritual achievements of medieval bishops, Flambard's stands alone: here was a man who had bored God.

The half-built cathedral into which Cuthbert's coffin was conveyed was not like other churches. From outside, its walls seemed impossibly high, with apparently three stages to the aisles alone, which had a zigzag profile created by dozens of tiny gables.[19] The lowest stage was a blank arcade, a decorative feature seen outside the apses of some European churches; this one, exceptionally, ringed the building, as if the whole church was a shrine. The church also had a blank arcade inside, a rare and expensive feature that was new to England. At Durham it took the unique form of an interlacing pattern of arches, an elaborate design with possible Anglo-Saxon roots; the emphatically stepped bases to the walls were also perhaps Anglo-Saxon in inspiration.[20] The massive piers, like the legs of elephants, were covered in carved patterns – chevrons, diamonds and spirals. Columns had been carved before, perhaps imitating the 'marbling' painted on to them in some churches,[21] but the combination of carved pattern and colossal, tubular pier was new, and its power was enhanced by the unerring, abstract regularity with which the patterns themselves were applied to the columns (see p. 222). Everything was bare, unpainted.[22]

There is force in the result – the kind of muscular force that the Normans had been developing over the previous decade at cathedral rebuilds such as Winchester, enriched with motifs from the latest buildings in the Germanic lands across the North Sea. But this was also the most richly decorated new building in England, and the decoration contained a message. Six enormous spiral-patterned columns stood out in the eastern half of the church. This was a direct reference to the shrine of St Peter in Rome, the holiest site in Europe and symbol of the power of bishops, which was famously associated with six Roman spiral columns. Above these columns curved what was perhaps the first-ever rib vault.[23] This brilliant invention would become the defining feature of medieval architecture. It evoked both the vaults of heaven and the canopies of saints' shrines. In effect, the whole of Durham's east end – with its blank arcades, spiral columns and vaulted roof – was a saint's shrine turned into architecture.[24]

For many, Durham is not merely a great romanesque church: it is *the* great romanesque church. Its architecture has two messages: the overwhelming importance of Cuthbert, and the combining of Anglo-Saxon and Norman traditions. To find the roots of these messages we must look further back, to what happened before this church was built.

The see was founded in 635, with its cathedral on Lindisfarne, 60 miles north. Lindisfarne now is a place of wild beauty; then, together with nearby Bamburgh, it was the centre of power in an independent kingdom of Northumbria. Bamburgh was the seat of the king, Lindisfarne of the bishop. Cuthbert was both a monk and sixth bishop of Lindisfarne. The discovery of his incorrupt body in 698 just eleven years after he died triggered the creation of a grand shrine, the writing of new lives of the saint and the making of the Lindisfarne Gospels, which accompanied the community from then on, sitting talismanically on the cathedral's high altar (illustrated p. 43).[25] After repeated raids by the Danes, the island was abandoned in 875, and the refugee monks and their bishop spent eight years wandering northern England. The very presence of the saint among Cuthbert's people must have brought hope in trying times. In 883 they settled in Chester-le-Street, which became the site of the cathedral for almost a century. But the Danish incursions grew more severe, and Cuthbert and his community went on the move again.

One day, in 995, the coffin suddenly refused to move. At that moment a nearby cow bolted: its owner chased it onto a high promontory, surrounded by a swift river. Cuthbert (via the cow) had selected this place as his home. The community set about building the see's third cathedral here, at Durham; alongside it, the local earls established a fortified settlement. In 999 Cuthbert was translated into a large Anglo-Saxon cathedral that became known as the White Church. This, the first Durham cathedral – 'so admirable it pointed the way to the finer church to come'[26] – was thus about seventy years old when the Normans invaded.

For some time, the cathedral had been staffed by a group of secular clergy – men who had wives and children, and engaged with the world around them. The first Norman bishop, a man from Lorraine called Walcher, found himself in an unusual situation. On the one hand, this community seemed ripe for reform. On the other, thanks to the Anglo-Saxon kings, his church had an unusually wide range of powers, both political and spiritual. It was also isolated: thanks to the Vikings, Durham was one of the few religious communities to survive north of York. Indeed, it was not properly in

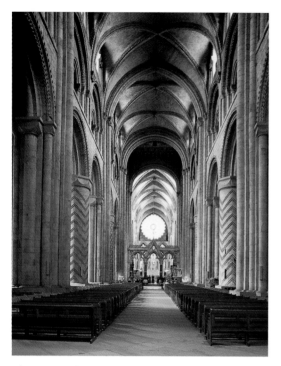

The nave: Durham's rib vaults are among the first in the world

England at all: Domesday ignored the area, and the kings of Scotland were just as significant to local politics as those of England. Its heritage as an independent kingdom was still very much alive, and was embodied by its saint. But any plans Walcher may have had for his cathedral were forestalled. In the late 1060s the earl of Northumbria rebelled against the Normans. William the Conqueror had him beheaded, and made Walcher earl of Northumbria as well as bishop of Durham. Sadly for him, Cuthbert was yet to be won over: Walcher was murdered by local Anglo-Saxon lords in 1079, and the culprits vanished into a dense fog that appeared from nowhere.[27]

William's next choice as bishop was William of St-Calais, a man who was both a monk and a canny politician. He was open to the fluidities of local politics, allowing the kings of Scotland to be key secular sponsors of his plan to rebuild his cathedral, and accepting the advances of an intriguing and useful group of Anglo-Saxon refugees who came from the distant abbey at Evesham.[28] To these monks, who had a particularly intolerant Norman abbot, Northumbria must have seemed like a haven of Anglo-Saxon culture. They had approached Walcher with the idea of reviving the long-ruined monastery of Jarrow, former home of St Bede and others, but got nowhere. Now St-Calais welcomed them: a group of orthodox Benedictines was just what he needed.

St-Calais helped these monks repair the ruins of Jarrow. Then, in 1083, he told the secular community of his cathedral that they could only stay if they abandoned their families and became monks. When only one accepted, St-Calais installed the community of Worcestershire monks in his cathedral, appointing as prior Turgot, himself an Anglo-Saxon. Between them St-Calais and Turgot reopened ancient sites of Northumbrian monasticism – Jarrow, Monkwearmouth, Lindisfarne and Tynemouth – as daughter houses of Durham.[29] Turgot was truly the bishop's deputy: St-Calais made him archdeacon as well as prior, giving him enormous powers in the see as well as within the cathedral.[30] The two men began to build a monastic complex at their new cathedral priory.

As a renewed institution that could also claim to have inherited Cuthbert's commitment to monasticism, Durham was at once both young and old, both Anglo-Saxon and Norman. In 1083 a new *Life* of the saint was written, which portrayed the new community as the natural inheritors of Cuthbert's authority, contained new miracles that indicated his approval of the new order and reinvented the saint as a misogynist.[31] Ten years later, after St-Calais had returned from a period of exile and high politics far from Durham, the rebuilding of the cathedral church began.

This romanesque cathedral was designed by a master of Brunel-like genius, a man familiar with some of the latest buildings in Europe, innovative and far-sighted in his engineering, and able to translate a complex brief into jaw-dropping architecture. Men like Prior Turgot and St-Calais must have played a key role in guiding him: the building's aim, to evoke the unity of rival traditions under the talismanic power of a saint, are the aims of churchmen, not masons. But this is not the architecture of 'prince-bishops': St-Calais was a high-flying bishop and royal servant,[32] not an earl of Northumbria, and in fact he was rarely in Durham. Durham's vision is syncretic rather than combative; it uses the uniqueness of Durham's heritage to help support the new regime. By fusing native and European traditions, as the Lindisfarne Gospels (illustrated p. 43) had done several centuries earlier, it coined an architecture with the power to evoke an intense sense of sanctity.

———

Cuthbert's tomb has been opened twice since 1541.[33] His coffin was found to be decorated just as had been described in the twelfth-century report. The objects it contained were in an astonishing state of preservation: the material described in 1104 as something 'not fully understood' is now known to be a ninth-century silk from imperial Constantinople, covered in pagan imagery.[34] These finds are now displayed in the Treasures of St Cuthbert museum at the cathedral. The body itself lies beneath the feretory floor. It is a disarticulated skeleton, but when last seen the bones had a 'deep brownish tint' and a 'membraneous covering or layer' on them, suggesting that the body had once been mummified – a relatively simple process in the dry, salty sands of Lindisfarne. Although Cuthbert's body can never have looked as if it had just fallen asleep, it may have long remained a striking sight.

While Cuthbert has not quite had the last laugh – women have been walking around his church for centuries now, without causing discernible disasters – at least the monks come out of the story with some of their claims intact. And without their faith in him, we would have no Lindisfarne Gospels, and no Durham cathedral. Human creativity driven by faith is a powerful thing; indeed, for such works, 'miraculous' is not a bad word.

WHAT TO SEE

St Mary and St Cuthbert, now Christ and St Mary, Durham
Monastic cathedral founded 635; later became secular; arrived in Durham 995; Benedictine monastic cathedral from 1083; secular cathedral from 1541.

Church: Norman architecture throughout, perhaps the period's masterpiece; later, more graceful Galilee (with wall paintings); evocative shrine area; thirteenth-century Chapel of the Nine Altars; fourteenth-century Neville screen.

Close: Durham castle (bishop's castle-cum-palace); monastic complex, including kitchen and library; setting on a cliff-edge promontory above the Wear.

ELY

It was time to put Christ in his place. Here, some 46 metres above the ground, John of Burwell and his assistants were positioning a great carving. It was 1340, and this, the last boss in the highest vault of an extraordinary building, was the culmination of eighteen years' work. John of Burwell, a jobbing East Anglian wood carver,[1] was perhaps the last man to look down through the Christ-shaped hole in the middle of Ely's Octagon.[2]

From the hole into which the boss was lowered, fifteen wooden ribs fanned outwards and downwards; beneath these, eight great windows hung, apparently suspended in the air. Then an enormous octagonal void opened out, like some great gothic dome. The supports for this structure – four enormous arches and four window-filled walls – could be made out far below, enriched with niches and tabernacles shaped more like distended pieces of metalwork than anything made of stone.

John had been paid two shillings, perhaps a quarter of his weekly pay, to make this great image of Christ in heaven, displaying his wounds.[3] Around and beneath him work was under way on one of the most vainglorious building programmes of the Middle Ages: half a great monastery and its cathedral church were being rebuilt simultaneously.

This complex, already ancient, utterly dominated the town that clustered around its walls, and ruled much of the watery landscape beyond like an independent state. Within it, fifty-odd monks led lives of elaborate discipline. Among them were the

cloisterers who had few responsibilities other than to eat, sleep and worship together (see chapter six), which they would do beneath the Octagon when it was complete. Many of their buildings were being renewed or rebuilt, including the infirmary, where prayers and herbs were the main medicines and a fire was permitted throughout the year, and a 'painted chamber' where female relatives of monks

The Octagon, stone-and-wood hymn to a Virgin saint; all lines converged on John of Burwell's carving of Christ

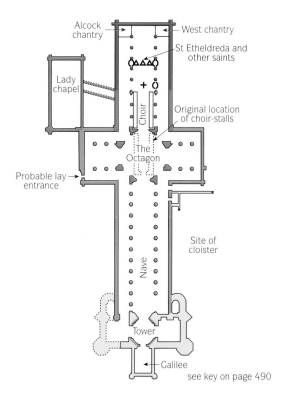

see key on page 490

The romanesque nave, glimpsed through the richly carved Prior's Door

could stay. Then there were the twenty or so obedientaries who ran the monastery, many of whom had real power in the world beyond its walls. The sedge master, for example, was one of the lowliest among them, yet twenty-three account rolls survive for his office alone, detailing the acquisition of the peat and dried grasses used to heat, insulate and roof much of the cathedral priory.[4] Other obedientaries included such senior figures as the sacrist, Alan of Walsingham, and the prior, John of Crauden.

Like other sacrists, Alan of Walsingham oversaw the 'stage management' of a complex liturgical diary, the purchase of provisions and the progress of building works. But at Ely his role went much further. Alan effectively governed much of the town itself and the lands around,[5] gathering rents, letting manors, and acting as judge. He maintained the three causeways that connected Ely to the world beyond, and the four granges from which Ely's farming projects were administered. Now his residence was being rebuilt, as well as a new office complex with exchequer room, bakehouse, kitchen, store, and accommodation for the Salomons, Ely's hereditary family of goldsmiths.[6]

As for Prior Crauden, priors of Ely had been known to attend Parliament, entertain royalty, and even wear a bishop's mitre. He was effectively chief executive of one of England's richest Benedictine monasteries.[7] His staff of twenty men helped manage an income of about £1,200 a year. His residence had also been rebuilt, with a great hall

The great church at Ely dominated its landscape politically, economically, spiritually and architecturally

filled with Italianate paintings, a sumptuous series of VIP guest rooms, a private study and a tiny chapel of great richness.[8]

There was another side to Ely: the world of the bishop, John Hotham. As at other monastic cathedrals, his palace and its staff – senior churchmen themselves – were almost totally separate from the monks, and focused on the needs of the see rather than those of the cathedral priory. At Ely, however, the monks' responsibilities extended unusually far into the governance of the see, and Hotham had made it his business to influence the appointment of key figures in the monastery.

Hotham's was one of the richest bishoprics in England.[9] He ruled a compact (and thus easily governed, if strategically sensitive) see, which included Cambridgeshire as well as the Isle of Ely. The bishops of Ely were invariably chancellors of Cambridge University.[10] But the heart of his domain was the Isle of Ely, not, as now, a hill in a flat expanse of enormous fields, but 'an island . . . surrounded by marshes or by water'[11] This 'Isle' was really a great expanse of marshland, reaching almost to the Wash, in which lay an archipelago on whose largest island the monastery stood. It was entirely owned by the church – mostly by Ely itself – and throughout it all justice and many taxes were due not to the king or any secular lord, but to the cathedral priory. Only Durham dominated its see more completely (map p. 175).[12]

The Isle was also England's Achilles heel, 'a most dangerous place in case any sedition should arise'.[13]

Etheldreda rests as her staff flowers: from a carving in the Octagon

In 1071 an insurgency based there nearly toppled the Normans; in the 1140s inflated sheepskins had to be used to construct causeways in order to break a siege during the civil wars of Stephen and Matilda; and another siege in 1216, during the rebellion against King John, was only broken when the waters around the Isle froze over. None of this prevented the Isle being a military focus again in the 1250s, during the baronial rebellion against Henry III. Whoever was bishop of Ely, Henry once said, 'should be a man of tried and trusted loyalty'.[14] Hotham was Edward II's chancellor.

———

Ely's special privileges, its watery domain, its ancient monastery and its architectural grandeur were owed ultimately to one sacred figure. Uniquely among the cathedrals[15] this great saint was female; she pre-dated by 400 years the appearance of a bishop on the Isle.

Ely had been a monastery long before it became a cathedral. It was founded in the seventh century by Etheldreda, an Anglo-Saxon queen who had fled there from her husband, the king of Northumbria. Etheldreda was the daughter of one of the most powerful kings in Britain, and St Wilfrid himself (see p. 40) was her mentor. She had committed herself to religion and to celibacy, although her husband was determined that things would be otherwise. En route from the north-east she had rested overnight in Lincolnshire, putting her staff into the ground, and woken the next morning to find that it had flowered.

Eventually Etheldreda reached the Isle of Ely, which had come into her possession as part of her wedding dowry. Here she founded a monastery in 673, a mixed community of men and women, and here she died a virgin, to be succeeded as abbess by her sister. Her body was believed to be 'as uncorrupt as if she had died and been buried that very day'.[16] Bede presented her as a uniquely important figure, a kind of English model for the Virgin Mary herself.[17] Alongside Cuthbert and Thomas Becket she was perhaps the most important English medieval saint. Ely also held the remains of four other royal Anglo-Saxon virgin saints,[18] the disputed relics of St Alban, and at least one minor cult around the tomb of an Anglo-Saxon bishop.

Etheldreda's church was probably abandoned during the Danish conquest of East Anglia in the 860s. When one Viking attempted to ravage her tomb, his eyes were torn out by supernatural forces. A group of priests later returned to the site, and one of them also tried to penetrate the tomb to see if Etheldreda's body really was incorrupt: he and his family all died of plague. For a nun, the virgin queen could be surprisingly ferocious.

Ethelwold, the reforming tenth-century bishop of Winchester (see p. 44), turned Ely into a Benedictine monastery with the support of King Edgar, who around 970 confirmed that the community owned the 'the Liberty of St Etheldreda' or Isle of Ely, free of interference from the Crown.[19] Ely now became a kind of spiritual eastern outpost of the newly united English kingdom. Kings, archbishops and local noblemen gave lands to it; the abbots of

Ely were royal chaplains. King Cnut was moved to poetry after he heard the chanting of the monks of Ely from a boat on the Fens, and legend had it that Edward the Confessor himself was educated there. The monastery was packed with the magnificent gifts of its royal patrons (see p. 48).

Ely put itself in the firing line during the Norman Conquest. The last Anglo-Saxon abbot, Thurstan, was a local boy, steeped in the abbey's traditions, and Archbishop Stigand of Canterbury and the abbot of St Albans both fled to Ely in 1066. In 1071 a band of rebellious English nobles and their soldiers, accompanied by the bishop of Durham, chose to launch an insurgency there and were soon joined by a Danish naval force. This was a serious threat. William the Conqueror surrounded the Isle and built causeways for his army. Some of the monks then lost their nerve; only one middle-ranking Anglo-Saxon, Hereward the Wake, refused to negotiate, and disappeared into the marshes with his band of followers.[20] Thurstan was fined and many of his lands were seized.

In 1082 the abbacy was given to Simeon, brother of Walkelin, bishop of Winchester.[21] Simeon immediately followed his sibling's example, demolishing what must have been one of the most magnificent of Anglo-Saxon churches and re-building it on an exceptional scale. The new Ely abbey was a slightly smaller younger cousin to 'brutalist' Winchester cathedral, then one of the largest structures on earth. Just a single pin survives from the riches of its predecessor.

Simeon died in 1093, aged 100, and for seven years the abbot's income went to William II. Building work was put on hold; when it restarted the stylistic harshness had softened slightly. The effortlessly strong-limbed architecture that resulted was to spread throughout East Anglia: it is the ultimate source for the designs of Norwich and Peterborough alike.[22]

Henry I appointed Abbot Richard on the day of his coronation. Together they dealt with a problem that had arisen almost immediately after 1066. Anglo-Saxon abbots of Ely had been careful never to defer to the bishop of Dorchester, in whose diocese it lay, but from whom it claimed independence.[23] The first Norman bishop, Remigius, was a man of action: he moved the diocesan seat from Dorchester to Lincoln, and had no truck with Ely's traditional autonomy, forcing subsequent abbots to make the trip to Rome to avoid being consecrated by him. To Abbot Richard, there was a simple solution. Since the Isle was too important to be independent of a bishop's control, the abbey's powers on the Isle were greater than those of many cathedrals, and the see of Lincoln was unwieldy in size, Ely should itself be a bishopric.[24] In 1107 King Henry chose Hervey, a former bishop of Bangor, as Richard's successor.[25] Papal approval was received for Richard's idea, and in 1109 Cambridgeshire was taken out of the diocese of Lincoln – its bishop received a manor in compensation – and added to the Isle of Ely to form a new see.

The monks, who had spent several centuries avoiding bishops, now had one of their own. Though their last abbot had been behind the idea, the creation of a see at Ely was not entirely to their benefit: the monastery's lands had to be divided in order to provide the bishop and his office with a separate income; the bishop, reminding his prior that monks were sworn to poverty, took an enormous two-thirds of the abbey's total endowment. The monks continued to be proud of their heritage: new lives of the Ely saints were written, an Ely monk wrote an account of the exploits of Hereward the Wake, and Ely's chronicle included a detailed account of the lost treasures of the Anglo-Saxon church.

Under the bishops, rebuilding of the church continued without pause, and everything except the west front was complete by the 1140s.[26] The latter was the work of Bishop Ridel (a bitter enemy of

The lady chapel's flickering walls were originally inhabited by hundreds of richly painted statues

Thomas Becket), who was appointed in 1169. Ridel's extraordinary early gothic west front,[27] with its wing-like western transepts (one of which collapsed around 1500) and tower-block like western tower, is the nearest thing surviving in England to the 'westwork' that is such a feature of German cathedrals.[28] Ridel also repainted the church and enriched the east end. All building work stopped after 1208, when his successor went into exile during the interdict; he died soon after his return and left money for the addition of the early English Galilee porch (illustrated p. 94).[29]

In 1229 Ely acquired one of its few monk-bishops in Hugh Northwold, formerly abbot of Bury St Edmunds, 'the abbot of abbots . . . the bishop of bishops'.[30] In 1234 he began a new presbytery – the

easternmost part of the east end, 'most notable for the rich and magnificent marble carvings'.[31] He personally contributed over £5,040 to the project, an estimated three-quarters of the total cost. It is a particularly ornate work of late Early English, thick with swags of stiff leaf and columns of polished stone, vaulted throughout and with a squared-off plan which was to be highly influential.[32] When built, it must have seemed as rich as a heavenly palace compared to the Norman choir with which it connected. This east end contained both Northwold's own tomb and the shrines of St Etheldreda and her companions, whose cults were the source of its aesthetic drive. In 1252 Northwold rededicated the church in the presence of Henry III, with St Etheldreda joining St Mary and St Peter among the dedicatees. The position of her shrine is marked in the building by a roof boss showing the virgin queen herself, and by a motif that, once recognized, provides one of the more quietly heart-stopping moments in an English cathedral (illustrated p. 326).[33] On one side of her shrine, the cone-like corbels that separate the arches of the main arcade are carved into wintry, dry, stick-like sprays of stiff leaf foliage; on the other they have burgeoned into ebullient life. The stone itself seems to be blossoming. The virgin queen and her flowery symbols were beginning to permeate Ely's architecture.

The next phase of building at Ely was even more innovative. John of Hotham was provided to the see of Ely in 1316, and was soon chancellor of England. But in 1320, after a run of defeats in the Scottish wars, he fell from grace, and was replaced as chancellor by his colleague, Bishop Salmon of Norwich, himself a native of Ely. Hotham retreated to his diocese, from which he helped Queen Isabella prepare her revolt against Edward II (see p. 122).[34] He also had time to launch a building programme that eclipsed his rival Salmon's magnificent Norwich cloisters, and apparently filched some of its best talent. At the same time he engineered a level of harmony between bishop and monks that was rare in monastic cathedrals, by placing hand-picked men in key posts in the monastery: men like Prior John of Crauden and sacrist Alan of Walsingham.[35]

Alan of Walsingham had already been given some key tasks. First, in 1314, Edward II himself came to decide whether Ely really held the relics of St Alban, as it had claimed since 1045,[36] and Alan – then best known for being 'remarkable for his skill in goldsmith's work' – was entrusted with the delicate task of opening the shrine. In a major blow to Ely's credibility, the king then declared that the true bones of Alban were at St Albans.[37] Second, Alan had also been 'keeper' of the lady chapel,

which stood in the south choir aisle, causing real problems for the monks: as early as 1300, Bishop Walpole had pointed out how 'the . . . contemplation of the monks is interrupted by the entry of the laity; and most especially, of women' there, and ordered a screen to be built to separate monks from lay visitors. Eventually, in 1321 it was decided to build a new lady chapel in a better location, which would result in a standalone structure on the other side of the church, its building overseen by a monk called John of Wisbech. Alan was finally appointed to his key post, along with Prior Crauden, when the previous prior of Ely had to be sacked for financial incompetence. The two men had only been in office a few months when the Norman central tower collapsed.

At first, Alan was at a loss, 'not knowing which way to turn nor what to do'.[38] Yet within six months, the rubble had been cleared, adjacent bays of the church demolished, and stone suitable for foundations found 2.5–3 metres below ground level. Work had begun on the Octagon. And, Bishop Hotham announced, half of the east end would also be rebuilt. In two years, Ely had launched a new lady chapel, central tower and choir, and at the same time the monks were also rebuilding large portions of the monastic buildings. It was a display of rude good health after the setbacks of the previous years, and a refocusing on Etheldreda after the St Alban denouement.

The results were certainly impressive. Hotham's choir bays were built by Norwich masons,[39] among them perhaps the up-and-coming master-mason William Ramsey, a key figure on the Norwich cloisters who in less than a decade would be one of the inventors of the Perpendicular style. The choir was a luscious updating of Bishop Northwold's work to its east and the intended setting for grand tombs to both Hotham and Crauden, a rare honour for a prior and one that acknowledged the 'special relationship' underlying these works.[40]

The lady chapel was a simple rectangular box of stone, a virtually freestanding building off the north choir aisle, a location that allowed easy access for pilgrims – who probably entered the church via the north transept – and also evoked East Anglia's great Marian shrine, the House of Our Lady at Walsingham, another rectangular structure that stood off the north side of its church. Special access passages were built so as to allow monks and laywomen to come and go without coming into contact.[41] When they arrived in the lady chapel, such visitors found themselves in one of medieval England's more breathtaking buildings. Its walls flickered with tabernacles so curvaceously layered that they felt alive, organic. In these niches stood 147 life-size statues and an exquisite frieze telling the story of the Virgin Mary's life and miracles. The chapel was carved by a team from Lincolnshire, where there was a tradition of richly carved stone fittings;[42] when covered in red, blue, green and gold paint, with its large windows packed with glass, it would have possessed a greenhouse-like architectural heat. Both it and the Octagon had one foot in the goldsmith's world of shrines and censers.

The Octagon was also carved and overseen by Norwich masons. But it was surely the brainchild of its project manager, Alan of Walsingham, himself. It was a brilliant trope: towers are usually square, but there is no reason why they have to be. By clearing away a bay each from the transepts, nave and choir that surrounded the former central tower, a spectacular octagonal space was created, providing space both for the choir-stalls and for the circulation of pilgrims.[43] But most of all, this octagonal vault with a lantern rising from it was rich with metaphor: in form it was both flower and crown, both Etheldreda and the Virgin Mary, an image of permanent intercession for those beneath it.[44]

Alan may have had a brilliant vision, but he needed professional help to make it a reality. William Hurley, master carpenter for the king's

works south of the Trent, was brought in. The stone part of the Octagon is a simple sheath of walls, broken up by niches and arches, but on it sits[45] an elaborate structure, made of 450 tons of solid oak. This alone justified Hurley's £8 a year pay packet, twice that of anyone else on site.[46] Wood 'had to be sought far and wide, found with much difficulty, bought at great price, and carried to Ely by land and water' (see p. 219).[47]

All this was enormously expensive: £7,000–£8,000 has been estimated, with the Octagon alone costing at least £2,400 6s 11d.[48] Indeed, more money may have been spent on Ely's architecture in the 1320s and 1330s than at any other single building 'moment' described in this book. A cathedral rebuild normally required funds over an extended period: at Ely, three ambitious parts of the church went up simultaneously, while changes were also being made to almost every part of the conventual buildings.[49] Everything was of the highest quality, and the designs were demanding to produce – richly carved, inventive and labour intensive.

It must have helped that John of Hotham earned over £3,000 a year and had suddenly found himself with no 'day job'. But there were other factors, too. A bronze pot of old coins was 'miraculously' found while foundations for the lady chapel were being dug. Money was borrowed and debts called in. John of Crauden made a fundraising tour of the diocese. Donations came from sources as diverse as Bishop Salmon of Norwich (£13 6s 8d) and the monks' pittancer (£16), and the monks gave up some of their luxuries – pocket money, wine and sweets. Alan's Ely parishioners lent a hand, and were rewarded with small amounts of food and cash. By the late 1330s the monastery was even able to pay off large outstanding loans from its Italian bankers.[50]

Good management was equally important. For

England's model for Mary herself, Etheldreda is glorified in the tenth-century Benedictional of St Ethelwold

once, the monastic system aided great gothic architecture (see p. 248),[51] allowing each officer – Alan of Walsingham with the Octagon and the monastic buildings, John of Wisbech with the lady chapel, John of Crauden with his chapel and other works and Bishop Hotham with the choir – to worry about his own comparatively devolved task. They co-operated – for example, Alan of Walsingham paid for sharpening the axes of the bishop's masons in 1323–4 – and all made donations to the works from their own budgets. As a result, all did well.[52] Prior Crauden nearly became bishop in 1337, and Alan of Walsingham succeeded him as prior in 1341.

Choir and Octagon were finished during the 1340s; completion of the lady chapel was delayed by the Black Death. No 'pure' Perpendicular appeared inside the church for many decades, though late medieval bishops installed larger windows in many places.[53] In the 1390s an octagonal lantern was built on the western tower, purely to give the exterior of the church a more balanced appearance. It is a structure of skinlike thinness: perhaps its builders were worried about adding too much weight to the westwork.[54] In about 1500, one of the western transepts beneath it collapsed altogether. The late fifteenth-century Bishop Alcock, an important man and a keen builder (he founded Hull grammar school and Jesus college, Cambridge), spent over £1,490 on a new bishop's palace, employing the same mason on his 1488 chantry chapel.[55] (His chapel may have been planned for his previous cathedral at Worcester, for it looks as if it had to be cut back to squeeze into Ely.)[56] Nicholas West, who became bishop in 1515, built a sumptuous, dense, almost continental chantry, utterly gothic in spirit yet thick with early Renaissance details, which makes a fine pair with that of Bishop Alcock. The son of a Putney baker and a protégé of Cardinal Wolsey, he had a staff of over 100 servants and fed 200 poor people a day.[57]

Bishop Goodrich, appointed in 1534 and at the helm when the monastery was dissolved, left a more destructive legacy. A future chancellor of England, after 1541 he proved to be one of the most thorough of iconoclasts. Every one of the tiny figures in the lady chapel was beheaded; the statues of Anglo-Saxon kings and other subjects that stood high in the Octagon were taken down, and only the eight corbels bearing the legend of St Etheldreda were left behind. Here Etheldreda's bushy staff can still be glimpsed germinating behind her slumbering figure, helping support the stem-like shafts that rise and spread to form the great Octagon.

———

Today it is the Octagon that visitors come to see, but once upon a time it was Etheldreda herself. Every summer a constant stream of pilgrims and VIPs came to visit this great cathedral priory and its saint. The church was packed during the three great fairs associated with her.[58] Boys from the

Carved cones of foliage turn from wintry stiffness to the full bloom of summer either side of the site of St Etheldreda's shrine

cathedral school were paid 3 shillings apiece to manage the crowds, 'calling up the pilgrims and minding the candles'.[59] The pilgrims could take away bright silk necklaces called 'St Audrey's chains' or other souvenirs: the range of pilgrim tat available at Etheldreda's fairs was so great that it has given rise to our word 'tawdry', a corruption of 'Audrey', which is a diminutive for Etheldreda.

The Octagon was closed to these people. It loomed ahead as they entered the church via the north transept, but William Hurley's choir-stalls, which have since been moved further east, blocked access to it. Instead, ahead of them was the back of the stalls, and a series of fake 'tombs' of Ely's Anglo-Saxon benefactors,[60] reminders of Ely's history and permanent encouragements to give.[61] They toured the lady chapel and the shrines, concentrating on Etheldreda herself; one man is known to have spent seven nights there. Those with eye diseases would touch their heads on the site of her tomb, which was separate from the main shrine; other sights included the Black Rood, the fetters from which a criminal had been miraculously freed by the saint, and the Crux ad Fontem, where she had made a miraculous spring appear.[62] As they circulated, more tantalizing glimpses of the Octagon might be had: from some angles John of Burwell's carving of Christ might just peek down at them. But the great starburst view from directly beneath the Octagon could only be seen from within the choir. It was a view reserved for the monks, and a powerful reminder of who did what in the world, even of the reason Ely existed at all: to enact a sacred liturgy on behalf of the rest of humanity.

All the lines of the Octagon converged on the opening into which John of Burwell eased his carving that day in 1340. Everything must have seemed to connect up as the great wooden Christ slipped home. Yet the figure whose presence imbued this structure was not Christ but Etheldreda. She was the driving force behind Ely's dramatic story, apparently combining virginal purity with powers of fecundity, queenly authority with cloistered modesty. These contradictory qualities are effortlessly resolved in the architecture of her church.

WHAT TO SEE

St Peter and St Etheldreda, now Holy Trinity, Ely Monastery (for monks and nuns) 673; became secular; Benedictine monastery c. 970; monastic cathedral 1109; secular cathedral 1539.

Church: romanesque nave; late twelfth-century west front; Hugh of Northwold's presbytery; breathtaking fourteenth-century sequence of Octagon, lady chapel, choir, Prior Crauden's chapel and other surviving conventual buildings.

Fittings: monuments; stone carving in the gothic parts of the church.

Setting: though much of the monastic complex is gone, Ely retains much of the feel of a small city dominated by a single great church; and the approach to it from the surrounding Fens is unforgettable.

EXETER

Like an iron fist in a velvet glove, Bishop John Grandison sat within his throne. This place called Exeter was a long way from the papal court at Avignon, or his ancestral castle in the foothills of the Alps. His predecessor-but-one had been murdered by a London mob; the next bishop had only been in post a few months before he, too, dropped dead; and all this at a time of civil war. Now Grandison had been sent to the edge of the world, as he put it to his friend the pope.[1] He would have to balance firmness and magnificence if he was to surmount the problems here.

The pope himself had given Grandison this job. He was there to do what he believed in most: the work of the Church. In a diocese this size, containing some thousand parishes, in which Cornish and English were as commonly spoken as French and Latin, it was a job worth doing. Yet perhaps the biggest cause for hope of all was embodied in the throne that rose above him.

He had never seen anything like it. It was taller than a saint's shrine – taller than a small church – yet so delicate it looked almost weightless. Wooden angels swept down over his head, bearing a censer, a chalice and other items, all reminders of the supernatural authority with which he was to be vested.

It was a sultry August day in 1328. Grandison was about to be made bishop of Exeter: never had a piece of furniture made a bishop's authority seem more noble or profound. But then this job made him the local embodiment of the authority of the

apostle Peter; it made him a key link in a chain of spiritual power without which no human being could receive the sacraments. Only a bishop could bless chrism oils; only a bishop could make men priests.

Grandison loved beautiful things: some of his personally commissioned private books and carved ivories still survive (illustrated pp. 212, 232). Yet it was happenstance that brought him to a half-built church. Within the previous ten years it had been given a set of fittings which impressed him greatly. Thomas of Witney, their designer, was soon to become 'a dearly loved member of our household',[2] and Exeter sculptors would be asked to produce

Triumph of Decorated: the walls of Exeter's nave were once richly coloured

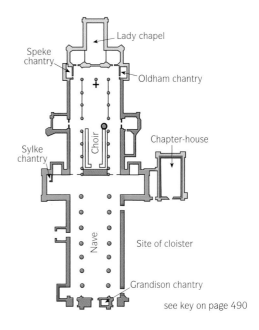

Lady chapel

Speke chantry

Oldham chantry

Choir

Chapter-house

Sylke chantry

Nave

Site of cloister

Grandison chantry

see key on page 490

Fourteenth-century Exeter, seen here from the north side of the close, is dominated by its twin twelfth-century towers

ivories for him influenced by the latest ideas from fourteenth-century Italy.[3]

The half-built church itself did not have the gravity-defying proportions of the great churches of France, but it had a unique spirit of its own. Its columns were made of Purbeck limestone, polished not to a glossy black but to a subtle, bluish-grey gleam; its bosses were so delicately painted that individual hairs were picked out, despite being invisible from the ground.[4] The overall effect was warm and human in scale, as well as ornate and magnificent. And most satisfying of all, the entire church was dedicated to St Peter, bringing full circle the themes of authority and power embodied by the bishop in his throne.

———

Exeter is exceptional. It was the last cathedral to be rebuild effectively in its entirety, over a period of about sixty years. The result is, with Salisbury and Bath, the most visually coherent of all cathedral interiors. It went up during English art's most creative years, exemplifying the style we call Decorated.[5] We know more about how it was built than about any other cathedral, including the way the project was funded and the names of many of its craftsmen.

But Exeter's story begins long before its great fourteenth-century rebuilding. It was a Roman city with a Christian community, and apparently had a church again from the late seventh century. It only became the seat of a see in 1050, when Bishop Leofric united the two sees of Cornwall and Devon. The cathedrals of St Germans and Crediton were moved to a single, more urban, site at Exeter; the new community occupied a small monastic house, which was now secularized, following a continental constitution in which priests emulated something of the communal lifestyle of monks.

So, exceptionally, the Normans found at Exeter a church that had already been reformed, if not rebuilt. Yet Exeter was the last of all post-Conquest cathedral rebuildings.[6] Perhaps, like other late projects at Hereford (1108) and Carlisle (1122), it was both a rather poor community and a little too near the edge of the Norman domain; Cornwall was only marginally less foreign than Wales. Or perhaps, having been based in its existing church for under twenty years, there was no great rush to do more.

The Norman cathedral was begun in 1112 or 1114. Its distinctive towers survive: two great rectangular piles, covered in ornamental patterns and positioned halfway down the church, so that their interiors double up as its transepts.[7] Their presence has remained a guiding feature of the cathedral's development: even today, the sight of the low, reddish building between these two strong, stumpy white verticals is instantly recognizable. From the outside at least, the visual signature of Exeter is a Norman creation.

A century or so later, more change was afoot at Exeter. In accord with the reforming spirit of the times, Bishop Brewer, who took office in 1224, overhauled his community.[8] He used his own lands to fund the creation of key dignitaries, such as a dean and a chancellor, but uniquely left the canons with Leofric's common fund, from which each took his share, rather than independent prebends of their own. Brewer's architecture focused on the needs of his newly reformed chapter: he is the likely builder of the bishop's palace, the deanery and the choir-stalls, of which the misericords, the oldest set in England, survive. He certainly built the chapter-house,[9] the rectangular plan of which is unique among the secular cathedrals and perhaps

a reflection of its members' communal constitution.

This constitution, a fusion of the pre-Conquest and the high medieval, gave Exeter a distinct identity. With twenty-five members, the chapter was small, but it had an unusually low number of absentees.[10] The lack of a prebendal system dissuaded career churchmen from adding an Exeter canonry to their portfolio, only to spend their life elsewhere. And it was surely easier to direct a proportion of the canons' common fund into building work than, as at other secular churches, to tax each of a large group of separate prebends, each effectively 'owned' by an even more disparate group of individuals.

Despite the potential of this arrangement, the Exeter cathedral we see today began as a conventional project. Piecemeal work to extend the east end and upgrade side chapels, led by Bishop Bronescombe, was under way by 1279; among other things, a new lady chapel was soon complete. Bronescombe probably expected that his work would lead to the gradual rebuilding of the entire church, as funds became available. But as the project developed it became something more remarkable. Bronescombe's work was funded, as far as we know, from donations from various collecting boxes and collections. His successor, Peter Quinil, created a special fund for the new fabric, and was remembered as 'the first founder of the new work'. As a result, a sluggish project became an energetic one. But it was under the next bishop, Thomas Bitton, that the funding of Exeter's rebuilding moved into new territory. In 1298 the bishop and his chapter agreed to an extraordinary 50 per cent annual tax on their own incomes. For two decades, the resulting £187 18s a year was paid into the project, making long-term planning possible.[11] In effect, the backbone of Exeter cathedral's construction fund came through an enormous and self-imposed 50 per cent corpor-ate income tax.[12] By 1300, therefore, the man lucky enough to be master-mason at

Exeter found that in addition to his standard pay – £6 a year plus a house in the close – his was a project with exceptionally long-term funding and strong support from its patrons. A hard stone of corporate commitment had developed at the heart of the project, and was now to gather plenty of velvety stylistic and iconographic moss.

By now work had moved on to the choir. Here, under Roger, master-mason from 1299, the architecture became both richer and less conventional than in the eastern chapels. Roger had various fixed points: the new eastern chapels, the Norman towers with the transepts within them, and an existing chapel at the west end. These defined the proportions of his church, suggesting a building that would be long and wide rather than narrow and high, and – as it had no central tower – with a potentially unbroken view from west to east. His design thus emphasizes richness and horizontality over weightlessness and height. Everywhere, forms are bundled together in clusters: the piers are composed of sixteen attached columns; the vault has a never-again-matched twenty-two tierceron shafts curving up each bay. Together they march from one end of the building to the other in an avenue-like sweep, the longest uninterrupted span of vaulting in the world.[13] There was pattern everywhere, in richly carved bosses and vault corbels and broad windows filled with the most inventive displays of tracery ever seen.

To emphasize the horizontal yet further, Roger took the radical step of omitting a middle storey or triforium; no cathedral, and few great churches, had done this before. The result must have been treelike in effect, emphasizing a quality that marks out Exeter to this day. There is something organic about the building, as if it has been planted rather than constructed: it seems to evoke the swaying strength of a great wood rather than the supernatural airiness of Heaven, the glory of creation rather than that of the Creator, a verdant paradise rather than a heavenly city.[14]

Bishop Stapeldon, Bitton's replacement in 1307, maintained the financial commitment of his predecessor, and expanded the project from one restricted to the cathedral community to one 'owned' by the entire diocese. In 1310, all clerics in Devon and Cornwall were asked to make contributions to the works for three years: a healthy £90 was raised in 1312. This later became a 'diocesan tax', a regular, systematic collection in which every parish was engaged.[15]

The east end was completed by about 1310, by which time work had been under way on the transepts for some time, and by the 1320s the nave had been begun. But attention was now focused on commissioning fittings for the new choir. The bishop and chapter wanted something rather special, and they appointed a consultant simply to help choose timbers for their new bishop's throne. This man, Thomas of Witney, had a reputation for creating rich furnishings (see p. 227).[16] In 1316 he moved from his work at Winchester cathedral to take up the post of master-mason at Exeter.

Witney immediately set to work. The breathtaking results are each miniature works of architecture in their own right. The wooden bishop's throne alone took three years to complete. By 1319 a stone pulpitum, reredos and sedilia had all also been begun. The reredos (now lost) was so elaborate that it required a separate set of accounts of its own:[17] it originally contained up to forty-eight separate statues arranged between three delicate tabernacles, and 12,800 sheets of gold foil were used in its decoration. Likewise the enormous rood, which once stood over the pulpitum, involved another 2,000 sheets of gold and silver foil.[18] Few groups of structures anywhere show a more brilliantly unreined creativity.

Architectural changes were also made. Someone must have had cold feet about the two-storey design of the choir – perhaps the fittings made it

Fitting that defines a church: a detail of Thomas of Witney's great cathedra *or bishop's throne at Exeter*

look inappropriately downmarket – because in 1318 Thomas returned to Roger's east end and deftly inserted a triforium into the elevation where none had been before.[19] The resulting design was then followed throughout the building. Thomas also added delightful vaulted galleries in the transepts, high up above the ground, where choristers could be positioned (the famous minstrel's gallery in the nave, though installed later, is one of them). There are sightlines between these galleries and the high altar, pulpitum, and west end of the church, making it possible for choristers to fill the church with co-ordinated singing from high above. Exeter was being turned into a kind of living shrine, not to a saint or a miracle-working object – for it had neither – but to the liturgy itself, and by extension the authority of its bishop.[20]

There was lateral thinking involved here. At Ely the Octagon and choir were a great hymn to the cathedral's in-house saint. Hopeful candidates for sainthood had fuelled new architecture at Hereford and Wells, where Witney had also been master-mason and had designed the setting for an intended shrine. Yet canonization bids were expensive, and success could not be guaranteed: the bid from Wells, like others at this time from Worcester and Norwich, was to fail. In any case, Exeter had no obvious candidate. But what it did have was a liturgy as unique as its constitution: the Use of Exeter was exceptionally elaborate.[21]

So, instead of conjuring up a saint, this cathedral's architecture would equip the church for spine-tingling ritual events. Voices would tumble from high above and from unexpected corners; the rituals at the high altar would take place in a setting that outdid the magnificence of the greatest shrine.

The bishop's throne – the one furnishing unique to a cathedral – would glorify its occupants. This church would reinforce both the church's core function, to perform the liturgy, and its unique status, as the seat of the man who made that liturgy possible. The bishop represented the authority of St Peter, the first bishop, throughout the see of Exeter, and this church was dedicated to that very saint. The thinking behind the fittings installed in the 1310s and 1320s at Exeter is as brilliant as the resulting structures themselves, the approach taken at once canny and brave,[22] and the result utterly convincing. Exeter on a major feast day would have been worth the trip for the rituals and their setting alone. No wonder Grandison was impressed by what he found.

Had it not been for Exeter's remarkable funding arrangement, the events of the 1320s, when the cathedral was unexpectedly and violently caught up in national politics (see p. 122), might have disrupted the building programme that Grandison inherited. Bishop Stapeldon was one of Edward II's most trusted administrators,[23] who by 1320 was treasurer of England, only to be sacked a year later when he advised the king to bow to the will of Parliament and exile the hated Despencers.[24] In 1321, both Despencer and Stapeldon were back – and England was sliding towards civil war. Stapeldon made huge efforts on behalf of a collapsing regime. He seized the lands of Queen Isabella, who was said to be plotting to depose the king, negotiated a thirteen-year truce with Scotland, and ruthlessly overhauled government accounts to help fund the king's wars. In the process he attacked some of the privileges of the people of London, earning their enmity.

There is spooky prescience as well as dogged loyalty in Stapeldon's story. As early as 1322, he had begun making elaborate preparations for his own death. In 1325, instead of his annual 50 per cent payment to the cathedral fabric fund, he made a massive cash donation of 1,000 marks.[25] That same year he took the future Edward III to France on a diplomatic mission, where he began to suspect an imminent invasion by Queen Isabella and her lover, Roger Mortimer. Fleeing to London in 1326, Stapeldon was recognized while riding down Cheapside. He was pulled from his horse, and he and his nephew and valet were slaughtered. The bishop of Exeter was decapitated with a bread knife, his head sent to Isabella, and his body dumped.[26] It was not long afterwards that Edward II was murdered. After some delay, Isabella – now ruling the country with Mortimer – returned the bishop's battered body to his cathedral.

Two strange years followed Stapeldon's murder, during which the one thing it had so brilliantly sidestepped – a saint's cult, albeit a minor one – fell into its lap. A junior member of the Berkeley family, loyal servants of the Mortimers, was made bishop of Exeter.[27] But James Berkeley died in his turn, of natural causes, after just a few months in the job, and for reasons unknown, rumours of miracles circulated around his tomb.[28]

Stapeldon cannot have known he was soon to die, yet thanks to his generous donation of 1325 the cathedral's building programme had a financial cushion. It continued unabated through the difficult years after his death, shielded from the crises that engulfed the cathedral. Even his tomb is suffused with a kind of bitter foresight. It is a furnishing in itself, built into the choir screen – the good bishop's nose almost brushing up against a vivid painting of Christ displaying his wounds. But opposite it in the aisle is a contemporary monument, widely assumed to be that of Stapeldon's brother. The knight is accompanied by a noble young man and a horse with a valet. It is curious that the dramatis personae present at Stapeldon's death are shown in a carving just a few metres away from him.[29]

It was after Bishop Berkeley's death that

Grandison took on the see. He was alienated from his chapter: Bronescombe, Quinil, Bitton and Stapeldon were all Devon men, elected by their peers from within the chapter, but Grandison was an outsider, born in Herefordshire but of a noble family from the Swiss-French border, and a man more at home discussing theology with future popes than running a suddenly troubled English diocese.[30] At least his throne was impressive.

John Grandison moved quickly to show his support for the building of Exeter cathedral. In 1328, the year he was enthroned, he donated silver statues of St Peter and St Paul and a pyx, in which the consecrated host would hang. They were the finishing touches of the reredos; he dedicated the high altar, and the new choir was ready for use.[31]

But Grandison was not as wealthy as his predecessors. He owed money to the papal court, and did not have vast estates at his disposal. He seems not to have continued the regular payments made by his predecessors. Cheaper colours began to be used to paint sculptures, and in the nave the walls were built up from their Norman predecessors, so avoiding complete demolition.[32] His priority was to get the job finished: as he himself put it, Exeter was 'marvelous in beauty', 'destined to exceed in glory all other churches of its class in England and France if only it could be brought to perfection

and completed'.[33]

Grandison turned out to be a stringent, committed bishop. His tastes are characterized by a kind of extravagant humility: in spite of his professed poverty, he added hugely to the bishop of Exeter's powers of patronage, increasing the size of the bishop's collegiate church at Crediton and founding a new one at Ottery St Mary. There, he built a kind of mini-Exeter cathedral in which ceaseless prayers would be said for the bishop and his relatives. The bishop of Exeter was also patron of the large college at Glasney in Cornwall, and an Oxford college. He thus had four foundations from which he could reward the senior churchmen of a large see.

The new collegiate church at Ottery St Mary was almost certainly the work of Thomas of Witney's protégé William Joy, who became master-mason at Exeter in 1342. Initially there was less room for Joy's individualistic creative style in the cathedral itself – with most aspects of the design already set, all he could do was draw up new patterns in window tracery and design porches and doors[34] – until Bishop Grandison made it clear that he wanted to place his personal stamp on the church in its west front (illustrated pp. 26, 124). Here, the row of five arches intended by Witney were filled in, and a stone screen was built across them. The new Exeter west front was to be a massive piece

The famous elephant depicted on Bishop Brewer's thirteenth-century misericords

A riot of foliage on Exeter's fourteenth-century pulpitum

of stone furniture built against a pre-existing wall, supporting a display of sculpture, like a diminutive Wells west front; from it choristers could sing at Palm Sunday services and other events (see p. 97).[35] One of Witney's arches was left open, though this was only visible from inside the church; and here, in the gap between the west wall of the church and the new stone screen, a unique chantry chapel was built for Grandison himself, in which the bishop's brass effigy stared up, in a twist on the image of Stapeldon's tomb, at a carving of the risen Christ. The open arch to the nave has since been blocked, the brazen effigy has long been lost and the chapel is generally closed to the public, but the image of Christ within is one of the largest such carvings to have survived the Reformation.

Grandison left elaborate instructions for his funeral. Huge candles were to burn around his body 'which is corruptible and hath weighed down my soul'; a night's vigil would be kept, in which 'all drinking of spiced wine' would be forbidden 'under pain of divine displeasure'. The main invitees were to be visiting bishops – no members of his family or local aristocrats – and they would have their travelling expenses paid and be given a souvenir mitre and pontifical ring to take away. Grandison's collection of European artworks and

specially commissioned books was to be distributed among his friends, colleagues and the religious houses of the see, especially the cathedral and Ottery St Mary. One hundred poor people would be clothed. His body was to be buried in its tiny, ornate chapel with a lead plate upon it: 'here lies John Grandison, the piteous bishop of Exeter, most miserable servant of the Mother of Mercy'.[36]

Grandison did not in fact die until 1368: he was still bishop when William Joy oversaw the installation of the first statues on the west front. Yet in 1348 the project stopped in its tracks, half-finished, and William Joy was never heard of again; the Black Death had swept him away, and at the same time the impetus that had sustained building work for seventy years evaporated. The cathedral itself was effectively complete,[37] and apart from the building of stone screens in the side chapels, a thundering Perpendicular tomb chest for Walter Bronescombe, and the rebuilding of the upper parts of the chapter-house after a fire in 1413, there was little further building work thereafter.[38] The biggest casualty was iconographic: although work restarted on the west front in the 1370s, it was not fully equipped with statues until the fifteenth century, and in 1390 the cathedral's main east window was 'amended and repaired'. The glazier, Robert Lyen, moved much glass from the old window and added new scenes (he was paid 20 pence a foot), making a mess of its original meaning.[39] As a result the key clues to the building's imagery are hard to decipher, and both the great east window and the west front's north door are unexpected outbreaks of Perpendicular in a church that is otherwise stylistically homogeneous. In such details lie the traces of the moment a great cathedral project was struck by the plague.

Exeter's fifteenth-century bishops managed another near-saint: after Bishop Lacy died in 1455, there were rumours of miracles at his tomb.[40] And in the decades before the Reformation, Exeter saw something of a mini-rebirth. Bishop Oldham indulged in reform and education, giving the vicars a common hall in 1508 and the chantry priests a college of their own as late as 1528. In 1518 and 1519 Oldham and a local magnate, Sir John Speke, built themselves a pair of intimate, richly patterned chapels in the east end. Oldham's robust effigy in his chantry chapel exemplifies the lordly extravagance of late medieval bishops. There is little piety but plenty of character in its blocky, gaudy carving. Oldham was said to have had 'more zeal than knowledge, and more devotion than learning', and to have been 'somewhat rough in speeches but friendly in doings', though he helped found educational colleges in Manchester and Oxford.[41] The stone owls that pepper the chantry's walls are a pun on his name. Oldham's precentor, Sylke, created another fine chantry chapel in the north transept, where his shrivelled corpse is dominated by a huge painting of the Resurrection, a further extension of the idea featured on the earlier tombs of Grandison and Stapeldon.

The Reformation was comparatively kind to Exeter. Although anti-Reformation rebels laid siege to it in 1549,[42] the church got one of the sixteenth century's more admirable bishops, in the shape of Miles Coverdale, in 1550. During the Commonwealth the church was divided: Presbyterians held their meetings in one half, Independents in another.[43] The reredos, rood and much stained glass and painting have been lost, but the cathedral still has one of the best collections of medieval fittings in the country. Two bays of the choir and adjacent chapels were destroyed on 4 May 1942, when the Luftwaffe flattened much of historic Exeter; fortunately most of the cathedral's fittings and much of its glass were in safekeeping.

Exeter today stands alongside Wells and Ely as a breathtaking and loveable monument to English architecture's most extraordinary years. It has wonderful architecture and first-rate monuments, painting, glass, fixtures and fittings. Yet it is most powerfully an insight into what could happen when brilliant designers worked with committed patrons. Inside, from the medieval cat door in the tower to the towering bishop's throne, there is a place for everything, and everything has its place. It is as if all nature is contained within the church.[44] That all this life is trapped in stone seems fitting, for this beguiling building is ultimately a statement of order and power, something rock hard falling over itself to seem benign and beguiling – an iron fist in a velvet glove.

WHAT TO SEE

St Peter, Exeter
Secular cathedral, moved to Exeter 1050.

Church: Decorated architecture; romanesque towers.

Fittings: one of the best collections in the country. Choir fittings, including misericords, bishop's throne, sedilia and pulpitum; tombs, including those of Stapeldon and Bronescombe; chantry chapel to precentor Sylke and bishops Speke and Oldham; wall paintings in north transept and choir ambulatory.

Carvings: rewarding sculptural detail throughout, from the west front (look out for the Nativity scene in the southern doorway) to the choir ambulatory (look out for a boss in which caterpillars are apparently indulging in synchronized salad-munching).

Setting: the close is the best historic area in much-bombed Exeter, though it has lost several churches and chapels, as well the once-grand cloister.

GLOUCESTER

Death stalks Gloucester. If it were not for some of the darker twists and turns of royal history, the abbey of St Peter there might have become nothing more than a pile of rubble in a faintly run-down county town. It is thanks to these burials that it has survived: a building full of ground-breaking architectural experiments and murderous narratives, and the most rewarding of all the monasteries that became cathedrals at the Reformation. Fittingly, its history is closely bound up with a remarkable series of tombs.

The abbey's royal associations are ancient, but never straightforward. It was founded in the seventh century by Osric, prince of the Hwicce tribe.[1] The city in which it stood became a prosperous trading centre in the see of Worcester, but its royal associations remained significant: Gloucester, along with Winchester, was the only venue for the Anglo-Saxon kings' annual crown-wearing ritual, which was continued by the Normans.[2]

The first Norman abbot, Serlo, came from Mont-Saint-Michel in 1072. He found the church newly rebuilt,[3] but monastic standards in decline. There were just two monks and six novices; the last abbot had responded to the challenge of the new regime by going on pilgrimage to Jerusalem. Serlo's first priority was reform rather than architecture, but when he did start to rebuild, he did so on an exceptional scale. Three hundred years after his death, the monks at Gloucester still remembered that

The murdered King Edward II is depicted as youthful, almost Christ-like, on his tomb at Gloucester; scene of miracles that transformed medieval architecture

Serlo's 'decisions were swift' and that 'with lightness of manners he did not please himself'.[4] He was certainly a man of action. He attracted donations of land from Norman mag-nates.[5] He enlarged the community rapidly, reaching one hundred monks before later stabilizing at around fifty. At its peak, Gloucester was one of the largest monasteries in the country.

Something of Serlo's hard-headedness is revealed in his church, begun in 1089. No mason would have designed a church whose choir and nave elevations were entirely different, with a gallery in the east end and a triforium in the nave. The tiny gallery in the nave is apparently copied from that at Mont-Saint-Michel; the design must have been

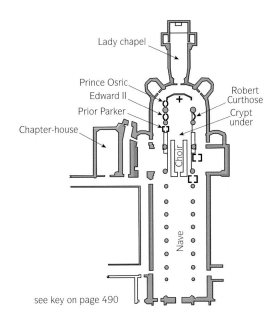

see key on page 490

339

Birth of Perpendicular: a taut grid of lines cover Gloucester's south transept

insisted on by Serlo, for reasons unknown.[6] His masons had probably worked on the Bishop's chapel at Hereford and the new cathedral at Worcester, both individualistic buildings that played with a wide range of influences.[7] Gloucester shares features with both, and like Worcester and only a handful of other churches it has the ambitious combination of radiating eastern chapels *and* a crypt. But Gloucester took such motifs further. Its masons experimented at every turn with geometry, for example in the many types of arch used in the process of vaulting the crypt. Its choir may also have been vaulted in stone, with a series of rib-like arches fanning down over the eastern apse; and as the nave went on to be vaulted, too, this was perhaps one of the first churches anywhere to be vaulted in stone throughout.[8]

Gloucester's designer loved to play sophisticated games with polygons. The eastern end of his church was semicircular outside, but three-sided within; the angles of its sides were derived not from a hexagon – which would be logical – but from three sides of an invisible octagon.[9] And in the elephant-leg columns of his nave, he coined one of the signature motifs of Anglo-Norman architecture, a self-conscious evocation of Roman Gloucester, where the bath house had columns of almost exactly the same height.[10] Serlo's church was dedicated in 1100, and its nave was perhaps finished over the next couple of decades (one of its fittings illustrated p. 73).

The abbey's first post-Conquest brush with ambivalent royalty took place in 1135. Robert Curthose, duke of Normandy and eldest son of William the Conqueror, had spent much of his life struggling to wrest the English Crown from his brothers, William II and Henry I. He spent his last twenty-eight years imprisoned in Cardiff castle, and asked to be buried at Gloucester. His wooden, painted effigy now sits in the ambulatory. But this tomb was made decades later, during Gloucester's next encounter with royal history.

At the death of King John in 1216, the court moved fast to anoint his young son Henry as his successor. John was buried at nearby Worcester; London was politically off-limits, so the nine-year-old boy was hastily crowned in St Peter's. In the ensuing decades the abbey was given an Early English makeover, while shoring up its royal associations.

Under the guidance of the sacrist, Elias, two towers were built, one in the centre of the building and one at the west end (both now lost). New monastic buildings went up, the convent's water supply was upgraded, a (lost) lady chapel was built and the Early English nave vault was completed in 1242; the church was even rededicated.[11] The exquisite 'treasury' screen now in the north transept may have been the pulpitum, a fitting climax to the updated nave.[12] Finally, the abbey's history was celebrated in two 'fake' retrospective effigies. That of Robert Curthose helped to emphasize the monastery's royal associations; that now on a bracket in the choir is probably of Serlo himself, posing as the church's founder.[13]

This brief heyday did not last. From the 1240s until at least the 1280s, Gloucester was badly in debt, at least partly because of over-generous hospitality to VIPs, and was often in dispute with the bishops of Worcester.[14] The nave vault was badly bodged – the monks, it was said, had to dismiss the masons and complete it themselves.[15] But by 1318 Gloucester was back in the black, and had some serious architectural catching up to do. A cluster of local monasteries were rebuilding their east ends in the Decorated style at this time,[16] and Gloucester had problems of it own: the nave, which ran over the site of the ditch outside the Roman city wall, was in structural trouble. A team of masons from the Marches covered a nave aisle with ball-flower ornament; another from Bristol began a characteristically eccentric update of the gallery chapels. Both focused on the south side of the church, which faced the lay cemetery and the town. Perhaps it was hoped to continue by renewing the east end.[17]

But at this moment, Gloucester experienced an extraordinary event. The burial here of Edward II

Gloucester's east window contains one of the greatest expanses of medieval stained glass in England

Even Gloucester's stalls respect its revolutionary tracery patterns

important abbey in the see already had some suitable royal connections.[18] The Crown took full control of the funeral. The young Edward III and Isabella were there in person. Images of gold, including eight angels swinging golden censers, surrounded the hearse, which was followed by a 'procession consisting of the entire town'. Perhaps it was hoped that things would end there; but there was something totemic about a murdered king. Miracles began at the tomb; 'the offerings of the faithful . . . were such that the city . . . could hardly hold the multitude of people flowing there from the cities, towns and hamlets of England'.[19]

In 1330 the young Edward III asserted his kingship, pushed aside his mother and her lover, and set about repairing the political damage of the previous decade. He had already visited his father's tomb, and made a series of donations both to the abbey and the incipient 'shrine'. He even fuelled the cult, claiming that he had been delivered from a storm at sea after invoking his father, and presenting the abbey with a golden boat as a thanks-offering. Such senior figures as the Black Prince, the Queen of Scotland and Queen Philippa, among 'a variety of lords and ladies', also gave expensive jewels to the 'shrine'.[20] Clearly, the dead king needed a suitable tomb. Here a delicate balancing act had to be struck: was this the tomb of an uncanonized saint or of an unpopular king?

The resulting structure comes as close to being a saint's shrine as a tomb can without actually being one: it is also the single most breathtaking English royal tomb of any age. Standing on the north side of the choir, it is a thing of bewildering beauty. A sheath of dark polished stone encloses the tomb chest, into which recesses of pale limestone are let. These recesses once held statues; they are also deep enough to be used by people seeking miraculous cures. Lying on the tomb chest, his eyes wide open, Edward's body is far from the tortured form it must have taken at its death: here is the

was the fulcrum around which turns the architecture not just of St Peter's, Gloucester, but all late medieval England. As with Robert Curthose, the story begins unhappily and in Wales.

The fleeing Edward II was captured by his barons in November 1326 on a Welsh hillside. They imprisoned him in Berkeley castle, just 15 miles south of Gloucester, and after a few months had him murdered there. It was the end of two years of civil war, and the first time an English king had been murdered by his own barons. For a time the country was run by Edward II's widow, Isabella, and her lover, the great Marcher lord Roger Mortimer. The king's body was far too sensitive to be buried in Westminster abbey (or, more to the point, Worcester cathedral), but luckily the most

king incorrupt, ready for the moment of resurrection. He gazes up into a maze of tabernacles and exotically stretched ogee arches, imprisoned in a world halfway between a cage of stone and a glimpse of heaven. This is court-related work of the highest order. It marks both an apogee and a cusp in medieval art: the end of a story of a taste for objects of ever-increasing inventiveness and elaboration, which went back a century or more. Its precise date is unknown.

In 1331 or 1332, soon after Edward III seized the reins of power, work began again on the southern side of the building. This time there is nothing provincial about the architecture. Over three years, the south transept was transformed into something breathtakingly new, funded by offerings at the dead king's tomb. The aesthetic fracture-line at Gloucester lies precisely here, between the tomb of Edward II and the south transept. In the Gloucester south transept the flowing lines and richly carved detailing have gone: instead, a simple grid of stone is imposed on the building. It is as if the vertical mullions separating the panels of the window have been turned from necessary evils into the starting point for an entirely new style of architecture. When they have finished doing their usual job – holding panels of glass – they run on, over stretches of wall and open voids, like the tightened strings of some great stone instrument.

To do this, the architect of the south transept had skinned several inches off each wall of the Norman church, and then grafted his new design over the top. This is plastic surgery, yet it has a deep respect for the skeleton beneath. The entire south wall of the transept was taken down and re-erected, with a new window placed within it but the Norman designs in the gable above intact; twelfth-century chevron patterns are reused – some short new stretches even created – to decorate the arches of the transept's windows.[21]

The Gloucester south transept is arguably the most brilliant of the many extraordinary English buildings of the 1320s and 1330s (see chapter four). It was certainly the most influential, not least at Gloucester itself. The community went on immediately to rebuild their choir on the same lines 'at vast expense' and paid for entirely from pilgrims' offerings.[22] Extraordinarily, there is no sign of a pause at the time of the Black Death; the choir was complete by 1367 (illustrated pp. 129, 229).

Perhaps not unexpectedly, the theme of this choir is sacred kingship. The single, glass-filled space of the choir makes it a giant descendant of royal chapels, themselves designed to look like saints' shrines.[23] The glass of the east window confirms the theme, laying out the entire feudal order like a management chart, from the heraldry of local barons at the base, running through the

The new technique of fan vaulting was shown off to spectacular effect in Gloucester's cloisters

Gloucester's Perpendicular central tower was a magnificent addition to the Norman structure beneath

church had been recased in the new architecture, and a new cloister was well under way, generating yet more architecture that is at once utterly new, utterly perfect, and apparently leaping fully formed from nowhere.[26] The cloister was glazed throughout, an expensive luxury, and in it the Gloucester masons produced the ultimate architectural expression of the style they were coining. The 'fan vault' took the underlying philosophy of Gloucester's architecture and applied it to a roof, creating long corridors whose smooth-coned vaults echo the patterns on window and wall, creating an extraordinary sense of enclosure and unity. The idea had, it seems, been tried in the chapter-house of Hereford cathedral. Although its full potential would not be realized for a century,[27] the fan vault would eventually be reborn in some of the greatest buildings of the medieval age.

Gloucester's fourteenth-century designs have their roots in a tiny circle of masons involved with the court, fuelled by a series of recent West Country experiments. The same motifs were used at almost exactly the same time in St Paul's cathedral chapter-house, a few years later at Edward III's new works in Windsor, and then at an increasing number of other buildings. By the time the cloisters were complete in 1412, the motifs coined at Gloucester in the 1330s dominated English architecture completely, forming the style we now call Perpendicular. It seems that a close circle of people around the young Edward III had helped move taste decisively away from the excesses of his father's years, while suitably honouring his memory.

St Peter's abbey was now at a high point in its fortunes. Richard II maintained Edward III's interest in Edward II: indeed, he seems to have positively identified with him, making generous offerings at the tomb-shrine and trying hard (and unsuccessfully) to have him canonized. Richard's crest of a white hart can still be seen painted on the Norman capitals near Edward II's tomb. After implementing

bishops (and, pointedly, abbots) who ran the English church, through the saints and the apostles, to Christ in Majesty at the top, all centred around a scene of Christ and Mary sitting regally in heaven.[24] In the vault, a small angel choir plays eternal praises. The designer of all this had a distinct aesthetic vision, and applied it to every aspect of his building. The glass of the east window was filled with air bubbles during the glass-making process, creating a shining quality that softens its colours and makes it very different in effect from the dense tones favoured in other churches (compare illustrations pp. 341, 439). The choir-stalls use the same straight-edged tracery patterns found in the windows.

Now the abbot gave £444 – over half of the total cost[25] – so that work could continue on the north transept. By 1373 the entire Norman east arm of the

an unpopular poll tax, Richard held a Parliament in Gloucester in 1378; once again, a contentious royal activity was held in Gloucester rather than London. The abbot was mitred, giving him procedural parity with bishops, in 1402; and the proud abbey commissioned its own history, the *Historiola*, at about the same time.[28]

If it were not for the extraordinary events of the fourteenth century, the church at Gloucester – if it existed at all – would be remembered for some Norman work of importance to the cognoscenti, and for some tremendous crowd-pleasers of the fifteenth century: the central tower, begun 1450–7, powering upwards draped in panelling of lace-like richness, the thick, linear loveliness of the lady chapel, begun 1468–82, and several chantry chapels. The sumptuous retiling of much of the east end (illustrated p. 226), and the rebuilding of the western bays of the nave, suggest the real possibility that the church would have been gradually made entirely Perpendicular in style.[29] Yet these later works are themselves a testimony to the significance of fourteenth-century Gloucester: nearly two hundred years after the south transept was built, architectural style had barely moved on at all. The story of the choir, transepts and cloister leaves these otherwise tremendous buildings rather badly upstaged.

Gloucester looked to its history again as Reformation loomed. In the late fifteenth century the effigy of Robert Curthose, which by then lay centre stage in the middle of the choir, was given added prominence in the shape of a new tomb-chest;[30] and in the 1530s a retrospective tomb to Prince Osric, the abbey's seventh-century founder, was placed next to that of Edward II, in a pointed and well-timed reminder of Gloucester's royal pedigree ('Osricus Rex' was written on it).[31] As late as 1540 a chantry chapel for William Parker,[32] the last abbot, was completed, though he died after the Dissolution and was never buried there.

Gloucester's tombs did their job: Henry VIII was shown around the church in 1535 by Abbot Parker, and in 1541 decided to make it a new cathedral, because of the 'many famous monuments of our renowned ancestors, kings of England' that were buried there.[33] Yet the tombs hide a curious fact: only one is what it appears to be.[34] Those of Curthose, Serlo and Osric are not tombs but retrospective monuments; Parker's chantry is empty; and Edward II's tomb wants us to believe that its occupant is a saint (and one conspiracy theory says that the king is not there at all).[35]

Here is a building whose very history is partly guided by its series of empty or ambivalent tombs, and whose revolutionary architecture involves the simultaneous death and reinvention, skinning and reclothing, of the church itself. There is a very medieval kind of thinking wrapped up in Gloucester cathedral; without the faintly grisly story of its tombs and the architecture they inspired, the entire church might have vanished forever.

WHAT TO SEE

St Peter, now Holy Trinity, Gloucester Monastery/nunnery founded c. 681; secular minster by 823; Benedictine monastery from c. 1022; secular cathedral 1541.

Church: Norman crypt and nave arcade; Early English nave vaults and thirteenth-century 'treasury' in north transept; fourteenth-century reinvention of the east end, especially the south transept and choir; fan vaults in the cloisters; fifteenth-century lady chapel and central tower.

Fittings: tomb-shrine to Edward II and other effigies/chantries; choir stalls; stained glass in the east window.

HEREFORD

Edith the 'furiosa' of Hereford was carried into the cathedral shortly before Easter 1287. She was suffering from fits: she had bitten her mother and attacked her husband. For a week she was carried between the church's two most promising healing sites, the lady chapel and the altar of the Holy Rood in the nave. Then 'a certain cleric' suggested the tomb of the previous bishop, Thomas Cantilupe, which stood in the lady chapel. At first her visit there seemed to have had no obvious effect. But back at the Holy Rood altar, Edith's fury left her. It was Thomas, she claimed, who was responsible.[1]

Edith's cure was something of a triumph for the cathedral authorities, because thanks to her, the most brazenly manufactured of English cathedral saints' cults was born. Its story links the local – little villages such as Madley and Sugwas, the city of Hereford itself – to Rome, Lyons and London; its architectural traces are by turns self-consciously continental and narrowly provincial. Much the same could be said of the cathedral as a whole.

———

This church had its roots in the kingdom of the Magonsaetan, squeezed between the Mercians and the Welsh, which is known to have had a bishop in Hereford by the eighth century.[2] This cathedral acquired the head of St Ethelbert, king of the East Anglians, murdered by King Offa of Mercia and

Hereford's distinctive Romanesque west front, fourteenth-century western tower and central spire – all now lost – are depicted in this nineteenth-century window in the cathedral

dumped near the River Lugg. But his relics were lost, along with the recently rebuilt 'glorious minster' itself, in 1055, when the cathedral was burnt down by Saxon rebels and their Welsh allies.[3]

In 1079 Robert of Lotharingia became the first new bishop after the Norman Conquest. His private chapel 'of elegant form' was modelled on Charlemagne's chapel in Aachen and other palace chapels of Robert's native Germany.[4] A single wall remains. In spite of his architectural interests and his energetic reform of the chapter, Robert was one of the only Norman bishops *not* to rebuild his cathedral.[5] Perhaps local concerns were more focused on establishing William the Conqueror's authority in the Marches than with cathedral building. The power of the local aristocracy was

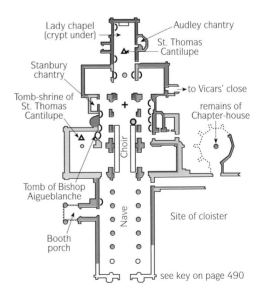

see key on page 490

long to be an important factor in these borderlands, and Hereford's cathedral never dominated its city like some others did.

It was Reinhelm, bishop between 1107 and 1115, who began to build a new cathedral. It took about thirty years to complete.[6] Originally the church had towers to the east and west as well as the centre,[7] and some of the carving in its many surviving romanesque parts is influenced by the local Herefordshire school of masons, who evocatively melded the art of the Celts, Anglo-Saxons, Vikings and French.[8]

Hereford's east end was rebuilt in the years around 1200. Dimunitive chapel-like eastern transepts, a retrochoir/ambulatory where the shrine of St Ethelbert stood, and a lady chapel with a crypt were added, and the choir itself vaulted and given a new clerestory. The break between the early gothic retrochoir and the rich twilight world of the Early English lady chapel may mark the period of Bishop de Braose's flight to France during the interdict (see p. 93). The crypt is unusual in position and late in date for such a structure; its function is not known.[9]

This church attracted an intellectual chapter. Hereford was called a 'city of philosophers' in the 1190s.[10] Residency here was high: between 25 and 50 per cent of the canons at a time might be resident in the close. The prebends of the thirty-three members of chapter were low in value, while the rewards for residency included free bread from the communal bakehouse. This system discouraged careerist 'prebend collectors' and attracted those with local connections or academic interests:[11] men like Bishop Robert himself (d. 1095), who could read Arabic and compiled astrological tables based on records of eclipses gathered in Islamic Toledo, Oc-speaking Marseilles and Anglo–Saxon–Norman–Welsh Hereford itself; or Bishop Gerard (d. 1108), said to have been a slave to evil practices because of his suspicious interest in classical authors;[12] or Robert Grosseteste (d. 1253), the translator of Greek

classics, philosopher and later bishop of Lincoln, who did much of his most important work while an administrator for the bishop of Hereford.[13] Even in the fifteenth century, 30 per cent of the canons had doctorates and two-thirds were local men.[14] They acquired vicars only gradually, often as a result of lay donations of land. The cathedral reflects this: small in scale, with many piecemeal alterations and one of the largest and oldest medieval libraries in existence.

The century after 1240 was the most dramatic in Hereford's history. Peter d'Aigueblanche (d. 1268) came from Savoy, a European centre of learning and art. In 1240, after having only been in England a year, he became keeper of the King's Wardrobe and bishop of Hereford. Henry tried several times to have Aigueblanche translated to more fitting bishoprics – Lincoln, St Paul's and Durham – and his repeated failure is perhaps a symptom of the bad feeling this bishop generated.[15] Aigueblanche spent much of his time on royal business in Gascony, Naples, Toledo, Rome or Canterbury, where he worked for the Savoyard archbishop. He helped Henry III develop a series of projects that demanded ever-increasing taxes of the church, culminating in a planned English invasion of Sicily in 1256. This foolish scheme left the king bankrupt, helping trigger the baronial rebellion led by Simon de Montfort. The king's Savoyard placemen were widely hated as a result (see p. 114).

Aigueblanche did a decent job as bishop of Hereford. The cathedral's statutes and liturgy were revised and codified.[16] But his reputation had been tarnished by national events, reflected locally in the appointment of about twenty Savoyards to the Hereford chapter.[17] De Montfort's power base was local, among the Marcher lords, and in 1252 Hereford's Gascon dean was murdered at the high altar; in 1263, they arrested Peter himself in the cathedral.

The bishop was ageing, and once released, he began to prepare for his own death. He had founded a collegiate church in his home town of Aiguebelle in the south of France,[18] where he originally planned to be buried. However, probably by 1257 he had begun to build a new north transept at the cathedral,[19] and before he died, one November night in Sugwas in 1268, he changed his mind and asked to be buried at Hereford.[20]

Aigueblanche's north transept bends over backwards to look sophisticated and cosmopolitan, sticking archly out from a battered Herefordshire barn of a cathedral. It is an independent-minded version of Henry III's Westminster abbey, itself the most French building of its age. With its painfully thin shafting, near-triangular arches and geometrical game-playing, there is a self-conscious stiffness about it. It is hard not to read it as one-in-the-eye for the barbarian barons of the Marches, with Aigueblanche's beautiful tomb as its climax.

Meanwhile Hereford's next-but-one bishop, Thomas Cantilupe, had come to prominence. He was briefly chancellor of England in 1265, part of the council forced on Henry III after de Montfort's rebellion. A cosmopolitan lawyer and administrator, Thomas had spent much of his life in the universities of Oxford, Paris and Lyons as well as in the service of the king, but he also had local connections: his sister had married into the local aristocracy, and his uncle was bishop at neighbouring Worcester.[21] When he became bishop in 1275, it might have seemed more a home-coming than a posting to the outer reaches.

Thomas was a man who did everything properly – perhaps a little too properly. He was fastidious and self-controlled in his habits, be they the approval of state documents or the giving of scraps from his table to the poor. For a man like John Pecham, the Franciscan archbishop of Canterbury, he must have epitomized the worldly proprieties of the secular church. Pecham dressed only in a battered habit, and once walked barefoot to a meeting in Pavia; Cantilupe may have secretly suffered

A man wrestles a bear in a twelfth-century manuscript from Hereford's library, creation of an exceptionally scholarly chapter

in his hair shirt, but outwardly he entertained lavishly, with all the rich trappings of his station. Not surprisingly, Thomas and the archbishop fell out badly. Pecham was using every power he had to interfere in the affairs of his bishops, mostly because he wanted to reform them; Thomas saw this as an infringement of his rights, and fought his ground.

After one particularly frosty meeting in Lambeth palace, Thomas found he had been excommunicated. He went to Rome twice in an effort to get the sentence lifted. His objection was not merely that it was unjust: there were procedures for these things, and Pecham had not followed them. Now around sixty years of age, he died near Rome in 1282, his Hereford *familia* at his bedside. Being a bishop, excommunicate, and far from home made his burial something of a challenge. His colleagues boiled his body,[22] burying the flesh in a monastery

The controversial Bishop d'Aigueblanche built Hereford's self-consciously sophisticated north transept

near Orvieto, and brought his heart and bones back home to England, where the heart was buried with a small monastic community. When they entered England, Thomas' bones quietly began to shed blood. After delicate negotiations, Pecham allowed them to be buried at Hereford.

Cantilupe's supporters saw him as a kind of martyr, albeit for episcopal propriety rather than the burning flames of faith. One of them, Richard Swinfield, was appointed his successor. With Pecham still archbishop, the bishop's men at Hereford stewed over their former master's death. If Cantilupe had a cult at this stage, it was restricted to his bitter friends: only they ever claimed to have noticed miracles when he was alive, and few even claimed

that he was an especially virtuous man.[23] But a couple of years after his death, Swinfield and his colleagues began to encourage prayers for the dead bishop's soul and praise him to local clergy. Enquiries were even made to see whether any miracles had occurred at the site of his heart burial.

In 1287, Swinfield decided to give the bishop's bones a far higher profile. A grand translation was planned for Easter Monday, into a shrine-like tomb next to that of Bishop d'Aigueblanche in the new north transept (illustrated p. 115).[24] Even bishops with substantial posthumous cults were rarely given such treatment. Then, a few days before the translation, Edith of Hereford arrived in the cathedral. She had clearly not heard of the bishop, and even her claims that Thomas was the agent of her healing sound faintly unconvinced. But that did not stop Robert Chevening, one of the bishop's officials, reacting quickly. The cathedral bells were rung; the Te Deum was sung. Rumours must have spread immediately. The priests of the diocese were sent slips of parchment confirming that a miracle had occurred. Suddenly, Hereford was at the centre of things.[25]

The next day was Good Friday, a busy day at the cathedral. Chevening sat hopefully by his former master's tomb. He was not disappointed. A woman called Juliana appeared, carrying her crippled daughter in a wicker basket. Gilbert the Minstrel was carried in on a stretcher. Both had heard of Edith's good fortune; both were walking within minutes. Another Te Deum was sung; more bells were rung; more priests got excited; more pilgrims came. Three days later, the great translation took place.

It was like throwing fuel on a fire. Initially, Chevening got his fingers burnt: Thomas was an excommunicate, and co-opting him as a saint was, as far as Archbishop Pecham was concerned, just the kind of game that cathedral clerics played. Chevening was suspended for a week. But even

Bishop Swinfield must have been astonished by what happened next. Seventy more miracles occurred over the next month: all involved local people, mostly women, and all were healed during visits to the tomb itself. Over the next year there were ninety more, mostly involving people who lived within 70 miles or so of Hereford who had also visited the shrine in person, and a further 310 were recorded over the next fifteen years.

Swinfield and his chapter responded on two fronts. First, they initiated an energetic lobbying campaign in Rome, the first result of which was the arrival in 1307 of papal commissioners, investigating Cantilupe's claims to sainthood. By this time St Thomas was intervening miraculously far from the actual shrine site: people as far afield as Cornwall, Ireland and Yorkshire had successfully invoked him without visiting Hereford. His shrine had been visited by the king and queen, and alternative pilgrimage sites associated with Cantilupe's life were developing.[26] Between 2,400 and 9,600 extra pilgrims a year were passing through Worcester on their way to Hereford.[27] At Thomas's tomb-shrine in the north transept the commissioners counted the offerings left by those who had been cured: 211 ships, most of them silver, left by those rescued from peril at sea; over 1,500 images of men or their limbs, left by those cured or ailments and injuries, and 77 more of 'animals and birds of diver species' left in thanks for cures to valued livestock; 108 crutches; wooden vehicles (left by cured cripples); nightgowns, jewellery and other clothing; and a 'multitude' of wax eyes, breasts and ears, chains, anchors, lances and arrows.[28] Even as they sat to count the offerings, 85 more were left. The cult's original context of high politics had been left far behind; the multilingual populace of the Marches had found a healing cult that united them.

The commissioners went on to cross-examine those involved in 205 of the most likely sounding miracles and return a vast amount of paperwork to Rome, where Swinfield maintained the pressure. But the bishop had already begun the second, architectural, flank of his response to the cult. As early as 1290–1, three-quarters of the cathedral fabric fund came from offerings at Cantilupe's tomb; by the time the commissioners arrived in 1307, the cathedral had a new central tower, a renewed western tower, and an upgraded pilgrim route, featuring a new north porch (the main entrance from the city), and updated architecture along the nave aisles. Work had also begun on upgrading the choir aisles, in anticipation of a successful outcome in Rome and a translation of St Thomas to a grand new shrine back in the lady chapel. Here, windows and other details were also updated – in the aisles, where the pilgrims would have seen them, rather than the more exclusive choir – and the route was lined with a series of ten 'retrospective' bishops' tombs, a reminder of Hereford's long history.[29]

Ironically, by this time the cult had peaked;[30] in 1312 only one miracle was recorded. But Swinfield and his associates had already gathered written testimonials from the great and the good, and had Cantilupe's excommunication examined and declared null and void. Now they sent Chevening himself to the papal curia, where he doggedly lobbied on Hereford's behalf. Finally, in 1320, three years after Swinfield's death, the pope declared himself satisfied. Thomas Cantilupe had triumphed over other English putative saints such as Robert Grosseteste of Lincoln and Walter Suffield of Norwich to become the last but one 'official' English cathedral saint of the Middle Ages.

A shrine was immediately commissioned, and liturgy devised for the new saint's feasts.[31] Cantilupe would be moved back to the lady chapel. But although at least £120 was spent, the translation did not finally take place until 1349. Edward III was healed on his way to the ceremony; the bones were kissed by the VIPs; it was even claimed that the Black Death abated afterwards. All this had

Funded by the dramatic cult of Bishop Cantilupe, Hereford's central tower is covered in the fourteenth-century ornament known as ballflower

little impact on the cult itself: by 1386, offerings amounted to no more than 26 shillings in a year.[32]

Between Edith's cure in 1287 and the early fourteenth century, a kind of charismatic revival had swept over the Marches, and its architectural traces are still evident in Herefordshire today. At Madley, where an image of the Virgin attracted pilgrims, the parish church was rebuilt on a grand scale, while elsewhere other local cults were promoted, dozens of churches reconstructed. Architecture in a Decorated style identical to that at the cathedral can be seen in perhaps half of all Herefordshire churches.[33]

This architecture has a great story, but it is not great architecture. There is something rather utilitarian about these designs in dense red sandstone.

At their most ambitious, they spread like a rash: the central tower at Hereford picked up the fruit-like motif known as 'ballflower' from the new Wells chapter-house, and from there it spread contagiously to Leominster, Gloucester and elsewhere.[34] There is a perceptible fall-off in ambition between Hereford's central tower and its remodelled east end, perhaps reflecting the fact that the expected income had not been sustained. And perhaps, like Bishop Swinfield, who rarely left his diocese,[35] this is architecture whose main concern is its locality: the polar opposite, oddly enough, of Bishop Aigueblanche's cosmopolitan transept in which most of the miracles took place. This is local architecture for local people.

Hereford is a relatively humble, multi-period building: view from the north transept (d'Aigueblanche's tomb, left) into the south

After the Black Death, Hereford's story was less dramatic. There was clearly a certain amount of pride among the chapter in the wake of the creation of their new saint, for in the mid-fourteenth century they installed the fine wooden choir-stalls and bishop's throne that still stand in their choir, and by 1337 they had began work on a ten-sided chapter-house, only for it to be interrupted by the plague. In 1364 work restarted, now with what was possibly England's first fan vault.[36] This was a wonderful building, and a fitting end to England's great run of polygonal secular cathedral chapter-houses. It has been in ruins since the eighteenth century.

The vicars choral, formed into a college in 1395, had a close built for them in 1472. This pleasant cloister of houses has a covered walkway to the cathedral, preventing the vicars from being 'so distant from the church that through fear of evil doers and the inclemency of the weather' they could not get to midnight services.[37]

Like all secular cathedrals, Hereford did not need a main cloister; but one was built anyway, very slowly, from around 1412 (illustrated p. 241) It helped create an exclusive burial area, 'Our Lady's Arbour', enhancing the setting of one of the cathedral's most staunchly protected rights: a complete monopoly on burials in the city. Hereford's parish churches lack churchyards to this very day. The south transept was given up-to-date Perpendicular windows in the early fifteenth century; but the really significant fifteenth-century additions to Hereford are its distinctive and delightful bishops' chantry chapels. Bishop Stanbury's fan-vaulted chapel is the first; he died in 1480. Bishop Audley's chantry, built before 1502, is an oriel-like polygonal attachment to the lady chapel with two floors, influenced by the royal college of St George's, Windsor, where Audley was a canon; after 1516 he became bishop of Salisbury, where he built a second chantry chapel. The Booth Porch, a lovely extension to the main lay entrance to the cathedral, was built by 1519 – apparently to enable pilgrims to access an image of the Virgin in a little chapel above it. Bishop Booth's tomb was placed in the nave aisle nearby.[38]

Cantilupe's shrine was destroyed at the Reformation, but his bones were rescued. In later years they were even processed at night through the city, to ward off the plague; fragments are still honoured at Downside and Belmont; one has even been returned to a revived shrine in the cathedral.[39] In 1786 the Norman west front, with its distinctive single tower rising over an ornate facade, collapsed; much of the cloister and nave was destroyed. As a result, the nave is a bay shorter than originally planned, and much of the western half of the church dates from the late eighteenth century onwards.

Yet somehow, Hereford's modern additions only add to its organic charms. It is the architectural equivalent of the softly moulded sandstone hills in which it is set, an 'ordinary' cathedral, a very local embodiment of an international authority. Its history is as much a story of remarkable people as of grand architecture. Relative poverty, and consequent reliance on the communities around it, make it a fitting, if only fitfully inspiring, monument to the diocese in which it sits.

The story of Hereford cathedral is exemplified by its greatest treasure, the *Mappa mundi*. The *Mappa* appears to have been created for a canon of Lincoln who died in 1278 – the expensive, learned conversation piece of a wealthy churchman. It came to Hereford during the cathedral's post-Cantilupe heyday, perhaps as a gift, and there it was given a magnificent altarpiece-like setting; it may have become an added attraction of the pilgrim route. This great map of the world shows such exotica as the barns in Egypt where Joseph stored his wheat; the people of the east who lived on the scent of apples alone; and Jerusalem itself, spiritual and actual centre of the universe.[40] And in one corner, as near to the 'foreigners' of *Walha* as to *Anglia*, a little city sits on a stumpy River Wye.[41] Hereford, typically, is at once on the edge of the world, and at the very heart of it.

WHAT TO SEE

St Mary and St Ethelbert, Hereford
Secular cathedral, founded c.676

Church: lady chapel; Bishop d'Aigueblanche's north transept; tomb-shrine of St Thomas Cantilupe and associated works (central tower, bishop's tombs); *Mappa mundi* and chained library (post-medieval in its current form); woodwork (bishop's throne and choir-stalls); late medieval additions (Booth Porch, Audley chantry).

LICHFIELD

Two Irish pilgrims, Simon Simeon and Hugh the Illuminator, were on their way to Jerusalem in 1323 when they visited Lichfield cathedral. They found a building that was 'uncommon in its beauty, with towers of stone and the loftiest and most noble of belfries; the interior wonderfully furnished and adorned with murals, carvings, and other lovely and spiritual devices'.[1]

Some of this was unfinished; much of it was the work of a man in disgrace. Bishop Walter Langton, sometime treasurer of England, had spent the last thirty years turning Lichfield into a kind of fantasy cathedral, and had endured imprisonment, disgrace, and even an accusation of witchcraft in the process.[2]

Langton was bishop of an ancient church. Bishop Chad had moved the young (and hitherto peripatetic) see there in 669.[3] He spent much of his life converting pagan members of the Mercian royal family to Christianity, assisted by the occasional miracle. A century later, under King Offa, Mercia was at its height and Lichfield briefly the seat of an archbishop.[4] By the Conquest the complex included at least two churches and a magnificent shrine to St Chad, on which sat the beautiful Lichfield Gospels.[5]

Yet Lichfield was never a rich cathedral. The last Anglo-Saxon bishop resigned after the Normans accused him of being married; and the seat of the see was moved, first to Chester in 1075 and then to monastic Coventry sometime between 1087 and 1102, though the bishop remained patron of the Lichfield chapter. At some point between 1083 and 1100, rebuilding of the church began. In spite of this, the community may have almost completely disintegrated. Lacking a substantial 'common fund' with which to reward resident canons, this was always a cathedral with many absentees.[6]

Lichfield's fortunes improved from the mid-twelfth century. In the 1130s the Lichfield chapter was reformed, and in 1148 Lichfield became co-cathedral with Coventry. In 1189 one bishop tried (by force) to turn Coventry itself into a secular community; in 1222 and 1321 the Coventry monks tried to establish their right to elect bishops alone; on both occasions, papal decisions insisted on Lichfield's parity with Coventry.[7] Throughout this time the canons of Lichfield continued a gradual rebuilding process, each stage of which appears to

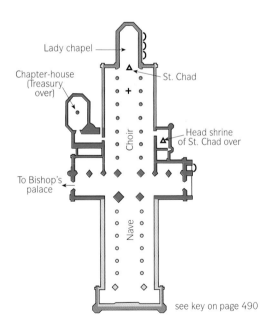

Lady chapel

Chapter-house (Treasury over)

St. Chad

Choir

Head shrine of St. Chad over

To Bishop's palace

Nave

see key on page 490

show greater self-confidence. The east end was extended in the mid-twelfth century and again, with much greater ambition, a few decades later:[8] the west end of the choir and the transepts were being rebuilt in the 1220s, the nave around the 1260s.

The chapter's ever-increasing power is most clearly expressed by two ancillary structures of the 1220s. The frothy little chapter-house was polygonal, perhaps inspired by that of Lincoln.[9] It is a two-storey building, shaped like a stretched octagon, with a secure room for the storage of archives, books and other treasures above a womb-like vaulted meeting room. The chapter at this period won the right to elect their own dean (rather than have him chosen by the bishop); his seat extends, throne-like, into the space, with room (just) for the then twenty-five canons.[10] The man responsible, Dean Mancetter, incorporated his own tomb into an unusual chapel of St Peter on the other side of the church, which seems to have been a sacristy-cum-office complex with shrine-like associations.[11]

The 1260s nave was grander still: it is poised, rich, refined work, one of the building's highlights.[12] The proportions of its elevation respected those of the choir, giving internal consistency to the building, which now had an entirely gothic interior.

Walter Langton became bishop in 1296, a reward for his role as Edward I's treasurer: he was known as the king's 'right eye'.[13] The scale of his work at Lichfield suggests that such bishops now saw the secular church as their main seat, though both Coventry and Lichfield had equal weight in electing new bishops.

As a career royal servant who was rarely in the see, Langton did not make an obvious builder-bishop; indeed, the see was not an obvious choice for such a high-profile man, although it did contain

Melding chivalric fantasy and New Jerusalem, Lichfield still makes a striking sight from Stowe Pool to its east

the strategic routes into recently conquered Wales.[14] Yet he completed the church, the west front of which stood half finished, and rebuilt the east end yet again, while from 1299 he turned his close into a great fantasy castle.

Langton placed a battlemented wall round the close,[15] and built houses for the canons, a smaller close for the vicars (1315) and a 'large and fair' bishop's palace (3,980 nails were bought over several years; two weeks were spent landscaping the gardens).[16] Langton's palace was remarkable for showing more interest in the recent and political than the timeless and the spiritual: it was a kind of miniature copy of Caernarfon castle, itself the result of some highly fanciful myth-making,[17] and decorated with 'very lively' paintings of the coronation, marriage and wars of Edward I.[18]

If all this suggests a certain lavish defensiveness, it was not without good reason. Langton had made enemies, not the least of whom was the king's son, the future Edward II (see chapter four). As early as 1301 Langton was accused of an extraordinary, presumably symbolic, range of crimes – adultery with his stepmother, murdering his father, and communicating with the Devil – as well as various kinds of ecclesiastical corruption. He was arrested almost immediately after Edward I's death in 1307.[19] His vast fortune, including estates worth over £5,000 annually, went to the Crown, much of it to the king's favourite, Piers Gaveston. He was later rehabilitated, even becoming treasurer again, but never acquired the pre-eminence he had had under the former king.

Before his imprisonment in 1307, Langton spent £2,000 on a new shrine to St Chad, bought from the goldsmiths of Paris using a loan from his Italian bankers, the Ballardi. After his 1312 rehabilitation he began building the glorious lady chapel as a setting for this shrine. In his will of 1322 he left £604 to ensure its completion[20] – money immediately 'borrowed' by the king to pay for his wars in

Walter Langton's spectacular lady chapel

Scotland. He must already have completed the west front and the cathedral's distinctive three spires. The west front is an extraordinary, dark confection of decorative patterns, virtually drawn on to the surface of the church; the three spires are its visual signature, and perhaps a riposte to Coventry's earlier screen facade and many-spired profile.[21]

But Langton's lady chapel is the church's highlight, an architectural homage to Edward I's greatest work of church architecture, St Stephen's chapel in the palace of Westminster,[22] itself abandoned as the king's wars became increasingly expensive. This apsidal-ended cage of glass rises the full height of the cathedral, creating a continuous vista from one end of the church to the other that belies the building's comparatively small size. Statues of the Wise and Foolish Virgins (now lost) once gazed down on performances of the lady mass; at the chapel's entrance, screened off from the high altar, stood St Chad's new shrine.

The barons now rebelled against Edward II, triggering a civil war. It took fifty years for the cathedral to get Langton's money back. The lady chapel was left only half-connected to the choir and presbytery, themselves in the process of being rebuilt. Not long after work restarted the Black Death struck, killing the brilliant master-mason, William Ramsey (who in 1337 was receiving £1 for each site visit, plus 6s 8d travelling expenses for himself and his servants). It was perhaps not until the 1360s that the presbytery, choir and lady chapel were complete, yet successive masters made a brave job of connecting the two in a way that harmonized both nave and lady chapel.

The essence of all this work – the renewed close, the bishop's palace, west front, spires, shrine and lady chapel – would have been a thrilling site to men like Simon and Hugh, approaching in 1323 from a recently subjugated Wales along ancient Watling Street. They would have entered the large diocese as soon as they reached Cheshire,[23] and not left it until they had passed through Warwickshire several days later. There were important outposts of episcopal authority at St John's, Chester as well as the cathedral priory of Coventry. But Lichfield itself was unmistakable. Home of the see's patron saint, its three blood-red spires rising above a castellated wall dominated by a Caernarfon-like palace, it must have appeared as much a chivalric fantasy as it did a New Jerusalem. On Palm Sunday, choirs sang from a hidden passage in the west front (see p. 197).[24] And the pilgrimage route round the church, still incomplete in 1323, had several highlights: the shrine of St Chad, the lady chapel and a head shrine, sited vertiginously above St Peter's chapel. Here the head of St Chad, which – as at many cathedrals – had its own shrine separate from his body, could be displayed to watching pilgrims.[25]

The Dean's stall has pride of place in Lichfield's crowded and ornate chapter-house

Charles II oversees restoration of the cathedral, battered in the Civil War: from a Victorian window at Lichfield

By the end of the fourteenth century the cathedral had been completed; unusually, few changes were made to the building in the fifteenth century. However, its later history was more turbulent than most: Lichfield today is partly a monument to the English Civil War, when it was besieged and stormed no fewer than three times. On each occasion the close held a garrison: the Parliamentarians were reported to have stabled their horses in the church, playing hunting games and holding mock baptisms. Both armies probably looted the tombs and sacristies. In the course of the Civil War, Lichfield lost its central spire, most of its vaults, and almost all its fittings and glass. In 1651 Parliament decided to 'dispose' of the cathedral altogether, to help the poor. Luckily the threat was never carried out, and during the reign of Charles II work began on restoring the church instead: it now has seventeenth-century nave vaults and other features.[26]

Lichfield's rust-dark sandstone ages poorly: much of its carved detail is Victorian, and occasional fragments of paint and stained glass, and some battered effigies, are the only medieval decorations and fittings. Yet thanks to the architectural energy generated by its thirteenth-century comeback and its fourteenth-century bishop-in-disgrace, it remains a consistent and alluring work of medieval architecture, capable of having almost as great an impact on us as it did on Simon Simeon and Hugh the Illuminator in 1323.

WHAT TO SEE

St Mary and St Chad, Lichfield
Secular cathedral, founded after 669; archbishopric 785–803; see moved to Chester in 1075 and then between 1087 and 1102 to Coventry; see held jointly with Coventry from mid-twelfth century to the Reformation.

Church: Early English chapter-house and (later) nave; Decorated lady chapel.

Anglo-Saxon treasures: Lichfield Gospels and recently discovered Lichfield Angel (illustrated p. 49).

Close: well-preserved secular close. Views of the three spires from nearby lakes.

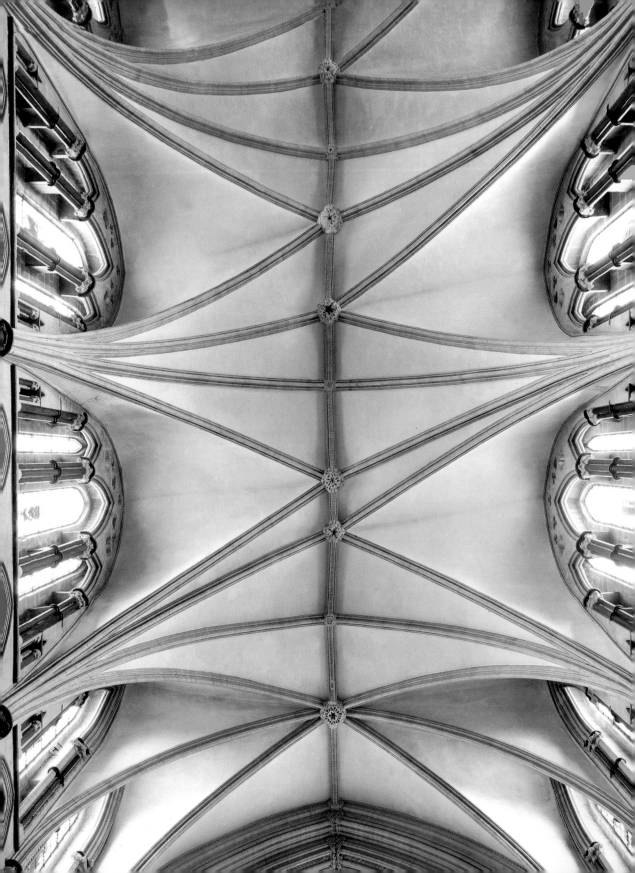

LINCOLN

It took five days to transport the body of Bishop Hugh from London to Lincoln. For much of that time the cortège moved across the vast diocese over which he had ruled, and on which he had had such an impact.

Their route roughly followed today's A1: hardly an easy journey in late November 1200. Yet the lights on the bier seemed inextinguishable: whenever one was blown out, another would light it. And 'everywhere, immense crowds of persons of every rank, class and profession collected . . . everyone's great ambition was to touch the coffin', as Hugh's chaplain, who was there, put it. At Biggleswade 'the crowd of weeping villagers by the bier was such that a man's arm was broken'. The injured man fell into a deep coma, where 'he had a vision of Hugh touching his arm'. When he came around, the pain had gone, the bone had set, and the arm had healed.[1]

Hugh had made a point of engaging with his diocese. It was the size of a small country, containing 'more than nine counties, with many large cities and a big population, indeed it would be difficult to find a larger or more populous one'; it contained up to 1,700 parishes.[2] He had stayed with the incumbents of tiny churches, confirmed children and inspected monasteries. His inspections of ordinary parish priests are the earliest to survive. He must have come as a shock to many: Lincoln had had no active incumbent for eighteen years, and the idea that bishops could engage with

'Like a flying creature jostling the clouds', the 'crazy vault' is the climax of St Hugh's eccentric and extraordinary choir at Lincoln

ordinary people in this way was itself, for the twelfth century, a novel one.

Hugh developed something of a reputation. He was said to have performed miracles in Cheshunt, Alconbury and Lincoln, and to have arrived late for a meeting with the king because he had stopped to ensure that a body found by the roadside was properly buried. There is a hint of insanity in the

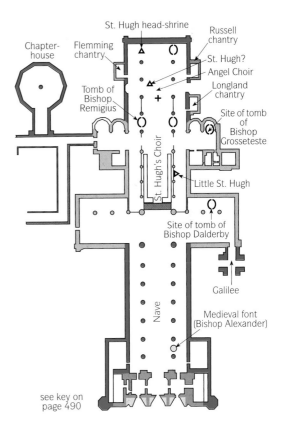

see key on page 490

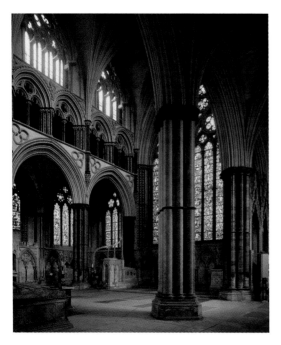

Setting for saints: the ornate Angel Choir

stories of him biting a mouthful from the arm of St Mary Magdalene – an exceptionally precious relic – wearing fragments of the bodies of thirty saints on a ring the width of four fingers, and kissing lepers on the mouth. Hugh stood up to kings, yet somehow managed not to alienate them. He and Henry II were so close that people wondered if they were related, yet after one argument with Henry, he theatrically grabbed the king in front of the court and forced him to exchange the ritual 'kiss of peace'. He was a holy man, for whom normal rules did not apply: rumours of sainthood crackled around him like electricity.[3]

Hugh's arrival in England was a side effect of Becket's assassination in 1170. As one of his acts of expiation for the murder, Henry II had founded the first monastery in England of the ascetic Carthusian order of monks;[4] Hugh, the procurator of a Carthusian house in the Italian Alps, was suggested to the king as a possible prior. Before taking up this comparatively outward-facing role, he had lived at least ten years of his life alone in a cell, fasting three days a week, leaving only for services and occasional acts of charity.

When he first learned of his new job, Hugh was worried. Surely he was unworthy of such a role, when he had not even conquered bodily lust. The thought triggered a dark night of the soul, in which he sought divine help – and a saint appeared in his dreams. The saint reached into his bowels, withdrew something red and hot, and threw it away. Hugh never again desired sex; and he had had his first encounter with the miraculous.

Hugh became bishop of the secular cathedral of Lincoln in 1186. In 1192 he began to rebuild his church, which, having apparently been damaged in an earthquake a year before he took office, was as battered as the moribund bishopric itself. It had been one of the earliest and most interesting Norman cathedrals (see pp. 56, 74, illustrated pp. 50, 59), with a west front that doubled up as a kind of castle; it had already been magnificently enriched once. Hugh's 'immense zeal for the beauty of the house of God'[5] would result in the most dangerously unhinged of English cathedrals, the starting point for decades of ostentatious architecture at Lincoln itself.

The famous 'crazy vault' zigzags giddily down Hugh's choir: it originally resolved itself in a half-hexagonal apse. The vault is completely asymmetrical, and every inch of the wall surface below it is filled with a manic restlessness, 'hard without but like a honeycomb within' as one of Hugh's biographers put it.[6] Tiny decorative openings are punched into walls for no apparent reason. There were originally fake painted openings, too.[7] Two wall arcades, one on top of the other, are syncopated so that the columns of one come down in the middle of the arches of the other. As if to confuse further, carved busts poke out where the hidden tops of the rear arcade should be. The quantity of polished stone bewildered contemporaries: 'people's minds are in suspense as they wonder whether it is jasper or marble . . . it presents a starry brilliance to the dazzled sight', said the same source. The widespread use of the pointed arch in this early gothic building would have been just as thrilling: with its aid the vault 'spread broad wings of its own, and like a flying creature jostled the clouds'. A layman of the 1190s must have imagined himself lost in the heavenly Jerusalem itself. Such liberal expense implies strong support from a bishop. In Hugh's case, this went further than usual. He 'carried the hewn stones and the lime mortar' for the church. He healed a crippled hod-carrier, and a mason's brother.

This building was an extraordinary cousin to the new east end at Canterbury, a building itself suffused with the edgy sanctity of the recently murdered St Thomas. It is full of decisions taken without regard to their consequences. Perhaps its designer[8] was over-excited by having a patron who was a *living* saint. Indeed, a wave of enthusiasm seems to have swept over the whole see in connection with Hugh and his building. The evidence, though fragmentary, suggests a wave of new donations of land, often small gifts from lowly people. A farmer might give half an acre, placing a symbolic sod on the high altar. The story of the Swineherd of Stow – a poor pig herder who gave to Lincoln and was carved onto a gable top in remembrance – has uncertain origins, but the right flavour. A works chantry guaranteed prayers for the soul of those who contributed.[9] Just as crucially, the chapter's own lands were divided so as to create a permanent fabric fund.

Although personally ascetic, Hugh was no enemy of ornament. Lay people could only approach God through their senses: 'Eat well, drink well and serve God well', he declared, laying on 300 deer at his installation feast, and providing entertainers at his banquets, while he himself wore a hair shirt

and observed as far as possible the ascetic fasts of his order.[10] 'Sculptures or pictures were at the entrances to churches for a very good reason, reminding people of the truths of their faith and encouraging them to seek forgiveness', he said to King John of a great French church portal.[11]

Lincoln had only been the seat of a cathedral since the 1070s. It lacked both age and sanctity. Hugh and his chapter worked hard to give it a saint. They focused on Remigius, the ambitious Norman monk who had relocated the cathedral from Dorchester in Oxfordshire, and laid the financial foundations for its large, rich chapter (which grew to over fifty canons, making it among the largest in England; at Hugh's period and later it was also

The Last Supper, from a romanesque carving on Lincoln's west front

The Angel Choir's beautiful east front

joined the throng, 'lamenting him aloud as the faithful servant of the one God'. 'Here lies Hugh, model of bishops, flower of monks, friend of scholars, and hammer of kings', it said on his tomb.[14]

Building work did not stop at St Hugh's east end. As the thirteenth century opened, work continued into the transepts and then, perhaps after a pause, it was decided to rebuild the nave as well.[15] No sooner was this complete than the east end was rebuilt a second time. At every stage the architecture that resulted was of the most sumptuous magnificence.

A series of gifted master-masons rose to the challenge of St Hugh's choir, ironing out its eccentricities and drawing on its strongest ideas. In the transepts the obsessive-compulsive double blank wall arcades were replaced by an elegant single arcade. Two great rose windows, then almost unique in England, gaze out with an air of authority and 'clerical surveillance'[16], as it has been put, over Lincolnshire on one side and the close on the other: later generations called them, appropriately, the Bishop's Eye and the Dean's Eye.

But it is the nave that finds a new gear. The Church as a whole had been through two difficult decades after Hugh's death. His canonization in 1220, when twenty-nine miracles were cited, was one of the key moments of that triumphant year (see p. 100). The then bishop, Hugh of Wells, would have known the euphoric new architecture at Wells and Salisbury, for his brother was the bishop behind the Wells west front. Lincoln's nave, perhaps the most perfectly beautiful of English cathedral interiors, mature and assured, reflects the political, spiritual and architectural normalization that had taken place since the 1190s.[17]

It is a work of mature Early English architecture, hugely influential in its magnificently decorous nobility. The architect took the vault-as-ornament

one of the most intellectually weighty).[12] Rumours of sweet smells and healings hovered hopefully around Remigius' tomb, and Gerald of Wales was commissioned to write a 'holy life' of the bishop. Unusually, he added a brief life of his employer, Hugh. It seems the incumbent bishop, rather than the dead one, was of interest too.

By the time of Hugh's funeral in 1200, the new east end was virtually complete.[13] His body had been met at Lincoln by an immense crowd. The kings of England and Scotland helped carried the bier, as others vied for the honour of joining them. The crowd followed them up Steep Hill, knee deep in mud, the bells of the city ringing as they passed. A knight whose arm was 'eaten by cancer' touched the body and was healed. The Jews of Lincoln

idea implicit in St Hugh's 'crazy vaults' and made it symmetrical (and less mad) by adding further 'decorative' ribs known as tiercerons. The choir's horizontal ridge rib, invented to cope with the unusual geometry of St Hugh's vaults, was employed now simply for its aesthetic qualities. Soon designers everywhere would be copying these motifs, many of which were anticipated in the ten-sided chapter-house. Indeed the Lincoln chapter-house, its beauty 'rivalling Solomon's Temple in stonework and architecture',[18] was itself an influential structure, launching an 150-year fad for spectacular, polygonal, secular cathedral chapter-houses.

By 1235 works on the interior were drawing to a close.[19] Apart from the romanesque west front, the church was now gothic from end to end. But then another 'living saint' happened along. This bishop was one of the great intellectuals of his age, and also a man of stiff principle. Robert Grosseteste (see p. 109) had spent much of his life in comparatively lowly roles at the cathedrals of Hereford and Lincoln.[20] He did not have the security of a benefice until he was in his fifties, and was teaching at the young university of Oxford (itself in the see); indeed, he may have been its first chancellor. But in 1229 this rising academic became archdeacon of Leicester, one of the most senior roles in the diocese of Lincoln. He was famously 'low born', and made a name for himself as an original thinker: he was one of the first men in Europe to see the significance of the works of Aristotle.

In 1229, Grosseteste heard one of the first friars in England preach at Oxford. The friars' back-to-basics message of poverty, preaching and populism struck a chord. He gave up his archdeaconry and his stable income, and became 'lector' to the newly established community, while writing books on everything from morality to the natural world. He must have been as shocked as anyone when he was elected bishop of Lincoln.

'As soon as I was made bishop, I considered myself to be the overseer and pastor of souls', he later told the pope. Within six months he had toured his huge see, 'causing the clergy to be called together . . . and the people to be warned . . . that they should be present with their children to be confirmed'. He would preach, while a group of friars energetically heard confessions. It was the kind of thing advocated by both the Franciscans and the Fourth Lateran Council (see p. 104) – and presaged by St Hugh. He could also be fierce: in these first months, he had seven abbots and four priors dismissed from their jobs. This kind of thing ruffled feathers: 'some came to me to find fault . . . saying "my lord, you are doing a new and unaccustomed thing"', he put it, with some understatement.[21]

Grosseteste's troubles really started when he told his chapter that he was about to inspect *them*. He had already prevented Lincoln canonries from being handed out to career churchmen. The result was a ferocious six-year dispute with his own cathedral, during which his only known physical impact on the building occurred.[22] In 1237 or 1239 one of the canons was preaching against his own bishop, and as he came to the words 'if we should hold our peace . . . the very stones would cry out on our behalf', the tower fell down.[23] Clearly, the cathedral disliked its bishop as much as its canons did. Teams of masons were then working on the fringes of the church: a spectacular ceremonial Galilee porch, facing the bishop's palace, and two cliff-like wings, studded with empty niches, surrounding the eleventh-century west front. Now they had to repair the tower as well.

For Grosseteste, the Church was there to care for human souls. Resources that went into anything else were contrary to the will of God. He went to the papal court twice, assuming the see of St Peter would support him in such battles. But the papal court did not see things so simply. Rich cathedrals like Lincoln were relied on to fund the lawyers and administrators who were indispensable to the

Church. On his second visit, Grosseteste realized that he was getting nowhere.[24] He announced to the court that the Church was riddled with 'antichrists and limbs of Satan masquerading as angels of light'.[25] This astonishing face-to-face attack on the very heart of papal authority later made him a Protestant hero.

Grosseteste spent the rest of his life a bitter man. He was not against the Church's institutions, merely how they were run: 'to defy the gospel by giving the care of souls to those who are inadequate either in learning or in commitment is heresy in action. Many defy the gospel in this way, the pope most of all; and it is the duty of all faithful persons to oppose such a person',[26] he said on his deathbed.

This is strong stuff. Some hated him; others thought they heard a strange music in the sky as he lay dying. People started to make pilgrimages to his tomb.[27] Perhaps Lincoln was about to gain another saint.

In the event, it did gain another saint – of a kind. Two years after Grosseteste's death, in 1255, a young boy called Hugh was playing with some Jewish friends when he fell down the well in their Lincoln home and died. The house's owner was imprisoned. Rumours spread: the boy had been imprisoned for days, perhaps weeks; a gathering of Jews had come to witness the child's crucifixion. The helpless homeowner was dragged to the gallows; eighteen Jews were murdered when the story reached London.[28]

In its combination of child-abuse scare and xenophobia, the story is depressingly familiar (Grosseteste himself was actively anti-Semitic); but it has a medieval twist. Miracles were rumoured around the boy's body. The bishop sent a procession to bring it to the cathedral. Now Lincoln had two possible – and controversial – new saints.

That very year, 1255, building restarted.[29] The king was approached for permission to breach the city wall.[30] Having only recently completed the west

end of the church, the bishop and his chapter would now go back and extend St Hugh's east end. They were working together in a way that had been impossible under Grosseteste.[31]

The Angel Choir[32] was thus the third new east end since the 1070s. It replaced the multiple polygons of Hugh's apsed building with a vast flat-ended box, leaving his choir, now known as St Hugh's Choir, and eastern transepts standing. It contained the high altar, St Hugh's shrine, processional paths and a lady altar, thus fusing presbytery, feretory, retrochoir and lady chapel in one spacious structure, filled with a stone-carved choir of angels. It has the earliest surviving window tracery in an English cathedral, taken from Rheims via Westminster abbey, and an east window of mind-boggling size for the period. Monuments to the great – bishops, Eleanor of Castile and Katherine Swynford, mistress and third wife of John of Gaunt – would eventually be placed among its shrines.

Much ink has been used trying to decode the carvings that grace the triforium of the Angel Choir. The stained glass and inscriptions that would have helped to provide a key are lost (see p. 164). The clues are tantalizing: a Christ and a Virgin Mary are among the angels above the high altar, where there are also many emblems of the Passion. The angels over the shrine area carry musical instruments, but one, bizarrely, appears to be about to go hawking (hunting in heaven?). However, a few hints can be traced of the poetic layers of image and allusion, presumably coined by members of chapter, that originally filled the building. The image of angel orchestras comes from Psalms 146–150, and among the figures is a winged carving of the psalmist, King David. It is surely not a coincidence that the psalms were sung in their entirety at dawn each day at Lauds in the choir below. The harping king turns his head towards the vast east window: in this service he is called 'the light of morning at sunrise'.[33]

In 1280, the body of St Hugh was translated into a new shrine in the heart of the new choir. King Edward I and his wife Eleanor were present, along with 230 knights: the gutters of the bishop's palace ran with wine for a week.[34] As those present carefully lifted Hugh from his previous burial place, noting his wonderfully well-preserved body – a sign of saintliness – its head fell off. The head was promptly given to an archbishop to carry on a silver platter; six bishops carried the body behind. But when they reached the new shrine, it was discovered to be too small by the size of a head. God, it seemed, had miraculously adjusted the saint's corpse to compensate for some mason's error.[35] Now there were two shrines in the Angel Choir – that of Hugh, and that of his head – both attracting pilgrims, prayers and donations.

The Angel Choir can seem overblown, as if spun from icing sugar rather than limestone. But its builders believed that real angels gathered wherever mass was performed, that transubstantiation occurred daily at the high altar, and that the air of heaven itself emanated from the shrine of Hugh and, some said, the tombs of both Remigius and Grosseteste.[36] Neither Remigius, nor little St Hugh, nor Grosseteste was ever to be canonized, but no one knew this at the time. All had cults of some description; three had been alive in living memory. No other cathedral could boast this.[37] The Angel Choir was a place where heaven and earth met.

Grosseteste in particular may be the ghost at this architectural feast. He was, for example, particularly devoted to King David.[38] And the magnificent Judgement Porch – a French-style ceremonial door into the Angel Choir[39] – shows an unusual image of Christ displaying his wounds; Grosseteste had famously preached on the theme of Christ's blood at Westminster abbey.[40] He had even left 100 marks to the fabric fund in his will. Nonetheless, although the dead Grosseteste could only be an asset to Lincoln, Rome never forgave him. Canonization papers were sent to the popes in 1286, 1288 and 1307. But 'in no way . . . have they been able to make progress – for what reason God knows'.[41]

Little St Hugh was not forgotten, either. The setting for his shrine survives as a particularly elaborate stretch of choir screen, probably paid for by Edward I, who ejected the Jews from England in 1290.[42] By the 1330s Hugh was still receiving an average of twenty-two visitors a day, although a century later it was half that.[43] Around this time Bishop Dalderby (d. 1320) became yet another

Angelic inscriptions, now lost, would have provided the key to the Angel Choir's meaning

Angels co-ordinate the resurrection of the dead: from the Angel Choir's south door

The passage from church to chapter-house and deanery was turned into a cloister from 1296

Lincoln bishop with a cult: he had cured the 'men from Rutland who could only bark like dogs', and even had liturgy written for performance at his tomb-shrine.[44] Canonization papers went to the pope three times, again without success. But the beautiful flowing tracery of the Bishop's Eye in the south transept, installed at around this time, must have made a grand backdrop to Dalderby's tomb-shrine (see p. 230).[45]

Lincoln's building programme had come back to life with the Angel Choir; now it was drawing slowly to an end. Bishops Sutton, Dalderby and Buckingham completed the building by adding towers and installing choir fittings: the central tower, once topped by a colossal spire almost 160 metres high, went up in 1307–11;[46] the exquisite

Decorated screens and a pulpitum, separating the choir from lay people, are of the late thirteenth and earlier fourteenth centuries. Remigius was given a shrine-like 'founder's' tomb by the high altar, doubling up as a liturgical stage set or tomb of Christ, from which the Eucharist would miraculously emerge on Easter Day. More imitation stone Easter sepulchres can be found in the parish churches of Lincolnshire and Nottinghamshire, marks of a diocese that took early to the feast of Corpus Christi.[47] The cloister was created from 1296; little closes for the cathedral's vicars and choristers were added, and were soon joined by several small chantry foundations. In the mid-fourteenth century there is a pause in this story that may mark the disruption caused by the Black

Death; but then in the 1360s and 1370s, some 200 years after Hugh began rebuilding, the western towers[48] were built under Treasurer Welbourne, a new base was created for Hugh's head shrine (after the head itself had been stolen and recovered) and a fine set of choir-stalls were added, in place by 1372. The cathedral was complete – just as it began to face its first financial troubles. Bishop and chapter fell out under the difficult Dean Macworth, though amends were made in the shape of a new cathedral constitution, created after his death in 1439.

Lincoln was now architecturally and institutionally fully evolved. Bishops, including Flemming in 1427, founded chantries and university colleges (Lincoln college at Oxford) rather than building anew at their cathedral. The last pre-Reformation bishop was Henry VIII's confessor, John Longland, who built himself a chantry, but died after chantries were made illegal in 1547, so could never use it as intended; it remains empty.[49]

The Reformation was deeply felt at Lincoln. The cathedral treasurer joined the anti-Reformation Pilgrimage of Grace in 1536–7 and was executed in York. The gold shrine of St Hugh and the silver one of Bishop Dalderby were taken down in 1540. The spire fell in 1549. The enormous diocese had long had a centrifugal tendency: Cambridgeshire had been lost to the new see of Ely as early as 1109; the abbeys of Eynsham, St Albans and Peterborough saw themselves as 'mother churches' on their own lands. Peterborough and Oxford became seats of sees in their own right in the 1540s. St Albans eventually followed in 1890.

Yet throughout the medieval period, processions from across the see had made their way to their cathedral, bearing the payments that were exchanged for chrism oil (see p. 202). They came every Pentecost to this great building, high on its limestone ridge – a 'strong church in a strong place'[50] – which, when topped by its spires, was probably the highest structure on the planet.

Every stage of this church's construction had been carried out to the most luxurious standards. The ultimate explanation for this extraordinary outpouring of resources must lie in the size of the diocese. Its lands sustained the largest chapter in the country. Unlike other large dioceses, the bishop had no smaller colleges which might divert his wealth.[51] Lay contributions, however small, if they came from many people would also result in large sums in such a see. Lincoln's bishops also seem to have been unusual for their quality and commitment: this bishopric 'demands personal residence', as a bishop of Worcester once said.[52] By maximizing the spiritual assets latent in some remarkable human stories, Lincoln had made up in immediacy what it lacked in venerability. The cults of Lincoln – like the architecture itself – were a palpable reminder to the people of this great see that heaven was just around the corner.

WHAT TO SEE

St Mary, Lincoln
Secular cathedral; seventh-century see; moved to Lincoln by 1075.

Church: eleventh-century west front (with additions); certifiable St Hugh's Choir; beautiful nave and chapter-house; Angel Choir.

Fittings and carvings: choir fittings (Christ's tomb/tomb of Remigius, pulpitum, choir-stalls); tombs and chantries, especially St Hugh's head shrine; many finely carved details throughout.

Close: setting on a ridge; bishop's palace (English Heritage); close proximity to Norman castle.

NORWICH

One day in 1095, three men stood on a busy Norwich street corner. The market place in front of them was packed and noisy. They were going to cut it in half, obliterating the town centre, and build a cathedral in its place. The faultline that resulted survives to this day, embodying the uneasy relationship between a medieval city and its church.

They can hardly have blended into the scenery, these three. All were Norman by birth. Walkelin, bishop of Winchester, was already working on one of the largest cathedrals ever built; Roger Bigod had been sheriff of Norwich for many years, and his castle had obliterated some 25 hectares of the town. Ralph the Chaplain sounds insignificant by comparison, but he may have been Ranulph Flambard, the colourful future right-hand man of William II and bishop of Durham.[1]

This prosperous Anglo-Scandinavian town was being made into the focus of Norman power in East Anglia. Norman settlers had been moved into a purpose-built suburb, the 'French Borough'. The chief Norman aristocrat in the region had been styled the earl of Norwich. The castle was first built in the 1060s.[2] Now Walkelin, Bigod and Ralph were meeting to 'inspect and cause to be surveyed' the lands where a new cathedral would stand.

The Normans had already merged the Anglo-Saxon bishoprics of Norfolk (based at Elmham) and the lesser see of Suffolk (based at Hoxne),[3] moving them to Thetford in 1075. For a decade the

Thanks to the guilt of bishop Herbert de Losinga, shown on this wall painting in the cathedral buying his bishopric, one of Europe's great Romanesque churches was created

bishops had acquired land in Norwich while also attempting to take over the mighty abbey of Bury St Edmunds.[4] Their designs on Bury had been frustrated, however, and by 1086 Norwich was becoming the main focus of their plans. The energy with which these plans were driven through was down to one man: Herbert de Losinga.[5]

De Losinga was the archetypal ambitious Norman monk-cum-imperialist. As prior of Fécamp he had been second-in-command at an important Norman

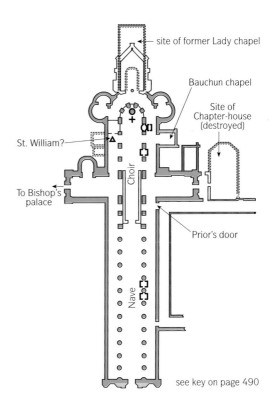

see key on page 490

abbey. William II brought him to England, where within a few years, 'practised in the art of flattery', he had paid the colossal sum of 1,000 marks in exchange for the new bishopric of East Anglia (as well as an abbacy in Winchester for his father). This unusually blatant act of simony flew in the face of church reform, the very cause the Normans were promoting. 'Oh grief, the church is let to sordid hire/the son a bishop, abbot is the sire', went a satirical rhyme.[6]

De Losinga became bishop in 1091. In 1094 he seems to have experienced a crisis of conscience, and set off to Rome to seek papal forgiveness. Within two years our high-powered band of royal advisers had surveyed the cathedral's proposed site and de Losinga had started signing himself 'bishop of Norwich'.[7]

The fact that the proposed cathedral site took up much of the town centre does not seem to have bothered them. Roads were blocked; houses and shops were demolished. The sloping site was levelled, an enormous project in itself. In 1096 de Losinga laid the foundation stone of today's Norwich cathedral. The community of priests who had formed the staff of the church was replaced by some fifty to sixty monks; work began on a large monastery on one side of the church and a bishop's palace on the other. 'Alms extinguish sin as water does fire', de Losinga said:[8] he was going about it in the grandest way imaginable.

The new cathedral close bisected Norwich's main market place, the 'Tombland' or 'empty land' (map p. 190). Taxes from lucrative events such as the weekly market and nine-day Whitsun fair were due to the landlord, but where in this open, busy area did the precise limits of the cathedral's territory lie?[9] Such questions were left unresolved, providing potential flashpoints between the fast-

Norwich's handsome spire has been rebuilt at least twice

developing city and its cathedral priory that would dominate the centuries to come.

Perhaps conflicts between city and priory would never have arisen had Herbert de Losinga been in a little less of a hurry. 'The work drags on, and in providing materials you show no enthusiasm,' he wrote.[10] 'Behold the servants of the king and my own are really in earnest – gather stones, carry them to the spot when gathered, and fill with them the fields and ways, the houses and courts, and meanwhile you are asleep with folded hands.' As well as his cathedral he managed to build further sub-priories or cells of the cathedral in Yarmouth, Lynn and Norwich itself, and also founded a large hospital.[11]

As they built, de Losinga's masons coined a distinctive decorative style, applying starkly muscular decorative patterns over selected walls of their buildings. The result, also applied to Norwich castle when it was rebuilt in stone in the twelfth century, gave the city a distinctive Norman corporate stamp that still marks it today. The combination of castle and cathedral made Norwich unequivocally the capital of an entire region. By the time the cathedral was finished (in 1145 at the latest), the cathedral had become one of the biggest landlords in East Anglia, and the single biggest institution of any kind in Norfolk. Its enormous cloister may have housed one of the earliest known schools in England, and its capitals were soon to be covered in educative scenes, full of classical allusions.[12]

The church remains one of the most complete romanesque great churches in Europe. To imagine the original building, it is simply necessary to replace the stone vaults with an open wooden roof[13] and omit all the tracery from the windows. The walls, it seems, were unplastered and un-painted, just as they are now.[14] On the outside, the crossing tower, with its distinctive patterning, was much lower than today, but the profile of the church as a whole was given added drama by the provision of perhaps twenty small turrets, since lost.[15]

Yet the new cathedral had a credibility problem. It had no in-house saint, its site lacked both age and sanctity, and the its creation must have caused bad feeling among the townspeople. De Losinga – and his successor, Eborard – needed to remind people that the see's history, in spite of many relocations, could be traced back to the seventh century, that it had been founded by saints (even if their relics were elsewhere) and that it was the home of a divinely ordained authority. To do so, they focused on two parts of the church: the bishop's palace and its connection with the cathedral, and the bishop's throne or *cathedra*, in the east end.

For a church built by a man expiating his own guilt, de Losinga's cathedral was very happy to aggrandize its bishop. One of his first acts was to build a keep-like palace on a raised terrace, from which construction could be observed; its large private chapel replaced an Anglo-Saxon city church.[16] He created a spectacular ceremonial entrance from the palace into the church, surrounding it with an unprecedented display of surface decoration. This included a large carving of a bishop giving a blessing, probably meant to represent St Felix, the seventh-century founder of the see. Above this doorway were distinctive triangular decorations that recalled the architecture of the Anglo-Saxons.[17]

The easternmost part of the church evokes the power of bishops even more emphatically. Much about the arrangement recalls the shrine spaces of the early church. Behind the high altar, a platform was built which stood high above the floor of the apsed east end. The ambulatory that curved behind it was sunk into the ground by nearly a metre, emphasizing the height of the platform still further. On this vertiginous location stood a new throne made from carved fragments of an ancient one, presumably a previous throne of East Anglian bishops. A hidden flue beneath the seat of the chair led to a niche in the ambulatory, where sacred objects or relics were probably displayed to pilgrims. It was as if sacred authority was being visibly directed quite literally up to the seat of the bishop.

Other parts of the cathedral appear to reflect the needs of the diocese as a whole. The nave was the longest in England, and the nave altar was given an unusually dramatic visual emphasis. It was surrounded by four enormous drum-like piers, their spiral designs evoking the shrine of St Peter in Rome (as did those of Durham and Canterbury – see pp. 313 and 68). De Losinga held synods of the priests and other churchmen of his see twice a year; Eborard initiated Pentecostal processions from the parishes of the see.[18] Thus the bishops began to draw together the churches of the large and populous diocese. Perhaps the nave was the venue for such events.

But all was not well in the city the Normans had divided. Norwich – with perhaps 5,000–10,000 inhabitants, and forty-three parish churches by 1086[19] – was well on the way to being one of the country's two or three largest and most prosperous settlements. But its new French Borough and old Anglo-Scandinavian centre did not even share a single legal system,[20] and a cathedral and a castle had been dropped on the town as if from the heavens, carving up the city centre. If Norwich was a brewing storm of ethnic and institutional tensions, in 1144 they found a lightning rod.

The events of that year are an all too modern story of child abuse witch-hunt and xenophobia. The near-naked body of an eight- or nine-year-old boy called William was found in Thorpe Wood on the edge of the city. Crowds descended on the site amid waves of rumour and counter-rumour. It was said that a stranger had arrived at William's home, claiming to be from the new cathedral. He offered the boy a job there, and offered payment upfront as a token of good faith. The boy's mother had misgivings, but let the pair go. On their way to the church, they visited the boy's uncle, a local priest. The next day – according to the uncle, who had previously been trying to stop his nephew from playing with Jewish children – they were apparently seen entering the house of a Norwich Jew.[21]

The boy's body was found in the wood on Good Friday, wearing only a cloak and shoes. He had apparently been tortured. Once again the priest-uncle is the protagonist, interrupting Bishop Eborard's Easter synod in the cathedral and accusing the Jews of Norwich of the murder. They had crucified William, he claimed: the Jews practised such Christ-mocking rituals every Easter; the little boy was a martyr. This is the first recorded example of the 'blood libel', a perverted twisting of Passover rituals into one of Europe's more long-lasting anti-Semitic fantasies.

To their credit, neither Bishop Eborard nor the sheriff of Norwich believed the priest. The sheriff took the Jewish community into his castle for safekeeping as the citizens attacked their part of the city. But Eborard's prior, Turbe, supported the growing cult surrounding the boy, and in 1147 he replaced Eborard as bishop. William's tomb was moved to ever more high profile parts of the church, and soon the crowds that flocked to it disturbed services there. Yet William was never canonized, and his *Life* goes out of its way to defend the cult from those who 'are entirely uncertain and doubtful by whom and why' the boy was murdered. (A modern investigator might ask some hard questions of Church figures in the story – the man from the cathedral, for example, or the boy's priest-uncle.)[22]

William of Norwich's cult flourished dramatically, and later collapsed almost completely. Two-thirds of known visitors to his shrine in its peak year, 1150–1, came from Norwich itself; at that time a miracle was being claimed every ten days or so. The shrine survived the Middle Ages – it was given an expensive nine-week refurbishment in 1305,

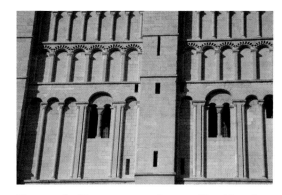

The muscular Norman patterns that cover Norwich castle echo those at the cathedral

fifteen years after the expulsion of the Jews from England – but by then it often only attracted a few pence in offerings each year.[23] There is little to see of it in the cathedral today, unless the roughly built arch known as the Treasury, near the site of the shrine, is in some way connected with it.

St William was one of the first signs that the 'new age of saints' was flickering into life. Norwich's encounter with the great events that followed – in which a flood of miracles, human and architectural, washed over the country, English bishops achieved unprecedented levels of power and the east end of almost every church in this book was rebuilt – would be almost as ignominious. Three bishops in succession had little to do with the church. A fire occurred in 1171; the cathedral was later given what was perhaps its first coat of paint.[24] An attempt to join the early thirteenth-century craze for new east ends came to little: in 1245 Bishop Suffield gave up after building a fine new lady chapel, sadly demolished after the Reformation,[25] though he also founded a hospital just outside the close.

Then, in 1272, the faultlines between the cathedral and the city resurfaced. The citizens had to pay the priory simply to trade in Tombland. Tolls taken at the great Pentecost fair there went straight into the cathedral coffers. Citizens also had to pay

The Norwich cloisters contain some of the finest stone carving in England

the cathedral to graze their animals on various lands outside the city. All this was bitterly resented, but various royal decisions on the matter had simply contradicted each other.[26]

In June there were scuffles in Tombland between the townsmen and the prior's men. The prior got 'men from Yarmouth' to fortify the cathedral's bell tower, a standalone structure near Tombland itself. To the citizens this was not self-defence but provocation: in August, calling the bell tower 'an illegal fortress', they 'assembled together and decided to arrest' those defending it. Between them and the tower stood the gate of the close: they burned it down. They took the tower and used it to fire on the cathedral itself. 'The fire spread, burning the bell tower and all the monastic buildings – and even, as some say, the cathedral church.'[27] Thirteen

people are known to have died in the ensuing riots, which lasted three days. Reports of the numbers of townspeople involved vary from 173 to 13,000, including many women and priests. In punishment, about thirty citizens were dragged through the streets by horses until they were dead. The woman who had set fire to the close gate was burned at the stake. The city was ordered to pay a colossal 3,000 marks in compensation, and was still paying the debt as late as 1342.

The priory spent this new wealth on repairing damaged parts of the building in the new Decorated style. Those that went up first were probably those that had been most severely affected: the chapter-house and adjacent cloister bays (helped by funds from a loyal layman, Richard Uphall of Tasburgh, given as early as 1272),[28] parts of the central tower and the separate bell tower (both now lost). Several burned books were replaced; meanwhile the Norwich monk Bartholomew Cotton's new *Historia Anglicana* just happened to include a detailed account (from the cathedral's point of view) of these events.[29] During this rebuilding process, in 1278, the church was rededicated.

Some forty years after the riot, at a time when much of the country was being rocked by famine, war and rebellion (see chapter four), John Salmon (bishop from 1299) and the monks began a range of initiatives that were a more explicit architectural reaction to the troubles of 1272. Salmon was a high flier – a future chancellor of England, and to some a potential saint[30] – as well as a former Norwich monk.[31] Since the cathedral was 'located in the centre of a well-known city', the bishop said, 'a great many of the unlettered are wont to come into the church on a variety of pretexts'.[32] It was time to point out that 'Forgive and forget' was not among the cathedral's mottos. So in 1317 the burnt Ethelbert Gate was rebuilt, at a cost of £115 8s 5d.[33] Despite its rich decoration, the new structure was eminently defensible, and was dominated by a dramatic carving of a citizen defending himself from an angry dragon: 'Don't try it again', the citizens might have concluded as they walked past it to the Tombland shops (illustrated pp. 119, 126).[34]

The lay community had long preferred the city's parish and Mendicant burial grounds to the lay cemetery outside the cathedral west front. Salmon founded the grand Carnary college there (1316), a chantry for his own soul and 'a repository for human bones buried in the city of Norwich'. His aim was to attract burials away from the city's overflowing graveyards, and bring pious lay mourners into the cathedral close.[35]

He also began a grand rebuilding of the cloister, a project that would drag on until well into the fifteenth century. At first the focus was on the east walk, the exclusive zone of the monks. Here, from 1316, Salmon and the monks sowed the seeds for 200 years of Norwich art, with a series of bosses and other carvings encoded with stories and messages. Their climax was the Prior's Door, through which the monks entered the church.[37]

The spicily inventive canopies carved on to this door make it look more like metalwork than stone, as if they were soldered on to the arch beneath (illustrated p. 126). The figures they bear sum up much of Christian theology in just six scenes. Moses is accompanied by St Peter, St Edmund the Martyr and St John the Baptist: two prophets (one Old Testament, one New) and two martyrs (one the biblical founder of the entire Church, the other post-biblical, royal and local). At their centre is Christ, exposing the wound in his side. Beneath each figure squirms a tiny adversary. Thus are evoked the different, but con-nected, worlds of the Old and New Testaments, and the victory over sin and death embodied by Christ himself: the key turning points of human history.[38]

The vault that starts above Christ's head is studded with bosses that expand on this theme, telling the story of the Passion, like an unfolding strip cartoon. Such scenes are built for the eyes of processing monks, cleverly designed to be 'read' whether one is coming from or going into the church itself.[39] This idea – using vault bosses to tell a story – would become Norwich's great contribution to late medieval art.

The cloister bosses went on to develop something of an obsession with the story of the Apocalypse, which they repeated twice over, to the extent that scenes of John holding his book of Revelations, plagues striking, and whores of Babylon accompanying terrible beasts seem to recur again and again. Given the tenor of the times, the sculptors, such as John Horn and William Reppys, and designers, among them the up-and-coming Ramsey dynasty of masons,[40] must have wondered whether such prophecies were coming true. In 1348, the monks had just bought a book of the Apocalypse, presumably to use as source material, when plague struck. Work on the cloister stopped in its tracks. It took another century to complete, mostly in a great push during the 1420s. At its completion, layman – who entered the church via a door in the west cloister walk – would be faced en route by a spectacular reminer of how time would end.

Meanwhile, in 1361–2, the timber spire that topped the cathedral's central tower collapsed in a hurricane. The roof, clerestory and choir-stalls of the east end were wrecked. With a papal indulgence, a £400 grant from the bishop and contributions from Norfolk grandees, all was rapidly replaced.[41] The choir's new clerestory windows were double the height of their predecessors, encircling the ancient apse with walls of glass and delicate tracery. The roof above was still, presumably, of wood.

Norwich was a focus of the Peasants Revolt of 1381. The men of Thetford, Lynn and Yarmouth assembled outside the city; the citizens within prepared to join them. But the then bishop, Henry Despencer, had worked as a mercenary in Italy, and made short work of the rebels before celebrating his victory by getting his knightly colleagues to club together for a new cathedral altarpiece. The thirty coats of arms on the Norwich Retable (illustrated p. 135) include those of Sir Stephen Hales, captured by the peasants, Sir Oliver de Calthorp, one of the post-rebellion commissioners for peace, and the Cavendishs – Sir John the Elder, killed by the rebels, and Sir John the Younger, who in his turn killed their leader Wat Tyler.[42]

Yet the underlying trend was in favour of the citizens. In 1404 Bishop Despencer's great rival Sir Thomas Erpingham helped the city gain county status, and the newly empowered merchants of the city gratefully revived their disputes over Tombland. Erpingham was born into a gentry family, and through his competence and effective soldiering rose to become a powerful and trusted figure at court; he may have created a unique monument to his achievements in the shape of the Erpingham Gate, which frames the cathedral's west front as seen from Tombland. The gate's massed display of images loomed grandly over the market place, displaying to all the emblems of Sir Thomas and his wives; the see of East Anglia and the cathedral priory of Norwich; and the Trinity, the crucifixion and the Eucharist. It was as if profound religious ideas and the souls of local grandees could together defeat the new forces abroad in the world: the Norwich heresy trials of the 1420s had fiercely defended such images, and in particular the mystery of the Eucharist.[43]

In 1443, during one of many disputes over Tombland and associated issues, the citizens signed a settlement that went badly against their interests. The result was another attack on the cathedral, one that invoked both the citizens' burgeoning civic-religious culture and their new-found status. Like some East Anglian Trojan horse, a certain John Gladman rode through the city streets dressed as the King of Christmas, as 'ever has been the custom in any city throughout this realm', on Shrove Tuesday.

But *this* festive king came accompan-ied by an armed entourage of twenty-seven men on horse-back, all also dressed up, 'and a hundred other unknown persons, some on horseback and some on foot . . . carrying bows and arrows and swords'. It seems the 'commonality of the city . . . planned to make a common insurrection and disturbance . . . they believed too that because the city formed a county . . . the king would neither dare nor be able to punish them by his law'.[44]

Within three days the citizens had taken control of Norwich. Now three thousand of them headed for the cathedral. The Ethelbert and Erpingham gates were of little defensive use: the citizens simply tunnelled beneath them. 'Let us burn the priory and kill the prior and monks', they shouted, aiming to terrorize the community and seize the deeds and charters they felt were so unjust. In the end, they simply 'forcibly removed . . . a certain evidence belonging to the prior which was sealed with the city's common seal'. No one died.

Now the townsmen prepared their city for reprisals, 'with closed gates and in a state of arms, like a city at war with the lord king'. On 4 February, after a week's siege, the duke of Norfolk retook Norwich, and put the prior of the cathedral in temporary charge of the entire city. A £2,000 fine was imposed, plus another £1,500 on various individuals, all of whom were excommunicated. It was three years before Norwich's liberties were restored.

But both sides had become more sophisticated since the 1270s. The citizens had acted tactically, clothing their rebellion in a display of piety and pride and focusing on controversial charters rather than random violence; the bishop in his turn deferred the excommunications and refused to lay the city under an interdict. And this time the cathedral's response was an exercise in architectural inclusion.

A wave of change now engulfed the lay cemetery outside the west front. A fair was instituted there, held every year at Pentecost; a group of permanent shops was built, together with a preaching cross (1469). It was as if the area, already enriched after the last rebellion, was being enhanced as a public space; a sacred version of nearby Tombland. Norwich's lay guilds and religious fraternities used the cemetery for meetings;[45] processions of at least five of Norwich's nineteen guilds climaxed here. At these events scenes from sacred texts were re-enacted: the *Creation of the World* (staged by the mercers and drapers); *Hell Cart* (the play of the glaziers, carpenters and others); and *Paradise* (the grocers and tallow chandlers).[46] The cathedral's unpre-possessing west front was the backdrop to all this: now Bishop Alnwick aggrandized it with a new Perpendicular west door and great west window, the latter paid for in his will of 1449.

But it was Alnwick's successor, Bishop Lyhart, who displayed a particularly populist streak. In this he seems to have been sincere: he wanted his funeral, for example, to be not 'superfluous and excessive', and to give more to the 'sick and needy' than 'the rich and well-founded'.[47] Now, taking his artistic cue from the cloisters, he turned the nave into a mystery play in stone. He gave the church its first stone high vault, and by starting in the nave upended half a millennium of tradition, in which east ends were always grander than naves (see pp. 134–7).[48] The 339 carved bosses that studded the vault expanded with robust populism on the themes so esoterically portrayed on the Prior's Door (illustrated p. 143). In Lyhart's vault, Genesis runs chronologically from the east, and the Last Judgement from the west, ensuring that Old Law turns to New halfway down the nave. At every stage, Old Testament events are shown to have been God's planned prefigurements of New Testament ones: Noah and the Ark prefigure Christ's baptism; Joseph, cast into the pit three bays from the end of the Old Testament scenes, prefigures Christ's crucifixion, three bays from the end of the New.

The Erpingham Gate gave the cathedral a permanent landmark overlooking controversial Tombland

Thus the most uneducated visitor could see how all history unfolded in a symmetrical and preordained pattern, one whose images matched those in the *biblia pauperum*, the little religious primers filled with woodcuts, that were then becoming popular. For the better-informed viewer, each bay had fourteen side-images which were variations on the theme of its central boss, depicted as little vignettes, or the scenes of a play.[49] Just to make sure everyone knew who had made all this possible, Lyhart's rebus – a visual pun on his name, a deer (or 'hart') lying down on water ('Walter') – was carved on to the supports of the new vault.

In 1460 another such vault was added to the Bauchun chapel, scene of the bishop's court, and

Four hundred years separates the walls and the vault of Norwich's choir

was damaged again (this time it was struck by lightning), and as a result yet another fire broke out in the east end. Lyhart had left 2,200 marks for the choir to be vaulted; now Bishop Goldwell, his successor, built these vaults. After yet another fire in 1508, Bishop Nix vaulted the transepts. Unlike that in the nave, Goldwell's choir vault is little more than a colossal stone obit to the bishop himself, with ninety-four copies of his rebus – a little golden well – on its 128 bosses; the bosses in the transepts are even less interesting.

After three centuries when there had been little building in the church itself, Norwich had now been vaulted in stone throughout. Apart from helping protect the cathedral from further fires, the stone vaults somehow work aesthetically: the combination of Norwich's richly textured Perpendicular high vaults and the muscular plasticity of its romanesque walls are its most memorable feature.

Yet the cathedral's east end might easily have been made entirely Perpendicular, thanks to the easing of tensions between cathedral and city, perhaps a mark of their mutual prosperity. Goldwell, with financial support from the up-and-coming Boleyn family, recased and strengthened its fire-damaged presbytery arcade, and began to work on the gallery as well.[51] The number of bequests made to the cathedral in city wills doubled (from a quarter to a half) in the second half of the fifteenth century. In 1524, after long and costly negotiation, town and cathedral came to a final and mutually acceptable agreement over their retrospective rights.[52] By now, though it feigned monkish isolation, the cathedral was heavily embedded in the local economy, as employer, landowner and land manager, and several prominent lay people lived with their families in the close itself.[53] The cathedral began to fill with the tombs of local lay people. Alongside a grand collection of chantry chapels – not all of which survive, although those of Bishops Goldwell (d. 1499) and Nix (d. 1536), and Prior Bozoun (d. 1480)

arguably the place where lay and cathedral power most vividly intersected. The Corrector General of Crimes in the diocese, William Seckington, paid for thirty-two scenes telling the story of the empress of Constantinople, falsely accused of crimes and rehabilitated thanks to the intercession of the Virgin Mary.[50] Now no other cathedral interior so loudly addressed the ordinary late medieval layman, just as no other cathedral had had quite such a traumatic relationship with the city in which it stood.

The later fifteenth century saw more rebuilding, punctuated by further disasters. In 1463 the spire

are among those that do – there were chantries to Thomas Erpingham, Elizabeth Clere and Sir James Hobart, the Boleyn-sponsored east end arcades, and over one hundred brasses, presumably to monks and laymen alike, most now lost.

Shortly before his death, Bishop Nix issued prayers for Henry VIII and Anne Boleyn throughout his diocese; but by 1536, the woman whose great-grandparent's arms adorned the choir walls was dead. Nonetheless, the end for Norwich cathedral priory, fretted over apocalyptically on its roof bosses and fought against from its gates for 150 years, came not with a bang but with a whimper. In 1538, before any other cathedral priory had been dissolved, the monks wrote to Henry VIII requesting their own 'transposition'.[54] All bar three of them became canons. With an air of surrender, the work of Herbert de Losinga had been undone, and the cathedral became a college of secular priests.

Though its medieval statues and glass are lost, Norwich cathedral remains exceptionally well preserved. Only the west front, lady chapel and south transept facade have been greatly altered (or in the case of the lady chapel, completely rebuilt) since the Reformation. Even the bishop's palace – now Norwich school – contains the stones of de Losinga's original within it. The cathedral looks simple at first: twelfth-century architecture, fifteenth-century vaults. Consistent in design, complementary in effect, the two seem at ease with each other, reflecting the fact that for 500 years this church was served by its monks, who maintained a constant round of worship while making forays into learning and good works. For most of the time it was respected, if perhaps not loved, by the citizens of the burgeoning city (see p. 217).

Yet conflict with these very people is the hidden key to its architecture. If this tension has been sucked out of the heart of the church itself, it is everywhere on its periphery: in the cloister, in the roof vaults, on the gates that seal it from troubled Tombland. Even today this is an unhappy part of the city: a sterile zone of fast-moving traffic that divides bustling city centre from quiet cathedral close. The bishops of Norwich presided over the creation of a city, and then struggled to catch up when their creation developed a mind of its own. The consequences of bullish Norman planning are with us still.

WHAT TO SEE

Holy Trinity, Norwich
See founded c. 630; moved to Norwich and made Benedictine monastic cathedral 1094–6; secular cathedral 1538.

Church: near-complete Norman church with spectacular Perpendicular vaulting.

Sculpture, fittings and decorations: bishop's throne in the apse; thirteenth- and fourteenth-century wall painting in the treasury and nave aisles; painted Norwich Retable in St Luke's chapel; Prior's Door and carved bosses in the cloister, nave and Bauchun chapel – one of the best displays of medieval sculpture in England.

Close: belligerent gates on to Tombland and the city; Carnary chapel and bishop's palace facing west front; ruined infirmary and other monastic buildings in an enormous enclosure whose open land – once farmland for the monks – runs down to the Wentsum.

OXFORD

Before Oxford was a town, let alone the home of a world famous university, there was a ford across the River Thames. This area of low islets was a perfect place in which to settle; it was also a perfect place in which to hide.

Frideswide wanted to do the latter. Algar, a local king, was coming for her. He wanted to capture and if necessary 'defile God's vessel', force her into marriage and acquire the little settlement here which she had inherited from her father, another local king. So she hid in the church she had founded by the ford and prayed. She had planned to spend her life here, in the settlement by the wide river, the virgin head of her community.

Suddenly, something told Frideswide to run. Out of the church she went, down the grassy bank to its south, towards the river. She found a boatman waiting there, and was struck by his perfect appearance. They rowed for an hour upstream, until he put her ashore near Bampton. Here she hid in an abandoned, overgrown hut. The mysterious boatman vanished.

King Algar reached the settlement soon afterwards. He planned to burn the whole place down; but suddenly some invisible force blinded him. Frideswide and 'Oxford' were safe.

Frideswide spent much of the rest of her life as a hermit, living near the river at Bampton and Binsey, and only returning to her community to die. By then she had cured Alward of Seacourt –

Oxford has a long tradition of clever-clever architecture, from the late twelfth-century elevation to the stupendous vault of around 1500. The east wall is Victorian

burned by his own axe while trying to chop wood on a Sunday – and the blind girl of Bampton, her sight restored by the water in which Frideswide washed her hands. After she died, in the year 727, Frideswide was acclaimed a saint.[1]

No account of Frideswide's life survives before the early twelfth century: she may be an invention. Yet the geography of her story is accurate.[2] And by 1066 Oxford had become the sixth most important settlement in England,[3] with two Anglo-Saxon minster communities among its churches. Nonetheless, despite the fact that a large Norman castle was sited here, Remigius, first Norman bishop of nearby Dorchester-on-Thames, relocated his cathedral to Lincoln, leaving Oxford far from diocesan control.[4] It was to be several centuries before St Frideswide's church became Oxford cathedral.

Twelfth-century aristocrats turned Oxford's minsters into Augustinian priories: Oseney abbey was to become the richer, but St Frideswide's age, shrine and fordside location gave it a cachet of its own. Refounded by 1122, and much later valued at

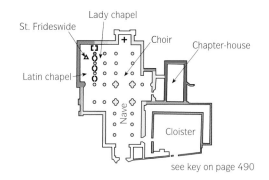

see key on page 490

The Anglo-Saxon nun Frideswide hides among Thames-side undergrowth: from her late thirteenth-century shrine

£220, it is the poorest religious institution described in this book; yet it became an architecturally dense building, with a story that embodies the roots of the famous city in which it lies.

For its first fifteen years, the community was virtually stillborn. Its reputed founder, 'warlord' builder Bishop Roger of Salisbury (see p. 74), directed its income into his own pocket, only asking on his deathbed that 'whatever I have taken from them unjustly' be restored.[5] When Robert of Cricklade became prior in 1139, he inherited a church that dated back to 1002. Leaving well enough alone for the time being, he began conventual buildings for his eighteen canons.[6] In the course of the twelfth century Oxford became the centre for a unique number of advanced teachers, each operating independently, as well as a third religious community in the shape of a collegiate church based at the castle. St Frideswide's, Oseney abbey and the

college of St George attracted scholarly churchmen, including Geoffrey of Monmouth[7] and Robert himself, who was already the author of a theological work, with a wide reputation for his preaching. Robert went on to write one of the most important early accounts of the life and miracles of Thomas Becket, after experiencing a miracle cure at the Canterbury shrine.[8] Perhaps this helped stimulate the rehabilitation of Oxford's virgin saint.

Before Robert could rebuild his church, he wanted to be sure its ancient saint was really there. After fasting for three days the canons entered their church at night, and – after some hard digging – found a skeleton beneath an empty stone coffin. One of those present pointed out that particularly precious remains were often hidden in this way.[9] As if in agreement, the candles around them went out and reignited again. St Frideswide had been found.

This spot of earth became a kind of tap root for the new church that was built in the last decades of the twelfth century. Work began to the north of the old church, the site of which was not disturbed until the north transept of the new one had been constructed. The transept reaches over the site of its predecessor like an arm over a sleeping body, and on its eastern side a square shrine-chapel was built covering the spot where Frideswide had lain. Yet even as the new church was being built, plans were changed, as if to accommodate more pilgrims than expected, and half the shrine-chapel was swallowed by new transept aisles.[10] Frideswide's cult was going through a remarkable revival, fuelled by the wave of interest in saints that followed in the wake of the Becket cult (see chapter three). Eighty-five new miracles were recorded; Robert wrote his *Life* of the saint, emphasizing her role as the city's protectress. The archbishop of Canterbury and the bishops of Winchester, Ely, Norwich, St David's and St Andrew's attended her translation of 1180, 'with a great crowd of clergy and people standing around and rejoicing'.[11]

The new church featured the 'giant order', a playful, knowing motif, popular in Scotland, where Robert had intriguing connections;[12] its up-to-date foliage shows awareness of the latest work at Canterbury. The giant order was invented in the 1090s at Tewkesbury abbey, in an attempt to follow the classical author Vitruvius.[13] With its burgeoning cult, intellectual prior and clever-clever architecture, twelfth-century St Frideswide's is a tantalizing window on Oxford at the moment the university was gestating.

Robert died before the translation. A fire in 1190 left the building 'without a roof and open to the assaults of the air and wind',[14] and as the building continued west there was a perceptible lowering of quality. St Frideswide's was to spend the next few hundred years in constant financial crisis.[15]

It was in the thirteenth century that the 'university' became an institution: it had a chancellor (often the bishop of Lincoln) from 1214 (see pp. 96, 106–7). St Frideswide's played an important symbolic role in this process: in 1228 the city's annual six-day fair was dedicated to her, and by the 1260s the university was making Ascension day processions to the priory as its 'mother church' – an expression usually reserved for cathedrals.

In the 1230s the canons built themselves a lovely Early English chapter-house; its timber roof may be the earliest surviving in Oxford.[16] Around the same time they added a short, narrow aisle between shrine-chapel and choir, perhaps intended to function as a lady chapel. And between 1289 – when St Frideswide was translated into the shrine that stands today – and 1334, the area was extended at least twice more in the Decorated style, one result being the Latin chapel. A complex of architectural accretions had thus billowed around the area on the north side of the church where Frideswide's tomb had lain; some are only known to exist from a handful of mouldings and other clues; and the twelfth-century shrine-chapel had been engulfed as completely as that chapel had replaced its Anglo-Saxon predecessor.[17]

The priory spent most of the fourteenth century locked in a series of unedifying, occasionally violent disputes: with the citizens of Oxford, with the many new academic colleges being founded in the university and within itself.[18] St Frideswide's had become just one of many competing institutions, its canonries and guest houses used by 'poor scholars'.[19] Yet the area around the shrine became packed with tombs.

Fifteenth-century Oxford was, as it remains, a medium-ranking city dominated by the university, the site of magnificent academic institutions such as New and Magdalen colleges. St Frideswide's benefited greatly in the slipstream of this: its cloister was funded by Robert Sherborn, dean of St Paul's and future bishop of Chichester, in 1489;[20] in 1504 a local notary left £30 for the north transept to be 'adorned' in the Perpendicular style, and for his own burial 'below the window he had had built'; and the famous Oxford mason William Orchard was buried in the church.[21] The pendant vault in the choir, which is closely related to Orchard's designs for the university's divinity school,[22] gave Oxford a dramatic late medieval vault that – like much of the church beneath it – combines cleverness and eccentricity.

In 1518 Katherine of Aragon visited St Frideswide's shrine, desperate for a baby boy.[23] Had the saint heard her prayers, history would have been very different. Perhaps she was concentrating on self-preservation. The Reformation destroyed almost every other church of comparable size, but Frideswide's survived – by the skin of its teeth. In 1524, in an experiment in dissolution, Cardinal Wolsey closed a dozen small monastic houses and used their income to fund a grand new Oxford college. Cardinal college was to be one of the richest ever created, and it was to lie partly on the site of one of these churches, St Frideswide's. Oxford's

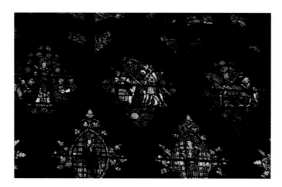

St Augustine, St Thomas and St Martin glow among grotesque creatures in this fourteenth-century window in the Lucy chapel, Oxford

nates Christ Church quad. Oseney abbey, by contrast, lies beneath Oxford railway station; Tom Tower, the gate to Christ Church, was built to house its famous bell.

Frideswide has proved good at hiding. Her bones still lie somewhere in the east end of Oxford cathedral. Although her shrine was destroyed at the Reformation, it has been re-erected, having been rediscovered in 1875, lining a well.[26] One end of her church billows around its ancient site, like one of the tumours she might have been expected to cure. The other has been truncated by the very university her priory helped to create. The church remains, a monument to the power of saints at their most talismanically local, and to the sudden ending of the world that made them.

oldest (and perhaps holiest) church would be entirely replaced by its newest and grandest college.

By 1529 three bays of the church's nave and one walk of its cloister had been demolished, and the masons were ready to take down its spire;[24] but in that year it was Wolsey's power rather than the tower that came crashing down. Building work ceased; a year later, Wolsey was dead. In his place the king picked up the pieces of the project, which was soon renamed King Henry VIII college.[25] The remaining two-thirds of St Frideswide's became the college chapel. This ancient church thus survived the Reformation, when the city's other non-academic religious houses were dissolved.

Sitting in one corner of the over-large diocese of Lincoln, Oxford was one of the more obvious candidates for a new see. For five years the former Oseney abbey was the chosen site, but then in 1547 Oseney cathedral was merged with the new King Henry VIII college; the new institution was renamed simply Christ Church. Oseney was abandoned, and the remaining portion of the former St Frideswide's began to fulfil a unique combinination of roles, both college chapel and England's smallest cath-edral. Wolsey's unfinished cloister still domi-

WHAT TO SEE

St Frideswide, now Christ Church, Oxford
Anglo-Saxon minster church (early eighth century, reformed mid-eleventh century); Augustinian priory 1122; chapel of Cardinal college and its successors King Henry VIII college and Christ Church, 1524; also cathedral from 1547.

Church: twelfth-century choir, nave, transepts and spire; thirteenth-century chapter-house; fourteenth-century Latin chapel; sixteenth-century choir vaults.

Fittings: St Frideswide's shrine (1289) and associated monuments; medieval glass in Latin chapel and St Lucy's chapel. Laudian and later fittings and glass.

Setting: Christ Church quad and the rest of the college are worth visiting as a vivid embodiment of Wolsey's ambitions; and the entrance to the cathedral, fittingly enough, involves walking along the edge of the Thames floodplain and coming in via the cloister.

PETERBOROUGH

Peterborough has reinvented itself several times. One of the most sweeping of these changes came in the twelfth century, when both the building we see today and the town around it were created; another came in 1541, when St Peter's abbey became a cathedral.

But these were not the first. A church was founded in the fenside town of Medeshampstede in 665; the fire with which the Vikings flattened it in 870 was said to have burned for fifteen days. Ethelwold, the great tenth-century reforming monk-bishop of Winchester (see p. 44), discovered 'the stalls of cattle and sheep'[1] among the ruins. Between 966 and 972 he founded a Benedictine monastery there dedicated to St Peter, and rebuilt the town in a great rectangle around it.[2] This settlement's wealth led it to be known as the Golden Borough: the monastery alone had an income of £1,050.[3]

By 1055 the Golden Borough had also acquired a precious relic: the arm of St Oswald. Oswald was a Northumbrian king who had been ritually dismembered by pagan Mercians in 642. By the time of the Conquest his head was at Durham, his left arm in Gloucester, and his right arm – fabled for its healing powers and incorruptibility – had been stolen from Bamburgh and brought to St Peter's.

The abbey suffered at the Conquest. The abbot, Leofric, died of the wounds he received at the battle of Hastings. The prior fled from the Normans, hiding at Ely, the great monastery on the other side of the Fens, with Oswald's arm buried in the straw of his bed. The monastery's income fell to £500; the town suffered equally badly.

Leofric's successor Prior Brand turned to the Anglo-Saxon pretender to the throne, Edgar Atheling, rather than the king, William the Conqueror, for his ritual blessing.[4] He was fined a rather restrained 40 marks. Meanwhile Hereward, an Anglo-Saxon tenant of the monastery's lands, had returned from Europe to find his brother

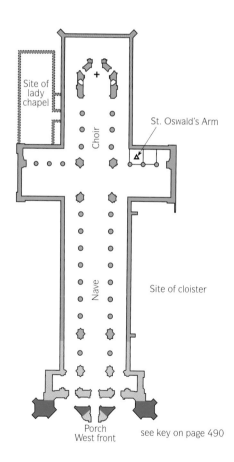

Site of lady chapel

Choir

St. Oswald's Arm

Nave

Site of cloister

Porch
West front

see key on page 490

murdered and his lands taken by Normans. Provocatively Brand knighted him; Hereward began gathering anti-Norman followers.[5]

After Brand's death in 1069, King William appointed a Norman abbot, Turold, who brought 140 knights with him. 'All manner of evils befell the monastery from that time onward.'[6] When an insurrection erupted at Ely, Hereward and his followers crossed the Fens to join it – and then, when the other rebels had been defeated, returned and attacked Peterborough itself. Finding that Abbot Turold was in Stamford, they sacked his monastery. Only the church and a single house were left standing.[7]

Turold and and the king came down hard on Peterborough, insisting that the abbey support sixty knights out of its income: this was more than anywhere bar Glastonbury, and consumed 46 per cent of the abbey's resources.[8] Hereward's rebellion had left Peterborough with a heavy burden of feudal obligations, and a ruin that would take decades to repair. None of this, however, prevented the monks from continuing the Anglo-Saxon tradition of maintaining a regular chronicle of events as they unfolded, and doing so with a virulent anti-Norman bias. Perhaps it was all they could do: Turold remained abbot for twenty-eight years, though 'being a stranger he neither loved his monastery nor his convent him'.[9]

When Turold died, the monks gave William II 300 marks in exchange for the right to elect their own abbot, and promptly elected Brand's brother. He was deposed a year later, accused of simony by Archbishop Anselm (see p. 67). No replacement was found for several years. But Anselm wanted to see Peterborough revived. In 1107 he made Ernulf, his energetic and cultured prior, the new abbot.[10]

By now cathedrals had been created at Lincoln

(in the diocese of which Peterborough lay) and Ely, and these, like the region's great abbeys at Bury St Edmunds and St Albans, had been rebuilt. Ernulf began his own rebuilding, but became bishop of Rochester in 1114,[11] only for his work at Peterborough to be destroyed as a result of a moment's irritation in August 1116. The new abbot's servant could not get the fire to light: 'The Devil take it!' his master shouted. The fire shot straight through his roof, and spread rapidly to both the church and the town. Soon, yet again, there was little left of either.[12]

Work restarted soon after,[13] and the result was a building in the grand East Anglian romanesque tradition of Ely and Norwich, incorporating a series of recent innovations: chevron decoration, intersecting wall arcades, a sanctuary marked out by inventive pier designs and double-aisled transepts. The galleries and passages that pierce its upper parts helped create a refreshingly light and noble effect, building on that explored at Ely and Norwich. But this building is not a pace-setter. This is architecture which has found a solid state, and is a proud part of the status quo.

The east end was in use by 1137, and much of the nave by 1175. It did no harm that the monks owned the quarries at Barnack, one of the best sources of stone in the country. But no English building project was free from the knock-on effects of 1170 and 1208 – the Becket murder and the interdict (see Chapter 3). After the Becket cult took off, where many churches focused on their in-house saint, Peterborough focused on Becket himself. Even before he was canonized in 1173, a hospital at the abbey gate seems to have been dedicated to him.[14] Four years later Benedict (d. 1193), another prior of Canterbury and Becket's main biographer, became abbot, bringing with him precious relics: finding himself alone in Canterbury cathedral, he had acquired two of the flagstones on which Becket had fallen and some of his blood.[15]

Abbot Benedict began an abortive project to

Peterborough's west front, building of which was perhaps disrupted by a clerical strike, is a work of glorious confusion

The Victorian painted ceiling is the climax of England's most complete romanesque great church east end

reinvent the near-complete abbey, perhaps inspired by the new Canterbury east end. Every mason for seventy years had followed the romanesque designs of 1118; now Benedict introduced early gothic. He tried (and failed) to vault the entire church. He lengthened it by two bays,[16] and built the back wall of 'that magnificent work' – a west front consisting simply of seven vast arches.[17] But something went horribly wrong with Abbot Benedict's plan; perhaps the interdict interrupted. Certainly Abbot Robert de Lindsey (*c.* 1214–22) works restarted, but now with a west front of only three great arches: as with so much post-interdict architecture, this was more imposing, and significantly higher, than Benedict had planned. Yet somewhere in the geometry of tying Benedict's seven-arch back wall to the new three-arch front, the central arch of the west front ended up narrower than the outer two, an effect that subverts normal compositional logic, while the gables above the arches were stuffed with decorations apparently intended for some different design. The thrilling and eccentric result looks as though it has been completed by someone with all the parts of a kit, but none of the instructions.[18] Nevertheless, these changes make the junction between Peterborough's nave and west end a living monument to one of the faultlines in medieval art: from Anglo-Norman romanesque, a style of architecture forged in the heat of invasion, to gothic, the architecture of a new age of saints, at once aggrandised and hopelessly confused by the interdict.

The west front is probably designed for Palm Sundays, when the church became a great theatrical model of the heavenly Jerusalem (see p. 197). A 'loud voiced clerk' stood on the abbey gate, to be answered from high in the west front itself: perhaps some of the openings in the gables were for a choir to sing through. Great banners were hung in front of the arches. The little fourteenth-century porch that stands within the central arch may have helped further choirs, who were to be positioned 'in modum castelli'.[19]

By 1222, Abbot de Lindsey and his sacrist had glazed the building and whitewashed the church and conventual buildings, and in 1237 the church begun 120 years earlier was dedicated. The wooden ceiling of the nave was soon painted, with the gallery of grotesques that survives today.

St Peter's spent much of the rest of the medieval period as a medium-to-large monastic community, with sixty-four monks before 1348 and about two-thirds of that number thereafter,[20] sustained by estates that included Stamford, Oundle and other lands mostly within 10 miles of Peterborough. But its most important possession was Peterborough itself. The Normans had relocated the entire town creating a new market place immediately west of the church and leaving the previous urban boundary to become the border of the abbey precinct. Thus was born modern Peterborough.[21] It was a settlement utterly dominated by its monastery: the inhabitants owed the abbot service and paid him obeisance; they could not even marry without his approval.[22] In return, the monks used perhaps 3 per cent of their resources to run two hospitals and give to the poor. During the fourteenth century the townsmen grew more vocal in their demands: the abbot built the first bridge over the Nene in 1308, only to enter a long dispute as to whether monastery or town should maintain it. Although such disputes turned to violent confrontations several times, in 1401–2 abbey and town united to build the parish church in the middle of Peterborough.[23]

Few other major changes were made to the church after the west front was complete. By 1272 – in spite of being fined for supporting Simon de Montfort, and an expensive legal battle with the king – the monks were able to afford a magnificent new lady chapel off the north transept. Fourteenth-century additions included a new central tower with an octagonal lantern, presumably influenced by that at Ely (both lady chapel and octagon have gone).[24] Almost all the windows were updated, in a gradual process that has left Peterborough with a virtual history of tracery design from the late thirteenth to

Fine tomb of a twelfth-century Peterborough abbot

the mid-fifteenth century. The cloister was renewed, and the delightful porch was inserted like a little house between the legs of the central arch of the west front.[25]

There is something urbane and worldly about late medieval Peterborough. In 1402 Pope Boniface IX mitred the abbey, placing the abbot on a par with bishops in certain areas. In the 1440s an abbot was found to have three lovers, all wives of townsmen, while under Abbot Kirkton (d. 1528) a monk was found to have stolen jewels from Oswald's shrine to give to local women.[26] Abbot Kirkton decided to turn the lay cemetery to the north of the church – former site of the Golden Borough – into a deer park for his influential friends, depriving the townspeople of both a cemetery and grazing land. Its grand entranceway is covered with heraldry intended to flatter his friend Lady Margaret Beaufort, mother of Henry VII.[27] Kirkton acted without the consent of town or convent – he even had to demolish a few houses – and the people of Peterborough invaded the precinct; legal arguments went as far as Star Chamber. Yet he also built the fine retrochoir known as the New Building, the first addition to the east end since it was built, 400 years earlier. Its magnificent fan vaults are probably by John Wastell, who designed those at King's college chapel, Cambridge.[28]

St Peter's was one of the monastic churches that were converted into cathedrals after the Dissolution. It may have been the presence of Katherine of Aragon that influenced Henry VIII's decision to save the church: when she died, cut off from her husband, at nearby Kimbolton in 1536, St Peter's was the nearest house of any stature, and she was buried here in an unmarked grave.[29] The huge diocese of Lincoln also needed to be broken up; whatever his reasons, in 1541 Henry founded 'the King's new college at Peterborough' – a cathedral for Northamptonshire.

St Peter's has lost almost all its medieval fittings.[30] With the honourable exception of the New Building, it is basically a monument to the period between about 1120 and 1220, and one that has lost much: an echoing piece of architecture rather than a piece of living history. Peterborough as a settlement has also become, once again, a kind of New Town. Yet the gaping west front of its former abbey still gazes over its shopping centre, a constant reminder of a church that has remade the town around it several times.

WHAT TO SEE

St Peter, now St Peter, St Paul and St Andrew, Peterborough
Monastery, founded c. 665; destroyed 870; Benedictine monastery c. 966; secular cathedral 1541.

Church: Norman architecture; thirteenth-century west front and painted ceiling of about same date; sixteenth-century New Building (retrochoir), with fine set of fan vaults.

Setting: view of the church from the town; cloister and traces of other monastic buildings.

RIPON

Ripon is a baby York minster, the cathedral that wasn't. As one of the archbishop of York's 'deputy cathedrals', this collegiate church was architecturally in thrall to York throughout the Middle Ages. It belatedly became a cathedral in its own right in 1836. Yet even when it was founded, over 1,100 years earlier, it was rather more than an 'ordinary' religious community, if rather less than a cathedral.

Ripon began life as a monastery on the Irish model in the 660s, soon reformed to follow the Roman rite by the bullish Wilfrid, abbot and later saint (see p. 40). He built an extraordinary church here, remained abbot when he became bishop of York, and was buried here; but Ripon was technically only a cathedral for five years in the 680s, during one of Wilfrid's periods of exile.

Astonishingly, the crypt of Wilfrid's church, dedicated in 672 with the Northumbrian kings in attendance, survives beneath the crossing of the present building (illustrated p. 40). With its sister crypt at Hexham, also built by Wilfrid, it is the oldest still-roofed part of a church in England. A barrel-vaulted room is reached through a disorientating series of passages; with recesses for lamps in its sides and a prominent niche in its east wall, it was probably a relic chamber beneath the high altar of Wilfrid's church, like those he had seen in Rome. Its walls are built of stones recycled from nearby Roman ruins, and its ceiling is still covered in hard Roman plaster.[1]

The crypt remained sacred for medieval Ripon, containing an altar to St Wilfrid.[2] One of its alcoves collapsed, leaving a hole known as St Wilfrid's Needle, where a woman's virginity could be tested: if she could climb through it, she was considered 'intact'.[3]

Wilfrid's cult at Ripon was powerful locally but never quite seemed to reach the heights of the other great northern saints. The problem started in c. 948, when Wilfrid's monastery was destroyed in a battle between the English and the Danes. Archbishop Oda of Canterbury visited its ruins four years later, and took away what he believed to be St Wilfrid's relics. Then Oswald, bishop of Worcester and archbishop of York (see p. 44), refounded and rebuilt the church, translating the bones which *he* believed to be Wilfrid's into it in 992. The Canterbury monks claimed that these bones actually belonged to Wilfrid II, bishop of York from 718.[4]

At the Norman Conquest, Ripon was a secular community, a typical minster church of seven priests, serving an area about 15–20 miles across,

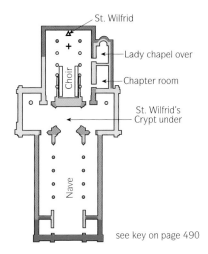

see key on page 490

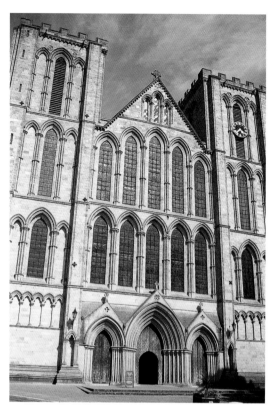

Deputy cathedral: Archbishop de Gray of York helped create one of England's finest Early English facades at Ripon

dust from Wilfrid's shrine to be used on sickening cattle, and the shrine itself to be carried from the church for an annual procession around the boundaries of the minster's lands, followed by local people (see p. 205). Ripon's priests administered the sacraments, and officiated at the Epiphany blessing of the ploughs of 'St Wilfrid's territory' (at a charge of one penny a plough); they oversaw the picking of yellow sallow and ivy from the archbishop's park, for use each Palm Sunday, as well as the burning of the previous year's palms and the anointing of the people with their ashes on Ash Wednesday.[6] Much of this work was carried out not by the canons, but by those they employed. Successive archbishops of York tried to encourage Ripon's canons to be resident, and after its twelfth-century rebuild the church had seven side altars, just right for each canon to say mass once a day. But only one canon was obliged to live in Ripon, and each employed several other men to do such work for him. It was these men – vicars, to sing in choir and do parish work, and proctors, who sat in chapter – who made Ripon tick. By 1303 some of the vicars had formed a sub-community of their own.[7]

Throughout the Middle Ages, the minster had a special relationship with the archbishop of York. He chose its canons, and had a symbolic seat in choir. He had a palace at Ripon, and owned more land there than the canons themselves. Ripon was a 'bishop's seat' and a 'mother church', it was said – terms usually reserved for cathedrals.[8] The arrangement, comparable with those at Southwell and Beverley, gave the archbishop of York a foothold at one extreme of his large diocese, and influence over the presentation of one of his sainted predecessors. As a result, builder-archbishops such as Roger of Pont l'Evêque and William de Gray sponsored ambitious architecture at Ripon, creating a church there that grew in step with its elder sibling at York.

The Anglo-Saxon church was rebuilt in the 1170s after a £1,000 donation from Archbishop Roger

like hundreds of others that once existed across England. By the thirteenth century most such establishments had been replaced by parish churches, but Ripon survived, the mother church for a huge 'parish' known as Riponshire. Its seven canons were responsible for the village churches of the 'shire' as well as for worship in the minster itself; their income, never particularly great, came from seven of these churches and a 'Liberty' in and around the town of Ripon.[5]

Ripon's community and its saint – rather like a more local version of Cuthbert – played an important part in life in the 'shire'. The canons permitted

of Pont l'Evêque.[9] The church that resulted was almost a two-thirds scale model of the then York minster. The plan of its western half imitated the distinctive aisleless nave built at York almost a century earlier, while the style of the building as a whole copied the revolutionary new east end at York then being constructed by Archbishop Roger himself (see p. 80), making it one of the earliest structures in the gothic style in England.

Another church with early gothic details stood even nearer to Ripon: the Cistercian abbey at Fountains just 3 miles away, founded in the 1130s. The birth of this community had been controversial, leading indirectly to the death of William fitz Herbert, archbishop of York (later a saint: see p. 78), and perhaps helping stimulate his successor, Archbishop Roger, to rebuild the York east end. The richness of this new east end at York and of Roger's work at Ripon was something of a riposte to the spare tastes of the Cistercians. Yet in spite of the troubled relationship between York and Fountains the canons of Ripon and the Fountains monks reached an agreement not to encroach on each other's lands as early as 1134.[10] The Cistercians' industrious conversion of wasteland to sheepwalk was to be the making of the town's economy and by the 1180s there was a wool industry there.

It seems that Roger's church was designed to focus attention on Ripon's saint, much as the new east end of Canterbury did on Becket after 1174.[11] This was done by locating the shrine at the east end of the nave, close to Wilfrid's crypt, which lay beneath the crossing of the new church.[12] The aisleless nave thus made a dramatic setting for the saint's crypt: a comparable arrangement to that around the tomb of archbishop William of York. Roger originally planned to vault the entire building in stone, though this was never carried out; when he died in 1181, the interior was nearing completion.

There was no archbishop at York for nearly a decade after Roger's death, or for the nine years of

The unfinished Perpendicular nave obscures a key early gothic design

the interdict (see p. 93). Ripon's west front, the base of which had been begun, appears to have been mothballed. But in the 1220s Archbishop William de Gray built a colossal set of transepts at York minster, improving the setting of the shrine of the newly canonized St William; and in 1225 he issued an indulgence encouraging pilgrimages to the shrine of St Wilfrid at Ripon, translated just a month earlier. Soon Ripon's west front had been completed in a mature Early English style. It is one of the most straightforwardly beautiful facade designs in England, with its noble arrangements of lancet windows echoing the famous Five Sisters window built by de Gray and his chapter in the north transept at York. Both made a striking setting for the approach of pilgrims to the shrine of a sainted archbishop.

Roger of Pont l'Evêque's determination to have the crossing of his church placed above the crypt of St Wilfrid proved unwise. It had forced the east end of his church to be dangerously close to the steep slope beyond, and in 1280 the east end collapsed, taking much of the presbytery with it. By 1286 rebuilding had begun, and a beautiful early Decorated east window was soon in place.[13] The east end is very much in the contemporary French-influenced vein of York's new chapter-house and nave. Even the new high vault, the first in the church, copied York's, in that it was made of wood.[14] In 1318 the Scottish army, with 'horrid deeds and hostile savagery',[15] burned the choir-stalls and other wooden fittings of the church, and the east end only finally neared completion in 1354.

There was a major collapse of the central tower in 1450: rebuilding began in 1459. The pulpitum screen, under way around 1472–6, attempted the grandeur of the one at York, but with clunky detailing by a very average team of masons.[16] The magnificent choir-stalls were built by William Bromflet and his two assistants between 1489 and 1494;[17] he supplied almost identical stalls to the monasteries at Jervaulx and Bridlington and the collegiate churches at Manchester and Beverley. By 1502 the aisleless nave was 'very much in ruins':[18] Christopher Scune, who had worked at Durham cathedral and the wealthy parish church of Louth in Lincolnshire, was appointed to rebuild it. He produced an anonymously handsome piece of late Perpendicular design, firmly rooted in the tradition of the grand mercantile parish church.

The early sixteenth century was not a good period for either town or church. Yorkshire's woollen industry was collapsing – 'Idleness is sore increased in the town and cloth-making almost decayed'[19] – while the last resident canon, Marmaduke Bradley, also abbot of Fountains, was a wealthy and simonous man. At the Reformation the college of canons was dissolved, and the minster became the parish church for Ripon.[20] Wilfrid's shrine, now located behind the high altar, was taken down; forty-nine service books and six 'great tablets of alabaster' were saved by being buried in the church, where they were rediscovered in 1871. Ripon was left unfinished, its nave dominated by a striking piece of stopped-in-its-tracks architecture: a single, massive supporting pier intended to support a new tower, its capitals crammed uncomfortably against the arch it was meant to replace.[21] Over the next few centuries the church lost its original three spires; but in 1836 northern Yorkshire finally got the cathedral that in some ways seems to have been waiting in the wings since the seventh century.

The collegiate church of Ripon began life as one of the most magnificent pieces of (not quite) cathedral architecture in Britain, and its subsequent story, from the miraculous to the mundane, reflects its status as a church at once in thrall to York minster and focused on one much smaller locality, known as Riponshire, and its saint. It remains a miniature homage to the architectural power of cathedrals, even when the cathedrals themselves were elsewhere.

WHAT TO SEE

St Peter and St Wilfrid, Ripon
Monastery founded mid-seventh century,
reformed by 672; cathedral 681– 6; abandoned
c. 948; refounded 972– 992; collegiate from
sometime thereafter to 1547, then a parish church;
became a cathedral in 1836.

Church: Wilfrid's crypt; original twelfth-century early gothic design visible in parts of the choir, transepts, and most clearly at the extreme east and west ends of the nave; Early English west front; Decorated east end and dramatically unfinished Perpendicular work in the nave; choir-stalls and other fittings.

ROCHESTER

A potent brew of politics, pride and poverty bubbled away in Rochester, resulting in one of England's more characterful little cathedrals. Long in thrall to Canterbury, it is a place at once bolshy and evasive, the architectural equivalent of a murder mystery in a Medway back street. Indeed it was a murder that gave Rochester its unlikely saint, the Scottish baker William of Perth.

The first mystery is why the diocese is there at all, squeezed as it is between the sees of Canterbury and London. In 604, just a few years after he had founded Canterbury, Augustine set up two new bishoprics. London was an obvious choice, being the former capital of Roman Britain and the intended site of his metropolitan church; but Rochester, an abandoned Roman city just 24 miles from Canterbury, perhaps had a political motiv-ation, for it is possible that east and west Kent had only recently been united into one kingdom.[1] Or it may be that the river crossing near the site of the cathedral was as important in the seventh century as it had been in Roman times, when the bridge across the Medway was first built. As a result Rochester was a key location on most journeys from London to Canterbury and on across the English Channel, and the history of cathedral, city and bridge were to remain profoundly interlocked. Whatever the reason, Canterbury and Rochester remained England's smallest dioceses throughout the Middle Ages. For Canterbury this was not a problem, since it had vast landholdings and regal powers over the English Church. But Rochester was one of England's poorest sees: Canterbury owned more land in the diocese than did Rochester itself.

The new cathedral was staffed by three to five priests and a bishop. A cult developed around Paulinus, third bishop of Rochester and first bishop of York. Rochester's strategic location made it vulnerable, however, and the cathedral's early history is marked by occasional bursts of warfare: the Mercians attacked in 676, the men of Wessex ten years later, the Danes five times between 842 and 981, and the Normans took a large portion of the town in order to create Rochester castle.[2]

When the last Anglo-Saxon incumbent died in 1076, Archbishop Lanfranc chose Gundulf (d. 1108), a close colleague and fellow Norman monk, as the new bishop. By 1083, he and Gundulf had begun to 'rebuild the church of Rochester from the founda-

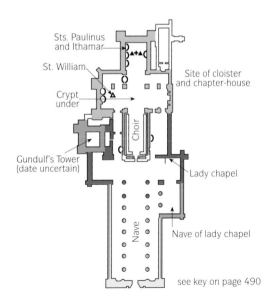

see key on page 490

The figure of Synagogue, her broken lance signifying the end of the Old Law, on the fourteenth-century door built by bishop Hamo de Hethe

unmistakable remains of an intriguing early Norman cathedral.[6] Gundulf had a reputation as a builder, responsible not least for the White Tower in the Tower of London,[7] and his church was distinctive in various ways. The simple, block-like capitals are an early example of the cushion capital, a Germanic import which would soon become a signature feature of Norman architecture. The flat-ended east end is even more prescient. Again, the precedents appear to lie across the North Sea.[8] This plan-form is unique among the post-Conquest cathedrals,[9] yet it was later to become one of the most distinctive features of English great churches.

In some respects the church was a smaller copy of Lanfranc's Canterbury. But in other ways it was a reaction to it, allowing more space for the monks and more latitude for architectural experimentation.[10] Such sincere imitation, if not quite flattery, of Canterbury was appropriate, for Rochester was a kind of Canterbury-on-Medway. Both were monastic cathedrals, created or supported by Lanfranc and adopting his constitutional arrangements. Rochester was already dependent on Canterbury,[11] but Lanfranc took the arrangement further. Rochester's bishop was to be chosen by the archbishop of Canterbury; he was to stand in for the archbishop when the latter was away on business (receiving an extra 20 shillings a day for the privilege); even his lands were held 'of the archbishop' rather than 'of the king'. Canterbury's estates in the diocese were 'peculiars', beyond the serf-cathedral's control. Rochester, in short, was Canterbury's feudal vassal.[12]

This arrangement worked well during the heyday of monasticism. The bishops were invariably also monks: Gundulf's successor was the brilliant Ernulf, prior of Canterbury under Anselm, where he created the sumptuous new east end; he became bishop in 1114 after seven years as abbot of Peterborough. But later hardly any monks or priors of Rochester went on to higher things, whether as

tions up', and 'established there the reverent religion of monks'.[3] Twenty-two Benedictine monks were moved in. The community reached sixty by 1100, before levelling off at between twenty and thirty.[4]

The church built by Gundulf and Lanfranc has mostly faded into the Medway fog, a casualty of later rebuildings and incompletely recorded archaeological investigations. How much of it can be attributed to Gundulf, long thought to have been among the most interesting of Norman cathedral builders, has been a matter of much recent debate. One recent author believes almost all the man's achievements are myths cooked up by later Rochester monks.[5] This is taking things too far, because down in Rochester's small crypt lie the

bishop of Rochester itself or as a senior figure in another monastic house.[13] The cathedral and its priory inhabited separate worlds, one focused on the high politics of Canterbury, the other inward-looking and fiercely self-protective.

Ernulf (d. 1124) had added a set of conventual buildings to the church.[14] His successors – an archbishop's nephew, another archbishop's brother – continued the building work, as a result of which the nave, perhaps first completed in the early twelfth century, was greatly reworked in the 1150s or 1160s along with the grand west front[15] and the exquisite (but now rather battered) east range of the cloister.[16] Rochester's west front, which contains several forms newly minted at St-Denis and Chartres, is one of the finest of its period in England.

But the cracks in the relationship between bishop and monks were starting to show. On Ernulf's death the archbishop installed a non-monk as bishop; the monks feared they would be the next to go. The long-lost relics of St Ithamar[17] were suddenly 'found',[18] and lives were written of him, St Paulinus and Bishop Gundulf, whose *Life* is often contradicted by known facts: in promoting their founding monk-bishop, the community's main aim was to create a potential stick with which to beat his successors. The monks also forged the documentation for almost every scrap of land and sliver of traditional rights they could find, creating in the process a great compendium, the *Textus Roffensis*. Soon bishop and monks had so little trust in each other that each created a separate copy of any decision, documents that often disagree.[19] The monks even tried to abandon their obeisance to Canterbury: it was traditional to place a dead bishop's staff of office on the high altar there until a replacement had been appointed, but during the 1180s the monks made this impossible by burying it with him. It was around this time that the bishops concocted a plan to replace the monks altogether;[20]

Bishop Glanville had to give up this plan after the death of Henry II in 1189, but the resulting tension between Glanville and the monks – and the febrile context of post-Becket Canterbury – fuelled an eventful period at Rochester.

With the murder of Thomas Becket, Rochester suddenly found itself on a pilgrim route of international importance.[21] Having failed to throw out the monks (but succeeded in helping his archbishop fight the monks of Canterbury – see p. 91), Bishop Glanville founded a hospital for weary travellers, with a new stone quay, right where the main pilgrim route from London crossed the Medway, staffed by priests rather than monks, and paid for out of the monks' lands.[22] Their assault on his plans dragged on for thirteen years.[23]

It was in this potent context that Rochester's most famous medieval murder occurred, and its most ambitious architecture was begun. Both seem

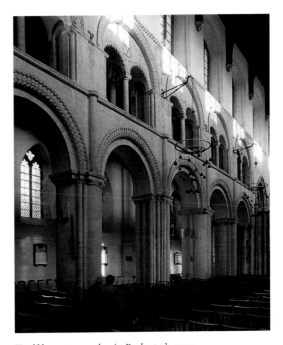

Twelfth-century arches in Rochester's nave

Rochester's early gothic east end: irascible project of a church at war with itself

to be at once in thrall to Canterbury, and desperate to demonstrate their independence from it.

William of Perth, a Scottish baker, went on pilgrimage to the Holy Land in 1201. He was on his way to Canterbury, having visited the shrines at Rochester, when his servant turned on him in a wood and cut his throat. After a local madwoman was healed by contact with his dead body,[24] local people took the 'martyred' corpse to the cathedral.

Every other cathedral saint was a former bishop; William was a commoner.[25] His cult came served with a large side order of local politics, emphasizing as it did Rochester's role on the route to Canterbury and beyond, just as its bishop was fighting to establish a refuge for pilgrims like William. Funds from the cult also conveniently helped the bishop pay for a new, early gothic east end.[26]

This east end, which is difficult to date precisely,

has a two-storey design, perhaps going out of its way to emphasize Rochester's subservient status;[27] yet its combination of both crypt and eastern transepts is an extravagance shared only by Canterbury and York.[28] Like the Canterbury east end it is a tense, stretched, restless design, covered in pipe-like shafts of polished stone, like the blackened veins of a martyr's corpse. Yet unlike Canterbury, it has almost no decorative carving, apart from the dogtooth ornament that runs like teeth in the mouths of its lancet-thin arches. The twin shrines of St Paulinus and St Ithamar were placed on a platform behind the high altar; that of William of Perth stood in the north-east transept.[29]

Work may have ceased altogether at the interdict (see p. 93): Glanville fled to Scotland and then France, and in the civil war that followed Rochester castle was placed under siege by the forces of

King John, who looted the cathedral. Glanville was eventually buried in an elegant tomb of polished stone – comparable to that built in Canterbury by his archbishop – positioned between the high altar and the shrine of the bludgeoned Scots baker whose death he had exploited.

Most cathedral building projects were boosted in the 1220s. But at Rochester – perhaps because of the interdict – works ceased, and never recovered their old vigour. The choir was completed by 1227,[30] but an attempt to create a grand vaulted space in the south choir aisle was abandoned, leaving a wooden-roofed area that remains the most oddly shed-like space in any English cathedral. The transepts were rebuilt, but not vaulted for a century; a projected rebuilding of the nave was abandoned after just two bays.[31] The choir-stalls are among the oldest in the country.

Meanwhile the monks continued to squabble with bishops and local citizens alike, in spite of the fact that they won the right to elect their own prior in the late thirteenth century, and in the decades that followed several monks even went on to become bishop.[32] There was the question of the *xenium*, the donation of food from Rochester's lands each St Andrew's day. This was no token gift: it included sixteen suckling pigs, thirty geese, 1,000 lampreys, 1,000 eggs and more.[33] Bishop and monks fought over its division. Then the monks locked the people of Rochester out of the church. Since the cathedral nave was used as the parish church, access at all times was vital, for without the holy oils stored at the parish altar no man could die in peace. The bishop eventually forced the monks to build a small parish oratory off the nave aisle, followed in 1423 by the parish church that still stands next door to the cathedral.[34]

All this litigation was expensive. Rochester was badly in debt for much of the thirteenth century;[35] building work happened only fitfully thereafter. The one exception, the relatively peaceful episcopate of Hamo de Hethe, proves the rule: as a monk and

Hopeful with optimism, a figure rises up the Wheel of Fortune, a thirteenth-century painting in the Rochester choir

former Rochester prior, he made high quality contributions to the building. Hamo became bishop in 1320: he created new shrines for St Paulinus and St Ithamar, had the choir richly repainted and built a new central tower, refectory and dormitory.[36] The main survival of all this is the magnificent Decorated door that dominates the darkest end of the south choir aisle, as covered with rich carving as the page of an illuminated manuscript. A little carved image of Hamo's naked soul entreats the prayers of the processing (and probably grumbling) monks; the door now leads to the Chapter Library.[37] Hamo also had financial problems, and endured complaints of simony from his monks.[38] Some people are never grateful.

In the fifteenth century the nave received a clerestory and roof that would be run-of-the-mill in a Perpendicular parish church, let alone a cathedral. A new window was punched through the twelfth-century west front.[39] Perhaps Rochester had given up being anything more than a medium-sized community run by a deputy archbishop. There are worse fates, especially as many late medieval bishops of Rochester were worthy theologians rather than careerist administrators.[40]

Rochester's last architectural gasp was left unfinished, but it might just have been the initiative of one of these men. It is a glorious attempt to give the church a suitable lady chapel. Rochester's lady altar stood against the east wall of the south transept, and was a popular place of burial, at first for bishops but later for laymen, too. Now an extension was built for it between the transept and the nave aisle.[41] The sweeping verticals of its walls suggest that a thrilling Perpendicular design was planned, but never completed.[42]

It is tempting to see this as the brainchild of Bishop Fisher, theologian, anti-heretic, founder of

St John's college, Cambridge, and one of the martyrs of the Reformation. Fisher refused to accept the split with Rome, and was deprived of his see, imprisoned in the Tower and beheaded in June 1535. His head was set on a spike over London Bridge, where it grew rosier and more alive every day; the authorities quickly had it thrown in the Thames. He was canonized by the Catholic Church in 1935.[43]

In 1539, after almost half a millennium fighting this very possibility, Rochester's irascible monks left the building, though some returned as secular canons. The conventual buildings became a royal residence. Yet in a sense Rochester – Canterbury's starveling, feisty little brother – has had the last laugh. It contributed some of the first and last saints in English history, and in the process has survived from the dawn of Roman Christianity to the present.

WHAT TO SEE

St Andrew, now Christ and St Mary, Rochester Secular cathedral 604; Benedictine monastery by 1083; secular cathedral 1541.

Church: eleventh-century western portion of crypt; ambitious twelfth-century west front; thrillingly tense Early English east end and transepts; Perpendicular additions including lady chapel.

Fittings: fine collection of tombs and other decorations and fittings, especially from the thirteenth and fourteenth centuries, including well preserved polychromy on the effigy of Bishop Sheppey; wall paintings in the choir; ancient choir-stalls; Chapter Library door; vault and roof bosses.

Setting: view of the whole church (and Medway) from the castle (English Heritage).

ST ALBANS

This strange, battered church is as much a work of archaeology as of architecture. The remains of dozens of ruined Roman buildings are locked up in its walls, along with bits of an abandoned Anglo-Saxon monastery; it became half-ruined after the Reformation; and the great shrine-base of St Alban has since been rebuilt from 2,000 pieces. Even its status as a cathedral is a reworking of the past: this once mighty abbey only became the seat of a bishop in 1878.

St Alban himself is the binding force in this complex stratigraphy. He was the protomartyr – the first man in Britain to die for his faith. This combination of venerability and martyrdom is the great theme of his church.

Yet the man himself is obscure. He is said to have died in the Roman city of Verulamium, the ruins of which lie a short walk from the abbey. He had saved the life of a fleeing British priest, St Amphibalus, by impersonating him. He was beheaded by the Romans; God plucked out the eyes of his executioner. We know his cult existed by 429, and that it somehow survived the Anglo-Saxon invasions; we also know that a great Pagan hero was worshipped nearby long before the Christian shrine was founded, in a cult that also associated a heroic figure with severed heads.[1]

For medieval people, the story of St Albans abbey also began with archaeology. King Offa of Mercia, it was said, excavated the tomb of St Alban in 793, and refounded the monastery. The truth is again unclear.[2] What is certain is that by the late tenth century the saint had moved a city. Roman Verulamium lay abandoned in its valley; modern St Albans grew up around the new church,[3] which

was centred on the site of the martyr's tomb in a suburban Roman cemetery, near the great road known as Watling Street.

In 1005 a major building project began at this monastery. The abbots were given permission to use stone from ruined Verulamium.[4] A new structure was begun, not far away but in a more commanding hilltop position.[5] Soon the monks had adopted a

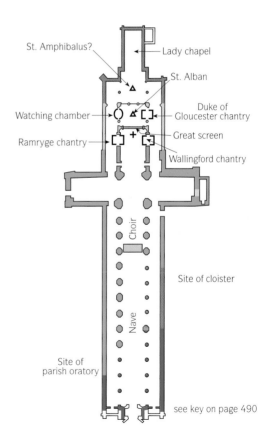

see key on page 490

special prayer to hallow some of the many classical vases they found and wanted to reuse: 'Cleanse these vases, fabricated by the art of the gentiles, that they may be used by believers in peace.'[6]

Although this church was probably never completed, St Albans remained one of England's richest abbeys, and in 1066 it became a focus for English resistance. It was said that William the Conqueror considered doing away with it entirely. Instead Paul, nephew of Archbishop Lanfranc of Canterbury, was made abbot in 1077, and began rebuilding the church almost completely (see p. 55). This was one of the earliest Norman rebuilding projects, and the first whose ambitions outstripped any church in Normandy itself. It may also be a pointed completion of the unfinished project of 1005.

The relocation of the church, away from the tomb of St Alban to a hilltop site overlooking both the approach from London and the Roman ruins, was now complete. Its ambitious architecture included a tunnel-vaulted east end and a row of seven apses, lined up on the hillside beneath a bright coat of whitewash. Perhaps Paul and Lanfranc, initially suspicious of Anglo-Saxon saints and religious practices (Paul called the monks 'uneducated simpletons'),[7] had decided that here at least was one saint they could invest in.

Master Robert, Paul's mason, 'excelled all masons of his time':[8] he was certainly a competent engineer.[9] The great arches of the crossing have now been standing for nearly one thousand years. Yet in terms of detail this is barely architecture at all. The arches are so plain that they are more like walls with holes in; there is no carving, barely even a chamfer, to relieve the eye. The church was built from countless reused Roman tiles, its interior relieved only by a few bold Anglo-Saxon balusters

Bare eleventh-century arches give way to unforgiving extensions of later centuries in the nave of the once-mighty St Albans abbey

from the abandoned building of 1005. Paul was completing on a grand scale what the Anglo-Saxon abbots had left undone – and making a building out of Roman materials, to house a Roman saint. St Alban was translated into a new shrine in 1129; the building around it was patched and extended many times but, in spite of the abbey's wealth, never rebuilt. Perhaps the abbots of St Albans, with their special claim to an ancient saint, actually wanted their church to look archaic.

In 1156 Pope Adrian IV granted mitred status to St Albans, giving it independence from the diocese of Lincoln and a direct reporting line to Rome itself.[10] Adrian came from Abbots Langley in Hertfordshire, so St Albans was his 'home' abbey. It must have seemed like a moment of great triumph. The monastery's lands included much of south-east Hertfordshire; it had daughter houses as far away as Tynemouth. But turf wars ensued: St Albans fought its dependent priories, it fought the bishop of Lincoln and it fought the neighbouring monastic houses at Westminster and Ely (which claimed to have returned someone else's relics, after protecting those of St Alban from the Danes). In order to avoid the risk of implying subservience to an English bishop, abbots had to make (or pay a proctor to make) the expensive trip to Rome to be invested, while the pope found he could approach St Albans directly when in need of cash. St Albans had expanded from fifty to about one hundred monks in about 1200, but soon fell back to about fifty again; it was often in debt.

Perhaps such problems lie at the root of St Albans' patchy architectural story, which is typified by its response to the challenge set by the post-Becket 'saint fever' of the years after 1170. St Albans' initial response was, as ever, archaeological. In 1178, the body of Alban's companion Amphibalus was 'found' and a new shrine created for him. About the same time, a new *Life* of Alban himself was written, now including Amphibalus – said to be Britain's

The central tower is built almost entirely of recycled Roman brick

first evangelist, as Alban was its first martyr. The monks began work on an ambitious early gothic west front. It was never to be completed. Despite the building fund's right to a sheaf of corn for every acre sown on abbey lands, 'a hundred marks and much more were spent and yet the foundation wall had not risen to the level of the ground'.[11] The project had to be abandoned, perhaps because the monastery was fined 1,100 marks after its abbot clashed with King John. A half-finished rebuild of the nave beyond was also stopped. There are few architectural junctions more brutal than that between the solid Norman piers of the abbey's nave and the shafted Early English columns of its still-born replacement.[12]

The optimism of the post-John era (see p. 99) was embodied at St Albans not by architecture but by decoration. William of Colchester, the famous sculptor, painter and goldsmith, became sacrist in 1213. He covered much of the church with new murals, sculptures and fittings as well as helping to make St Thomas's shrine at Canterbury. Another thirteenth-century St Albans monk was the artist and author, Matthew Paris: he produced new biographies of both Alban and Amphibalus, and may just have been the brains behind an antiquarian wheeze that gave weight to the latter's cult. A cross was bought at great cost from a London family,

where it had 'long lain hidden'; it was claimed that this was the 'cross of St Amphibalus' – the first crucifix ever to enter Britain.[13]

With the first martyr, the first evangelist *and* the first cross in England inside its doors, the abbey reordered its decorations around the all-embracing image of the crucifixion. By 1224, the shrine of St Amphibalus had been moved from the east end to a more accessible location in the nave, right beneath the great rood.[14] Three other roods had been installed, so that every arm of the abbey was dominated by one.[15] The church was whitewashed and reglazed, a spire added, and 'retrospective' tombs created for two local hermits with saintly reputations. All this helped to create a church that, 'illuminated with the gift of fresh light, seemed almost like new'.[16]

Later rebuilding work at St Albans was usually born of necessity rather than ambition or design. In 1257 large cracks appeared in the side of the eleventh-century presbytery, which triggered the replacement of much of the Norman east end: a new presbytery was built by around 1290, and a new retrochoir and richly decorated lady chapel by 1327 at the latest. The east end (and possibly also the west end) had now both been extended since the church was built, turning St Albans from long to lanky – almost as long as St Paul's and Winchester cathedrals, the longest churches in Europe.

The new east end was to be a powerhouse of sanctity. St Amphibalus was moved back into it and given a fine new shrine, fragments of which survive. In 1309 St Alban was given a 'marvellous tomb of splendid workmanship', which has become England's best-preserved shrine of a major saint.[17] The area became a magnet for high-profile fittings and tombs: the Watching Loft, built by 1420, from which one of the abbey's tenants acted as the shrine's security guard; the Duke of Gloucester's Chantry (see below) of about 1443;[18] and the chantry of Abbot Ramryge, who died in 1521. The result is the most evocative medieval shrine setting in England, even without the eagle with outstretched wings and the two suns with gold-tipped rays that once topped the shrine itself.

Then, in October 1323, fourteen years after St Alban had received his new tomb, 'there was a great crowd of men and women in the church to pray or to hear mass . . . suddenly two great columns on the south side . . . fell successively to the ground with a terrible noise and crash . . . laity and brethren came running together from all sides, stupid with terror.' Soon much of the south side of the nave lay in ruins.[19] Excavations have revealed an elaborate Saxon structure beneath this area;[20] perhaps St Albans was brought down by its own archaeology. In any case the mason, Henry Wy, could only make the best of a bad job. Part of the nave was Early English and the rest was from the 1070s, so whatever he designed would jar with something. In the event he built a near-copy of the Early English part of the nave. The cloister was also rebuilt. As a result, the bewildering nave at St Albans contains work of the 1330s on one side, pretending to be work of the 1220s; and on the other, work of the 1220s that suddenly stops, revealing arches of the 1070s, themselves constructed of materials made by the Romans. This is indeed archaeology.

The Black Death killed the abbot, the prior and forty-seven of the monks.[21] Thomas de la Mare (d. 1396), who became abbot in 1349, moved quickly to shore up morale. He rebuilt much of the monastic complex, including an enormous fortified gatehouse, and commissioned his own sumptuous brass, which is still one of the most impressive

A painting of St William of York in the feretory at St Albans, England's most evocative shrine space. The retrochoir and lady chapel stretch beyond

Grotesques and saints side by side in this detail from the magnificent brass of the reforming abbot de la Mare

objects in the church. He revived learning in the monastery, and worked hard to emphasize the role of the abbey and its saint among the townspeople. Each year, for example, on St Alban's feast day, the saint was carried around his town by twelve monks, who theatrically put it 'down a while at the market cross'; then, when 'the monks assayed to take it up again, pretending that they could not stir it', the abbot placed his crosier on the relic, saying 'Arise, arise St Alban and get thee home to thy sanctuary', at which point it yielded.[22] He also enforced the rules of monastic life so strictly that many of the remaining monks left. From de la Mare's time until the Reformation, St Albans had around fifty monks, supported by perhaps forty servants and advisers.[23]

Perhaps displays like the feast day procession reflected the tension between the church and the town it owned. The men of St Albans fought the abbey in the 1270s, the 1320s and 1340; the precinct was walled (or perhaps rewalled) from 1357.[24] In 1381 St Albans was the focus of the Hertfordshire contingent of the Peasants' Revolt; in 1417 heretics

were active there.[25] These late medieval troubles, set in a context of widespread political unrest and rapid social change (see chapter four), stimulated a virulent response from the monks. In the decades around 1400, the townsmen's claims to independence – their settlement had been founded by the abbey's masons, they said – were demolished. Bede himself was rewritten and re-edited to focus more fully on the figure of St Alban; sixty new miracles were claimed for the saint. A vast 'Book of the Benefactors' was compiled, and new *Lives* portrayed Alban as a princely, chivalrous martyr and Amphibalus as his proto-humanist, royal-blooded companion. To suit their upwardly mobile status both saints acquired coats of arms, which were then used by Abbot Wheathamstead in the decoration of the church.[26]

All this might have been designed to appeal to the abbey's friends in the aristocracy. Its location meant a constant stream of high-profile visitors – the Black Prince and the king of France to name but two – to all of whom it offered hospitality.

By the fifteenth century the abbey's guest hall was equipped with its own teams of huntsmen and falconers for the amusement of such guests.[27]

In the 1420s one such figure developed a particular devotion to St Alban. Humphrey, duke of Gloucester – Protector and Defender of the Realm of England – visited many times (once with a retinue of about 300 retainers).[28] He used both saint and abbey as extensions of his campaign to be made regent, setting St Albans up as a potential alternative to Westminster abbey. Around 1443 Humphrey built himself an extraordinary chantry chapel at St Albans. This three-storey chantry was on an unprecedented scale, a church-within-a-church with a tiny crypt, where Humphrey's tomb stood alongside an altar and a painting of the crucifixion. Here mass was read daily for Duke Humphrey's soul by two priests. On his annual deathday, thirteen poor men carried torches round the tomb. Humphrey died in 1447: poisoning by his dynastic enemies was suspected.[29]

In 1484 a Great Screen, like those at Winchester and Southwark (see p. 149), was built by Abbot Wallingford at a cost of 1,100 marks. The silver image of the crucifix at its centre made a dramatic setting for the raising of the host; it also hid the shrine – which had been a visual focus behind the high altar for 500 years – completely, directing all eyes towards the Eucharist.[30] Both shrine and Eucharist could also be glimpsed close-up through the screens of lordly tombs: Wallingford's chantry, by the high altar, and the duke of Gloucester's, by the shrine.

Two key battles of the Wars of the Roses – in 1451 and 1461 – were fought at St Albans, but the abbey's role in national life was fading.[31] After the Dissolution it was no longer clear that the building had any kind of future at all. A road was driven through the retrochoir, leaving the lady chapel an independent structure; it was converted by the former abbot into a school. The shrine-base was broken into over 2,000 pieces and built into the wall that divided the road from the church. The conventual buildings were sold for building stone; the abbey church became the parish church of St Andrew, a vast structure that could barely support a single priest. Eight metres of the nave collapsed in 1832. But thanks to men like Lord Grimthorpe, the building was rescued by the Victorians; it was during this process that the fragments of the shrine of St Alban were found. In 1872 it was rebuilt in its original location, and in 1992 – after £150,000 had been raised – re-erected once again.

Thanks to at least 2,000 years of rebuildings, alterations and half-finished projects, St Albans can seem at once oddly hollow and a little brooding. Yet 100,000 candles a year are consumed at the 'shrine' here.[32] The feretory is visited by a quiet stream of pilgrims of indeterminate faith, seeking healing as much psychic as physical, focusing on a reconstructed medieval fitting that until very recently contained no relics[33] – the distant echo of a man who himself may have been invented. The power of St Alban has been replaced by the power of archaeology.

WHAT TO SEE

St Alban, St Albans
Origins in the third to fifth centuries; Benedictine monastery founded 793; parish church after 1539; cathedral from 1878.

Church: Norman architecture, incorporating reused Roman and Saxon stonework; Early English and Decorated alterations, especially choir and lady chapel.

Fittings and decorations: wall paintings, especially in the nave; feretory, including reconstructed shrine of St Alban; Watching Chamber; chantry chapels.

Setting: view of the abbey from the ruins of Verulamium.

ST PAUL'S

'Paulsbury' was once as familiar a name to Londoners as Camden, Soho, or the City are to us. Thousands gathered in this enclosure for rule-of-thumb exercises in open-air democracy, mass displays of urban pride, or to make offerings to the special saints of the capital. At the heart it was the colossal church – one of the largest structures on earth – we call Old St Paul's. This cathedral dwarfed the one that stands on the same site today; its spire was every bit as iconic as Wren's great dome.

A whole section of this close, to the north and east of the cathedral, was a focus for London life. Here stood the site of the 'Folkmoot', whose separate bell tower summoned Londoners to mass meetings, and Paul's Cross, where bishops preached the downfall of King John and Lollards argued for the end of the established church. Here were the cathedral school, London's main concentration of bookshops, and the workshops where prelates on a shopping trip could commission a new funeral effigy or altarpiece. Here also was the tomb of Thomas Becket's parents, which became the centre of the Pardon Churchyard, a unique lay enclosure where Londoners – from paupers with no parish affiliation to mayors and merchants – could be buried. In the fifteenth century a unique lay 'cloister' was built around it, painted with the Danse of Paul's – a 'dance of death' that was one of the sights of medieval London. In 1549 over 1,000 cartloads of bones were taken from here to Finsbury Fields.[1]

This 'people's' zone' funnelled lay visitors towards the northern entrance of the cathedral itself.

Old St Paul's as painted in 1616

Today the north transept is the most easily ignored entrance to the cathedral: once, it must have been one of the most charged locations in London.

Here, from the fifteenth century, stood a statue of the wonderful St Uncumber, a kind of spiritual refuge for battered wives. Uncumber was a trans-sexual saint: she had miraculously grown a beard to avoid a forced marriage, and was crucified by her

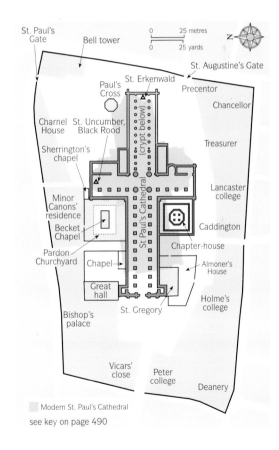

Modern St. Paul's Cathedral
see key on page 490

411

Wren's great church, 'model' cathedral of Anglicanism

was really dead; those killed in the battle of Barking in 1471 were also brought to the church for public display. The nave where these grisly events took place was almost an extension of the close outside: men looking for work as jurors gathered at the font; twelve 'scriveners' nearby[4] wrote contracts and official documents on demand; painted boards described the history of the venerable church itself.

The history of St Paul's marches in step with that of London itself: capital of Roman Britannia, with a bishop by 314; a near-abandoned city in 604, when St Augustine established a new cathedral, the intended seat of an archbishop; a settlement of growing importance in the late seventh century, when St Erkenwald established the first known church on the current site. This was followed by five hundred years during which London developed from an important Anglo-Saxon trading port into the uncontested political and economic capital of England, alongside Cologne the 'leading urban phenomenon of northern Europe'.[5] The last attempt to make London (if not St Paul's) the seat of an archbishop came in the 1190s.[6]

One cult underlay all others. Uniquely, 'London cathedral' is named for its patron, not for its city. St Paul was the capital's special protector: 'Paul provides for you in temporal things',[7] the chapter was taught; the citizens assembled before his banner in time of war. The cathedral and its close were literally his. The name Paulsbury[8] is pre-Norman: later documents simply talk of events happening 'at St Paul', as if cathedral, close and saint were one and the same.[9]

By the Reformation, St Paul's cathedral was, at 196 metres, the longest church in Europe.[10] It had a romanesque nave and transepts and a Decorated gothic east end, rebuilt from 1258. Imagine Norwich cathedral, with an east end rather like the nave of York, but bigger than either. The building had two great architectural signatures: the spire, which was perhaps 158 metres high (nothing taller was built

father as a result. Women in abusive relationships came here to pray. With her beard, crucifix and 'gay gown and silver shoes', Uncumber was one of the first targets of the Reformation.[2]

Just inside the transept was the Crux Borealis or Rood of the North Door, believed to have been brought to England by Joseph of Arimathea, Christ's uncle, and later miraculously washed up at Paul's Wharf.[3] The tombs of wealthy Londoners were packed around this relic. Other St Paul's cults were by turns London-centric and daringly political: Londoners loved Becket, the London boy and former canon of St Paul's who defied the king; and in 1322 Edward II tried to suppress the cult here of his recently executed opponent Thomas of Lancaster. The cathedral's bishop-saints Erkenwald and (uncanonized) Niger were given sumptuous new shrines shortly afterwards, perhaps in an effort to direct attention elsewhere. The body of Richard II was displayed in the church in 1399, to prove he

in London until the Telecom Tower in the 1960s); and the east window, combining a rose window with probable ogee-arched vertical lights,[11] the pattern of which was so popular that Chaucer describes 'Poule's window' being used as a decorative pattern on a clerk's shoes.[12]

Despite this grandeur, St Paul's was by no means England's richest cathedral, nor did it have an ecclesiastical monopoly over the city around it.[13] London contained 110 parish churches and seventeen or more other religious houses, including several of national importance. In the suburban fields of Southwark, Westminster, Holborn and the Strand stood the grand palaces of many English bishops. As many Londoners – about 15 per cent – gave money to London Bridge as to their mother church.[14] However, the cathedral did own the rich countryside now comprising Tower Hamlets, Hackney, Islington and Camden, and much else besides;[15] and its Pentecostal processions were organized in a way that suggests a deep-seated engagement with the citizens (see p. 203).[16] In 1075 it was declared the third most important church in England.

The thirty-one members of chapter were proud of their institutional uniqueness. Where other cathedral chapters were gatherings of equals, that of St Paul's divided its members into two ranks.[17] Prebends were not huge in value and residency was expensive, but with it came a house in the capital and membership of a very high-status corporation. St Paul's had low levels of absenteeism.[18] The chapter made the south and west sides of Paulsbury into an exclusive area, the base where perhaps 300 churchmen lived.[19] Here stood the bishop's palace, the deanery and the houses of the canons, as well as purpose-built colleges for minor canons, vicars choral, chantry priests and others. The most remarkable structure here was William Ramsey's chapter-house of 1332, which poked a stiff, scintillating octagonal profile above the high, windowless external walls of a tiny two-storey cloister (see p.

130). Admission to chapter was no one's right – not even new canons could assume membership without written permission from the dean.[20]

Old St Paul's was demolished after the Great Fire of London of 1666; some of its stones were used to build both the present crypt and Somerset House,[21] two Renaissance masterpieces recycled from a gothic one. By this date it had become a crumbling dinosaur, its architecture corroded by pollution, its spire lost after a fire of 1561, its shrines destroyed at the Reformation, and the west front and other areas already replaced in Renaissance style.[22] The Victorians might have turned such a building into a bland 'restoration' of the medieval cathedral – death by a thousand cuts. Instead we have Wren's magnificent Baroque church, the first purpose-built cathedral after the Reformation, itself partly a homage to its predecessor.[23]

In a sense, it is Paulsbury that is the greater loss than Old St Paul's itself, at least in the form that we would have inherited it. Wren's great church is caught in an arm-lock of tourists and traffic, and London has lost something unique, a sacred enclosure fitting for the energetic, many-voiced, populist spirit of the capital itself.

WHAT TO SEE

St Paul's, London
Secular cathedral, founded 604 (though London was also a bishopric under the Romans); refounded c. 675–93.

There is virtually nothing to see that is medieval; just walk around St Paul's and imagine a bigger, older church surrounded by an extraordinary complex. A lump of stone from the chapter-house can be seen near the south nave aisle; the Museum of London displays more material, including a wonderful pre-Conquest tombstone.

SALISBURY

Salisbury is the perfect failure. This 'model' cathedral was built in the 1220s, at the moment the English Church emerged in triumph from decades of trauma. Its small imperfections only make it a more vivid time machine to the period in which it was built.

It was also the completion of an old project. The see had been looking for a natural home since 705: by 1058, Herman, the last Anglo-Saxon bishop, had already incorporated his see of Ramsbury with that of Sherborne without resolving the issue.[1] After the Conquest a very Norman solution was found to the problem. If there was no obvious city that made a more suitable 'capital' for this diocese of Dorset, Wiltshire and Berkshire, one would have to be created. An Anglo-Saxon hilltop town, strategically placed in an Iron Age hillfort on the edge of Salisbury Plain, was turned into a fortified settlement containing both a castle and a cathedral: Old Sarum. The cathedral began relocation there, from Sherborne, in 1075.[2]

Old Sarum was in a perfect defensive position, but it was no place for a city. People could not come and go without permission from the castellan. Fresh water had to be carried in by hand. There were complaints of constant colds, of being blinded by the castle.[3] This is not as odd as it sounds: the motte was a 12-metre mound of gleaming white chalk. By 1199, Bishop Herbert Poore had decided to move again.[4]

The strict clerical logic of Salisbury's design is broken by the fourteenth-century bracing arches that dominate this view across its eastern transept

But almost immediately, the times turned against him. Church, barons and state were virtually at war; during the interdict (see p. 93), Archbishop Stephen Langton and other English bishops went into exile. Things only began to change after 1215: returning from exile, Langton helped draft Magna Carta; a year later the king was dead. By 1220 the pious boy-king Henry III had reconfirmed Magna Carta, the country was controlled by a bishop-dominated

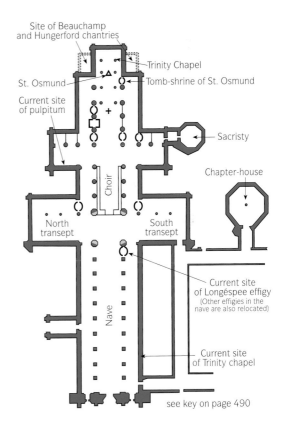

Site of Beauchamp and Hungerford chantries

Trinity Chapel

St. Osmund

Tomb-shrine of St. Osmund

Current site of pulpitum

Sacristy

Choir

Chapter-house

North transept

South transept

Current site of Longéspee effigy
(Other effigies in the nave are also relocated)

Nave

Current site of Trinity chapel

see key on page 490

council, and everywhere the militant architectural projects of the 1190s became the triumphalist one of the 1220s (see p. 99).

These were also heady years for Richard Poore, Herbert Poore's brother and former second-in-command at Old Sarum. He had been taught by Archbishop Langton at the university of Paris, and had been Herbert's dean for fifteen years; in 1215 he became bishop of Chichester.[5] Both he and Langton were at the Fourth Lateran Council that year (see p. 104). In 1217 Richard replaced his brother as bishop of Old Sarum, and he and his chapter applied to the pope for permission to relocate their church:[6] in 1219 it was granted. 'Let us descend joyfully to the plains, where the valleys abound in corn, where the fields are beautiful, and where there is freedom from oppression', as one canon put it.[7]

The new site must almost have selected itself: a crossing-point of two roads and a river, on land that already belonged to the bishop, in the wide Avon valley just 2 miles south of Old Sarum. The bishop asked the entire community to move by November. The cathedral at Old Sarum, one of the very first to be built after the Conquest (and magnificently extended only seventy or so years later, see p. 74) was abandoned, as Sherborne and Ramsbury had been before it.

Everything crystallized in the year 1220. Henry III had been crowned in haste in the middle of a civil war: now he was crowned properly. The long-delayed translation of Thomas Becket was held; Stephen Langton and Richard Poore were the only two men allowed to peer inside the coffin.[8] And at Salisbury, Richard, accompanied by the earl of Salisbury, laid the foundation stone for a completely new cathedral, as a crowd of onlookers wept and made more offerings 'with a ready mind'.[9] The king was late: but then he was just thirteen.

This was to be a model cathedral for the new era. The project embraced everything from town planning to theology. A new city was laid out around the church (illustrated p. 12);[10] at a series of meetings of much of the chapter,[11] Poore published a new constitution and liturgy for his church. Much about this constitution reflects the Fourth Lateran Council, while the liturgy – the Use of Sarum – was the result of fifteen years' work.[12] It would be the most influential summary of the Latin rite in the English Middle Ages.

Poore launched an aggressive fundraising campaign. The cathedral's vicars were supposed to tour the country seeking donations, but 'not one of them would undertake the task'.[13] So his canons went instead, some of them with real determination: one even spent Christmas asking for donations in Scotland. They perhaps had at their disposal a poem, *De Translatione*, which we can imagine them reciting during such encounters. It presented the relocation to Salisbury as a model of the Church's own move from captivity to emancipation, from a place without the solace of nature to a paradise that Adam might have preferred to Eden.[14] More prosaically, a seven-year tax of 25 per cent was imposed on the incomes of the canons.[15] Henry III, who was using masons from the same source to rebuild his favourite palace at nearby Clarendon, made donations of lavish generosity, including hundreds of oaks from royal forests (see p. 243).[16]

By 1225 the first 22 metres of the 144-metre church were complete, and probably the foundations of the entire building. They were dedicated in another grand ceremony: the archbishops of Dublin, Canterbury and other VIPs were entertained for a week, and the king made an appearance again.[17] In just five years, the church's easternmost chapels had been brought into use, and the key features of its design agreed. After about forty years' further work, the entire church was complete.[18]

Poore had behind him an extraordinary chapter. With around fifty-two members, it was one of the largest in the country; one member, Edmund Rich, was a future archbishop and saint. But Poore's

From his home at Leadenhall, Elias de Dereham could watch the cathedral being built; a similar view was later painted by John Constable (illustrated p. 16)

achievement at Salisbury is more than anything else due to Elias of Dereham – another close associate of Stephen Langton – who became a canon in 1220. Elias was an 'incomparable artist'[19] with an unusual range of skills: he had co-directed the translation of St Thomas and was executor to at least three archbishops and two bishops. Elias was the 'rector' of the entire project: when Richard Poore gave him the offerings from the 1225 consecration to look after, he said he 'had confidence in no one else'.[20] Elias even built himself a canon's house, the Leadenhall, built as an 'exemplum' to the other canons in 1232.[21] Elias, it seems, was a project manager: a networker, fundraiser and design guru who could appoint and brief craftsmen (such as

the possible master-mason, Nicholas of Ely), and perhaps come up with some ideas himself.

Salisbury is a textbook example of Early English, a defining expression of the style, combining calm reasonableness with self-assured authority. But much about it is also individual. Salisbury proposed coolness after decades of architecture overheating; it has a spare refinement lacking in its contemporaries. Yet beneath its air of graciousness lurk unexpected moments of wit and eccentricity. There is a cheerful oddness about the giant cusped arches that clasp many of the exterior windows. Sudden changes of elevation on the inside are the result of self-imposed rules followed through with forensic strictness.[22]

It is these very features that allow us to peer inside the minds of its makers. They wanted a building that could be completed rapidly; the reliance on easily replicable mouldings and shafts, rather than individually carved details, must have helped. Nonetheless, Salisbury was not a cheap building: it cost £28,000 besides the £40,000 of Westminster abbey, but that was the most expensive building of the age.[23] And though it has plenty of carved decoration, all of it is purposeful: it is used to help define the different parts of the building. Ornamentation increases subtly between nave and choir, choir and presbytery.[24] This approach – analytical, taxonomic – reflects not just the codifying mindset that created the Use of Sarum, but the way in which graduates such as Poore and his chapter were taught to think. It is the kind of approach that a sophisticated, intellectual chapter might impose on a master-mason. Salisbury was thus designed at least partly by committee,[25] which is perhaps why its beauty falls just short of perfection. Almost all its aesthetic failures – the cramped design of its triforium, the sudden jumps in elevation design – are the very features that reflect ideas insisted on by a group of non-masons sitting round a table.

Such men always sought authority in the past. The modernity of the building is a chimera: it is the completion of a failed project and the embodiment of an authority that went back centuries, coded throughout with references to its predecessor at Old Sarum. The tombs of eleventh- and twelfth-century bishops were carefully 'translated' to the new church. The triforium has a cramped design, best explained as a gothicized version of the romanesque gallery at Old Sarum. Even the building's proportions appear to be partly driven by an interest in evoking the church it replaced. If the

An angel from Salisbury's pulpitum, exquisite reminder of the colour that once covered cathedral sculpture

columns in the Trinity Chapel are mapped on to the apse of Old Sarum, the two align perfectly.[26] Only the canons and God himself can have known this: it is as if the authority of the old church could be passed to the new using mathematics alone.

Salisbury is also a 'machine for worshipping in',[27] planned with precision. Its beautiful and enormous cloister had little practical function, apart from the occasional procession such as that which, according to Poore's Use of Sarum, required its use on Palm Sunday. His constitution asked for at least one-third of the canons to be in residence at any one time; these men were obliged to perform mass at least once a day, so his church was provided with fifteen side altars.[28]

Salisbury's measured architecture stands in marked contrast to the most important achievements of the previous fifty years, a period when England's greatest cathedral projects had increasingly tried to dramatize the miraculous powers of their in-house saints (see chapter three).[29] Poore worked hard to build a cult around Osmund, yet there is a measured calibration of effect between his tomb-shrine – which now stands not far from its original location in the Trinity Chapel – and the grandeur of the area around the high altar.[30] The focus at Salisbury is not on saints but on the liturgy, and specifically the Eucharist.[31] The cathedral puts forward with quiet authority one of the core messages of the era: that correct performance of the Eucharist, and regular participation in it by all men and women, was a fundamental obligation of all humanity. Whole passages from Poore's constitution closely match the proclamations of the Fourth Lateran Council; here, the same ideas are turned into architecture.

It is still just possible to recapture how this building was intended to look. Its windows were filled with silver-grey carpets of grisaille glass (illustrated p. 99). In important locations, however, such as the eastern wall of the Trinity Chapel, the windows could be packed with colour. The way in which the church was painted was likewise carefully controlled. The walls and vaults bore the simplest patterns – thin red lines to simulate ashlar blocks, relieved by occasional sprays of foliage – and only in the east end was the temperature allowed to increase. Here, images of prophets and sibyls, Christ in Majesty and the Labours of the Months were painted on the vaults. The east end also contained fine oak choir-stalls and a restricted and self-effacing collection of monuments to bishops and earls of Salisbury, most of them again in the Trinity Chapel: Osmund's tomb-shrine, the other tomb-slabs from Old Sarum, and the effigy of William Longespee, one of the earliest knight's effigies in England. Salisbury's tombs later became

The elegance and poise of its east end would have impressed visitors to Salisbury's dedication in 1225

more dramatic in design, but they always doubled up as choir screens and other fittings. The nave, by contrast, was unfurnished, apart from the great rood and a magnificently carved pulpitum, originally filled with statues of English kings.[32]

An astonishing amount of this survives, albeit moved to new locations in the church. A large amount of grisaille window glass is intact, while the glass from the Trinity Chapel's east window, which depicted the Jesse Tree in exquisite reds and blues, is now in a window in the south nave aisle. The vault paintings in the choir were repainted rather mechanic-ally by the Victorians, but still give an impression of the original design; the choir-stalls, if not their canopies, are original. Many of the cathedral's monuments, including those of Old Sarum's bishops and William Longespee on a later tomb chest, now stand in the nave; the heavenly wall of stone that was the pulpitum fills a wall in the north-east transept.

But it was the Trinity Chapel that would have dominated the scene at the dedication of 1225. It already contained the tomb-shrine of Osmund, the tomb slabs of the bishops of Old Sarum and presumably the Jesse window; architecturally it remains the most ravishing part of the interior. The Use of Sarum's daily mass of Our Lady was celebrated here, and this was where those hoping for a miracle at Osmund's tomb-shrine came. With side aisles the same height as its central vessel,[33] the chapel would have looked to contemporaries more like a secular hall than a church, and the breathtakingly thin columns that separate these aisles make its roof seem almost weightless – at once chaste and exquisite. The Use of Sarum described the Virgin as the 'Hall of Seemliness':[34] it is as if the unique qualities of the Virgin were being made architecturally visible.

By 1258 much had changed. Elias of Dereham and Richard Poore were dead. Poore's plan to have Osmund canonized had failed; the chapter apparently omitted to forward the papers to Rome.[35] Before his death, Poore had moved to Durham: 'I would . . . have chosen rather to leave this body than to have been thus suddenly snatched away from the church at whose breast I was suckled.'[36] He died in 1237 and was buried in his Dorset birthplace,[37] where he had founded a house of Cistercian nuns.

Poore's immediate successors maintained their commitment to the project: two out of three of them were elected to the post from within the chapter. Bishop de Bridport even made a bid to make Salisbury a second Oxford, taking advantage of the flight to his city of many Oxford teachers after riots there in 1238 and 1264. He founded a small college in 1262, 'the House of the Valley of Scholars', which proved as early a model for the academic college as Poore's cathedral had been for an episcopal one.[38]

But at some point after Poore's death, Salisbury lost its aesthetic nerve. Its stylistic message had been ignored: architecture continued to move towards greater elaboration rather than greater restraint. When de Bridport's predecessor, Bishop William of York, imported masons and a new *custos fabrice* from Yorkshire in 1247,[39] they brought a busier, fussier Early English with them. Only the display of balanced pattern and elegance in the cloister, using the new technique of window tracery, is a complete success; the chapter-house[40] – and even more so, the west front – is anything but. De Bridport's tomb was one of the most scandalously shrine-like of all English bishops' tombs, complete with little carvings of the good bishop's life.[41] Poore, by contrast, had absented himself from the church completely.

From the 1270s, Salisbury ran into trouble. Aside from its proximity to the palace at Clarendon – not favoured by subsequent kings as it had been by Henry III – there was nothing inherently significant about it; it became a middle-ranking cathedral, plagued by the same internal disputes and absen-

The fourteenth-century tower and spire perfectly completed a church a century old

teeism as any other. For a while, Salisbury had shone 'like the sun in full orb, shedding her beams on every side so as to make up for the shortcomings of other churches';[42] but the light had begun to fade.

Salisbury had two more periods in the sun. First, under Bishops de Gandavo[43] (1297–1315) and de Martival (1315–30), internal political wounds were briefly healed and the Decorated tower and spire, with its almost uncannily perfect proportions, were probably built: William Joy of Winchester, Exeter and Wells was one of the master-masons.[44] Then, in the first half of the fifteenth century, Salisbury became nationally prominent again. The Use of Sarum was becoming standard throughout the province of Canterbury (it was finally made official policy in 1534),[45] and a second canonization bid for Bishop Osmund was launched. Its success in 1457 is only partly a reflection of the £713 spent on arguing the case in Rome: in 1450 Bishop Aiscough had been murdered as part of a rebellion linked to the Wars of the Roses. The well-defended gate to the city was one reaction to this traumatic event; the attention-grabbing new shrine to a former bishop perhaps another.

This period also saw the building of a Perpendicular library above the cloister, the construction of strainer arches beneath the tower and the creation of the sumptuous new shrine for St Osmund in the heart of the Trinity Chapel; the new shrine was so substantial that it took twenty-five days to take it apart in 1539. On either side of St Osmund's new shrine were elaborate chantries to Bishop Beau-champ (who doubled the size of his nearby palace) and Robert, Lord Hungerford, both of which were demolished in the eighteenth century.[46] The sumptuous chantry to Bishop Audley – doubling up as an Easter sepulchre – is perhaps the least magnificent of the four Salisbury originally had.[47]

Despite these late flourishes, Salisbury's failures are several. The restrained model proposed by its original architecture only resurfaced from time to time:[48] it had more in common with Brunelleschi or Mies van der Rohe than most other medieval buildings. Salisbury abandoned its own model in its later years, and even in its pure form suffered aesthetically from the meddling of an over-intellectualizing committee. And it had taken 250 years for Osmund to be canonized.

Nevertheless, the city invented along with the cathedral is a town planner's dream (see p. 12). It had become the sixth richest city in England by 1337, and remains a thriving and pleasant place to this day. The close – cleared of its tombs and standalone bell tower, and made less exclusive – has become an iconic English scene. The collegiate principle championed by Richard Poore at Salisbury was arguably the medieval cathedrals' greatest contribution to the modern world. And since

Thomas Cranmer took Poore's Use of Sarum as his starting point for the new Book of Common Prayer, his liturgy has influenced worship throughout the Anglican communion ever since. Not bad for a failure.

WHAT TO SEE

St Mary, Salisbury
Secular cathedral; see founded 705; moved to Salisbury 1219.

Church: thirteenth-century building (Trinity Chapel and cloister are particularly exquisite), topped perfectly by fourteenth-century spire.

Fittings and decorations: exquisite thirteenth-century pulpitum against west wall of north-east transept; choir-stalls and woodwork including doors, roofs and scaffolding (all visible by taking a Tower Tour); glass, traces of wall paintings; good collection of tombs; Magna Carta in chapter-house.

Setting: no cathedral close more fully embodies the gracious lives of the canons; several houses retain medieval work. The city, too, is worth exploring as a creation of the bishops; iconic setting by Avon water meadows.

Old Sarum: this evocative site 2 miles north of Salisbury is in the care of English Heritage; the Salisbury and South Wiltshire Museum in the cathedral close contains many finds from the cathedral there, as well as material on medieval Salisbury.

SOUTHWARK

Medieval Southwark was a town like no other, a human and architectural logjam at the wrong end of London Bridge. Here were prostitutes' 'swells' and bishops' palaces, inns for pilgrims and sanctuaries for criminals;[1] and here, pilgrims embarked for Canterbury.

The Augustinian priory of St Mary Overie – 'St Mary-over-the-Bridge' – stood at the heart of all this. Its church has only survived by chance, and much of it is Victorian; it did not become a cathedral until 1905. It is a precious survival nonetheless: one of the only remnants of the dozens of great churches that once clustered in and around London.

Medieval St Mary's was a multi-functional place. The London palace of the bishops of Winchester, in whose diocese Southwark lay, stood next door: it often doubled up as their London church (and court room), with a now lost 'bishop's chapel' off the retrochoir.[2] St Mary's also incorporated one of Southwark's five parish churches, and in its close was a hospital, dedicated early to Becket himself. St Thomas's moved away in search of 'better air' as early as 1215; it now stands, rather enlarged, opposite the palace of Westminster.[3]

The fifteen to twenty canons of St Mary's were stuck between London's red light district and its main late-night drinking zone.[4] They were asked not to leave the priory by themselves, and were forbidden from allowing taverns or 'other dishonourable trades' to occupy their Southwark properties. From their properties in London they had an income of nearly £625: St Mary's was thus as wealthy as some smaller cathedrals.[5]

Men of influence also lived at St Mary's, installed in 'grace and favour' accommodation by high-placed patrons. One earl of Arundel used the priory's 'suitable apartments' when in London; the poet John Gower, a good friend of Chaucer, lived here with his wife, made generous contributions to building work and probably used the church's scriptorium and library. His brash, heavily restored tomb in the church shows him using his three main works as a pillow.

St Mary's building history is a roll-call of influential bishops of Winchester.[6] Its origins are obscure, but a minster may have been built here by the Anglo-Saxon bishop-saint Swithun.[7] Another bishop helped two Norman knights found the priory in 1106: only a few bare arches of this building remain.[8]

In 1212 a fire took place in Southwark in which 1,000 were said to have died. Bishop Peter des

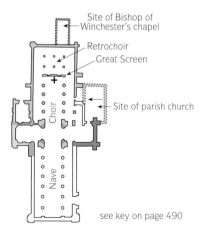

Site of Bishop of Winchester's chapel

Retrochoir
Great Screen

Site of parish church

Choir

Nave

see key on page 490

423

Reaching out towards London's only medieval bridge, Southwark's east end has witnessed centuries of revelry and riot

Roches, 'warrior of Winchester, up at the exchequer, keen on finance, slack at the scriptures',[9] rebuilt the church, which shares with contemporary Winchester cathedral a hall-like retrochoir; in spite of later clutter it remains a spare and beautiful building. The urbane Early English choir shows knowledge of the latest French architecture; des Roches also founded several monastic houses and went on to build in Jerusalem and Acre.[10]

Both the nearby ruined palace of the bishops of Winchester and the north transept of St Mary's itself have court-influenced work from the cusp between Decorated and Perpendicular. Bishop William of Wykeham is said to have started the Perpendicular tower after a fire of 1373; the bells were installed under Cardinal Bishop Henry Beaufort in time for a royal wedding in 1424. His arms decorate the former entrance to the parish church of St Mary Magdalene in the south transept.[11] The cliff-like Great Screen reredos is said to be the work of the conservative Bishop Richard Fox (d. 1528): it is virtually a copy of its older siblings at Winchester

and St Albans (see p. 149). Finally, the anti-Protestant Bishop Gardiner helped the people of Southwark to buy St Mary's in 1539, turning it into a parish church.

By the eighteenth century 'Old Moll', as it was known, was half-ruined. Its nave is Victorian; the few medieval fittings are heavily restored. Yet it remains a potent reminder of a vanished medieval London.

WHAT TO SEE

St Mary Overie, now St Saviour and St Mary Overie, Southwark
Anglo-Saxon church; Augustinian priory 1106; parish church after 1539; cathedral 1905.

All heavily restored: thirteenth-century choir and retrochoir; monuments and carvings (thirteenth-century oak knight, fifteenth-century Gower tomb); late medieval bosses displayed in nave.

SOUTHWELL

Among the leaves of oak, maple and hawthorn that decorate the late thirteenth-century chapter-house of Southwell minster, little stone pigs snaffle acorns from the ground and hunting dogs wrest a rabbit from its burrow. Such scenes would have been familiar to the men who used this ceremonial meeting room, for their wealth depended on the land.[1]

These canons had reason to be proud of their church and its estate. The minster was not a cathedral until 1884, but it was one of the richest collegiate churches in England. Within its territory – the 'Peculiar of Southwell' – the only churchman with greater power than the canons was technically the pope in far-off Rome. Each of the canons derived his income from a portion of these landholdings, which took up about a quarter of Nottinghamshire. The Peculiar was to a large extent the minster's private domain.[2]

Yet the initiative and inspiration for the chapter-house here came from York, 80 miles to the north. Southwell lay in the southern reaches of the see of York, near the main road to London and the important centres of Newark and Nottingham. The archbishops of York devolved certain powers to it, declaring Southwell the 'mother church' for the counties of Nottinghamshire and Derbyshire. Every year at Pentecost, processions from across these counties made their way here to receive the archbishop-blessed chrism oil that was essential for performance of the Eucharist – a role usually reserved only for a cathedral.[3]

Like the other 'deputy cathedrals' of the see, Beverley and Ripon, Southwell was originally one of the minster churches that dominated the English landscape before parishes were created. The large Roman villa known to lie near the church perhaps suggests that the area has always been special, and that the minster has deep roots in the landscape that sustained it.

Southwell's recorded history begins in 955, when King Eadwig gave the estate to the archbishop of York. By the mid-eleventh century there was a church here with the relics of one St Eadburh and canons who were living a communal life; a refectory was built sometime between 1060 and 1069. Both saint and refectory vanished with the Conquest: all that remains of Saxon Southwell is a tessellated pavement.[4]

It was at this time that Southwell was reinvented as a kind of proxy York minster. Between 1108 and 1114, 'Archbishop Thomas' (probably Thomas II) of

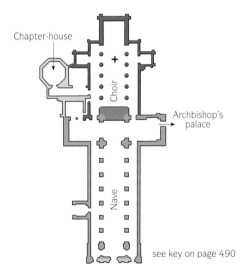

Chapter-house

Choir

Archbishop's palace

Nave

see key on page 490

York issued an edict to the parishes of Nottinghamshire, encouraging them to 'assist with their alms to the building of the church of St Mary at Southwell', and allowing them in return to visit Southwell, rather than York, to collect their chrism oil each year. St Mary's was then rebuilt.[5]

Romanesque Southwell is a spirited exercise in the energetic power of the semicircular arch, by a man well informed enough to have built rib vaults (in the nave aisles) within a decade or so of their invention. His arches jump down the nave gallery in colossal bounds as if competing in some synchronized hurdle race. Semicircular arches also hold up the tower with an Apollonian energy, carved with bobbin-like shapes that look rather like a massive, coiled rope. Others make a sunburst of the Norman north door, which was the ceremonial entranceway for the canons and the probable endpoint of Pentecostal processions (see p. 202). Here each community handed over a pre-set payment: £3 annually from each of the deaneries of Nottingham, Newark, Bingham and Retford, and a cut-price £2 0s 6d from the Peculiar of Southwell.[6]

Southwell's special status as a secular sub-cathedral of York continued to be reflected in the thirteenth century. In the 1230s Walter de Gray, archbishop of York – an energetic reformer and rebuilder – issued a series of indulgences to aid ambitious new works at each of his sub-cathedrals: that for Southwell was issued in December 1233.[7] Like many other early thirteenth-century great churches, Southwell was about to build a new east end, double the size of its predecessor.[8] This Early English structure was complete, along with a new chapel off the north transept, by 1260. But although the initiative came from York, this is not York architecture. Here, three miles north of the Trent, we may technically be in the north of England, but

Twentieth-century glass and fifteenth-century tracery fill Southwell's twelfth-century west wall

we are spiritually in the Midlands. The 'easy amplitude'[9], as it was recently called, of the church's radical two-storey elevation comes from Pershore, 80 miles to the west.[10] The tensely lavish decoration – razor-sharp runs of nailheads in the arches and a newly invented ridge rib in the vault – comes from Lincoln, 12 miles to the east (illustrated p. 223).

In 1288 Archbishop John le Romeyn reformed the Southwell community and added two prebends, bringing to a close a process that had seen the number of canons grow from at most ten in 1100 to sixteen by 1291. At this point few if any non-cathedral chapters were larger; none was richer, and the chapter's constitution was said to be based on that 'which the church of York is known to have had and still to have'.[11] At the same time, to match the status of this community, the archbishop ordered the construction of a chapter-house. The resulting building was closely modelled on the new one at York, an octagonal structure with enormous windows, its gravity-defying vault unsupported by a central column. The delicious carvings within provide a vivid window on the lives of the Southwell chapter members (illustrated p. 120).[12]

It is easy to imagine these senior churchmen gathered in such a room. The stalls are all identical, reflecting the egalitarian nature of the chapter, which at Southwell had no dignitaries and no dean. There are thirty-six such seats, perhaps allowing room for vicars as well as canons on those occasions when complete convocations of the community took place.[13] The carvings that surround each stall are based on a close study of the natural world, just the kind of observation then being encouraged in the universities at which these educated men had studied. So-called naturalistic carvings in other buildings of the age show idealized versions of various plant forms, but at Southwell botanists have identified individual strains of oak.[14]

Yet this imagined gathering is a fiction. Each canon employed two vicars, one of whom sang on

Substantial portions of the twelfth-century minster survive

of Southwell, in other words, are prebends in stone.

This does not make the carvings banal. They are emblematic of the ambivalent bond between medieval people and the natural world. For these people there would have been no distinction between good land management and the glorious variety of God's creation. It is this very inclusivity – at once down-to-earth and profound, witty and serious – that makes the leaves of Southwell at once so medieval and so wonderful.

The minster was given permission to transport stone through Sherwood Forest free of charge in 1337, around the time when the new stone sedilia (much altered in the nineteenth century) and an extraordinary pulpitum were installed.[18] Many East Midlands churches were given such ornate new stone fittings at this period. These works, in the Decorated style, can be almost exhausting to look at: like a richly illuminated manuscript, not an inch is left undecorated. But the Southwell pulpitum is a cut above the average. It conjures up a surreal world of spaces that should be solid, cusps that turn into little heads, and arches that sprout stylized, crinkly foliage – an aged, overripe version of the fruitfulness in the chapter-house.

Building work in the later Middle Ages further underlined Southwell's links with York. The archbishops had long had a palace next door to the church, from which they reached their nearby hunting parks or stayed overnight on their journeys south. Now it became one of their favourite residences, and apart from the fine set of Perpendicular windows installed in the minster nave during the fifteenth century, all surviving work of the period focuses on the palace. We have lost the chantry chapel built in the nave of the minster for Archbishop Booth, who died in the palace in 1464.[19] Also gone is the vicars' college, rebuilt in 1379. What we have is the rebuilt archbishop's palace itself. Archbishop Kemp poured huge funds into this between 1426 and 1452.[20] Much of the current

his behalf in choir and one of whom ministered to the parishioners in his part of the Peculiar.[15] With these vicars to do their work for them – supported by clerks and bailiffs, and the sweat of countless forgotten peasants – the canons did not need to be in Southwell at all. In both 1260 and 1361, for example, only one of the sixteen actually lived there. Like the archbishop, the members of chapter were usually far away,[16] and this chapter-house was always meant to be empty. It is a stand-in for a community united only by the source of its wealth: the lands of the Peculiar.

The plant types shown in the chapter-house have one thing in common: each is cited in medieval sources for its importance to a well-managed estate.[17] The neat stone borders are thus filled with the very plants that sustained the canons' careers in York, London, Rome and elsewhere. The leaves

Prebends in stone, the carvings in the chapter-house evoke a vanished world

building dates from 1907, but the handsome ruins of the eastern half remain, and demonstrate that this palace was almost as big as Southwell minster itself. Cardinal Wolsey himself retired here in 1530 after being disgraced, and died a few months later.

Perhaps Southwell's popularity with the archbishop helped the Reformation come quietly here. The college was refounded in 1543 rather than abolished, and the Peculiar survived virtually unreformed until 1840. But the church had less luck in later iconoclasms: the area was one of the epicentres of the Civil War, and perhaps because of this almost no medieval glass, paintings or monuments survive. After 1840 the minster became an overgrown parish church for forty years before, in 1884, Nottinghamshire (and at that date, Derbyshire) finally got a bishop of their own.

Southwell is one of England's most satisfying medieval buildings, just imperfect enough to be loveable as well as beautiful. It is as if it mattered just enough to the absent archbishop and chapter for them to employ first-rate master-masons, but not so much that they interfered overmuch in the resulting designs. The church is in fact full of bodges, as if few of its designers spent much time

on site. The east end, for example, might be a noble experiment by one of the architects of Lincoln cathedral, but it contains a spectacular 'bad join': two teams of jobbing masons, each a dozen or more strong,[21] built around the outside of the existing east end, and where the two parts meet, it looks as if they were working in the dark.[22] The chapter-house likewise lacks the expensive micro-architecture and polished marbles of its sibling at York: instead, one gifted carver was employed to make a set piece of the capitals.[23] A special window was even installed in the vestibule in order to throw chlorophyll-stimulating light on his spectacular entrance door.

Southwell's geographical and constitutional identity runs through its architecture like DNA. This is nowhere better reflected than in the community's corporate and spiritual home, the chapter-house. Here, among stone leaves which seem to pulse with the sinews of real sap, is one of the more quietly diaphanous spaces in which to get closer to medieval England.

WHAT TO SEE

St Mary, Southwell
Collegiate church, founded by mid-eleventh century; became a parish church 1840; cathedral 1884

Church: Norman transepts, nave and north porch; Early English choir; Decorated chapter-house and pulpitum.

Fittings and carvings: miraculous sculpture in the chapter-house and on the pulpitum.

Setting: both town and Peculiar are worth exploring for occasional clues to their medieval origins; the Perpendicular remains of the archbishop's palace, visible from the churchyard, are most impressive.

WELLS

No comeback was ever more beguiling. In 1090 Wells' status as the cathedral for Somerset, which went back to 909, was wrested from it. The church was to spend the next two centuries fighting to become a cathedral again: some of the greatest architecture in England was the result.

The church at Wells had roots deep in the Somerset landscape. Its site by St Andrew's Well, a spring at the foot of the Mendips, has been significant since at least late Roman times. Archaeologists have found a complex series of structures there, the most recent of which was an Anglo-Saxon chapel dedicated to Our Lady, which was later joined to the Anglo-Saxon cathedral to its west.[1] Wells thus has much in common with its local monastic competitors: Bath, by the famous healing spring in its Cotswold valley; and Glastonbury, with its hallowed Tor and Chalice Well, set on its island in the Levels. These three great religious houses – two ancient monasteries and one secular cathedral – were to spend much of the Middle Ages locked in institutional rivalry.

It was the first Norman bishop, John of Tours, who moved his seat from Wells to the monastery at Bath, despite the fact that his predecessor had reformed the Wells community, imposing something of the communal life of monks and building a group of conventual buildings. In an apparent reversal of these reforms, John of Tours demolished the canons' cloister and made his brother 'provost'

Before its towers were added, in the late thirteenth century, the screen-like west front at Wells must have looked even more extraordinary

to watch over them.[2] Wells had thus been demoted to a large collegiate church sited on the bishop's lands, its canons living in houses in the town and the income of its bishop diverted to Bath, where a large new cathedral church was begun. But the canons never forgot their history, and from the mid-twelfth century their bishops, too, began to see the advantages of Wells. Unlike a monastery it could provide canonries for their staff; it was in any case near the centre of the see; and perhaps just as important, it was close to mighty Glastonbury, one of the richest and most powerful churches in the

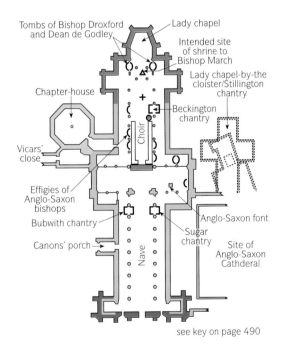

see key on page 490

Wells literally sprang from St Andrew's Well, to the south-east of the modern church

land, which operated a virtual statelet of its own from its island site in the middle of the county (see map, p. 191).[3]

In 1136 Bishop Robert of Lewes re-established the chapter at Wells.[4] Reginald fitz Jocelin, who became bishop in 1174 at the age of just thirty-four, up and coming and well-connected,[5] was generous to both church and city at Wells, and tried to bring Glastonbury under his wing by giving the abbot a place on the Wells chapter. His successor (and relative) Savaric went further, attempting an all-out takeover of Glastonbury and styling himself bishop of Bath and Glastonbury from 1195. The support Savaric got from the Wells chapter – who helpfully imprisoned some rebellious monks – must have done them no harm at all. The next bishop, Jocelin of Wells, who succeeded Savaric in 1206, resolved the

issue in Rome: he surrendered his claim to be bishop of Glastonbury but, crucially, co-opted the abbot of Glastonbury on to the Wells chapter, and took several of the abbey's manors in compensation. The acquisition of these manors must have had an immediate impact on the finances of a cathedral whose landholdings were scattered throughout the see, and already included the cities of Wells and Bath, along with much of the surrounding countryside.

Jocelin was a native of Wells, and had come up from within the chapter. The canons at Wells participated in his election to the bishopric in 1206, and in 1220 the pope permitted him to use the title of bishop of Bath and Wells, which is still used today. Although this decision does not appear to have been widely broadcast, to all intents and purposes Wells had now become a cathedral again, and a greatly enriched one at that.[6]

These crucial years in Wells' history were accompanied by remarkable architectural developments. Robert of Lewes had updated parts of the Anglo-Saxon church, but almost immediately after Reginald fitz Jocelin took up office[7] it was demolished and an entirely new building begun almost next door. At around the same time, the canons wrote a history of their church that emphasized how Wells had acquired and lost its cathedral status and the many sufferings the chapter had borne as a result; they also perhaps forged various papal bulls that claimed the right to elect bishops jointly with Bath.[8]

But it is the church itself that forms the most determined statement of their claims.[9] The canons' knowledge of their own history was reflected in every aspect of it; the result is a kind of manifesto in stone for cathedral status. It was replete with features normally accorded only the most magnificent buildings,[10] yet it was built by a community that had only recently been sidelined and impoverished. A battery of techniques was used to display its age and history. Although the Anglo-Saxon cathedral was flattened,[11] in 1196 a decision was made to preserve its ancient lady chapel, to be accessed via the new church's cloister as if it were some ancient and exclusive relic associated with St Andrew's Well.[12] The great cloister itself, which had little practical function to a chapter who each had prebends of their own, may be something of a one-in-the-eye after the demolition of its predecessor a century earlier.[13] The font of the Anglo-Saxon cathedral, perhaps originally also associated with the ancient spring, was translated inside the new one.[14] An ambitious series of invented 'effigies' of the Anglo-Saxon bishops of Wells was commissioned, and perhaps lined up above the high altar with the relics of the bishops themselves, moved from the old cathedral.[15] It was a display which the cathedral priory at Bath, with its collection of

bishops' tombs only a century old, could never hope to match.[16]

Finally, the church played some bizarre stylistic games, in an apparent attempt to put clear blue architectural water between Wells and its monastic competitors. Glastonbury abbey had recently been sumptuously rebuilt, using lavish quantities of polished stone and carved decoration; such motifs were transforming English architecture via the new east end at Canterbury.[17] Wells goes out of its way to avoid them (illustrated p. 218).[18]

Yet the church built at Wells after 1174 – of which part of the choir, and all of the transepts and nave, survive – was not a backward building. It may be the first church anywhere to dispense entirely with the semicircular arch.[19] This, combined with the lack of polished stone, chevron and other then-fashionable motifs, gives it a unique, cool clerical

The early gothic nave; the spectacular scissor arches are later insertions, probably by William Joy

The west front is the greatest gallery of medieval sculpture in England

quality of its own. The smooth horizontal energy of Wells' interior is as characterful as it is hard to categorize, at once rooted deeply in the past (it is, in effect, a 'gothicizing' of local romanesque practice) and strikingly modern. With no saints to rival Glaston-bury, and Bath still officially the cathedral, Wells had fallen back on its history – on its 'cathedralness'.

It took about sixty years to complete this church – years punctuated by the loss of the architect's favoured source of stone (monopolized by the monks of Glastonbury after a fire there in 1184 led to further rebuilding) and by the flight of Bishop Jocelin into exile during the interdict (see p. 93), during which the nave stood unfinished for several years.[20] All this must have thrown into sharp relief the triumphant mood in the English Church after the accession of Henry III in 1216. A key adviser

to the new king, Jocelin was then at the height of his political powers,[21] while the chapter revelled in being effectively that of a cathedral once more. The architecture likewise goes from defensive uncertainty to a proclamation of triumphant self-confidence.

By the time the nave was nearing completion, early gothic had developed into Early English. Some of the motifs that Wells had rejected, such as polished shafting, had become indispensable parts of the national style. The new master-mason, perhaps Adam Lock, flexed his own muscles in the north porch, cloister[22] and above all, finally, the west front. Far from eschewing polished stone, this structure is covered in a pipelike scaffolding of the stuff.

The west front has nothing to prove. It is happy to stand alongside the greatest works of gothic art. This colossal outdoor multimedia installation serves not only as a medium for theology, architecture, sculpture and painting, but also as a backdrop for the actual events, both ritual and supernatural, that were to take place there. Stretched out in front of it, the cathedral's lay cemetery filled the open green,[23] giving the facade a very public role at the burial ceremonies of the people of its see. This backdrop had at its climax a depiction in stone of the very event that people believed might occur at any moment in the cemetery itself: the Resurrection. And at least once a year the facade itself came to life for one of the most important, and public, rituals of the church year: the Palm Sunday re-enactment of Christ's Entry into Jerusalem, when the facade was transformed into the walls of Zion themselves, and resounded to singing and trumpet blasts from choristers hidden behind and above its stone angels, each painted with bright, hyper-real colours (see p. 197; illustrated p. 199).[24]

On such occasions the boundary line between architecture, sculpture, liturgy and theatre would have blurred. For people who had no access to other art forms – no cinema, no theatre, no easy access to books – it must have been quite mind-blowing. One wonders whether crowds flocked to witness the Palm Sunday celebrations at Wells.

The key figures among the 176 enormous statues of the west front (149 of which survive) are arranged around its central axis: Christ and the Virgin and their Old Testament prefigurements, Solomon and Sheba, embodied the loving relationship between Christ and his church.[25] But this great gallery of figures was also designed to communicate a more sophisticated message. The precise intent may have gone, along with the names once attached to each statue[26] but the most recent theories establish some of the outlines of the scheme. There is a chronological dimension to the west front: it may even present the entirety of human history, with the Old Testament on the left or north side, the New Testament and post-biblical times on the right or south side, and the Resurrection – the end of time – bursting out of the top.[27] Most of all, it is an image of the city of God, the metaphor for the Church first developed by St Augustine of Hippo, an image contemporary scholars often depicted as a great church facade filled with symbolically arranged figures.[28] Yet among such grand ideas lurk bullish statements of Wells' place in the state of things, such as statues of the cathedral's claimed Anglo-Saxon royal benefactors bearing the church's foundation charters.[29]

Jocelin of Wells also rebuilt the close (map p. 191),[30] with his grand bishop's palace to the south

The spectacular tierceron vault of the Wells chapter-house

The canons of Wells rise from the dead in the glass of their chapter-house

of the church, much of which still exists, and an ample complex of canons' houses to the north, facing the north porch or Great Gate of the Canons through which they entered the church.[31] The close as a whole was part of a wider district known as the Liberty, a place were the canons could live 'free of secular demands',[32] separate from the city of Wells itself. Jocelin's magnificent palace and west front were emphatic statements of where the balance of power now lay between Wells and Bath; another was the size of his chapter. With fifty-four canons by the time of his death in 1242, Wells had the second largest chapter in the country.[33]

The monks at Bath had been remarkably patient throughout the gradual resurgence of the community at Wells, but now they got their own back, and in 1244 – five years after the church at Wells was dedicated, with the last touches still being put on the west front – everything ground to a halt for twenty years.[34] On Jocelin's death the monks of Bath elected a new bishop without consulting Wells; the resulting litigation in Rome led in 1244–5

to final and unequivocal papal support for the role of Wells as co-cathedral electing its bishops jointly with Bath; financially it nearly crippled both churches.[35] Work on the west front slowed almost to a standstill, and was finally abandoned around 1250. The statues in the topmost gable, and much of the painting of the facade itself, were never completed; work ceased on a new chapter-house on the north side of the cathedral, with only the crypt-like ground floor completed. But Wells had already fulfilled its own architectural prophecy, and had been magnificently rebuilt in the process.[36]

Its institutional status confirmed, the chapter's interests now turned inwards.[37] In 1258 Dean de la Knoll procured new levels of independence for himself and his colleagues; the bishop even surrendered his right to appoint new canons. As if in reflection of this, between the 1280s and the 1340s the community not only completed its chapter-house, but also rebuilt and extended the east end of the church. In 1286 Bishop Burnell, chancellor of England, went to Gascony on royal business, leaving his masons, who were working on a magnificent chapel and great hall at his Wells bishop's palace,[38] to restart work on the chapter-house. In the event, however, they only completed the stairway that leads to the building's main meeting room before they were supplanted by an entirely different team, perhaps one favoured by the canons.[39] The resulting structure, complete by 1306, was one of the most complete statements of the new Decorated style, with an extraordinary thirty-two rib tierceron vault and innovative and early use of motifs, such as ogee arches and ballflower ornament, that would dominate architecture for decades to come.

The octagonal chapter-house literally set in stone the body politic of the cathedral itself. It had exactly as many seats as there were canons, and a series of carvings symbolizing their management structure, in which each seat for a chapter dignitary was carved with the head of his superior (illustrated p. 171). In the windows, the chapter installed images of the Resurrection above depictions of the specific canons who had helped pay for the building, each accompanied by a favoured saint. Chapter meeting itself included prayers for every member of the community who had gone before; here, therefore, the entire community, living and dead, gathered.[40]

In this room, under Dean John de Godley, the canons continued to enhance their independence.[41] In the 1320s Bishop Droxford[42] (d. 1329), keeper of the Privy Seal for Edward II (and only known to have spent twenty-two days in Wells in the fifteen years of his episcopate),[43] almost completely surrendered his right to inspect the chapter, and allowed various funds to go to the fabric of the church rather than his own pocket. It was against this background that work on the new east end began.

The result was a veritable shrine in stone, whose subject is Wells cathedral itself and the sacred authority it embodied. The seven effigies of Anglo-Saxon bishops carved in the 1180s were repositioned along the aisles of the new choir; the tombs of subsequent bishops (such as Jocelin, before the high altar) were put back in equivalent positions to those they had occupied in the old east end. And two identical new monuments were created: the paired tombs of Bishop Droxford (illustrated p. 235) and Dean de Godley. For a dean's tomb to be granted the honour of a carved effigy was rare; for it to be identical in design and equivalent in location to that of his superior was unique. It strongly suggests that de Godley was the driving force behind this building.

Indeed the chapter appears to have made an above-average financial contribution to the new east end. The bishop gave his visitation fees and published indulgences. The canons taxed their own income from 1325 onwards, reviewing and renewing the commitment on a five-yearly basis

until at least 1338; each also paid for his own choir-stall. A 'Fraternity of St Andrew' encouraged lay involvement; five collection boxes positioned around the church gathered cash from visitors.[44]

The Wells east end is one of the greatest creations of an extraordinary decade in English architecture (see chapter four). The lady chapel, probably designed by Thomas of Witney (see p. 227), was complete by 1326. It is a stretched octagon, like a distended chapter-house, its vault an exact semi-circle in section, its walls a carpet-like expanse of glass. The choir to its west, completed in 1337, was probably designed by Witney's junior colleague William Joy;[45] it plays with straight lines in a way that shows its designer was aware of the latest ideas – these are precisely the years in which the new Perpendicular style was coined – but was happy to take them in his own direction.

Jewel-like scenes are depicted in the stained glass of the two most important windows of the new east end: the choir east window, above the high altar, and – hanging hazily beyond it among a forest of columns – the east window of the lady chapel. These windows form an extended meditation on the way in which the authority of the Old Testament was transferred to that of the new, via the two figures who form the bridge between these two traditions: Christ and his mother. Lurking among these heavily restored images are subtle and poetic ideas: the intertwining ancestry of Christ, with his human mother (celebrated in the lady chapel) and divine father (worshipped at the high altar); the analogy between that ancestry and a tree – a half-human, half-divine 'family tree' – that itself evokes the cross on which Christ died. All this shimmers suggestively in tones of silver and green above the high altar, where Christ is nursed by his mother before suffering on a green cross as silver tendrils curl around figures of his spiritual and corporeal ancestors; and in the lady chapel, where Old Testament figures are depicted in powerful blues and reds.

Also in the lady chapel is glass that contains images of the Church, depicted first as a kind of ancient family and then as a patrician peer group for the bishops and canons of the cathedral: on one side of the east window are depicted the sons of Jacob, patriarchs of the tribes of Israel, an Old Testament 'model' for the Church; and on the other, the bishop-saints who mattered most to the Wells community. Pointedly, Dunstan, sainted abbot of Glastonbury, takes centre stage among these, but he is depicted as archbishop of Canterbury rather than as a monk. These questions of authority, of the Church over humanity, bishops over monks, cathedrals over abbeys, went to the heart of the history of Wells itself. Yet there is nothing obviously defensive about their depiction here: the images hover sustainingly over worshippers' heads, set in architecture that embraced the Wells community like a great stone womb.

The retrochoir above all is worth coming back to again and again. Yet something is missing in the walk through this vaulted sequence of triangles, hexagons and squares that links the choir and the lady chapel (illustrated p. 125). Six columns of polished stone at the centre of the space were intended as the setting for the one thing Wells did not have: a saint's shrine. As the building went up, Bishop Droxford was campaigning to have his predecessor, Bishop William March, turned into a saint.[46] As treasurer to Edward I, March had retired to Wells in disgrace after being blamed for heavy taxation of the Church. There he salved his conscience with some conspicuous acts of charity (or, at least, lent the chapter £1,000),[47] and after his death there were said to be miracles at his tomb. An unusual monument was created for him in the south transept, perhaps designed to encourage such offerings. But a corrupt politician and a few second-rate miracles do not a saint make. The possibility that the cathedral might acquire a saint was

used to help raise funds for the east end, but the campaign itself was dropped on Droxford's death in 1329, leaving the shrine space without a function.[48]

After Dean de Godley's death in 1333, support for the rebuilding project wavered. The western parts of the choir were completed to a less exacting standard under Dean London, and kitted out with fittings – a (much-restored) bishop's throne and a pulpitum – which do not quite match the quality of the architecture. Thirteen of the stalls have unfinished misericords.[49]

The Wells chapter-house, choir and lady chapel are elaborate spaces suffused with a very human warmth, at once glorious and enfolding. These buildings evoked the chapter's superiors and predecessors alive and dead, absent and present, symbolic and actual, in a way that – in a world where bishop and chapter alike spent much of their career away from the cathedral – reality would never match. Perhaps a certain insecurity lurks behind their grandeur: perhaps the canons could never forget that religious cuckoo-in-the-nest of their diocese, Glastonbury, with its plethora of *real* saints and its monks who *really* ate, slept, worked and worshipped communally.

———

By the late fourteenth century, Wells had evolved into a closely regulated religious institution, a hieratic series of communities and sub-communities – the canons themselves, their vicars, the boy choristers, other chaplains and chantry priests (see pages 180–3). The architecture of this complex religious corporation is still reflected in the buildings around the cathedral. The houses of the canons line the north side of the close (most have been rebuilt), with larger plots for key figures such as the dean. By 1348 redevelopment of one of these plots had begun: it was to be the site of a miniature college for the vicars, designed to remove them 'from the hurley burley of everyday life and the ostentation and temptations of the world'.[50] Two rows of houses were constructed, facing each other over a narrow passage. Although this looks to us like a street of terraced houses, it was not a street but a religious enclosure, like a cloister or Carthusian monastery, squashed into a narrow strip of land. Eventually it was sealed at each end by a chapel-cum-library and a hall-cum-treasury; and, a century later – after the vicars were still found to be taking too much interest in life outside the close – the Chain Gate was built to direct them straight past the chapter-house and into the cathedral. Similarly, the chantry priests had Monteroy college (after 1400), with rooms for fourteen chaplains and their servants, and a chapel doubling up as a chantry to its founder, Bishop Erghum; and the choristers had a 'beautiful dwelling' just west of the cloister, (now part of the new cloister and restaurant complex) with their school next door.[52]

As the world beyond the close seemed to become less secure (see chapter four), so Wells' architecture turned once again to self-defence: in 1336 reports of attacks on strangers and chapter members led the close to be walled anew.[52] Heresy was in the diocese early, and in 1428 a Bristol priest was imprisoned in Wells after having been told five times to stop his heretical preaching.[53] In 1450 Bishop Beckington, alarmed by the murder of the bishop of Salisbury by his citizens, appointed extra Welsh arrowmen to act as security; he built the enormous defensive gateways to cathedral and bishop's palace that still dominate the city market place.[54]

Beckington was a classic late medieval bishop, installing a sumptuous chantry chapel by the high altar some fifteen years before his death – he even said mass at the altar himself – and spending some £6,000 on architectural improvements to cathedral

Rods, trees, virgins: the lady chapel glass at Wells is rich with poetic images

The fourteenth-century vicars' close: chimney stacks were added a century later

and city. His improvements to the city were suitably paternalistic, including a new water supply (the mayor was directed to pray at Beckington's chantry in return) and a group of speculative developments around the market place. A former keeper of the Privy Seal and the first Wells native to be bishop since Jocelin, he is in good company with Bishop Stafford (who went on to become archbishop of Canterbury), Bishop Stillington (a Lancastrian chancellor of England who died a prisoner of the Yorkists) and Bishop Adriano Castellesi, an Italian cardinal who never went near Wells: Castellesi was so embroiled in Vatican politics, mainly as a representative of the Tudor court, that he was the victim of two attempted murders (the second was successful).[55] Such men appointed heavyweight chapters, including celebrated humanists and musicians.[56]

Towers, chantries and cloisters were the architectural themes of these years. We do not know whether Adam Lock had intended his west front to sprout towers, but they were built in 1386 and 1424 to a Perpendicular design by William Wynford, architect of the Winchester nave and New College, Oxford (see p. 232).[57] Their long, vertical windows inspired a series of magnificent variations on the theme in parish churches across the diocese, known as Somer- set towers.[58] Both they and the central

tower (from 1315) were originally topped by spires, resulting in a church that convincingly dominated the landscape of Mendips and Levels around it just as the bishops utterly dominated medieval Wells.[59] The cloister was rebuilt, with new first floor levels that incorpor-ated both a school and the largest cathedral library in England.[60] Off it stood the Lady-Chapel-by-the-Cloister, greatly enlarged since its preservation in the 1190s and packed with tombs, but still containing the walls of an Anglo-Saxon building, and still pointing like a finger at St Andrew's Well, along the axis of the lost cathedral of which it had once been such an important part.[61]

Between 1477 and 1486 this complex structure was replaced by a church-sized chantry chapel for Bishop Stillington. This was one of the most ambitious chantry chapels in England, and a mark of the extent to which the inventive designs explored in such buildings were beginning to transfer to large-scale architecture. In this case, as a cruciform, fan-vaulted miniature church, the chapel was perhaps an inspiration for Bath cathedral priory, the belated rebuilding of which was largely the work of Stillington's successor,[62] Bishop King. Yet the extent to which Stillington's lady-chapel-cum-chantry obliterates the building that preceded it is also a sign that Wells had, in its maturity, apparently forgotten the significance of this ancient site.[63] Stillington's chantry also unwittingly contained the seeds of its own destruction. Chantries became illegal in 1547, and the sixty-year-old chapel was carted away in pieces a few years later.[64] Had it remained simply an ancient lady chapel, it might well be with us today, a tap root for Wells as a whole.

In 1539 Wells' ancient competitors at Bath and Glastonbury were dissolved amid great trauma: the abbot of Glastonbury was hung on Glastonbury Tor, and the cathedral priory of Bath was demoted, in mid-rebuild, to a parish church. Wells was now the uncontested senior church of Somerset. Its early

The communities of Wells have been climbing the chapter-house steps for seven hundred years

Renaissance pulpit, with its English inscription, is a physical reminder that the privileged world embodied by its east end was being replaced by a far more public kind of worship.

Getting to know Wells cathedral today is an intimate experience, like watching a great collective psyche growing into maturity. The child-Wells that was born out of St Andrew's Well existed before memory, yet it shaped the modern building; that of the 1180s is a pushy adolescent, becoming an ambitious, over-achieving young adult in the 1220s. Wells spent the fourteenth century celebrating its independence, only settling into secure middle age in the fifteenth. This was more than a church, more than a large institution: it was a community, as fractious and contradictory as any extended family.

Wells continues to be shaped in the most subtle ways by all who encounter it. The famous chapter-house steps, built for the canons in the 1280s and spliced in the 1450s so as to take processions of vicars en route from close to cathedral, have been carved into a subtle, organic series of dips and curves by 600 years of human feet. The tread of every modern visitor deepens them minutely: simply by exploring this great church, we join the community of souls that has shaped it.

WHAT TO SEE

St Andrew, Wells
Church first recorded in 766; secular cathedral from 909; moved to Bath 1090; reinstated c. 1170s/1240s; see then held jointly with Bath until the Reformation; still retains the title Bath and Wells.

Church: experimental early gothic architecture in the transepts and nave (and exquisite north porch, the Great Gate of the Canons); Early English west front (largest display of medieval sculpture in Europe); 'palm tree' vault of the Decorated chapter-house; exquisite late Decorated east end and central tower; Perpendicular cloister and western towers.

Tombs, fittings and carvings: heavily restored stained glass in lady chapel and choir; excellent collection of monuments and chantries, including twelfth-century tombs of Anglo-Saxon bishops and Bishop Beckington's chantry with its cadaver; first-rate incidental sculpture, especially on bosses in the transepts and nave; the west front.

Close: approach from the city market place, once an open space in front of the Anglo-Saxon cathedral, in its current form largely the work of Bishop Beckington; vicars' close and canons' houses of the Liberty; bishop's palace, one of England's finest medieval lordly houses, and open to the public; St Andrew's Well in the palace grounds.

WINCHESTER

Winchester sits in its Hampshire valley like some great sacred beast. This has been the site of a cathedral since the seventh century; it has been patched and extended constantly, and completely rebuilt at least once. Yet what remains most visible today are the architectural bookends of the middle ages: the twin stories of the Norman Conquest and the Reformation, played out side by side. Winchester was the richest bishopric in England: 'Canterbury had a higher seat but Winchester was more succulent', as one bishop put it.[1] More bishops of Winchester were chancellors of England than at any other cathedral.[2] These men were politicians of regal power; but they could also become semi-detached from their cathedral, whose liturgical needs were met by the monks, and from their comparatively small diocese, which comprised Hampshire and Surrey, and could easily be administered on the bishop's behalf by his own staff.[3]

For the Normans, however, Winchester was as close to a capital city as anywhere in England. William claimed to be the legitimate inheritor of the Anglo-Saxon crown: here, in the cathedral known as the Old Minster (see pp. 44–7), he continued the Anglo-Saxon tradition of holding an annual crown-wearing. Here, his bishop Walkelin built the most emphatically all-conquering of all the Norman cathedrals.

Walkelin's Winchester, begun in 1079, was, at about 157 metres long and 25 metres wide, one of the largest structures on the planet.[4] It was the

Though shorn of its many towers, Winchester still remains a powerful presence in its Hampshire valley

first Norman cathedral whose architecture was not simply an import from Normandy. Instead Winchester took ideas from the most ambitious buildings in pre- and post-Conquest England, Empire Germany, Lombardy and France. It neatly reproduced the dimensions of St Peter's, Rome.[5] And it coined an architectural brutalism as thrilling as an

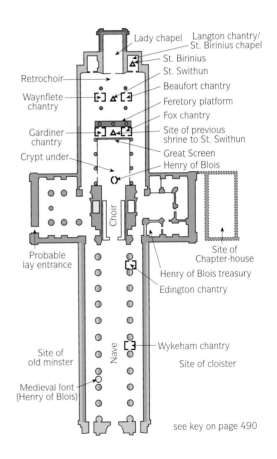

see key on page 490

443

Winchester's eleventh-century crypt has provided inspiration for Anthony Gormley, whose Sound II is installed there

engraving by Piranesi, as harsh as a 1970s car park.

The transepts and crypt are the places to see Walkelin's architecture. Their muscular effects are unforgettable (illustrated p. 61). But most of the rest of the church is also his work, made over by later architects. The cathedral was built using foundations of oak and concrete, but the site was a potential swamp and in later centuries there were structural problems, especially in the east end. The parts of this church that have since vanished are perhaps ten towers,[6] the mighty 15-metre wide west front, and the eastern apse and side chapels. It was into these that the treasures of the Old Minster – the shrine of bishop-saint Swithun and the bones of the Anglo-Saxon kings of Wessex and England – were translated in 1093.

Walkelin was a former royal chaplain, and his project surely had the support of the king. But the bishop's role was crucial. He made his post fabulously wealthy by separating his income from that of the monks, taking at least half for the bishopric,[7] and he shocked the king by demolishing in three days a 'delectable wood' offered as a possible source for building materials.[8]

By the mid-twelfth century, the monastic revival championed by the Normans had turned into a mini-renaissance. At the centre of English taste, like a queen bee in a great hive, stood one man, a close relative of three kings, monk of magnificent Cluny and purveyor of high politics – 'part pure and part corrupt . . . part monk and part knight' – Henry of Blois, bishop of Winchester, abbot of Gloucester and papal legate (see pp. 74–5).[9] Henry played a key role in the dynastic war known as the Anarchy, treating his cathedral enclosure as a castle and burning to the ground several of the city's churches, including the great abbey of Hyde.

Henry was a man of almost unimaginable wealth. In 1143 he visited Rome with the aim of creating a new province in England, one that would cover historic Wessex, have Winchester for its cathedral and himself as its first archbishop. His request was refused; instead he indulged in some extravagant comfort-shopping, combing the city for classical statues and shipping them back to Hampshire to decorate Wolvesey castle, his palace in the close.[10]

Henry's only architectural contribution to the cathedral comprised two arches in the south transept, but he left the church with over sixty precious objects – altar frontals, candlesticks and such exotica as the 'hoof of a griffin'.[11] He may have commissioned the Winchester Bible, made from 250 pieces of calfskin – one calf per page – which remains in the cathedral library.[12] He may have installed the font and built the Holy Sepulchre chapel, which contains magnificent murals of thirteenth century and the 1170s.[13] He certainly rearranged and redisplayed the shrine of St Swithun which stood behind the high altar, with its associated tombs of Anglo-Saxon kings.

Twelfth-century Winchester was home to some of the finest craftsmen of the era. It was the third richest city in the country; a place where – in addition to a royal palace, Wolvesey castle and several smaller monastic houses – many members of the aristocracy retained high-status pieds-à-terre. Henry built St Cross hospital (1135–7) here to house thirteen poor men and feed one hundred more each day – a far cry from the eighteen brothels he licensed on his recently acquired lands at Southwark, south of the Thames, where nearby he built a London palace.[14]

From around 1202, the eastern chapels of Walkelin's cathedral were being rebuilt and extended by Bishop de Lucy and his successor Peter des Roches, right-hand man to both King John and the young Henry III. The sumptuous hall-like retrochoir that resulted is an elegant work in the emerging Early English style. The function of this space is a mystery: it stands between the lady chapel and St Swithun's shrine, on its platform in the apse. Like many buildings of the era (see chapter three) the retrochoir partly created a dramatic approach to this shrine, for it was from the retrochoir that pilgrims accessed the Holy Hole that led beneath the relics of St Swithun; it may be that there was an unrealized intention to move the shrine itself into the retrochoir.[15]

It is a beautiful, oddly hesitant building, and it marks the start of Winchester's architectural problems. It is full of pauses and changes of mind. The building would have taken a decade at most complete, yet its floor – an extraordinary survival – appears not have been laid until sixty years later.[16] The monks described men like Bishop des Roches as 'hard as rocks'; there were frequent disputes between him and the sixty-strong community.[17] In any case, they did not need to worry about the cathedral fabric. The monks had a dedicated obedientary in charge of buildings maintenance, with the income from two manors to spend.[18] Perhaps such maintenance included the repainting programme of the thirteenth century,[19] and the gradually renovation of many side chapels in the fourteenth-century Decorated style.[20]

In 1305, a Winchester prior became bishop for one of the only times in the cathedral's history.[21] This man, Henry Woodlock, was a native of Norfolk; he borrowed from John Salmon of Norwich (another monk-bishop) a carpenter named William Lyngwode who in 1308 was working on Winchester's rumbustious choir-stalls.[22] About a decade later, the Norman apse was replaced, a delicate operation that squared off the eastern wall without destroying the eleventh- and thirteenth-century structures around it, resulting in a Decorated east end of which the most obvious remains are the arcades, as well as the squaring-off of the shrine area behind the high altar. The tabernacled screen surrounding this is an early achievement of its mason, Thomas of Witney (see pp. 227).[23]

In the wake of the Black Death, the bishops of Winchester started, once again, to make large-scale changes to their cathedral. London had now been

The Holy Sepulchre chapel provides a rare opportunity to enjoy the kind of painting which once covered great churches

the nation's capital for a century or more. Winchester was well on the way to being overtaken by Southampton as the richest town in Hampshire, let alone England. The cathedral priory and royal castle dominated the city, with bishops' foundations stretching down the Itchen: St Cross Hospital (1137), St Elisabeth's college (1301) and Winchester college (1378).[24]

Three fourteenth-century and eight fifteenth-century bishops of Winchester were chancellors of England; six treasurers also held the post.[25] Their palace at Southwark was thus a medieval Downing Street, the adjacent priory of St Mary Overie (now Southwark cathedral) their grand London church. Such men ran large offices, quite independent of the monks; diocesan work continued while the bishop got on with running the country.

The story of these men and their architecture is virtually a history of the late Middle Ages. Their chantry chapels spiral in magnificence as they march in pairs down the building: through them one can watch architectural and political ideas being passed like a baton through the Perpendicu-

The Winchester Bible, one of the lavish works of the twelfth-century bishop Henry of Blois

lar age of heresy, civil war and Reformation.

William Edington was the first of these. Keeper of the Wardrobe, treasurer and finally chancellor of England, he overhauled the royal finances, helping fund expensive wars in France and Scotland while barely leaving his desk.[26] Edington had been bishop for just three years when, in 1348, the plague struck. Over half of Winchester's sixty monks died; numbers never again rose much above forty.

After centuries of adaptations to the east end,[27] in the 1360s Edington focused architecturally on the western half of his cathedral.[28] The enormous Norman west front was demolished; its unassuming replacement was begun. The Perpendicular style his masons used was known to few outside the royal court. Edington founded a chantry to go with his tomb: the stone screen around it, containing an altar, makes it the first known 'cage' chantry chapel (illustrated p. 137).[29] In his will he earmarked substantial funds for the building of a new nave. 'A man with a career instead of a life',[30] he had helped sponsor a new architectural style, and with it some of the defining innovations of late medieval cathedral architecture – magnificent new naves and chantry chapels.

His successor, William Wykeham, combined the accumulative determination of the self-made man, the enlightened vision of the philanthropist and the tough intelligence of the politician. He was also one of the greatest patrons of architecture of the English Middle Ages. A local boy, William had made his name in royal building projects:[31] by 1359 he was in charge of Edward III's ambitious works at Windsor castle. Within four years he had moved into high politics. He collected and traded church preferments like a property magnate, becoming hugely rich in the process. He became bishop of Winchester in 1366 and chancellor of England a year later. 'Everything was done by him, and without him nothing was done', it was said.[32] He certainly ran a tight diocese, on one occasion

By entering the 'Holy Hole' pilgrims could position them-selves near the sacred relics of St Swithun

inspecting every church and religious house in his see in a single year.[33]

Wykeham lived in stormy times.[34] Despite his impeachment in 1376 in the last years of Edward III's reign, he made his way with skill through difficult political waters, entertaining Richard II (and 180 'followers') at Wolvesey castle and presiding at the marriage of Richard II's usurper, the young Henry IV, in the cathedral.[35] He saw for himself how both the clergy and the civil service (the two overlapped hugely) were being depleted by war, plague and wage disputes.

Between 1378 and 1380 Wykeham founded a 'grammar school' at Winchester, designed to create a flow of educated local boys into a new university college of St Mary at Oxford (illustrated p. 138). Unlike previous cathedral schools, Winchester college was a large and independent institution. 'New' college, Oxford was a model institution, set up on a grand scale. With combined endowments worth over £1,700, Wykeham's two foundations rivalled the greatest cathedrals in wealth.

Winchester college had seventy pupils, all local boys, who were to be educated free of charge by nine priests and three clerks; his Oxford college had ten priests and seventy scholars. Wykeham expressly wanted his colleges to respond to the 'deficiency in the numbers of educated clergy due to war and pestilence';[36] promising but low-born himself, perhaps this self-made man wanted to ensure others could also better themselves.

Wykeham had meant to continue Edington's work. But in 1371 the 'ashlar blocks and unhewn stone, lime, cement and scaffolding poles' of the nave were stolen (the robbers surely 'feared neither God nor men').[37] Over the next twenty years Wykeham was occupied by arguments with the monks, with Parliament, and by his educational projects. In 1393 he kick-started work on the nave by carrying out a 'visitation' of his own cathedral priory. The nave was unfinished, it was announced: the prior and convent should pay £700 and 700 marks a year respectively towards it. Further massive contributions came from his own pocket. Work restarted within a year.

Instead of taking down Walkelin's massive nave and rebuilding it from the foundations, Wykeham's masons – led by his favourite designer, William of Wynford – simply reinvented it.[38] At first they carved the eleventh-century walls until they were transformed into their own crisp, linear Perpendicular designs: later, they scraped several inches off their surface and then applied a skin of stone to their own design. The proportions of the old

William Lyngwode's energetic choir stalls are among the finest of their era

building governed those of the new, but every other aspect of its former self was hidden. The gallery was torn out, creating a tall arcade; arches were turned from round to pointed; the wooden roof was replaced by a glorious, fountain-like lierne vault, upstaging the east end considerably. In the middle of it was Wykeham's elegant chantry, as richly appointed as a tiny church.[39]

At his death in 1404 Wykeham left money for the completion of the nave: 2,500 marks of an estate worth an astonishing £6,000 or £7,000 even after he had given New College a cash reserve of £2,000 and set up a whole branch of his family as substantial local gentry.[40]

It was left to Bishop Henry Beaufort to complete this nave. Here was a Henry of Blois without the taste. He shared much with his predecessor besides a given name and royal blood.[41] Both were the richest man of their age (Beaufort lent the Crown and others £80,000–100,000 during his career),[42] and both had grandly multiple roles: Beaufort was chancellor of Oxford, chancellor of England and papal cardinal. The lives of both were dominated by dynastic wars. Beaufort even refounded Blois' St Cross Hospital. A man like Wykeham might have turned this charitable institution into an educa-

tional one: Beaufort merely made it into an old people's home for his own staff.[43]

Beaufort had visited Venice and other cultural centres of the early Renaissance; his portrait was painted by Jan van Eyck.[44] But rather than importing the latest artistic innovations, he spent much of his life in Europe, stamping out heresy – burning Joan of Arc and leading armies against proto-Protestant reformers.[45] In 1447 he left huge amounts of gold and silver to the convent (and £1,000 to the fabric of Canterbury cathedral), and asked to be buried next to St Swithun.[46] The money helped pay for a sumptuous new set of architecturally scaled furnishings: a sumptuous chantry to Beaufort himself, a new grand shrine to St Swithun and probably the 12-metre high Great Screen behind the high altar, which dramatized the raising of the host and gave the church the visual climax it lacked.[47] All were built under Beaufort's successor Bishop Waynflete, headmaster, humanist and anti-heretic.[48]

On St Swithun's day 1476 the saint's relics were processed around the city, a sermon was preached in English in the cathedral, and the saint was deposited in his new home, where Waynflete, other assembled bishops and a few brave aristocrats kissed the mouldering bones 'with great devotion'.[49] Such gestures – as well as the Great Screen itself – were all ways of responding to the threat of heresy, making saints more accessible and emphasizing the Eucharist; Waynflete founded Magdalen college, Oxford with the same aim.

The spectacular twin chantries of Bishops Waynflete and Beaufort were built either side of the new shrine, making lavish use of polished stone from the Isle of Purbeck (illustrated p. 209).[50] They were the last great surviving cathedral structures to be made from a material which Henry of Blois had done much to promote some 300 years earlier.

By the early sixteenth century Winchester had more monks than at any time since the Black

Winchester's choir extends into the nave (left) which around 1400 was reinvented as a Perpendicular structure without any rebuilding being necessary (right)

Death. But the seeds of its very different future were everywhere. They were in the lady chapel, filled by the priors with choir-stalls and wall-paintings, making it a suitable setting for polyphonic music:[51] in such places, early music began its long evolution into classical music. They were present in the chantry chapel of Bishop Thomas Langton (d. 1501), which included some of the earliest, hesitant, Renaissance details in England: he had spent much time in Padua, Bologna and Rome.[52] And they were evident in the works of Bishop Richard Fox (d. 1528), who founded Corpus Christi, Oxford for his monks, but then realized they would soon be a thing of the past, and made it a secular college instead.[53] It was Fox who attempted to turn his

church – which by now had a Perpendicular nave and west front, Norman transepts, Decorated choir and early gothic retrochoir and lady chapel – into a building that was Perpendicular throughout. His plans were stopped by the very forces he helped unleash, leaving Winchester's east end a monument to the makers of Reformation.

Fox's diplomatic work in Rome won the then prince of Wales the right to marry Katherine of Aragon; his Oxford college, Corpus Christi (1517), was the first place in the country where Ancient Greek was formally taught.[54] Yet he was an instinctive conservative, and working for the Tudor kings left him with 'a cold stomach, little sleep, pale visage, and a thin belly'.[55] In 1516 he retired to his

This painting by Jan van Eyck, recently claimed to be of Cardinal Beaufort, bishop of Winchester, is one of the earliest surviving portraits of an Englishman

represent his episcopal career in stone, and leaving money in 1513 for new vaults in other parts of the building.

When Fox died in 1528, to be briefly replaced by the infamous Cardinal Wolsey, he left more money to ensure his ambitious architectural plans were completed. Work on the stolidly Perpendicular choir aisle vaults and windows was still under way in 1532, and Walkelin's mighty transepts had been reroofed pending the start of similar work there; Fox's will makes it clear that the entire church was soon to be given a Perpendicular vault.[59] Given the baton-passing of projects and legacies that had taken place over the previous 150 years, Fox might have assumed his project was in safe hands, and would result in a building that was Perpendicular in style from one end to the other. But it seems that both Cardinal Wolsey and his successor, Bishop Gardiner, had bigger problems to contend with.

The new shrine of St Swithun had only been in place some sixty years when, early one morning in September 1538, two of Henry VIII's officials 'made an end' of it. They recovered huge quantities of fake jewels and 2,000 marks of silver.[60] Soon, over half a millennium after St Ethelwold had ejected them from the Old Minster (see p. 46), the canons were back.

The Reformation runs like a faultline through the life and architecture of the then bishop, Stephen Gardiner.[61] His shuttle diplomacy over the king's divorce grew increasingly desperate as its implications became clear. Henry VIII called him 'much bent to the Popish party', and had him spied on. After the coronation of Edward VI he retired to his diocese, where he came down hard on outbreaks of image-breaking and mounted a letter-writing campaign against Archbishop Cranmer's Protestant plans. In 1544 his secretary was executed for denying royal authority over the church. Not long after, Gardiner himself was imprisoned. Released on condition that he gave a sermon that

diocese, 'whereby I may do some satisfaction for twenty-eight years negligence'.[56] He was slowly going blind, and in 1518 built his own chantry chapel (probably designed by the royal mason William Vertue)[57] near the high altar.

Fox and his priors built new presbytery screens, on which were placed 'Fox's boxes': miniature Italianate coffins where the mixed-up bones of the Anglo-Saxon kings, moved and repackaged several times since the close of the Dark Ages, found their final resting place. He gave the east end what could have been its first high vault in four hundred years,[58] studding it with bosses whose arms – Exeter, Bath and Wells, Durham, Winchester –

endorsed the regime's religious policies, Gardiner came dangerously close to doing the opposite,[62] and was imprisoned again. In 1551 he was deprived of his see.

Gardiner responded to the accession of Catholic Mary in 1553 with indecent haste. Triumphantly restored to his post, he gave the dead Protestant king a full Catholic requiem mass and tried to get Parliament to reverse all its Protestant reforms, triggering riots in London. He died in 1556, leaving £700 for the erection of a tomb at Winchester 'that I may be prayed for'.[63] His chantry chapel – Winchester's last – was, thanks to the Chantries Act of 1547, technically illegal. Inside, its vault is full of the spiky energy of late Perpendicular, interrupted rudely if elegantly by a well-composed classical reredos, full of details fresh from the courts of Renaissance Europe: Ionic capitals, fluted colonnettes, and Roman-style round-headed arches, beneath which statues pose with a relaxed elegance only recently coined by men like Donatello and Michelangelo (illustrated p. 163).

In the richly decorated space of Stephen Gardiner's chantry, a new way of seeing – a new world – explodes within an old one. The semicircular arches of this chapel are the first in Winchester cathedral since the days of the Conqueror, and they make a fitting end to the cathedral's story. Gardiner's refusenik chantry is as eloquent a monument to Reformation as Walkelin's church was to Conquest.

Were it not for the Reformation, we might think of Winchester as a great Perpendicular cathedral. Yet no one would wish for the pragmatic, conservative architecture of Richard Fox over what has survived instead: Wykeham and Wynford's nave, one of the most glorious in the Perpendicular style; the brutalist vision of Walkelin's transepts and crypt, time-machines to the years of the Conquest; the hesitant genius of the early gothic retrochoir; and the fragile palimpsest of projects and additions that have accrued around the high altar and feretory behind it. This, the most sacred part of the cathedral, may be aesthetically inconclusive; but here little Renaissance boxes house the bones of the kings who invented England, and the end of a world is built into the very stones that gave birth to it.

WHAT TO SEE

St Peter, St Paul, St Amphibalus and St Swithun; now Holy Trinity
Secular cathedral 662–3; Benedictine monastic cathedral 964; secular cathedral from 1541.

Church: brutalist Norman transepts and crypt; beautiful early gothic retrochoir; Perpendicular nave.

Tombs and fittings: high romanesque font; wall paintings in the Holy Sepulchre and Guardian Angels chapels; fourteenth-century choir-stalls; collection of seven chantry chapels.

Bishops' foundations: Henry of Blois' Hospital of St Cross (usually open); Wykeham's Winchester college (tours most days); bishop's palace at Wolvesey castle (English Heritage).

WORCESTER

Bishop Wulfstan ordered the destruction of his twin cathedral churches, and wept as it was carried out. It was 1084: he was almost England's last surviving Anglo-Saxon bishop.[1] 'We miserable people have destroyed the work of saints', he sobbed; 'We neglect our souls, so we can pile up stones.'[2]

These churches were indeed the work of saints. One had been built by the great monk Oswald, bishop of Worcester and archbishop of York,[3] over a century earlier. St Oswald's shrine of 1002 stood there still. Wulfstan had lived among these buildings since adolescence; he had been prior before he became bishop; and he had built the bell tower the remains of which lay among the ruins in front of him.[4]

Wulfstan might have seen parallels between himself and his predecessor.[5] The first cathedral here, dedicated to St Peter, had been founded with a community of priests in 679–80.[6] When Oswald arrived, probably in 961, he could have marched in and replaced these men with monks;[7] instead he built the monastery of St Mary next door,[8] and preached and persuaded until so many flocked to it that in 969 the priests gave the monks the keys to their church. Oswald spread monasticism throughout his see: soon much of Worcestershire (and parts of Gloucestershire) was owned by one monastic house or another, while the cathedral's lands – the 'triple hundred' of 'Oswaldslow' – made Worcester a rich institution.[9]

St Oswald had used the latest continental ideas to

Worcester's central tower of 1377: finest product of the nave rebuilding programme

reform monasticism, and had created one of the first cathedral priories as he did so (see p. 44). Now, thanks to the Norman invaders, such ideas were everywhere: there was more good practice from overseas, further monastic cathedrals were being created,[10] and flagging monastic houses in his own see were being reformed and revived.[11] None of this was a bad thing. At the age of seventy-four, Wulfstan could not match the bitterly anti-Norman abbots who had so recently ruled Ely, Peterborough and elsewhere. He would work with what was good about the new regime, and quietly preserve what was good about the old.[12]

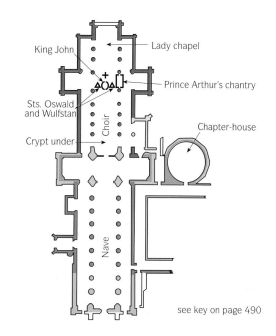

King John

Lady chapel

Prince Arthur's chantry

Sts. Oswald and Wulfstan

Crypt under

Choir

Chapter-house

Nave

see key on page 490

Wulfstan's church, as reconstructed in 1994

Wulfstan was one of the first Anglo-Saxon bishops to make an oath of fealty to the Norman king. He 'minded' the see of Lichfield while King William was looking for a new bishop there. He worked closely with Bishop Herbert de Losinga at Hereford and Abbot Serlo of Gloucester, both Norman appointees, especially on matters of architecture.[13] The Norman archbishop of Canterbury, Lanfranc, had offered him support when, for months at a time, he had gone to Bristol – the great port on the edge of his diocese, which seemed to grow wealthier every year[14] – to preach against the lucrative local trade in English slaves for export to Ireland. Quietly, too, Wulfstan encouraged his monks to maintain their traditions: to keep writing their chronicle in English, long after other attempts to do so had been abandoned, and to keep writing biographies of recent bishops and saints, a tradition the incomers did not have.[15]

Without Wulfstan, such traditions might have died out altogether. Instead, as the tension of Conquest slipped into the past, others began to recognize their value. By the time he died, in 1095, he was the grand old man of Anglo-Saxon culture, 'above all imbued with knowledge of the ancient customs of the English'.[16] He had reformed religion throughout his diocese, and expanded Worcester from just twelve monks to nearly fifty.[17] The size of his community alone justified a bigger church: in 1089 he translated St Oswald into the choir of his new cathedral. There was nothing half-hearted about this building: it was 'marvellous . . . in single details and singular in all parts'.[18]

This building is full of glimpses of a man trying to keep the past alive without rejecting the present. It eschewed the brutal triumphalism of some Norman cathedrals; yet it was also by far the most ambitious new church in the English West Country, its combination of ambulatory, radiating chapels and crypt placing it among the greatest churches in the land, in elaboration if not in size.[19] Its crypt and chapter-house are among the most ambitious structures of their period, yet both seem to be inspired by the past. Among the crypt's muscular forest of columns, many recycled from the lost Saxon cathedral, services to St Mary – beloved by the English – would be held.[20]

Wulfstan's chapter-house, planned before his death and built around 1110–20, is unlike any other of its age. The best explanation for its unique circular design is that it evokes some vanished Saxon building.[21] Its function was after all suffused with the monastery's history: here the community remembered their past members and buried their bishops. The adjoining passage that led to the monks' graveyard was even constructed out of more reused Saxon stone.[22]

Wulfstan's innovations outlasted him. His church had massive circular piers and unusual amounts of architectural decoration: both would become leitmotifs of Anglo-Norman architecture.[23] The circular chapter-house, in its polygonal form, would develop into one of the most spectacular building types in English architecture. The art forms of chronicle-keeping and the writing of biographies would be reborn in the twelfth century.

Wulfstan himself was acclaimed a saint. After the murder of Becket in 1170, many communities found that the old English saints had been badly upstaged, and so sought ways of raising their profile. The reaction at Worcester combined high farce and low politics. In 1198 the bishop heard that St Wulfstan

The innovative chapter-house may have its roots deep in Worcester's Anglo-Saxon past

was appearing in visions, asking to be translated to a new shrine. He got the monks to carry out Wulfstan's request at night, but died soon afterwards, whereupon St Oswald appeared to the monks and informed them that the bishop's death was no coincidence. Wulfstan had been 'raised irreverently and by night', Oswald said; moreover, no one had sought papal approval for the plan.[24] St Oswald, it seemed, was acting as a standard bearer for the papacy's efforts at the time to exert as much control as possible over the making of saints (see p. 97). The monks put the body back, and sent a deputation to the pope: in 1203 the canonization was announced. But just a year later the monks were fined 300 marks by King John for taking the side of the barons against him, and the shrine was melted down to raise this money.[25]

This must have incensed the king, who was devoted to the saint. To John, St Wulfstan symbolized the rights of kings over bishops.[26] In 1216, lying ill in Newark-on-Trent and at war with his barons, John asked to be buried at Worcester, between the bodies of St Oswald and St Wulfstan (illustrated p. 95). His body was carried across the country and buried in the cathedral. The nine-year-old Henry III was hastily crowned in Gloucester abbey, using a bracelet from his mother's arm.

In 1218 an extraordinary gathering took place at Worcester, comprising Henry III, the papal legate, his regent and his council, ten bishops and seventeen abbots.[27] They were there to 'dedicate' Worcester cathedral, even though it had not recently been rebuilt. In fact, the gathering seems to have been a high level post-war governmental conference, aiming to draw a line under the troubles of the past (see chapter three).[28] Wulfstan was finally translated into a suitable shrine. St Peter, St Oswald and St Wulfstan were added to St Mary as the cathedral's dedicatees, between them a kind of potted history of the church itself. There were elements of farce at this event: the shrine turned

out to be too small, so Bishop Sylvester of Worcester took an axe to the bones so as to fit them in. Archbishop Stephen Langton made off with poor Wulfstan's arm for Canterbury's relic collection; Abbot William de Trumpington of St Albans took one of his ribs 'by industry'.[29]

The cathedral, too, was perhaps drawing a line under the previous decades, during which – in addition to the mishaps over Wulfstan's shrine – it had been placed under siege during the war with John and the shrine had been melted down a second time.[30] The interdict (and two serious fires) had further impeded thirty years of architectural improvements: a new west end in experimental early gothic[31] and the repainting of the church, replacing plain white plaster with elegant patterns and biblical scenes.[32] Now, in the optimistic atmosphere of the 1220s, Bishop William of Blois reformed the church and won new lands for the convent. With their saint in his shrine and the troubled years of King John in the past, it was time to build a church that deserved its rededication, its saint and its new status as a royal burial place.

From 1224 Bishop William, perhaps spurred on by efforts by the Cistercian monks of Beaulieu to have John reburied in their church,[33] rebuilt the east end, and the result was a pure, elegant exercise in Early English gothic, at once rich and restrained.[34] The design is filled with a certain stretched tension, most emphatically in the great, long, single-light windows – some of which have shafts of polished stones no less than 21 metres long – and in the syncopated arches of his triforium, an idea borrowed from Lincoln. Tiny, faintly distended carvings enriched many surfaces: the Last Judgement and life of St Mary in the wall arcade; kings, angels, saints and prophets in the triforium.[35] These features, and the church's then unusual flat-ended plan, made a

Though much restored, Worcester remains an impressive sight from the nearby Severn

palatial setting for the highlights of the building: the high altar, the shrines of St Oswald and St Wulfstan, the tomb of King John and the lady altar against the east wall. In 1232 John was moved into a tomb of chilly magnificence (illustrated p. 95).

The thirteenth century was marked by petty struggles, as the convent struggled to limit the bishop's powers and expand their own. Then, as the century drew to a close, Worcester was again over-shadowed by outside events. Up to nine-and-a-half thousand pilgrims a week were flowing through the city, heading for the miracle-working new shrine of Thomas Cantilupe at neighbouring Hereford. His cult had stimulated considerable rebuilding at Hereford, and equally impressive works were under way at the nearby abbeys of Bristol, Tewkesbury and Gloucester, each striving to outdo the others architecturally. The Worcester monks[36] decided to rebuild the remaining Norman part of their build-ing, which comprised the crossing and much of the nave, so as to make the church gothic from end to end. For some time, the bishop refused to help, but work had begun by 1309–10.[37]

It was a troubled campaign, especially from the late 1330s. Resources might be diverted to grand conventual buildings, such as the prior's VIP guest house,[38] the swaggering Edgar Gate (illustrated p. 136), a refectory that must have dwarfed the forty or so monks who dined there, or the chapter-house, which was brought architecturally up to date.[39] As all this was drawing to an end in the 1370s and 1380s, work began on rebuilding the cloister, though this may have taken a century to complete. Throughout, the monks imposed a conservative brief on their designer: the new nave and crossing were built on the half-demolished ruins of the old building, and the design is a less magnificent emulation of the thirteenth-century east end, only with Decorated details (later turning to Perpen-dicular). Only the lovely central tower was allowed to be free of this stricture.[40] Yet the result was then

the only monastic cathedral in the land to have an entirely gothic interior.

Life at Worcester cathedral priory in the late fifteenth century would have been unrecognizable to Oswald or Wulfstan. The prior had been hon-oured with mitred status during the fourteenth century (see p. 169). His monks worked in a newly completed cloister that was more like a lavishly appointed business suite than a place of austere reflection. Stained glass windows made it warm and free of draughts, and were filled with heartening depictions of the monastery's benefactors, each accompanied by the names of the estates they had given to it.[41] Comfortable carrels between each window provided workplaces for the monks.

Meanwhile, Bristol had become second only to London in wealth. In the 1450s Bishop Carpenter rebuilt the small but ancient collegiate foundation associated with the bishop at Westbury-on-Trym, not far from the city, and appointed the great proto-capitalist merchant, mayor and Bristol MP William Canynges as his dean (see p. 147).[42]

By the end of the century, it seems, the see could function perfectly well with a bishop who rarely visited Worcester itself. Four late fifteenth-century bishops of Worcester were Italians, members of the papal curia based in London or Rome. Yet the Reformation might not have happened at all, had a chance virus not robbed us of a future King Arthur (illustrated p. 153), giving us his younger brother Henry VIII in his stead. Arthur's death was to provide Worcester with another royal tomb.

As prince of Wales, Arthur had impressed the court at his castle in Ludlow. His marriage to Katherine of Aragon in November 1501 had been a great diplomatic coup. The couple lived in their new Shropshire base for six months; then, suddenly and unexpectedly, the handsome, intelligent prince caught a fever and died. He was just seventeen.[43] Although Henry VII and his queen, Elizabeth of York, were too devastated to attend the funeral,[44]

£566 16s was spent on an occasion of appropriate grandeur. Over the ensuing years one of the most magnificent of all late medieval chantry chapels was built around Arthur's tomb, in its sculptural richness a kind of miniature workout for the greatest of all late medieval works of English architecture, Henry VII's chapel at Westminster abbey, but architecturally unique in its delicacy of design.[45]

In 1540 the monks of Worcester surrendered their ancient institution and its saints quietly. Perhaps they had grown comfortable in their all-mod-cons cloister; perhaps they had been suitably prepared by their new bishop, the committed Protestant John Latimer. In 1541 Worcester became, ironically, what it had first been when St Peter's cathedral was founded: a college of secular priests, headed by a bishop, albeit of a see whose size and significance were greatly reduced. Two of the great churches in the diocese, St Augustine's, Bristol, and St Peter's, Gloucester, became the cathedrals for two new sees: both might otherwise have been lost.

Today, Worcester is England's most Victorian medieval cathedral. All its main facades, all its cloister tracery and most of its fittings are nineteenth-century.[46] Much of the monastic complex survives within King's School, but the layman's approach from the city has almost disappeared. Medieval visitors from the city passed the bishop's palace, a parish church, a grand cemetery chapel and a standalone bell tower before they reached the church: today, they have to cross a dual carriageway. There is no sign of the fourteenth-century chapel of St Mary in the nave, with its miracle-working image of the Blessed Virgin,[47] nor of the shrines of Wulfstan and Oswald. Worcester's heyday as one of the centres of Anglo-Saxon civilization is invisible. What survive are the royal tombs, structures of the highest quality, to men whose deaths changed the course of history.

WHAT TO SEE

Christ and St Mary, Worcester
Secular cathedral 679–80; Benedictine monastic cathedral c. 969; secular cathedral after 1541.

Church: eleventh-century crypt and twelfth-century circular chapter-house; early gothic bays at the west end of the nave; thirteenth-century east end with fine original sculpture; Decorated work between the two, including new central tower.

Monuments: tomb of King John; chantry of Prince Arthur.

Setting: picturesque views from the River Severn; some fine monastic buildings have become part of the King's school.

YORK

To get to grips with medieval York we have to reimagine this genteel city as a teeming metropolis. We have to remember that it was at once England's second city,[1] the seat of one of the country's largest dioceses, and the headquarters of the senior church-man in northern Britain.[2] Canterbury may have been the headquarters of English Christianity, but as a city and a see it was little but an adjunct to its archbishop. York, by contrast, was truly the 'capital' of the north; and the presence of an archbishop was among the things that set it apart. It is no surprise, then, to find that one of the largest medieval churches in Europe still dominates the city.

Yet this cavernous building is easy to misread, and much the same could be said of the province over which it ruled. Much of the north was moun-tainous and poor. The archbishop ruled over just three sees, compared to Canterbury's fourteen:[3] York itself; the young and impoverished see of Carlisle; and mighty Durham, almost as venerable, arguably as powerful, and something of a cuckoo in the nest. Border politics, sometimes violent, could dominate life here when it was but distant thunder in the south. The archbishops of York spent dispro-portionate amounts of energy trying to prove their parity with (and independence of) their colleagues in far-off Kent.

But the north had strengths, too. The Danish invasions had left it a *tabula rasa* for monasticism:[4] as a result, by 1300 the province was packed with some sixty-five young and independent-minded

Only completed decades before the Reformation, York dominates its city to this day

houses of monastic orders new and old. The see of York was large, and also contained a unique series of 'deputy cathedrals': collegiate churches at Southwell, Ripon and Beverley with a special rela-tionship to the archbishop and many episcopal responsibilities in their part of the see.[5] Ripon and Beverley even held the shrines of sainted former archbishops; their architecture of all three churches

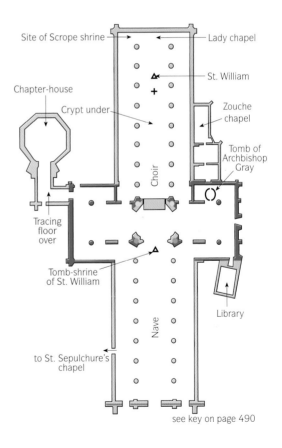

Site of Scrope shrine

Lady chapel

St. William

Chapter-house

Zouche chapel

Crypt under

Tomb of Archbishop Gray

Choir

Tracing floor over

Tomb-shrine of St. William

Library

to St. Sepulchre's chapel

Nave

see key on page 490

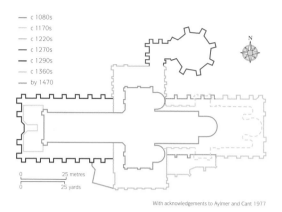

— c 1080s
— c 1170s
— c 1220s
— c 1270s
— c 1290s
— c 1360s
— by 1470

N

0   25 metres
0   25 yards

With acknowledgements to Aylmer and Cant 1977

York has grown around itself several times over

is often on a cathedral scale, and moves in step with that of the minster itself.[6]

York minster dominated its city. In 1327, the richest layman in the city was worth just £26 a year.[7] The prebends of the minster, by contrast, had an average value of £40 each; individual officers such as the dean might earn as much as £373, and the prebend of Masham was the richest in England. Churchmen from all over Europe competed to possess these posts. Influence over the disposal of such resources gave the archbishop extraordinary powers of patronage. Via the chapters of Ripon, Beverley, Southwell, the minster itself and its adjacent 'St Sepulchre's chapel',[8] the archbishop had over eighty separate sources of income that could be directed into the pockets of senior churchmen.[9]

Absenteeism was a particularly serious issue in York. Throughout the Middle Ages, the minster rarely had more than seven of its thirty-six canons resident;[10] in the early fourteenth century, between a third and a half of its chapter were foreigners.[11] This level of absence perhaps stimulated the development of England's earliest series of sub-colleges: the vicars first had a close of their own as early as the mid-thirteenth century. And in some ways absenteeism actually enhanced the powers of

the York chapter, giving the minster community complex and wide-ranging connections deep into the heart of royal and Church power. But absenteeism also meant that the riches of the region went into the pockets of generations of senior administrators who were based elsewhere. York's wealth could be a weakness.

All this explains much about the minster, which combines huge size with a certain emptiness. With its host of sainted archbishops, York should be as steeped in sanctity as Canterbury, but it has seeped relics to other churches like a holy colander,[12] while its main in-house cult, St William, was of little more than local significance. Competition with Canterbury and the great churches of the north was a powerful incentive to stay ahead of the game architecturally, and for at least 300 of the 470 years between the Norman Conquest and the Reformation, the minster was largely a building site. Much of the rebuilding was carried out around the outside of the preceding structure, creating a 'hollow Russian doll' effect: the minster has swallowed its own history several times over.

———

York's history is nonetheless its greatest obsession. It is a story that starts early. Pope Gregory the Great knew little about England, but he had heard of York. Constantine, before he made the Roman Empire Christian, had been proclaimed emperor in the city, and there had been a bishop in York in the fourth century. Gregory wanted to make this once great city the base for one of England's two archbishops. His mission to the English of 597 made it a priority to send a missionary, Paulinus, to the kingdom of Northumbria (see p. 38). The king was successfully converted, and built a wooden baptistery among the Roman ruins by 627, soon to be replaced in stone. Paulinus became bishop; the see later lapsed (it was refounded by Wilfrid – see

p. 40) and the archbishopric Gregory wanted to set up was not fully established until 735. Subsequently a major centre of scholarship developed at York, which came to an end when the Vikings took the city from 868;[13] it went on to become one of the most important settlements in the Danelaw. By 1066 the cathedral complex here included churches dedicated to St Mary and the 'Holy Wisdom' as well as the grand, ancient church of St Peter built by St Wilfrid, and served by seven canons.

What happened next was to replace these buildings so utterly that even their site is no longer certain.[14] In 1068, William the Conqueror put down a rebellion in the north with uncompromising ferocity. He then made Thomas, the treasurer at Bayeux cathedral, archbishop of York. On his arrival, Thomas found 'everything deserted and waste'.[15]

Within twenty years, 'the archbishop . . . divided some of the lands, which were still waste, into separate prebends, to leave room for a growing number of canons, each of whom might be eager to build on and cultivate his own share for his own sake'. A 'model' secular cathedral constitution, its essentials imported from the best practice in Normandy and northern France, was adopted. The chapter that developed gave its individual members exceptionally good incomes, for 'above all he desired to have good and reputable clerks'.[16] Thomas also fought a bitter battle against Canterbury's primacy over York and rode a wave of monastic foundations, many of which could be seen as threatening York's interests, including the cathedral priory at Durham and the important new abbey of St Mary in York itself.

This door in the nave is all that remains of St Sepulchre's chapel, private college of the archbishop

At some point in this process – probably in 1079–80 – Thomas began to rebuild his cathedral church. The resulting building was the most unusual of all the Norman cathedral rebuilds.[17] At over 105 metres long, it was vast by the standards of its age, but completely aisleless.[18] It would have seemed as hall-like to contemporaries as the much bigger nave is to us today and, with no aisles, far more distinctive. This building aimed to be self-consciously different (perhaps among other things, self-consciously secular): different from such new monastic foundations as St Mary's and Durham, and different from Canterbury, with which Thomas and his successors were locked in near-warfare.

By the twelfth century, the political issues that influenced the creation of this building had subsided. But new challenges faced the archbishop. A Burgundy-based breakaway movement within Benedictine monasticism inspired a desire for greater austerity among some of the monks of St Mary's abbey. In 1132 the prior and thirteen monks – with the backing of the then archbishop, Thurstan – left their rich urban abbey for the wilds of north Yorkshire to found the monastery at Fountains, from which the Cistercians (see p. 78) became a major force in the land.

These monks wanted to take the Church back to original ideals. Working with other senior church-men in the province, they made an example of the worldly archbishop of York, William fitz Herbert, who had succeeded Thurstan in 1141 (see p. 79). As a result, William spent six years in exile in Sicily and Winchester, becoming something of a hero in the process. William's return in 1154 was greeted by miraculous events; he died in his cathedral soon afterwards, possibly after the Eucharist itself had been laced with poison The scandalous nature of his death made William a martyr in the eyes of some; the background to it, charged with intra-church politics, made the story even more controversial. A potential saint was waiting in the wings,

even if in life William had been remarkable more for his 'lightness of morals' than for any special holiness.[19]

William's replacement, Roger of Pont l'Evêque, must have known St Anselm's 'glorious choir' in Canterbury well (see p. 69). In York he found an out-of-date church that had been damaged in a fire of 1137, and a see riven by conflict. Equally alarming was the fact that his rival, Thomas Becket, had replaced him as archdeacon of Canterbury;[20] Becket must already have seemed to be heading for the southern archbishopric.

After he took up office in 1157 Roger of Pont l'Evêque poured resources into his church. The building that resulted, which has also almost disappeared – only part of the crypt survives – was one of the most important structures of its age. Roger gave the minster an inventive and magnificent new east end which used the pointed arch in a way that was new to England, not simply as an occasional decorative motif, but as a key to the 'feel' of his architecture: in other words, the building could be called gothic, perhaps the first gothic building in the country. The richness of its decoration was equally extraordinary: it probably included more lavish use of polished stone than at any previous church, and had an unusual plan that may have culminated in a circular eastern chapel.[21] In addition Pont l'Evêque replaced the transept chapels and built a new west front, also now lost, which was covered in figurative sculpture.[22] Knowledge of gothic had come to northern England via the Cistercians, yet Roger's ornate architecture, created at a time when York had a controversial potential new saint on its hands, flew directly in the face of their ascetic tastes.

Soon England seemed to be awash with new saints and with ever more magnificent buildings in

Archbishop de Gray's colossal transepts were the main lay entrance to the church

the new style. By the 1220s it was time to make rather more of William fitz Herbert. At this date the archbishop was Walter de Gray, a man who had been King John's chancellor and was rumoured to have paid £10,000 for the archbishopric. In spite of this, he was an exemplar of the enlightened post-John years, even attending the epochal Fourth Lateran Council in Rome in 1215 (see p. 104)

Gray arrived to find an institution which had been poorly led since the death of Roger in 1181.[23] He drew up new statutes for the church, reforming many aspects of its institutional life. And in 1223 he applied to Rome for the canonization of William fitz Herbert – a bid supported, it was said, by a further large cash payment. Walter de Gray, it seems, knew that fitz Herbert was no Thomas Becket or Hugh of Lincoln. The canonization was secured in 1227; it was time to upgrade the shrine's setting.

About 1225, Gray began fundraising for the rebuilding of the transepts of Thomas of Bayeux's cathedral. He took on the south transept, and John le Romeyn, the Italian sub-dean and later treasurer[24] (a post recently enriched as a side-effect of Gray's reforms), took on the north one, as well as the building of a new central tower. Thus began a long tradition of architectural patronage by York's exceptionally rich treasurers.[25]

Gray's enormous transepts are multi-purpose structures, designed to impress a wide public. They use the northern version of Early English, in which rich mouldings and tight yet stately arrangements of giant lancet windows create an effect of lavish elegance. The transepts were so wide that a plan to vault them in stone was abandoned.[26] Wood was used instead: it would remain the preferred option for minster vaults for the next 300 years.

While the central door of the west front was reserved as a ceremonial entranceway for important visitors (see p. 167), ordinary lay visitors entered via the south transept, which lay closer to the city centre. The decision was made in mid-construction

to make its main facade as high and impressive as possible, resulting in one of the first gothic rose windows in England, which still dominates the approach from the south today. As soon as they entered the church, pilgrims were faced by a glorious, shimmering series of stepped lancet windows in the far wall of the north transept, today known as the Five Sisters and still filled with their thirteenth-century grisaille glass. They then approached the shrine of St William, which stood at the east end of the nave, passing as they did the tombs of archbishops of York, starting with that of Gray himself, who died in 1255. By impressing a wide audience, providing an approach to the shrine and acting as a mausoleum for subsequent archbishops, Gray's transepts reflected many of the classic themes of post-Lateran IV architecture.[27]

Gray had helped make his chapter a rich, proud and independent religious corporation, even though he was not a member himself (to join one had to be in receipt of a prebend).[28] By around 1280 work had begun on a chapter-house suited to the chapter's status. Like the transepts before it, this octagonal chapter-house was unusually flexible in function. With eight more seats than there were canons and two special 'thrones' (perhaps for the use of exceptionally important visitors such as the king and archbishop) either side of the west door, it could double up as the city's most high-status meeting room. Instead of an archbishop's seat on the east wall, there was a row of six equal and specially enriched seats for the dignitaries, reflecting the 'first among equals' principles of the York chapter. With no central column to impede proceedings, the building could also be an appropriate setting for convocations of the northern province, or even the Parliament of England itself.[29] Architecturally it is designed to astonish and overwhelm, outdoing all previous polygonal chapter-houses (illustrated pp. 214, 226).

The York chapter-house is a work of rich, integrated beauty and high symbolism. Playful polygonal canopies, clever geometrical patterns and rich colours combine to spectacular effect. The chapter-house is perhaps the first major part of a cathedral to be unequivocally in the new Decorated style which had burgeoned from within Early English, and it remains one of the most complete medieval interiors in England, with rich (if much restored) incidental sculpture and eight wall-like expanses of glowing medieval glass. Parts of the giant painted figures which once dominated the vault have survived, and are on display in the minster undercroft.

As well as displaying many of the saints that mattered to York, the decoration of the chapter-house included a great swathe of shields representing great northern families, such as Clare and Ros, who included among their numbers several members of chapter. These sacred and secular themes, explored in some complexity in the main windows, were united by one overarching idea: the protection and intercession offered by the Virgin Mary. She guards the entrance, and is evoked in the proud poem painted immediately inside the door – 'the rose of roses, and the house of houses' – which symbolically unites Mary and the chapter-house itself in a single metaphor.[30]

For all its exclusivity, York is the most outward-looking of all cathedral chapter-houses. The carved animals which crouch along its parapet, many gazing north, are said to be the bears of Berwick ('bear-wick'), the focus of vital negotiations over the Scottish kingship in 1291. The man who designed its vestibule knew about pace-setting buildings in far-off France: one window in particular is a direct copy of one built at St-Urbain at Troyes (Burgundy), begun less than twenty years earlier. John le Romeyn, archbishop of York from 1285–6 (and illegitimate son of the John le Romeyn who was Gray's treasurer), was a great scholar who had trained at Paris, and visited Troyes in 1291.[31]

In the 1290s the focus of English politics began

Crystalline and continental, the nave evokes a symbolic gathering of northern knights

to move north, as Edward I's bid to control the succession to the Scottish throne moved from diplomacy to full-scale invasion. It was at precisely this period that Archbishople Romeyn initiated a grand building project which would be even more cosmopolitan in design and even more proudly local in message: a new nave that would be perhaps the most notable display of secular power in any cathedral. As early as 1284 St William's body had been moved from the nave to a more traditional position in the east end, behind the high altar.[32] This was a major event – the king himself helped carry the body. Although the nave remained the setting of a shrine at William's original tomb, access to it was no longer essential to maintain the cult. The assembled nobility of northern England were perhaps then canvassed for their contributions to the re-building, and in 1291 le Romeyn, with his dean, precentor and other residentiary canons, laid the foundation stone of the new nave.[33] It was the start of nearly 200 years of grandiose projects, which proceeded in fits and starts until by the 1470s the entire central body of the church, from the west front to the east wall, had been rebuilt, leaving only Gray's transepts standing from its predecessor and no romanesque fabric visible in the church at all.

This nave is almost completely continental in style.[34] It is a work of crystalline, almost brittle grace, and it was also the setting for a richly coloured decorative scheme in glass and sculpture that is emphatically secular in its interests. The arms of the northern nobility line the arcades;[35] lifelike statues of knights and civilians[36] people the triforium. All were probably vividly painted. The families whose badges line the walls may have given money to the project, but they also formed a community: the great families of the north, whether their members were lay or ecclesiastical, were bound together in complex webs of power and patronage. Thanks to the war with Scotland they were also increasingly at the centre of national politics, and the arms of their leader Edward I take centre stage throughout the nave's decoration;[37] in the stained glass windows of the nave aisles, installed from about 1306,[38] they show us something of themselves.

These were men like Stephen de Mauley, archdeacon of Cleveland and a member of the York chapter. De Mauley was a churchman whose family was important to him: he paid for a stained glass window in the nave in which he, his father and brothers are depicted alongside a swaggering display of their coats of arms. The unknown donors of the Pilgrimage Window were lay people who wanted to be known for their piety: like a huge page from an illuminated manuscript, their glass is packed with sacred images, surrounded by piously light-hearted marginalia. Perhaps most evocative of all

is the window in which one of the citizens inserts himself among this lordly gathering: that of the craftsman Richard Tunnoc, goldsmith, bell-founder and sometime mayor of York. Tunnoc was one of just three ordinary York citizens to found chantries in the cathedral in the Middle Ages; in his glass he himself presents a window to St William (illustrated p. 242). All around such scenes hang the bells that had made Tunnoc's fortune. His window is a very medieval combination of touching piety and brazen self-promotion.[39]

Architecturally, the York nave stands apart, talking a language from overseas that had few local sources.[40] But its imagery was secular and local. It was as though the doors of the church had been thrown open, and the aristocratic community of the province (with a few upwardly mobile hangers-on) had come rushing in, just as they would have gathered in the nave itself for St William's translation in 1284 or the royal wedding of 1328. This pious company of knights defends the praying canons to the east.

Within a couple of years of Edward I's invasion of Scotland in 1296, York had become the temporary capital of England. But in the 1310s things began to go badly for the English, and as they did, so building work at the cathedral slowed down. After his defeat at Bannockburn in 1314 – at which several of those whose arms are displayed in the nave died[41] – King Edward II became caught up in struggles with his own knights. Key churches like Carlisle and Ripon were attacked by the Scots. Edward III turned the tide of the war – with glorious architectural consequences in Durham – but politically France, not Scotland, was increasingly the prize. Then came the Black Death. The archbishop, de la Zouche, retired to his country manor and appointed a deputy (himself the absentee archbishop of Damascus) to do his work.

As warfare and plague engulfed the north, the minster's strong links with the lay community became less prominent in its architecture. The northern knights had symbolically abandoned their nave; with no new sponsors forthcoming, twelfth-century stained glass had to be reused to complete the windows of the clerestory. Archbishop William Melton (1316–40) helped to stop the rot, and chose to celebrate the minster's own proud history above all else.[42] He refurbished St William's tomb-shrine in the nave and in 1338–9 filled the glorious curvilinear Decorated tracery of the 'Heart of Yorkshire' west window with glass, using images that depicted former bishops and archbishops of York as the 'apostles' of northern England. His window also helped complete one of the triumphs of the nave campaign: the new west front.

With its rich surface decoration and handsome, two-towered design, York's west front seems so inevitable that it is easy to overlook how unique it is. It was intended to be as richly decorated, and presumably as replete with meaning, as west fronts such as Wells,[43] yet it lacks the compositional oddness of these screen facades, opting instead for the logic of the two-towered arrangement more common at monastic cathedrals such as Durham and Canterbury. Even though it is the product of many designers (the towers were not completed until the fifteenth century), it is arguably the most satisfying cathedral west front in the country.[44]

Nevertheless, by 1345 the unfinished nave was leaking and morale among the workmen was low. Fortunately the cathedral received the boost it needed when in 1352 Edward III had his chancellor, John de Thoresby, made archbishop.[45] Like Gray, de Thoresby was as much senior civil servant as churchman, but within four years he had resigned from national life. Also like Gray, he came to a diocese in need of reform, and used architecture as a tool in that process. His attention focused initially on the destruction caused by the Black Death. He recruited new priests and prevented others from deserting their parishes. He reached out to lay

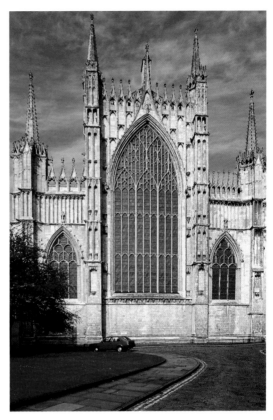

The east front is one of several glorious facades at York

people by creating a religious manual in English, the Lay Folks' Catechism of 1357; in the spirit of the Fourth Lateran Council over a century earlier, he wanted to make sure the restive populace understood their faith.

From 1359 de Thoresby gave money 'for the more speedy consummation of the fabric',[46] rapidly completing the seventy-year-old nave project. In 1361 he announced the rebuilding of Roger of Pont l'Evêque's east end, a project that had been in the air since at least 1349. The whole church would have a 'uniform beauty',[47] it was announced, as well as a suitable space for performance of a daily lady mass. The options of the master-mason, William Hoton, and his successors were restricted, however, by the contradictory brief: to respect the design of the nave, but also keep pace with the new Perpendicular style. Only where they had room to breathe – as in the east window – were these designers able to flex their muscles, proposing a softer, more decorous alternative to the new style for the south.

De Thoresby's priority was to simplify the complex plan of the former east end, forming a vast square-ended lady chapel whose east wall would rise the full height of the church.[48] He paid £200 a year towards it from 1363 until his death in 1373, perhaps contributing one-third of the total cost.[49] As a result, a process that had taken nearly seventy years in the nave took just a decade in the lady chapel.[50] But in 1373 de Thoresby died, and work ground to a halt before a choir could be built that would finally replace Pont l'Evêque's east end and join the lady chapel on to the rest of the church. As a result the building was not glazed for several decades. It eventually became a kind of Lay Folks' Catechism for the importance of York minster, complete with a series of large written notices – for public consumption – describing the history of the church.[51] Its glass spelled out the course of human history, with special emphasis on York's unique place in the history of British Christianity; retrospective 'tombs' of previous archbishops were commissioned to fill the space beneath.

———

Over the next century, the Church came increasingly under the control of the king, while the monarchy was rocked by a series of dynastic crises (see chapter four). Both themes were to be reflected in the architecture and decoration of the minster, and royal politics began to intrude sharply on minster life. Archbishops of York had often been political appointees, but between 1388 and 1500 not a single archbishop came from within the York chapter, while deans often worked in Rome.[52] Edmund Stafford was an exception: he restarted building work on the choir, employing a team of twenty-four masons by 1399.[53]

In 1379 Richard II made gifts to the minster,[54] and gave county status to the city – a privilege at that point shared only with Bristol and London. Yet the only sign of these gestures of friendship is a solitary white hart – Richard's emblem – carved in the choir aisles; unlike his predecessors', Richard's coat of arms is absent from the carved heraldry that had remained a theme of the church's decoration.[55] By 1399 he had been deposed: the house of York had been replaced by the house of Lancaster. The consequences for the minster were dramatic. Archbishop Richard Scrope had worked loyally for the deposed king, as had several members of both his chapter and his family; he had even been sent to Rome by Richard II to pursue the case for canonizing King Edward II. Initially loyal to the new regime, he can never in his wildest of dreams have imagined that he, too, would become the subject of a controversial cult.

The events that followed would have been watched with increasing amazement by the glass painter John Thornton. In 1405 this Coventry glazier had received the commission of a lifetime: to fill the 156 square-metre east window of York 'with historical images and other painted work in the best manner and form that he possibly could'.[56] The ostensible subject of the window[57] was the beginning and end of time, as embodied in the books of Genesis and Revelations, but in actual design the window was dominated entirely by the apocalyptic themes of the latter book. Its creation gave Thornton a ringside view of events that must have made him wonder whether the end of time was indeed imminent.

In 1403, a group of northern barons rebelled

against the new king Henry IV. Within a year, Archbishop Scrope – distinguished lawyer, close colleague of two kings – suddenly turned himself into a politician of a very un-medieval kind: a populist, a whipper-up of crowds.[58] In 1405 he pinned a manifesto to the doors of the minster and around the city.[59] Church and clergy were being abused, it said; lay people were being heavily taxed; money was going into the wrong hands. The people should rise up against the king. Scrope preached in the minster against royal taxation. He walked the streets of York, crozier in hand, urging rebellion. He got what he asked for.

In late May the archbishop rode out of York dressed for combat. Behind him were eight or nine thousand people, townsmen and country folk of York and its vale. Their presence transformed the rising from a piece of dynastic power politics into 'a "crusade" for good government'.[60] As a result the king turned against his archbishop, while the expected armies of the northern barons failed to reach York in time to support the latter. After waiting for three days, Scrope was imprisoned by the king in his own palace at Bishopsthorpe. Archbishop Arundel of Canterbury rode through the night to seek an audience with the king, and after arriving exhausted at the palace was reassured that nothing untoward would happen. But in another room, the archbishop of York was being sentenced to death by a hastily convened court.

The next day Scrope was led through the streets of York to a field outside the city – 'that there should be no prayer made for him'[61] – and beheaded. Five blows of the axe, the rumour later went: five wounds of Christ. It was 8 June 1405: St William's day.

The pope excommunicated Henry IV; in Canterbury, Arundel – trying to keep a lid on things – 'forgot' to publish the bull that announced this. Back in York, four vicars choral brought Scrope's headless body into the minster and buried it in an

The beast of Revelations, *as depicted in John Thornton's fifteenth-century east window*

eastern corner of the new lady chapel. The minster had spent several hundred years encouraging the people of its city to pray for the souls of dead archbishops, and that is what they now did. Some left money and offerings, as if the tomb was a shrine. The following year, the barley field in which Scrope had been beheaded brought forth a bumper crop. It was said that the king had fallen ill immediately after the beheading, 'was smight with a leprosy . . .', and that this fulfilled Arthurian prophecies of the downfall of a king with rough, scaly skin: soon 'Almighty God soon after wrought many miracles'.[62]

Things were getting out of hand. Henry IV ordered that the entire area round the tomb be blocked with logs and stones, but an old man named John Sibson, inspired by a vision of the dead archbishop, moved them away single-handed. The publishing of news of miracles was banned, though

The lantern vault of the central tower, built from the proceeds of a suppressed cult

the tower without stopping work on the choir. Indeed, it gave them something to do with their controversial source of funds.[66] Meanwhile, Henry IV decided to use the event to make a gesture to the minster: he took one of his senior master-masons, William Colchester, off work at Westminster abbey and sent him to York. The arrival of a southerner caused serious resentment among the masons of York; members of the York lodge were accused of a conspiracy to attack Colchester, in which one of his assistants was injured.[67] But undeterred, Colchester went on to build the handsome, four-square central tower of York which, paradoxically, is both one of the city's defining structures, and an uncharacteristic outbreak of sober southern Perpendicular in a building which otherwise resists architectural influence from the province of Canterbury. 'St' Richard Scrope, though, has been airbrushed out of it: the central tower credits Henry IV and Bishop Skirlaw of Durham in its coats of arms, despite the fact that the great majority of the costs must have come from Scrope's cult. The sum of £73 8s was transferred from shrine to fabric fund in 1415–16, enough to pay eight masons for a year; a further £150 was transferred in 1418, serious money by any standards.[68] York's sober icon is therefore the result of a potent brew of politics, violence and superstition (not to mention suspicion of much that emerges from south of the Trent).

The cult of Richard Scrope gradually became an accepted part of minster life. Henry V even removed the royal ban against pilgrimages to the archbishop's tomb. Soon Scrope even eclipsed William: in 1415–16 income at St William's shrine was 2s 10d, while in the same year no less than £78 was collected at Scrope's tomb.[69] By 1500 Scrope's chapel – though it contained no formal shrine – was packed with offerings from Yorkshiremen who had received miraculous assistance, alongside the tombs of other members of his family. In the 1440s the uncanonized archbishop had even been

not without some opposition from city officials who supported the cult.[63] 'By private means of money the matter was ceased', as one chronicler put it:[64] in 1408, after what was rumoured to be a massive transfer of funds to Rome, the pope published a new bull absolving the king of the murder, while asking him to found three new monasteries as a penance. The political teeth of Scrope's incipient cult were drawn, even if it could not be fully controlled.

Then, in 1407, the thirteenth-century tower of the minster – rendered unstable by centuries of building work on all sides of it – collapsed.[65] John Thornton, who had come to York to paint 144 scenes from Genesis and the Last Days only to find the area beneath his window the focus of a dangerous cult and treasonous prophecies filling the land, now saw the heart of the church collapse before his eyes. His head must have been spinning.

The result is one of the great ironies of medieval cathedral history. Thanks to the offerings generated by Scrope's cult, the chapter could afford to rebuild

depicted with a nimbus in a stained glass window in the minster.[70]

With the accession of Edward IV in the 1460s, the house of York finally seized the throne back, and Scrope's stand for good governance against a Lancastrian king was co-opted into Yorkist mythology. In 1467 a canon of Ripon even left twenty gold nobles to be spent on the building of a shrine to Scrope 'when God grant that he should be translated'.[71] But it was not to be. In 1462 a meeting of the province of York, perhaps aware that the cult raised issues that were by no means dead, decided against pursuing canonization; and today, Scrope's extraordinary story is but a footnote in York's history, and the site of his tomb in St Stephen's chapel at the east end of the north choir aisle, is a relatively anonymous corner of the minster.

The next cult to overtake York minster was, perhaps surprisingly, that of a king. Convocation's decision not to pursue Scrope's canonization was a wise one, for now it was the Lancastrians who were the underdogs. In 1471 their claim to the throne was violently defeated when Henry VI was murdered.

Yet again, the minster's decoration became the subject of high politics. In the intervening years, the minster had acquired a grand potential focus for devotion in its pulpitum, a grand work of propaganda in stone (illustrated p. 149). Erected by 1450 to divide choir from nave, this presented to lay visitors a gallery of statues of English kings shown in unbroken historical succession, despite the violent usurpation that had brought the Lancastrians to the throne.[72] In 1472, people began to make devotions at the last statue on the new pulpitum, which was in a very public position near the south transept[73] – that of the saintly Henry VI himself. In 1479 the archbishop ordered that it be taken down. But for the Tudor kings, Henry VI was unquestionably a saint; the magnificent Henry VII chapel in Westminster abbey was built in the hope that Henry VI would be canonized. By 1516

there was even an altar to Henry VI in the choir. The statue may have been re-erected, only to be destroyed at the Reformation (when the other statues were left untouched).[74] The current Henry VI statue was installed in 1810, rendering invisible another of the minster's highly political fifteenth-century cults.

Meanwhile, John Thornton and his team had completed their east window and gone on to turn the choir into a gallery of the great figures of English Christianity in the north. The two enormous windows that filled the new east end's eastern transepts and lit the site of the high altar were filled with glass, depicting the life of St William, paid for by Beatrice, Dowager Lady Ros, in 1414, and the life of St Cuthbert, paid for by Thomas Langley, another ambitious bishop of Durham, in 1440.[75]

Looking up and across in the eastern transepts

Other works also marked the gradual completion of building work: bells (one of which survives) were hung in one of the western towers in 1466; in 1479 crockets and gargoyles were added as finishing touches to the outside of the church.

In 1469–70 the final great work was commissioned: a mason named Robert Spillesby and his servant were sent on a twenty-eight-day hunt for the finest 'marblers', to create a new shrine for St William. This mighty structure – perhaps the largest shrine-base in medieval Europe, and York's final show of strength through size – must have helped to refocus minds away from more controversial saints. Large sections survive in the Yorkshire Museum, exquisite carvings of polished stone from Frosterley in County Durham.[76]

On 22 September 1472 five bishops, two dukes, four earls and many others witnessed the translation of William to his new shrine, and the consecration of the church as a whole. A rebuilding process that had been going on since at least the 1270s[77] – with significant pauses as Scotland and England went to war, plague ravaged the land, the chapter vanished overseas on business, archbishops morphed into saints and towers collapsed – was complete.

Over the same period, the city of York was beginning its slow but inexorable slide from capital of the north to tourist attraction-cum-university town. Henry VII was welcomed to the city with a grand pageant, but York was rarely an epicentre of national politics after that. The city's population halved during the fifteenth century.[78] When the last minster master-mason was not replaced in 1558,[79] the cathedral became an ancient monument rather than a building in progress.

———

There is something corporate about the minster today. Its decorative schemes are more secular than those that survive in any other cathedral;[80] its saint and near-saint, the archbishops William and Scrope, are distinguished more by politics than by piety; its most perfect interior – the chapter-house – is also the part of the building with the most corporate function.[81]

But this slight coldness is also an accident. It is hard to guess from the architecture that the cults of

WHAT TO SEE

St Peter, York
Secular cathedral: see founded 625–7 (though York was also a bishopric under the Romans); refounded c. 664.

Church: enormous Early English transepts; exquisite Decorated chapter-house and icily beautiful nave; Perpendicular eastern arm and towers. York also has the most beautiful collection of facades in England: the two transepts present contrasting exercises in Early English composition, while the west and eastern fronts, despite their design being altered several times in the course of construction, are two of the finest in the country.

Fittings and decorations: the greatest collection of medieval stained glass in England, forming a history of the medium from the twelfth century (nave clerestory) to the fifteenth century (choir); sculpture in the nave and on the pulpitum; fully carved and glazed medieval interior in the chapter-house; fascinating collection of objects, as well as remains of the romanesque church and Roman York in the Undercroft and Crypt museum.

Setting: approaching the south transept from the city, or viewing the minster itself from the city walls, one comes close to the experience of medieval pilgrims; on the north side of the church are the expansive, if fragmentary, remains of the 'cathedral quarter', including the archbishop's palace.

St William and Richard Scrope even existed, yet by 1500 St William had the largest shrine in Europe. Modern eyes do not 'read' the heraldry and statues that made the nave such an extravagant display of secular power. And while vaults are the aesthetic climax of most medieval great churches, at York barely a ceiling in the entire church is as its architect designed it. Thanks to the minster's preference for wood vaults and the four disastrous fires which have taken place since the Reformation, together with sweeping change in the eighteenth century, most of the originals have been destroyed, as have most other fittings.[82] Only the unparalleled collection of glass survives.

The minster is the oldest community with an unbroken existence described in this book,[83] yet it only achieved its current swaggering appearance fifty years before the Reformation, at a time when York's importance in other ways was in rapid decline. Yet it dominates its city with convincing and evocative authority. The minster has succeeded in at least one aim: it is hard to find another church so deeply loved by the people of the county and the city in which it is set. 'Northern pride' has ancient roots indeed.

OTHER ENGLISH CATHEDRALS

A number of medieval parish churches have gained cathedral status since the late nineteenth century. Architecturally, culturally and historically they belong to a different milieu from the churches in this book, though several – Portsmouth and Manchester in particular – would be indispensable to any review of smaller medieval churches. Brief details on each are given here. All other English cathedrals, both Anglican and Catholic, are post-Reformation buildings: again, they tell a different story.

BRADFORD

Bradford's main medieval parish church has details of 1200, after 1327, 1430 and 1493. Sculpture includes a fifteenth-century font cover and a tenth-century carving. Bradford was made a cathedral in 1919. Many additions were made from 1832–3 on, including an east end in the 1950s.

BURY ST EDMUNDS

One of Bury's medieval parish churches, its history was caught up with the abbey next door. The church stood within the abbey precinct; the eleventh-century building was demolished to make way for the abbey west front, and the abbey's Norman gate later served as the parish bell tower. The current building dates from c. 1510–1530 and later, and is perhaps by the great master-mason John Wastell (Bell Harry tower, Canterbury; Peterborough retrochoir, King's college, Cambridge).

Manchester's fifteenth-century arcades are emblazoned with the heraldry of local families

Some medieval fittings survive (glass and altarpieces) mostly from other churches. The Victorian roof is by Scott. The church was made a cathedral in 1914, and a new east end and many other parts were built then. The abbey next door was one of the few monastic houses that gave the greatest cathedrals a run for their money; perhaps the mightiest of the great romanesque churches of East Anglia, it stubbornly refused cathedral status for itself.

CHELMSFORD

A fifteenth-century urban parish church, Chelmsford has a fine west tower and eighteenth-century lantern; the tower and the south porch feature splendid late medieval East Anglian limestone-and-flint 'flushwork' decoration. Additions of 1801 and 1873 leave little of earlier interest in the interior. It was made a cathedral in 1913 and was given a new east end and other additions in 1923.

DERBY

Derby's main parish church was a small collegiate foundation. It has a magnificent sixteenth-century tower, and two average-quality late medieval monuments to sub-deans, designed by John Otes, a pupil of John Wastell. The rest was rebuilt by James Gibbs in 1723–5, with fine fittings of the period; there were several subsequent restorations, and a new east end was begun in 1967. Derby became a cathedral in 1927.

LEICESTER

A late medieval parish church, Leicester contains thirteenth-century arcades, two medieval tombs and a fifteenth-century sedilia. Fragmentary indications of a twelfth-century church also survive. The tower and spire are nineteenth century. Leicester became a cathedral in 1927.

MANCHESTER

Manchester has been an important settlement since Roman times. Its parish church, of ancient origin, was made a collegiate community of eight canons in 1421, and was rebuilt. It became a cathedral in 1847, but retains many important features of a large urban collegiate church built by aristocratic founders. Like many new colleges of the fifteenth century, this was effectively an exceptionally generous chantry for the family of its founder (the rector of Manchester) and others. With four clerks and six lay choristers, the foundation was also able to meet the needs of the many guild communities and chantry foundations in the rich merchant town of Manchester.

The church was built from 1422 (east end) and 1465 (nave), then fitted out in 1485 by James Stanley, bishop of Ely, son of an earl of Derby and stepson to the mother of Henry VII. He donated the exceptionally fine rood screen and choir-stalls, and his illegitimate son added the Derby chapel, with a separate chantry chapel-like tomb for his father (now lost). Other local grandees and guilds added aisles in the early sixteenth century, too, in a fashion typical of town churches across the country (see Cirencester, Gloucestershire and Grantham, Lincolnshire). Thus Manchester is partly a monument to the patronage of late medieval bishops, who often gave magnificently to the main church in their birthplace.

Apart from the fourteenth-century arch to the lady chapel (the chapel itself was bombed in the Second World War), the design is all of one piece: it is architecturally impressive if standard issue for its date. The only thing that marks it out as a collegiate foundation rather than a well-endowed parish church is the scale of the choir-stalls and the existence of an attractive little chapter-house and an eastern lady chapel. There are also two late medieval brasses, one fragment of Anglo-Saxon sculpture, and a rich collection of Victorian furnishings, reflecting Manchester's Victorian pride. The church was heavily restored in the nineteenth century, with additions then and during the twentieth century.

NEWCASTLE

The parish church of the important medieval town of Newcastle, in the see of Durham, was founded with its eponymous castle in the eleventh century. Most of the church is fourteenth-century and later, with some fragments of earlier work: the Norman church had a vaulted chancel, indicating a building of some pretension. The fourteenth-century work was financed from the 1340s on, including an interesting crypt and a 'planned' series of tomb recesses (compare Hereford, Bristol and such contemporary parish churches as Winchelsea and Aldthorpe). The striking 'crown'-type tower was financed by Robert Rhodes MP and finished by 1448. Although this design appears to have been invented at St Mary-le-Bow in London, it really took off in Scotland (St Giles; Edinburgh); it seems Newcastle is the link between the two. There is a medieval font with a fine cover; several medieval monuments, including a giant double brass of after 1411, imported from the Low Countries; a brass lectern; and a rich collection of post-medieval monuments and glass. The library dates from the eighteenth century. There are many Victorian additions and restorations; Newcastle became a cathedral in 1882.

PORTSMOUTH

One of a breed of exceptional local churches built in rapidly-growing English ports around 1200 (compare St Mary Redcliffe, Bristol; St Margaret, King's Lynn; St Nicholas, New Shoreham),

Portsmouth was founded by the wealthy shipowner John de Gisors as a chapel-of-ease and known to be under construction in 1185. This phase is among the best early gothic work in the country; a vaulted choir and transepts poking toy-like out of one of England's oddest religions buildings. The church gained a parish of its own in 1320.

Things to see include a fine thirteenth-century painting of Christ in Majesty. The seventeenth-century nave and the west tower, built to designs by Ambrose Stanyford after Civil War damage, are now the cathedral choir and central tower. The large nave and aisles were built from 1935 by Sir Charles Nicholson after the church was raised to cathedral status in 1927. The west front, by Michael Drury, was completed in 1991.

SHEFFIELD

The parish church of the town of Sheffield became a cathedral in 1914. Mostly fifteenth-century to the eye, it probably incorporates older work. The fine spire and Shrewsbury chantry chapel both date from around 1538; there is a collection of late medieval aristocratic monuments, and the wooden sedilia are fifteenth-century. Many of the other fittings and additions are post-medieval, especially parts of an intended new east end built in the 1940s, and the completed new west end of the 1960s.

WAKEFIELD

This late medieval parish church became a cathedral in 1888. The fine spire was under construction in the 1420s; the chancel was complete by 1458, but the arcades inside are a complex combination of the twelfth and later centuries. There are medieval choir-stalls with misericords, and an unusual collection of seventeenth-century fittings (the font and rood screen).

TRURO

Most of Truro parish church has vanished under Pearson's great cathedral of 1876, Cornwall's first since the tenth century (when the seat of the see was at St Germans). The remaining (heavily restored) south aisle of 1504–18 is now an outer aisle off the choir. This suggests a building that would have stood shoulder to shoulder with such major churches as St Petrock's, Bodmin and St Mary Magdalene, Launceston, ambitiously decorated in a manner associated locally with the Trecarrel family (see Place, Fowey and St Mary Magdalene, Launceston).

With acknowledgements to Pevsner & Metcalf 1984

CHARTS

Other maps and plans in this book

THE CATHEDRALS: SIZE AND WEALTH

Left table

Cathedral*	Who	How many†	What	Income‡
BATH	Bishop (shared with Wells)		Bishop	see Wells
	Benedictine monks	(1205) 41, (1377) 17, (1525) 22	Priory	£617
Bristol	Augustinian canons	(Pre 1348) c.25+, (1353) 18, (1498) 24, (1511–12) 18		£670
CANTERBURY	Archbishop		Archbishop	£3233?
	Benedictine monks	(c.1080) 60, (c.1146) 100, (by 1349) 80, (1534) c.70	Priory	£2349
CARLISLE	Bishop		Bishop	£577
	Augustinian canons	(c.12) 26, (1366) 13, (1540) 23	Priory	£418
Chester	St Werburgh's: Benedictine monks	(by 1249) 40, (1382) c.24, (1538) c.25		£1003
	St John's: (cathedral briefly late c12; role in see thereafter)			
	Prebends, etc	9–8		£119
	Priests, etc	10–7		
	Clerks, etc	6+		
CHICHESTER	Bishop		Bishop	£698
	Prebends, etc	27–31	Chapter	£310
	Priests, etc (Vicars' college 1396, 1465)	23–34		
	Clerks, etc	12–18+		
COVENTRY	Bishop (shared with Lichfield)		Bishop	see Lichfield
	Benedictine monks	(1016) 24, (1256) 31, (1478) 26	Priory	£808
DURHAM	Bishop		Bishop	£3138
	Benedictine monks	(1215) 45–7, (c.1290) c.69, (1372) 56, (1501) 43	Priory	£1366

* Non-cathedral churches are lower case   † Dates given in brackets   ‡ Net

Right table

Cathedral	Who	How many	What	Income
ELY	Bishop		Bishop	£2134
	Benedictine monks	(1093) 72, (1349) 53, (1377) 48, (1427) 44, (1534) 33	Priory	£1084
EXETER	Bishop		Bishop	£1566
	Prebends, etc	25	Chapter	£1179
	Priests, etc (Vicars' college by 1387)	24	College	£204
	Clerks, etc	30		
Gloucester	Benedictine monks	(1078) 80, (1104) c.100, (1284) 50, (1339) 46, (1380) 54, (1534) 35		£1430
HEREFORD	Bishop		Bishop	£831
	Prebends	33	Chapter	£426
	Priests, etc (Vicars' college 1395, 1472)	12–27	College	£88
	Clerks, etc	11+		
LICHFIELD	Bishop (shared with Coventry)		Bishop	£795
	Prebends, etc	28–35	Chapter	£275
	Priests, etc (Vicars' college 1241)	29–21	College	£199
	Clerks, etc	19+		
LINCOLN	Bishop		Bishop	£2095
	Prebends, etc	54+	Chapter	£575
	Priests (two ranks; Vicars' college +1277 and 1441)	37–20	Colleges…	£358
	Choristers (poor clerks' house)	19–24		
	Cantilupe college (chantry) 1367	8–2		£41
NORWICH	Bishop		Bishop	£1050
	Benedictine monks	(1101) 60, (1348–9) 67, (1381) 50, (1441) 56, (1526) 39	Priory	£874
	Carnary college (chantry & charnel house) 1316			
	Priests	4		
Oxford	Augustinian canons	(after 1160) 18, (1445) c.17, (1520) 9		£220
	(6 canons served parishes)			

Cathedral	Who	How many	What	Income
Peterborough	Benedictine monks	(1124) 60, (pre 1348) 64, (post 1349) 32, (1437) 47, (1534) 41		£1679
Ripon	Prebends, etc	7		
	Priests, etc (Bedern 1303, 1411)	6		
	Clerks, etc	12		£334
ROCHESTER	Bishop		Bishop	£444
	Benedictine monks	(1079) 22, (1108) 60, (1210) 60, (1385–6) 24, (1534) 20	Priory	£486
SALISBURY	Bishop		Bishop	£1507
	Prebends, etc	36–54	Chapter	£601
	Priests, etc (Vicars' college 1409, 1422)	52	Colleges…	£272
	Clerks, etc	12–20		
	Vaux college (academic) 1260	3–6 priests, 20–11 choristers		£94
	St Edmund's (chantry) 1269	7–13–6		£102
Southwark	Augustinian canons	(1304) 19, (1501) 14+		£626
Southwell	Prebends	7–16		
	Priests (two ranks) (Vicars' Hall by 1291, 1379)	16–17, 13–17		
	Clerks	10		£516
St Albans	Benedictine monks	(1190) 50, (c.1210) 100, (1380) 54+, (1396) 51, (1529–30) 54		£2102
ST PAUL'S	Bishop		Bishop	£1207
	Prebends, etc	31	Chapter	£725
	Minor canons ('Pettie' college 1353, 1395–6)	12		
	Chantry priests (St Peter's college, 1318)	32+	College	£244
	Vicars by 1273	30		
	Clerks, etc	71+		
	Holmes' college (chantry) 1386	7		
	Lancaster college (chantry) 1403	several		
WELLS	Bishop (shared with Bath)		Bishop	£1939
	Prebends, etc	10–24–54	Chapter	£729
	Priests, etc (Vicars' college 1348–54)	53–50	Colleges…	£100
	Chantry priests (New/Mountery College +1400, 1459)	14–17+		£120
	Clerks, etc	12–13		
WINCHESTER	Bishop		Bishop	£2873
	Benedictine monks	(1262) 62, (1325) 64, (1409) 42, (1533) 43	Priory	£1507
	St Elizabeth's college (chantry) 1301	Priests 13–11, Clerks 7		£112
	St Mary's college (educational) 1378	Dean, Priests 10, Scholars 70, Choristers 12–16, Commoners 10–100	£947	£639+/
WORCESTER	Bishop		Bishop	£1106
	Benedictine monks	(c.1100) 50, (1381) 37, (1401) 44, (1530s) 41	Priory	£1290
YORK	Bishop		Bishop	£2035
	Prebends, etc	7–36	Chapter	£747
	Priests, etc (Bedern c.1250, 1421)	36	Colleges…	£255
	Chantry priests (St William's college 1455)	23–27		£22
	St Sepulchre's college ('chantry') 1154–61	13–17		£165
	Clerks, etc	7–12+		

Note: The aim of this chart is to give some idea of the size, wealth and structure of the community living in each cathedral close by the Reformation. To these figures should be added the bishops' staff of professional churchmen (at the monastic cathedrals this figure was a larger 'extra' than at the seculars, where members of the bishop's staff held prebends); neither does it include lay advisors or servants, many of whom might live in the close.

It is hard to compare wealth across the board (but see chart, p.486), as the bishop's income was utterly separate from that of the chapter, especially in the monastic cathedrals; while the sub-colleges popular at the secular cathedrals might or might not be financially independent. Edited and updated from Knowles and Hadcock 1971, whose figures are mostly from the last assessment of wealth, the *Valor Ecclesiasticus*, made c.1535.

What	Where and when	How much
A new Westminster Abbey (not including half the nave)	1245–1272	£40,000
A new Salisbury Cathedral (not including spire)	Salisbury, 1219–1258	42,000 marks, or £28,000
National Royal revenue (that is, the budget of 'central Government')	Twelfth century / Thirteenth century	£12,000 / £20,000
Half a new eastern arm	Ely, 1234–1252 (Lady Chapel) / York, 1361–1373 (Lady Chapel) / Ely, 1322–1340s (Bishop Hotham's choir)	£6–7,000 / £6,000 / £2,034
A senior aristocrat's wealth	Duke of Gloucester 1314	£6,000+ pa
A bishop's wealth	Archbishop Savage of York, c15 Value of goods at death	£4,037
	Bishop of Ely, 1298 / Bishop of Ely, 1171–2	£2,550 / £920
A new Ely Octagon	1322–c.1340 (total cost of contemporary works at Ely £7–8,000)	£2,400
A prior's budget	Ely, 1320s (John Crauden)	£1,200 pa
A recased transept	Gloucester, by 1373	£781 0s 2d
A 'Great Screen' reredos	St Albans, 1484	1,100 marks = £733 6s
A Royal funeral	Prince Arthur, Worcester, 1502	£566 16s
A top of the range chantry chapel	The Hungerford Chantry, Salisbury (now lost) after1459	£497
A business trip to Rome	The abbot of St Peter's Gloucester, 1449	£400
A dean's income (More like personal wealth and less like a departmental budget than a prior)	York, 1290	£373
A new wooden lead covered spire	St Albans, 1297	£248
A manor (ie rights to much of the produce from an area of land)	Manor of Mepal, bought by the monks of Ely in 1361	£236 plus gifts to officials
Canon's incomes These prebends might be expected to cover many cathedral costs; while the canons might have additional sources of income	All York, c14/c15	£233 Treasurer (Prebend of Newthorpe) / £68 Archdeacon of York / £42 Archdeacon of the East Riding / £33 Prebend of Wilton
A very rich mason	Hugh Grantham, York 1410 He had £52 worth of stone and malt in store, and cows and sheep at pasture	£180 value of all goods
Offerings at a shrine at the peak of a cult	Archbishop Scrope of York, 1418	£150
A sumptuous private chapel	Ely, 1324–6 (Prior Crauden's Chapel and associated study)	£138
A new gatehouse	Norwich, 1317 (The Ethelbert Gate) / Wells, c.1450 (The Bishop's Eye)	£115 17s / 200 marks = £133 6s
A new mitre	Gift from Henry III to Bishop d'Aigueblanche of Hereford	£82
Candlewax (Supplies most lighting; also essential for ritual purposes)	Canterbury 1468-8 2,311 lb of wax (in bulk 5d–7d /lb) / Norwich c14 'wax budget' / A single candle that will burn for a year	£62 13s 4d / £30 p.a. / 13s 8d
An expensive new book	Rationale Divinorum, Lincoln c14	£60 6s
Remodel a chapel	Bauchun chapel, Norwich 1460 revaulting, new windows	£48 17s 4d

What	Where and when	How much
An executive home	Worth of master mason Hugh Grantham's house, York 1410 It had a great hall, two bedrooms, a cellar and a kitchen	£30
A rich citizen's wealth	Worth of all the goods owned by the richest layman in York, 1327	£26
	Likewise 1319 (he was Mayor)	£33
Annual pay of a parish priest	Lincolnshire, 1535	£11 plus lodging (curate, £5)
	'Minimum wage' for priests, 1222	5 marks p.a
The pay of a senior master carpenter	1334 William Hurley, working at Ely	£8 a year
A new seal for the prior	Canterbury, 1233	£7 6s 8d
A mid-range tomb	Prior Selyng, Canterbury, 1487 Bought from a marbler in St Paul's churchyard; the brass might be extra	£4 13s 4d
Glazing an east end	Exeter, 1304 3950 feet of glass by Walter the Glazier	£4 10s
Some payments a parish made a bishop	Reconsecrate the churchyard (after ritual pollution, for example bloodshed)	£3 6s 8d
	Contribution per parish for chrism oil (a farthing per hearth)	7 d
The pay of a 'consultant' master mason (Both projects run at the same time)	William Ramsey, Norwich cloister, 1338–9	£1 1s a year and a robe worth 16s 8d
	The same master, Lichfield presbytery 1337	£1 per visit plus 6s 8d travelling expenses for himself and his servants
Some paintings and statues	Norwich, c15 Image of St Thomas adorned with stones	117s
	'The story of the blood of Christ in English'	3s 4d
A choir stall	Sponsorship per stall asked of Wells canons, 1325	30s

What	Where and when	How much
Weekly bills and food	William Savernak, Bridport, 1453–60 Including food, light and fuel for a small household comprising two priests and a servant	40d
Feeding the monks of Winchester	Winchester, 1492 Plus food from the monks' own kitchen garden Higher price is for festivals	8s 6d, or 10s and 9d per day
Carved bosses	One great central boss (wood, Ely Octagon, 1339–40)	2s
	16 vault bosses (wood, York, 1370s)	£4
Felling 620 alder trees	Lichfield Bishop's Palace 1308–9	29d
A labourer's day rate	Exeter, c1300 Rate varies with the season	8d–11d
Lay offerings in a parish church	Deeping St James, Lincolnshire, 14th/15th century Figure is total offerings from parish	3d Christmas 2d Easter 2d Whitsun 1d Dedication
		1d each person for each sacrament: Burials, marriages, churchings. Baptism free
	Contribution per parish for chrism oil (a farthing per hearth)	7 d
A loaf of bread	1266–7, Henry III Act 51	½ d

Note: The aim of this chart is to give a general sense of the relative values of things. Individual figures are very hard to assess without knowing precisely what they cover, especially as not all transactions involved cash alone. Larger figures are rounded down, usually to the nearest shilling.

Prices and wages (and the relationship between them) fluctuated enormously, especially in the fourteenth and fifteenth centuries, but when flattened out to form an overall mean the result is almost flat compared to modern 'inflation'. See Phelps Brown and Hopkins 1966a and 1966b. There are 12 pennys in a shilling, 20 shillings in a pound, and one mark is worth two-thirds of a pound or 13s 4d.

English cathedrals by wealth
(1535 data)

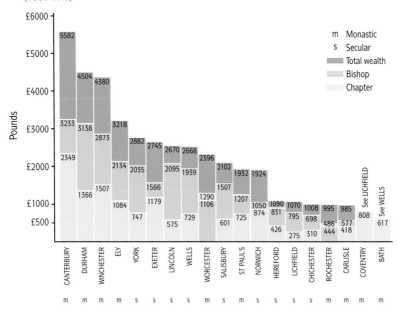

Legend:
- m — Monastic
- s — Secular
- ▮ Total wealth
- ▮ Bishop
- ▮ Chapter

Pounds (y-axis): £6000, £5000, £4000, £3000, £2000, £1000, £500

Cathedral	Total	Bishop	Chapter	Type
CANTERBURY	5582	3233	2349	m
DURHAM	4504	3138	1366	m
WINCHESTER	4380	2873	1507	m
ELY	3218	2134	1084	m
YORK	2882	2035	747	s
EXETER	2745	1566	1179	s
LINCOLN	2670	2095	575	s
WELLS	2668	1939	729	s
WORCESTER	2396	1290	1106	m
SALISBURY	2102	1507	601	s
ST PAUL'S	1932	1207	725	m
NORWICH	1924	1050	874	s
HEREFORD	1090	831	426	s
LICHFIELD	1070	795	275	s
CHICHESTER	1008	698	310	s
ROCHESTER	995	486	444	m
CARLISLE	985	577	418	m
COVENTRY	See LICHFIELD		808	m
BATH	See WELLS		617	m

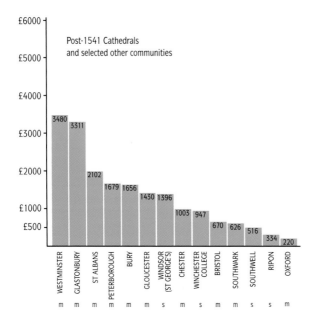

Post-1541 Cathedrals and selected other communities

Pounds (y-axis): £6000, £5000, £4000, £3000, £2000, £1000, £500

Community	Value	Type
WESTMINSTER	3480	m
GLASTONBURY	3311	m
ST ALBANS	2102	m
PETERBOROUGH	1679	m
BURY	1656	m
GLOUCESTER	1430	m
WINDSOR (ST GEORGE'S)	1396	s
CHESTER	1003	m
WINCHESTER COLLEGE	947	s
BRISTOL	670	m
SOUTHWARK	626	m
SOUTHWELL	516	s
RIPON	334	s
OXFORD	220	m

486

Estimated overall architectural activity at the English cathedrals
(Church building only)

All cathedrals

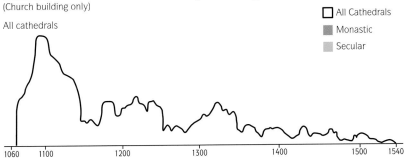

Secular cathedrals only

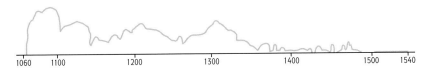

Monastic cathedrals only

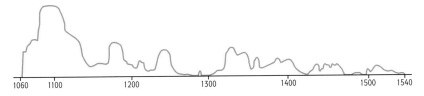

Members of religious communities in England

Monastic
Secular

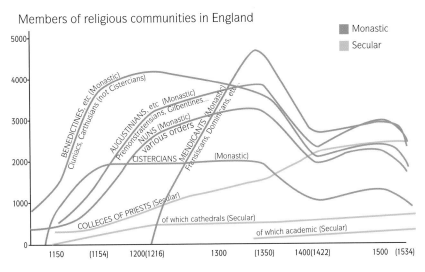

487

Architectural activity at the English cathedrals

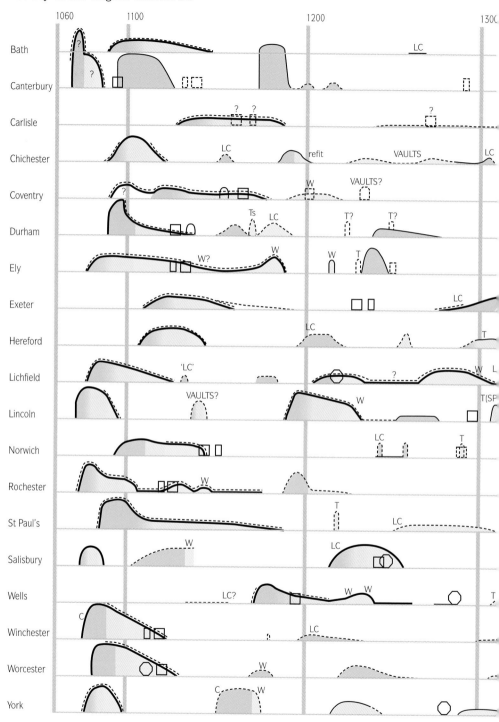

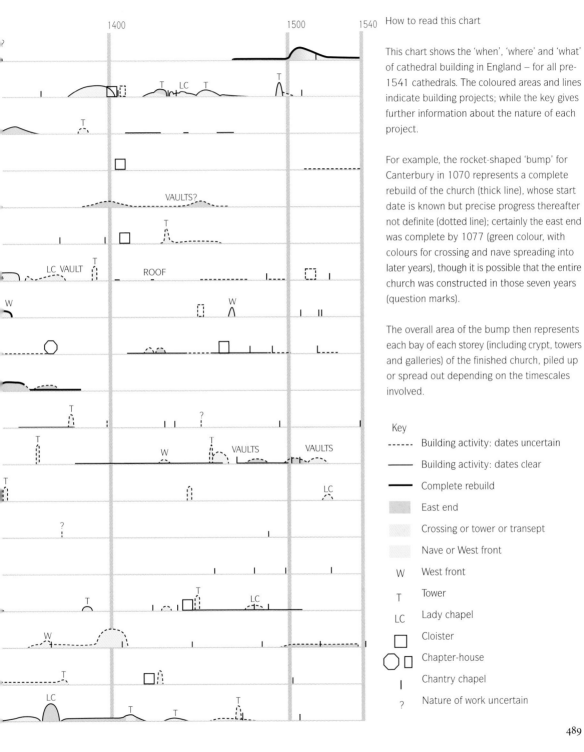

1400   1500   1540

How to read this chart

This chart shows the 'when', 'where' and 'what' of cathedral building in England – for all pre-1541 cathedrals. The coloured areas and lines indicate building projects; while the key gives further information about the nature of each project.

For example, the rocket-shaped 'bump' for Canterbury in 1070 represents a complete rebuild of the church (thick line), whose start date is known but precise progress thereafter not definite (dotted line); certainly the east end was complete by 1077 (green colour, with colours for crossing and nave spreading into later years), though it is possible that the entire church was constructed in those seven years (question marks).

The overall area of the bump then represents each bay of each storey (including crypt, towers and galleries) of the finished church, piled up or spread out depending on the timescales involved.

Key

- - - - -   Building activity: dates uncertain

————   Building activity: dates clear

━━━━   Complete rebuild

▨   East end

▨   Crossing or tower or transept

▨   Nave or West front

W   West front

T   Tower

LC   Lady chapel

□   Cloister

⬡ □   Chapter-house

| Chantry chapel

?   Nature of work uncertain

489

Parts of a cathedral

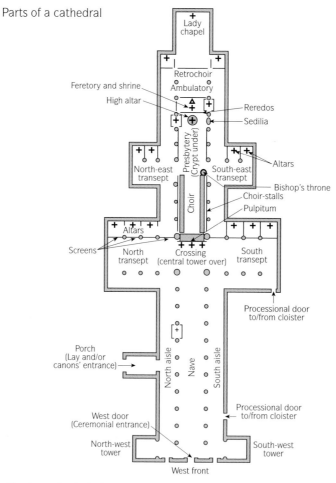

Key to cathedral plans

- Conquest 1066-1130 (Norman/Romanesque)
- Transformation 1130-1170 (Norman/Romanesque, roots of gothic)
- Miracles 1170-1220 (Early gothic/Early English)
- Triumph 1220-1255 (Early English)
- Prosperity 1255-1307 (Decorated)
- Unrest 1307-1348 (Decorated/early Perpendicular)
- Politics 1348-1485 (Perpendicular)
- Rebirth 1485-1538 (Perpendicular/Tudor)
- Post-Reformation/Modern

Dates indicate period work began. Plans are schematic. Two colours indicate a wall in which substantial surviving parts are of more than one period.

+   Altar (High altar on cathedral plans)

▲   Shrine

[ ]   Chantry chapel

( )   Key tomb

○   Medieval Bishop's throne

—   Medieval screens (Screens, choir stalls etc. are only shown where medieval examples survive)

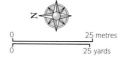

0   25 metres
0   25 yards

GLOSSARY

abbot: the head of a *monastic* house; his church is known as an abbey.

ambulatory: see east end

Anglo-Saxon: the peoples from northern Europe, principally Angles and Saxons, who colonized what is now England (literally, Angle-Land) in the wake of the fall of Rome; their architecture is generally simply called *Saxon.*

apse: when an arm of a church has a curved end rather than a flat, cliff-like wall (see *facade)* or series of flat-ended chapels it is called an apse. Side chapels may also be 'apsidal'. Particularly common in the *east ends* of *romanesque* churches.

arcade: a row of arches separated only by columns or piers, allowing virtually free movement between the parts of a building. A **blank arcade** is positioned against a wall and is thus entirely decorative.

archbishop: a senior *bishop*, with authority over other bishops, who are known as his **suffragans.**

Augustinian: monastic order at the height of its popularity in the twelfth century. Augustinians were always *priested* and therefore often focused on ministering to the needs of lay people; their Rule, which they claimed had been written by St Augustine of Hippo, was relatively flexible, but obliged them to live communal lives, that is, to be monks. Augustinians were not centrally organized but – being priests – were meant to accept the authority of the bishop of whichever see they were in. Members of the order are known as *canons regular.*

Benedictine: a monk who follows the Rule of St Benedict. This gives detailed regulations for a communal life devoted to worship, a withdrawal from worldly matters and a commitment to poverty and celibacy. For many centuries there was no other Rule and, however varied their practices and independent their houses, all who aspired to a religious life were ultimately reliant on this Rule. The idea of a Benedictine type or order of monasticism only emerged to distinguish these older monastic houses from the emerging reformed orders such as the *Augustinians, Cistercians* and *Mendicants,* none of whom

saw themselves as rejecting the Rule of St Benedict so much as taking monasticism back to first principles. Benedictine houses were originally independent of one another but gradually accepted some degree of mutual co-ordination in response to the challenge set by the reformed orders.

bishop: the senior type of churchman, with power to make priests, bless oils and govern the religious standards of his *diocese*. His church is a *cathedral.* Both archbishops and popes while senior to ordinary bishops, are themselves a type of bishop.

canon regular: an Augustinian monk, called a canon because he is a *priest*, and regular because unlike a *secular canon*, he lives according to a Rule. In this book simply called a canon; where the house is *Augustinian* this will be clear from the context.

canon (secular): member of chapter in a *collegiate* church, always a priest, and usually the possessor of a *prebend* from which he draws its income. In this book, simply referred to as a canon.

canonization: the process of declaring a dead person officially a saint, with powers to intercede in heaven on behalf of those who invoke him in prayer. Once the process was embedded, during the thirteenth century, only the pope could confirm sainthood in this way; other cult figures were not officially saints. A great number of saints, however, survived from the centuries before the process was widely accepted.

Carthusian: a monastic order whose monks live in separate houses within the monastery like hermits, only coming together in their church.

cathedral: any church that is the main seat of a bishop, containing his throne or *cathedra.*

central vessel: the central space of a church, with aisles either side of it; these are almost always lower in height. Running east–west along the church, the parts of this central vessel are the *nave, choir* and *presbytery*; the main space in the north–south *transept* is also technically a central vessel.

chantry: a mass said regularly, usually once a day (but with particular elaboration on the anniversary of a person's death), for the soul of a specific named individual or individuals. These people can be laymen or churchmen; a chantry can be held at any altar selected by its founder, though from the fourteenth century standalone *chantry chapels* began to be built.

chantry chapel: an architectural space – a room or enclosure of screens containing a tomb and an altarpiece – designed primarily for the holding of *chantry* masses.

chapter: the meeting of all the members of a religious community; also the group of people entitled to be part of that meeting. The meeting itself takes place in a *chapter-house*. In a monastic community all the *monks* are members of chapter. In a *secular* or *collegiate* community only the canons are members: their *vicars* and others such as choristers and chantry priests are not. The meeting has some executive power, for example to elect its main officers. It is also a semi-ritualized event that includes a reading of a 'chapter' from the Rule followed by the house – hence the name.

chapter-house: the main meeting room of a religious community. While real, practical business was done in these rooms, there was a ritual element to gatherings there, and some of the functions of the chapter-house were part of the liturgy. Here, for example, was kept the record of all deceased members of the community; they were prayed for by name on a regular basis as part of chapter meeting. Confessions were made here and punishments announced for any member of the community who had erred. The chapter-house is invariably the most architecturally elaborate building outside the church itself.

chevron: zig-zag ornament characteristic of Norman/Romanesque architecture from the early twelfth century.

choir: although not strictly its correct usage, the term choir is often used to refer to the entire central vessel in the *east end* of a church, itself subdivided into choir and presbytery. More accurately, 'choir' describes the part of that central vessel in which the main part of the community sings during services. This choir is usually in the western half of the east end; sometimes, especially in earlier churches, it extends under the *crossing* and even a short way into the nave.

Cistercian: monastic order at the height of its popularity in the twelfth century. The Cistercians were a back-to-basics movement within Benedictine monasticism,

spreading across Europe from the monastery at Cîteaux which was their headquarters. Cistercians cut themselves off from worldly matters to a greater extent than the mainstream Benedictines, seeking out isolated places in which to live lives of strict discipline and poverty. They were centrally co-ordinated from Cîteaux itself.

clerestory: the upper storey of the *central vessel* of a church, rising above the aisles and filled with windows that allow light into that area.

cloister: a quadrangle of covered passages that lay at the heart of most monastic complexes. The monks' communal buildings were all positioned off it, as was the church itself. In imitation of this, secular communities (and indeed some lay aristocrats) often also built cloisters, though the significance of these was as much symbolic and liturgical as practical: the cloister of a secular or collegiate religious community rarely provides direct access to anything other than a chapter-house.

close: the area, almost always enclosed by a wall, within which a religious community lives and works. The complex thus includes various *conventual* buildings, the most important and largest of which is the church.

Cluniac: the Benedictine monastery at Cluny came to prominence in the eleventh century, distinguished by an exceptionally lavish and elaborate liturgy (with architecture to match) and a strong corporate ethos which insisted that all the abbey's *daughter-houses* owed fealty to Cluny rather than their local bishop (and Cluny answered only to the pope). The Cluniacs were more the ultimate expression of Benedictine monasticism than a fragmentation of it, and are thus not seen as a separate order, though they were an important precursor to the reformed orders that came later.

collegiate: a community of priests, the individual members of which do not follow a strict rule and usually do not live communally. Its members are thus more independent and flexible than monks; indeed they may be so busy with worldly matters that they have to employ *vicars* to perform the liturgy on their behalf. The English contraction 'college' appears in the late fourteenth century, about the same time that colleges began to be founded in a great variety of sizes. Their members were dedicated to a range of functions (though worship was always paramount), such as education or the singing of *chantry* masses. Prior to this the largest and richest collegiate churches were all cathedrals. These are often called *secular* cathedrals; indeed a secular community and a collegiate one are the same thing. A college is headed by a *dean*, who has beneath him a group of **dignitaries** who have specific responsibilities within the church. The members of the college are known as *canons*; all of them sit on chapter, but their vicars do not.

conventual buildings: the buildings used communally by a religious community, including a dormitory or (in old English) dorter; an eating room, the refectory or frater; a hospital or infirmary, a *chapter-house* or meeting room, and other buildings. All are grouped around a *cloister*. Most of these buildings are only needed by monastic communities, but secular churches sometimes built a cloister and both had a chapter-house.

crossing: the place where north–south *transepts* cross the main east–west arm of a church, usually surmounted by a tower, which often has windows throwing light down-wards into the church itself, a device known as a **lantern**.

cross-vault: the simplest kind of *rib vault*, with four ribs following the main lines of the *groins* of the vault. See *vault*.

crypt: vaulted space underneath the central vessel of a church, usually beneath all or part of the east end and partly or wholly underground. Like the *gallery*, the crypt was a common feature of *romanesque great churches* that declined dramatically in significance with the emergence of *gothic*; some crypts were even abandoned in the thirteenth century.

cushion capitals: a type of capital that became popular very soon after the Norman conquest; it originated in northern Europe. The cushion capital in its original form is very simple – a block shape bulging at the sides as if bearing a great weight. During the twelfth century these capitals began to be richly carved; they had disappeared by about 1200, and are thus synonymous with Norman romanesque architecture.

daughter-house: smaller monastic house, branch of a main monastery or mother-house, founded in a new location, and subservient to it.

dean: the head of a collegiate or secular religious community, subservient to the bishop of his diocese.

Decorated: the second phase of English *gothic* architecture, emerging in the mid- to late thirteenth century and dying in the mid- to late fourteenth. Decorated is more a series of evolutionary waves than a single definable style; at its height it is given to spectacular architectural effects. It emerged out of *Early English* only gradually, and has two phases. From around 1240 ribs were added to vaults to make *tierceron* vaults; *tracery* patterns were developed in ever-increasing variety; and *stiff-leaf* foliage began to be replaced by other kinds of foliage, first naturalistic and later 'crinkly' or 'seaweed'. By the 1260s and 1270s a new style had clearly emerged, at this stage known as **geometrical Decorated**. Then around 1300 smaller ribs known as *liernes* began to be used to make decorative patterns among the tiercerons of a vault, while sinuous and curvaceous patterns started to dominate window tracery and carving alike. The defining invention of this second phase, known as **curvilinear Decorated**, was the *ogee* arch, with its flowing S-shaped curves.

dignitary: senior officer of a collegiate church or secular community.

diocese: the area of land in which a *bishop* has authority and in which the cathedral is the ultimate 'mother church'; also known as a *see*.

Dominican: *mendicant* order founded by St Dominic in 1214–16.

east end: the entire area east of the transepts of a church, containing all the most important altars. It is the focus of liturgical activity, and its most sacred area is the *high altar*, location of the **pyx** where the consecrated **host** is kept. The precise layout of east ends varies, and the details of their medieval configuration – such as the location of the high altar or of any shrines – may not always be obvious from the architecture. In all cases the central vessel contains a *presbytery* – a sacred area around the high altar – with a *choir* to its west, from which the religious community performs most of the liturgy. The area immediately behind the high altar is particularly important: if there is a saint's shrine it will probably be here, perhaps in a *feretory*; beyond there may be an important eastern chapel, perhaps a *lady chapel*. All these spaces, and any others such as side chapels and *eastern transepts,* are accessed via proces-sional aisles which pass behind the high altar to form an *ambulatory*; here the space may open out to form a small hall-like area or *retrochoir* (also spelt retroquire). Architecturally the east end starts east of the transepts, but functionally it might start further west and be defined by screens rather than by major divisions in the architecture; the choir and presbytery in particular are always screened off. The most important of these is the pulpitum, which divides the choir from the nave. The term east end is also sometimes used to refer to the area around and to the east of the high altar, where the many side chapels and other important spaces focused, rather than the entire eastern arm of the church.

Early English: the first *gothic* style of architecture. Once fixed, around 1200–20, its forms are very specific: the pointed arch becomes universal, simple *cross vaults* are used, all foliage is of the *stiff-leaf* type, and windows are simple in form, sometimes arranged in patterns of single-light *lancet windows,* later developing into the earliest forms of *tracery.* Arches are sometimes extremely thin, known as *lancets*; *polished stone* is used to pick out decorative shafts.

early gothic: used in this book in preference to the traditional term Transitional, to describe any building in which the aesthetic and engineering potential of the pointed arch is having a discernible and palpable effect on the architecture's overall aesthetics qualities. This was an experimental phase in architecture, in which the elements that became *Early English* evolved but had yet to settle into a fixed style. It is first discernible in a few buildings of the mid-twelfth century; by around 1200–20 it had developed into Early English.

elevation: the design of one vertical flank of a building, whether internal or external. A *facade* has an elevation; as do most other parts of a church, internal or external. The elevation of the *central vessel* of a medieval *great church* is usually divided into three storeys: *arcade, triforium* or *gallery,* and *clerestory*; the precise configuration varies greatly.

Eucharist: the sacred and miraculous event at the heart of high mass, during which, via a priest, consecrated wine and unleavened bread – the **host** – become the blood and body of Christ.

facade: flat, or mainly flat, expanse of wall; in a church this is usually at the end of one of the arms of the building: that is, the *west front,* the east front if the church has a flat east end; and the *transept* facades. The facades of *great churches* are almost always decoratively enriched.

fan vault: a type of *vault* associated with the *Perpendicular* style, originating in the 1360s–70s. In their purest form, fan vaults do not have ribs but are pure trumpet-like sheaves of stone covered in carved *panelling.* See *vault, perpendicular.*

feretory: the part of a church, usually in the *east end* often immediately behind the high altar, in which the shrine of a saint is held; also a word for the shrine itself.

four-centred arch: an arch drawn using four segments of imaginary circles: two outer circles of smaller diameter are linked by segments of two large circles, whose centres are far below those of the two outer circles. The

low-slung (and hence comparitively horizontal) effect made this arch type popular among *Perpendicular* designers.

Franciscan: *mendicant* order founded by St Francis in 1209–21.

gallery: when the middle storey of a church is really a first-floor aisle, containing rooms for processions and altars, rather than simply a roof space above an aisle *vault,* it is known as a gallery rather than a *triforium.* A standard feature of *romanesque great churches,* the gallery had been almost completely replaced by the triforium by the end of the twelfth century; side altars were instead positioned in the chapels of *east ends* of ever-increasing complexity.

friar: the member of a *mendicant* order.

Galilee: an extension to a church, usually at its western end, sometimes associated with special liturgical events.

gothic: architectural style, at the core of which lies the aesthetic and engineering potential of the pointed arch. It developed in France, then England, during the twelfth century, and spread across Europe in the thirteenth; in its wake came changes in almost every form of art, from painting to metalwork. Its possibilities were explored in a series of stylistic phases and national variants until the *Renaissance* of (in England) the sixteenth century. The main gothic styles in England are *Early English, Decorated* and *Perpendicular.*

great church: a particularly ambitious type of church associated with specific architectural attributes, such as (from the thirteenth century) stone vaults throughout and an elaborate east end with a lady chapel.

groin vault: a groin vault is formed by two tunnel vaults crossing each other at right angles. See *vault.*

high altar: the most important altar in a church, positioned at the *east end* of the *presbytery*; that is, at the eastern end of the *central vessel* of the church.

lady altar: an altar dedicated to the Virgin Mary – usually the second most important altar in a church after the *high altar.*

lady chapel: strictly speaking, any chapel dedicated to the Virgin Mary; but as the Marian liturgy became increasingly complex and important – and especially after many churches began to celebrate a daily **lady mass** in the course of the thirteenth century – many cathedrals constructed elaborate chapels, usually called lady chapels, for its celebration. A lady chapel was usually an eastern extension to the church, sometimes positioned off the north transept, and occasionally located elsewhere.

lancet: a pointed arch of exceptional thinness; also a window with a pointed head but no other decorative features. Almost always associated with *Early English* architecture.

lay: life outside the Church.

lierne: short decorative vault-rib: see *vault*.

mark: a mark is worth two-thirds of a pound, that is 13s 4d (*see also shillings*).

mendicant: a group of monastic orders that emerged in the early thirteenth century and constituted the last great monastic reform movement of the Middle Ages. They combined a strict emphasis on the core monastic values of poverty, celibacy and communal living with an equally powerful commitment to minister to the needs of ordinary lay people, living in the heart of Europe's rapidly-expanding urban settlements. They quickly became very popular among lay people; the main two mendicant orders, the *Dominicans* and *Franciscans*, won the right to complete independence from the power of their local bishop.

minster: originally an *Anglo-Saxon* term for religious communities of all kinds, the term survived in the names of many northern great churches. It also has a more narrow meaning, describing a church in which a group of priests served an area perhaps 15–20 miles in diameter. This was the main kind of church in Anglo-Saxon England before **parishes** were created in the eleventh and twelfth centuries, a process that made minster churches superfluous in their original form. Many became parish churches *or Augustinian* houses; a few survived as ancient *collegiate churches*.

monastic: a religious community that lives communally, sharing all property; its members surrender themselves to a Rule that prescribes much about their daily life. These **monks** or **nuns** are ruled by an *abbot* (abbess); the second in command is the *prior* (prioress). In some cases the monastery is ultimately ruled by a mother house, in which case its local ruler is the prior and the de facto abbot is elsewhere. In monastic cathedrals the bishop is also abbot and the prior effectively runs the monastic side of the institution. Beneath the prior, the obedientiaries have specific jobs to do with running the monastery; but all the monks, obedientiaries or not, are members of *chapter*. Monasticism developed from the fifth century and from the eleventh century fractured

into many different orders: see *Augustinian, Benedictine, Carthusian, Cistercian, Cluniac, Mendicant*.

nave: the central vessel of the western half of a church, and (with any associated aisles and sometimes the western part of the transept) the only part of it to which lay people have free access.

nave altar: the main altar in the *nave* of a church, usually beneath the *rood* and in front of the *pulpitum* and thus often dedicated to the Holy Cross. The most important altar in the church after the *high altar* and *lady altar*, and the only one at which lay people could witness the offices without peering through screens.

Norman: used in England to describe *romanesque* architecture after the Conquest. It is divisible into two phases: the architecture imported in the 1060s from the European mainland, which gradually acquired unique 'Anglo-Norman' characteristics; and the architecture of the twelfth century, in which innovations of around 1100 – including the development of a wide variety of decorative motifs, such as the *chevron*, and the invention of the *rib vault* – helped create an architecture of ever-increasing ornamentation and lightness of effect.

obedientiary: the officer of a *monastic* house.

offices: the main services of the liturgy, of which high mass, the ritual centred around the sacred moments of the *Eucharist*, is the most important. On an ordinary day a religious community would celebrate the offices for some eight hours.

ogee: a sinuous form of arch, featuring two 'S' curves, that appeared in the late thirteenth century. While it remained in use until the Reformation, it was a defining feature of the later phase of the *Decorated* style. The adjective is *ogival*.

panel: a rectangular decorative motif with a simple arched head to it, used in large numbers in *Perpendicular* buildings to create repeated patterns laid out in a grid.

pendant vault: a type of *fan vault* in which the *voussoirs* are extended and then carved so that they look like an extension of the vault; dropping down from above, these pendants have a gravity-defying effect. See *vault*.

Perpendicular: the third style of gothic architecture, emerging in the mid-fourteenth century, unique to England and universal from late in that century until the Reformation. Originally one of the many varieties of *Decorated*, Perpendicular explored the decorative potential of the straight line – the polar opposite of then-dominant *curvilinear* tastes. At the heart of the style lies the idea of a grid of narrow stone ribs extending over all surfaces in a building. The individual cells of this grid are rectangular motifs with simple tracery carved at the top, known as *panels*. Attempts to apply the idea to the curved surfaces of *vaults* led to the invention of the *fan vault*; arches also became flatter through the adoption of the *four-centred arch*. In spite of this many earlier motifs, such as *lierne* vaults, 'seaweed' foliage and *ogee arches* remained in use. Although Perpendicular changed more slowly than other styles, it became richer in decorative effects from the mid-fifteenth century, eventually entering its last **Tudor** phase, in which the gravity-defying *pendant vault* was developed as a subset of the *fan vault*, and the *Tudor arch* developed as an even straighter version of the four-centred one.

polished stone: certain stones, often fine-grained limestones, take on a dark hue and a dull gleam when polished. The resulting effects were reminiscent of precious stones. The most widely used of them came from the Isle of Purbeck in Dorset and are known as Purbeck marble. Explored throughout the medieval period, they were particularly crucial to the *Early English* style.

pope: today the head of the Catholic Church, for medieval people the pope was the senior authority in the western Church and the most important religious leader in western Europe. The pope alone had the power to make *bishops* and *archbishops* (though kings often tried to circumvent this) and to declare saints; his court, known as the **curia**, was the ultimate legal court for Church matters. The pope was also a type of *bishop*, one whose see was all of Christendom and his **suffragans** the archbishops and bishops within it. Based in Rome (with a period when there was an alternative pope in Avignon), the pope was considered to have inherited the authority of St Peter, as in a sense had all *bishops*.

prebend: the patch of land and the products of that land that are set aside to form the income, or part of the income, of a canon or other secular churchman.

presbytery: the eastern half of the central vessel of the *east end* of a church, in which the high altar sits; a sacred place entered only by the handful of churchmen involved in leading the *offices*.

prior: the deputy to an *abbot* of a monastic house; his nearest equivalent in a collegiate community is the *dean*. If a church is subservient to another house it is known as

a priory, if the abbot is present it is an abbey, if he is a bishop it is a cathedral priory.

priest: a person who has been ordained that is, priested, by a bishop, permitting him to perform the *Eucharist* and other sacraments (such as baptism, confirmation and confession). *Monks* or *seculars* could become priests, but women could not.

pulpitum: a substantial screen, often containing an altar or altars, separating *nave* from the *choir* and *presbytery* of a church. Pulpitums are wide enough to support choristers or a small organ; they always have a central door through which processions can enter the *east end*.

relic: object associated with a saint and believed thus to be a vehicle for miraculous powers. The object could be an item of clothing, a fragment of bone or even a piece of furniture; but apart from those associated directly with Christ such as the Holy Blood, the most important relics were the entire bodies of saints, often believed to be incorrupt.

Renaissance: the rediscovery of **classical** – i.e. ancient Greek and Roman – art and learning from the fifteenth century onwards. In England the intellectual Renaissance began in the fifteenth century, and painting was to some extent affected by this, but architecture did not begin to respond until the sixteenth. An earlier wave of rediscovery in the twelfth century is known as the **twelfth-century renaissance**.

reredos: substantial decorative furnishing, usually including carved or painted images and scenes, standing above an altar. Developed from the thirteenth century on.

reticulated: a specific *tracery* pattern associated with the *curvilinear Decorated* style, in which a simple shape formed of *ogee* curves is tessellated or repeated many times over, rather like a honeycomb drawn with a compass rather than a ruler.

retrochoir (or retroquire): an open area in the *east end* behind the *high altar* and any *feretory* or *ambulatory*, separating these from any eastern chapels.

romanesque: architecture pre-dating gothic, featuring semicircular arches and motifs ultimately derived from Roman *classical* designs. In England it was imported around the time of the Norman Conquest and is often called *Norman* or *Anglo-Norman*.

rib vault: any vault in which the ceiling is supported, or appears to be supported, by narrow stone aches or ribs. See *vault*.

rood: a great carving of Christ on the cross, mourned by St Mary and St John, which stood at the eastern extremity of the nave of every church and thus dominated the western parts of that church. In great churches the rood usually hung over or to the west of the *pulpitum*; sometimes there was a separate screen below it; a rood altar or *nave altar* was always associated with it.

Saxon: English architecture before the Norman Conquest. With two main phases: the stylistically varied rebirth of stone architecture from about 600 to the Viking invasions in the ninth century; and the distinctive architectural style developed during and after these invasions. Hardly any buildings of the first period survive.

secular: can refer to life outside the Church as well as to *collegiate* religious communities. In this book it is used solely in the latter sense, and the word *lay* is used solely to refer to the world beyond the Church.

sedilia: group of throne-like chairs (usually three of them) to one side of the *high altar*, for use by the main celebrants in the course of the daily offices.

see: old English word for *diocese*.

shilling: there are 12 pennies in a shilling, and 20 shillings in a pound.

shrine: a decorative and protective structure in which a saint's *relics* are preserved and displayed. Shrines could be small and highly portable, but a major relic such as the entire body of a saint would sit on a distinctive structure, in which the coffin was covered with a hat-like canopy and raised high above the ground on a stone **shrine-base**, usually with openings in it that pilgrims could use to draw close to the body itself.

stiff-leaf: distinctive kind of carved foliage that emerged with *gothic* architecture and was used universally in the early thirteenth-century *Early English* style, gradually fading into near-oblivion thereafter as other kinds of foliage were developed. Stiff-leaf foliage is like a stylized fleur-de-lis with three bulbous symmetrical leaves, the central one having a pronounced stamen.

tierceron vault: a vault with many ribs fanning out palm-tree like from a single point; each of these ribs is a tierceron. See *vault*.

tomb-shrine: a *shrine* associated with the site or former site of the tomb of a saint, the very earth in which he or she had been buried being considered holy and potentially a vehicle for miracles. Though none survive, many churches had a separate tomb-shrine in such a

location even after the saint's body had been *translated* to a main shrine, an event that usually only occurred after he or she had been *canonized*. But uncanonized 'saints' – men or women who were the subject of cults but whose status as saints was not officially recognized by the Church – might remain in their original place of burial, and acquire shrine-like tombs: these are also called tomb-shrines in this book.

tracery: the use of thin ribs of stone to form elaborate patterns in a window-head; the emergence of the technique in the 1240s marks the beginning of the evolution of *Early English* into *Decorated*.

transepts: the north–south cross-arms of a church, between the east end and the west end. Usually there are chapels or an aisle on the east side of them, and occasionally also an aisle on the west side. In the twelfth and thirteenth centuries it was popular to construct a second pair of transepts, known as **eastern transepts**, halfway down the *east end*, often parallel with the junction between *choir* and *presbytery*. These enabled the provision of more altars and emphasized the status of the east end as an exclusive church-within-a-church.

translation: the ritualized transfer of the dead body of a significant person from one location to another. The term is usually applied to saints, but important bishops could also be translated.

triforium: the middle storey of the *elevation* of the *central vessel* of a *great church*, in which decorative arches or panels are used to mask the roof space above the aisle vaults. If it is truly a separate storey – that is, if the space behind it is a first-floor aisle, containing room for processions and altars, rather than a roof space, then it is a *gallery*. The emergence of the triforium is one of the markers of the development of *gothic* architecture.

Tudor arch: a late kind of arch in which two of the curves of the four-centred arch are in fact straight lines.

tunnel vault: the simplest kind of stone-vaulted ceiling: a simple semicircle of stone, like a tube cut in half.

vault: a way of creating decorative effects on a curved ceiling, usually of stone (and if of wood, imitating the appearance of stone). Vaults have a striking architectural effect, and were developed mainly for their weightless aesthetic impact (it is worth remembering that for medieval people the sky itself was a curved vault-like skin). They can also support great weights – making it possible to build churches on top of stone-vaulted crypts – and, when installed in the *central vessel* of a church, they can impede the spread of fire. The simplest kind of vault, the *tunnel vault*, is effectively a tube cut in half. But this kind of vault restricts the design of complex buildings. The *groin vault*, which developed from this, is like two tunnel vaults intersecting at right angles, and allows windows or arches to surround the vault on all four sides; the corners formed by their intersections are called **groins**. Groin vaults create geometrical problems: it is hard to build a smooth curve where the two imaginary tunnel vaults interpenetrate, particularly if the sides of the vault are not of equal length. Ribs were developed mainly to cover this bad join, i.e. for aesthetic reasons, but they also helped support the vault itself, enabling the construction of higher and wider vaults. *Rib vaults* begin to appear in the late eleventh century, and although they were initially used to aggrandize the presbytery or apse of a church, soon after 1100 a few designers attempted to vault entire churches in stone using the technique. Such exploration of vaulting techniques also led to more experimentation with the geometry of the arches supporting these vaults; it quickly became clear that the pointed arch was easier to lay out across spaces of varying dimensions than any other kind of arch, helping generate yet more ambitious vaults and a widespread exploration of the other engineering and aesthetic qualities of the pointed arch itself. The two went hand-in-hand, so that by about 1200 the semicircular arch was a great rarity and all self-respecting great churches aspired to being rib vaulted throughout; the gothic style had been born. The simple X pattern formed by the ribs dominated *Early English cross vaults*, but as the *Decorated* style emerged in the 1230s–1260s extra ribs were added, fanning out from the springing-point of the vault and running uninterrupted outwards and upwards. These ribs, known as *tiercerons*, suggested the possibility that vaulting ribs could be used to create a variety of decorative effects, much as ribs were also making a range of decorative patterns possible in windows. About 1300 designers therefore began to add short ribs that ran between tiercerons, known as *liernes*; using these an almost infinite variety of patterns was possible. As vaults became more and more densely packed with these short ribs, the distinction between the ribs and the groins behind them began to be of little significance, and *Perpendicular* designers began to explore ways of applying the panels which were a leitmotif of their style to vaults, resulting in the conoid form of the fan vault,

invented in the 1360s, which in its purest form has no ribs or groins but is simply a trumpet-shaped expanse of panels carved into a single piece of stone. The designs of lierne and fan vaults cross-fertilized throughout the fifteenth century (and simpler tierceron and even cross vaults were still built from time to time), until towards the end of the century a group of designers began to create large fan vaults of exceptional ambition, sometimes with gravity-defying descending features known as pendants.

vicar: a deputy *priest*. A vicar worked as a stand-in for a more senior priest, either in a parish church or in a *secular* or *collegiate* community, enabling his senior priest – usually called a canon – to be free of the obligation to perform the *offices* daily.

voussoirs: the wedge-shaped pieces of stone which make up an arch; they are held in place by a *keystone* at the top.

west end: the western half of the church, including all those areas to which free lay access was allowed. The central vessel is the *nave*, usually with lower aisles either side of it and *transepts* at one end. There may be various altars in the west end, but the most important is the *nave altar*, situated in front of the *pulpitum* and/or *rood*. The main lay entrance to the church is also in the west end, but its position varies: it may be a door in the western walk of the cloister, a porch halfway down the west end, or a door in one of the transepts; occasionally it might even be a side door in the west front.

west front: the western facade of the church, and the structures that support it. In most churches this was the most important facade, richly decorated and the focus of such liturgical events as Palm Sunday celebrations. In England the development of the **screen facade** at the west end – see Wells, Lichfield and Exeter – often includes specific facilities used to stage these celebrations, such as hidden locations for choristers. There are usually three doors in the west front, the central one of which is reserved for important liturgical events or the semi-ritualized entry of visitors such as *bishops*, *archbishops* or royalty.

westwork: in the romanesque period, especially in northern Europe, the western end of a church can sometimes be as elaborately planned and grand in scale as the east end. This is the westwork, a German word used hesitantly to describe some particularly bloc-like romanesque west fronts in England.

NOTES

PREFACE

1 Salisbury's medieval core has an area of about 105 hectares; the cathedral close 42 hectares: RCHME 1980, 1993.
2 RCHME 1980.
3 The bishop's palace is an estimate based on its late medieval form and east–west dimensions.
4 According to the Book of Revelations.
5 John 41:2.
6 Revelations 21.
7 Salisbury cathedral *Annual Report*: http://www.salcath.co.uk/docs, accessed December 2006.
8 The disappearance of paganism as a range of practices consciously identified as non-Christian is a gradual process, hard to date, but surely complete well before 1200. During the twelfth century fair-sized Jewish communities developed in many English cities, though the Jews were expelled in 1290. There were no other non-Christian commu-nities in medieval England, though cultural contact with Islam continued in various forms, both negative and positive, through-out our period but, again, especially in the twelfth century.
9 Medieval abbey history or *Historiola*: Welander 1991, 129.

INTRODUCTION

1 A title made formal in the fourteenth century; earlier it was disputed by the archbishops of York.
2 Monks even preached in Latin, rendering their teachings incomprehensible to any but the most educated: James Clark, pers. comm. In spite of this, English was increasingly used for all purposes, but especially at the expense of French, from the late fourteenth century onwards.
3 Indeed it was increasing: James Clark, pers. comm.
4 Known as an archdiocese.
5 Clifton-Taylor 1967; Wilson 1990; in a similar vein, there were 131 in Gallia (roughly modern France), 56 in Germany, 33 in Spain and Portugal, 12 in Scotland and 34 in Ireland: Dobson 2005.
6 As a result, the word 'secular' has two meanings; throughout this book I have used it purely to distinguish one kind of churchman from another and 'lay' to mean the world outside the Church.
7 In some cases the seat was dependent on possession of a prebend rather than on simply holding the post of canon. So, in theory, though rarely in practice, it would be possible to be a canon and not have a place on chapter.
8 Of course the vast majority of monasteries were not bishop's seats, and were simply headed by an abbot. The virtually 50/50 balance between monastic and secular cathedrals throughout the Middle Ages appears to have been unique to England.
9 For example, in the diocese of Lincoln, the abbots of Ely (before it became a cathedral) and to a lesser extent Eynsham, Peterborough, Crowland, Thorney and St Albans all had various privileges normally exclusive to bishops: Owen 1984.
10 Such as communism, fascism or religious fundamentalism.
11 In particular, many places were bi-polar, dominated by two major establishments alongside smaller religious houses and parish churches. This was particularly true of Canterbury (Christ Church and St Augustine's abbey); London (St Paul's and Westminster abbey); York (York minster and St Mary's abbey), and the sees of Worcester (which included the powerful abbeys of Evesham and Gloucester) and Bath and Wells (which contained Glastonbury abbey).
12 This prejudice eroded during the fourteenth century. Winchester is an early case, though here its complex structural history and uncertain foundations may be as much the cause as any aesthetic consideration.
13 Wilson 1990. Bristol and York could both claim to be an economic second city, though York had the political edge.
14 Only bishops or members of the royal family could assume the right of monumental burial in a cathedral, although this principle eroded later in our period. Even the presence of aristocrats who were not royal or churchmen who were not bishops is the exception rather than the rule, and worth further study when it does occur.
15 The cathedrals of Lichfield and Worcester (and among the churches that later became cathedrals, Chester, Peterborough, Southwark and Southwell) have very few surviving medieval fittings; while others, including Exeter, Wells and Canterbury, and among the post-Reformation cathedrals, Oxford and Gloucester, are exceptionally rich in surviving furnishings and decorations.
16 William of Malmesbury 2000, 259–61.
17 Canterbury, Salisbury and others are also known to have had these scenes in their east end.
18 Others, especially Tim Tatton-Brown, have put the distinction itself to the forefront of their accounts of these churches, or studied aspects of the two institutional types in isolation from one another, but I am not aware of anyone else drawing my general architectural-sociological conclusions from them.
19 The issues underlying such a project are eloquently outlined in Morris 1996.
20 Most of these are multi-author projects, while Salisbury, Peterborough, Gloucester and Worcester have highly authoritative, recent analyses by single authors (that of Worcester in German). St Albans, Southwell and Ripon have more general recent histories; Carlisle and Lichfield so far await monographs, but have BAA volumes. At the other extreme, even the basic literature for some cathedrals, including Norwich, York, Durham and Canterbury, includes several important works of scholarship. In addition, there are articles on all these buildings in a wide range of academic journals.
21 The analogies between history and therapy this suggests are not entirely out-of-court; individual buildings such as Wells can be portrayed as a community 'individuating' over several centuries, while there are rich pickings indeed lurking for anyone brave enough to venture through the theoretical minefield suggested by issues of sexuality and gender at the cathedrals.
22 It is worth remembering that the cathedrals of countries that remained Catholic were also substantially rebuilt and refitted, some-times even more so than those in England.

PART 1: LIFE AND HISTORY

CHAPTER 1: BIRTH

1 Bishops from London and York attended the Council of Arles in 314, a century before the Roman withdrawal; after that, it seems only a few cult sites, such as that around the tomb of a martyr named Alban on the edge of the ruined Roman city of Verulamium, managed to survive in what became England. The church built at Whithorn in Galloway in the fourth century, later the site of a Northumbrian cathedral, was an important

example of a British church.

2   Blair 2005 is a landmark overview of such matters; Etchingham 1994 debunks the myth that this was also true in the Irish Church.

3   The term *bretwalda* is now considered an anachronism.

4   Carver 2001.

5   St Martins-by-Canterbury: Taylor and Taylor 1965.

6   It is possible that Gregory felt a personal calling to evangelize the English: there is a famous story of the Anglians he saw for sale as slaves, whose beauty he compared to angels; and, even before the mission of Augustine, we know he was seeking out English slaves to be bought and converted.

7   Bede 1965, 66.

8   Lesley Abrams, pers. comm.

9   Blair 2005.

10 The East Saxons (Essex), the East Angles (Sussex), the West Saxons (Wessex), the Middle Angles of Mercia (the Midlands), and Northumbria (north of the Humber), and the Hwicce (Worcestershire and Gloucestershire), later joined by the shadowy, Kingdom of Magonsaeton (Herefordshire).

11 Remains of it were discovered during excavations in the present nave in 1979–80; though very fragmentary, they can be fitted onto the very standardized plan known from other churches built subsequent to the mission of St Augustine.

12 Pre-650 cathedrals in former Roman cities: Canterbury, Rochester, London, York, Dorchester. Not in former Roman cities: Lindisfarne, East Anglia (?). None of these went to the Rome-copying extremes of Canterbury, with its twin communities.

13 Fernie 1982.

14 Bede 1965, 185, which gives Scottorum as Scots. I am grateful to Lesley Abrams for pointing out that in this context Scots means Irish.

15 Collinson and Sparks 1995; Knowles 1963. Seven of the ten chapters of the joint statement clarified and affirmed the powers of bishops and the diocesan structure that they worked within.

16 Wilfrid's biographer Stephanus in Webb 1965, 156.

17 The twelfth-century William of Malmesbury in Fernie 1982, 61: a remarkable statement considering the scale of the architecture he was used to.

18 Stephanus writing of Hexham in Webb 1965, 154–5.

19 Hexham and Ripon: Taylor and Taylor 1965; Fernie 1982; Bailey 1996.

20 And perhaps Lincoln, though if so it was abandoned long before Lincoln cathedral was founded.

21 The word minster is simply old English for monastery, though the word was applied to any religious community, cathedral or not, monastic or not. This is the origin of its use in the north, such as at York minster and Southwell minster. But it also has acquired

narrower meaning as historians piece to together the pre-parish system of regional churches described here.

22 Blair 2005.

23 Two survivors of this system are today cathedrals: the minsters of Ripon and Southwell, which throughout the Middle Ages remained communities of priests serving a large area. Most others have become parish churches, their former status discernible only by clues such as an exceptionally large parish.

24 Old Minster: Biddle 1976; Kjølbye-Biddle 1993. It is thanks to the Biddles' excavations that so much is known.

25 Lapidge and Winterbottom 1991.

26 Aelfric in Knowles 1963, 41.

27 Wulfstan, Ethelwold's biographer, in Knowles 1963; Willis 1984; Lapidge and Winterbottom 1991.

28 Wulfstan in Willis 1984, 12–13.

29 And part of a complex that took up an entire quadrant of Roman Winchester, including the royal palace; the New Minster and a nunnery, both royal churches; and what was possibly England's first bishop's palace, later known as Wolvesey castle.

30 Or, to give it its full title, 'The Agreement to follow the Rule (of Saint Benedict), for the Guidance of the Monks and Nuns of the English Nation'.

31 Blair 2005. There were nearly a hundred parishes in London by the late eleventh century.

32 At St Albans, the balusters in the transept galleries; at Worcester, columns reused in the slype and cloister.

33 Canterbury: Blockley et al 1997. Alongside the buildings already noted, featureless pre-Conquest walls survive in the Durham and Westminster abbey cloisters; at Bristol (later a cathedral) there is a fine pre-Conquest stone carving; and archaeology has (so far) uncovered parts of Anglo-Saxon cathedrals at Hexham, Lichfield, Rochester and Wells and, among the great churches that were later cathedrals, St Albans, Southwell and Peterborough.

34 Sherborne: Gibb 1975.

35 William of Malmesbury in Tatton-Brown 1989, 47.

36 Ely's chronicler in Keynes 2003, 25.

37 Canterbury, Durham, Dorchester, Elmham, Exeter, Hereford, Lichfield, London, Rochester, Selsey, Sherborne, Wells, Winchester, Worcester and York.

CHAPTER 2: INVASION

1   William of Malmesbury, writing some sixty years after the event. Only small parts of the cloister and associated buildings survive above ground. William of Malmesbury, trans J A Giles 1847.

2   The narrative sequence of Anglo-Norman architecture is summarized in Fernie 2000.

3   William of Malmesbury, trans J A Giles 1847,

257.

4   Maccarini 1984.

5   Keynes 2000, 47.

6   Marner 2000.

7   Our description of the fire is from the monk Eadmer, who saw it, and says that the damage was so severe that services had to be held in the open air: Eadmer in Southern 1962.

8   Woodman 1981, 28. This may relate to the east end rather than the entire church.

9   Lanfranc in Klukas 1984.

10 Eadmer in ibid, 51.

11 Scholars have combed contemporary documents for clues as to their location: it seems likely that they were placed in galleries in the transepts; the important shrines of St Dunstan and St Alphege stood either side of the high altar in both the old building and in that which later replaced Lanfranc's, but their location in the cathedral of the 1070s is unknown.

12 This taste for order over elaboration is true of Lanfranc's architecture and ritual alike. Klukas 1984 gives detailed comparisons between the rites recommended by Lanfranc and those in the *Regularis Concordia*.

13 The Germanic cushion capitals used in the one surviving wall of the crypt are the only known detail in the building that is not Norman. They suggest that someone on the team knew about architectural practice in other parts of Europe. A flood of ideas from Germany and the Low Countries would appear in the buildings of the ensuing decades.

14 Klukas 1984, 145.

15 In many Norman monastic churches the choir extended beneath the crossing and into the nave, if perhaps not as far into the nave as at Canterbury. One result of this was that Lanfranc's nave was quite small.

16 First quote is Lanfranc himself; the second is Eadmer; both in Klukas 1984, 135.

17 Most of the Anglo-Saxon bishops were replaced at their death; apart from Stigand, only the bishops of Selsey and Elmham were deposed.

18 Rubinstein 1999.

19 At Berkhamsted.

20 How much of this Anglo-Saxon church was completed remains uncertain: Biddle and Kjølbye-Biddle 2002 argue that the entire church was completed, yet we know from Matthew Paris that building materials were gathered for a projected rebuild of 1005 which was never finished; these stones are the presumed source of much of the current building, especially the Anglo-Saxon balusters in the transepts.

21 Gibson 1995.

22 Fernie 2000.

23 With Worcester the only post-1066 cathedral rebuild to be initiated by an Anglo-Saxon bishop.

24 Henry of Huntingdon in 'Remigius' *DNB* 1975.

25 Bates 1992. Not all agree this story is true.

What is certain is that, as almoner at Fécamp, he had been in charge of a significant budget, which he is said to have run with unusual sophistication.

26 It seems they were crowned by the archbishop of York instead.

27 Real threats: both the attempted Danish invasion and the Ely insurgency took place in the Lincoln diocese.

28 Cowdrey 2004b.

29 Bates 1992.

30 Gem 1986.

31 Ibid; one recent opinion (David Stocker and Alan Vince: David Stocker, pers. comm.) suggests it was built before the rest of the cathedral, and may have been the first Norman stone building in Lincoln. Not all accept the 'castle' interpretation.

32 The Lincoln canon Henry of Huntingdon in Gem 1986, 9.

33 As Quiney 2001 points out, they would make the corners almost pre-undermined: poor strategy in a siege.

34 This suggestive detail relates to a city gate rather than the cathedral, but at Peterborough in the diocese banners were hung from the west front on Palm Sunday, and the design of the west front there also features a row of enormous arches.

35 One arch from Roman Lincoln stands in the city to this day, while Remigius and his companions would have seen spectacular classical remains when they visited Rome in 1071.

36 Remigius tried to build a special relationship with the monasteries at Stow and Eynsham; some have wondered if he at one stage considered using Stow to create a monastic cathedral.

37 Along with St Albans, Battle (founded by the Conqueror) and St Augustine's, Canterbury, are important non-cathedral great churches known to have been begun in that decade: Fernie 2000.

38 For example, Stigand and his associates were deposed at the Council of Winchester in 1070.

39 The most obvious larger structure is the prayer hall of the great mosque at Cordoba. But the statement as a whole is dependent on the expanses of roofing essential in a temperate climate. Several centuries before this, Chang'an and Baghdad, for example, were far larger than any city in medieval Europe, and both China and what is now Iraq contained vast palace and mosque complexes; but these were courtyard-based structures, whose largest spaces were not roofed over.

40 Fernie 2000. The analogy is appropriate considering William had gone from being a duke to being a king as a result of the invasion. In 1091, when the Normans acquired Sicily, it would indeed be appropriate to talk of an empire.

41 The complete disappearance of the west end means that the precise number of towers is not certain. In addition the central tower

was rebuilt early in the twelfth century and some of the others were probably never completed. Massive west ends are common in Germany, but among the English cathedrals only Ely and the original Lincoln west front survive.

42 The joints were probably picked out: Park and Welford 1993.

43 Fernie 2000; Gem 1983. The arrangement of alternating columns was a borrowing from the presbytery at Westminster.

44 Fernie 2000.

45 Klukas 1984.

46 The ceremony, whose precise location and frequency both before and after the Conquest are a little unclear, continued until at least 1108: Klukas 1984.

47 Plant 2006. Gundulf was an able assistant to both Lanfranc and his successor Anselm, and a keen builder. He was said to have helped construct the White Tower in the Tower of London.

48 During the nearest comparable period, the 1220s, four were under way at the same time: Lincoln, Salisbury, Lichfield and Wells. Subsequently, the rebuilding of Exeter, in the late thirteenth to mid-fourteenth century, and of Bath, from the late fifteenth century, were separated by over a hundred years.

49 Fernie 2000. A building whose archaeological traces are still yielding fresh insights and interpretations, and on which important research was being completed as this book went to press.

50 William of Malmesbury, quoted in Gem 1990, 52.

51 Later versions of York and Lincoln were arguably as ambitious as Winchester, but only as a result of separate building initiatives.

52 Such as the polygonally ended chapels and perhaps the circular chapter-house. Anglo-Saxon columns were reused in the crypt and the slype.

53 The related work of the Lotharingian bishop of Hereford, who built a remarkable bishop's chapel modelled on those of Germany, is the first obvious sign of this.

54 St-Calais made him his archdeacon, meaning Turgot was effectively the bishop's deputy in the see as well as in the monastery: Barlow 2004c.

55 St Paul's and Bury St Edmunds abbey were probably also in the same tradition.

56 Or perhaps thirteen.

57 Of these, the churches at Canterbury and Old Sarum were probably complete. It is not known when the rebuilding of Coventry began.

58 In the Marches, a series of mighty earldoms were created to help protect the borders with Wales; these newly enriched aristocrats founded important abbeys, such as St Werburgh's, Chester (later a cathedral). Perhaps the bishop's church was less of a priority in an area with such a focus on martial, lordly power.

59 Eadmer, Anselm's biographer, in *DNB* 1975,

490.

60 Eadmer in Southern 1962.

61 'Anselm' *DNB* 1975; Woodman 1981.

62 For example, at York, Lichfield and Lincoln.

63 William of Malmesbury, trans J A Giles 1847, 289.

64 Gervase of Canterbury in Holt 1957.

65 The Anglo-Saxon cathedral had an entire western apse dedicated to her; there was a lady altar in the nave by 1130 that could be of Lanfranc's period: Sparks 1997.

66 The French abbey that was rapidly outstripping Winchester in size.

67 The motif itself has Anglo-Saxon roots; intriguingly, an early and ungainly version of it has recently been pointed out on the transepts at Winchester, just as the crypt of Lanfranc's monastic dormitory included an early attempt at the patterned columns of Durham.

68 Kahn 2001.

69 Gibson 1995.

70 Gervase's phrase: Holt 1957, 53.

71 Kahn 2001.

72 Woodman 1981.

73 Of course, at Salisbury relocation made this essential. Even Bath and Wells, the nearest other contenders, deliberately preserved important parts of the former church (Wells) or incorporated stretches of its walls (Bath).

74 Dimensions. From the late twelfth to early thirteenth centuries, Wells (126 metres), Salisbury (144 metres), Lichfield (121 metres) and Lincoln (156 metres); these dimensions include the later lengthening of all but Salisbury. Exeter (128 metres) and Bath (69 metres, but intended to be longer) came later. Bath was the only one of these cathedrals that was monastic rather than secular and here the rebuilding actually reduced the size of the church.

75 Fernie 2000.

76 The wood is in Willis 1984; the 'bad year' in Savage 2002.

77 Keynes 2003.

78 Among the churches in this book, Ripon, Wells and Oxford (at least) were all Anglo-Saxon buildings in 1130, and of the three only Oxford had ceased to be a minster community. By this time reform and rebuilding had been completed at all the cathedrals.

79 St Albans because it was no longer the primary monastic house in its area (the boundary between the lands of the two was to be contested for centuries); Winchester because Westminster proposed an alternative focus for the English kings.

80 Carlisle was created in 1123.

81 Remigius may have considered creating a monastic cathedral (see n.36); at Old Sarum, the bishop created a secular cathedral to replace the monastic one he had left at Sherborne.

82 Before the Conquest, monasteries could be sizeable, but secular religious communities, whether minster or cathedral, seem to have

often been communities of seven to a dozen priests (for example, York, Rochester, Ripon, Wells). Yet Lincoln, for example, had grown to forty-two canons by 1123. Dobson 2005 sees the process of the creation of prebends already in evidence at Lincoln, York and Salisbury in around 1090, and discernible at the other secular cathedrals within a generation.

83 Both of which were connected to the power of bishops: Southwell as a kind of deputy cathedral of the archbishop of York, Crediton as a former cathedral that, in spite of its size, was not at all wealthy.

84 The earliest figure we have for Ripon is rather later, but is likely to be accurate: Knowles and Hadcock 1971. The figure for vicars is Dobson 2005, Barrow 2005.

85 Subsequent kings were buried at Reading, Fontevrault and Worcester. Henry III rebuilt Westminster abbey as a royal mausoleum.

86 Peterborough abbey is the most emphatic example of this; elsewhere, as at Ely, for example, work stopped with the nave functioning but with the west front effectively still to be built.

87 The Burgundian Radulfus Glaber, writing of 1000.

88 The periods are comparable in other ways. Both were marked by political turmoil and the gradual emergence of cultural trends that went on to transform society.

89 As Henry of Huntingdon said of Henry of Blois: King 2004.

90 *Gesta Stephani*, quoted in Hudson 2004.

91 A continuation of the Anglo-Saxon Chronicle in Savage 2002, 265.

92 Gem 1986, 11, translated rather differently. The date of this work is not certain (the dating of the frieze in particular is much debated); it may have made Lincoln the first church after Durham to be rib-vaulted throughout.

93 I have been unable to establish his relationship to Herbert Poore, bishop in the late twelfth century, or Herbert's brother Richard, bishop in the early thirteenth; *ODNB* simply names him Roger of Salisbury.

94 Exquisite carvings from it can be seen in the Salisbury and South Wiltshire Museum, Salisbury.

95 Savage 2002, 268.

96 Its precise date is not known.

97 Kusaba 1988.

98 His interest in these stones may have encouraged English craftsmen to identify local sources for them, for some of the earliest English polished stones can be seen on Blois buildings: Blue Lias at Glastonbury abbey, which he rebuilt; Purbeck marble at St Cross.

99 Riall 1994.

100 See comparable material in cathedral essays for citations.

101 William is the likely source of the Islamic ivory box in the minster; Hubert Walter was given 'handsome presents' by Saladin and gave Canterbury a fine carpet.

102 Becket's privy seal as an up-and-coming churchman was an antique intaglio of Mercury: McNeil 2006a.

103 Gransden 1978. The other well-known continuation, at Peterborough, was damaged in a fire in 1120; in the 1130s the Peterborough monks acquired a copy of the Worcester version to help with their work.

104 Ely chronicler in Maddison 2000a, 23.

105 Lewes in the diocese of Chichester, Thetford in that of Norwich, and Bermondsey in the see of Winchester are three early Cluniac houses in England.

106 J Franklin 2004.

107 The only further developments were the return to cathedral status of Wells, in partnership with Bath; of Lichfield, jointly with Coventry; and the move from Old Sarum to Salisbury, all over the next century. Attempts to move Canterbury to various locations and Worcester to Westbury led nowhere. The number of sees remained unchanged until 1541.

108 Bernard of Clairvaux in Stalley 1971, 81.

109 Bernard of Clairvaux in James 1957, 145.

110 Bernard of Clairvaux in James 1957, 146.

111 William of Newburgh in Burton 2004.

112 William fitz Herbert: Burton 2004; French 1999; Hill and Brooke 1977.

113 French 1999.

114 Until very recently, the cult was seen as having been entirely manufactured in the 1220s: French 1999. Norton 2006 shows that the first known miracle occurred in 1177. I have been unable to see the detail of his discussion before this book went to press.

115 See Norwich essay; though something comparable happened at Gloucester in 1168 and Lincoln in 1255 without this context.

116 Hearn 1983.

CHAPTER 3: TRIUMPH

1 We do not know if any English cathedral cult had ever had such wide appeal. The popular impact of the seventh- and eighth-century saints, about whom our knowledge is dependent almost entirely on the mediation of Bede, is beyond our reach; their successors seem to have mattered most to the communities of their own churches (for example, in the case of St Ethelwold of Winchester: Lapidge and Winterbottom 1991).

2 The linked popularity of pilgrimage to Canterbury and crusade to the Holy Land was made explicit by Bishop Glanville of Rochester, who in 1192–3 founded a hospital on the main pilgrimage route to Canterbury, the priests of which would pray for the restoration of Christianity in the kingdom of Jerusalem. Ten years later the Rochester saint, William of Perth, was en route to Jerusalem via Becket's shrine when murdered nearby.

3 Installation of this in the Trinity Chapel was delayed until the 1220s, when the previous site, Becket's tomb in the crypt, became a separate focus for pilgrims. Other shrines included the site of the martyrdom itself and Becket's head shrine, probably in the Corona at the east end.

4 Many modern commentators have played down the significance of this new type of arch at the time, suggesting that its widespread acceptance was more of interest to masons than to their patrons.

5 The pointed arch was known to the Romans, and indeed to Norman architects, but purely as an engineering technique. Islamic designers had been exploring its aesthetic potential for some centuries (at the very least, crusaders would have seen independent confirmation of its effectiveness). The essence of gothic lies in the synergy between these two aspects of the pointed arch, one structural and the other aesthetic.

6 The latter dimension was more to the fore in England, in marked contrast to the situation in France. While aspects of both Canterbury and Lincoln demonstrate that their designers understood the engineering possibilities of the new architecture, they equally make it clear that exploitation of these was not their designer's primary interest. In engineering terms, Wells is basically a romanesque building.

7 Complete east ends: Canterbury, Carlisle, Ely, Lincoln, Rochester, Southwell, Worcester; retrochoirs: Chichester, Durham, Lichfield, Winchester; Hereford; lady chapels: Bath, Chester, Norwich, Oxford (and chapter-house); complete rebuilds: Wells, Salisbury, Lichfield, Lincoln, Southwark. Other major additions include transepts: York; and west fronts: Peterborough, Ripon, Coventry, St Albans (failed, plus part of nave). Also: Bristol (lady chapel off transept), Gloucester (vaulting and possible lady chapel), Exeter (chapter-house). St Paul's had a new east end later in the century.

8 By cathedral saint, I mean the main in-house relic of a cathedral, canonized or not (St William of Perth may never have been formally canonized).

9 The local bishop, Reginald fitz Jocelin of Bath and Wells, had just begun the gothic rebuilding of Wells, to be discussed shortly.

10 Page 1906a.

11 Page 1906a, 232.

12 Though there was some very smart architectural trickery relating to an ancient site associated with the Virgin Mary: see Wells essay.

13 It was rebuilt yet again, still rich with chevron and polished limestone, after a fire of 1184.

14 After a failed attempt to take over the ancient monastery altogether by giving the abbot of Glastonbury a place on the Wells chapter (an arrangement that was not to last).

15 From the late twelfth century until the Reformation, the bishops of Wells spent

their building budget at Wells rather than Bath. The one exception to this, the rebuilding of Bath in about 1500, was funded by the imposition by the bishop of cuts to the monks' income rather than directly by the bishop himself. Likewise, a new bishop's palace was built at Wells in the 1220s that outshone any known equivalent at Bath; the same could be said of Lichfield vis-à-vis Coventry in about 1300.

16 Or, to be precise, near Westminster, now the main centre of the royal court.

17 Much of the modern geography of this part of south-west London is the result of initiatives, such as the plan to build a hospital at Southwark and a new metropolitan cathedral at Hackington, that occurred in the backwash of Becket's martyrdom, but were subsequently revised.

18 Complete is a relative term: in contrast to the post-Conquest rebuilds, work at Wells and Lincoln involved the preservation of important sections of the previous church (the former cathedral's lady chapel in the case of Wells, its west front in the case of Lincoln).

19 The parallels between the two churches, obscured by Salisbury's comparative architectural maturity, are many. The phrase 'episcopal style' was coined in Jansen 1996; the 1170s Canterbury crypt and 1190s incarnation of Lambeth Palace may have played a key role in defining this architecture: Tatton-Brown 2000.

20 Initiated by his predecessor, in 1202.

21 Stroud 1996.

22 The alternative view, that the architectural impact of the interdict is uncertain, is advanced in Draper 2006a.

23 Including many of the fruits of his heavy taxation of the Church, the 'cursed tollage upon the churches of England'.

24 Jocelin and his brother spent some of the interdict together in sunny Bordeaux.

25 Garton 1986, 56.

26 And the universal acceptance that a fully equipped great church should have rib vaults throughout.

27 Dobson 1995a.

28 Peter des Roches at Hales in Worcestershire, Titchfield, Selborne and Netley in Hampshire and at Clarté Dieu, near his birthplace in the Touraine: Vincent 2004b. Poore founded a Cistercian nunnery at Tarrant in Dorset, his birthplace.

29 In the late twelfth century, 24 to 38 per cent of the students at Paris were from England. By the mid- thirteenth century, graduates of the young universities made up 42 per cent of the chapter of Lincoln cathedral, 47 per cent of that of St Paul's and 50 per cent of that at Salisbury: Binski 2004.

30 Woodman 1981.

31 Apart from the revival of her cult at the time, described in the cathedral essay, T A Heslop has noted in Blair 1990a that the priory's seal of this period portrays St Frideswide as a patroness of learning.

32 See the Worcester essay for an account of this story.

33 Gilchrist 2005.

34 Whether they actually *did* cease to have a sex life is of course harder to say, but in earlier centuries secular churchmen were openly married; not any more.

35 The abbot of St Albans in 1230, quoted in Sparks 1997, 123; also see Draper 1995.

36 The first building certain to have been associated with a daily lady mass was the, since rebuilt, eastern chapel at the new Wells cathedral: Draper 1995. Other important Marian buildings of these years included the Durham Galilee and the Salisbury Trinity chapel.

37 Previously dean of Old Sarum and bishop of Chichester.

38 Sampson 1998. Some of the sculptures may be test pieces by carvers drawn from as far away as Yorkshire.

39 Statues were not added to Salisbury until the fourteenth century, and only a few were ever installed; Exeter was stopped in its tracks by the Black Death and not finished until afterwards, and to a slightly different scheme. Even Wells was left with a few sculptures not installed and much of their painting barely begun. The niche-filled facades built around the Norman west front at Lincoln seems never to have been seriously intended to display statues. That at York minster still has battered portions of a substantial sculptural scheme.

40 Binski 2004.

41 The image is used, for example, by Hugh d'Avranches as early as the 1220s.

42 The implications of which can be explored by reading Binski 2004 (who points out that, by his death, Northwold was the only monk-bishop in the country) and Draper 2006a.

43 Stroud 1996, 6. A detailed discussion of its reception and artistic implications can be found in Binski 2004.

44 Page 1906a; Dobson 2005.

45 In this case issued by Archbishop de Thoresby of York.

46 Polygonal chapter-houses were not unusual among the greater monastic houses – Westminster abbey is the most complete survival – but not a single one was built at a cathedral priory.

47 All perhaps derived from more ancient models: Old Sarum had a cloister; Wells had communal buildings before the Norman reforms; Exeter's communalized constitution suggests it would have had them too. Here the cloister, rebuilt in the fourteenth century, has since been demolished.

48 Four of these were at Oxford and two at Cambridge. By the Reformation, Oxford had fifteen colleges, nine founded by bishops (three by bishops of Winchester, two by bishops of Lincoln, and the remainder by the archbishop of Canterbury and the bishops of Exeter, London and a bishop-to-be of Rochester) and Cambridge had sixteen, five founded by bishops (two by the

bishops of Norwich, two by those of Ely and one by a bishop of Rochester assisting his royal patron): Knowles and Hadcock 1971.

49 As early as 1214, when the post was created, it was intended that the bishop appoint whoever was to fill it. There was a subsequent struggle with the masters of the university, who wanted to make the appointment themselves; it later became usual for the bishop to take on the role.

50 Barrow 2000.

51 Page 1906c.

52 Harper-Bill 1996.

53 The structural value of even the simplest rib vaults is not clear. Although they appear to support the vault above them, modern engineers have found that they do not. Rather, they mask geometrically messy elements of these vaults; indeed, painted ribs may have been used to do this long before stone ones were created (John Goodall, pers. comm.). In other words, the addition of ribs was led from the first by visual rather than structural considerations.

54 The completion of the west front, and the creation of the Galilee, an exquisitely vainglorious ceremonial porch for the bishop, may just date from these years too: Draper 2006a.

55 Sampson 1998.

56 For a deeper exploration of the imaginative landscape that created such art, see Binski 2004.

57 Other examples: Chichester was given 150 trees between 1226 and 1240, Gloucester 100 oaks from the Forest of Dean in 1232, both gifts presumably connected to the vaulting of these churches. Lichfield was given 20 oaks from Cannock in 1221 and Carlisle 20 good oaks from Inglewood in 1219–21.

58 Colvin 1963.

59 Draper 2006a gives the total spend as £50,000, comparing it to the £7,000 he spent on Dover castle and £113,000 spent on castles and houses in general.

60 Keene 2004.

61 With the very belated exception of Osmund of Salisbury (canonized 1457), Cantilupe was the last official cathedral saint of the middle ages; while highly politicized unofficial cults would be a major theme of the centuries to come.

62 Aaron the Jew is known to have helped finance a new shrine at St Albans, for example.

63 Sadly, such events occurred in a culture of widespread anti-Semitism. The Fourth Lateran Council itself recommended that Jews be visibly marked out, while Bishop Grosseteste's dislike of Jews went well beyond the norms of his age.

64 Adapted from Pevsner's account: Pevsner and Metcalf 1985, I.

65 Some would date the new style to the advent of tracery per se; for them the Angel Choir is very early Decorated.

66 Bath was rebuilt in the years around 1500, but this was a much smaller project and was

not completed until after the Reformation.

67 It is worth noting that an interest in a lay audience can be discerned in the clues to nave iconography that survive in other cathedrals. The fifteenth-century vault at Norwich is the best survival after York, but the fourteenth-century bosses and corbels at Exeter and triforium corbels at Worcester should also be taken into account, alongside the fragmentary thirteenth-century paintings on the vault at Lincoln, which include the names of local mayors: Draper 2006a.

68 Orme 1991.

69 1277–1301.

CHAPTER 4: CHANGE

1 Maddison 1993a. There is little to see of Langton's bishop's palace, but that built by his mentor, Bishop Burnell of Wells, is a spectacular sight to this day.

2 Later commentators assumed the king was homosexual, and that this was at the core of the enmity he inspired. This may well be the case, but contemporaries focused on his military and political failures, and his refusal to observe the proprieties of his station, reflected in his treatment of favourites.

3 The famous and grisly story that a red-hot poker was inserted in his anus is not contemporary; the equally famous story that he was spirited overseas to live out his life as a hermit remains unexplained.

4 Dobson 1995a.

5 Page 1907c.

6 Summerson 2004.

7 Brown and Hopkins 1966a and b.

8 To extend a metaphor of Nikolaus Pevsner's.

9 To extend another metaphor, this time coined by Nicola Coldstream.

10 At Ely, the sacrist was Alan of Walsingham, supported by prior John Crauden; at Wells, Dean de Godley. See cathedral essays and chapter 7.

11 Wilson 1995; Denton 2004b.

12 Coldstream 1976; she sees the source for this wave of renewal as the opulent shrine built for Edward the Confessor at Westminster abbey (1268).

13 The porch lady chapels at Westminster abbey and St Mary Redcliffe, Bristol, which focused on popular devotion to cult images of the saint, are among less widely known examples.

14 Nilson 1998, 158.

15 One, Roger Niger, was uncanonized.

16 Archbishop Winchelsey of Canterbury criticized such bishops on precisely this basis: Denton 2004b.

17 John Goodall, accessed 2007.

18 One reason for this may be the death of many masons in 1348, leaving a dearth of skilled men and a legacy of early Perpendicular design templates, to adapt a theory suggested by John Goodall, pers. comm.

19 The deepest formal exploration of the birth of Perpendicular is by Christopher Wilson in his University of London PhD thesis of 1980. It is currently being prepared for publication.

20 Chantries: Kreider 1979; Brown 1995.

21 De Thoresby, future builder of the York lady chapel, speaking as vicar-general at Worcester cathedral. Page 1906c, 32.

22 Page 1906a.

23 Page 1913.

24 Doubleday and Page 1903, 33.

25 Woodman 1996.

26 Salzman 1948.

27 Page 1906a.

28 Ibid, 38.

29 They had been charging as much as 10 marks a year.

30 Troubles at Oxford, often breaking into violence, ran from the 1330s to the 1370s; Chester was more than once placed under government control during a series of scandals running from the mid-fourteenth to the early fifteenth centuries.

31 Indenture announcing the rebuilding of the York east end: Brown 2003, 164.

32 Woodman 1981, 151.

33 Sudbury material: Walker 2004b.

34 Salzman 1948.

35 The prison is known to have been there by 1541.

36 Page 1906c, 106.

37 Walker 2004b.

38 Hughes 2004a; spelling modernized.

39 Nilson 1998; see chapter 5.

40 There had been several attempts at creating structures designed for the tomb-and-altar combination implied by the founding of a chantry mass, among them de Gray's thirteenth-century tomb at York, positioned so its effigy gazes at the altar chosen for his chantry, and, at the peak of the chantry craze, such varied structures as the tomb of Roger Waltham in St Paul's, the Berkeley chapel in St Augustine's, Bristol, and the Grandison chantry buried in the Exeter west front.

41 The count includes all the great churches covered by this book.

42 There had been one previous attempt at a feeder and university college arrangement: Malden, Surrey, feeder for Merton college from 1263. The precise evolution of the architecture and planning of academic colleges is an important subject for detailed study.

43 He had also been to Rome in 1330 seeking canonization of his former patron, Thomas of Lancaster.

44 Hughes 2004b.

45 Purvis 1964.

46 Brown 2003 makes a reasonable case for the iconography being de Thoresby's idea.

47 Park 1983.

48 John McNeill, pers. comm.

49 This extraordinary culture has been most vividly brought to life in the work of Eamonn Duffy.

50 McAleer 1999, 161.

51 Strayer 1970; Lyon 1980; Denton and Dooley 1987; Brown 1989; Sherborne 1994.

52 Depending on which year one chooses as the Reformation and counting Thomas Audley as the last: ODNB.

53 In 1388.

54 The venue is assumed to be the nave; such plays were non-liturgical enough to require the purchase of a clock and pairs of gloves as props, and the presence of a vicar as stage manager and producer: Bowker 1994.

55 An angel was made for Norwich in 1454–60: Woodman 1996; an angel and dove for Lincoln: Bowers 1994.

56 The dating of the vault, before or after a fire of 1462, is not agreed.

57 This prioritising of nave over east end was true to a slightly lesser extent of Winchester in the 1390s and to a greatly lesser extent of York in the 1290s, whose twelfth-century choir was hard to upstage. At Norwich it seems that, although the choir clerestory was rebuilt in the late fourteenth century, no vault was created for it. This was eventually done after, rather than before, the vaulting of the nave, a reversal of priorities that would have shocked earlier cathedral-builders. However, by this date many parish church naves had been lavishly rebuilt, usually with money from the lay community, often leaving the chancel, which the parish priest was expected to maintain, untouched. This might have softened the visual shock of the Norwich volte-face on previous architectural priorities.

58 Fleming 2000.

59 Particularly strong connections have been seen between the designs of Perpendicular architects and those of Peter Parler and others in northern and central Europe, and have been explored by Paul Crossley.

60 Quoted in Gillingham and Griffiths 2000, 151.

61 Of the other saints with nationwide appeal, Etheldreda and Cuthbert were hieratic figures from the past, and strongly connected to the locality where their shrine lay; Becket was associated with the Church, Edward the Confessor with the Crown.

62 A process begun under Edward III.

63 This did not prevent ongoing patronage on a smaller scale, nor investment in these churches through the founding of chantries. Patronage in the Benedictine houses of the era is discussed in detail in Luxford 2005.

64 James Clark pers. comm; Davis 2004b.

65 Although most vicars' colleges were founded in the thirteenth century, starting with that at York, it is during the late fourteenth and fifteenth centuries that they were formally incorporated and rebuilt wholesale. What little is known of their predecessors, for example at York and Lincoln, suggests a more communal arrangement, in other words, a complex that imitated a small monastery more than it did a small religious college: Stocker 2005.

66 Kettle and Johnson 1970, 165.

67 Leedy 1980.

68 Surviving massive late-medieval gatehouses include the sixteenth-century one at Canterbury as well as those at Norwich, Lincoln, Ely, Worcester, Salisbury and Wells.

69 As does the poorer-quality diminutive copy of the York pulpitum at Ripon minster. Pulpitums decorated with English kings were themselves nothing new: that at Salisbury had borne just such a scheme in the thirteenth century.

70 The identity of each king is less certain at Canterbury than at York.

71 Humphrey, duke of Gloucester, 'Protector and Defender of the Realm' and would-be regent tried to do something more focused on his own interests at St Albans.

72 Salzman 1948.

73 Page 1907b.

74 Fan vaults were a West Country phenomenon and had rarely been built to cover main spans.

CHAPTER 5: END

1 The roods have utterly vanished, bar a few fragments, from every church in the land; among the cathedrals, Durham and Winchester have medieval high altar reredoses, though these have lost their statues; not a single cathedral retains a substantial part of its most important shrine, though these have been reconstructed at the former abbeys of St Albans, Chester and Oxford.

2 Thomas Wrothesley in Crook 1993c, 66.

3 Dr John Caius in Maddison 2000a, 102–3.

4 It is often the most communally focused buildings, such as the cloister and chapter-house, that were destroyed (Ely and Winchester, for example, retain neither), making it harder for anyone to turn back the clock on the dissolution.

5 That is, there were 33 members of the community, but 10 of them were novices, leaving 23 fully professed monks, men who had probably been priested too: Salzman 1948.

6 Bentham in Salzman 1948, 174.

7 As well as the royal burial church Westminster abbey, which was a cathedral from 1541 for ten years and remains a unique kind of royal collegiate church.

8 And, for much of this period, bishop of Lincoln, Bath and Wells, Durham, Winchester and Tournai; dean of York and abbot of St Albans: Tatton-Brown 1989.

9 And three times bigger than that of St Frideswide's.

10 If Henry VIII's first intentions had been seen through, we might also have Shrewsbury, Fountains, Bury St Edmunds and Bodmin cathedrals, which would have presumably meant the loss of St Werburgh's, Chester, and possibly that of Ripon minster, and no need for Truro to be built: Tatton-Brown 1989.

11 Scarisbrick 1994, 165.

12 Thacker 2004a, 122.

13 As the proto-Protestant Bishop Goodrich of Ely put it as early as 1541, quoted by Bentham in Salzman 1948, 166.

14 Woodman 1981, 233.

15 Forster 1993.

16 Peterborough's losses occurred in 1643. Southwell: Summers, 1984. Here the enormous stone pulpitum and the built-in sedilia survive.

17 Bowker 1994.

CHAPTER 6: WORKERS AND WORSHIPPERS

1 A gift from Henry III to Bishop Aigueblanche of Hereford: Toulson 2000.

2 York minster's fourteenth-century statutes in Dobson 1977.

3 Hill 1950 of Bishop Sutton of Lincoln.

4 Page 1906c.

5 Harper-Bill 1996.

6 The precise figure is 58 per cent: Bowker 1968.

7 Page 1906c, 38.

8 Bowker 1968.

9 Page 1906c.

10 Thompson 2004.

11 Dobson 1977.

12 Their presence on chapter cannot be assumed: the precise arrangement varied from place to place. But at York, for example, each archdeaconry came with a specific prebend attached to it. This meant that, no matter how independent of the archbishop the chapter was as a corporate body, five of his most important diocesan officers were also members of it: Dobson 1995a.

13 Maddison 2000a.

14 Bowker 1968.

15 Wollaston 1996, 29.

16 Dunning 1982.

17 Ibid.

18 Ibid.

19 Page 1906a.

20 Harper-Bill 1996; Virgoe 1996.

21 Mate 2004.

22 Salzman 1948. Ely installed hermits at the bridges on these causeways and thus an ancient tradition of solitary monasticism was combined with the practicalities of bridge-maintenance and toll-gathering.

23 Matthew 16, 13–19.

24 Keefe 2004.

25 Not all of which actually had an incumbent priest at any one time.

26 The number would have varied greatly and accurate counts are rare. The 1379 clerical subsidy at Lincoln found ninety people in the close, including everyone from the lowliest chorister to the most senior residentiary canon, but not including lay staff, servants or non-resident canons. At monastic Norwich the estimate of 270 staff, of whom sixty were monks, does include such people: Gilchrist 2005; but it is less clear whether it takes account of the bishop and his staff.

27 They were the cathedral's in-house

carpenters and odd-job men; the sweeping took place each Passiontide: Owen 1994b.

28 Dobson 1995a; MacDowdy 1974.

29 Gilchrist 2005.

30 Dobson 1977.

31 Some figures from ODNB. S Ellis, 'Percy, Henry, fourth earl of Northumberland': £4,044 a year gross from lands; R W Hoyle, 'Percy, Henry Algernon, fifth earl of Northumberland': a clear income after deductions of about £3,600.

32 Barr 1977.

33 Barrie Dobson's phrase: Dobson 1977.

34 Kettle and Johnson 1970.

35 Page 1913.

36 Keene 2004; Dobson 1977.

37 Swanson and Lepine 2000, 23.

38 Even this constitutional principle had an architectural dimension. It was known as 'four-square': at many cathedrals, the choir-stalls were arranged in a rectangle with one stall for a dignitary on each corner, and separate larger thrones for the dean and the (usually absent) bishop.

39 Dobson 1977. Precise roles and titles might vary from place to place.

40 Ibid.

41 Harper 2005.

42 The first known mention is in York in 1138–42: Dobson 2005.

43 For an example of this, see the entry for London (St Paul's) in Knowles and Hadcock 1971.

44 Gransden 1982, 38.

45 Pugh and Crittall 1956.

46 Dobson 1977.

47 Dobson 2005.

48 As six poor clerks at Lincoln did in 1516: Bowker 1994.

49 The most architecturally elaborate is at Wells: see also York, Hereford, Chichester.

50 Some vicars at Lichfield in the fourteenth century are known to have been there for thirty to forty years: Dobson 2005.

51 Barron and Rousseau 2004; deathday is my coining.

52 King 1996.

53 Gransden 1982, 40.

54 Knowles and Hadcock 1971: of which twenty-seven were cathedrals or their sub-colleges and over thirty were academic/educational.

55 A statement directly reflected in their architecture: even such comparatively wealthy colleges as Crediton, Warwick, Manchester and Wimborne owed as much to grand parish church architecture as they did to the great church tradition; perhaps only Beverley and to an extent Southwell and Ripon could ever have been mistaken for a small cathedral.

56 Until the development of new orders in the eleventh and twelfth century, no one talked of being Benedictine: there was simply monasticism, with the rule of St Benedict as its model text.

57 My etymology may be weak, but the implications are suggestive: a senior monk

is obedient, a senior canon dignified.

58 The exceptions, Lichfield and York, perhaps had particular reason to look emphatically unlike their rival cathedral priories, Coventry and Canterbury respectively.

59 Gilchrist 2005.

60 Ibid.

61 Ibid.

62 Sampson 1988; Tringham 1993.

63 Simply a cross-section of the church with a large window and some extra ornamentation, though that at Rochester was richly ornamented. Those at Worcester and Durham are in more visible locations but remain simple compositions when compared to the screen facades.

64 Full meetings did occur. There were between seventeen and thirty-nine canons present at some of the meetings of general chapter at which Richard Poore and his colleagues set in train the building of Salisbury: Pugh and Crittall 1956. Wells appears designed with one stall for each canon, and steps below each stall for a vicar and other juniors, as if its patron wanted the entire cathedral community to enter on rare, presumably ceremonial, occasions

65 All bar Worcester are rectangular, sometimes with apsidal east ends. Worcester, Canterbury and Durham are romanesque with later refurbishments. The others have been destroyed, but archaeological evidence suggests romanesque with later refurbishments at Coventry and less conclusively at Ely. While Winchester and Rochester have surviving romanesque entrance arches, Norwich's are gothic: this is the most likely case of a complete rebuild (following the 1272 riot). I am not aware of evidence for those at Bath and Carlisle. By contrast all the secular cathedral chapter-houses are entirely new structures dating between the 1220s (Exeter) and the 1360s (Hereford) and only Exeter, perhaps the earliest of the sequence, is not polygonal.

66 The biggest exceptions to this were Durham and Ely, whose huge range of powers gave some of the monks some very worldly responsibilities. For a time, the prior of Durham was also the bishop's main archdeacon; while the sacrist of Ely was effectively mayor of the surrounding township and its inhabitants.

67 Gilchrist 2005.

68 In this respect it was more like the household of an aristocrat: large and powerful, but without any corporate existence independent of its head.

69 According to Gerald of Wales: Hastings 1997.

70 From the 1290s monks elected two or three of their number to put forward to the archbishop, who chose one of them: Dobson 1995a.

71 Owen 2003.

72 Anon 1593.

73 Gilchrist 2005.

74 Owen 2003.

75 Dodwell 1996b.

76 Doubleday and Page 1903.

77 Proud 1990.

78 Gibson 1995, 46.

79 Anon 1593.

80 Ibid.

81 Glazed inscriptions are said to have noted the names of estates and the kings who had given them: Craze 1986/7.

82 Page 1926; Dobson 1995a.

83 Page 1906c, 110.

84 Dobson 1995a.

85 Ibid, 89.

86 Bates 1994.

87 Ramsay 1995, 352. Looking at the architectural response to fires or structural collapses, such as the Canterbury fires of 1067 and 1174 and the collapse of the central tower at Ely in 1321, it is possible to argue that the degree of actual damage was exaggerated, and that the community was not unprepared for an ambitious building project.

88 Page 1907b.

89 Harper-Bill 1996.

90 Dobson 1995a.

91 Craze 1986/7; anon 1593.

92 Dobson 1995a, 112.

93 At Wells (Draper 1981) and elsewhere.

94 At Canterbury every door-sill was asperged weekly: Sparks 1997; at Wells tombs were sometimes censed: Ayers 1996.

95 Tudor-Craig 1982. Hidden choristers' passages have also been identified at Peterborough, Salisbury and Lichfield.

96 Matthew 1994.

97 Craze 1986/7.

98 Certainly for all the craftsmen, labourers and tradesmen involved with the cathedrals: Erskine 1981.

99 Bowers 1994.

100 Harper 2000.

101 Harper 2005.

102 The first known polyphonic singing in England was at St Paul's cathedral in the 1220s.

103 Braytoft came from the Westminster abbey lady chapel; he was to be Master of the Song School: Bowers 1994.

104 Page 1906b.

105 Owen 1994b.

106 This visitation was carried out by the abbot of Colchester: Harper-Bill 1996.

107 Keene 2004.

108 Owen 1994b.

109 Wilson 1905.

110 Ayers 1996.

111 Tillott 1961.

112 Stroud 1996.

113 Sparks 1997; Tim Tatton-Brown 1997.

114 See chapter 3, note 00.

115 Binski 2004 argues that the altars that gradually filled St Albans nave are a sign of lay 'colonization' of part of the abbey church.

116 Ayers 1996.

117 Ripon did not have a separate chapterhouse.

118 Forster 1993.

119 Barron and Rousseau 2004.

120 Anon 1593, 88.

121 Bowker 1968.

122 McAleer 1991.

123 Pevsner and Metcalf 1985, II.

124 Harper-Bill 1996.

125 Owen 1994b.

126 Ibid.

127 Page 1910.

128 Catto 1982.

129 Durham: Page 1907a; Winchester: Doubleday and Page 1903; Norwich: Gilchrist 2005.

130 Gilchrist 2005.

131 Rex 2004.

132 Salzman 1948.

133 Thacker 2004a.

134 Salzman 1948.

135 Anon 1593.

136 Serjeantson et al 1906.

137 Anon 1593, 76.

138 Nilson 1998. Uncited saint-related facts are all from him.

139 Jancey 1982a.

140 Nilson 1998; Willis-Bund 1924, 42. Oswald seems to have been particularly good at helping with the weather: fifty years later the relics were processed again, this time 'for ceasing of such continual rain' and later again 'for peaceful air'.

141 Forster 1993.

142 Sadgrove 1994, 170–1.

143 Douie and Farmer 1961, II, 230.

144 Stroud 1983, 52.

145 Garton 1986.

146 Nilson 1998, 142.

147 Woodman 1981. Very important visitors could hire proxy pilgrims, as Elizabeth of York did in 1502: two separate pilgrims were sent to visit a dozen or more shrines around England at a 10d day-rate: Nilson 1998.

148 Nilson 1998, 27.

149 Durham: Anon 1593.

150 Nilson 1998, 137.

151 Brown 1999.

152 Anon 1593.

153 Malden 1901.

154 Nilson 1998; Tanner 1996.

155 Mainly to this image.

156 Wilson 1995.

157 Owen 1971.

158 St Hugh of Lincoln seemed to pass dead paupers in the road almost every time he went for a walk.

159 Vivid and grisly examples can be seen at York, Exeter and Wells, though the depiction of the worms is rare in England.

160 Lubin and Barker 1990. Worcester had a monopoly on burials in the city.

161 Tanner 1996.

1 Hewett 1974.
2 Purcell 1973; MacDowdy 1974; these particular trees are more likely to have been used for scaffolding than for the vault itself.
3 Coldstream 1979.
4 Ibid. Coldstream identifies the region from which certain motifs originate, but only implies that the masons came from that area.
5 Numbers of labourers: the lower figure is for 1299–1300, when there were fifteen masons, three carpenters, a quarryman and a 'daubere' on site; the higher figure is for 1329–30, when the labourers were among thirty-two people on site: Erskine 1981. Pay of labourers: the top summer rate in 1334 was 11d a week; the lowest winter rate 8.5d; in 1348–9 ditch-diggers were earning 7d to 10d a week: Erskine 1983.
6 Allen 1981.
7 Purcell 1973.
8 Exeter: quarrying of Salcombe stone, 2d a ton; haulage from Topsham to Exeter after initial transport by water, a further 9d a ton: Allen 1981.
9 Tringham 1993.
10 Brown 2003. The 3,980 nails needed at the Lichfield bishop's palace (Tringham 1993) were divided into types: lednails, lath nails, board nails, shingle nails, spikings.
11 MacDowdy 1974.
12 Erskine 1983.
13 Dendrochronology has identified a lot of Baltic pine in the cathedrals: the thirteenth-century ceiling at Peterborough is one example. Ireland was another important source of wood.
14 Knoop and Jones 1967.
15 Bony 1990.
16 Knoop and Jones 1967.
17 John David, York minster, pers. comm.
18 Knoop and Jones 1967.
19 See note 4.
20 Fawcett 1996.
21 Such as the chapter-house.
22 Kettle and Johnson 1970.
23 Alexander 2004.
24 Not all such stones in English churches necessarily come from the Isle of Purbeck; some are not even limestone. Hence the use in this book of the phrase 'polished stone'.
25 Blair and Ramsay 1991.
26 Wilson 1995; Brown 2003.
27 Everyone got a week off at Christmas, Easter and usually Pentecost: Erskine 1981.
28 William fitz Stephen describing twelfth-century works on the Tower of London. Knoop and Jones 1967, 3–4.
29 King 1996; Jenny Alexander, pers. comm.
30 Woodman 1996.
31 Pevsner and Metcalf 1985, II.
32 Brown 2003.
33 Ibid. Dr Jenny Alexander, pers. comm., suggests that these sheds are more likely to have been used to lay out window tracery

34 Holt 1957; Sparks 1997.
35 John David, York minster, pers. comm.
36 Lucy Rutherford, York minster, pers. comm.
37 Hereford and Worcestershire Earth Heritage Trust, no date.
38 Geddes 1996.
39 King 1996, 402.
40 Heslop 1982.
41 Brooks 1991b.
42 Ayers 1996. Some buildings, such as the 1080 incarnation of Rochester, do not even seem to have been particularly well designed for worship: Plant 2006.
43 The Dominican friar Nicholas de Briari: Fernie 1993. 59.
44 Uncited biographical material for Witney: Harvey rev. Ayers 2004; for Hurley: Harvey 1975.
45 Erskine 1981.
46 Pevsner and Metcalf 1985 II.
47 Harvey 1975; Courtney 2004.
48 Morgan 1982, 152.
49 Binski 2002, 35.
50 Or it may just suggest the designers were very well travelled.
51 Harvey 1994.
52 I am grateful to John David of York minster mason's yard for showing me round this evocative space.
53 Harvey 1968.
54 I am grateful to Dr Jenny Alexander of the University of Nottingham for showing me this; she has published it: Alexander 1996.
55 Brown 2003.
56 Lindley 1985.
57 Plus a few shillings of rents: Erskine 1981 (boxes); 1983 (indulgences).
58 Maddison 2000a.
59 Lindley 1985.
60 Less easy to assess is the role of loans in the cathedral-building economy. Bishops played an important role themselves as money-lenders (without interest, theoretically); before 1290 the Jewish community and later the great Italian banking families also played an important role in the supply of financial capital, glimpsed from time to time in cathedral records.
61 Hayes 2004.
62 Harvey 1977; this means that the mason was a guest at Wykeham's table, with the rest of his household and *familia*: dinner-for-two had not been invented.
63 Page 1909.
64 Dodwell 1996a; my quotes.
65 Woodman 1981.
66 Gilchrist 2005; Fernie 1993.
67 With his successor, Prior Conrad, who is more often credited with it.
68 Luxford 2005.
69 Beaufort's money paid for his own chantry chapel and perhaps for the great screen in the cathedral.
70 Page 1906c.
71 Exactly the same could be said of Norwich from Bishop Alnwick on.

72 Kjølbye-Biddle 2001, 98.
73 Dobson 1977.
74 Brown 2003.
75 MacDowdy 1974; Purcell 1973; Harvey 1975.
76 Matthew Paris in Woodman 1981, 135. Elias is also known to have been involved in, among other things, the great hall at Winchester castle and a tomb for Henry III's sister.
77 Malone 2004.
78 A mindset most subtly recovered in Binski 2004.
79 Woodman 1996.
80 Brett 1996.
81 Kettle and Johnson 1970.
82 The most ambitious project, the taking down of Walkelin's apse, re-working of the feretory platform, and creation of a new set of choir-stalls certainly involved the bishop, who helped appoint the carpenter who built the stalls. Nevertheless, as a former monk, he might have been acting on the convent's initiative, while even the ambitious replacement of the apse might just have been presented as maintenance in a part of the building that was unstable.
83 Among monastic cathedrals, Durham and Rochester are among the clearest examples; among other monastic houses, Peterborough and Gloucester stand out.
84 Lindley 1985.
85 Dobson 1995a. Eastry's two largest works, the refurbishment of the chapter-house and the installation of choir screens, cost £839 between them.
86 Erskine 1983.
87 Barron and Rousseau 2004.
88 Brown 2003.
89 Ibid.
90 These examples, all in or near the cathedral lady chapel, are the only monumentally expressed lay female tombs I have come across in the cathedrals.
91 Ibid.
92 Pugh and Crittall 1956; Brown 1999.
93 As the bishop put it: Cherry 1995, xxx; Gee 1995.
94 Page 1907b.
95 Simpson 1996.
96 See chapter 3, 'triumph'.
97 Nilson 1998; see Chapter 6.
98 Morris 1974.
99 Durham 1093–1104; Norwich 1096–1119.
100 Begun from 1082; translation 1102.
101 Wilson 1990; Allison 1989; Tillot 1961.
102 Although the initial rebuild here from 1192 was done quickly, the design changed three times; it is the addition of the Angel Choir and the towers that puts Lincoln in the 'long' category.
103 Hastings 1997.
104 Wilson 1990.
105 Haines 2004a.
106 But not always: at the east end of Wells, the roof was put on after the vaults: Tatton-Brown 1989.
107 Traces of a fad among West Country masons to start rebuilding on the south side rather than the east end can be seen at Bristol,

Gloucester and other local churches.

108 And before them the early seventh and late tenth centuries.

109 Harvey rev. Ayers 2004; Courtney 2004.

110 St Paul's to match the dynastic capital at Winchester, just as key royal functions are being located in London; York to match Canterbury, just as the two are locked in combat over the primacy of their archbishops.

111 Lichfield may contain stretches of wall, but nothing that could be called architecture.

112 Some with apsidal ends. See Chapter 6, 'Working in the cathedral'.

113 Canterbury: Dobson 1995a; Ely: Ayers 1996.

114 Eric Fernie's phrase.

POSTSCRIPT

1 Gillespie 1997, 212–14.

2 One wonders if it is completely coincidental that the two cathedrals we have lost, Coventry and St Paul's, are also in the only two medieval cathedral cities that were not sidelined by the Industrial Revolution.

3 Gerald of Wales quoted in http://www.bwpics.co.uk/quotes/index.html; accessed 2005.

4 The Norman cathedral relocations of Chichester, Bath and Lincoln selected former Roman settlements when others might have done just as well.

5 MacDowdy 1974.

6 Binski 2004; Garton 1986, 56–8.

7 The top landowners in Britain are, in order of size of landholding, the Forestry Commission, the Ministry of Defence, the royal family, the National Trust, insurance companies, the utility companies, the Duke of Buccleuch, the National Trust for Scotland, the Dukedom of Atholl, the Duke of Westminster and the Church of England; but as several of these landowners own large estates in Scotland, the Anglican Church is far more significant in England itself. Of course, many of the non-Church estates were partly acquired from the Church at the Reformation. http://www.who-owns-britain.com, accessed 2005.

8 Norwich: Atherton and Holderness 1996; St Paul's: Morrin 2004; Canterbury: Appendix 2, 'Estates' in Blockley et al 1997.

9 In this sense, a society that bears more resemblance to that of the seventh century than has been true at any other time.

PART 2: THE CATHEDRALS

BATH

1 Perhaps a community founded by Osric of the Hwicce (see Gloucester, Worcester).

2 As Matthew Paris put it: Davenport 1996, 19.

3 Ibid.

4 Central and western towers may have been built in the 1320s or 1340s, when the new east end at Wells was being built, though the

figure we have for these towers, 100 marks, suggests repairs rather than a rebuild.

5 Monckton 1999, 255. It appears they had raised nearly £500 for a new refectory, while doing little for their church: Luxford 2000.

6 They were asked to make a report on the 'state and forwardness' of the church in 1502, and finally appointed as master-masons in 1506: Monckton 1999.

7 Leedy 1980.

8 The enormous fan vaults at these three buildings – Bath, King's college chapel and Henry VII's chapel – were all conceived at almost exactly the same time: so close that working out which came first is a rather academic problem, especially as the master-masons involved, John Wastell and the Vertue brothers, were interconnected via the king's projects. Leedy 1980 gives the most detailed account of each project.

9 And punning inscription, 'trees going to chuse their King/said 'be to us the Olive King'.

10 Or Castello.

11 Luxford 2000 and 2005. Jacob promised to give one-tenth of his wealth to God after he awoke, a passage often used to justify tithe-giving. St Benedict had used the image of his Ladder to illustrated the dangers of pride.

12 Page 1911, 77.

13 Ibid, 78.

14 The chancel roof was vaulted and the west front complete by 1518; plans for a conventional east end with a lady chapel were then abandoned. The prior was buried in his (today heavily restored) chantry in 1525. The church was still unfinished in the 1830s. Monckton 1999.

15 Monckton 1999; Luxford 2000.

BRISTOL

1 The other richest cities were London, Norwich and York, but Bristol in some ways is better compared with Southampton and Newcastle, also major ports with no dominant great church.

2 Such close relations between one abbey and one family rarely lasted more than a few generations. St Augustine's is exceptional for the long duration of Berkeley patronage. Golding 1986.

3 Keen 1997, vii, quoting the anonymous twelfth-century author of the Gesta Stephani.

4 Oakes 2000.

5 See, for example, the 'trepanned' heads biting off the end of each main stretch of string course, a sign that the stonework was carved to dimensions that proved to be a few inches out when the structure was actually erected.

6 The fullest analysis to date is Morris 1997.

7 Cannon (forthcoming).

8 Brown 1997.

9 Pevsner 1958; Foyle 2004.

10 Morris 1997 detects no fewer than three

phases, each involving subtle changes of design. He also points out that the south-west bay of the choir aisle is of a different design from the others – perhaps it went up in the '1298 campaign' – and that the Berkeley chapel and ante room have both a complicated history and a complicated relationship with the main east end. Fourteenth-century work in the Elder Lady Chapel also needs to be fitted into the picture, while the Berkeley chapel must pre-date the east end itself; the Berkeley context (especially the family's inability to intervene between 1322 and 1326) is crucial: see Cannon 2004; Cannon and Williamson forthcoming. The pro-1298 case – the date widely accepted before Morris's article – is to be published by Christopher Wilson in 2011.

11 Morris 1997.

12 Wells-Furby 2004.

13 Maclean 1883; Wells-Furby 2004; Cannon (forthcoming).

14 Fleming 2000.

15 Jeayes 1899–90.

16 Warren 1897–9.

17 William Joy designer of the Wells choir, the Exeter west front and the collegiate church of Ottery St Mary knew the Bristol work well. The Wells strainer arches, Exeter north porch and Ottery St Mary itself are among the closest comparators for its style.

CANTERBURY

1 After the Conquest, that is.

2 One thinks of Edgar and Dunstan, William the Conqueror and Lanfranc.

3 Barlow 2004a.

4 Caesarius in Staunton 2001, 239. The ensuing sources are also all roughly contemporary.

5 Ibid, 238.

6 Herbert of Bosham in ibid, 183.

7 William fitz Stephen in ibid, 187.

8 Garnier in ibid, 189.

9 Edward Grim in ibid, 199.

10 William of Canterbury in ibid, 200.

11 Edward Grim in ibid, 201.

12 Ibid, 202.

13 Ibid, 203.

14 Benedict of Peterborough in ibid, 204.

15 William fitz Stephen in ibid, 184.

16 Edward Grim in ibid, 203.

17 Benedict of Peterborough in ibid, 204–5.

18 William fitz Stephen in ibid, 205.

19 Ibid.

20 Lambeth Anonymous in ibid, 210.

21 Draper 2006a gives an outline of the trajectory: the early embrace by common-born laymen, substantially underground until the king had been seen to accept it in 1172; then the monk Benedict began to record miracles as they happened from 1171; by 1174 he needed a full-time assistant to keep up.

22 Duggan 1982.

23 Ibid.

24 Draper 2006b. Becket's story itself is one of the stereotypical secular churchman –

careerist, worldly – who suddenly starts to behave like a monk.

25 Edward Grim in Staunton 2001, 217.
26 Gervase of Canterbury in Holt 1957. Gervase's account is unique in Europe as a detailed account of a medieval building campaign by someone – in this case a Canterbury monk – who was clearly closely involved with it. His account is all the more significant because the building concerned is a landmark structure in a new style of architecture. It has been pored over for information on how medieval builders worked and how their work was viewed by others involved. Its very existence, in an age not given to the sudden coining of new literary genres, amounts to a kind of hagiography of the building to match that being created for its saint.
27 The estimate of up to 32 metres was made in Blockley et al 1997.
28 Blair 2005.
29 He had refused to allow a ransom to be paid, and was murdered at Greenwich.
30 Woodman 1981: seventeen saints out of sixty-eight archbishops before the Reformation; the only post-Conquest saints were Anselm and Becket.
31 46 and then 57 metres long by perhaps the eleventh century; 65 metres by 1066. Blockley et al 1997.
32 Lanfranc is said to have found the monks holding services by the tomb of Dunstan, huddled under a cloth. But Lanfranc's Ground Zero approach is likely to tell us as much about him as it does about the state of the building. It would be odd if this was the only cathedral fire in this book that genuinely necessitated complete demolition (one might cite London in 1666, but in that case it took a fire that devoured an entire city to do irreparable damage to its church). As the works of the 1170s at Canterbury, and comparable stories at Chichester, Carlisle and elsewhere demonstrate, it is perfectly possible to design a replacement for a fire-damaged church that retains or evokes key features of its predecessor.
33 Brooke 1993.
34 The peak aimed at by Lanfranc; numbers had reached 100 by 1090 and were still growing: Woodman 1981. Dobson 1995a gives detailed figures thereafter.
35 Gervase of Canterbury in Holt 1957.
36 All quotes from Gervase of Canterbury in Holt 1957.
37 Anselm's choir in Woodman 1981: 22.25 metres high; 1174 choir was 25.92 metres high.
38 Woodman 1981 and other works: extra Ancestors of Christ had to be made for the clerestory glass as a result, while the wall arcade of the previous building still stops in mid-flow where its extension bursts eastwards. It has recently been speculated that the extension here was always intended to be grand, but that a large circular chapel was first intended: research under way as this

book went to press suggests that something similar may have existed at the recently built east end of York; and another was built as the setting for a saint's shrine at Trondheim cathedral, a building hugely influenced by English early gothic architecture.
39 Kidson 1993a has entertainingly wondered if the fire might have been an act of arson by the monks themselves, and whether William of Sens was anything but the lucky winner of a piece of open competition.
40 Binski 2004, noting the stripped-back architecture of the new crypt, sees two 'visions' of Early English deriving from Canterbury: the elaborate model of St Hugh's, Lincoln from the Trinity Chapel, and the elegant and spare model of Salisbury from the crypt. Each space was of course the setting for a different shrine.
41 Draper 2006a; Binski 2004.
42 Binski 2004.
43 In 1513: Woodman 1981, 223. The evidence for the Corona as the location for Becket's head-shrine is compelling, but not proven.
44 Gibson 1995 and other works.
45 Tatton-Brown 1982, 2000.
46 Woodman 1981.
47 Once the costs of employing shrine-keepers and of buying candles and other goods were subtracted.
48 Both in Nilson 1998.
49 Brilliantly decoded in Wilson 1995. Other fourteenth-century additions include new windows in St Anselm's chapel, a fine series of choir screens and the refurbishment of the chapter-house by Prior Eastry.
50 The prior of Canterbury was no ordinary figure: 'the priors of Christ Church excel all other priors in England in dignity and honour', it was said (Page 1926, 88). Likewise, among the archbishop's staff, the archdeacon of Canterbury was effectively bishop of east Kent.
51 As Leland said of Prior Chillenden: Tatton-Brown 1997, 135.
52 Eastry and Chillenden figures are from Dobson 1995a.
53 Detail on the nave is from Tatton-Brown 1997.
54 The earthquake is said to have coincided with the precise moment that John Wyclif's trial for heresy began. It is said to have damaged several monastic buildings, including the cloister, which would shortly be rebuilt.
55 For Arundel's approach to Lollardry see Hughes 2004a.
56 Wilson 1995.
57 My summary from Blockley et al 1997 and Woodman 1981.
58 Sparks 1997.
59 Quotation from Woodman 1981. The date at which this 'clocarium' was constructed is unknown, but its existence is not recorded before 1421. It has since disappeared.
60 Sparks 1997.
61 Wilson 1995. The chantry is now used as a French Protestant church and is rarely open

to the public.
62 Ibid.
63 Woodman 1981 gives 864 for the cloister: then there are the transepts, nave, towers and south porch.
64 Woodman 1981.
65 John McNeill, pers. comm.
66 As Erasmus put it; Woodman 1981, 199.
67 Woodman 1981, 233.
68 My summary from Woodman 1981; Dobson 1995a; Nilson 1998.
69 Nilson 1998.
70 Dobson 1995a, 157.
71 An atmosphere compellingly transmuted into post-Apocalyptic mythology by Hoban 2002.

CARLISLE

1 He contributed to its building in 1129–30.
2 For early and Norman history, see Summerson 1993, 1994, 2004; McCarthy 2004; Henig 2004.
3 Plant 2004.
4 We cannot be certain that its designer – working sometime before 1129 – knew it was going to be a cathedral at all, though it seems likely that Henry I had the creation of a diocese in mind when he founded the priory (and chose its prior).
5 It has good claim to be the most important church north of Chester and west of the Pennines.
6 J Franklin 2004.
7 Loosely translating Osbert of Clare: Summerson 1994.
8 i.e. ancient Cumberland.
9 Summerson 1994.
10 Ibid.
11 Ibid.
12 Tatton-Brown 2004, 258.
13 From 8.5 metres to 12.2 metres: Alexander 2004.
14 Ibid.
15 Summerson 2004.
16 Lanercost chronicle in Wilson 1905, 31.
17 With indulgences in 1293, 1306 and 1307 and gifts of wood from the king. Summerson 2004.
18 Wilson 1905.
19 And perhaps 1345: Tatton-Brown 2004.
20 Simpson 2004.
21 As at Chichester and Canterbury, the process shows how a fire in a wooden roof damaged the upper storey and the wooden fittings and arcades of a church disproportionately.
22 Alexander 2004.
23 Higham 2004.
24 Wilson 1905; McCarthy 2004.
25 Wilson 1905; Summerson 1993.
26 North and south of the high altar, perhaps in imitation of York. The Victorians later 'put back' a thirteenth-century design.
27 Tracy 2004; Park and Cather 2004.

CHESTER

1 Thacker 2004b.

2 Thacker 2000b; Harris 1979, III.

3 Lewis 2004.

4 It was an area where the bishop already owned property, and a diocese that might expand westwards if Norman expansion continued.

5 His neighbour to the south, the earl of Shrewsbury, had recently done likewise.

6 Harris 1979, III.

7 After 1098 there was little immediate possibility of westward expansion (though the earl managed to colonize distant but vulnerable Anglesey); indeed Chester itself might have seemed under threat from the Welsh.

8 Gem 2000. More early work survives in the monastic complex.

9 Lucian, in Harris 1979, III, 135; http://www.bwpics.co.uk/quotes/index.html, accessed 2005.

10 Written at a date when only Jerusalem and Rome were considered worthy of such attention: a description of London, the only comparable work in Britain, had been written perhaps twenty years earlier. Danbury 2000.

11 Higden in Danbury 2000, 107.

12 For this and subsequent accounts of the county's history, see Harris 1979, I.

13 Works were probably under way in 1277 and 1284.

14 Maddison 2000b.

15 Adam of Usk in Harris 1979, I; Lewys Glyn Cothi: http://www.bwpics.co.uk/quotes/index.html, accessed 2005.

16 Harris 1979, I.

17 Harris 1979, III, 139.

18 Harris 1979, III.

19 Ibid.

20 St Oswald's was initially based in the abbey enclosure and later moved into the church. Such arrangements were not uncommon.

21 Grosinger 2000; Harris 1979, III.

22 Harris 1979, III; Pevsner and Metcalf 1985, II.

23 Harris 1979, III. The diocese of Carlisle was the runt among medieval sees, and the archdeaconries of Richmond (in the diocese of York) and Chester (in that of Coventry and Lichfield) to its south were both semi-detached from their mother churches.

24 Pevsner and Metcalf 1985, II, 51.

25 Jansen 2000b.

26 Including a walk of the cloister and the south choir aisle.

CHICHESTER

1 Indeed it seems the king had already been baptized: Greenway 1994.

2 Kelly 1994.

3 By the eleventh century there was a minster church there. Selsey cathedral must have formed close ties with the growing settlement, Greenway points out (1994).

4 Such issues did not stop the Normans making dramatic relocations of other cath-edrals – Dorchester to Lincoln, for example.

5 Greenway 1994.

6 Ian Nairn, in Pevsner and Metcalf 1985, I, 85.

7 When a dedication took place. Most of the interior was done by the time Bishop Luffa died in 1123.

8 A complex story: Tatton-Brown 1994c and 1996a.

9 A similar pattern can be traced in post-fire 'plastic surgery' visible at Canterbury and Carlisle.

10 Binski 2004 points out that a canon of Chichester criticized such architectural sumptuousness in 1190, just as his bishop was building this retrochoir. People sometimes adorned their temples rather than their minds, Gervase of Chichester pointedly said.

11 A one-twentieth tax on their common fund.

12 Harper-Bill 2004c; Page 1907d.

13 My suggestion. The clear French influence is also a marker of Chichester's proximity to the Channel.

14 There was a separate shrine for his head.

15 He left £341 in his will.

16 He made many changes to his palaces; helped build a new tower at Portsmouth in 1494 and a new chapel for the English college in Rome in 1501; gave an enormous £500 to the fabric of St Paul's; and built new cloisters and paid for a new floor at St Frideswide's priory in Oxford. Tatton-Brown 1994c; Munby 1990; Harper-Bill 2004b.

17 Eighteen of the 140 canons known to have worked at the cathedral between 1500 and 1540, assisted by the four new prebends Sherborn endowed on the basis that they could only be occupied by other Wykhamists. Fines 1994.

18 The north one was a parish church by the fifteenth century: Tatton-Brown 1994c.

19 Tummers 1994. However, he may not have been pro-Reformation: see Harper-Bill 2004b.

20 Walcott 1879, 26; Tummers 1994; Page 1907d. The tomb looks heavily over-restored, but this was never what one might call a quiet colour scheme. It is also the only serious tomb in the building to have originated at Chichester. The very fine (if rather battered) lay tombs in the nave were (it is said) rescued from Lewes priory after the Reformation.

21 Kelly 1994; Brighton 1994; Fines 1994. One bay of Barnard's original decoration, in the lady chapel, survives in reasonable condition.

22 Tatton Brown 1994a. It gives a far better impression of the original appearance of such structures – which were once major features in several closes – than the other surviving example, Gundulf's tower at Rochester. The Leaning Tower of Pisa is of course a more famous cathedral campanile.

23 Or a relief that included it as well as surrounding walls. Zarnecki 1979.

24 The cult of Lazarus was at its height in the 1130s and 1140s.

COVENTRY

1 The clearest idea of medieval Coventry cathedral is given in Morris 1994. It would be odd for the lesser churches of St Michael's and Holy Trinity next door to have had such very breathtaking spires if the cathedral did not; and for similar reasons Lichfield's three suggest a similar arrangement at Coventry.

2 And consecrated in 1043.

3 As at Bath and Southwark, this may have been a nunnery; as at Ely, Oxford and Chester, Osburga was a virginal Saxon woman.

4 Stephens 1969.

5 Richard of Devizes in Franklin 1994, 136.

6 The pattern is replicated in many ways at Bath and Wells, where the differences between the two are more emphatic. Unlike Wells, Lichfield was a poor cathedral, and Coventry was arguably a more high-profile monastic house than Bath.

7 Scarisbrick 1994.

8 Morris 1994.

DURHAM

1 Anon 1998, 85–6. All subsequent direct quotes are from this account, written in 1593 by a retired member of the community, unless credited otherwise.

2 Battiscombe 1956. The bishop was in London at the time.

3 In most other churches, saints' bodies were simply discarded; Cuthbert is the only saint in this book whose remains lie on the site of his shrine. (St Edward the Confessor at Westminster abbey and St Wite at Whitechurch Canonicorum in Dorset are said to be the only others in England.)

4 Descriptions of fittings are all also from Anon 1998 unless credited otherwise.

5 The figure includes a few other items of far lesser significance: Nilson 1998.

6 Page 1907a; Marner 2000.

7 They even ran their own parliament and issued their own coinage. Page 1907a; Dobson 2003.

8 Also known as Bear Park.

9 Anon 1998, 20–1.

10 Klukas 1995.

11 Coldstream and Draper 1980. In addition, sometime in the decades before this, the whole cathedral received its first coat of paint, updating (and probably rather spoiling) the dour Norman interior – David Park, pers. comm. Only the faintest traces of this colour remain

12 Draper (2006a, 41) quotes a contemporary comment on du Puiset: 'the more anxious he was to build on earth the more remiss he was in building in heaven'. Other works by the bishop include additions to Norham Castle, the early gothic church of St Cuthbert in Darlington and perhaps the west towers of the cathedral itself.

13 Surely a piece of twelfth-century metalwork,

14 *viz* the Gloucester Candlestick, and thus here attributed to him, just as the sanctuary knocker has been previously.

14 Marner 2000.

15 As Harrison 1994 has shown, one aisle had its east end painted with sumptuous scenes that copy the arrangement of statues and other decorations at the high altar. The Galilee was also to become the setting for a separate shrine to St Bede and the chantry chapel of Bishop Langley, who greatly refurbished it.

16 Tudor 1994.

17 Quotes and description from the twelfth-century monks Simeon of Durham and Reginald of Durham in Simeon 1993, 779–85; Battiscombe 1956.

18 From now on, the bones of lesser saints would be displayed separately; only the head of St Oswald would be kept inside Cuthbert's coffin.

19 This alone made the church look very different from how it does now, but eighteenth-century restorers have also literally shaved 8 cm of surface from the entire exterior.

20 Thurlby 1994; Fernie 2000.

21 There was also the enormous new monks' dormitory at Canterbury cathedral, on to the columns of which ungainly zigzags were carved.

22 Park and Howard 1996.

23 Other rib vaults appear in northern Italy at almost exactly the same time. Durham's earliest high vaults have not survived: perhaps as a result of their experimental engineering, they threatened to collapse by the early thirteenth century. But the choir aisle rib vaults are original, and the high vault design was continued, improved in detail and unchanged in its essentials, in the nave.

24 Fernie 1994 and 2000; Perkins 1952.

25 It is probably the book described in the *Rites of Durham* (Anon 1998).

26 Barrow 1994; Matthew 1994.

27 Marner 2000.

28 For this period and its context, see Rollason et al 1994, especially contributions by Matthew, Barrow, Wall, Dalton and Aird.

29 Tynemouth was given, rather impractically, to St Albans in 1093.

30 Barlow 2004c.

31 An attempt to emphasize the ritual purity of the reformed community. Women who approached his church, it was said, suffered appalling fates. Foster 1994.

32 Durham stands with Ely, Canterbury and Winchester as the most popular bishopric to give to a chancellor or treasurer of the realm.

33 In 1827 and 1899. Material additional to Anon 1998 is in Battiscombe 1956.

34 Flanagan 1946.

ELY

1 There are Burwells in both Lincolnshire and Suffolk.

2 The lantern was as good as rebuilt in 1862–3, so it is just possible someone did so then.

3 Purcell 1973.

4 'Roscarius' was his title. Lindley 1985.

5 The Ely sacrist effectively governed the city parishes of Ely and had the responsibilities of an archdeacon in the Isle. Ibid.

6 Ibid. The exchequer was where clerks could count cash in and out. The complex remains a conspicuous part of central Ely. It has been speculated that both Bishop Salmon of Norwich and Alan of Walsingham had a special connection with the goldsmithing family: Salmon's surname and Ely origin imply that he may have been born into the dynasty, while Alan's known skill in the craft and the attention he gave its practitioners in his own office complex are also suggestive.

7 At the time of the Domesday survey it was the second richest in the country after Glastonbury.

8 Details from Salzman 1948; Lindley 1985. Priors attended late thirteenth-century Parliaments and were mitred from 1413. Crauden's chapel, completed in 1324–5, survives.

9 Hotham perhaps earned about £3,000 a year.

10 A colony of Oxford that, unlike Northampton, Salisbury and Stamford, survived.

11 Bede, quoted in Keynes 2003, 3.

12 Salzman 1948.

13 As the twelfth-century chronicle of Crowland abbey put it: Salzman 1948, 386.

14 Ibid, 389.

15 The other female saints of this book, Frideswide of Oxford and Werburgh of Chester, both contemporaries of Etheldreda – not to mention the obscure Osburga of Coventry and even more obscure Eadburh of Southwell – were the saints of abbeys (or in Southwell's case a collegiate church), not cathedrals.

16 Keynes 2003, 13. Historical material on pre-Conquest Ely is from this source unless cited otherwise.

17 Bede's stories of her life were told him by her mentor St Wilfrid himself.

18 Etheldreda and her companions were all descendants of the East Anglian King Anna: Binski 2004.

19 Although these privileges were said to go back to the days of Etheldreda herself, there is no record of them before Edgar's time.

20 Burning the abbey that is now Peterborough cathedral.

21 Prior to this there had been one short Norman abbacy followed by a period when there was no formal abbot.

22 Fernie 2003. The building break is in the transepts.

23 Instead it cultivated a long friendship with the neighbouring East Anglian sees – two bishops of Elmham were buried there – and for a period in the eleventh century even kept a kind of 'pet' bishop in-house, a retired native of Bremen with a rather shaky claim to episcopal status.

24 The process is described in Owen 2004a.

25 Hervey was a Breton; he had been bishop of Bangor but the rebellious Welsh were too much for him.

26 Etheldreda was translated into the completed choir in 1106.

27 Maddison 2003. It is romanesque at the base, turning more gothic as it goes up, and may originally have been topped with a pyramidal spire.

28 Such strapping glories, if of rather different design, once also stood at Lincoln, and perhaps – depending partly on how one defines the term 'westwork' – at Hereford and Winchester.

29 Bishop Eustace died in 1215 and is remembered as the builder of the porch, but stylistically it must be later: Maddison 2003.

30 Matthew Paris, quoted in Owen 2004b.

31 Matthew Paris, quoted in Draper 1979, 8, also the source for subsequent details. Translation by Kirstie Young.

32 Both the Angel Choir at Lincoln and the New Work at St Paul's are among buildings which imitated this idea.

33 Draper 1979.

34 The two careers are compared in Lindley 1985; also Buck 2004a and 2004c.

35 Lindley 1985 points out how decisively this appears to have been done.

36 They were stored there by the monks of St Albans when they were threatened by the Danes; Ely claimed to have returned someone else's bones instead.

37 Salzman 1948; Lindley 1985.

38 This took place in February 1322: MacDowdy 1974. Lindley 1985 wonders if the idea for the Octagon already existed, at least in someone's head. The monks had anticipated the collapse, moving their services into a side chapel before it occurred: they would have been foolish not at least to consider what to do when it happened. It is not known how badly damaged the replaced bays of the choir, transepts and nave actually were.

39 Coldstream 1979.

40 Just the same thing was happening at the same time at Wells, between Dean de Godley and Bishop Droxford, and at Canterbury with Prior Eastry.

41 'By means of which barrier the monks shall be concealed and protected from ill-intended interruption': Lindley 1985; translation by Kirstie Jackson.

42 Coldstream 1979; see Lincoln and Southwell.

43 Arguably more stable, too.

44 Rich possibilities explored thus far by Lindley 1985 and 1995; Maddison 2000a.

45 Quite literally: the whole thing rests by its own weight on the lip of the octagonal walls.

46 He was also paid a further £1 a year to make return visits with an eye to the structure's long-term stability (and to complete the choir-stalls).

47 As one of Ely's monks wrote. More wood came from the Baltic via the Wash.

48 Over twenty years; the choir cost £2,034

12s 8¾d; among the other buildings, Prior Crauden's chapel cost £138 8s 5d. Lindley 1985.
49 Probably: Dixon 2003.
50 All from Lindley 1985. By then Ely had begun to purchase new lands too.
51 That is, in its peculiarly divisive cathedral priory form: non-cathedral monasteries are another matter.
52 Signs of working stopping and starting in both choir and lady chapel suggest resources being moved from one part of the site to another.
53 Maddison 2003.
54 In 1405–7 the arches that supported it were shored up.
55 For more detail on the buildings see Schoeck 2004a; also Maddison 2000a, 2003.
56 Maddison 2000a.
57 Ibid.
58 Cult details from Nilson 1998. The two most important fairs were around 23 June and 8–13 September; income from one benefited the bishop and the other the monastery.
59 Salzman 1948, 207.
60 The Octagon was studded with images, only fragments of which survive. They included many images of now-forgotten Anglo-Saxon figures, yet another reminder of how seriously Ely took its history. The subject is also reflected in its long history of deriving architectural inspiration from its own past: Lindley 1986; Maddison 2003.
61 Lindley 1985.
62 Nilson 1998; Maddison 2000a.

EXETER

1 Stratford 1991, 146.
2 Morris 1991, 79.
3 Stratford 1991.
4 Sinclair 1991.
5 Though buildings like the Ely lady chapel better show the flowing lines that resulted as the ogee arch took over in the early decades of the fourteenth century.
6 Carlisle was not yet founded.
7 Thurlby 1991a and b. Others, including Fernie 2000 and Pevsner and Cherry 1989, see the towers as keep-like structures, not open to the church. The presence of an entrance arch of some kind is hard to disprove, and made more likely by the presence of eastern chapels in the towers themselves.
8 Thurmer 1991.
9 Beacham 1991. It pre-dates the great run of polygonal secular cathedral chapter-houses, though those of Lincoln and perhaps Lichfield probably existed by this date. With their rectangular chapter-house and unusually early secular cathedral cloister, the canons' buildings at Exeter have an unusually monastic quality that perhaps reflects the cathedral's constitution.
10 Thurmer 1991.
11 Most other examples taxed the chapter between one-tenth and one-fifth, and for a

fixed time period.
12 Erskine 1981, 1983, 1991a and b.
13 The lack of a crossing must in itself have provided a powerful impetus not to change the church's design between east end and nave.
14 To paraphrase Binski 2004.
15 Erskine 1982, 1983, 1991a and b.
16 Morris 1991; see the feretory screen at Winchester.
17 What may be a fragment survives in the chapel of St Andrew and St Catherine: the sedilia and Stapeldon tomb are in many ways extensions of the original reredos.
18 Eddie Sinclair, pers. comm.
19 Jansen 1991. It was done by altering the window splays and carving arches into the bare wall surface.
20 Sekules 1991a and b; Tudor-Craig 1991.
21 Sekules 1991a and b; Tudor-Craig 1991.
22 For no one could be certain that, of the over-hyped bishops of Hereford, Norwich, Wells and Worcester then also having their cases heard in Rome, only one would ever be canonized.
23 He moved around Europe on missions for the king in the 1310s, and did not miss a single Parliament from 1313 until the end of his life. Buck 2004d.
24 Buck 2004d: he had written a letter – famous among constitutional historians – advising the king not to fly in the teeth of a Parliamentary decision.
25 Erskine 1983.
26 Buck 2004d; Boggis 1922.
27 His older brother may have been the driving force behind the east end at what is now Bristol cathedral.
28 Sekules 1991a and b.
29 This tomb is usually said to be that of Stapeldon's brother, but its unusual design makes one wonder whether the subject merits further investigation.
30 Erskine 2004.
31 Sekules 1991a and b; Tudor-Craig 1991.
32 Sinclair 1991; Sekules 1991a and b; Tudor-Craig 1991.
33 Coldstream 1991, 205.
34 The north porch has much of the energy-filled oddness familiar from his designs at Ottery St Mary and elsewhere.
35 Allen and Blaylock 1991. This design would have made the west front a diminutive equivalent of Peterborough and Lincoln rather than (as it is now) of Wells and Salisbury. One could of course see the architecture of Exeter as an attempt to apply the idea behind the Wells west front – architecture dramatizing liturgy – to an entire church.
36 J Cherry 1991, 205.
37 With much less good reason, many other west fronts were left without statues installed – Salisbury and Lincoln, for example.
38 B Cherry 1991a; Brooks 1991b.
39 Brooks 1991b.
40 Brooks 1991a.
41 The contemporary Exeter historian John

Hooker, in Orme 2004b.
42 Youings 1991.
43 Erskine 1991b.
44 To stretch a metaphor in Swanton 1991a.

GLOUCESTER

1 Worcester and Bath also claim to have been founded by Osric. All three were Roman cities, yet it was at Gloucester (rather than the cathedral at Worcester) that Osric was buried.
2 A practice continued by the Normans at Winchester – there, the cathedral was partly designed as the venue for the event – though at Gloucester it is not clear whether the venue was St Peter's or a royal palace.
3 It has even been argued that the crypt is a late and very up-to-date Anglo-Saxon building rather than a Norman one: Fernie 1982.
4 From a history of the abbey known as the *Historiola*, written around 1400. Other medieval quotes are from this source unless cited otherwise. Welander 1991, 604.
5 Bates 1984
6 Wilson 1985, as are uncited further references to Serlo's architecture.
7 It is even possible that Herbert de Losinga, bishop of Hereford, played a role: Wilson 1985.
8 The evidence for these vaults is enjoyably contradictory: Wilson 1985 argues in their favour; Thurlby 1985 (in the same volume) argues against their existence. St Albans is the only surviving English church known to have already had a high choir vault; Durham and perhaps Lincoln early in the twelfth century were among the first anywhere to be stone-vaulted throughout.
9 Wilson 1985. Chapels with polygonal ends appear to have been a local Anglo-Saxon practice (e.g. at Deerhurst), also revived at Worcester.
10 Welander 1991. The columns were found in excavations in Westgate Street; the columns of the nave are 9.6 metres high. There is no way of knowing if they were visible in *c*. 1100.
11 In 1239.
12 The screen has clearly come from somewhere else, appears to have the characteristics of a pulpitum screen and would fit in the nave. Moreover, the nave pulpitum screen was replaced during the fourteenth-century choir rebuild – a perfect time for this one to be moved to the north transept, which was refurbished as a late part of the same campaign.
13 The fact that the figure is holding a church indicates that it is meant to be the church's founder. It could be Abbot Foliot, in charge of these works, but Serlo is a more obvious figure to be evoked in such terms. Welander 1991; Bazeley 1882–3.
14 Page 1907b.
15 Especially towards the east.
16 Winchcombe, Tewkesbury and Bristol, for

example.

17 The nave problems were caused by poor backfilling of the vallum of the Roman city, which runs beneath it. But this may be coincidental: Richard Morris has shown (1997; Morris and Shoesmith 2003) that the Bristol and Tewkesbury east ends also began at the south-west corner of the east end. The incentive to focus on this part of the building first at Gloucester was even greater, as it overlooked the lay cemetery and the approach from the city, to which the south transept contains a small but remarkable door.

18 The story that the body was first refused by the abbeys at Malmesbury and Bristol is now thought to be a later invention.

19 Quotes from *Historiola* in Welander 1991, 146.

20 Welander 1991. Quote is from the *Historiola* in Luxford 2005, 151, who gives further details about objects given to the tomb. The golden boat valued at £100 was displayed with pride above it (the bracket is still there).

21 Ashwell 1985. This kind of self-conscious reuse of older architecture was common at the period, but Gloucester is an extreme example.

22 *Historiola* in Welander 1991, 165.

23 Such as the Ste-Chapelle in Paris and St Stephen's chapel at the palace of Westminster.

24 Kerr 1985. The top now contains a later image of a pope (Welander 1985). It is often said that the aristocratic shields relate to comrades-in-arms at a specific battle; but these families were closely linked to many of the key events of the fourteenth century. More interesting is the political context at a time when Edward III was using techniques political and cultural to reinforce the bonds between Crown and barons after the disastrous end to his father's reign.

25 The cost to the convent was £781 0s 2d (Luxford 2005); the resulting total cost of over £1,200 seems enormous considering the project itself was a recasing rather than a rebuilding.

26 The east walk was already complete in 1377 and the rest finished off – with unusual rapidity for a cloister – by 1412.

27 The technique was at first restricted to the West Country and there almost entirely to small-scale settings: Leedy 1978 and 1980. It is not certain that the Hereford chapter-house was in fact fan vaulted.

28 All Welander 1991.

29 Luxford 2005. Abbot Seabroke's tiles can still be seen in the choir gallery, when it is open to the public. It seems Abbot Morwent's death was all that prevented the complete rebuilding of the nave.

30 Much like King John at Worcester.

31 Luxford 2005. It would no longer do only to have the effigy of a monk-founder (Serlo) on display…

32 Also known as Malvern.

33 Luxford 2005, 122.

34 The small chantry chapel of Abbot Seabroke in the south nave aisle was built around the time of his death and contains his body – the basic expectations one would normally have of a tomb.

35 Some have argued that he was in fact spirited away to become a hermit in northern Italy, in which case the shrine-like design is a bare-faced lie: without relics, a shrine is nothing.

HEREFORD

1 Facts and figures about Cantilupe's cult are from Finucane (1977, 1982a and 1982b) unless cited otherwise.

2 Bede says the area was evangelized mid-century; 676 is the traditional but unproven date for the creation of a bishopric. Worcester, in another edge-of-Mercia sub-kingdom, was founded at about the same time.

3 Keynes 2000; Jancey 1994.

4 Shoesmith 2000; Boüker 1998.

5 He may have played a role in the rebuilding of St Peter's, Gloucester (Gloucester cathedral), whose architecture has much in common with his palace chapel, and at the dedication of which he played a key role.

6 With Exeter, another diocese on the western fringes; it is the last of the 'Norman' cathedral rebuilds.

7 Thurlby 1995.

8 Their work can be seen in a group of churches, especially Kilpeck, along the Welsh borders.

9 Only the crypt added to St Paul's later in the thirteenth century is later. Hereford's is also the only crypt to be purely beneath a lady chapel. Possible functions include as the site of a parish altar for those who lived in the close; as an attempt to reinvigorate the cult of St Ethelbert (a biography of whom had been commissioned from Gerald of Wales in the 1190s, in spite of the lack of any relics); or as some kind of evocation of a space known to have existed in the lost Saxon church.

10 Canon Simon de Freine in Burnett 1995, 7.

11 Residency peaked during the cathedral's thirteenth- and fourteenth-century heyday: Barrow 2000.

12 Burnett 1995.

13 Southern 2004.

14 Barrow 2000.

15 All from Vincent 2004a.

16 Incidentally obliging the canons to contribute to future building works.

17 Barrow in Aylmer 2000; Vincent 2004a. Two-thirds of his thirty appointments to chapter came from Savoy, causing widespread bad feeling.

18 Which as a result practised the Use of Hereford for many centuries.

19 Morris 2000.

20 Gardner 1995 claims he asked to be buried in Savoy only; his eventual burial site caused dismay there and about 200 years later the canons of Aigueblanche created a founder's tomb. Morris 2000, Vincent 2004a.

21 Cantilupe biography from Finucane 1982a, 1982b and 2004; Martin 1982. His brothers also had senior roles nearby, at Brecon and Gloucester.

22 So as to separate the bones from the flesh.

23 Thirteen out of 205 respondents: Finucane 1977.

24 The tomb-shrine has a miniature arcade around the top, inviting the insertion of ailing limbs and visual comparison with shrines. The knights who surround the base may be Templars, the order of which Cantilupe was provincial grand master, though they may also form a generalized reminder that he died, in the view of the Hereford community at least, defending the Church.

25 Accounts of Cantilupe's cult and its development are Finucane 1977 and 1982a, based on his analysis of the voluminous canonization records in Rome. It seems to me that evidence for it being manufactured is strong.

26 The bishop of Lincoln had tried to quash pilgrimages to one unauthorized site.

27 An estimate based on figures for offerings at the shrines in Worcester cathedral, known to have been due to traffic on its way to Hereford: Finucane 1982a.

28 Full details are in Nilson 1998.

29 Architecture: Morris 1974, 2000: he shows that offerings were £178 10s 7d, plus £30 15s from an alms box; the fabric fund income that year was £286 18s 5d. See Coldstream 2000 and Lindley 1995 for more on architecture; Finucane 1977 and 1982a for the spread of the cult.

30 There were 160 recorded miracles in 1287; 34 in 1288; 9 in 1300; 1 in 1312. Finucane 1977.

31 Barrett 1982.

32 Morgan 1982.

33 Morris 1974, 2000.

34 Morris 1985.

35 Hoskin 2004b.

36 Morris 2000 is hesitant. Only a vault springer survives from the work commissioned from Thomas Cambridge in 1364, and the reconstruction drawing done by Stukeley in 1721 may be rather imaginative.

37 Shoesmith 2000, 307.

38 Morris 2000.

39 Barrett 1982.

40 Bailey 1993. The central part of the map's altar-like setting still survives – indeed it was only identified recently, and its design is very close to Hereford architecture of the early fourteenth century.

41 It has even been suggested that Hereford was inked in after the *Mappa* arrived there. There are various connections between Hereford and Lincoln: Swinfield himself had been at Lincoln before he became bishop (Reed Kline 2003). For more on the *Mappa* (apart from works already cited) see Westrem 2001, Harvey 2000, and much else.

LICHFIELD

1 Maddison 1993a, 80. Translation by Kirstie Jackson.
2 Haines 2004b.
3 It was only thirteen years old.
4 For sixteen years, from 785 to 801.
5 Another possible original location for this precious manuscript is the high altar.
6 Kettle and Johnson 1970.
7 Franklin 1994.
8 First in high romanesque and then in early gothic, the latter still visible in the choir aisles and the transepts; further east all the chapels were squared off.
9 Lincoln is probably a few years earlier.
10 The chapter eventually grew to thirty-five or so.
11 Rodwell 1989, 1993, 1996. It perhaps included both vestries and a cathedral court (Kettle and Johnson 1970). One turret had a well at its base. St Chad's head shrine was later in the upper storey. A monument to a dean is a very rare thing at this date: this may be the earliest in any English cathedral. 'Monuments in the wall' are a rather curious Lichfield theme, perhaps arising from the slope on which the church is built.
12 Influence here from both Westminster abbey and the Angel Choir. The nave is vaulted, and the early gothic east end almost certainly was too, so the entire church was now vaulted in stone.
13 Biographical details from Haines 2004b.
14 Watling Street, the main road to northern Wales, went right by the city; the armies mustered at Chester, in the north of the diocese.
15 Licence to crenellate the close was granted in 1299; some turrets were over 18 metres high: Maddison 1993a.
16 Tringham 1993.
17 Colvin et al 1963.
18 As the antiquarian Sampson Erdeswick put it when he saw them in 1590: Tringham 1993.
19 The king's son had long held a grudge against the bishop, who had been a critic of his relationship with Piers Gaveston.
20 Maddison 1993a. As well as a gold chalice, two phials (worth £80), and a bejewelled gold cross (worth £200): Haines 2004b.
21 Without their presence our pilgrims of 1323 would surely not have described the church as having 'the loftiest and most noble of belfries'. Morris 1994 explores the architectural relationship with Coventry.
22 And to the Royal Ste-Chapelle in Paris, inspiration for St Stephen's chapel.
23 Though in spite of the bishop's foothold there, the County Palatine was often semi-detached from episcopal authority.
24 See Wells and Salisbury.
25 Probably built by Bishop Streeton sometime in the period 1360–86: Pevsner and Metcalf 1985, II.
26 Cocke 1993.

LINCOLN

1 Adam of Eynsham, Hugh's biographer, who witnessed many of these events. Douie and Farmer 1961, II, 219–29.
2 By 1500 (Bowker 1968): presumably rather fewer in 1200. Quote is from Douie and Farmer 1961, II, 93.
3 Leyser 1987. Other biographical details from Douie and Farmer 1961 and Mayr-Harting 2004.
4 At Witham in Somerset, where part of the monastery he built remains as the parish church.
5 Douie and Farmer 1961, II, 190.
6 Quotes from the description of his cathedral written by Hugh d'Avranches in the *Metrical Life of St Hugh*, c. 1220. Garton 1986, 56–7.
7 Park 1986.
8 Long held to be Geoffrey de Noiers, though Draper 2006a points out that this individual may have been a canon in charge of project management rather than a master-mason.
9 Draper 2006a; Douie and Farmer 1961, I (Introduction); Hill 1948.
10 Page 1906a, 83.
11 Douie and Farmer 1961, I, 140; II, 174–84.
12 Including a former lecturer at the university of Paris and the famous author Gerald of Wales: Binski 2004.
13 The magnificent oaks in the roof above the vault were felled in 1202–3.
14 Douie and Farmer 1961, II, 225, 228, 232. The crowd had included 'three kings, three archbishops, nine bishops and 200 or more nobles and magnates; a throng of abbots and a crowd of priors'.
15 Kidson 1986 and 1994; Draper 2006a.
16 Binski 1997. Both contain medieval glass.
17 Fragments of names painted either side of the ridge rib seem to evoke the lay great and good of the area, including two mayors of Lincoln. Draper 2006a.
18 Garton 1986, 57–8. The ridge rib was not invented at Lincoln (Jenny Alexander, pers. comm.) but it is in the nave vault that its aesthetic potential is first fully displayed. It was to become a standard feature of all English vaults.
19 The date when oaks, presumably for the roof, were left by the then bishop in his will. The eastern chapels were being completed in c. 1228–30. Draper 2006a.
20 He received his first employment in the see during St Hugh's episcopacy. Details of his life are from Southern 2004.
21 Quotes from the *Anglia Sacra*, quoted in Page 1906a; life is from Southern 2004.
22 Draper 2006a wonders if the Galilee porch was built under Grosseteste.
23 Owen 1994b.
24 Indeed the pope had already been 'got at' by the Templars of his diocese.
25 Southern 2004.
26 Matthew Paris in Southern 2004.
27 Which – when built – was unusually shrine-like in design: Stocker 1986b.
28 Lorrey 2004a.
29 If indeed it had ever stopped.
30 An enormous crack is still visible in the roof

space, showing how the building slumps as it crosses the vallum of the Roman wall – Jenny Alexander, pers. comm.
31 For the rest of the thirteenth century, and into the next, every new bishop was elected by the chapter from within the cathedral's ranks, rather than being imposed by the king or the pope: an exceptional fact for such a wealthy institution.
32 Technically the 'choir' is the remaining part of Hugh's east end, and the Angel Choir is a multi-purpose space for the high altar, shrines and lady altar.
33 Binksi 1997.
34 Nilson 1998.
35 Ibid.
36 The former by the high altar, the latter in the south-east transept.
37 Ely and Canterbury had more saints, but – apart from Becket's – their relics were all ancient.
38 Binski 1997.
39 One of the most complete displays of thirteenth-century sculpture in England, it is just the kind of door that Hugh had praised to King John some sixty years earlier.
40 Vaughan 1984, 39; Roberts 1986; Stocker 1986b.
41 As Canon John de Schalby wrote, Srawley 1966, 12.
42 Stocker 1986b.
43 Nilson 1998.
44 Owen 1971, 126; Binski 1997.
45 Suggested as the likely location in Kidson 1994.
46 In two intense bursts, about 1296 and 1307.
47 Sekules 1986.
48 And the carved gallery of kings over the west door.
49 His body was buried at Eton, where he was probably educated, and his heart before the cathedral high altar.
50 As the Lincoln canon Henry of Huntingdon put it in the twelfth century. Gem 1986, 9.
51 Such as at York (Southwell, Ripon and Beverley), Lichfield (St John's, Chester) and Exeter (Glasney, Crediton and Ottery St Mary). The bishops had a 'special relationship' with the abbeys of Stow and Eynsham.
52 As the Italian Bishop Gigli of Worcester told Cardinal Wolsey: Bowker 1968, 7. There were fewer absentee bishops than at, say, Winchester or Durham; and a sophisticated group of suffragans and vicars-general evolved to ensure diocesan work was supported.

NORWICH

1 Dodwell 1996a; Wollaston 1996. The meeting was described in the First Register, 150 years after it was said to have taken place.
2 Historical material for the period, and the planning of the precinct: Fernie 1993; B S Ayers 1996; Gilchrist 2005.
3 The complex story of pre-Conquest East Anglian cathedrals includes periods when both Suffolk and Norfolk had cathedrals of their own, and a century or so after the

beginning of Danish invasions in which there may have been no bishops at all. Scholars still argue over the location some of East Anglia's early cathedrals.

4 The bishop's lands at Thetford itself were never firmly in his hands.

5 De Losinga: Atherton et al 1996, especially Wollaston 1996; Harper-Bill 2004a.

6 Quoted by William of Malmesbury: Wollaston 1996.

7 Or sometimes, until about 1103, 'bishop of Norwich and Thetford'.

8 Harper-Bill 2004a.

9 De Losinga erected a cross on the edge of his lands as 'a cautionary landmark': Fernie 1993, 163.

10 Wollaston 1996, 32–3.

11 De Losinga also rebuilt the chapels at his manors of North and South Elmham, at least one of which had been the site of an Anglo-Saxon cathedral.

12 Franklin 1996. Only a few battered carvings survive.

13 We know the roof was designed to be open, rather than ceiled, because certain paint and architectural features appear designed to be seen through the timbers.

14 Park and Howard 1996.

15 For the architecture, Fernie 1993; various essays in Atherton et al 1996; Gilchrist 2005.

16 Gilchrist 2005. Compare the Lincoln west front (Chapter 2). Elsewhere in the precinct he avoided demolishing old churches, even as he flattened the city centre itself.

17 Some of this is a late addition, perhaps in time for the consecration of Eborard in 1121.

18 Dodwell 1996a; Preface in Atherton et al 1996. The synods, at least, may have been held in the nave by the mid-twelfth century.

19 Gilchrist 2005.

20 Anglo-Scandinavian law in one part of the city, Norman-French law in the other.

21 Lorrey 2004b; Jessop and James 1896.

22 Jessop and James 1896. Thomas of Monmouth's account is partisan, as are all saints' Lives. It was written about fifteen years after the events.

23 Ninepence in 1304–5; twopence in 1363–4; there was a brief late medieval revival when Norwich's guild of pelterers adopted William as a patron. Nilson 1998.

24 Park and Howard 1996.

25 The one there now was built in 1930–2. Fernie 1993 demonstrated that Suffield's plans went much further.

26 Accounts from Tanner 1996; Fernie 1993; Page 1906b.

27 Tanner 1996, 259–60.

28 Gilchrist 2005. The Treasury Arch in the north choir aisle is often assumed to be a place of secure storage, hastily created in the wake of the riots; but Park and Howard 1996 demonstrate that the earliest phase of its magnificent wall paintings pre-dates 1272.

29 Cotton also wrote the First Register of the cathedral, from which much of the cathedral's earlier history is drawn. As in many cathedrals at a moment of triumph

or crisis, the cathedral archives, which included all that body's property claims, were comprehensively reclassified and reordered at around this time: Tanner 1996.

30 A cult was focused on his tomb after his death.

31 Its significance revealed by Gilchrist 2005.

32 Lindley 1985; translation by Kirstie Jackson.

33 Fernie 1993.

34 For example, only slit windows face onto the city. Gilchrist 2005 suggests that the 'citizen' is St George.

35 Gilchrist 2005, 34.

36 Ibid.

37 For the cloister, see Fernie 1993; Woodman 1996, Rose 1996, Sekules 1996 (all in Atherton et al 1996); Gilchrist 2005. The east walk was their route to their church, chapter-house, cemetery and infirmary, and the apartments of the prior.

38 Woodman 1996.

39 Sekules 1996.

40 Rose 1996; Woodman 1996.

41 Woodman 1996.

42 King 1996. It may be, of course, that these men were also connected in many other ways.

43 Sekules 1996; Gilchrist 2005. The latter questions the gate's association with Erpingham

44 Tanner 1996, 264ff is the main source, quoting three contemporary accounts.

45 One met in the Carnary chapel and another had a hall in the cemetery itself.

46 Page 1906b; Rose 1997. The venues of specific plays are unknown.

47 Schoeck 2004b, rendering his name 'Lyhert'.

48 High stone vaults were invented in the mid-eleventh century to make east ends grander; no one had vaulted a cathedral nave before its east end before (though Winchester, another Perpendicular nave, may be an exception). See Chapter three. Alnwick began work on the west front before 1436 – that is, before the riots – but his window is post-1449 and Lyhart's vault is later, probably about 1454–60 (Woodman 1996). Fires did their damage towards the east of the nave and in the east end but not, it seems, to the nave proper.

49 Rose 1996.

50 Ibid.

51 Woodman 1996.

52 Tanner 1996.

53 Gilchrist 2005.

54 Houlbrooke 1996, 507.

OXFORD

1 Twelfth-century account adapted from Blair 1987, with interpretation of the landscape based on Blair 1990b and c.

2 Bampton and Oxford were both sites of Anglo-Saxon minsters; Binsey still has Frideswide's chapel and well; Oxford remains a gravelly floodplain pierced by watery tributaries of the Thames, albeit one with some very urbane buildings on top

of it.

3 It probably first acquired some kind of urban character as part of Alfred's great wave of 'burgh' planning.

4 As a centre of population that was still close to the cathedral's lands – compare Chichester – Oxford would have made a reasonable alternative location.

5 Blair 1990b; Halsey 1990.

6 Halsey 1990; Blair 1990b. He had to move Oxford's city wall several metres towards the Thames to make room for them. The chapter-house door of the 1140s or 1150s, tinged red by a fire of 1190, remains from this campaign.

7 Page 1907c. Geoffrey of Monmouth was the historian and rediscoverer/reinventor of King Arthur, who was on the staff of St George's collegiate chapel in Oxford castle.

8 Robert of Cricklade in A J Duggan 2004.

9 Blair 1990b.

10 All suggestions about the previous church are based on very fragmentary archaeology: Sturdy 1990; Blair 1990b. The 'Frideswide chapel' may have been centralized, perhaps in imitation of the Tomb of the Virgin in the Holy Land. Double-aisled transepts are rare even in the greatest cathedrals: St Frideswide's southern transept only had aisles because the north one did, strongly suggesting that the saint is the cause of the expansion.

11 Account in Blair 1987, 117. Story: Crossley 1979; A J Duggan 2004.

12 He visited Scotland in the 1160s; he may have written a life of St Magnus of Orkney; his most famous (though lost) work, a Life of Becket, got as far as Iceland, where it was turned into the Thomas Saga; King Malcolm of Scotland gave land to far-off St Frideswide's. It is probably a coincidence that Jedburgh abbey in Scotland has another example of the 'giant order' motif. Page 1907c; Halsey 1990; A J Duggan 2004.

13 St Frideswide's was the last attempt at such an elevation before the 'real' Renaissance of the eighteenth century.

14 Sermon by Alexander Neckham in Blair 1990a, 134.

15 Page 1907c.

16 Ashdown et al 1990.

17 Morris 1990a.

18 Page 1907c.

19 The medieval phrase: Salter and Lobel 1954; examples in Crossley 1979.

20 Walcot 1879.

21 Halsey 1996. Orchard: Crossley 1979.

22 It has long been assumed to be by Orchard himself.

23 Blair 1990b.

24 Biddle 1990. A wooden belfry was built in the cloister for the bells, the spire was about to come down, and there would be little left of St Frideswide's but rubble had work gone on much longer.

25 The college's endowment of £2,000, though

smaller than that planned by Wolsey, still made it richer than some cathedrals.

26 Halsey 1990. The shrine was put back together and re-erected, in a rough approximation of its most recent location.

PETERBOROUGH

1 Reilly 1997. Most uncredited historical and architectural material is from this source, and quotes are from the Peterborough version of the Anglo-Saxon Chronicle.
2 Mackreth 1999.
3 Reilly 1997. It was the tenth richest in England at Domesday.
4 Roffe 2004 .Their excuse? 'The local people expected that he would be king'.
5 Ibid.
6 Reilly 1997, 46–7.
7 'He swore in after times that they had done this of good intentions, because he supposed they were conquering King William and would themselves possess the land': ibid, 47.
8 Higham 1999.
9 'Gunton' in Serjeantson et al 1906, 86.
10 Whose monuments include the magnificent crypt at Canterbury.
11 As the prior of Christ Church Canterbury was effectively abbot of England's chief monastery and the bishop of Rochester was a deputy to the archbishop, these are more or less sideways moves.
12 Serjeantson et al 1906. It was said that only the chapter-house and the dormitory survived.
13 Reilly argues that the scale of the fire was exaggerated and that the current church was begun by Ernulf. What is certain is that either he or his successor began it sometime between 1107 and 1118.
14 Higham 1999. It was in existence by 1174.
15 Nilson 1998. The flagstones were used as altarpieces.
16 These bays respect the romanesque design.
17 Reilly 1997, 59. The blind pointed arches intended to frame Benedict's vault can still be seen above the romanesque ones of the nave clerestory.
18 The connection to the interdict is my suggestion: the building is undated, though the details in the gables look to me like work of the 1190s or 1200s and the overall composition and most of the arches a decade or so later, which fits.
19 In the fourteenth century great white banners bearing a red cross were hung from them. The Lincoln west front, which also features a great row of arches, might have been designed for comparable rites.
20 Serjeantson et al 1906.
21 Mackreth 1999; Higham 1999.
22 Higham 1999.
23 Mackreth 1999.
24 The current tower is nineteenth-century.
25 It may have had a liturgical function – see above – but it may also have been intended to buttress an arch which still leans outwards by 0.6 metres.

26 Higham 1999.
27 Ibid.
28 Peterborough had got through 400 years without any expansion eastwards. Only Norwich can compare. Yet it never even had an ambulatory. Kirkton's east end has images of the Passion in its bosses, and three altars here also had Passion themes: it was probably simply intended to provide extra altar spaces.
29 On the north side of the presbytery; Mary Queen of Scots was later buried on the south side, before being moved to Westminster abbey by James I.
30 The fine set of monuments to twelfth-century abbots may not be in their original locations, though their grouping between St Oswald's shrine, the site of which in the north transept is marked by a shrine-watcher's tower, and the high altar makes sense.

RIPON

1 Bailey 1996.
2 Hearn 1983.
3 Bailey 1996. The story is first recorded in the sixteenth century. A collapsed alcove was seen in the nineteenth century, when piles of what may have been relic deposits were also found.
4 The argument of the Canterbury hagiographer Eadmer. Note that York was not the seat of an archbishop until 735.
5 Page 1913; Forster et al 1993.
6 All Forster et al 1993.
7 Page 1913.
8 Forster et al 1993. Most uncited historical material is from this source.
9 Hearn 1983.
10 Or just after. Fountains had then only been in existence for two years.
11 The Canterbury east end was itself modelled on Archbishop Roger's east end at York, and the role of St Wilfrid's crypt (and shrine above?) in the Ripon design is thus circumstantial evidence for the cult of St William having played a role in that of the York east end.
12 The location is identical to that of the tomb-shrine of St William in York, but it is unclear whether this would have been seen as a shrine when Roger began his building work at Ripon (or indeed at York). William was buried in 1154, but there is no evidence for a cult before at least 1177 or even 1220.
13 In 1296: Pevsner and Metcalf 1985, II.
14 Only the well-carved bosses survive; the rest is Victorian. Other fragments from this period include the ornate sedilia and fine pieces of stained glass gathered together in a window in the nave.
15 As the archbishop of York put it: Forster et al 1993, 11.
16 The canons voted half their common fund to the fabric in 1477.
17 He conveniently carved the earlier date at one end of the work and the later one at

the other.
18 Ripon's own account: Forster et al 1993.
19 Leland, quoted in ibid, 11.
20 Still in the see of York, despite being surrounded by the new see of Chester.
21 Sketches of where the next layer of worked stones was to be fitted are etched into its upper surface, invisible except from above.

ROCHESTER

1 Brett 1996. Small dioceses were also commonplace in Augustine's native Italy. Fragments relating to the Anglo-Saxon cathedral have been found outside the west end of the cathedral.
2 McAleer 1999.
3 Lanfranc's obituary in Flight 1997, 179.
4 Greatrex 2006.
5 The main proponent of this (Flight 1997) calls the result 'de-Gundulfisation'.
6 Plant 2006. The contradictory conclusions of McAleer 1999 and Flight 1997, both of whom rejected much of what had previously been written about Gundulf's church, appear to have been resolved by this work. It is a mark of the rude good health of medieval architectural history that no fewer than three major studies of a small building that disappeared 800 years ago have been published in just over a decade.
7 Other works attributed to him include Rochester castle itself (one of the earliest of Norman stone keeps), the nave of Malling abbey, and the chancel of St Margaret at Darenth. For more detail see McAleer 1999.
8 For example at Sainte-Gertrude, Nivelles, Belgium: Plant 2006.
9 It occurs in a rather different form in Bishop Roger's twelfth-century east end at Old Sarum.
10 Indeed it is hard to see how its east end worked, given that it allows little room for the monks to process behind the high altar.
11 Brett 1996.
12 Brett 1996; Oakley 1996.
13 Only four more Rochester monks became bishops between 1142 and the Reformation, all between 1278 and 1352: Greatrex 2006.
14 Rochester would have fitted twice over into the east end he had begun as prior of Canterbury.
15 Halsey 2006 shows how the gallery of Gundulf's nave, perhaps complete in 1107 and certainly by the dedication of 1130, was bizarrely reconstructed after a fire of 1137, taking out its floor so as to make the nave aisles two-storey in appearance on the interior. He argues that the basic footprint of the west front must have been determined by Gundulf, even though its current appearance is later, and speculates that the richness of the west front may reflect that of a lost twelfth-century updating of the facade at Canterbury.
16 McNeill 2006b.
17 Held to be the first native Englishman to have been bishop of Rochester.

18 Translated into a new shrine in 1128.

19 Flight 1997.

20 Oakley 1996.

21 Many people travelled by water from London to the Rochester docks, and overland from there; Glanville's hospital and quay were at Strood, by the Medway crossing.

22 The priests would devote themselves to prayer for the return of Jerusalem to Christianity and of Richard I from crusade: Blount 2004.

23 Page 1926, 'Strood Hospital'. As late as the 1290s a procession of monks across hospital land caused a violent confrontation.

24 She made a garland of honeysuckle for the corpse's head, then put in on herself and instantly became sane: Richardson 1906–7.

25 William's so-called canonization in 1256 seems to have been more a semi-official permission for the cult to continue (Oakley 1996; Flight 1997); it is also peculiar that there is no sign of there having been any interest in the cult in Scotland itself, despite an early response to the cult of Becket there and the existence of documented links between Rochester and Scotland: Richardson 1906–7.

26 It seems reasonable to assume that the monks could never afford ambitious architecture unaided; at Rochester it is even possible that bishops generally needed unusual amounts of outside support – for example, from their archbishop – to build on any scale. Nevertheless Rochester's records, usually written by the monks, tend to ascribe building work to the prior or sacrist – in this case in spite of the fact that Bishop Glanville's tomb is in the position usually reserved for a founder or rebuilder (Draper 2006b).

27 For tension over two-storey designs (and their later success), see (in chronological order) Rochester (subservient to Canterbury), Southwell (subservient to York), Chester and Exeter (two-storey designs proposed by masons and rejected, presumably by patrons) Lichfield (to make a link between lady chapel and three-storey nave) and Bath (final acceptance: although Bath could be regarded as subservient to Wells by this date, earlier designs in the Perpendicular style made it clear that the prominence of the middle storey no longer mattered; see the naves of Canterbury and Winchester). The main exception to the rule is Winchester, where the fourteenth-century design of the two-storey east end was the focus of much inconclusive architecture.

28 Worcester also has both features, but here the crypt was abandoned when the eastern transepts were built.

29 Crook 2006.

30 Draper 2006b.

31 McAleer 1999.

32 Draper 2006b; Greatrex 2006.

33 Brett 1996. It was converted to a cash payment in 1320.

34 Oakley 1996. The oratory was built in 1327.

35 For example, Archbishop Pecham removed a prior from office in 1283 for maladministration and debt.

36 The tower has since been entirely rebuilt. As at many monastic houses, a gradual programme to install up-to-date window tracery around the building was carried out over a century or so.

37 McAleer 1999. It was probably an entrance to the new dormitory.

38 Buck 2004b.

39 Bishops Langdon and Bourne gave money for new windows in the 1430s and 1440s.

40 Rex 2004.

41 St John Hope 1898. I am grateful to Jim Bugslag for this reference.

42 Work on it is usually assumed to be marked by payments to a carver in 1521–3: McAleer 1999.

43 Rex 2004. He was present at the first burning of books by Martin Luther, and survived an attempted poisoning by supporters of Anne Boleyn in 1531.

ST ALBANS

1 Sharpe 2001.

2 Crick 2001.

3 Though the site of the church itself was later to move slightly.

4 Niblett and Thomson 2005.

5 Biddle and Kjølbye-Biddle 2001 believe this structure was a new church and that this church may well have been completed and lies beneath the current nave.

6 Roberts 1993, 24.

7 Ibid, 35.

8 Binski 2002, 35.

9 Roberts 1993, 35.

10 Ibid (and ensuing uncited historical material); Wallingford 2004.

11 Roberts 1993, 76.

12 Binski 2004 cites the way in which the monks blamed these problems on the deceit of the master mason, Hugh of Goldcliff, and says that the plans included an intention to vault the nave.

13 Kjølbye-Biddle 2001.

14 Binski 2004 gives 1221 as the date and sees in the proliferation of altars in the nave an ever-increasing lay pressure on the nave, only finally resolved by the rebuilding of the east end.

15 Binski 2002.

16 St Albans chronicler in Roberts 1993, 89.

17 Ibid, 113.

18 Goodall and Monckton 2001.

19 Roberts 1993, 113.

20 The main evidence for the unfinished Saxon church.

21 Page 1914.

22 Clark 2001, 221; Clark 2004.

23 Page 1914.

24 Ibid.

25 Clark 2001.

26 Ibid.

27 Page 1914.

28 Ibid.

29 Goodall and Monckton 2001.

30 Lindley 2001.

31 Page 1914.

32 Verger in St Albans, pers. comm.

33 A fragment of the reputed relic of St Alban in Cologne has since been installed in it.

ST PAUL'S

1 Barron and Rousseau 2004; Cragoe 2004.

2 Barron and Rousseau 2004; Thacker 2004a; http://en.wikipedia.org/wiki/Saint_Wilgefortis, accessed 2005.

3 Barron and Rousseau 2004; Thacker 2004a.

4 In 1314. Keene 2004; the rest is Barron and Rousseau 2004.

5 Keene 2004 of the eleventh/twelfth century. In 1334 London was four times richer than England's 'second city', Bristol; it was the main focus of royal and administrative power by 1200.

6 Lambeth, then not really London at all, but opposite the royal palace at Westminster.

7 Thacker 2004a.

8 For example in 704–9 Paulesbyri, though Paulesbyrig is actually more common (Keene and Taylor 2004) so might equally well be modernized as 'Paulsburgh' or even 'Paulborough'.

9 Keene 2004.

10 The longest standing church, Winchester cathedral, is 169 metres long; Wren's St Paul's is 155 metres (and the dome 111 metres compared to Old St Paul's 152-metre-plus spire).

11 The ogees are not certain, but they would have been one of the earliest large-scale displays of this influential and distinctive form. The spire is used to indicate London in many images, from manuscript illuminations to graffiti; a copy of the window was installed at St Katherine Cree in the 1630s.

12 Cragoe 2004.

13 St Mary Overie, Southwark (now Southwark cathedral), St Bartholomew's, Smithfield and Holy Trinity, Aldgate all owned as much or more land in the City as did St Paul's.

14 Barron and Rousseau 2004.

15 Faith 2004.

16 Keene 2004.

17 Canons and minor canons (is the two-storey elevation connected to this?).

18 Keene 2004.

19 Barron and Rousseau 2004.

20 Page 1909.

21 Cragoe 2004.

22 Important works by Inigo Jones.

23 The chapter insisted Wren's design was made more cathedral-like, which made it more like a medieval cathedral. The false walls of his nave as a result hide a very un-Renaissance elevation: aisles, clerestory and flying buttresses.

SALISBURY

1 Sherborne had itself been the seat of a see

since 705; Ramsbury was much younger.

2 Sherborne had been a monastic cathedral, but Old Sarum was secular from the start: a unique case of secularization of a cathedral at a time when many others were being monasticized. Old Sarum was also unique as a Norman relocation overseen by an existing Saxon bishop rather than a 'new broom' Norman one.

3 Stroud 1996.

4 Pugh and Crittall 1956. House plots for canons were being laid out as early as this.

5 Brown 1999.

6 It seems the letter was written before Richard took up office: Stroud 1996.

7 Canon Peter of Blois, quoted in Pugh and Crittall 1956, 165; from a letter of 1200 apologizing for being unable to come to a distribution of houses.

8 Hastings 1997.

9 Most contemporary quotes are from the dean, William de Waude. Stroud 1996, 11.

10 A chapel had already been built and a market licensed to take place; it seems a settlement had been developing on this spot for some time: McNeill 2006a.

11 Pugh and Crittall 1956. Seventeen to thirty-nine canons were present.

12 And was itself based on a 'model' use by the first Norman bishop, Osmund.

13 Stroud 1996, 9.

14 Binski 2004.

15 Renewed in 1225: Hastings 1997.

16 Simpson 1996. The forests were Clarendon, New Forest, Chippenham and Trivelle in the Forest of Dean.

17 Stroud 1996.

18 Poore's successor Bishop Bingham brought the whole east end into use; Bishop Bridport consecrated the church in 1258.

19 Matthew Paris in Hastings 1997, 11.

20 Hastings 1997, 13. He was given both the common fund and the fabric fund to control: Binski 2004.

21 His house was in ruins in 1915, and has since been demolished (although parts may be incorporated in the current building). Binski 2004 says that Elias made careful provisions for future occupants, who had to contribute to the cost of building the house as well as feed 100 poor people annually on Elias' deathday.

22 For example, in both sets of transepts, arches that let on to chapels have different widths from those which let on to aisles. The most complete explorations of these qualities are Draper 1996; Sekules 1996; Kidson 1993b.

23 Such facts throw an interesting light on the relationship between the cost of a building, the amount of decoration it contained and the speed with which it could be erected. The east end at St Hugh's, Lincoln, for example, is as ornate and irregular as Salisbury is spare and repetitive, yet as far as we can tell Lincoln's rebuilding (1192–c.1230) was no slower than Salisbury's (1220–58).

24 Nailhead in the moulding of the arches after the crossing, foliage paterae in the clerestory

after the eastern transept.

25 Peter Kidson's phrase, in Kidson 1993b.

26 Kidson 1993b.

27 Fernie 1982 (referring to the Anglo-Saxon church at Deerhurst, Gloucestershire).

28 Thirteen side-chapels plus the nave and Trinity Chapel altars: Brown 1999.

29 Wells is the main exception to this rule, and is worth seeing as a precursor to Salisbury: see Chapter 3.

30 Osmund's tomb-shrine is almost identical to that of Thomas Becket: its late twelfth-century lid was perhaps created or recarved to help support its occupant's saintly reputation.

31 It is perhaps significant, then, that Henry III presented Salisbury with a magnificent silver pyx to hang in front of the high altar.

32 Brown 1999.

33 A quality noticeable at some other early buildings with important lady altars, such as the Durham Galilee.

34 Hearn and Willis 1996.

35 Perhaps they thought the scale of the cult around their bishop not convincing enough: the documentation gives accounts of just twenty-six miracles since 1180.

36 He wrote to Dean de Waude in 1228: Stroud 1996, 14.

37 Tarrant Keyneston.

38 Its constitution pre-dated that of Merton college, Oxford by two years; it was directly modelled on that of the university of Paris. Pugh and Crittall 1956, 'College of de Vaux'.

39 Brown 1999.

40 A vaulted polygonal chapter-house with wall-filling windows can never be ugly: but – compared to Westminster abbey, Lincoln or Wells – this one lacks conviction, in spite of the wonderful (and hugely restored) carvings of stories from the first books of the Bible that surround its walls.

41 Brown 1999.

42 Stroud 1996, 5.

43 Also known as Ghent.

44 Morris 1996b; Tatton-Brown 1996b.

45 Or 1542: http://anglicanhistory.org/essays/wright/ sarum.pdf, accessed 2006. All the cathedrals of Canterbury province bar Hereford had adopted it by 1325: Binski 2004.

46 Brown 1999. The current lower walls of the Trinity Chapel were subsequently rebuilt using finely carved Perpendicular coving from the abandoned chantries; at about the same time tombs of many periods were placed in serried ranks below the nave arcades.

47 Audley also built a fine chantry at his other bishopric, Hereford.

48 Though the differences between the 'restrained' and 'rich' mode of any given medieval style are both remarkable and fascinating: think of the Decorated Worcester next to the Decorated Ely lady chapel, or Perpendicular Bath cathedral priory next to Henry VII's chapel.

SOUTHWARK

1 Reilly 1998.

2 Added off the retrochoir, perhaps in the fourteenth century. Both ordinations and the bishop's court are known to have been held in St Mary's.

3 Something comparable happened on the other side of medieval London at St Bartholomew the Great, where a great Augustinian priory church also stands; here, the hospital stayed in the same place.

4 Bankside and Borough High Street respectively.

5 Malden 1905/Page 1909, as is most other uncited historical information.

6 See Winchester for more on all these bishops.

7 The last prior of Southwark claimed that a nunnery was established here as early as the seventh century, though his source for this is not known.

8 The knights were William Pont de l'Arch and William Dauncey. The oldest part of the church forms the entrance to the Harvard chapel off the north transept.

9 Contemporary satirical poem, quoted in Vincent 2004b.

10 Ibid.

11 First built by Bishop des Roches.

SOUTHWELL

1 Pevsner 1945; Givens 1998.

2 In the twenty or so parishes making up the Peculiar itself (and aside from the parts of the Peculiar which were the property of the canons of York). Here Southwell ran the ecclesiastical courts, stood in judgement over adulterers and murderers, and was at once landowner and ecclesiastical authority. Page 1910; Summers 1974.

3 Page 1910; Summers 1974.

4 Page 1910; Coffman 1998. The famous sculpture of St Michael, long thought to be Anglo-Saxon, is now held to be twelfth century.

5 Edict of Thomas of Bayeux: Coffman 1998, 1.

6 Ottey 2005.

7 Contemporary campaigns at Beverley and Ripon had similar support; and the archbishop was also rebuilding the transepts of York minster.

8 Though if the previous church had had altars at gallery level, the replacement arguably placed them all at ground level rather than increased their numbers.

9 John McNeill's phrase; for the east end, McNeill 1998.

10 And may just have been felt to be a little more appropriate in a kind of under-cathedral.

11 Summers 1974, 21. Southwell was only overtaken by larger collegiate foundations when large academic colleges began to be founded during the fourteenth century.

12 Summers 1974.

13 In 1248, for example.

14 Pevsner 1945; Givens 1998.

15 Summers 1974.

16 Ibid.

17 Givens 1998.

18 Summers 1974.

19 Ottey 2005.

20 Summers 1974.

21 Alexander 1998b. One team of nine to thirteen men, another of nineteen to twenty-two.

22 McNeill 1998; Alexander 1998b.

23 Even the rich carvings in the gables above the capitals are not of the same quality.

WELLS

1 Rodwell 2001, 1982a, 1981.

2 Page 1911.

3 Glastonbury was immune from the power of the local bishop.

4 Ramsey 2004a; Gransden 1982. The Wells chapter grew in size enormously during the twelfth century and may already have been one of England's largest non-cathedral collegiate churches.

5 He had been to Jerusalem with Henry II, sided with the king against Becket and with the monks of Canterbury against their planned relocation to Hackington, and helped bring the future St Hugh of Lincoln to England. On his death he was archbishop-elect; there were even rumours of saintliness. C Duggan 2004.

6 The pope asked his legate Pandulf to check whether Wells had a historic claim to the title, but it is not clear to what extent his instructions were acted on. Page 1911 (including entries for Bath and Glastonbury abbeys); Rodwell 2001; Gransden 1982; Ramsey 2004a; C Duggan 2004; Dunning 2004; Shaw 2004; T Ayers 1996.

7 Work had certainly begun by 1185, but each revisiting of the question has tended to push the actual date works began closer to 1174, and it now seems the east end of the church was functioning by 1180. Harvey 1982a; Sampson 1998; Rodwell 2001, etc.

8 Gransden 1982; Binski 2004.

9 Draper 1995; Sampson 1998; Harvey 1982a; Rodwell 2001.

10 Fully aisled transepts; the intention if not yet the detailed design for a grand west front.

11 The city still retains the ghostly imprint of this church, whose west front loomed over the space that is now Wells' market place; the church's axis can be followed by walking along the high street towards the market place, beyond which the cathedral extended in a line leading towards St Andrew's Well.

12 It was positioned off the east walk, en route to the bishop's palace – the location originally intended for the chapter-house: Rodwell 2001. This was all in spite of the fact that the new church had a lady chapel at the east end, perhaps the first in England for which there is documentary evidence to link its foundation to the adoption of a daily lady mass: Draper 1990.

13 The current one is a later rebuilding, masking the fact that it is unusually grand and early for a secular cathedral cloister.

14 Rodwell 2001 makes some fascinating suggestions.

15 Rodwell 1982a and 2001.

16 Binski 2004.

17 The fire that destroyed it had been witnessed by bishop fitz Jocelin: Harvey 1982a.

18 Draper 1995. It was also around this time that Glastonbury began to make a meal of *its* lady chapel and the myths around it, and creating 'heritage' effigies of figures in *its* ancient history, such as Arthur and Guinevere.

19 Harvey 1982a.

20 The fire is marked in the transept by an abrupt change from Doulting to Chilcote stone: the latter was on Wells land; the former belonged to Glastonbury. The interdict is marked by a series of subtle but significant adaptations to the design halfway down the nave: Sampson 1998.

21 Dunning 2004.

22 Fragments of which survive in the chapel of the vicars' close and the old rectory at Wookey known as Mellifont Abbey.

23 In 1243, as the west front was nearing completion, Jocelin issued a memorandum that reorganized the cemeteries around the church itself, specifying that the far west should be reserved for lay people, canons should be buried in the cloister, and other priests east of the Lady-Chapel-by-the-Cloister. Sampson 1998.

24 Tudor-Craig 1982; also Sampson 1998.

25 Of these, 149 life-size statues survive, plus sixty-eight of the ninety-plus smaller sculpted scenes and figures: Sampson 1998; Tudor-Craig 2004.

26 Wells was a richly inscribed building. There were messages in the chapter-house and lady chapel stained glass and a hidden 'key' relating to Jesse in the glazing of the choir east window (T Ayers 1996). The main survival is the inscription on the inner door of the north porch: a canon holding the invitation, 'Enter thou into the joy of thy Lord'.

27 Sampson 1998.

28 Tudor-Craig 2004.

29 Binski 2004. Both King Ine of Wessex and St Edward are cited in the *Historiola* and appear to be present, carrying scrolls that presumably represent the charters with which they founded and gave to the church respectively.

30 From as early as 1207.

31 Lay people probably entered via the west cloister door.

32 Jocelin or one of his officials: Page 1911, 164.

33 The bishops of Bath and Wells, who between 1090 and 1174 had focused their architectural spending on Bath, for the rest of the medieval period spent it on Wells, even forcing the monks to pay for Bath's belated rebuilding of the late fifteenth century.

34 The dean had been in charge of works (see Bristol); now he was sent to Rome.

35 In 1245 the canons were asked to pay off a debt of 1,775 marks 'contracted in the Roman courts'.

36 Soon afterwards Glastonbury slipped itself free of the bishop's control again, never to return.

37 Information historical and architectural for the chapter-house and east end is mostly from T Ayers 1996 unless cited otherwise.

38 They had already built him a country house at his Shropshire home of Acton Burnell, much of which still stands.

39 It is also possible that Bishop Burnell returned, restarted work on his palace, and asked for the return of his masons.

40 The glass is now in fragments in the lady chapel: T Ayers 1996.

41 There were decisions in favour of the chapter under deans de la Knoll in 1278 and 1298, and de Godley from 1331 and 1338.

42 Also known as Drokensford.

43 Dunning 1982.

44 These are only known to have existed in the fifteenth century: T Ayers 1996.

45 Precise dates much discussed: this is T Ayers 1996.

46 Also known as William de Marchia.

47 Jewell 2004.

48 Draper 1981.

49 Harvey 1982b.

50 Gransden 1982, 38. It was perhaps the first in the country to be formally instituted. Rodwell 2005 points out that the scheme fulfilled an earlier plan of Dean de Godley.

51 Gransden 1982; Rodwell 2001.

52 Dunning 1982. It had apparently first been walled by Bishop Burnell after 1286.

53 Page 1911.

54 Monckton 1999.

55 Mayer 2004.

56 Gransden 1982.

57 Wynford's patron, William Wykeham, was a canon of Wells as well as bishop of Winchester.

58 Monckton 1999. One wonders what Adam Lock would have thought of these: they gave the Wells exterior a stately grandeur but also detracted from the screen-like effect of the facade beneath them.

59 The spires may not have been part of the original design: Harvey 1982b argues that Wynford's Wells tower pioneered the idea of the tower with a horizontal profile, soon to be a standard feature of Perpendicular towers.

60 As with many late medieval cloister rebuilds (compare Norwich and Hereford), this was a slow process: work began in the 1420s and may not have been finished until 1508. Rodwell 2001 has much extra detail on the cloister and its development.

61 Rodwell 2001. It seems the bishop's consistory court was also based in the lady chapel.

62 Separated by two years by Richard Fox, later bishop of Winchester.

63 The new chapel was built parallel to the current cathedral, rather than lying on the axis of its predecessor, as the Lady-Chapel-

by-the-Cloister had done.

64　Page 1911.

WINCHESTER

1　The saying is attributed to Bishop Fox: C S L Davies 2004.
2　From the mid-fourteenth century, the bishopric virtually 'went with the job'.
3　As a result it included much of what is now southern London.
4　Fernie 2000; and see p. 59 n. 39. It seems the only roofed structure that exceeded it was the Great Mosque at Cordoba, though Winchester itself was overtaken within a decade by the monastery at Cluny. Since it was built, Winchester has lost its west end but gained an eastern extension: at over 169 metres long it remains the longest medieval cathedral in Europe.
5　Eleventh-century Winchester: Gem 1983; Crook 1993a.
6　The maximum possible total: towers (never completed) on each corner of the transepts (four); likely towers at the east ends of the aisles (two); three towers at the west end, like some of the greatest German cathedrals; and central tower (surviving but rebuilt): Richard Plant, pers. comm. Not all were ever built.
7　Greatrex 1993; M J Franklin 2004.
8　Winchester chronicler: Crook 1993a, 22.
9　Henry of Huntingdon in King 2004.
10　King 2004. This is his best-known visit to Rome, but the event could have occurred during another visit.
11　Kusaba 1988.
12　Donovan 1993b.
13　Park 1983.
14　Riall 1994.
15　The lady chapel – presumably always dedicated to St Mary – was rebuilt, too, but its eastern bays were later much adapted.
16　Woodman 1983; Draper 1986; Norton 1993.
17　Vincent 2004b.
18　Greatrex 1993. The manors were Nursling and Millbrook. The date this arrangement was developed is not clear.
19　Park 1983. Putting bright patterns of blue and gold and images of saints over altars and saints in blank arcades.
20　Russell 1983. Each is done differently, as if they were carried out piecemeal or individually funded.
21　Greatrex 1993.
22　Tracy 1993a.
23　Draper and Morris 1983.
24　Winchester bishops also funded new buildings elsewhere, such as Bishop des Roches' many monastic foundations (see p. 96 n. 27).
25　My counts from ODNB.
26　He founded a collegiate church at Edington, his home village in Wiltshire, in 1351, soon adopting it for a quasi-monastic order so fashionable that its only other known house was founded by the Black Prince.
27　Perhaps the result of that area's longstanding instability.
28　It is not impossible that work began in the 1350s.
29　See C Wilson, cat. 601 in Alexander and Binski 1987.
30　R G Davies 2004.
31　One of his first posts was at the royal castle in Winchester.
32　The French chronicler Froissart in Partner 2004.
33　The year was 1373. In his thirty-seven years as bishop he carried out over 5,300 ordinations; he also bought 113 new chalices and 100 sets of vestments for the parish churches of his see. Doubleday and Page 1903.
34　Biographical details from Partner 2004.
35　Greatrex 1993.
36　Wykeham in Partner 2004.
37　Crook and Kusaba 1993, 227.
38　A similar idea had been successfully completed at Gloucester abbey (now the cathedral).
39　The great Robert Willis was the first to realize this in 1845; the precise details and dating have been much discussed since.
40　Partner 2004.
41　Beaufort was the illegitimate son of Katherine Swynford and John of Gaunt.
42　Figure reached by totting up individual loans cited in Harriss 2004.
43　Harriss 2004.
44　Partner 2004.
45　Specifically the Hussites in Bohemia.
46　To be precise, £477 15s 1d in gold, £229 3s 2d in silver: Luxford 2005.
47　Stevenson 1993; Henig and Lindley 2001; Marks and Williamson 2003.
48　Davis 2004b. Waynflete was the first bishop in a century not to be royal chancellor. He was educated at Wykeham's Winchester college, later becoming head there. In the 1440s, he became Eton's first provost and bishop of Winchester. He founded the handsomely Perpendicular Magdalen college, Oxford, leaving it his 800-volume library. He even seems to have won the affection of the monks.
49　Memorandum by Archbishop Morton's staff: Crook 1993b, 64.
50　C Wilson (cat. 233) in Marks and Williamson 2003 sees all this work as Beaufort's initiative (rather than just the way his bequest was spent).
51　Bowers 1993; Park and Welford 1993; Tracy 1993b.
52　Biddle 1993; Wright 2004.
53　The story may be apocryphal: Orme 2004b.
54　C S L Davies 2004. Fox also drew up the iconographic programme for King's college chapel, Cambridge and (perhaps) Henry VII's chapel, Westminster abbey.
55　Fox in a letter to his successor Cardinal Wolsey, in ibid.
56　Fox in ibid.
57　Marks and Williamson 2003.
58　If Walkelin's apse had a groin vault, it was demolished by Thomas of Witney. Draper and Morris 1993 then assume a wooden roof. Fox's wooden vault avoided placing unnecessary weight on weak foundations.
59　Munby and Fletcher 1983. Fox's will said the money was to be spent on 'the makinge of a new vaulte of stone over St Swithun his shrine and of the new makinge and vaulting with stone of aisles upon the side of the said church & the vaulting of the cross-aisle [or transept] in the said cathedral church of Winchester with stone after the manner and form of the vaulting of the said cathedral church': Lindley 1993, 117. Apart from the Perpendicular nave, only the lady chapel, already substantially Perpendicularized, is not mentioned. However, Luxford 2005 points out that funds were only to be made available for all this when work on Corpus Christi was complete, perhaps greatly restricting what could actually be carried out.
60　Lindley 1993.
61　Armstrong 2004.
62　Ibid.
63　Ibid.

WORCESTER

1　Giso of Wells, was to die in 1088.
2　William of Malmesbury in Fernie 2000, 154.
3　Many Anglo-Saxon bishops of Worcester were also archbishop of York, and there are many connections between the diocese and the northern province.
4　In the 1050s: Gem 1978; Barker et al 1994.
5　'The age of that most happy man did not know how to build pompous buildings', declared the upset Wulfstan of Oswald: William of Malmesbury in Fernie 2000, 154.
6　The diocese originally covered the territory – roughly modern Worcestershire and Gloucestershire – of the Hwicce, a group on the fringes of the Anglo-Saxon realm, later swallowed up by Mercia. The abbeys of Bath and Gloucester in this territory were also founded at about this time.
7　As his colleague Ethelwold had done at Winchester.
8　Many Anglo-Saxon great churches comprised several separate buildings arranged in a line: perhaps that is the arrangement we can imagine here.
9　Five out of twelve Worcestershire hundreds were in church hands at Domesday: Page 1906c. Oswald built an important estate, but its consolidation into the 'Hundred' comes a little later: Brooks 2004.
10　Durham and Rochester were both new in 1084, and were the first new monastic cathedrals since the creation of Worcester, Winchester, Canterbury and Sherborne in the late tenth century.
11　In an enlightened way at Gloucester, a heavy-handed one at Evesham.
12　Uncited biographical material mainly Mason 2004.
13　The architecture of the three churches is interrelated.

14 Medieval Bristol history in Keen 1997.

15 Gransden 1978.

16 As the Canterbury monk Eadmer put it: Gransden 1978, 4.

17 Gem 1978. Wulfstan: 'more than twelve brethren were found by me, up to fifty have been gathered by me'.

18 William of Malmesbury in Gem 1978.

19 Among West Country great churches, only Old Sarum had then been rebuilt; Gloucester, Tewkesbury, Bath, Hereford and Exeter were all to come. And only mighty Winchester, Bury St Edmunds, St Augustine's, Canterbury, and Canterbury cathedral itself shared the ambitious combination of features that distinguished Wulfstan's church: Gem 1978.

20 Uniquely described as 'St Mary in the crypt' in 1092, making it the only attested cathedral lady chapel of the immediate post-Conquest years: Page 1906c.

21 The recently discovered circular foundations there have now been shown to be post-Conquest. But speculation concerning the roots of the chapter-house's design existed even before they were found: Stratford 1978.

22 Barker et al 1994.

23 Engel 2000; for example at Gloucester and Durham. Gloucester imitated its polygonally ended chapels, another motif with local Saxon precedents.

24 Nilson 1998; Page 1906c.

25 Craze 1986/7.

26 Thanks to his misunderstanding of one of Wulfstan's miracle stories.

27 Craze 1986/7; Page 1906c has nine bishops and does not mention the legate and council.

28 Singleton 1978.

29 Nilson 1998, 31.

30 Singleton 1978.

31 Probably after a tower fall of 1175: Barker et al 1994; Wilson 1978.

32 Barker et al 1994.

33 John had founded the abbey and had earlier expressed a desire to be buried there: Draper 2006a.

34 The only master known was named Alexander, in the late 1230s at the earliest.

35 Engel 2000.

36 Engel 2000; Morris 1978 assumes bishop's sponsorship, and dates the start of work to 1317–21.

37 Engel 2000.

38 Morris 1978: during its rebuilding the masons abandoned the cathedral for forty-one weeks.

39 With new windows, for example; by making it polygonal outside while leaving it circular within; and probably (but very respectfully) rebuilding its vault.

40 Morris 1978 has picked apart the stages of its growth, and demonstrated how many details show its designer's awareness of the latest fashions, and the emerging Perpendicular style. Though it is hard to see clearly, the incidental sculpture in the nave is of high quality and closely related to contemporary Bristol work.

41 Luxford 2005; a fourteenth-century glazing programme that apparently extended into the east end and vestry.

42 Page 1907b.

43 Material on Arthur: Craze 1986/7; Lloyd 2002.

44 Luxford 2005 says they were worried about catching plague.

45 Pevsner and Metcalf 1985 say the chantry was complete within two years, but Luxford 2005 points out that the altar was not dedicated until 1516–17. King John was given a new tomb base shortly after, in the 1520s; Gloucester is another local monastic house that found it politic to emphasize its royal roots at this time.

46 Though Engel 2000 argues that the renewals were extremely careful – and the Victorian fittings are some of the finest in the country.

47 Nilson 1998: a fifteenth-century cult that at least matched Worcester's older saints.

YORK

1 In terms of wealth it is hard definitively to rank York above Bristol as second city, but York was a far more emphatic centre of administrative power.

2 A title to which Glasgow competed after the fifteenth century.

3 Eighteen including Wales.

4 It has been said that in 1066 there was not a single functioning community north of the Wash apart from Burton upon Trent: Aylmer and Cant 1977.

5 Although the special relationship of these churches to the archbishop had ancient roots, their preservation as minster churches bears the traces of a conscious decision, taking place as it does at a time when dozens, perhaps hundreds, of comparable establishments across England were being turned into either parish churches or small Augustinian houses.

6 The resulting cathedral-scaled and ancient collegiate churches have no equivalents outside the diocese. Builder-archbishops of York such as Wilfrid, Gray and de Thoresby played a key role in the architecture in each of them. Ripon and Southwell became cathedrals in the nineteenth century.

7 Out of 800 citizens assessed for tax. Tillott 1961; in 1292–3 the city's entire revenue from tolls, rents taxes and court fees was £123 14s 9d.

8 A college of priests formally known as the chapel of St Mary and the Holy Angels, founded by Roger of Pont l'Évêque.

9 Prebends (with widely varying values): York: 36; St Sepulchre: 16; Beverley: 11–13; Ripon: 7; Southwell: 16.

10 Dobson 1977. At some points in the fifteenth century numbers were as low as two or three; York may have had the worst residency record of any English cathedral.

11 Page 1913.

12 The shrine of Archbishop Paulinus was in Rochester; that of Wilfrid in Ripon or Canterbury (or even Worcester), depending on whom you believed; John in Beverley; Wilfrid II at Ripon; Chad in Lichfield; the dismembered Oswald (the king) in Durham, Gloucester and Peterborough; and the whole Oswald (bishop and archbishop) in Worcester. Adjusted from Brown 2003.

13 York's library, built up by scouring Europe for texts, became one of the key sources for the development of scholarship throughout Europe, at least partly thanks to Alcuin, the York cleric who rose to become (from 768) one of Charlemagne's chief advisers.

14 They may even have been located in various parts of the city; recent scholarship, however, places these churches together in a single grand complex just north of the current minster, and on a different orientation, itself perhaps relating to the remains of the Roman principia: Norton 1998.

15 Hugh the Chanter in Hill and Brooke 1977, 25.

16 Both quotes: ibid, 26.

17 It is known only through excavations; description here from summaries in Fernie 2000 and Brown 2003; Stuart Harrison, pers. comm.

18 New research suggests a building about 19 metres wide and 15 metres high, with a large crypt, eastern towers and perhaps vaults in the eastern parts of the choir: Stuart Harrison, pers. comm.

19 William of Newburgh in Burton 2004.

20 One of the church's most senior jobs: right-hand man of the archbishop, effectively bishop of the Canterbury archdiocese or see.

21 These statements are the result of research by Stuart Harrison and Christopher Norton under way as this book went to press, and I am grateful to Stuart Harrison for sharing his discoveries with me. The architecture is revolutionary enough, but the context (the death of Archbishop William and the rise of the Cistercians) and the way the architecture itself was taken up (at Ripon, Canterbury and Lincoln, all in association with saints) are highly suggestive, if weakened by the lack of evidence for a cult of St William at this date. The alternative view, that Archbishop Roger was responding to the challenge set by Anselm's east end at Canterbury, and that the replacement of that building was itself soon mooted as a result, i.e. before Becket's death, is equally intriguing, if more suggestive of competing institutional and personal interests than a budding new age of saints.

22 Evidence for twenty-four figures survives, some reused in later parts of the building: Brown 2003.

23 There was no archbishop for ten years, and quarrels over the appointment of Archbishop Geoffrey Plantagenet were followed by the interdict.

24 Smith 2004.

25 Brown 2003. Few cathedrals have generated as much research as York; none has synthe-

sized it as completely as this remarkable book. Specific architectural facts not cited from here on can be assumed to derive from it.

26 Ibid.
27 Ibid. French 1999 suggests that the split emphasis between the shrine of St William and the intended tombs of the archbishops may imply that even in the 1220s there was a certain amount of ambivalence surrounding the validity of William's cult, which never spread far beyond York itself.
28 Indeed new canons could not join chapter until they had received a prebend, and on very rare occasions – usually absentees, and only three cases are known – even the dean never took one up: Dobson 1977.
29 In 1296, for example.
30 Brown 2003 gives the most detailed account of the iconography, emphasizing the Marian dimension as just one among many themes.
31 Smith 2004.
32 A new shrine was paid for by Bishop Bek of Durham in exchange for the privilege of being enthroned in the minster: French 1999.
33 Smith 2004.
34 The nearest detailed comparators are in France and Germany.
35 They hang from masonry brackets, in imitation of the way shields were hung from the walls of secular great halls, an idea that first appears a few decades earlier at Westminster abbey: Sarah Brown, pers. comm.
36 Brown 2003. Most of them carry falcons.
37 For example, the arms of Edward and his brother originally stood in the middle of all the clerestory windows, and head up the heraldry of the nave arcade: Brown 2003.
38 Ibid.
39 Ibid.
40 And one quickly taken up by such local monastic houses as St Mary's, York.
41 Brown 2003.
42 Iconography that has its ultimate roots in Bede.
43 It seems likely the sculptural programme was never completed: Brown 2003.
44 The Heart of Yorkshire window (a modern name), which seems slightly too small for the facade as a whole, is perhaps the facade's weakest moment. By contrast, the other windows and decorative details form a

veritable history of late gothic design, from Geometrical Decorated on the lowest storey through Curvilinear Decorated higher up to Perpendicular in the towers – yet the facade still manages to be balanced in appearance overall.

45 Hughes 2004b.
46 Terms of a gift of 1359: Brown 2003, 139.
47 York Fabric Rolls in ibid, 144.
48 A plan apparently invented at Ely in the 1234, and since tried at Lincoln and St Paul's.
49 Brown 2003.
50 The nave is seven bays long, the lady chapel four: the overall rate of construction had therefore more than doubled.
51 Purvis 1964.
52 Dobson 2003.
53 Brown 2003.
54 His 1395 gift of 1,000 marks appears to have initiated work on the new choir.
55 Brown 2003.
56 O'Connor and Haselock 1977, 364.
57 Paid for by Bishop Skirlaw of Durham.
58 Scrope: Tillott 1961; McKenna 1970; McNiven 2004.
59 Tillott 1961.
60 McNiven 2004.
61 McKenna 1970, 611.
62 Ibid, 612.
63 Tillott 1961; McKenna 1970.
64 McKenna 1970, 621.
65 The crossing was until recently thought to have been rebuilt, along with the tower itself, in the thirteenth century; but it now seems that beneath the many layers of alterations that had gone on in this area over the centuries, it remained basically an eleventh-century structure: Stuart Harrison, pers. comm.
66 McKenna 1970; Brown 2003.
67 Harvey 1977; Brown 2003.
68 Brown 2003, 205.
69 Nilson 1998.
70 Pointedly opposite an image of St William. The window is in the south-east transept.
71 McKenna 1970, 621.
72 Brown 2003.
73 So it is assumed that it was this image, rather than another in the minster, that was taken down.
74 Aylmer and Cant 1977; Brown 2003.
75 Brown 2003 suggests that much of this glazing still followed schemes drawn up

by de Thoresby.

76 Wilson 1977; Harvey 1977; Brown 2003 implies that this is not definite and that the marble was probably sourced in London, and points out (following French 1999) that the cult itself may have needed re-emphasizing, as the shrine must often have been inaccessible during the building of the lady chapel and choir.
77 Or even the 1220s, if one overlooks a ten- to twenty-year gap between transepts and chapter-house.
78 Tillott 1961.
79 Harvey 1977, 188. Today the minster once again has a master-mason.
80 This is partly because the nave scheme survives. See p. 118, n. 67.
81 Closely followed by the nave, the area with the most secular concerns.
82 The fires took place between 1711 and 1984; the lady chapel vault is now the only original high vault in the building. By contrast, during the Civil War General Fairfax went out of his way to protect the minster.
83 The main objection to this is that all deans and chapters were abolished during the Commonwealth. Apart from this, as a community, Canterbury has been radically transformed twice, from secular to monastic and back again; and while the closet competitor, St Paul's, was founded earlier, it was refounded a decade or two later than York. It also assumes, as seems likely, that the minster was not abandoned for a time at the height of the Viking invasions. Another contender would be Hereford, founded decades later but far less disrupted by events thereafter. All this in turn raises the possibility that the chapter of York minster, or failing that the chapter of Hereford or St Paul's, is the oldest institutional body with an unbroken existence in England.

ILLUSTRATION CREDITS

akg-images/ Musée Condé, Chantilly (ms 76/1362 f.3) 204/British Library (ms Royal 15 E III f.102) 221

T. Ball/reconstruction following R. Gem 59

Bodleian Library, University of Oxford (ms Bodley 691 f.1v) 212 right,

Bridgeman Art Library/Bibliothèque Municipale, Agen (ms 41 f.42v) 205/ Bibliothèque Municipale, Dijon (ms 170 f.75v) 79/ Bibliothèque Nationale, Paris (ms français 2643 f.97v) 309/British Library (ms Royal 16 G VI f.568v) 97, (ms Royal 15 E IV f.187) 123, (ms Add 42130 f.60) 127, (ms Add 10294 f.39) 131, (ms Harley 1319 f.12) 137 top, 161, (ms Add 23923 f.2) 168, (ms Add 27697 f.194) 215, (ms Cotton Nero D I f.23v) 228/British Museum 34 bottom, 232/Groeningemuseum, Bruges 22/Kunsthistorisches Museum, Vienna 450/Lambeth Palace Library, London (Reg.Courtenay f.337v) 220, (ms 209 f.2v) 237/Musée Condé, Chantilly (ms 65/1284 f.71v & f.72) 203 top left & 203 top right/Musée de la Tapisserie, Bayeux 52/New College, Oxford, courtesy of the Warden & Scholars (ms 258 f.3v) 138/The Earl of Pembroke, Wilton House, Wilts 157/Private Collections 136 bottom, 174, (courtesy of Philip Mould) 153/ St Bavo Cathedral, Ghent 14/San Francisco, Upper Church, Assisi 108/Society of Antiquaries, London 410/Trinity College, Cambridge (ms R 171 f.283v) 183/Victoria & Albert Museum, London 16, 73, 172

British Library, London (ms Harley 3860 f.48) 109, (ms Add 49598 f.90v) 325

Jon Cannon frontispiece, 13, 15, 21, 30–31, 32, 40, 50, 66, 82 84, 87, 89, 94, 99, 102, 110, 112, 119 left, 119 right, 120, 121, 124, 125, 126, 129, 133, 135, 136 top, 139, 141, 143, 146, 149, 154, 155 left, 155 right, 165, 171, 176, 179, 181, 187, 188, 195, 199, 207, 209 bottom, 212 left, 214. 216, 218, 219, 223, 226, 229, 230, 231, 235, 241, 243, 245, 252, 255, 257, 258–259, 262, 264, 267, 277, 283, 285, 286, 288, 290, 293, 294, 299 left, 299 right, 302, 314, 318, 322, 326, 333, 336, 340, 341, 342, 346, 350, 352, 353, 356, 359 left, 359 right, 363, 364, 367 left, 367 right, 368, 370, 375, 376, 379, 380, 384, 386, 390, 391, 394, 395, 398, 399, 400, 401, 406, 407, 408, 417, 418, 420, 421, 424, 426, 428, 429, 432, 435, 439, 440, 441, 444, 447, 448, 452, 455, 460, 462, 463, 469, 473, 476

© **Canterbury Archaeological Trust Ltd/**drawn by John Atherton Bowen 36/drawn by Ivan Lapper 47, 55

Canterbury Cathedral Archives (Lit ms E42 f.36v) 69 right

© **Stephen Conlin**, based on research by E. Sinclair 26

Continuum/Birmingham and Warwickshire Archaeological Society 303

John Crook 34 top, 45 bottom, 61, 83, 85, 92, 95, 113, 115, 137 bottom, 163, 193, 209 top, 260, 275, 296, 298, 310, 319, 328, 358, 360, 372, 414, 434, 442, 445, 449 right, 457

Crown Copyright. NMR 23, 436, 471, (Automobile Association Collection) 12

BIBLIOGRAPHY

ABBREVIATIONS

BAA = British Archaeological Association

CUP = Cambridge University Press

DNB = Dictionary of National Biography, OUP 1975 (original edition of 1908–9 plus supplements to 1960, reproduced micrographically)

ODNB = Oxford Dictionary of National Biography, OUP, 2004 (citations are all from http://www.oxforddnb.com)

OUP = Oxford University Press

RCHME = Royal Commission on the Historical Monuments of England

VCH = Victoria County Histories (short titles given below are usually preceded by 'History of the county of')

Alexander, J S 1995 'The Angel Choir of Lincoln cathedral and the shrines of St Hugh', *Journal of the BAA*, 148, 137–47

Alexander, J S 1996 'Masons' marks and stone bonding', in Tatton-Brown and Munby 1996, 219–36

Alexander, J S 1998a *Southwell and Nottinghamshire: medieval art, architecture and industry*, BAA

Alexander, J S 1998b 'Southwell minster choir: the evidence of the masons' marks', in Alexander 1998a, 44–59

Alexander, J S 2004 'The construction of the gothic choir of Carlisle cathedral and the evidence of the masons' marks', in McCarthy and Weston 2004, 106–26

Alexander, J and Binski, P (eds) 1987 *Age of chivalry: art in Plantagenet England 1200–1400*, Royal Academy

Allen Brown, R (ed) 1984 *Anglo-Norman studies VI*, Boydell and Brewer

Allan, J 1991 'A note on the building stones of the cathedral', in Kelly 1991, 10–18

Allan, J P and Blaylock, S R 1991 'The west front I: the structural history of the west front', in Kelly 1991, 94–115

Allison K J 1989 *VCH Yorkshire: East Riding* VI, Institute of Historical Research/OUP

Anon 1998 *Rites and monuments of the cathedral church of Durham*, Llanerch (facsimile of Surtees Society edn 1842)

Armstrong, C D C 2004 'Gardiner, Stephen', *ODNB*

Ashdown, J, Fisher, I and Munby, J 1990 'The roof carpentry of Oxford cathedral', in Blair 1990a, 195–204

Ashwell, B J 1985 'Gloucester cathedral – the south transept: a fourteenth century conservation project',

Antiquaries Journal, 65, 112–20

Atherton, I 1996 'The close', in Atherton et al 1996, 634–64

Atherton, I, Fernie, E, Harper-Bill, C, Smith, H (eds) 1996 *Norwich cathedral: church, city and diocese 1096–1996*, Hambledon

Atherton, I and Holderness, B A 1996 'The dean and chapter estates since the Reformation', in Atherton et al 1996, 665–87

Ayers, B S 1996 'The cathedral site before 1096', in Atherton et al 1996, 59–72

Ayers, T 1996 'The painted glass of Wells cathedral, *c*1285–1345', PhD thesis, Courtauld Institute of Art (since published as *The medieval stained glass of Wells cathedral*, Corpus Vitrearum Great Britain IV, British Academy, 2004)

Ayers, T (ed) 2000 *Salisbury cathedral: the west front: a study in history and conservation*, Phillimore

Ayers, T and Tatton-Brown, T (eds) 2006 *Medieval art, architecture and archaeology in Rochester*, BAA

Aylmer, G and Cant, R (eds) 1977 *A history of York minster*, Clarendon Press

Aylmer, G and Tiller, J (eds) 2000 *Hereford cathedral: a history*, Hambledon

BAA (ed) 1978 *Medieval art and architecture at Worcester cathedral*, BAA

BAA/Kent Archaeological Society 1982 *Medieval Art and Architecture at Canterbury before 1220*, Transactions of 5th BAA conference 1979

Backhouse, J (ed) 2003 *The medieval English cathedral*, Proceedings of the 1998 Harlaxton Symposium, Shaun Tyas

Bailey, D S 1981 'The Liberty, Wells', in Coldstream and Draper 1981, 54–61

Bailey, M 1993 'The Mappa Mundi triptych: the full story of the Hereford cathedral panels', *Apollo*, June 1993, 374–8

Bailey, R N 1996 'Seventh-century work at Ripon and Hexham', in Tatton-Brown and Munby 1996, 9–19

Barker, P, Wiltshire, K and Prentice, J 1994 *A short architectural history of Worcester cathedral*, Worcester Cathedral Publications 2

Barlow, F 2004a 'Becket, Thomas', *ODNB*

Barlow, F 2004b 'Leofric', *ODNB*

Barlow, F 2004c 'St Calais, William of', *ODNB*

Barnard, T c.2000 *St Chad and the Lichfield gospels*, R J L Smith and Associates/Chapter of Lichfield Cathedral

Barr, C B L 1977 'The minster library', in Aylmer and Cant 1977, 487–539

Barret, P 1982 'A saint in the calendar: the effect of the canonisation of St Thomas Cantilupe on the liturgy', in Jancey 1982b, 153–80

Barret, P 2000 'The college of vicars choral', in Aylmer and Tiller 2000, 441–60

Barrett, I 1982 'The relics of St Thomas Cantilupe', in Jancey 1982, 181–90

Barron, C M and Rousseau, M-H 2004 'Cathedral, city and state 1300–1540', in Keene et al 2004, 33–44

Barron, C M and Stratford, J (eds) 2002 *The church and learning in later medieval society: essays in honour of R. B. Dobson*, Proceedings of the 1999 Harlaxton Symposium, Shaun Tyas

Barrow, G W S 1994 'The kings of Scotland and Durham', in Rollason et al 1994, 311–24

Barrow, J 1994 'English cathedral communities and reform in the late tenth and eleventh centuries', in Rollason et al 1994, 25–39

Barrow, J 2000 'Athelstan and Aigueblanche, 1056–1268', in Aylmer and Tiller 2000, 21–47

Barrow, J 2004 'Robert the Lotharingian', *ODNB*

Barrow, J 2005 'The origins of vicars choral to c.1300', in Hall and Stocker 2005, 11–16

Bates, D 1984 'The building of a great church: the abbey of St Peter's Gloucester and its early Norman benefactors', *Transactions of the Bristol and Gloucestershire Archaeological Society*, 102, 129–32

Bates, D 1992 *Bishop Remigius of Lincoln 1067–92*, The Honywood Press/Lincoln Cathedral Publications

Bates, D 1994 'The forged charters of William the Conqueror and bishop William of St-Calais', in Rollason et al 1994, 111–24

Battiscombe, C F 1956 *The relics of St Cuthbert*, OUP for the Dean and Chapter of Durham cathedral

Baxter, P 1984 *Sarum Use: the development of a medieval code of liturgy and customs*, Sarum Script

Bazeley, W (ed) 1882–3 *Records of Gloucester cathedral* I, Gloucester Cathedral Society

Beacham, P 1991 'Buildings of the close', in Swanton 1991b, 19–28

Bede, the Venerable 1965 'Life of St Cuthbert', in *Lives of the saints*, ed and trans J F Webb, Penguin, 69–131

Bede, the Venerable 1977 *A history of the English church and people*, ed and trans L Sherley-Price, rev R E Latham, Penguin

Bettey, J 2000 'St Augustine's abbey', in Rogan 2000, 15–37

Biddle, M 1976 *Winchester in the early middle ages*, OUP

Biddle, M 1990 'Wolsey's bell tower', in Blair 1990a, 205–10

Biddle, M 1993 'Early Renaissance at Winchester', in Crook 1993c, 257–304

Biddle, M and Kjølbye-Biddle, B 2001 'The origins of St Alban's abbey: Romano-British cemetery and Anglo-Saxon monastery', in Henig and Lindley 2001, 45–77

Binski, P 1997 'The Angel Choir at Lincoln and the poetics of the gothic smile', *Art History*, 350–74

Binski, P 2002 'The murals in the nave of St Alban's abbey', in Franklin and Rubin 2002, 249–87

Binski, P 2004 *Becket's crown: art and imagination in gothic England 1170–1300*, Yale University Press

Blair, J 1987 'Saint Frideswide reconsidered', *Oxoniensia*, 52, 71–127

Blair, J (ed) 1990a *Saint Frideswide's monastery at Oxford: archaeological and architectural studies*, Alan Sutton

Blair, J 1990b 'St Frideswide's monastery: problems and possibilities', in Blair 1990a, 221–58

Blair, J with Mellor, M 1990c, 'Thornbury, Binsey: a probable defensive enclosure associated with Saint Frideswide', in Blair 1990a, 3–20

Blair, J 1996 'The archaeology of Oxford cathedral', in Tatton-Brown and Munby 1996, 95–102

Blair, J (ed) 2005 *The church in Anglo-Saxon society*, OUP

Blair, J and Ramsay, N 1991 *English medieval industries – craftsmen, techniques, products*, Hambledon

Blockley, K, with Sparks, M, Tatton-Brown, T and contributors 1997 *Canterbury cathedral nave: archaeology, history and architecture, I: the archaeology of Canterbury*, Dean and Chapter of Canterbury cathedral with Canterbury Archaeological Trust [Appendix 2: Estates, 566]

Blount, M N 2004 'Glanville, Gilbert de', *ODNB*

Boggis, R J E 1922 *A history of the diocese of Exeter*, W Pollard and Co

Bonner, G, Rollason, D and Stancliffe, C (eds) 1989 *St Cuthbert, his cult and community*, Boydell and Brewer

Bony, J 1990 'The stonework planning of the first Durham master', in Fernie and Crossley 1990, 19–34

Boüker, J 1998 'The bishop's chapel of Hereford cathedral and the question of architectural copies in the Middle Ages', *Gesta*, 37/50, 44–54

Bowers, R 1993 'The lady chapel and its musicians *c.* 1210–1559', in Crook 1993c, 247–56

Bowers, R 1994 'Music and worship', in Owen 1994a, 47–76

Bowker, M 1968 *The secular clergy in the diocese of Lincoln 1495–1520*, Cambridge Studies in Medieval Life and Thought, new series, XIII, CUP

Bowker, M 1994 'Historical survey 1450–1750', in Owen 1994b, 164–209

Brett, M 1996 'The church at Rochester, 604–1185', in Yates and Welsby 1996, 1–27

Brett, M 2004 'Gundulf', *ODNB*

Brighton, T 1994 'Art in the cathedral from the foundation to the Civil War,' in Hobbs 1994, 69–84

Brooke, C 1993 'Bishop Walkelin and his inheritance', in Crook 1993c, 1–12

Brooks, C 1991a 'The cathedral since the Reformation', in Swanton 1991b, 217–26

Brooks, C 1991b 'The medieval stained glass', in Swanton 1991b, 99–110

Brooks, N 1984 *The early history of the church of Canterbury: Christ Church from 597 to 1066*, Studies in the Early History of Britain, Leicester University Press

Brooks, N P 2004 'Oswald [St Oswald]', *ODNB*

Broughton, L 1996 *Interpreting Lincoln cathedral: the medieval imagery*, Lincoln Cathedral Publications

Brown, A D 1995 *Popular piety in late medieval England: the diocese of Salisbury 1250–1550*, Oxford Historical Monographs, Clarendon Press

Brown, A L 1989 *The governance of late medieval England 1272–1461*, Stanford University Press

Brown, E H Phelps and Hopkins, S 1966a 'Seven centuries of building wages', in Carus-Wilson 1966, 168–78

Brown, E H Phelps and Hopkins, S 1966b 'Seven centuries of the prices of consumables compared with builders' wage-rates', in Carus-Wilson 1966, 179–96

Brown, S 1997 'The stained glass of the lady chapel of Bristol cathedral; Charles Winston (1814–64) and stained glass restoration in the 19th century', in Keen 1997, 107–17

Brown, S 1999 *Sumptuous and richly adorn'd: the decoration of Salisbury cathedral*, RCHME/Stationery Office

Brown, S 2003 '*Our magnificent fabrick' York minster: an architectural history c.1220–1500*, English Heritage

Buck, M C 2004a 'Hotham, John', *ODNB*

Buck, M C 2004b 'Hythe [Hethe], Hamo', *ODNB*

Buck, M C 2004c 'Salmon, John', *ODNB*

Buck, M C 2004d 'Stapeldon, Walter', *ODNB*

Burnett, C 1995 'Mathematics and astronomy in Hereford and its region in the twelfth century', in Whitehead 1995, 50–9

Burton, J 2004 'William of York (St William of York, William fitz Herbert)', *ODNB*

Campbell, J 1989 'Elements in the background to the life of St Cuthbert and his early cult', in Bonner et al 1989, 3–20

Cannon, J 2004 'The absent figure: on authorship and meaning in … St Augustine's, Bristol', *Transactions of the Ancient Monuments Society*, 48, 21–48

Cannon, J (forthcoming) 'The tombs don't fit: aggrieved barons and the dating of the east end of St Augustine's, Bristol', in A Gomme, *Bristol: an architectural history* (revised edn)

Cannon, J and Williamson, B 2011 *An Enigma Explored: Medieval history, art and architecture at Bristol cathedral*, Boydell and Brewer

Carus-Wilson, E M 1962 *Essays in economic history* II, Edward Arnold (1966 edn)

Carver, M 2001 'Why that? Why there? Why then? The politics of early medieval monumentality', in Hamerow and Macgregor 2001, 1–22

Catto, J 1982 'The academic career of Thomas Cantilupe', in Jancey 1982b, 45–56

Chapman, F R (ed) 1907 *Sacrist rolls of Ely*, CUP

Cherry, B 1991a 'Flying angels and bishops' tombs, a fifteenth-century conundrum', in Kelly 1991, 199–204

Cherry, B 1991b 'Some cathedral tombs', in Swanton 1991b, 157–68

Cherry, J 1991 'The ring of Bishop Grandisson', in Kelly 1991, 205–9

Cherry, J 1995 'The rings of John Stanbury and Richard Mayo, bishops of Hereford', in Whitehead 1995, 150–6

Chibnall, M (ed) 1991 *Anglo-Norman studies XIV*, Boydell and Brewer

Churchill, I 1933 Josephine *Canterbury administration: the administrative machinery of the archbishopric of Canterbury, illustrated from original records*, I, SPCK

Clark, J G 2001 'The St Albans monks and the cult of St Alban: late medieval texts', in Henig and Lindley 2001, 218–30

Clark, J 2004 'Mare, Thomas de la', *ODNB*

Clifton-Taylor, A 1967 *The cathedrals of England*, Thames and Hudson

Cocke, T 1993 'Ruin and restoration: Lichfield cathedral in the seventeenth century', in Maddison 1993b, 109–14

Coffman, P 1998 'The romanesque east end of Southwell

minster', in Alexander 1998a, 1–23

Colchester, L S (ed) 1982 *Wells cathedral: a history*, Open Books

Coldstream, N 1976 'English decorated shrine bases', *Journal of the BAA*, 129, 15–34

Coldstream, N 1979 'Ely cathedral: the fourteenth-century work', in Coldstream and Draper 1979, 28–45

Coldstream, N 1991 'The great rebuilding, c.1270–1390', in Swanton 1991b, 47–60

Coldstream, N 2000 'The medieval tombs and the shrine of Saint Thomas Cantilupe', in Aylmer and Tiller 2000, 322–30

Coldstream, N and Draper, P (eds) 1979 *Medieval art and architecture at Ely cathedral*, BAA

Coldstream, N and Draper, P (eds) 1980 *Medieval art and architecture at Durham cathedral*, BAA

Coldstream, N and Draper, P (eds) 1981 *Medieval art and architecture at Wells and Glastonbury*, BAA

Coldstream, N and Draper, P 1982 *Medieval art and architecture at Canterbury before 1220*, BAA

Coldstream, N and Lindley 1995 Hereford

Collinson, P; Ramsey N and Sparks, M (eds) 1995 *A history of Canterbury cathedral*, OUP

Colvin, H R, Allen Brown, R and Taylor, A J 1963 *The history of the king's works: vols I and II, The Middle Ages*, HMSO

Courtney, L 2004 'Hurley, William', *ODNB*

Cowdrey H E J 2004a 'Lanfranc', *ODNB*

Cowdrey H E J 2004b 'Remigius', *ODNB*

Cragoe, C D 2004 'Fabric, tombs and precinct 1087–1540', in Keene et al 2004, 127–42

Craze, M 1986/7 *Lectures on Worcester cathedral* [no publisher]

Crick, J 2001 'Offa, Aelfric and the refoundation of St Albans', in Henig and Lindley 2001, 78–84

Crook, J 1993a 'Bishop Walkelin's cathedral', in Crook 1993c, 21–36

Crook, J 1993b 'St Swithun of Winchester', in Crook 1993c, 57–68

Crook, J (ed) 1993c *Winchester cathedral: Nine hundred years 1093–1993*, Phillimore

Crook, J and Kusaba, Y 1993 'The Perpendicular remodelling of the nave: problems and interpretation', in Crook 1993c, 215–30

Crook, J 2006 'The medieval shrines of Rochester cathedral', in Ayers and Tatton-Brown 2006, 114–29

Crossley, A (ed) 1979 *VCH Oxford IV*, OUP

Dalton, N 1917 *The collegiate church of Ottery St Mary* [no publisher]

Dalton, P 1994 'Scottish influence on Durham 1066–1214', in Rollason et al 1994, 353–68

Danbury, E 2000 'The intellectual life of the abbey of St Werburgh's in the Middle Ages', in Thacker 2000a, 107–20

Davenport, P 1996 'The cathedral priory church at Bath', in Tatton-Brown and Munby 1996, 19–31

Davies, C S L 2004 'Fox, Richard', *ODNB*

Davies, R G 2004 'Edington, William', *ODNB*

Davis, V 2004a 'The lesser clergy in the later Middle Ages', in Keene et al 2004, 157–61

Davis, V 2004b 'Waynflete, William', *ODNB*

Deanesly, M 1964 *Augustine of Canterbury*, Nelson

Demidowicz, G (ed) 1994 *Coventry's first cathedral: the cathedral and priory of St Mary*, Paul Watkins

Denton, J H 2004a 'Bronescombe, Walter of', *ODNB*

Denton, J H 2004b 'Winchelsey, Robert', *ODNB*

Denton, J H and Dooley, J P 1987 *Representatives of the lower clergy in parliament 1295–1340*, Boydell/Royal Historical Society

Dixon, P 2003 'The monastic buildings at Ely', in Meadows and Ramsay 2003, 142–56

Dobson, B 1977 'The later middle ages, 1215–1500', in Aylmer and Cant 1977, 44–110

Dobson, B 1995a 'The monks of Canterbury in the later Middle Ages, 1220–1540', in Collinson and Sparks 1995, 69–153

Dobson, B 1995b 'The protestant cathedral, 1541–1660', in Collinson and Sparks 1995, 154–203

Dobson, B 2003 'The clergy are well lodged: the transformation of the cathedral precinct at late medieval Durham', in Backhouse 2003, 23–40

Dobson, B 2005 'The English vicars choral: an introduction', in Hall and Stocker 2005, 1–10

Dodwell, B 1996a 'Herbert de Losinga and the foundation', in Atherton et al 1996, 36–58

Dodwell, B 1996b 'The monastic community', in Atherton et al 1996, 231–54

Dodwell, B 1996c 'The muniments and the library', in Atherton et al 1996, 325–38

Donovan, C 1993a 'The Winchester Bible', in Crook 1993c, 81–96

Donovan, C 1993b *The Winchester Bible*, Winchester Cathedral

Doubleday, H A and Page, W (eds) 1903 *VCH Hampshire and the Isle of Wight*, IHR (repr. Dawsons 1973)

Douie, D L and Farmer, H (eds) 1961 *Magna vita Sancti Hugonis*, 2 vols, Thomas Nelson

Draper, P 1979 'Bishop Northwold and the cult of St Etheldreda', in Coldstream and Draper 1979, 8–27

Draper, P 1981 'The sequence and dating of the

Decorated work at Wells', in Coldstream and Draper 1981, 18–29

Draper, P 1983 'William of Sens and the original design of the choir of Canterbury cathedral, 1175–1179', *Journal of the Society of Architectural Historians*, 42, 238–48

Draper, P 1986 'The retroquire of Winchester cathedral: evidence and interpretation', *Journal of the BAA*, 139, 68–74

Draper, P 1990 'Seeing that it was done in all the noble churches in England', in Fernie and Crossley 1990, 137–42

Draper, P 1995 'Interpreting the architecture of Wells cathedral', in Raguin et al 1995, 114–30

Draper, P 1996 'Paradigm or maverick', in Keen and Cocke 1996, 21–31

Draper, P 1997 'Interpretations of the rebuilding of Canterbury cathedral, 1174–1186: archaeological and historical evidence', *Journal of the Society of Architectural Historians*, 56, 1–22

Draper, P 2006a *The formation of English gothic: architecture and identity*, Yale

Draper, P 2006b 'The late twelfth-century east end of Rochester cathedral', in Ayers and Tatton-Brown 2006, 97–113

Draper, P and Morris, R K 1993 'The development of the east end of Winchester cathedral from the thirteenth century to the sixteenth', in Crook 1993c, 177–92

Duffy, E 1992 *The stripping of the altars*, Yale

Duggan, A J 1982 'The cult of St Thomas Becket in the thirteenth century', in Jancey 1982b, 21–44

Duggan, A J 2004 'Robert of Cricklade', *ODNB*

Duggan, C 2004 'FitzJocelin, Reginald', *ODNB*

Dunning, R W 1982 'The Bishop's Palace', in Colchester 1982, 227–44

Dunning, R W 2004 'Jocelin of Wells', *ODNB*

Edwards, K 1967 *The English Secular Cathedrals in the Middle Ages*, Manchester University Press

Engel, U 2000 *Die Kathedrale von Worcester*, Deutscher Kunstverlag

Engel, U 1998 'Two-storied elevations: the choir of Southwell minster and the West Country', in Alexander 1998a, 33–43

Erskine, A (ed) 1981 and 1983 *The accounts of the fabric of Exeter cathedral, 1279–1353*, 2 vols, Devon and Cornwall Record Society new series, 24 and 26

Erskine, A 1991a 'Library and archives', in Swanton 1991b, 193–202

Erskine, A 1991b 'The documentation of Exeter cathedral: the archives and their applications', in Kelly 1991, 1–9

Erskine, A 2004 'Grandison, John', *ODNB*

Etchingham, C 1999 *Church organisation in Ireland AD 650–1000*, Laigin Publications

Evans, S 1973 *The medieval estate of the cathedral priory of Ely*, Dean and Chapter of Ely

Faith, R 2004 'Estates and income, 1066–1540', in Keene et al 2004, 143–50

Fawcett, R 1996 'The influence of the gothic parts of the cathedral on church building in Norfolk', in Atherton et al 1996, 210–27

Fernie, E 1982 *The architecture of the Anglo-Saxons*, Batsford

Fernie, E 1993 *An architectural history of Norwich cathedral*, Clarendon Press

Fernie, E 1994 'The architectural influence of Durham cathedral', in Rollason et al 1994, 269–79

Fernie, E 1996 'The building: an introduction', in Atherton et al 1996, 47–58

Fernie, E 2000 *The architecture of Norman England*, OUP

Fernie, E 2003 'The architecture and sculpture of Ely cathedral in the Norman period', in Meadows and Ramsay 2003, 95–112

Fernie, E and Crossley, P (eds) 1990 *Medieval architecture in its intellectual context: studies in honour of Peter Kidson*, Hambledon

Fines, J 1994 'Cathedral and Reformation', in Hobbs 1994, 47–68

Finucane, R C 1977 *Miracles and pilgrims: popular beliefs in medieval England*, Dent

Finucane, R C 1982a 'Cantilupe as thaumaturge: pilgrims and their 'miracles'', in Jancey 1982b, 137–46

Finucane, R C 1982b 'The Canterbury–Pecham controversy', in Jancey 1982b, 103–24

Finucane, R C 2004 'Cantilupe, Thomas', *ODNB*

Flanagan, J F 1946 'The nature goddess silk at Durham', *Burlington Magazine*, 88 (523), 241–7

Fleming, P 2000 'Conflict and urban government in later medieval England: St Augustine's abbey and Bristol', *Urban History*, 27, 325–43

Flight, C 1997 *The bishop and monks of Rochester 1076–1214*, Kent Archaeological Society

Forster, B, Robson, B and Deadman, J 1993 *Ripon cathedral: its history and architecture*, William Sessions Ltd

Forsyth, M 2003 *Bath* (Pevsner Architectural Guides), Yale University Press

Foster, M 1994 'Custodians of St Cuthbert: the Durham monks' views of their predecessors, 1083–c.1200', in Rollason et al 1994, 53–65

Foyle, A 2004 *Bristol* (Pevsner Architectural Guides), Yale University Press

Franklin, J 1996 'The romanesque sculpture', in Atherton et al 1996, 116–35

Franklin, J 2004 'Augustinian architecture in the twelfth century: the context for Carlisle cathedral', in McCarthy and Weston 2004, 73–88

Franklin, M J 1994 'The bishops of Coventry and Lichfield c.1072–1208', in Demidowicz 1994, 118–38

Franklin, M J 2004 'Walkelin', ODNB

Franklin, M J and Harper-Bill, C (eds) 1995 Medieval ecclesiastical studies in honour of Dorothy M Owen, Boydell and Brewer

Franklin, M J and Rubin, M with Abulafia, D 2002 Church and city, 1000–1500: essays in honour of Christopher Brooke, CUP

French, T 1999 York minster: the St William window, OUP for the British Academy

Gardner, J 1995 'The tomb of Bishop Peter of Aquablanca in Hereford cathedral', in Whitehead 1995, 105–10

Garton, C 1986 The metrical life of St Hugh, Honywood Press

Geddes, J 1996 'The medieval decorative ironwork', in Atherton et al 1996, 431–42

Gee, E A 1974 York minster: chapter house and vestibule, HMSO (RCHME) (1980 edn)

Gee, L 1995 'Fourteenth-century tombs for women in Herefordshire', in Whitehead 1995, 132–49

Gem, R 1978 'Bishop Wullfstan II and the romanesque cathedral church of Worcester', in BAA 1978, 15–37

Gem, R 1983 'The romanesque cathedral of Winchester: patron and design in the eleventh century', in Heslop and Sekules 1983, 1–12

Gem, R 1986 'Lincoln minster: ecclesia pulchra ecclesia fortis', in Heslop and Sekules 1986, 9–28

Gem, R 1990 'The romanesque architecture of Old St Paul's cathedral and its late eleventh-century context', in Grant 1990, 47–63

Gem, R 2000 'The significance of the eleventh-century rebuilding', in Thacker 2000a, 1–44

Gibb, H P 1975 'The Anglo-Saxon cathedral at Sherborne', Archaeological Journal, 132, 71–110

Gibson, M 1995 'Normans and Angevins 1070–1220', in Collinson and Sparks 1995, 38–68

Gilchrist, R 2005 Norwich cathedral close: the evolution of the English cathedral landscape, Boydell and Brewer

Gillespie, V 1997 'Medieval hypertext: image and text from York minster', in Robinson and Zim 1997, 206–29

Gillingham, J and Griffiths, R A 2000 Medieval Britain: a very short introduction, OUP

Givens, J A 1998 'The leaves of Southwell revisited', in Alexander 1998a, 60–6

Golding, B 1986 'Burials and benefactions: an aspect of monastic patronage in thirteenth century England', in Ormrod 1986, 71–3

Gomme, A et al 1979 Bristol: an architectural history (revised edn forthcoming)

Goodall, J 2007 'St George's chapel: history', http://www.stgeorges-windsor.org/history/hist_index.asp, accessed 2007

Goodall, J and Monckton, L 2001 'The chantry of Humphrey, duke of Gloucester', in Henig and Lindley 2001, 231–56

Gransden, A 1978 'Cultural transition at Worcester in the Anglo-Norman period', in BAA 1978, 1–14

Gransden, A 1982 'The history of Wells cathedral, c.1090–1547', in Colchester 1982, 24–51

Grant, L 1990 Medieval art, architecture and archaeology in London, BAA

Gray, D 2004 'Gower, John', ODNB

Greatrex, J 1993 'St Swithun's priory in the later Middle Ages', in Crook 1993c, 139–166

Greatrex, J 2003 'Benedictine observance at Ely: the intellectual, liturgical and spiritual evidence considered', in Meadows and Ramsay 2003, 77–94

Greatrex, J 2006 'Who were the monks of Rochester?', in Ayers and Tatton-Brown 2006, 205–17

Greenway, D 1994 'The medieval cathedral', in Hobbs 1994, 11–24

Greenway, D 2004 'Historical writing at St Paul's', in Keene et al 2004, 151–6

Grossinger, C 2000 'Chester cathedral misericords: iconography and sources', in Thacker 2000a, 98–106

Haines, R M 2004a 'Gray, Walter de', ODNB

Haines, R M 2004b 'Langton, Walter', ODNB

Hall, R and Stocker, D (eds) 2005 Vicars choral at English cathedrals: Cantata Domino: history architecture and archaeology, Oxbow

Halsey, R 1990 'The twelfth-century church of St Frideswide's priory', in Blair 1990a, 115–68

Halsey, R 2006 'The twelfth-century nave of Rochester cathedral', in Ayers and Tatton-Brown 2006, 61–84

Hamerow H and Macgregor A (eds) 2001 Image and power in the archaeology of early medieval Britain: essays in honour of Rosemary Cramp, Oxbow

Harper, J 2000 'Music and liturgy, 1300–1600', in Aylmer and Tiller 2000, 375–97

Harper, J 2005 'The vicar choral in choir', in Hall and Stocker 2005, 17–22

Harper-Bill, C 1996 'The medieval church and the wider world', in Atherton et al 1996, 281–313

Harper-Bill, C 2004a 'Losinga, Herbert de', ODNB

Harper-Bill, C 2004b 'Sherborn [Sherborne], Robert', *ODNB*

Harper-Bill, C 2004c 'Wych, Richard of', *ODNB*

Harris, B E 1979 *VCH Cheshire* I and III, OUP for Institute of Historical Research

Harrison, F 1952 *Life in a medieval college: the story of the vicars-choral of York minster*, John Murray

Harrison, S 1994 'Observation on the architecture of the Galilee chapel', in Rollason et al 1994, 213–34 (and more recent unpublished conference paper on the same)

Harriss, G L 2004 'Beaufort, Henry', *ODNB*

Harvey, J H 1950 *The cathedrals of England and Wales*, Batsford (1963 edn)

Harvey, J H 1968 'The tracing floor of York minster', *Annual Report of the Friends of York minster*, 40, 1–7

Harvey, J H 1975 'William Hurley', *Dictionary of National Biography*, OUP

Harvey, J H 1977 'Architectural history from 1291 to 1558', in Aylmer and Cant 1977, 149–92

Harvey, J H 1981 'Perpendicular at Wells', in Coldstream and Draper 1981, 36–41

Harvey, J H 1982a 'The building of Wells cathedral I 1175–1307', in Colchester 1982, 52–75

Harvey, J H 1982b 'The building of Wells cathedral II 1307–1508', in Colchester 1982, 75–101

Harvey, J 1994 *Henry Yevele*, Batsford

Harvey, J H (rev T Ayers) 2004 'Witney, Thomas of', *ODNB*

Harvey, P D A 2000 'Mappa mundi', in Aylmer and Tiller 2000, 557–64

Hastings, A 1997 *Elias of Dereham: architect of Salisbury cathedral*, R J L Smith and Associates/Dean and Chapter of Salisbury

Hayes, R C 2004 'Alnwick, William', *ODNB*

Hearn, M F 1983 'Ripon minster: the beginning of the gothic style in northern England', *Transactions of the American Philosophical Society*, 73, pt 6

Hearn, M F and Willis, L 1996 'The iconography of the lady chapel of Salisbury cathedral', in Keen and Cocke 1996, 40–5

Heighway, C 1996 'The archaeology of Gloucester cathedral', in Tatton-Brown and Munby 1996, 73–80

Henig, M 2004 'The arts of Rome in Carlisle and the civitas of the carvetii and their influence', in McCarthy and Weston 2004, 11–38

Henig, M and Lindley, P 2001 *Alban and St Albans: Roman and medieval art, architecture and archaeology*, BAA

Henry, A 1991 'The west front III: the iconography of the west front', in Kelly 1991, 134–46

Hereford and Worcestershire Earth Heritage Trust (no date) *Explore Worcester cathedral building stones trail*

Heslop, T A 1982 'The conventual seals of Canterbury cathedral 1066–1232', in Coldstream and Draper 1982, 94–100

Heslop, T A 1990 'The iconography of the Angel Choir at Lincoln cathedral', in Fernie and Crossley 1990, 137–42

Heslop, T A and Sekules, V (eds) 1983 *Medieval art and architecture at Winchester cathedral*, BAA

Heslop, T A and Sekules, V (eds) 1985 *Medieval art and architecture at Gloucester and Tewkesbury*, BAA

Heslop, T A and Sekules, V (eds) 1986 *Medieval art and architecture at Lincoln cathedral*, BAA

Hewett, C A 1974 *English cathedral carpentry*, Wayland

Hibbert, C (ed) 1988 *The encyclopaedia of Oxford*, Macmillan

Higham, J 1999 'The relationship between the abbey and town of Peterborough, from 1200 to the Reformation', in Thompson 1999, 157–76

Higham, N J 2004 *A frontier landscape: the north west in the Middle Ages*, Windgather Press

Hill, J W F 1948 *Medieval Lincoln*, CUP

Hill, R M 1950 *Oliver Sutton bishop of Lincoln 1280–99*, Honywood Press (1982 edn)

Hill, R M and Brooke, C N L 1977 'From 627 until the early thirteenth century', in Aylmer and Cant 1977, 1–43

Hoban, R 2002 *Riddley Walker*, Bloomsbury

Hobbs, M (ed) 1994 *Chichester cathedral: an historical survey*, Phillimore

Hobhouse, Bishop Right Rev. 1889–90 'Map of Somerset showing the chief estates as recorded in *Domesday Book* a.d. 1086' *Proceedings of the Somerset Archaeological and Natural History Society*, 35

Hobley, B et al 1967–70 'Excavations at the cathedral and Benedictine priory of St Mary Coventry', *Birmingham and Warwickshire Archaeological Society Transactions*, 84, 46–139

Holdsworth, C 2004 'Langton, Stephen', *ODNB*

Holt, E G 1957 *A documentary history of art I*, Doubleday Anchor, 52–62

Hoskin, P 2004a 'Poore, Richard', *ODNB*

Hoskin, P 2004b 'Swinfield, Richard', *ODNB*

Houlbrooke, R 1996 'Refoundation and Reformation 1538–1628', in Atherton et al 1996, 507–633

Hudson, J 2004 'Nigel', *ODNB*

Hughes, J 2004a 'Arundel [Fitzalan], Thomas', *ODNB*

Hughes, J 2004b 'Thoresby, John', *ODNB*

Hulbert, A 1991 'An examination of the polychromy of Exeter cathedral roof-bosses, and its documentation', in Kelly 1991, 188–98

Hurst, A M 2004 *Diocese of Southwark 1905–2005: a centennial celebration*, presumed Dean and Chapter of Southwark

James, B S 1957 *Saint Bernard of Clairvaulx: an essay in biography*, Hodder and Stoughton

Jancey, M 1982a 'Appendix: a servant speaks of his master: Hugh le Barber's evidence in 1307', in Jancey 1982b, 191–202

Jancey, M (ed) 1982b *St Thomas Cantilupe bishop of Hereford: essays in his honour*, Friends of Hereford Cathedral

Jancey, M 1994 *St Ethelbert patron saint*, Hereford Cathedral Enterprises

Jansen, V 1991 'The design and building sequence of the eastern arm of Exeter cathedral *c*.1270–1310', in Kelly 1991, 35–56

Jansen, V 1996 'Salisbury cathedral and the Episcopal style in the early thirteenth century', in Keen and Cocke 1996, 32–9

Jansen, V 2000a 'Attested but opaque: the early gothic east end of St Werburgh's', in Thacker 2000a, 57–65

Jansen, V 2000b 'George Gilbert Scott and the restoration at Chester cathedral 1819–76', in Thacker 2000a, 81–97

Jeayes, I H (ed) 1889–90 'Abbot's roll of the abbots of St Augustine's abbey by Bristol', *Transactions of the Bristol and Gloucestershire Archaeological Society*, 14, 117–30

Jessop, A and James M R (eds) 1896 *Thomas of Monmouth: the life and miracles of St William of Norwich*, CUP

Jewell, H 2004 'March, William', *ODNB*

Kahn, D 2001 *Canterbury cathedral and its romanesque sculpture*, Harvey Miller

Keefe, T K 2004 'Henry II', *ODNB*

Keen, L (ed) 1997 *Almost the richest city: medieval art and archaeology at Bristol*, British Archaeological Association

Keen, L and Cocke, T (eds) 1996 *Medieval art and architecture at Salisbury cathedral*, BAA

Keene, D 2004 'From Conquest to capital: St Paul's *c*.1100–1300', in Keene et al 2004, 17–32

Keene, D, Burns, A and Saint, A 2004 *St Paul's: the cathedral church of London 604–2004*, Yale

Keene, D and Taylor, P 2004 'St Paul's as St Paul's', in Keene et al 2004, 1

Kekewich, M L 2004 'Aiscough, William', *ODNB*

Kelly, F (ed) 1991 *Medieval art and architecture at Exeter cathedral*, BAA

Kelly, S 1994 'The bishopric of Selsey', in Hobbs 1994, 1–10

Kerr, J 1985 'The east window of Gloucester cathedral', in Heslop and Sekules 1985, 116–29

Kettle, A J and Johnson, D 1970 *A history of Lichfield cathedral*, fascicule from *VCH Staffordshire*, repr. Staffordshire and Stoke-on-Trent Archive Service 2001

Keynes, S 2000 'Diocese and cathedral before 1056', in Aylmer and Tiller 2000, 3–20

Keynes, S 2003 'Ely abbey 672–1109', in Meadows and Ramsay 2003, 3–58

Kidson, P 1986 'St Hugh's choir', in Heslop and Sekules 1986, 29–42

Kidson, P 1993a 'Gervase, Becket and William of Sens', *Speculum*, 68, 969–91

Kidson, P 1993b 'The historical circumstances and the principles of the design', in Kidson and Cocke 1993, 37–91

Kidson, P 1994 'Architectural history', in Owen 1994a, 14–46

Kidson, P and Cocke, T 1993 *Salisbury cathedral: perspectives on the architectural history*, RCHME

Kidson, P and Cocke, T 1994 'Architectural history', in Owen 1994a, 14–46

King, D 1996 'The panel paintings and stained glass', in Atherton et al 1996, 410–30

King, E 1973 *Peterborough abbey 1086–1310: a study in the land market*, CUP

King, E 2004 'Blois, Henry de', *ODNB*

Kjølbye-Biddle, B 1993 'Old minster, St Swithun's day 1093', in Crook 1993c, 13–20

Kjølbye-Biddle, B 2001 'The Alban cross', in Henig and Lindley 2001, 85–110

Klukas, W A 1981 'The *Liber Ruber* and the rebuilding of the east end at Wells', in Coldstream and Draper 1981, 30–5

Klukas, W A 1984 'The architectural implications of the *Decreta Lanfranci*', in Allen Brown 1984, 136–71

Klukas, W A 1995 'Durham cathedral in the gothic era: liturgy, design, ornament', in Raguin et al 1995, 69–83

Knoop, D and Jones, G P 1933 *The medieval mason: an economic history of English stone building in the later Middle Ages and early modern times*, Manchester University Press (1967 edn)

Knowles, D 1961–2 *The religious orders in England*, vols I and III, CUP

Knowles, D 1963 *The monastic order in England*, CUP

Knowles, D and Hadcock, N R 1971 *Medieval religious houses*, Longman

Kreider, A 1979 *English chantries: the road to Dissolution*, Harvard University Press

Kusaba, Y 1988 'The function, date and stylistic sources of the treasury of Henry of Blois in the south transept of Winchester cathedral', *Winchester Cathedral Record*, 57, 38–49

Lapidge, M and Winterbottom, M 1991 *Wulfstan of Winchester: the life of St Aethelwold*, Clarendon Press

Leedy, W C 1978 'The origins of fan vaulting', *Art Bulletin*, 40 (2 June), 207–13

Leedy, W C 1980 *Fan vaulting: a study of form, technology, and meaning*, Scolar

Lewis, C P 2004 'd'Avranches, Hugh', *ODNB*

Leyser, K J 1987 'The Angevin kings and the holy man', in Mayr-Harting 1987, 62–3

Lindley, P G 1985 'The monastic cathedral at Ely, *c*.1320 to *c*.1350: art and patronage in medieval East Anglia', unpublished PhD thesis, Downing College, Cambridge

Lindley, P G 1986 'The imagery of the Octagon at Ely', *Journal of the BAA*, 139, 75–99

Lindley, P G 1993 'The medieval sculpture of Winchester cathedral', in Crook 1993c, 97–122

Lindley, P G 1995 'Retrospective effigies, the past and lies', in Whitehead 1995, 111–31

Lindley, P G 2001 'The great screen and its context', in Henig and Lindley 2001, 256–70

Lloyd, D 2002 *Arthur, Prince of Wales*, Fabric Trust for St Laurence, Ludlow

Lorrey, H J 2004a 'Little St Hugh', *ODNB*

Lorrey, H J 2004b 'St William of Norwich', *ODNB*

Lubin, H and Barker, P (eds) 1990 *The Worcester pilgrim*, Worcester Cathedral Publications I

Lucius, 'Description of the city of Chester', at http://www.bwpics.co.uk/quotes/index.html (accessed 2005)

Luxford, J M 2000 'In dreams: the sculptural iconography of the west front of Bath abbey reassessed', *Religion and the Arts*, 4 (3), 313–36

Luxford, J 2005 *The art and architecture of English Benedictine monasteries, 1300–1540: a Patronage History*, Boydell and Brewer

Lyon, Bryce W W 1980 *A constitutional and legal history of medieval England*, Norton

Maccarini, P A 1984 'William the Conqueror and the church of Rome (from the Epistolae)', in Allen Brown 1984, 172, 187

MacCulloch, D 2004 'Cranmer, Thomas', *ODNB*

MacDowdy 1974 *The monastic setting of Ely*, Ely Local History Publications Board

Mackreth, D F 1999 'Peterborough from St Aethelwold to Martin de Bec, *c*. 970–1155', in Thompson 1999, 137–56

Maclean, J (ed) 1883 *The Berkeley Manuscripts: lives of the Berkeleys …*, Bristol and Gloucestershire Archaeological Society

Maddison, J 1993a 'Building at Lichfield cathedral during the episcopate of Walter Langton 1296–1321', in Maddison 1993b, 65–84

Maddison, J (ed) 1993b *Medieval archaeology and architecture at Lichfield*, BAA

Maddison, J 2000a *Ely cathedral: design and meaning*, Ely Cathedral Publications

Maddison, J 2000b 'Problems in the choir of Chester cathedral', in Thacker 2000a, 66–80

Maddison, J 2003 'The gothic cathedral: new building in a historic context', in Meadows and Ramsay 2003, 113–42

Malden, A R 1901 *The canonisation of Saint Osmund*, Bennett Brothers/Salisbury Record Society

Malden, H E, 1905 *VCH Surrey* II, Constable

Malmesbury, William of 1847 *English Chronicle*, trans J A Giles, ed H G Bohn

Malmesbury, William of 2000 *A history of the Norman kings (1066–1125) with the Historia Novella or history of his own times (1126–1142)*, Llanerch (from translation by Sharpe, revised Stevenson 1854)

Malone, C M 2004 *Façade as spectacle: ritual and ideology at Wells cathedral*, Brill

Marks, R and Williamson, P 2003 *Gothic: art for England 1400–1547*, Victoria and Albert Museum

Marner, D 2000 *St Cuthbert, his life and cult in medieval Durham*, British Library

Marshall, G 1951 *Hereford cathedral: its evolution and growth*, Littlebury and Company

Martin, N D S 1982 'The life of St Thomas of Hereford', in Jancey 1982b, 15–20

Mason, E 2004 'Wulfstan [St Wulfstan]', *ODNB*

Mate, M E 2004 'Eastry, Henry', *ODNB*

Matthew, D 1994 'Durham and the Anglo-Norman world', in Rollason et al 1994, 1–22

Mayer, T F 2004 'Castellesi, Adriano de', *ODNB*

Mayr-Harting, H (ed) 1987 *Saint Hugh of Lincoln*, Clarendon

Mayr-Harting, H 2004 'Hugh of Lincoln', *ODNB*

McAleer, P J 1991 'The problem(s) of the St Edmund's chapel at Exeter cathedral', in Kelly 1991, 147–61

McAleer, P J 1996 'The medieval fabric', in Yates and Welsby 1996, 149–84

McAleer, P J 1999 *Rochester cathedral, 604–1540: an architectural history*, University of Toronto Press

McCarthy, M 1996 'The origins and development of the twelfth-century cathedral church at Carlisle', in Tatton-Brown and Munby 1996, 31–46

McCarthy, M 2004 'The roman town of Luguvalium and the post-Roman settlement', in McCarthy and Weston 2004, 1–10

McCarthy, M and Weston, D 2004 *Carlisle and Cumbria: Roman and medieval architecture, art and archaeology*, BAA

McKenna, J W 1970 'Popular canonisation as political propaganda: the cult of archbishop Scrope', *Speculum* XLV, 608–23

McNeill, J 1998 'The chronology of the choir of Southwell minster', in Alexander 1998a, 24–32

McNeill, J 2006a *Old Sarum*, English Heritage

McNeill, J 2006b 'The east cloister range of Rochester cathedral priory', in Ayers and Tatton-Brown 2006, 181–204

McNiven, P 2004 'Scrope, Richard', *ODNB*

Meadows, P and Ramsay, N (eds) 2003 *A history of Ely cathedral*, Boydell and Brewer

Monckton, L 1999 'Late gothic architecture in south west England: four major centres of building activity at Wells, Bristol, Sherborne and Bath', unpublished PhD thesis, University of Warwick

Morgan, N 2003 'Marian liturgy in Salisbury cathedral', in Backhouse 2003, 89–107

Morgan, P E 1982 'The effect of the cult of Thomas Cantilupe on Hereford cathedral', in Jancey 1982b, 145–52

Morrin, J 2004 'Estates and income 1714–2004', in Keene et al 2004, 335–42

Morris, R K 1974 'The remodelling of the Hereford aisles', *Journal of the BAA*, 3rd series, 38, 21–39

Morris, R K 1978 'Worcester nave: from Decorated to Perpendicular', in BAA 1978, 116–143

Morris, R K 1979 *Cathedrals and abbeys of England and Wales*, Dent

Morris, R K 1985 'Ballflower work in Gloucester and its vicinity', in Heslop and Sekules 1985, 99–115

Morris, R K 1990a 'The gothic mouldings of the Latin and lady chapels', in Blair 1990a, 169–84

Morris, R K 1990b 'The new work at Old St Paul's cathedral and its place in English thirteenth-century architecture', in Grant 1990, 74–101

Morris, R K 1991 'Thomas of Witney at Exeter, Winchester and Wells', in Kelly 1991, 57–84

Morris, R K 1994 'The lost cathedral priory church of St Mary, Coventry', in Demidowicz 1994, 17–66

Morris, R K 1996 'The style and buttressing of Salisbury cathedral tower', in Keen and Cocke 1996, 46–58

Morris, R K 1997 'European prodigy or regional eccentric?: the rebuilding of St Augustine's abbey church, Bristol', in Keen 1997, 41–56

Morris, R K 2000 'The architectural history of the medieval cathedral church', in Aylmer and Tiller 2000, 203–40

Morris, R K and Shoesmith, R 2003 *Tewkesbury abbey: history, art and architecture*, Logaston Press

Morris, R 1996 'The archaeological study of cathedrals in England, 1800–2000: a review and speculation', in Tatton-Brown and Munby 1996, 1–8

Munby, J 1990 'Christ Church, Priory House: discoveries in St Frideswide's dormitory', in Blair 1990a 185–94

Munby, J and Fletcher, J 1983 'Carpentry in the cathedral and close at Winchester', in Heslop and Sekules 1983, 101–11

Niblett, R and Thompson, I 2005 *Alban's buried towns: an assessment of St Albans archaeology up to AD 1600* English Heritage/Oxbow

Nilson, B 1998 *Cathedral shrines of medieval England*, Boydell and Brewer

Norton, C 1993 'The medieval tile pavements of Winchester cathedral', in Crook 1993c, 167–76

Norton, C 1998 'The Anglo-Saxon cathedral at York and the topography of the Anglian city', *Journal of the BAA*, 151, 1–42

Norton, C 2006 *St William of York*, Woodbridge

Oakes, C 2000 'Romanesque architecture and sculpture', in Rogan 2000, 64–87

Oakley, A 1996 'Rochester priory 1185–1540', in Yates and Welsby 1996, 29–56

O'Connor, D 2004 'The dim shadowing of the things which should be: the fourteenth-century doom in the east window of Carlisle cathedral', in McCarthy and Weston 2004, 146–74

O'Connor, D and Haselock, E J 1977 'Stained and painted glass', in Aylmer and Cant 1977, 313–94

Orme, N 1991 'The charnel chapel of Exeter cathedral', in Kelly 1991, 162–71

Orme, N 2004a 'Brewer, William Quinil [Quivil]', *ODNB*

Orme, N 2004b 'Oldham, Hugh', *ODNB*

Ormrod, M 1986 *England in the thirteenth century*, Proceedings of the 1984 Harlaxton Symposium, Boydell and Brewer

Orme, N and Cannon, J 2010 *Westbury-on-Trym: Monastery, minister and College*, Bristol History Society

Ormrod, M and Lindley, P (eds) 1996 *The Black Death in England*, Paul Watkins, Stamford

Ottey, J L 2005 *The story of Southwell minster* (self-published)

Owen, D 1971 *Church and society in medieval Lincolnshire*, History of Lincolnshire V, History of Lincolnshire Committee and Lincolnshire History Society

Owen, D 1984 'The Norman cathedral at Lincoln', in Allen Brown 1984, 188–99

Owen, D (ed) 1994a *A history of Lincoln minster*, CUP

Owen, D 1994b 'Historical survey 1091–1450', in Owen 1994a, 112–63

Owen, D 2003 'Ely 1109–1539: priory, community and town', in Meadows and Ramsey 2003, 59–76

Owen, D 2004a 'Hervey', *ODNB*

Owen, D 2004b 'Northwold, Hugh of' *ODNB*

Page, W (ed) 1906a *VCH Lincoln* II, Constable

Page, W (ed) 1906b *VCH Norfolk* II, Constable

Page, W (ed) 1906c *VCH Worcester* II, Constable

Page, W (ed) 1907a *VCH County Durham* II, Constable

Page, W (ed) 1907b *VCH Gloucester* II, Constable

Page, W (ed) 1907c *VCH Oxford* II, Constable

Page, W (ed) 1907d *VCH Sussex* II, Constable

Page, W (ed) 1909 *VCH London* I, Constable

Page, W (ed) 1910 *VCH Nottingham* II, Constable

Page, W (ed) 1911 *VCH Somerset*, Constable

Page, W (ed) 1913 *VCH County of York* III, Constable

Page, W (ed) 1914 *VCH Hertford* IV, Constable

Page, W (ed) 1926 *VCH Kent* II, St Catherine Press

Park, D 1983 'The wall paintings of the Holy Sepulchre chapel', in Heslop and Sekules 1983, 38–62

Park, D 1986 'The medieval painted decoration of Lincoln cathedral', in Heslop and Sekules 1986, 75–82

Park, D and Cather, S 2004 'Later medieval paintings at Carlisle', in McCarthy and Weston 2004, 214–31

Park, D and Howard, H 1996 'The medieval polychromy', in Atherton et al 1996, 379–410

Park, D and Welford, P 1993 'The medieval polychromy of Winchester cathedral', in Crook 1993c, 123–38

Partner, P 2004 'Wykeham, William', *ODNB*

Perkins, J B 1952 'The shrine of St Peter and its twelve spiral columns', *Journal of Roman Studies*, 42, 21–33

Pevsner, N 1945 *The leaves of Southwell*, Penguin

Pevsner, N 1953 *Medieval carvings in Exeter cathedral*, Penguin

Pevsner, N 1958 *The buildings of England: North Somerset and Bristol*, Penguin

Pevsner, N and Cherry, B 1989 *Devon*, Penguin

Pevsner, N and Metcalf, P 1985 *The cathedrals of England*, 2 vols, Viking

Pinder-Wilson, R H 1973 'The reliquary of St Petroc and the ivories of Norman Sicily', *Archaeologia* 104 (2nd series 54), 261–306

Plant, R 2004 'The romanesque fabric', in McCarthy and Weston 2004, 89–105

Plant, R 2006 'Gundulf's cathedral', in Ayers and Tatton-Brown 2006, 38–53

Prestwich, J O 1994 'The career of Ranulph Flambard', in Rollason et al 1994, 299–310

Proud, K 1990 *The prince bishops of Durham*, Keybar

Pugh, R B 1953 *VCH Cambridge and the Isle of Ely* IV, OUP

Pugh, R B and Crittall, E (eds) 1956 *VCH Wiltshire* III, OUP

Purcell, D 1973 *The building of Ely cathedral*, Dean and Chapter of Ely

Purvis, J S 1964 'The tables of the vicars choral', *Yorkshire Archaeological Journal*, 41, 741–8

Quiney, A 2001 'In hoc signo : the west front of Lincoln cathedral', *Architectural History*, 44, 162–71

Raguin, V, Brush, K and Draper, P 1995 *Artistic integration in gothic buildings*, University of Toronto

Ramsay, N 1995 'The cathedral archives and library', in Collinson and Sparks 1995, 341–407

Ramsay, N 2003 'The library and archives 1109–1541', in Meadows and Ramsay 2003, 157–68

Ramsey, F 2004a 'Lewes, Robert of', *ODNB*

Ramsey, F 2004b 'Savaric', *ODNB*

RCHME 1931 *An inventory of the historical monuments in Herefordshire: I south west*, 90

RCHME 1980 *Ancient and historical monuments in the city of Salisbury*, I, HMSO

RCHME 1993 *The houses of the close*, HMSO

Reed Kline, N 2003 *Map of medieval thought*, Boydell and Brewer

Reilly, L A 1997 *An architectural history of Peterborough cathedral*, Clarendon Studies in the History of Art, Clarendon Press

Reilly, L 1998 *Southwark: an illustrated history*, London Borough of Southwark

Rex, R 2004 'Fisher, John [St John Fisher]', *ODNB*

Riall, N 1994 'Henry of Blois, bishop of Winchester: a patron of the twelfth-century renaissance', *Hampshire Papers* 5

Richardson, J S 1906–7 'Saint William of Perth and his memorials in England', *Transactions of the Scottish Ecclesiological Society*, IV, vol 2 pt 1, 122–6

Roberts, E 1993 *The hill of the martyr: an architectural history of St Albans abbey*, Castle Books

Roberts, M E 1986 'The relic of the holy blood and the iconography of the thirteenth century north transept portal of Westminster abbey', in Ormrod 1986, 129–42

Robinson, P R and Zim, R (eds) 1997 *Of the making of books: medieval manuscripts, their scribes and readers*, Scolar Press

Rodwell, W 1981 'The Lady Chapel by the Cloister at Wells and the site of the Anglo-Saxon cathedral', in Coldstream and Draper 1981, 1–9

Rodwell, W 1982a 'The Anglo-Saxon and Norman churches at Wells', in Colchester 1982, 1–23

Rodwell, W 1982b 'The buildings of the vicars close', in Colchester 1982, 212–26

Rodwell, W 1989 'Archaeology and the standing fabric: recent studies at Lichfield cathedral,' *Antiquity*, 63, 281–94

Rodwell, W 1993 'The development of the choir of Lichfield cathedral: romanesque and Early English', in Maddison 1993b, 17–35

Rodwell, W 1996 'Archaeology and the standing fabric: recent investigations at Lichfield cathedral', in Tatton-Brown and Munby 1996, 81–94

Rodwell, W 2001 *Wells cathedral, excavations and structural studies*, 2 vols, English Heritage

Rodwell, W with Neale, F 2005 '"Begun while the Black Death raged …": the vicars' close at Wells', in Hall and Stocker 2005, 112–37

Roffe, D 2004 'Hereward [Hereward the Wake]', *ODNB*

Rogan, J (ed) 2000 *Bristol cathedral: history and architecture*, Tempus

Rollason, D, Harvey, M and Prestwich, M (eds) 1994 *Anglo-Norman Durham, 1093–1193*, Boydell and Brewer (1998 edn)

Rose, M 1996 'The vault bosses', in Atherton et al 1996, 363–78

Rose, M 1997 *Stories in stone: the medieval roof carvings of Norwich cathedral*, Herbert

Rubinstein, J 1999 'Liturgy against history: the competing visions of Lanfranc and Eadmer of Canterbury', *Speculum*, 74, 279–309

Russell, G 1983 'Decorated tracery in Winchester cathedral', in Heslop and Sekules 1983, 94–100

St John Hope, W 1898–9 'The architectural history of the cathedral church and monastery of St Andrew at Rochester', *Archaeologia Cantiana*, 23, 194–328; 24, 293–8

Sadgrove, Michael 'The theatre of the soul – liturgy then and now: worship in Coventry's priory church' in Demidowicz 1994, 169–180

Salter, H E and Lobel, M D 1954 *VCH Oxford* III, OUP

Salzman, L F 1948 *VCH Cambridge and the Isle of Ely* II, OUP

Sampson, J 1998 *Wells cathedral west front: construction, sculpture and conservation*, Alan Sutton

Savage, A (ed) 2002 *The Anglo-Saxon chronicles*, Greenwich Editions

Scamell, C V 1956 *Hugh de Puiset, Bishop of Durham*, CUP

Scarisbrick, J C 1994 'The dissolution of St Mary's priory Coventry', in Demidowicz 1994, 158–68

Schoeck, R J 2004a 'Alcock, John', *ODNB*

Schoeck, R J 2004b 'Lyhert [Lyhart], Walter', *ODNB*

Schofield, J and Keene, D 2004 'Before St Paul's', in Keene et al 2004, 2–4

Scull, C et al 1990 'Excavations in the cloister of St Frideswide's, 1985', in Blair 1990a, 21–74

Sekules, V 1986 'The tomb of Christ at Lincoln and the developments of the sacrament shrine: Easter

sepulchres reconsidered', in Heslop and Sekules 1986, 118–31

Sekules, V 1991a 'Early fourteenth-century liturgical furnishings', in Swanton 1991b, 111–15

Sekules, V 1991b 'The liturgical furnishings of the choir of Exeter cathedral', in Kelly 1991, 172–9

Sekules, V 1996 'The gothic sculpture', in Atherton et al 1996, 197–209

Serjeantson, R M, Ryland, W and Adkins, D 1906 *VCH Northampton* II, Constable

Sharpe, R 2001 'The late antique passion of St Alban', in Henig and Lindley 2001, 30–7

Shaw, D G 2004 'Button [Bitton], William', *ODNB*

Sherborne, J 1994 *War, politics and culture in fourteenth-century England*, Hambledon

Shoesmith, R 2000 'The close and its buildings', in Aylmer and Tiller 2000, 293–310

Simeon 1993 *Simeon's history of the church of Durham* Llanerch (*c.* 1105; from translation by Stevenson, 1855)

Simpson, G 1996 'Documentary evidence and dendrochronological evidence for the building of Salisbury cathedral', in Keen and Cocke 1996, 10–20

Simpson, G 2004 'The chancel roof of Carlisle cathedral: its architecture and historical context', in McCarthy and Weston 2004, 127–44

Sinclair, E 1991 'The west front II: The west front poly-chromy', in Kelly 1991, 116–33

Singleton, B 1978 'The remodelling of the east end of Worcester cathedral in the earlier part of the thirteenth century', in BAA 1978, 105–15

Smith, D M 2004 'Romanus, John [John le Romeyn]', *ODNB*

Southern R W 1962 *The life of St Anselm by Eadmer*, Thomas Nelson

Southern, R W 2004 'Grosseteste, Robert', *ODNB*

Sparks, M 1997 'The liturgical use of the nave', in Blockley et al 1997, 121–7

Srawley, J H (trans) 1966 *The book of John de Schalby canon of Lincoln 1299–1333 concerning the bishops of Lincoln and their acts*, Lincoln Minster pamphlets no 2

Stalley, R 1971 'A twelfth-century patron of architecture: a study of the buildings erected by Roger, bishop of Salisbury', *Journal of the BAA*, 3rd series, 24, 62–83

Staunton, M 2001 *The lives of Thomas Becket*, Manchester University Press

Stenton, F M 1971 *Anglo-Saxon England*, OUP

Stephanus, Eddius 1965 'St Wilfrid', in Webb 1965, 131–206

Stephens, W B 1969 *VCH Warwickshire* VIII, OUP

Stevenson, K 1993 'Liturgy and the fabric', in Crook 1993c, 47–56

Stocker, D 1986a 'The shrine of Little St Hugh', in Heslop

and Sekules 1986, 109–17

Stocker, D 1986b 'The tomb and shrine of Bishop Grosseteste in Lincoln cathedral', in Ormrod 1986, 143–8

Stratford, N 1978 'Notes on the Norman chapter-house at Worcester', in BAA 1978, 51–70

Stratford, N 1991 'Bishop Grandisson and the visual arts', in Swanton 1991b, 145–56

Strayer, J R 1970 *On the medieval origins of the modern state*, Princeton University Press (2005 edn)

Stroud, D 1983 'The cult and tombs of St Osmund', *Wiltshire Archaeological and Natural History Magazine*, 78, 50–4

Stroud, D 1996 *Richard Poore and the building of Salisbury cathedral*, Dean and Chapter of Salisbury Cathedral

Sturdy, D with Donald, N 1990 'Excavations in the Latin chapel and outside the east end of Oxford cathedral 1962/3', in Blair 1990a, 75–102

Summers, N 1974 *A prospect of Southwell: an architectural history of the church and domestic buildings of the collegiate foundation*, Kelham House Publications (1988 edn)

Summerson, H 1993 *Medieval Carlisle: The city and the borders from the late eleventh to the mid-sixteenth century*, 2 vols, Cumberland and Westmorland Antiquarian and Archaeological Society, extra series, 25

Summerson, H 1994 'Old and new bishoprics: Durham and Carlisle', in Rollason et al 1994, 369–80

Summerson, H 2004 'Medieval Carlisle: cathedral and city from foundation to dissolution', in McCarthy and Weston 2004, 29–38

Swanson, R and Lepine, D 2000 'The later Middle Ages 1268–1535', in Aylmer and Tiller 2000, 48–86

Swanson, R N 1994 'The priory in the later Middle Ages', in Demidowicz 1994, 139–57

Swanton, M 1991a 'Discovering the cathedral', in Swanton 1991b, 1–12

Swanton, M (ed) 1991b *Exeter cathedral: a celebration* Dean and Chapter of Exeter Cathedral

Tanner, N 1996 'The cathedral and the city', in Atherton et al 1996, 255–80

Tatton-Brown, T 1982 'The Great Hall of the archbishop's palace', in Coldstream and Draper 1982, 112–19

Tatton-Brown, T 1989 *Great cathedrals of Britain*, BBC

Tatton-Brown, T 1991 'Building the tower and spire of Salisbury cathedral', *Antiquity* 65, 74–96

Tatton-Brown, T 1994a 'Destruction, repair and restoration', in Hobbs 1994, 143–70

Tatton-Brown, T 1994b 'The buildings of the bishop's palace and the close', in Hobbs 1994, 225–46

Tatton-Brown, T 1994c 'The medieval fabric', in Hobbs 1994, 25–46

Tatton-Brown, T 1996a 'Archaeology and Chichester cathedral', in Tatton-Brown and Munby 1996, 47–56

Tatton-Brown, T 1996b 'The archaeology of the spire of Salisbury cathedral', in Keen and Cocke 1996, 59–67

Tatton-Brown, T 1997 'The rebuilding of the nave and transepts', in Blockley et al 1997, 128–46

Tatton-Brown, T 2000 *Lambeth Palace: a history of the archbishops of Canterbury and their houses*, Society for Promoting Christian Knowledge

Tatton-Brown, T 2004 'Rose castle', in McCarthy and Weston 2004, 257–69

Tatton-Brown, T and Munby, J (eds) 1996 *The archaeology of cathedrals*, Oxford University Committee for Archaeology

Taylor, H M and Taylor, J 1965 *Anglo-Saxon architecture*, CUP

Taylor, P 2004 'Foundation and endowment: St Paul's and the English kingdoms 604–1087', in Keene 2004, 5–16

Thacker, A (ed) 2000a *Medieval art and architecture at Chester*, BAA

Thacker, A 2000b 'The early medieval city and its buildings', in Thacker 2000a, 16–30

Thacker, A 2004a 'The cult of saints and the liturgy', in Keene et al 2004, 113–26

Thacker, A 2004b 'Werburh [St Werburh, Werburgh, Werburga]', *ODNB*

Thomas, J 1987 *Coventry cathedral*, New Bells Cathedral Guides

Thompson, B (ed) 1999 *Monasteries and society in medieval Britain*, Proceedings of the 1994 Harlaxton Symposium

Thompson, J B 2004 'Pecham [Peckham], John', *ODNB*

Thurlby, M 1985 'The elevations of the romanesque abbey churches of St Mary at Tewkesbury and St Peter at Gloucester', in Heslop and Sekules 1985, 36–51

Thurlby, M 1991a 'The romanesque cathedral circa 1114–1200', in Swanton 1991b, 37–46

Thurlby, M 1991b 'The romanesque cathedral of St Mary and St Peter at Exeter', in Kelly 1991, 19–34

Thurlby, M 1994 'The roles of the patron and the master mason in the first design of the romanesque cathedral at Durham', in Rollason et al 1994, 161–84

Thurlby, M 1995 'Hereford cathedral: the romanesque fabric', in Whitehead 1995, 15–28

Thurmer, J 1991 'The cathedral constitution', in Swanton 1991b, 13–18

Tillott P M (ed) 1961 *VCH Yorkshire: the city of York*, OUP

Toulson, W 2000 'The ornaments: the textiles', in Aylmer and Tiller 2000, 493–9

Tracy, C 1993a 'The fourteenth-century choir stalls', in Crook 1993c, 193–206

Tracy, C 1993b 'The lady chapel stalls', in Crook 1993c, 231–46

Tracy, C 2004 'The stylistic antecedents of the Gondibour screen at Carlisle cathedral', in McCarthy and Weston 2004, 175–98

Tringham, N 1993 'The palace of Bishop Walter Langton in Lichfield cathedral close', in Maddison 1993b, 85–100

Tsurushima, H 1991 'The fraternity of Rochester cathedral priory about 1100', in Chibnall 1991, 313–37

Tudor, V 1994 'Durham priory and its hermits in the twelfth century', in Rollason et al 1994, 67–77

Tudor-Craig, P 1982 'Wells sculpture', in Colchester 1982, 102–31

Tudor-Craig, P 1991 'Bishop Grandisson's provision for music and ceremony', in Swanton 1991b, 137–44

Tudor-Craig, P 2002 'The iconography of wisdom and the frontispiece to the *Bible Historiale*, British Library, Additional Manuscript 18856', in Barron and Stratford 2002, 110–27

Tummers, H A 1994 'Church monuments', in Hobbs 1994, 203–24

Use of Sarum:
http://anglicanhistory.org/essays/wright/sarum.pdf, accessed 2006

Vaughan, R (ed and trans) 1984 *The illustrated chronicles of Matthew Paris*, Alan Sutton with Corpus Christi Cambridge (1993 edn)

Vincent, N 2004a 'd'Aigueblanche, Peter', *ODNB*

Vincent, N 2004b 'Roches, Peter des', *ODNB*

Virgoe, R 1996 'The estate of Norwich cathedral priory 1101–1538', in Atherton et al 1996, 339–62

Walcot, M 1879 'The bishops of Chichester from Stigand to Sherborne', *Sussex Archaeological Collections*, 1–39

Walker, S 2004a 'Erpingham, Sir Thomas', *ODNB*

Walker, S 2004b 'Sudbury, Simon', *ODNB*

Wall, V 1994 'Malcolm III and the cathedral', in Rollason et al 1994, 325–38

Wallingford, R 2004 'Adrian IV [real name Nicholas Breakspear]', *ODNB*

Warren, R Hall 1897–9 'The choir of Bristol cathedral', *Clifton Antiquarian Club*, IV, 220–35

Webb, J F (ed and trans) 1965 *Lives of the saints*, Penguin

Welander, D 1985 *The stained glass of Gloucester cathedral*, Gloucester Cathedral (1993 edn)

Welander, D 1991 *The history, art and architecture of Gloucester cathedral*, Alan Sutton

Wells-Furby, B 2004 *A catalogue of the medieval muniments at Berkeley castle*, Bristol and Gloucestershire Archaeological Society

Westrem, S D 2001 *The Hereford map*, Brepols

Whetter, J 1988 *The history of Glasney college*, Tabb House

Whitehead, D (ed) 1995 *Medieval art, architecture and archaeology at Hereford*, BAA

Williams, D 2003 'Trouble in the cathedral close: Archbishop Boniface's 1259 visitation of the priory of Christ Church, Canterbury', in Backhouse 2003, 15–22

Willis, R 1845 *The architectural history of Winchester cathedral*, Friends of Winchester Cathedral (1984 edn)

Willis-Bund J W 1924 *VCH Worcester* IV, St Catherine Press

Wilson, C 1977 *The shrines of St William of York*, Yorkshire Museum

Wilson, C 1978 'The sources of the late twelfth century work at Worcester cathedral', in BAA 1978, 80–90

Wilson, C 1980 'The Neville screen', in Coldstream and Draper 1980, 90–104

Wilson, C 1985 'Abbot Serlo's church at Gloucester, 1089–1100: its place in romanesque architecture', in Heslop and Sekules 1985, 52–83

Wilson, C 1990 *The gothic cathedral: the architecture of the great church 1130–1530*, Thames and Hudson

Wilson, C 1995 'The medieval monuments', in Collinson and Sparks 1995, 451–510

Wilson, J 1905 *VCH Cumberland* II, Constable

Wollaston, D 1996 'Herbert de Losinga', in Atherton et al 1996, 22–35

Woodman, F 1981 *The architectural history of Canterbury cathedral*, Routledge and Kegan Paul

Woodman, F 1983 'The retrochoir of Winchester cathedral: a new interpretation', *Journal of the BAA*, 136, 87–97

Woodman, F 1996 'The gothic campaigns', in Atherton et al 1996, 158–96

Wright, D P 2004 'Langton, Thomas', *ODNB*

Yates, N and Welsby, P (eds) 1996 *Faith and fabric: a history of Rochester cathedral 604–1994*, Boydell and Brewer

Youings, J 1991 'John Hooker and the Tudor bishops of Exeter', in Swanton 1991b, 203–8

Zarnecki, G 1979 'The Chichester reliefs', in *Studies in Romanesque Sculpture* XII, Dorian Press, 106

INDEX